2024

（总第42期 No.42）

四川统计年鉴

Sichuan Statistical Yearbook

四　川　省　统　计　局

国家统计局四川调查总队　编

Statistical Bureau of Sichuan

NBS Survey Office in Sichuan

中国统计出版社

China Statistics Press

图书在版编目（CIP）数据
四川统计年鉴. 2024 = Sichuan Statistical Yearbook 2024 : 汉英对照 / 四川省统计局，国家统计局四川调查总队编. —— 北京 : 中国统计出版社, 2024. 12. —— ISBN 978-7-5230-0518-7
Ⅰ. C832.71-54
中国国家版本馆 CIP 数据核字第 2024RT6856 号

四川统计年鉴2024

作　　者 / 四川省统计局　国家统计局四川调查总队
责任编辑 / 姜　洋
执行编辑 / 宋　兰　汪小红　王　毅
出版发行 / 中国统计出版社有限公司
地　　址 / 北京市丰台区西三环南路甲6号　邮政编码 /100073
电　　话 / 邮购（010）63376909　书店（010）68783171
网　　址 / http://www.zgtjcbs.com
印　　刷 / 成都鑫达彩印印务有限责任公司
经　　销 / 新华书店
开　　本 / 890mm×1240mm　1/16
字　　数 / 1100　千字
印　　张 / 33.25　彩页 1
版　　别 / 2024 年 12 月第 1 版
版　　次 / 2024 年 12 月第 1 次印刷
定　　价 / 420.00　元　　　Price: 420.00　yuan(RMB)

本书附同版本 CD-ROM 一张，光盘内容以书面文字为准。
如有印装差错，由本社发行部调换。

《四川统计年鉴2024》

编委会和编辑部

SICHUAN STATISTICAL YEARBOOK 2024

Editorial Board and Staff

编 者 说 明

一、《四川统计年鉴2024》是一部全面反映四川省经济和社会发展情况的综合性统计资料年刊。本年鉴收录了全省和各市（州）、县（市、区）2023年经济和社会发展各方面的大量统计数据，以及历史重要年份和近年来的全省主要统计数据。

二、本年鉴正文内容分为22个篇章，即：1.综合；2.国民经济核算；3.人口；4.就业和工资；5.固定资产投资；6.能源；7.资源和环境；8.财政和物价；9.人民生活和社会保障；10.城市发展；11.民族自治地方概况；12.县（市、区）概况；13.农业；14.工业；15.建筑业；16.交通运输和邮电业；17.国内贸易；18.对外经济贸易和旅游；19.金融业；20.教育、科技和专利；21.文化、体育和卫生；22.其他社会活动。为方便读者使用，部分统计表下作了简要注释，并在各篇末附有主要统计指标解释。

三、与《四川统计年鉴2023》比较，本年鉴根据现行统计调查制度和统计工作开展情况，主要作如下修订：

1.为了满足统计调查划分经济类型需要，国家统计局会同市场监管总局对《关于划分企业登记注册类型的规定》（国统字〔2011〕86号）进行修订，联合印发《关于市场主体统计分类的划分规定》（国统字〔2023〕14号），本年鉴对相关分组按新标准作出相应调整。

2.本年鉴在"综合"篇，整理了新中国成立75年以来四川省经济社会发展总量、速度、比例和构成资料。

3.在"综合"篇，删除了"按地区和登记注册类型分企业法人单位数"表；在"就业和工资"篇，删除了"城镇登记失业人数及失业率"表和"各市（州）城镇登记失业人数及失业率"表；在"财政和物价"篇，删除了"商品零售价格总指数"表和"各市（州）城市商品零售价格指数"表；在"城市发展"篇，删除了"城市建设情况"表；在"国内贸易"篇，删除了"限额以上批发零售贸易法人企业主要商品分类销售额"表。

四、本年鉴中，涉及的部门统计资料均由省级相关部门提供。

五、本年鉴中涉及的历史数据，均以最新出版的本年鉴数据为准。

六、本年鉴中所使用的度量衡单位均采用国际统一标准计量单位。

七、本年鉴中部分数据合计数或相对数由于单位取舍不同而产生的计算误差，均未做机械调整。

八、本年鉴表中的符号使用说明："空格"表示该项统计指标数据不足本表最小单位数、数据不详或无该项数据；"#"表示其中的主要项。

Preface

Ⅰ. *Sichuan Statistical Yearbook 2024* is an annual statistics publication to reflect various aspects of Sichuan's economic and social development, which covers very comprehensive data series in 2023 and some selected data series in historically important years and the most recent years at provincial level, local levels of prefecture and level of county.

Ⅱ. The *Yearbook* contains twenty-two chapters: 1.General Survey; 2.National Accounts; 3.Population; 4.Employment and Wages; 5.Investment in Fixed Assets; 6.Energy; 7.Resources and Environment; 8.Local Government Finance and Prices; 9. People's Livelioods and Social Security; 10.Urban Development; 11.Survey of Minority Nationality Autonomous Areas; 12.Survey of County (City, District); 13.Agriculture; 14.Industry; 15.Construction; 16.Transportation, Postal and Telecommunication Services Industry; 17.Domestic Trade; 18.Foreign Trade and Economic Cooperation and International Tourism; 19.Finance and Insurance; 20.Education, Science Technology and Patents; 21.Culture, Sports and Public Health; 22.Other Social Activities. To facilitate readers, the brief notes below Some statistical tables, and Explanatory Notes on Main Statistical Indicators is attached to the end of each chapter.

Ⅲ. Compared with *Sichuan Statistical Yearbook 2023*, the *Yearbook* has made the following revisions based on the current statistical survey system and the progress of statistical work:

1.In order to meet the needs of economic classification in statistical surveys, the National Bureau of Statistics, together with the State Administration for Market Regulation, has revised the Regulations on the Classification of Enterprise by Registration Status (Guotongzi [2011] No. 86), and then jointly issued the Regulations on the Classification of Market Entity Statistics (Guotongzi [2023] No. 14). The *Yearbook* has made corresponding adjustments to the relevant groups according to the new standards.

2.Data on the aggregate, speed, proportion and composition of the main indicators of Sichuan's economic and social development since 1949 are sorted out in Chapter 1 "General Survey" of the *Yearbook*.

3.The table "Number of Corporate Enterprises by Region and Registration Type" has been deleted from Chapter 1 "General Survey"; The tables of "Number of Registered Unemployed Persons and Unemployment Rate in Urban Areas " and "Number of Registered Unemployed Persons and Unemployment Rate in Urban Areas by Region" have been deleted from Chapter 4 "Employment and Wages"; The tables of "General Retail Price Index" and "General Retail Price Index by Region" have been deleted from Chapter 8 "Local Government Finance and Prices"; The table "Basic Statistics on City Construction" has been deleted from Chapter 10 "Urban Development"; The table "Total Sales of Enterprises above Designated Size in Wholesale and Retail Trades by Category of Main Commodities" has been deleted from Chapter 17 "Domestic Trade".

Ⅳ. In the *Yearbook*, the relevant department statistics are provided by relevant departments at the provincial level.

Ⅴ. For updated historical date, please refer to the newly published version of the *Yearbook*.

Ⅵ. The units of measurement used in the *Yearbook* are international standard measurement units.

Ⅶ. Statistical discrepancies on totals and relative figures due to rounding are not adjusted in the *Yearbook*.

Ⅷ. Notations used in the *Yearbook*: "blanks space" means that the statistical index data is less than the minimum number of units in the table, the data is unknown or is not available; "#" indicates the main item.

目 录

CONTENTS

一、综 合
Chapter 1 General Survey

二、国民经济核算
Chapter 2 National Accounts

三、人　口
Chapter 3　Population

四、就业和工资
Chapter 4 Employment and Wages

五、固定资产投资
Chapter 5 Investment in Fixed Assets

六、能 源
Chapter 6 Energy

七、资源和环境
Chapter 7 Resources and Environment

八、财政和物价
Chapter 8 Local Government Finance and Price

九、人民生活和社会保障
Chapter 9 People's Living Conditions and Social Security

十、城市发展
Chapter 10 Urban Development

十一、民族自治地方概况
Chapter 11 Survey of Ethnic Minority Autonomous Areas

十二、县（市、区）概况
Chapter 12 Survey of County (City,District)

十三、农 业
Chapter 13 Agriculture

十四、工　业
Chapter 14　Industry

十五、建筑业
Chapter 15 Construction

十六、交通运输和邮电业
Chapter 16 Transportation and Post

十七、国内贸易
Chapter 17 Domestic Trade

十八、对外经济贸易和旅游
Chapter 18 Foreign Trade and Economic Cooperation and Tourism

十九、金融业
Chapter 19 Financial Intermediation

二十、教育、科技和专利
Chapter 20 Education, Science, Technology and Patents

二十一、文化、体育和卫生
Chapter 21 Culture, Sports and Public Health

二十二、其他社会活动
Chapter 22 Other Social Activities

年末户籍人口

（万人）
7000
6000
5000
4000
3000
2000
1000
0
6465
6317
6140
5997
5850
5753
5606
5598
5544
5512
2694
2785
2998
3116
3272
3347
3476
3496
3524
3560
2014年
2015年
2016年
2017年
2018年
2019年
2020年
2021年
2022年
2023年
城镇人口
乡村人口

就业人员

（万人）
5000
4500
4000
3500
3000
2500
2000
1500
1000
500
0
4638
4652
4657
4667
4690
4714
4745
4727
4706
4722
2014年
2015年
2016年
2017年
2018年
2019年
2020年
2021年
2022年
2023年

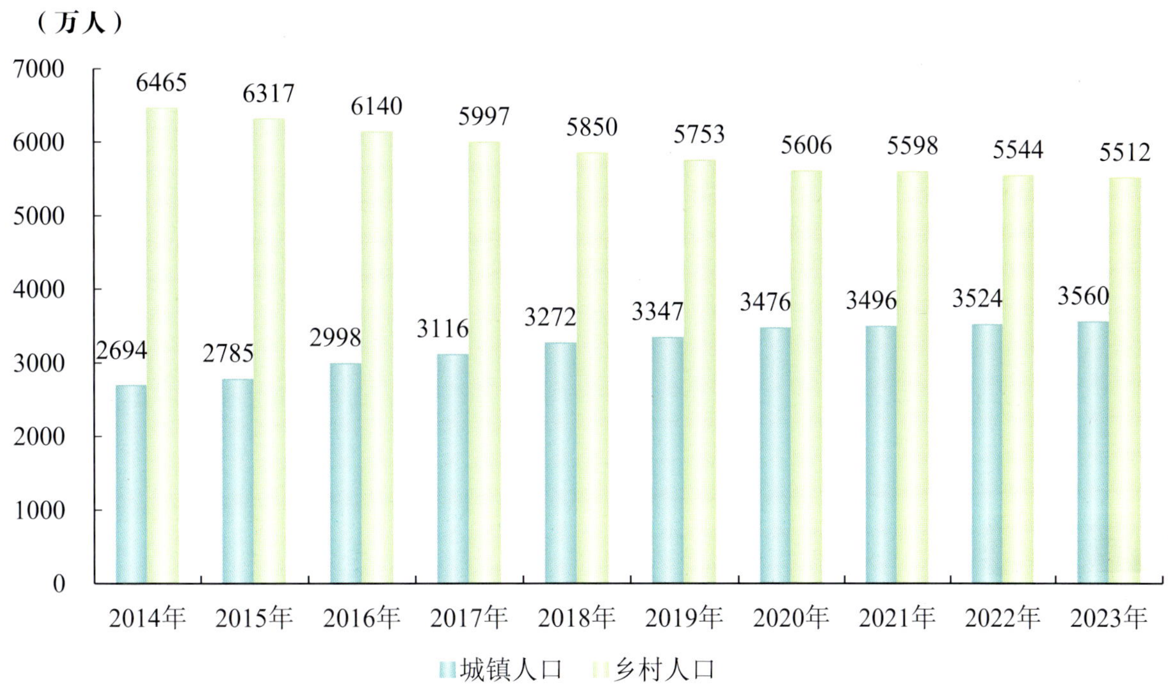

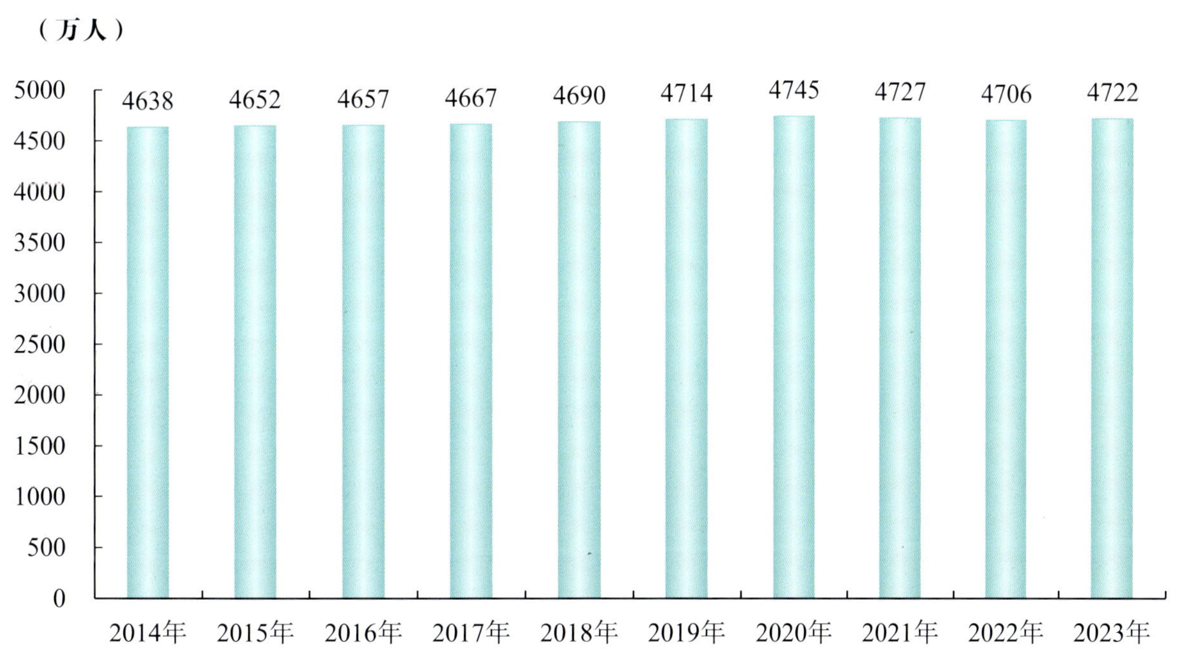

三次产业就业人员构成

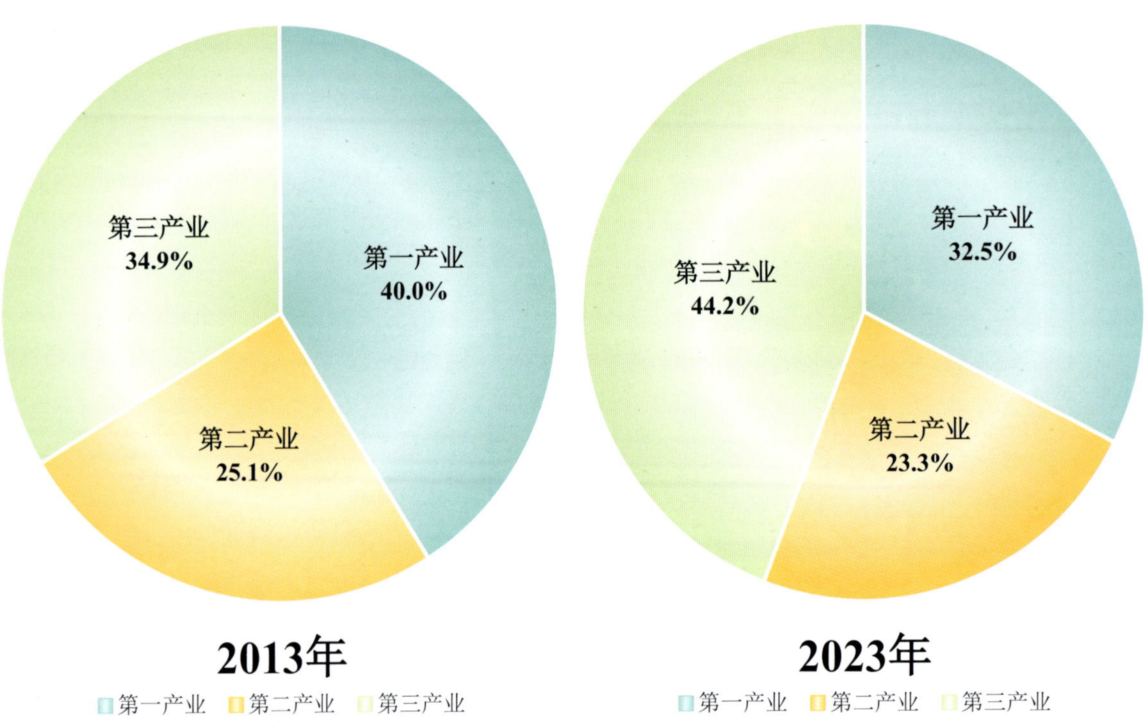

地区生产总值和增长速度

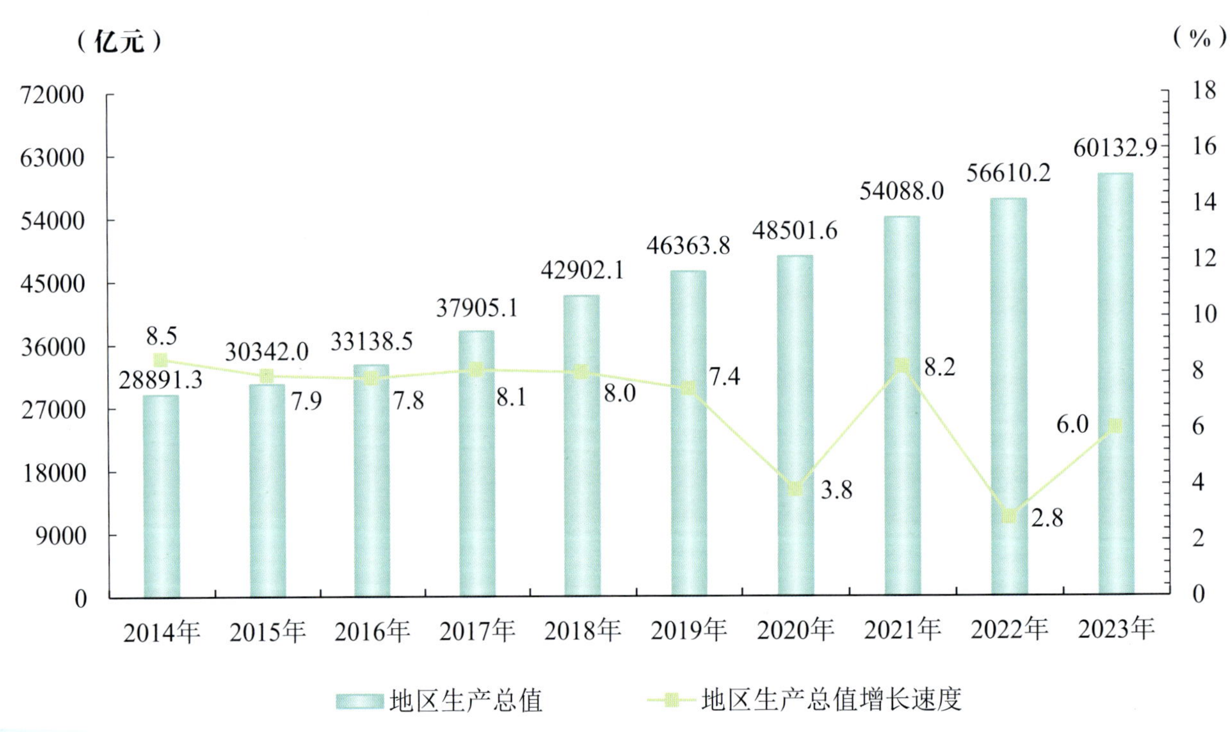

地区生产总值构成

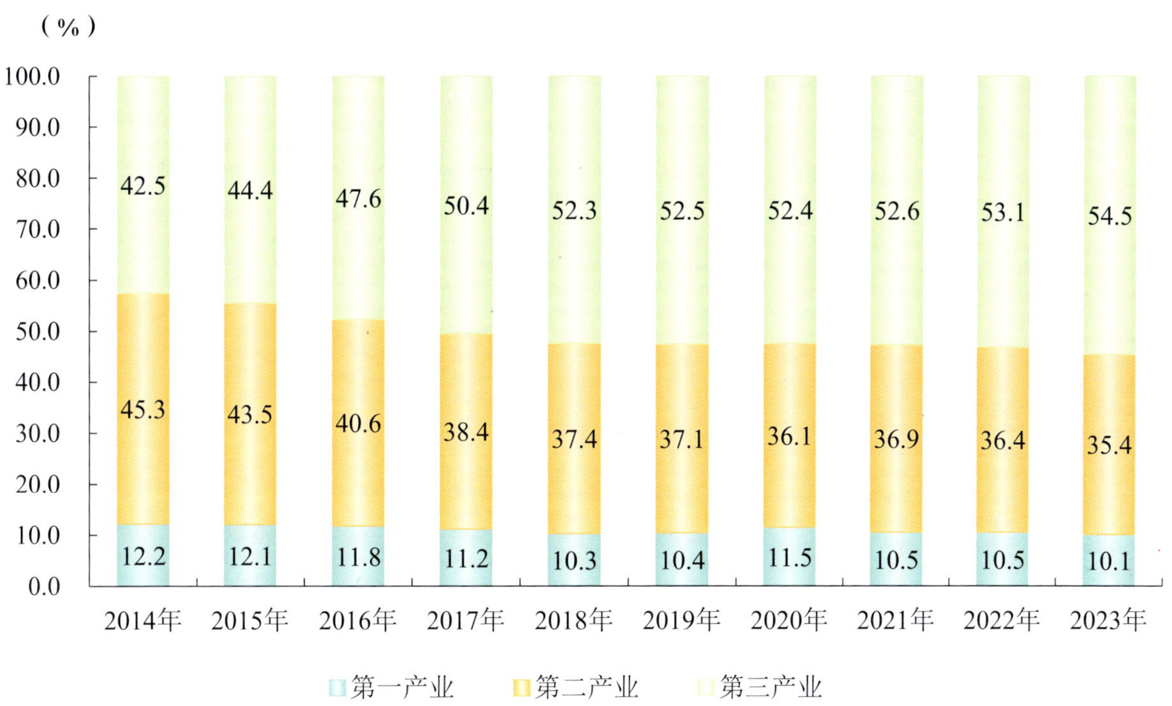

人均地区生产总值

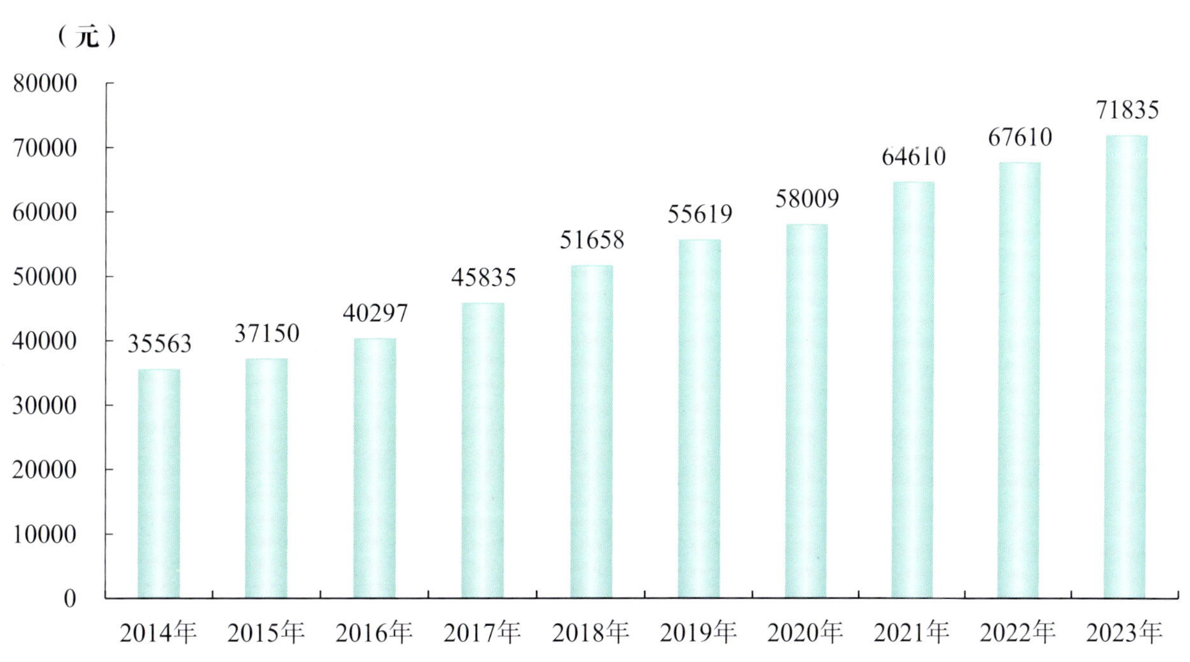

农林牧渔业总产值

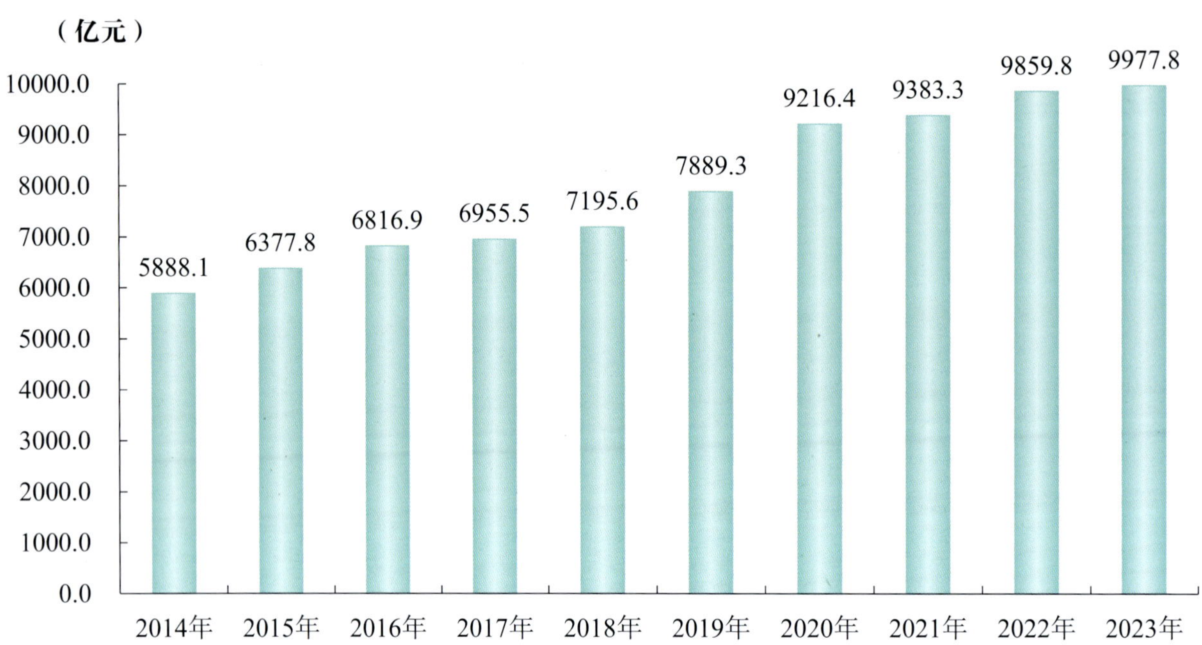

粮食作物和油料作物播种面积

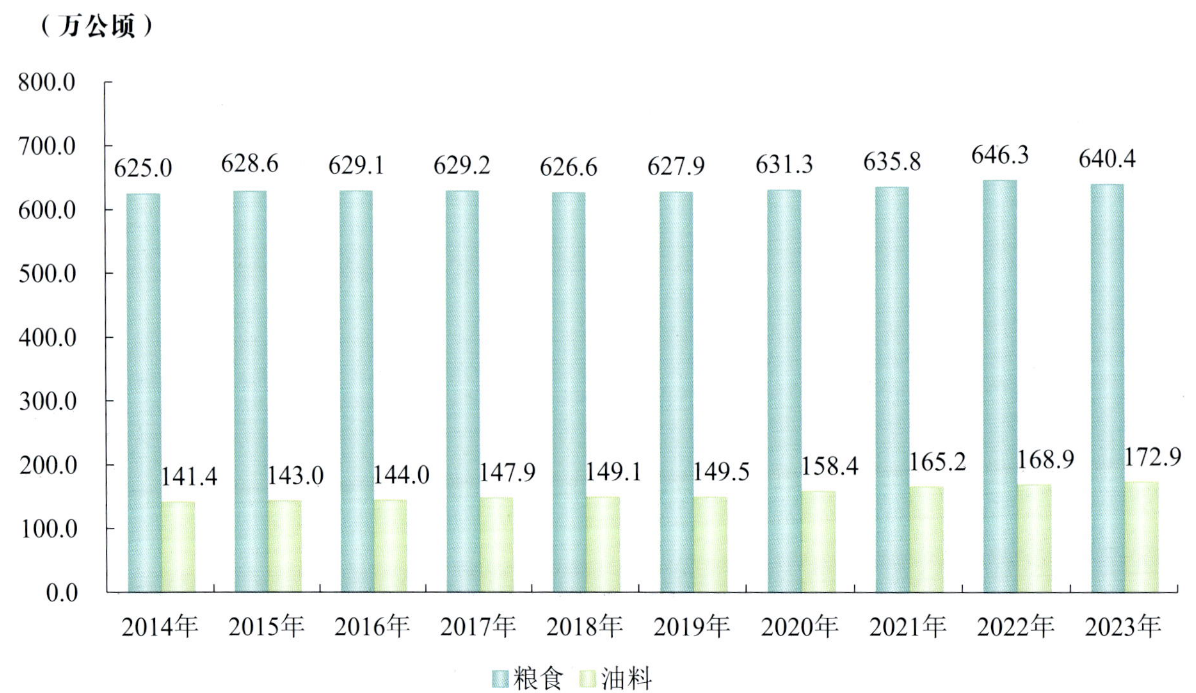

粮食产量和油料产量

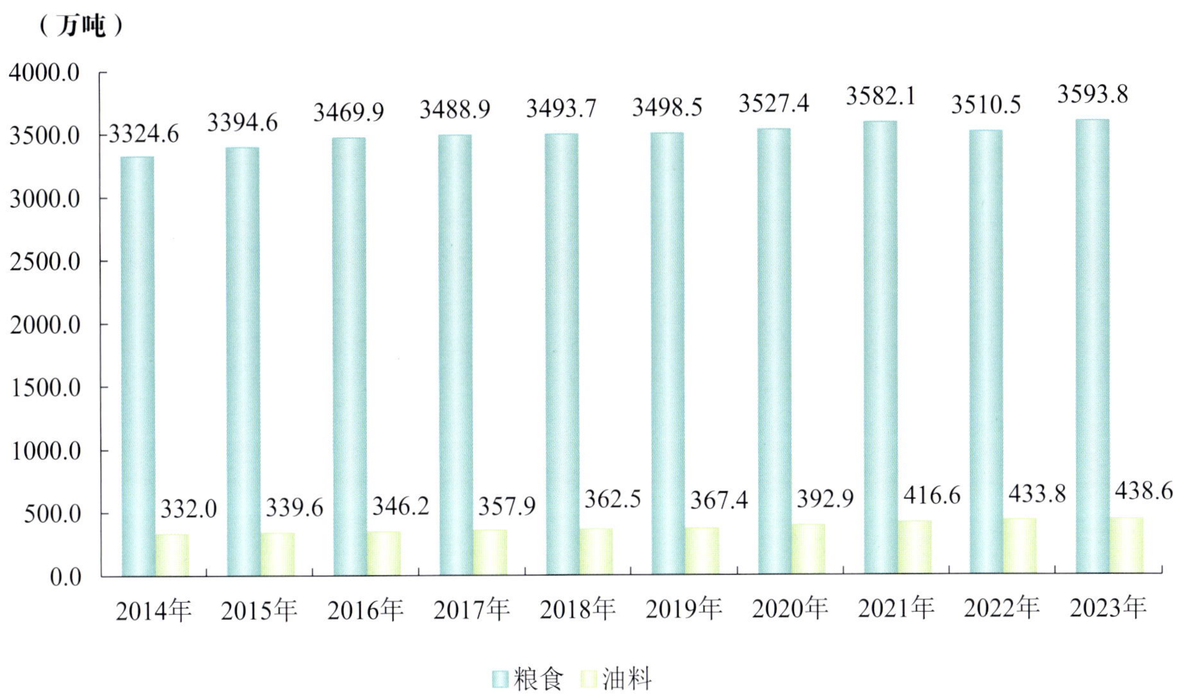

肉类总产量

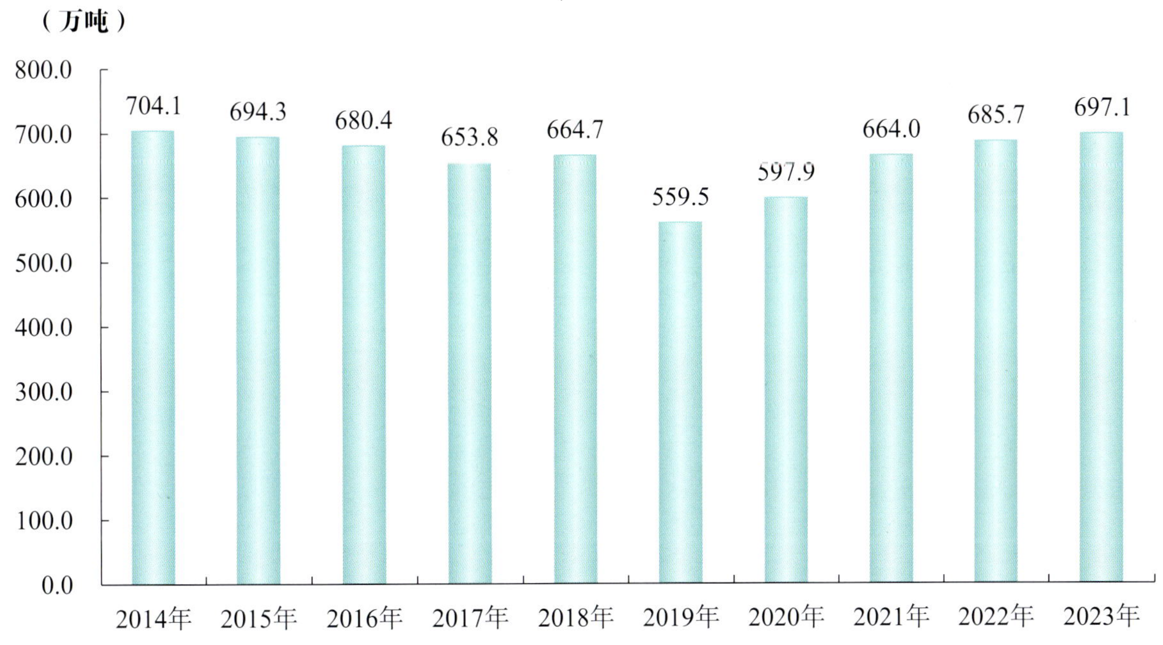

化肥施用量

（万吨）
300.0
250.0
200.0
150.0
100.0
50.0
0.0
252.1
252.1
249.0
242.0
235.2
222.8
210.8
207.2
204.4
202.2
2014年
2015年
2016年
2017年
2018年
2019年
2020年
2021年
2022年
2023年

工业增加值

（亿元）
18000.0
16000.0
14000.0
12000.0
10000.0
8000.0
6000.0
4000.0
2000.0
0.0
10703.8
10735.0
10790.9
11437.8
12360.1
13165.9
13401.0
15546.1
16188.7
16705.2
2014年
2015年
2016年
2017年
2018年
2019年
2020年
2021年
2022年
2023年

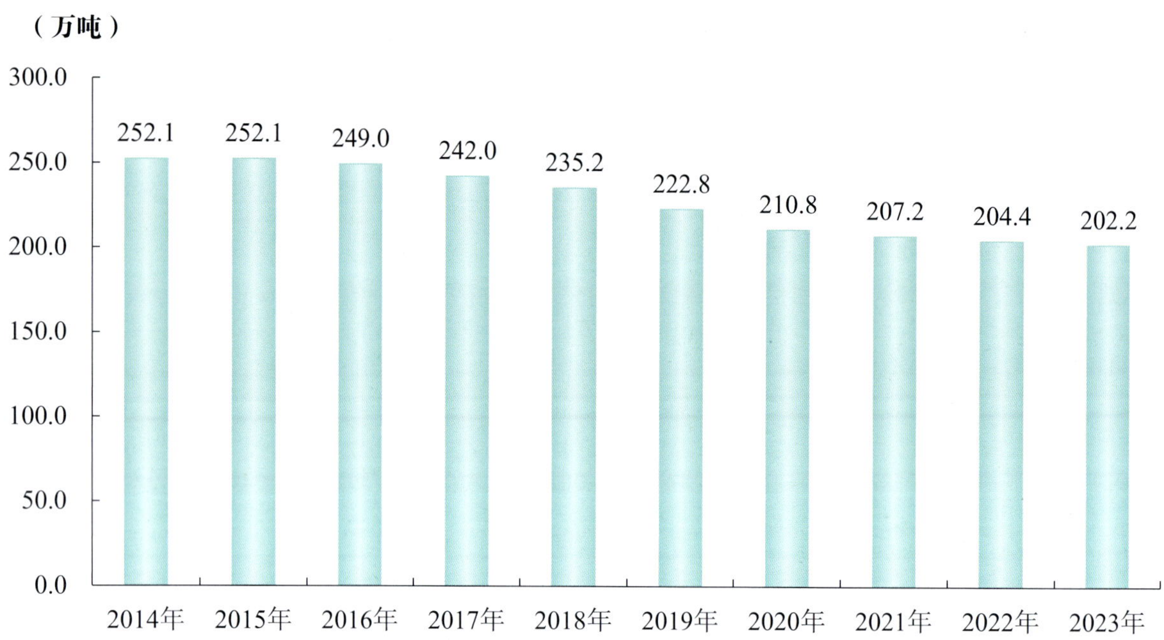

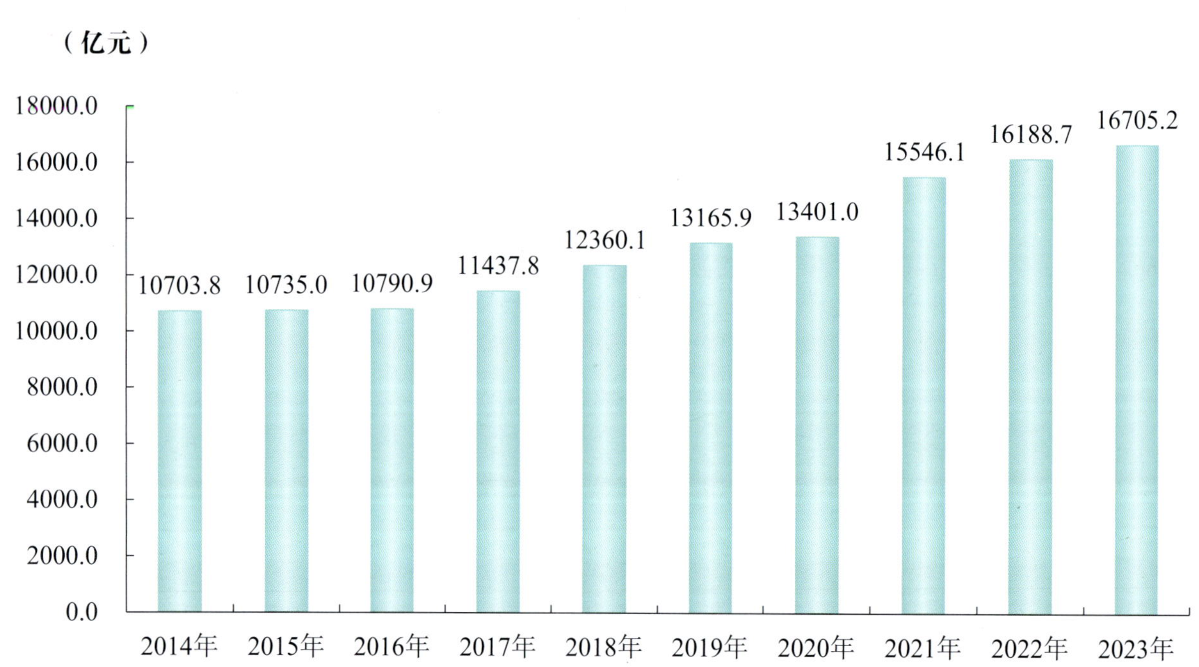

规模以上工业企业利润总额

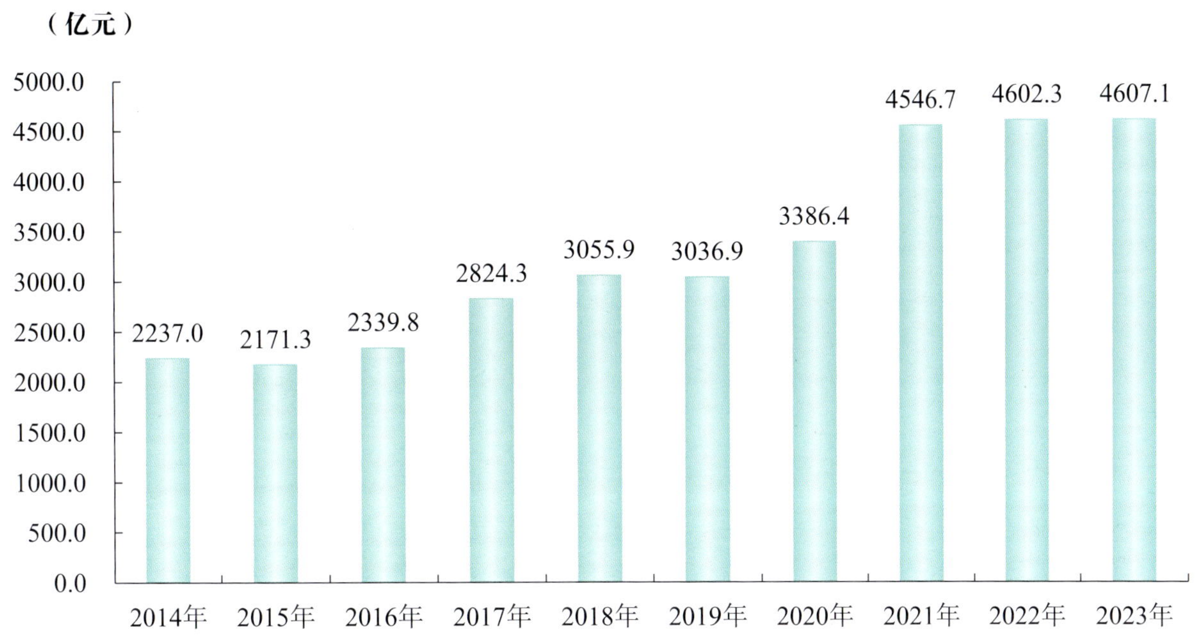

规模以上工业企业发电量

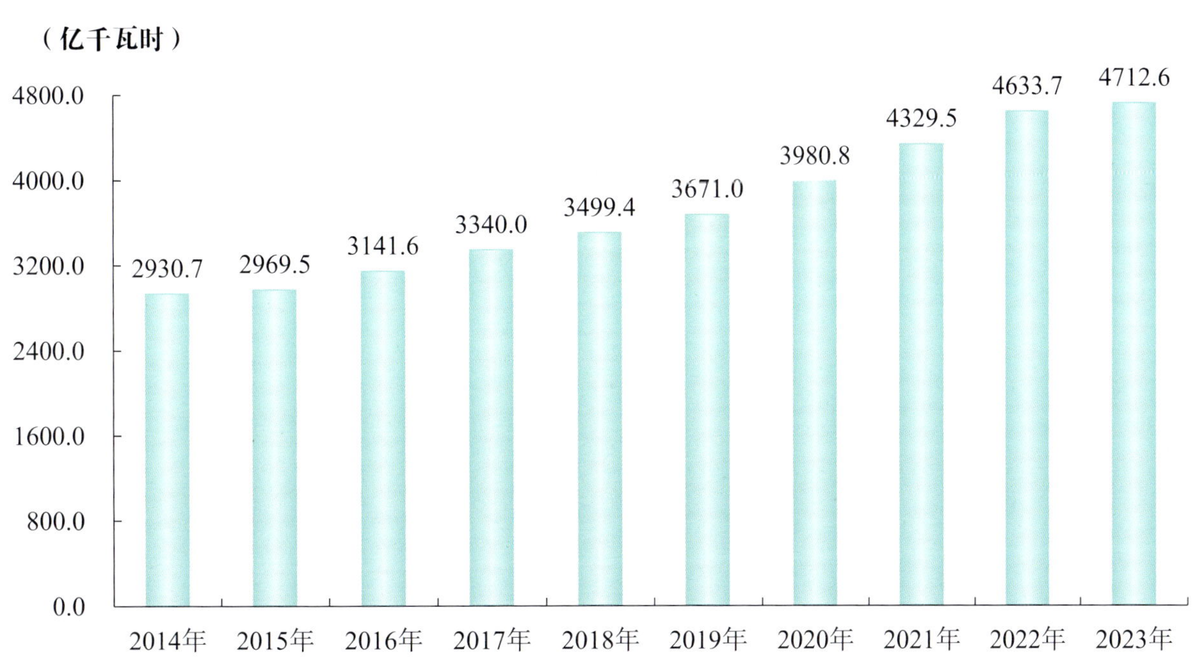

规模以上工业企业水泥产量

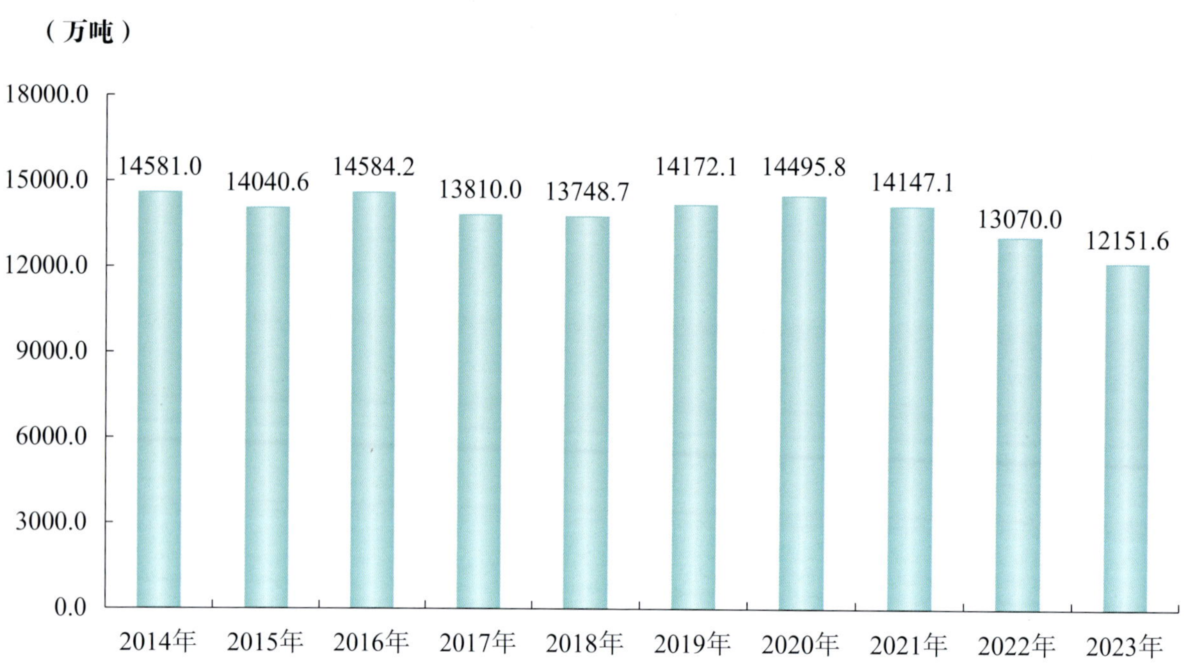

规模以上工业企业成品钢材产量

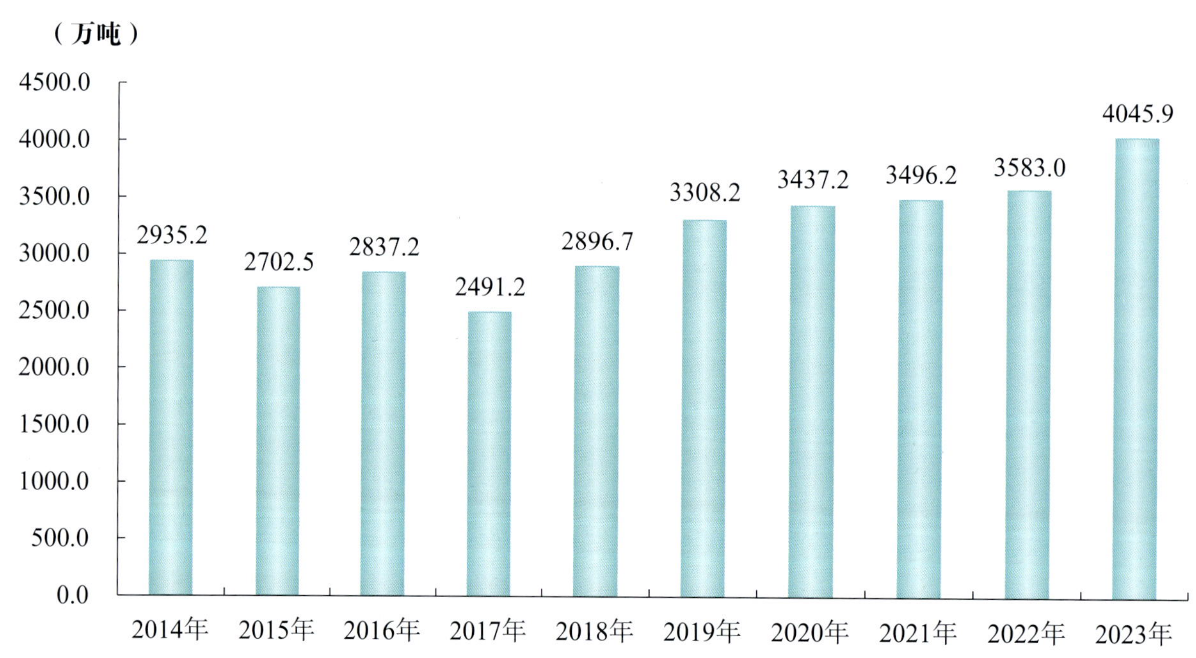

规模以上工业企业汽车产量

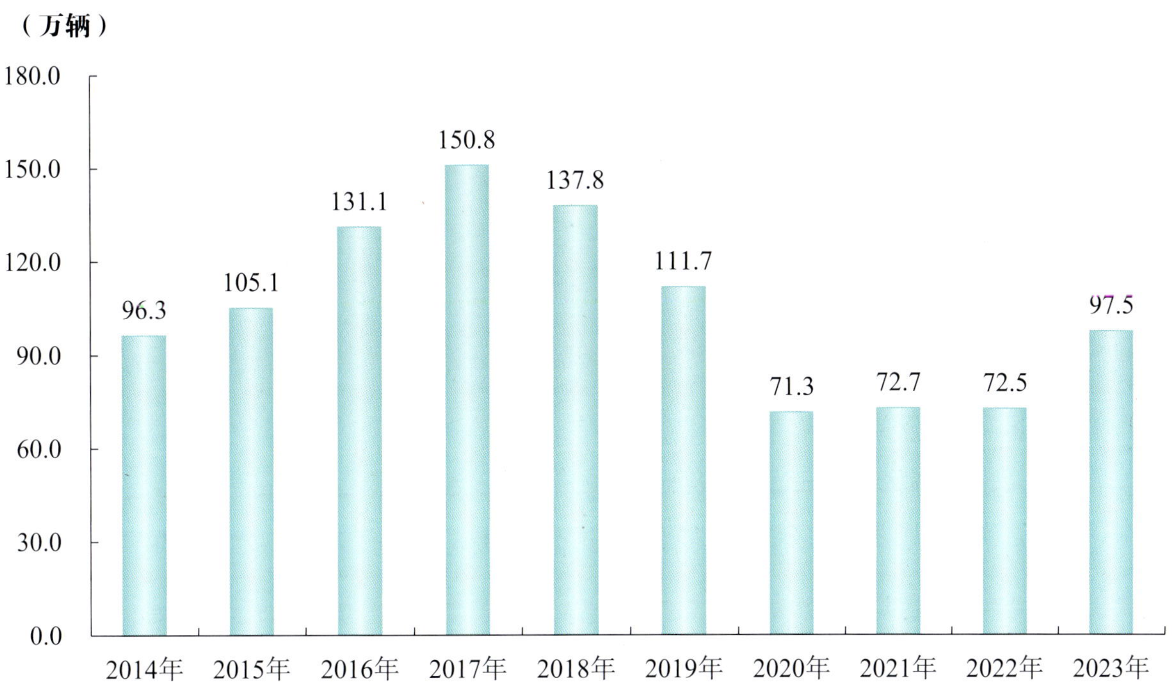

固定资产投资增长速度

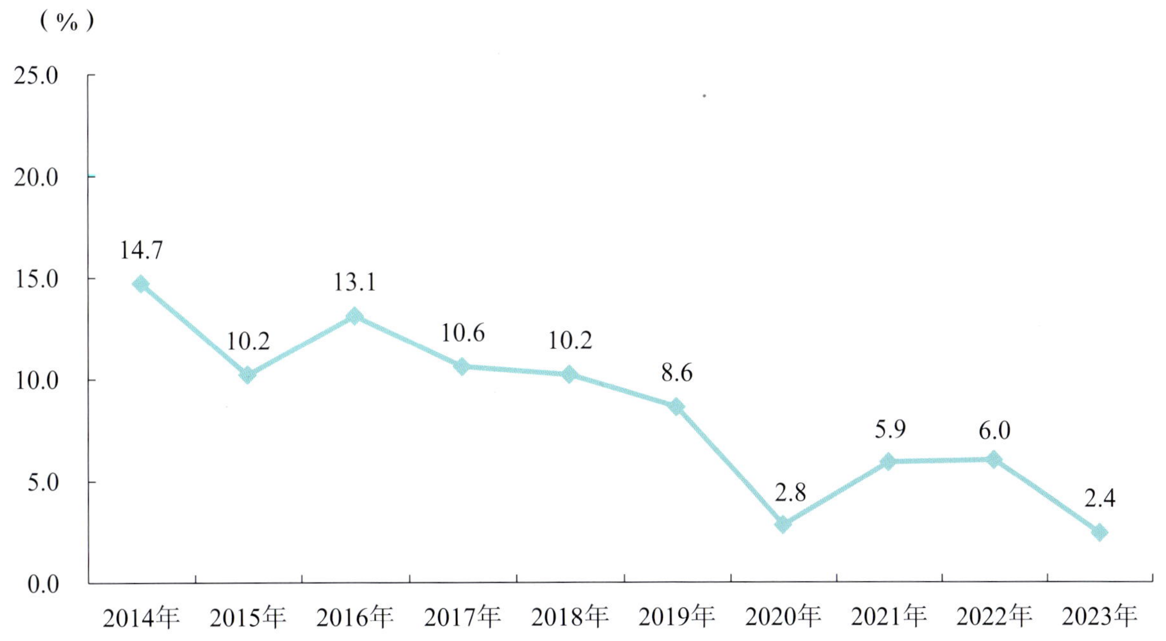

能源生产量和消费量

社会消费品零售总额

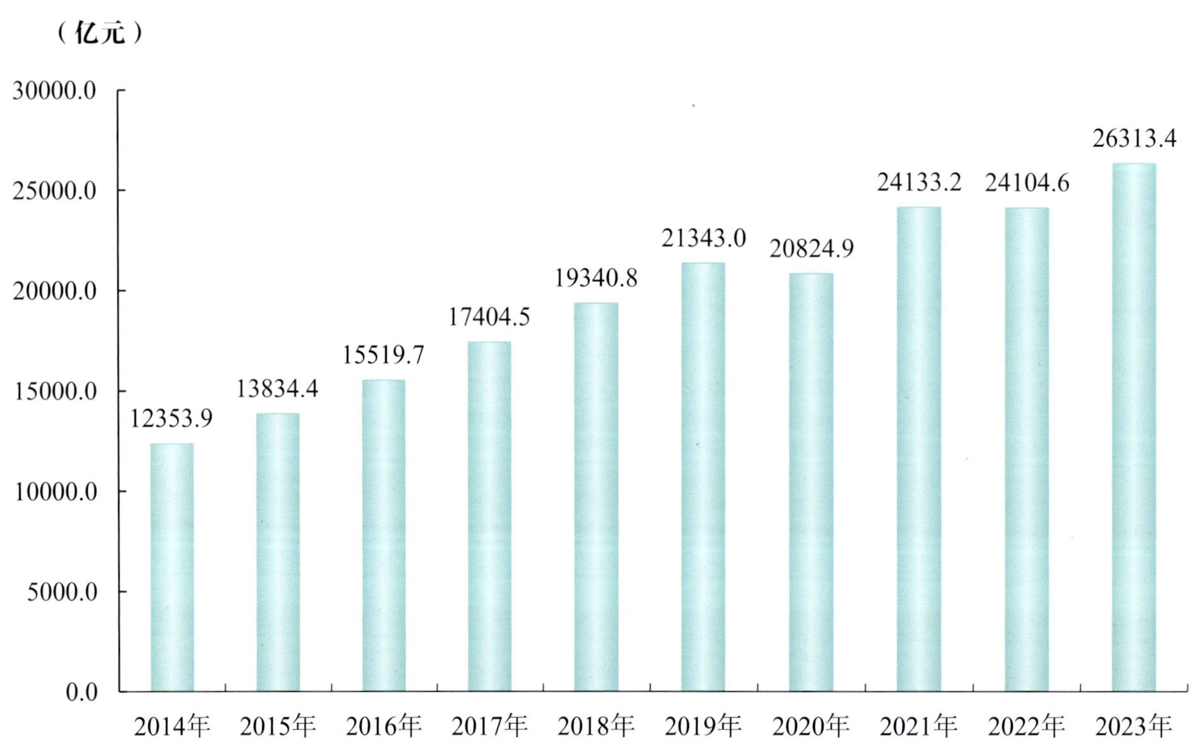

进口额和出口额

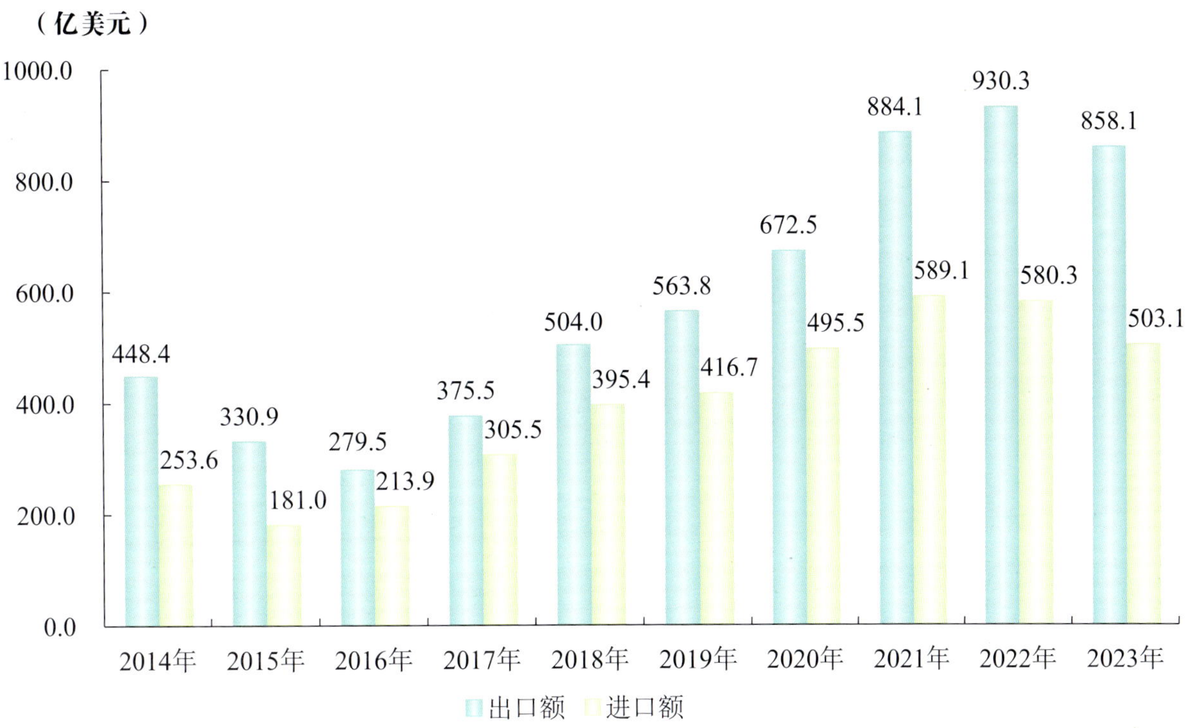

地方一般公共预算收入和支出

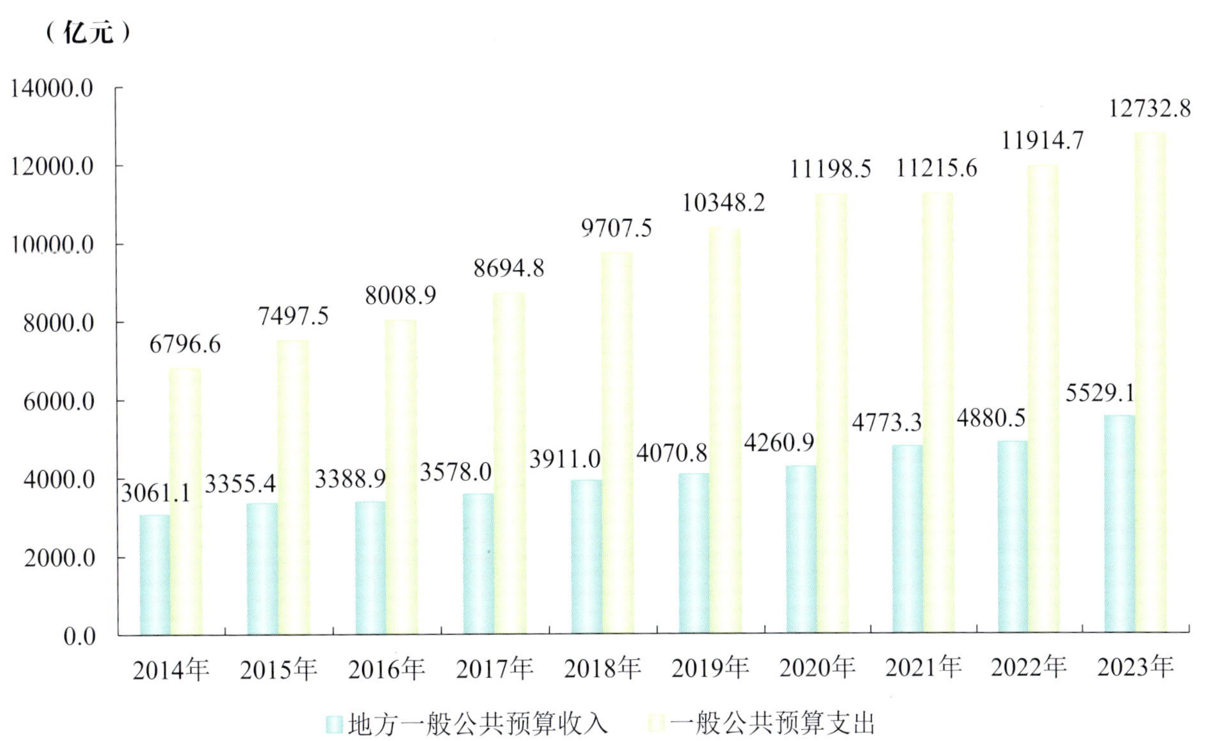

年末金融机构人民币各项存贷款余额

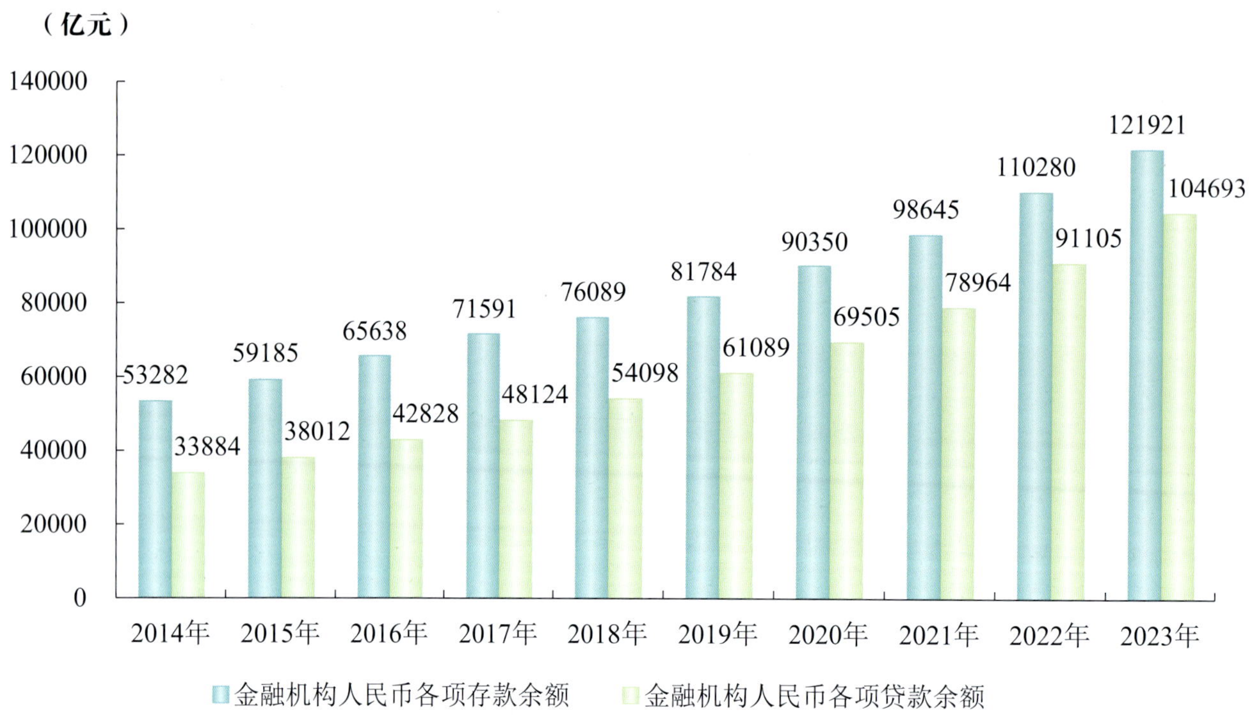

城乡居民人均可支配收入

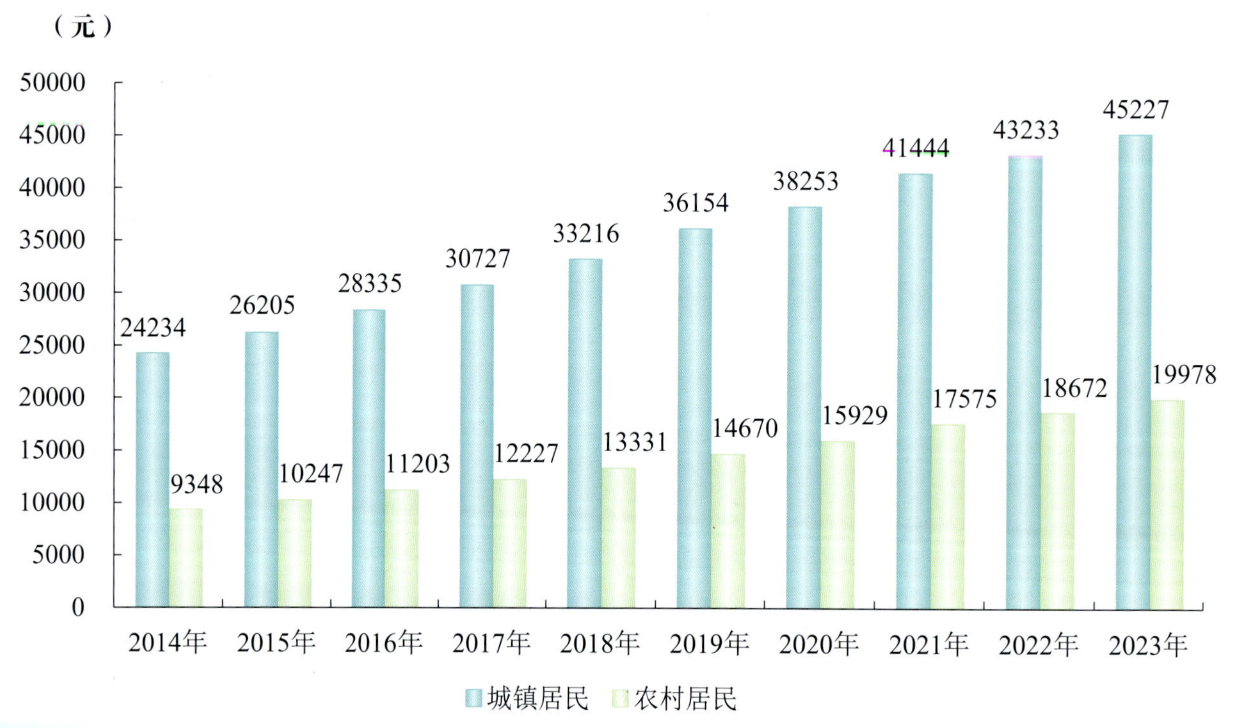

城乡居民人均消费支出

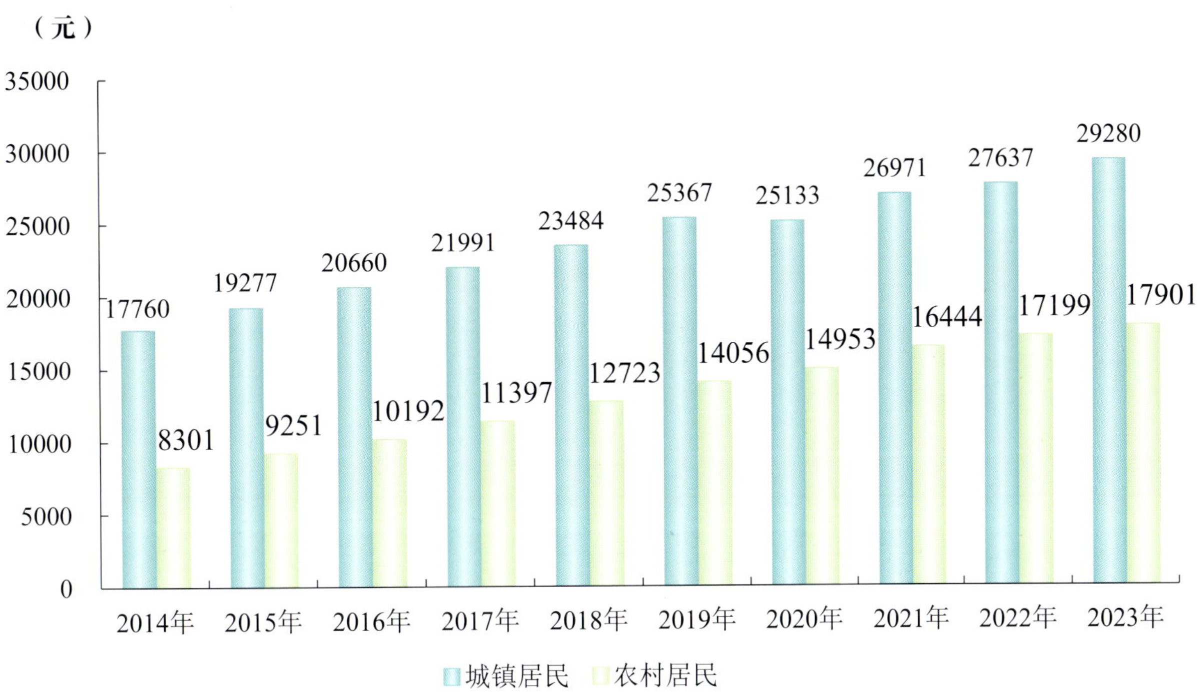

居民消费价格涨跌情况

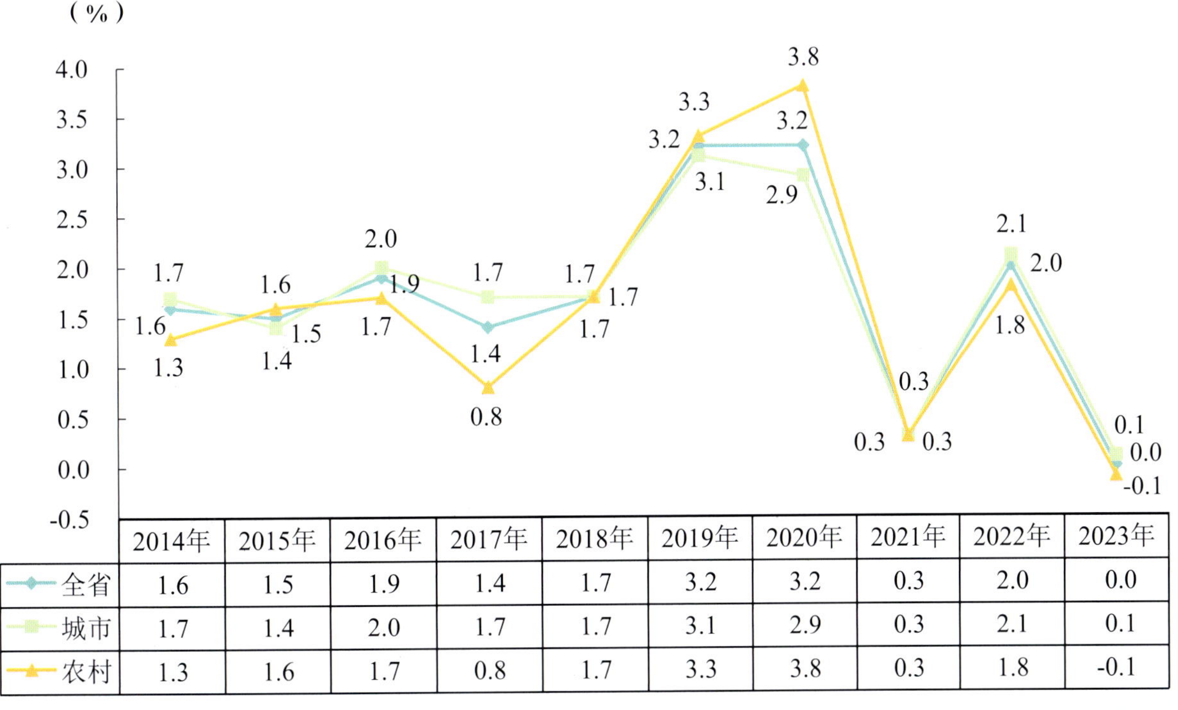

	2014年	2015年	2016年	2017年	2018年	2019年	2020年	2021年	2022年	2023年
全省	1.6	1.5	1.9	1.4	1.7	3.2	3.2	0.3	2.0	0.0
城市	1.7	1.4	2.0	1.7	1.7	3.1	2.9	0.3	2.1	0.1
农村	1.3	1.6	1.7	0.8	1.7	3.3	3.8	0.3	1.8	-0.1

工业生产者出厂价格涨跌情况

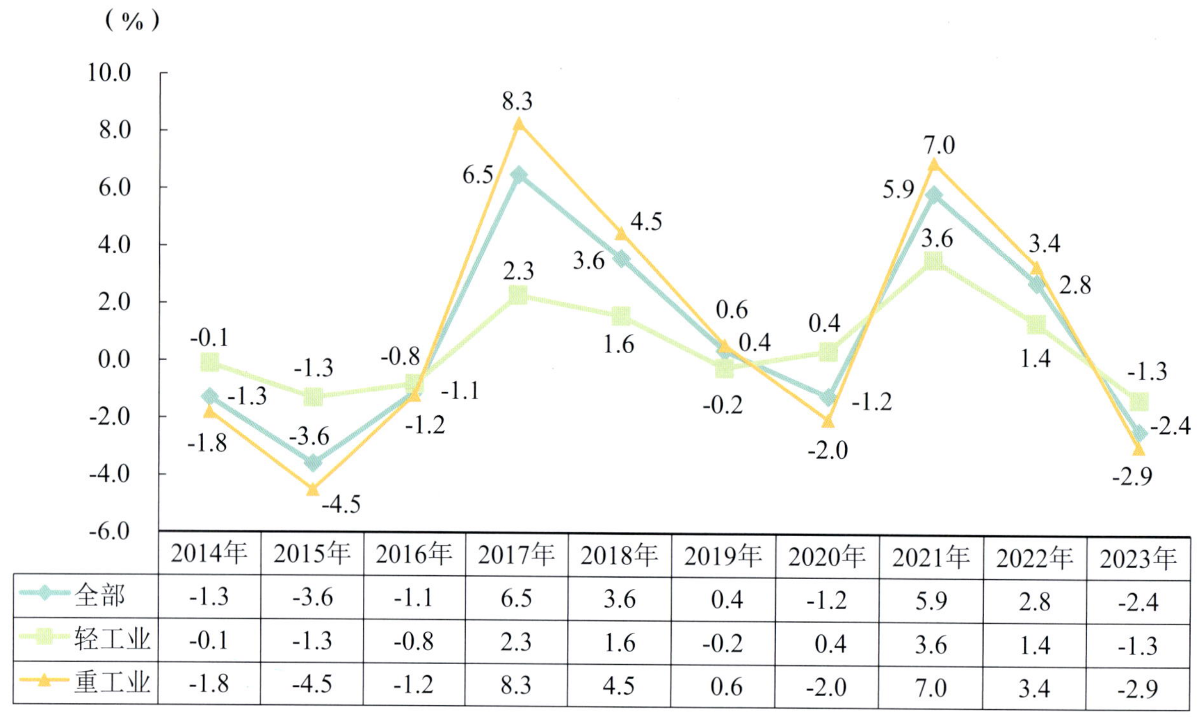

	2014年	2015年	2016年	2017年	2018年	2019年	2020年	2021年	2022年	2023年
全部	-1.3	-3.6	-1.1	6.5	3.6	0.4	-1.2	5.9	2.8	-2.4
轻工业	-0.1	-1.3	-0.8	2.3	1.6	-0.2	0.4	3.6	1.4	-1.3
重工业	-1.8	-4.5	-1.2	8.3	4.5	0.6	-2.0	7.0	3.4	-2.9

货物周转量和旅客周转量

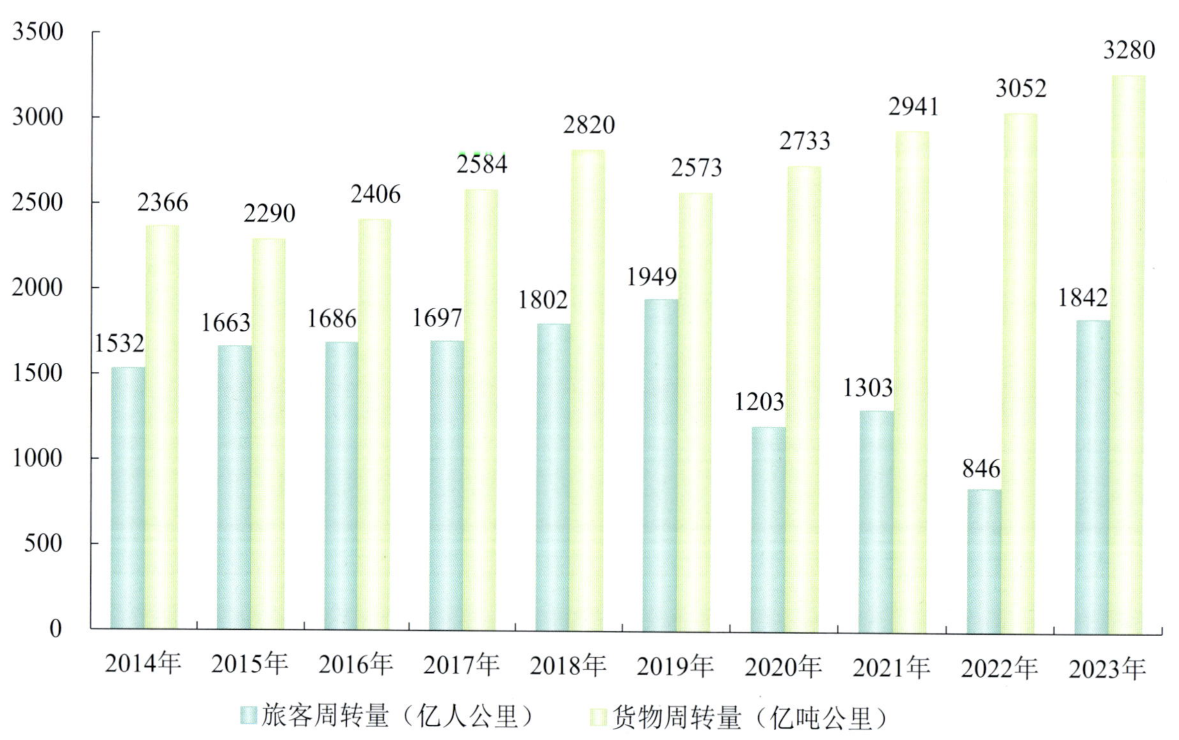

高速公路里程

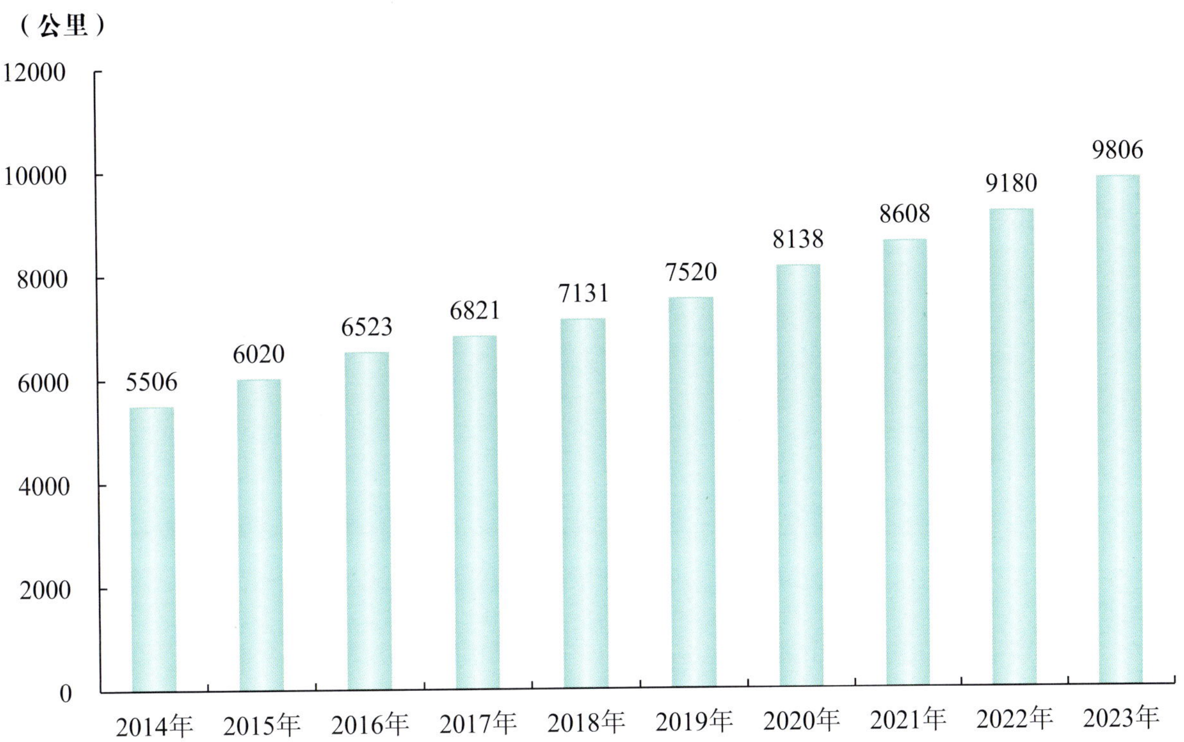

广播覆盖率和电视覆盖率

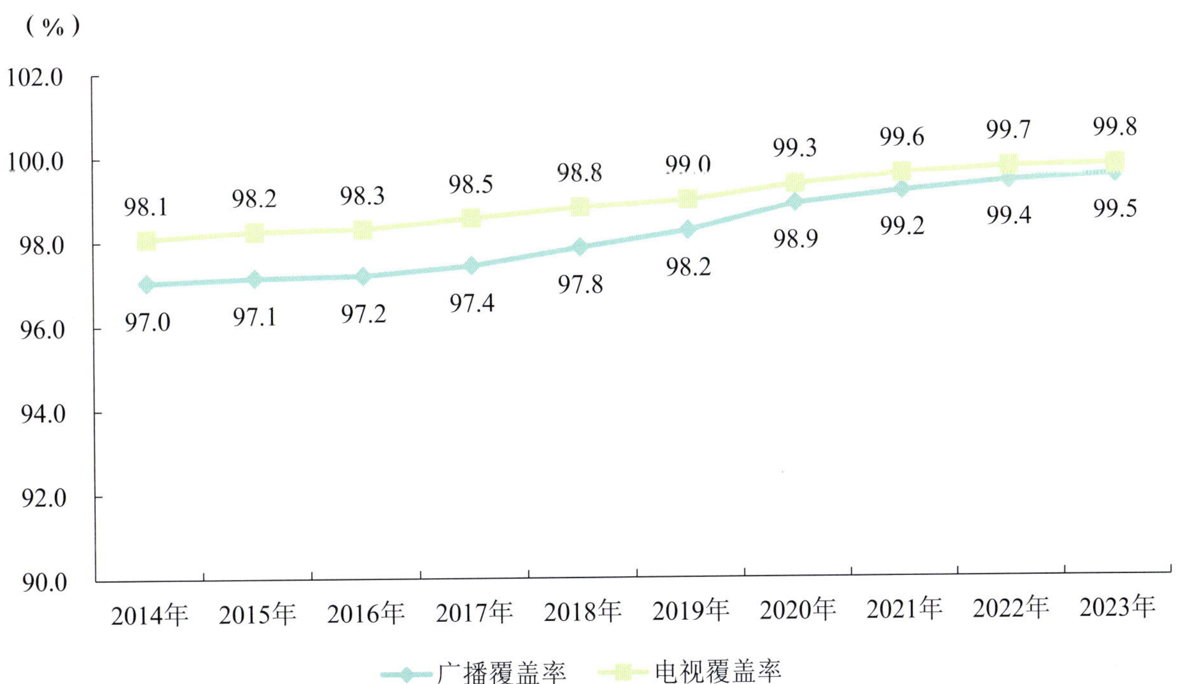

各类学校在校学生数

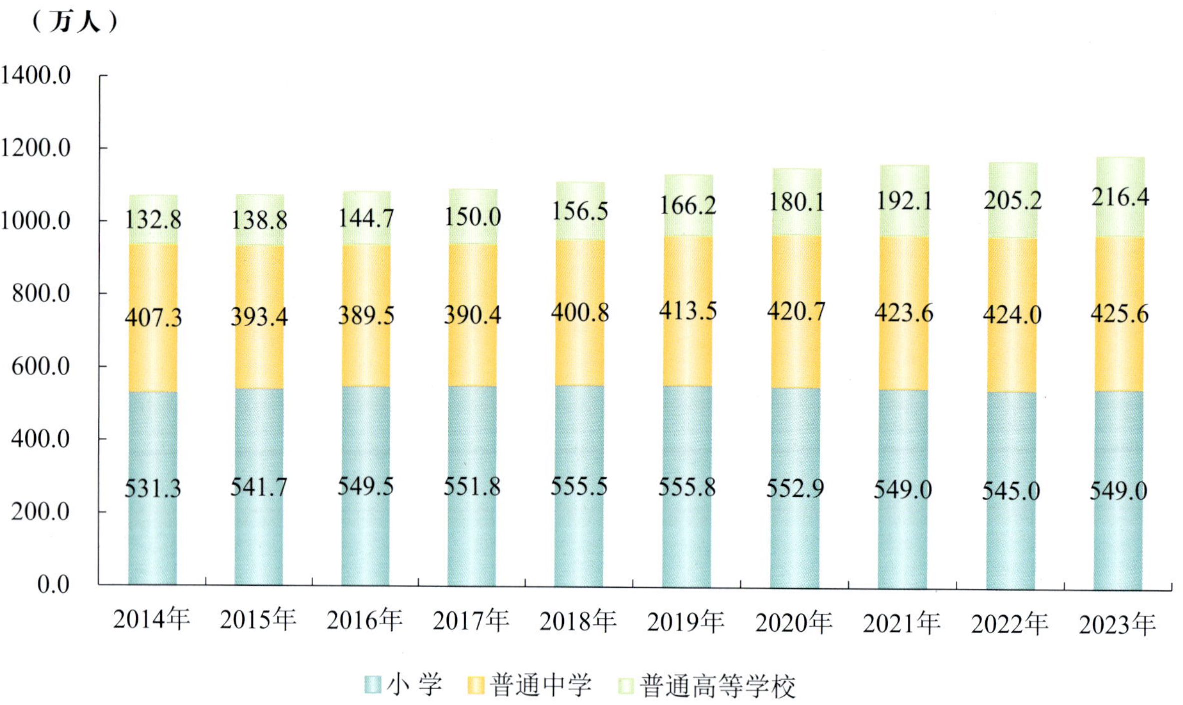

卫生机构床位数

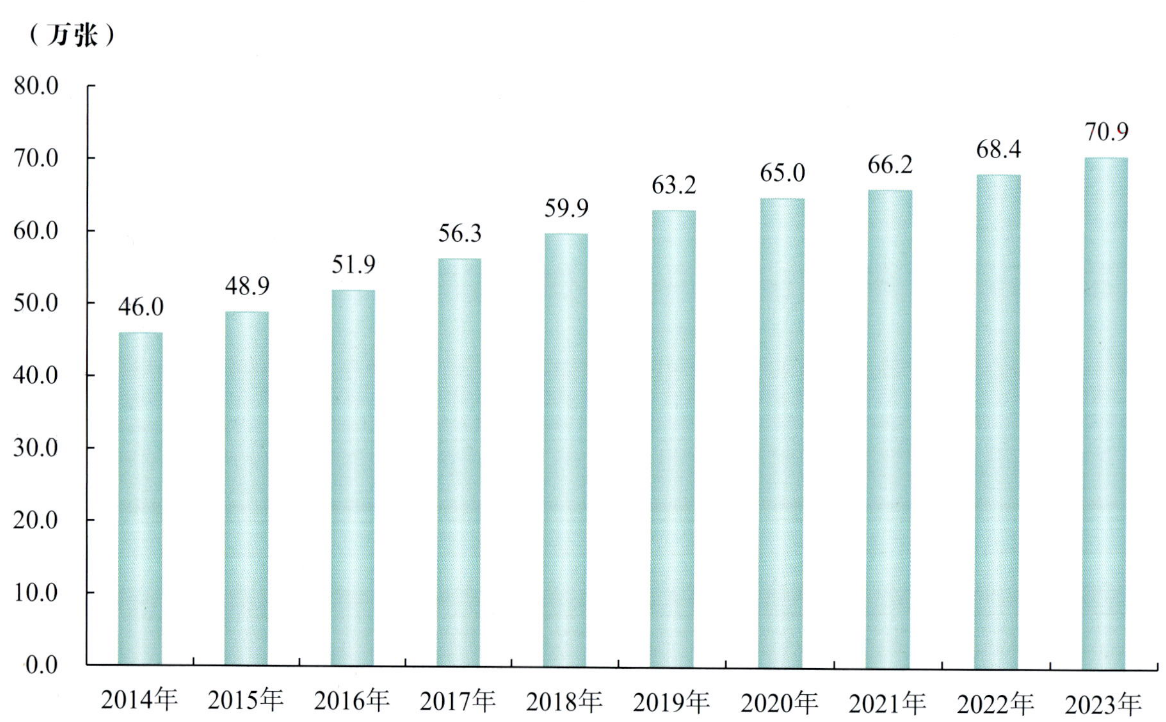

01 综 合
Chapter 1 General Survey

SICHUAN STATISTICAL YEARBOOK

1-1 各市(州)行政区划及辖区面积(2023年底)
Administrative Divisions and Area by Region (End of 2023)

单位：个、平方公里 (unit, sq.km)

市(州)	Region	县(市、区) Counties, Cities at County Level and Districts under City Administration					乡、镇、街道办事处 Township, Towns and Street Communities					辖区面积 Administrative Area
		合计 Total	市辖区 Districts under the Jurisdiction of Cities	县级市 Cities at County Level	县 Counties	自治县 Autonomous Counties	合计 Total	乡 Township	#民族乡 Ethnic Township	镇 Towns	街道 Subdistricts	
全省	**Sichuan**	**183**	**55**	**19**	**105**	**4**	**3101**	**626**	**83**	**2016**	**459**	**486052.3**
成都市	Chengdu	20	12	5	3		261			100	161	14332.3
自贡市	Zigong	6	4		2		90	2		63	25	4380.6
攀枝花市	Panzhihua	5	3		2		49	15	10	23	11	7401.4
泸州市	Luzhou	7	3		4		126	8	8	92	26	12236.2
德阳市	Deyang	6	2	3	1		84	4		67	13	5909.8
绵阳市	Mianyang	9	3	1	4	1	166	31	14	122	13	20248.4
广元市	Guangyuan	7	3		4		142	23	2	112	7	16311.1
遂宁市	Suining	5	2	1	2		95	3		72	20	5323.2
内江市	Neijiang	5	2	1	2		83			70	13	5384.7
乐山市	Leshan	11	4	1	4	2	132	18	2	103	11	12723.0
南充市	Nanchong	9	3	1	5		242	38	1	162	42	12477.2
眉山市	Meishan	6	2		4		80	5		62	13	7139.5
宜宾市	Yibin	10	3		7		136	17	12	105	14	13266.2
广安市	Guangan	6	2	1	3		124	10		99	15	6340.5
达州市	Dazhou	7	2	1	4		200	30	4	149	21	16582.0
雅安市	Yaan	8	2		6		96	29	13	57	10	15046.2
巴中市	Bazhong	5	2		3		139	6		116	17	12293.3
资阳市	Ziyang	3	1		2		89	13		67	9	5746.6
阿坝藏族羌族自治州	Aba	13		1	12		174	92	1	82		83016.3
甘孜藏族自治州	Ganzi	18		1	17		289	177	3	110	2	149599.3
凉山彝族自治州	Liangshan	17		2	14	1	304	105	13	183	16	60294.4

注：行政区划情况及辖区面积来源于《四川省行政区划简册（2023）》。

a) Data of administrative division and area are sourced from the "Sichuan Province Administrative Division Brochure (2023)".

1–2 各市(州)基层群众自治组织情况(2022年底)
Basic Statistics on Grass Roots Organizations by Region(End of 2022)

单位：个 (unit)

市(州)	Region	社区居委会 Community Neighborhood Committee	居民小组 Residents Unit	村民委员会 Villagers Committee	村民小组 Villagers Group
全省	**Sichuan**	**8285**	**59157**	**26083**	**155270**
成都市	Chengdu	1751	21512	1294	14197
自贡市	Zigong	284	954	703	6408
攀枝花市	Panzhihua	106	544	230	341
泸州市	Luzhou	344	2386	1143	10471
德阳市	Deyang	371	4199	816	8209
绵阳市	Mianyang	488	2310	1582	11695
广元市	Guangyuan	352	1016	1379	3403
遂宁市	Suining	336	1706	1109	8272
内江市	Neijiang	356	3519	924	11065
乐山市	Leshan	264	2021	1107	9275
南充市	Nanchong	789	3811	2215	6822
眉山市	Meishan	337	3171	510	4871
宜宾市	Yibin	309	1212	1792	9580
广安市	Guangan	349	2645	1366	13738
达州市	Dazhou	621	3581	1662	8352
雅安市	Yaan	105	491	554	1618
巴中市	Bazhong	493	273	1316	1384
资阳市	Ziyang	266	1844	963	6264
阿坝藏族羌族自治州	Aba	64	143	1090	3644
甘孜藏族自治州	Ganzi	70	73	2181	3285
凉山彝族自治州	Liangshan	230	1746	2147	12376

1–3 各市(州)行政区划一览表(2023年底)
Administrative Division Schedule by Region (End of 2023)

市(州) Region	县(市、区) Counties, Cities at County Level and Districts under City Administration
成都市 Chengdu	锦江区、青羊区、金牛区、武侯区、成华区、龙泉驿区、青白江区、新都区、温江区、双流区、郫都区、新津区 金堂县、大邑县、蒲江县、都江堰市、彭州市、邛崃市、崇州市、简阳市、 Jinjiang, Qingyang, Jinniu, Wuhou, Chenghua, Longquanyi, Qingbaijiang, Xindu, Wenjiang, Shuangliu, Pidu, Xinjin, Jintang, Dayi, Pujiang, Dujiangyan, Pengzhou, Qionglai, Chongzhou, Jianyang
自贡市 Zigong	自流井区、贡井区、大安区、沿滩区、荣县、富顺县 Ziliujing, Gongjing, Daan, Yantan, Rongxian, Fushun
攀枝花市 Panzhihua	东区、西区、仁和区、米易县、盐边县 Dongqu, Xiqu, Renhe, Miyi, Yanbian
泸州市 Luzhou	江阳区、纳溪区、龙马潭区、泸县、合江县、叙永县、古蔺县 Jiangyang, Naxi, Longmatan, Luxian, Hejiang, Xuyong, Gulin
德阳市 Deyang	旌阳区、罗江区、中江县、广汉市、什邡市、绵竹市 Jinyang, Luojiang, Zhongjiang, Guanghan, Shifang, Mianzhu
绵阳市 Mianyang	涪城区、游仙区、安州区、三台县、盐亭县、梓潼县、北川羌族自治县、平武县、江油市 Fucheng, Youxian, Anzhou, Santai, Yanting, Zitong, Beichuan, Pingwu, Jiangyou
广元市 Guangyuan	利州区、昭化区、朝天区、旺苍县、青川县、剑阁县、苍溪县 Lizhou, Zhaohua, Chaotian, Wangcang, Qingchuan, Jiange, Cangxi
遂宁市 Suining	船山区、安居区、蓬溪县、大英县、射洪市 Chuanshan, Anju, Pengxi, Daying, Shehong
内江市 Neijiang	市中区、东兴区、威远县、资中县、隆昌市 Downtown, Dongxing, Weiyuan, Zizhong, Longchang
乐山市 Leshan	市中区、沙湾区、五通桥区、金口河区、犍为县、井研县、夹江县、沐川县、峨边彝族自治县、马边彝族自治县、峨眉山市 Downtown, Shawan, Wutongqiao, Jinkouhe, Qianwei, Jingyan, Jiajiang, Muchuan, Ebian, Mabian, Emeishan
南充市 Nanchong	顺庆区、高坪区、嘉陵区、南部县、营山县、蓬安县、仪陇县、西充县、阆中市 Shunqing, Gaoping, Jialing, Nanbu, Yingshan, Pengan,Yilong, Xichong, Langzhong
眉山市 Meishan	东坡区、彭山区、仁寿县、洪雅县、丹棱县、青神县 Dongpo, Pengshan, Renshou, Hongya, Danling, Qingshen
宜宾市 Yibin	翠屏区、南溪区、叙州区、江安县、长宁县、高县、珙县、筠连县、兴文县、屏山县 Cuiping, Nanxi, Xuzhou, Jiangan, Changning, Gaoxian, Gongxian, Junlian, Xingwen, Pingshan
广安市 Guangan	广安区、前锋区、岳池县、武胜县、邻水县、华蓥市 Guanganqu, Qianfeng, Yuechi, Wusheng, Linshui, Huaying
达州市 Dazhou	通川区、达川区、宣汉县、开江县、大竹县、渠县、万源市 Tongchuan, Dachuan, Xuanhan, Kaijiang, Dazhu, Quxian, Wanyuan
雅安市 Yaan	雨城区、名山区、荥经县、汉源县、石棉县、天全县、芦山县、宝兴县 Yucheng, Mingshan, Yingjing, Hanyuan, Shimian, Tianquan, Lushan, Baoxing
巴中市 Bazhong	巴州区、恩阳区、通江县、南江县、平昌县 Bazhou, Enyang, Tongjiang, Nanjiang, Pingchang
资阳市 Ziyang	雁江区、安岳县、乐至县 Yanjiang, Anyue, Lezhi
阿坝藏族羌族自治州 Aba	马尔康市、汶川县、理县、茂县、松潘县、九寨沟县、金川县、小金县、黑水县、壤塘县、阿坝县、若尔盖县、红原县 Maerkang, Wenchuan, Lixian, Maoxian, Songpan, Jiuzhaigou, Jinchuan, Xiaojin, Heishui, Rangtang, Abaxian, Ruoergai, Hongyuan
甘孜藏族自治州 Ganzi	康定市、泸定县、丹巴县、九龙县、雅江县、道孚县、炉霍县、甘孜县、新龙县、德格县、白玉县、石渠县、色达县、理塘县、巴塘县、乡城县、稻城县、得荣县 Kangding, Luding, Danba, Jiulong, Yajiang, Daofu, Luhuo, Ganzixian, Xinlong, Dege, Baiyu, Shiqu, Seda, Litang, Batang, Xiangcheng, Daocheng, Derong
凉山彝族自治州 Liangshan	西昌市、会理市、木里藏族自治县、盐源县、德昌县、会东县、宁南县、普格县、布拖县、金阳县、昭觉县、喜德县、冕宁县、越西县、甘洛县、美姑县、雷波县 Xichang, Huili, Muli, Yanyuan, Dechang, Huidong, Ningnan, Puge, Butuo, Jinyang, Zhaojue, Xide, Mianning, Yuexi, Ganluo, Meigu, Leibo

1-4 新中国成立75年来四川省国民经济和社会发展总量与速度指标

指标		Item	
人口		**Population**	
年末常住人口	(万人)	Total Resident Population (year-end)	(10 000 persons)
年末户籍人口	(万人)	Total Registered Population (year-end)	(10 000 persons)
#男性	(万人)	Male	(10 000 persons)
女性	(万人)	Female	(10 000 persons)
#城镇	(万人)	Urban	(10 000 persons)
乡村	(万人)	Rural	(10 000 persons)
就业		**Employment**	
就业人员合计	(万人)	Employment	(10 000 persons)
按三次产业分		By Three Strata of Industry	
第一产业	(万人)	Primary Industry	(10 000 persons)
第二产业	(万人)	Secondary Industry	(10 000 persons)
第三产业	(万人)	Tertiary Industry	(10 000 persons)
按城乡分		By Residence in Urban and Rural	
城镇就业人员	(万人)	Urban Employees	(10 000 persons)
乡村就业人员	(万人)	Rural Employees	(10 000 persons)
国民经济核算		**National Accounting**	
地区生产总值	(亿元)	Gross Regional Product	(100 million yuan)
第一产业	(亿元)	Primary Industry	(100 million yuan)
第二产业	(亿元)	Secondary Industry	(100 million yuan)
第三产业	(亿元)	Tertiary Industry	(100 million yuan)
人均地区生产总值	(元)	Per Capita Gross Regional Product	(yuan)
人民生活		**People's Livelihood**	
全体居民人均可支配收入	(元)	Per Capita Disposable Income of Total Residents	(yuan)
#工资性收入	(元)	Income of Wages and Salaries	(yuan)
全体居民人均消费支出	(元)	Per Capita Living Expenditures for Consumption of Total Residents	(yuan)
#食品烟酒支出	(元)	Food, Tobacco and Liquor	(yuan)
全体居民恩格尔系数	(%)	Engle Coefficient of All Residents	(%)

Principal Aggregate Indicators on National Economy and Social Development and the Related Growth Rates of SiChuan Provence in 75 Years Since The founding of People's Republic of China

总量指标 Aggregate Indicator				指数(%) Index(%) (2023年为以下各年) (2023 as Percentage of the Following Years)			平均增长速度(%) Average Annual Growth Rate(%)		
1952	1978	2012	2023	1952	1978	2012	1953～2023	1979～2023	2013～2023
		8085.0	8368.0			103.5			0.3
4628.5	7071.9	9097.4	9071.4	196.0	128.3	99.7	1.0	0.6	
2357.9	3621.5	4685.0	4640.3	196.8	128.1	99.0	1.0	0.6	-0.1
2270.6	3450.4	4412.4	4431.1	195.2	128.4	100.4	0.9	0.6	
	784.2	2512.0	3559.9		454.0	141.7		3.4	3.2
	6287.7	6585.4	5511.5		87.7	83.7		-0.3	-1.6
2027.9	3087.0	4635.0	4722.0	232.9	153.0	101.9	1.2	0.9	0.2
1753.9	2524.2	1905.0	1535.0	87.5	60.8	80.6	-0.2	-1.1	-1.9
89.4	279.5	1173.0	1100.0	1230.4	393.6	93.8	3.6	3.1	-0.6
184.7	283.3	1557.0	2087.0	1129.9	736.7	134.0	3.5	4.5	2.7
196.3	465.5	1746.4	2545.0	1296.3	546.7	145.7	3.7	3.8	3.5
1831.6	2621.5	2888.6	2177.0	118.9	83.0	75.4	0.2	-0.4	-2.5
24.61	184.61	23922.41	60132.88	24072.0	6383.3	213.1	8.0	9.7	7.1
14.56	82.20	3142.55	6056.64	1450.7	823.3	155.8	3.8	4.8	4.1
3.67	65.55	11231.06	21306.70	164557.7	12975.9	210.4	11.0	11.4	7.0
6.38	36.86	9548.80	32769.54	60360.0	11537.3	230.7	9.4	11.1	7.9
53	261	29627	71835	13429.7	5398.1	205.2	7.1	9.3	6.8
		12753	32514			255.0			8.9
			16154						
		9837	23550			239.4			8.3
			7846						

1-4 续表 1

指标		Item	
城镇居民人均可支配收入	(元)	Per Capita Disposable Income of Urban Residents	(yuan)
#工资性收入	(元)	Income of Wages and Salaries	(yuan)
城镇居民人均消费支出	(元)	Per Capita Living Expenditures for Consumption of Urban Residents	(yuan)
#食品烟酒支出	(元)	Food, Tobacco and Liquor	(yuan)
城镇居民恩格尔系数	(%)	Engle Coefficient of Urban Households of Urban Residents	(%)
农村居民人均可支配收入	(元)	Annual per Capita Disposable Income of Rural Residents	(yuan)
农村居民人均生活消费支出	(元)	Expenditure for Consumption of Rural Residents	(yuan)
#食品烟酒支出	(元)	Food, Tobacco and Liquor	(yuan)
农村居民恩格尔系数	(%)	Engle Coefficient of Urban Households of Rural Residents	(%)
全部单位就业人员工资总额	(亿元)	Total Wages of Staff and Workers in all Units	(100 million yuan)
全部单位就业人员平均工资	(元)	Average Money Wages of Staff and Workers in all Units	(yuan)
财政		**Government Finance**	
地方一般公共预算收入	(亿元)	Local General Public Budget Revenue	(100 million yuan)
一般公共预算支出	(亿元)	Local General Public Budget Expenditure	(100 million yuan)
能源		**Energy**	
一次能源生产总量	(万吨标准煤)	Primary Energy Output	(10 000 tons SCE)
能源消费总量	(万吨标准煤)	Total Energy Consumption	(10 000 tons SCE)
房地产		**Real Estate**	
房地产完成投资额	(亿元)	Completed Investment of Real Estate	(100 million yuan)
农业		**Agriculture**	
农林牧渔业总产值	(亿元)	Gross Output Value of Farming, Forestry, Animal Husbandry and Fishery	(100 million yuan)
#农业	(亿元)	Farming	(100 million yuan)
牧业	(亿元)	Animal Husbandry	(100 million yuan)
粮食产量	(万吨)	Grain Yield	(10 000 tons)
油料产量	(万吨)	Oil Bearing Crops Yield	(10 000 tons)
蔬菜及食用菌产量	(万吨)	Yield of Vegetables and Edible Fungi	(10 000 tons)
水果产量	(万吨)	Yield of Fruits	(10 000 tons)
水产品产量	(万吨)	Output of Aquatic Products	(10 000 tons)
肉猪出栏头数	(万头)	Number of Slaughtered Fattened Hogs	(10 000 heads)
猪年末头数	(万头)	Number of Hogs (year-end)	(10 000 heads)
牛年末头数	(万头)	Number of Oxen (year-end)	(10 000 heads)

continued

总量指标 Aggregate Indicator				指数(%) Index(%) (2023年为以下各年) (2023 as Percentage of the Following Years)			平均增长速度(%) Average Annual Growth Rate(%)		
1952	1978	2012	2023	1952	1978	2012	1953～2023	1979～2023	2013～2023
	338	20180	45227		13380.8	224.1		11.5	7.6
			26228						
	314	14824	29280		9324.8	197.5		10.6	6.4
			9614						
			32.8						
	117	7432	19978		17075.2	268.8		12.1	9.4
		6265	17901			285.7			10.0
			6103						
			34.1						
	26.3	3772.4	13473.7		51192.6	357.2		14.9	12.3
319.0	590.0	35873.0	90220.1	28282.2	15291.5	251.5	8.3	11.8	8.7
	37.3	2421.3	5529.1		14819.3	228.4		11.7	7.8
	35.7	5451.0	12732.8		35646.1	233.6		13.9	8.0
	2552.0	14735.1							
	2552.0	18376.0							
		3266.4	5320.6			162.9			4.5
21.7	95.7	5433.1	9977.8	1774.3	861.3	159.6	4.1	4.9	4.3
18.5	73.9	2764.9	5821.7	905.3	484.6	166.0	3.2	3.6	4.7
2.8	18.2	2177.0	3035.6	6073.7	1980.3	141.8	6.0	6.9	3.2
1170.1	2381.8	3271.3	3593.8	307.1	150.9	109.9	1.6	0.9	0.9
25.2	52.8	315.9	438.6	1740.6	830.8	138.9	4.1	4.8	3.0
		3569.2	5417.9			151.8			3.9
10.3	17.8	791.4	1490.4	14469.4	8372.8	188.3	7.3	10.3	5.9
0.8	3.1	116.8	178.9	22082.0	5845.2	153.1	7.9	9.5	3.9
393.0	1614.0	7170.7	6662.7	1695.3	412.8	92.9	4.1	3.2	-0.7
943.0	3243.0	4718.5	3855.0	408.8	118.9	81.7	2.0	0.4	-1.8
		238.2	316.4			132.8			2.6

1-4 续表 2

指标		Item	
肉类总产量	(万吨)	Output of Meat	(10 000 tons)
#猪肉	(万吨)	Output of Pork	(10 000 tons)
农作物总播种面积	(万公顷)	Total Sown Areas	(10 000 hectares)
#粮食	(万公顷)	Sown Areas of Grain Crops	(10 000 hectares)
化肥施用量	(万吨)	Consumption of Chemical Fertilizers	(10 000 tons)
#氮肥	(万吨)	Nitrogen	(10 000 tons)
造林面积	(万公顷)	Afforestation Area	(10 000 hectares)
规模以上工业企业		**Industrial Enterprises above Designated Size**	
主要财务指标		Principal Financial Indicators	
资产总计	(亿元)	Total Assets	(100 million yuan)
负债合计	(亿元)	Total Liability	(100 million yuan)
所有者权益合计	(亿元)	Owners' Equities	(100 million yuan)
营业收入	(亿元)	Business Revenue	(100 million yuan)
营业成本	(亿元)	Business Cost	(100 million yuan)
利润总额	(亿元)	Total Profits	(100 million yuan)
平均用工人数	(万人)	Number of Average Employed Persons	(10 000 persons)
主要产品产量		Output of Major Products	
布	(亿米)	Cloth	(100 million m)
机制纸及纸板	(万吨)	Machine-made Paper and Paperboards	(10 000 tons)
原盐	(万吨)	Salt	(10 000 tons)
卷烟	(亿支)	Cigarettes	(100 million pieces)
白酒(商品量)	(万千升)	Liquor	(10 000 kiloliter)
天然气	(亿立方米)	Natural Gas	(100 million cu.m)
发电量	(亿千瓦小时)	Electricity	(100 million kwh)
#水电	(亿千瓦小时)	Hydropower	(100 million kwh)
生铁	(万吨)	Pig Iron	(10 000 tons)
粗钢	(万吨)	Crude Steel	(10 000 tons)
成品钢材	(万吨)	Steel Products	(10 000 tons)
水泥	(万吨)	Cement	(10 000 tons)
农用氮、磷、钾化学肥料(折纯)	(万吨)	Chemical Fertilizer	(10 000 tons)

注：2017年及以前营业收入、营业成本分别为主营业务收入、主营业务成本。

continued

总量指标 Aggregate Indicator				指数(%) Index(%) (2023年为以下各年) (2023 as Percentage of the Following Years)			平均增长速度(%) Average Annual Growth Rate(%)		
1952	1978	2012	2023	1952	1978	2012	1953～2023	1979～2023	2013～2023
17.10	78.00	663.16	697.09	4076.6	893.7	105.1	5.4	5.0	0.5
15.60	76.00	496.40	489.70	3139.1	644.3	98.7	5.0	4.2	-0.1
827.70	885.90	932.00	1026.44	124.0	115.9	110.1	0.3	0.3	0.9
686.30	744.10	625.60	640.40	93.3	86.1	102.4	-0.1	-0.3	0.2
0.40	62.50	252.80	202.16	50539.7	323.5	80.0	9.2	2.6	-2.0
0.40	46.40	127.91	74.47	18618.6	160.5	58.2	7.6	1.1	-4.8
2.13	20.05	11.22							
		30362.89	74351.86			244.9			8.5
		18721.46	41696.84			222.7			7.6
		11471.16	32653.12			284.7			10.0
		31427.16	50393.25			160.3			4.4
		25755.76	40861.66			158.7			4.3
		2333.76	4607.14			197.4			6.4
		391.44	304.40			77.8			-2.3
1.6	5.2	14.2	10.2	653.8	196.9	71.8	2.7	1.5	-3.0
1.6	26.4	237.1	343.7	21347.8	1301.9	145.0	7.8	5.9	3.4
42.6	127.7	476.4	545.2	1280.4	427.1	114.4	3.7	3.3	1.2
2.4	50.4	978.9	913.9	38079.2	1814.4	93.4	8.7	6.7	-0.6
		295.2	174.1			59.0			-4.7
0.1	60.8	242.1	594.8	991333.3	978.5	245.7	13.8	5.2	8.5
2.5	139.3	2002.4	4712.6	189259.4	3383.0	235.3	11.2	8.1	8.1
0.3	54.8	1410.7	3583.3	1279767.0	6541.3	254.0	14.2	9.7	8.8
9.2	224.0	1670.2	1983.6	21631.4	885.6	118.8	7.9	5.0	1.6
5.0	238.2	1674.3	2688.8	53992.0	1128.9	160.6	9.3	5.5	4.4
11.2	174.0	2281.6	4045.9	36027.6	2325.0	177.3	8.6	7.2	5.3
4.4	454.8	13342.1	12151.6	276172.7	2671.7	91.1	11.8	7.6	-0.8
	102.5	425.3	316.5		308.8	74.4		2.5	-2.7

a) The data of business revenue and business cost are revenue from principal business and cost of principal business respectively in 2017 and before.

1-4 续表 3

指标		Item	
贸易		**Trade**	
社会消费品零售总额	(亿元)	Total Retail Sales of Consumer Goods	(100 million yuan)
城镇	(亿元)	Retail Sales in Town	(100 million yuan)
乡村	(亿元)	Retail Sales in Rural	(100 million yuan)
进出口总额	(亿美元)	Total Import and Export	(USD 100 million)
出口总额	(亿美元)	Total Export	(USD 100 million)
进口总额	(亿美元)	Total Import	(USD 100 million)
交通运输		**Transportation**	
铁路营业里程	(公里)	Railways in Operation	(km)
公路里程	(万公里)	Highways	(10 000 km)
#高速公路	(公里)	Expressway	(km)
民用汽车拥有量	(万辆)	Possession of Civil Motor Vehicles	(10 000 units)
#私人汽车	(万辆)	Private	(10 000 units)
旅客周转量	(亿人公里)	Passenger-Kilometers	(100 million passenger-km)
货物周转量	(亿吨公里)	Freight Traffic	(100 million ton-km)
文化、教育和卫生		**Culture, Education and Health**	
图书出版总印数	(万册)	Total Printed Copies of Published Books	(10 000 copies)
杂志出版总印数	(万册)	Total Printed Copies of Published Magazines	(10 000 copies)
报纸出版总印数	(万份)	Total Printed Copies of Published Newspapers	(10 000 copies)
专任教师数		Full-time Teachers	
普通高等学校	(万人)	Regular Institutions of Higher Education	(10 000 persons)
普通中学	(万人)	Regular Secondary Schools	(10 000 persons)
小学	(万人)	Primary Schools	(10 000 persons)
在校学生数		Number of Students Enrollment	
普通高等学校	(万人)	Regular Institutions of Higher Education	(10 000 persons)
普通中学	(万人)	Regular Secondary Schools	(10 000 persons)
小学	(万人)	Primary Schools	(10 000 persons)
医院数	(个)	Number of Hospitals	(unit)
医院床位数	(万张)	Number of Beds in Hospital	(10 000 bed)

continued

总量指标 Aggregate Indicator				指数(%) Index(%) (2023年为以下各年) (2023 as Percentage of the Following Years)			平均增长速度(%) Average Annual Growth Rate(%)		
1952	1978	2012	2023	1952	1978	2012	1953～2023	1979～2023	2013～2023
14.00	61.60	9606.44	26313.40	187952.9	42716.6	273.9	11.2	14.4	9.6
		7874.90	21994.04			279.3			9.8
		1758.50	4319.35			245.6			8.5
	0.41	591.44	1361.14		334678.6	230.1		19.8	7.9
	0.19	384.69	858.08		450434.6	223.1		20.6	7.6
	0.22	206.75	503.06		232682.6	243.3		18.8	8.4
124	2813	3510	6471	5218.5	230.0	184.4	5.7	1.9	5.7
0.9	8.2	29.4	41.8	4496.8	507.5	142.5	5.5	3.7	3.3
		4334	9806			226.3			7.7
		493.2	1542.5			312.8			10.9
		408.9	1363.0			333.3			11.6
	86.7	1744.3	1841.9		2125.1	105.6		7.0	0.5
	215.8	2133.2	3279.7		1519.8	153.7		6.2	4.0
1481	24993	23587	43714	2951.7	174.9	185.3	4.9	1.3	5.8
565	562	9066	4589	812.2	816.5	50.6	3.0	4.8	-6.0
6799	51889	172573	90530	1331.5	174.5	52.5	3.7	1.2	-5.7
0.12	0.90	7.31	11.02	8972.5	1217.9	150.7	6.5	5.7	3.8
0.60	16.75	29.04	33.98	5707.2	202.8	117.0	5.9	1.6	1.4
11.12	34.27	30.49	35.20	316.5	102.7	115.5	1.6	0.1	1.3
0.91	3.57	122.37	216.41	23771.2	6059.4	176.9	8.0	9.5	5.3
15.53	383.88	455.84	425.58	2741.2	110.9	93.4	4.8	0.2	-0.6
380.78	1074.59	560.74	549.05	144.2	51.1	97.9	0.5	-1.5	-0.2
		1542	2479			160.8			4.4
		25.73	53.32			207.2			6.8

1-5 国民经济和社会发展比例和效益指标
Proportions and Efficiency Indicators on National Economy and Social Development

指标		Item		1952	1978	2012	2023
人口		**Population**					
出生率	(‰)	Birth Rate	(‰)	41.0	15.1	9.9	6.3
死亡率	(‰)	Death Rate	(‰)	18.2	7.0	6.9	9.4
自然增长率	(‰)	Natural Growth Rate	(‰)	22.8	8.1	3.0	-3.1
国民经济核算		**National Accounting**					
人均地区生产总值	(元)	Per Capita GDP	(yuan)	53	261	29627	71835
人民生活		**People's Living Conditions**					
城乡收入比(农村居民收入为1)		Urban and Rural Income Ratio(Rural Income as 1)			2.7	2.9	2.3
财政		**Government Finance**					
地方一般公共预算收入与地区生产总值之比	(%)	Local General Public Budget Income to GDP	(%)		20.2	10.1	9.2
一般公共预算支出与地区生产总值之比	(%)	Local general public budget expenditure to GDP	(%)		19.3	22.8	21.2
农业		**Agriculture**					
每公顷播种面积农产品产量		Output of Farm Crops per Hectare of Sown Area					
粮食	(公斤)	Grain	(kg)		3201	5229	5612
油料	(公斤)	Oilseeds	(kg)		1278	2308	2537
国内贸易		**Domestic Trade**					
人均社会消费品零售总额	(元)	Per Capita Retail Sales of Consumer Goods	(yuan)		87	11897	31434
金融		**Financial Intermediation**					
金融机构人民币各项存款与地区生产总值之比	(%)	Financial institutions RMB Bank Deposits as Percentage of GDP	(%)		34.2	171.9	202.8
金融机构人民币各项贷款与地区生产总值之比	(%)	Financial institutions RMB Bank Loans as Percentage of GDP	(%)		39.8	106.8	174.1
教育		**Education**					
每万人口普通高等学校在校大学生数	(人)	Number of College Students per 10000 Population	(person)		5.0	151.5	258.5
文化		**Culture**					
每百万人有公共图书馆	(个)	Number of Public Libraries per Million Persons	(unit)		0.8	2.3	2.5
每百万人有文化馆、文化站	(个)	Number of Cultural Centers and Stations per Million Persons	(unit)		2.6	59.4	51.0
人均年出版报纸	(份)	Annual Number of Newspaper Published per Capita	(copy)		7.3	21.4	10.8
人均年出版图书、杂志	(册)	Annual Number of Books and Magazines Published per Capita	(copy)		3.6	4.0	5.8
卫生		**Public Health**					
每万人口医院数	(个)	Number of Hospitals per 10000 Population	(unit)		0.1	0.2	0.3
每万人口医院床位数	(张)	Number of Beds of Hospitals per 10000 Population	(bed)		8.8	31.9	63.7

注：人均指标均按年平均常住人口计算。

a) The per capita data is calculated by average permanent resident population.

1-6 国民经济和社会发展结构指标
Composition Indicators on National Economic and Social Development

单位：%　　(%)

指标	Item	1952	1978	2012	2023
户籍人口结构	**Structure of Resident Population**				
城镇人口	Urban Population		11.1	27.6	39.2
乡村人口	Rural Population		88.9	72.4	60.8
就业人员结构	**Employment Structure**				
第一产业	Primary Industry	86.5	81.8	41.1	32.5
第二产业	Secondary Industry	4.4	9.1	25.3	23.3
第三产业	Tertiary Industry	9.1	9.2	33.6	44.2
地区生产总值结构	**GDP Structure**				
第一产业	Primary Industry	59.2	44.5	13.1	10.1
第二产业	Secondary Industry	14.9	35.5	46.9	35.4
第三产业	Tertiary Industry	25.9	20.0	39.9	54.5
进出口总额构成	**Composition of Total Import and Export**				
出口	Export		46.8	65.0	63.0
进口	Import		53.2	35.0	37.0
第一产业总产值构成	**Composition of Gross Output Value of Primary Industry**				
农业	Farming	84.9	77.2	51.8	60.0
林业	Forestry	2.3	3.3	4.4	5.0
牧业	Animal Husbandry	12.8	19.0	40.8	31.3
渔业	Fishery		0.4	3.1	3.7
旅客周转量构成	**Composition of Passenger-Kilometers**				
铁路	Railways		57.0	14.9	27.6
公路	Highways		39.2	57.6	12.3
水路	Waterways		1.0	0.2	0.1
民用航空	Civil Aviation		2.7	27.3	60.0
货物周转量构成	**Composition of Freight Ton-kilometers**				
铁路	Railways		84.8	32.5	30.1
公路	Highways		10.7	62.1	60.5
水路	Waterways		4.5	4.9	8.9
民用航空	Civil Aviation			0.5	0.5

1-7 按主要行业分法人单位数(2022年)
Number of Legal Entities by Sector(2022)

单位：个 (unit)

市(州)	Region	合计 Total	农、林、牧、渔业 Agriculture, Forestry, Animal Husbandry and Fishery	采矿业 Mining	制造业 Manufacturing	电力、热力、燃气及水生产和供应业 Production and Supply of Electricity,Heat, Gas and Water	建筑业 Construction	批发和零售业 Wholesale and Retail Trades
全省	**Sichuan**	**1595315**	**148381**	**4763**	**97886**	**7755**	**137005**	**392191**
成都市	Chengdu	715978	18241	187	35586	1129	69623	198359
自贡市	Zigong	33187	4036	127	3362	187	2402	7702
攀枝花市	Panzhihua	23112	2017	529	1416	232	1261	7394
泸州市	Luzhou	62076	5276	184	4681	378	5297	17292
德阳市	Deyang	57495	5077	103	9386	315	3967	12801
绵阳市	Mianyang	97631	11056	248	7738	426	9647	22140
广元市	Guangyuan	36204	6392	242	2104	159	3344	6034
遂宁市	Suining	39291	7151	68	2272	160	3419	8334
内江市	Neijiang	33206	5236	171	2388	225	1885	7301
乐山市	Leshan	41012	3836	342	2842	404	2980	10558
南充市	Nanchong	71226	10710	125	3618	282	7102	14322
眉山市	Meishan	47711	6653	103	3733	286	3710	9922
宜宾市	Yibin	55492	9019	340	3914	421	3935	12723
广安市	Guangan	34622	5477	100	2325	256	3143	7373
达州市	Dazhou	63265	12447	434	3675	394	3969	16298
雅安市	Yaan	27567	3135	303	2370	672	1746	6725
巴中市	Bazhong	32956	6873	75	1336	264	2671	5139
资阳市	Ziyang	25856	4003	5	1902	82	2270	6004
阿坝藏族羌族自治州	Aba	20426	6225	152	750	293	907	2697
甘孜藏族自治州	Ganzi	20779	3456	168	522	284	896	2588
凉山彝族自治州	Liangshan	56223	12065	757	1966	906	2831	10485

注：建筑业企业按照法人单位注册地原则进行统计。
a) Construction enterprises are counted according to the principle of the registered location of legal entities.

1-7 续表 1 continued

单位：个 (unit)

市(州)	Region	交通运输、仓储和邮政业 Transport, Storage and Post	住宿和餐饮业 Hotels and Catering Services	信息传输、软件和信息技术服务业 Information Transmission, Software and Information Technology	金融业 Financial Intermediation	房地产业 Real Estate	租赁和商务服务业 Leasing and Business Services	科学研究和技术服务业 Scientific Research and Technical Services
全省	**Sichuan**	**36222**	**32083**	**97501**	**5304**	**48671**	**234871**	**99577**
成都市	Chengdu	15688	14836	73952	2227	23061	121919	61602
自贡市	Zigong	802	630	981	140	799	3835	1572
攀枝花市	Panzhihua	1034	428	561	67	771	2309	941
泸州市	Luzhou	1683	1110	1896	185	1744	9679	2559
德阳市	Deyang	1362	829	1911	192	1865	7539	3357
绵阳市	Mianyang	2165	1938	4858	269	3141	12372	6675
广元市	Guangyuan	662	532	866	112	946	5785	1386
遂宁市	Suining	730	719	1127	162	1132	4771	1560
内江市	Neijiang	880	644	782	135	1073	3999	1387
乐山市	Leshan	1420	795	1017	144	1384	4878	1621
南充市	Nanchong	1475	1285	1983	253	2989	9347	2966
眉山市	Meishan	949	793	962	148	1968	8677	1884
宜宾市	Yibin	1077	1452	1078	176	1313	6685	2009
广安市	Guangan	585	520	914	149	1182	3609	1437
达州市	Dazhou	1098	1763	1372	214	1529	6398	1851
雅安市	Yaan	1022	597	625	110	559	3319	878
巴中市	Bazhong	483	541	612	83	929	4894	1246
资阳市	Ziyang	471	298	575	101	748	2980	905
阿坝藏族羌族自治州	Aba	564	626	255	65	248	1833	526
甘孜藏族自治州	Ganzi	513	609	289	159	203	2422	704
凉山彝族自治州	Liangshan	1559	1138	885	213	1087	7621	2511

1-7 续表 2 continued

单位：个 (unit)

市(州)	Region	水利、环境和公共设施管理业 Management of Water Conservancy, Environment and Public Facilities	居民服务、修理和其他服务业 Service to Households, Repair and Other Services	教育 Education	卫生和社会工作 Health and Social Service	文化、体育和娱乐业 Culture, Sports and Entertainment	公共管理、社会保障和社会组织 Public Management, Social Security and Social Organization
全省	**Sichuan**	**11333**	**36497**	**41901**	**22867**	**46780**	**93727**
成都市	Chengdu	4408	18313	13157	8495	24211	10984
自贡市	Zigong	344	669	1101	572	1007	2919
攀枝花市	Panzhihua	230	607	572	295	546	1902
泸州市	Luzhou	415	1432	1787	990	1599	3889
德阳市	Deyang	423	1176	1296	632	1373	3891
绵阳市	Mianyang	718	2418	2546	1205	2585	5486
广元市	Guangyuan	344	642	1206	546	904	3998
遂宁市	Suining	294	752	1371	725	1104	3440
内江市	Neijiang	205	667	1438	565	836	3389
乐山市	Leshan	348	872	1598	733	1163	4077
南充市	Nanchong	510	1530	2448	1458	2123	6700
眉山市	Meishan	415	863	1510	690	1232	3213
宜宾市	Yibin	445	1407	1913	850	1279	5456
广安市	Guangan	230	640	1473	628	956	3625
达州市	Dazhou	434	1475	2016	1173	1344	5381
雅安市	Yaan	265	526	838	451	765	2661
巴中市	Bazhong	287	631	1104	598	759	4431
资阳市	Ziyang	216	361	1235	548	432	2720
阿坝藏族羌族自治州	Aba	245	243	521	332	565	3379
甘孜藏族自治州	Ganzi	194	202	789	510	734	5537
凉山彝族自治州	Liangshan	363	1071	1982	871	1263	6649

1-8 分地区按三次产业和机构类型分法人单位数(2022年)
Number of Legal Entities by Three Strata of Industry and Type of Institutions(2022)

单位：个 (unit)

市(州)	Region	法人单位数 Number of Legal Entities	按三次产业分 Grouped by Three Strata of Industry			按机构类型分 By Type of Institutions			
			第一产业 Primary Industry	第二产业 Secondary Industry	第三产业 Tetiary Industry	企业法人 Business Entity	事业法人 Institution Entity	机关法人 Government Entity	社会团体 Social Organization
全省	**Sichuan**	**1595315**	**138252**	**245512**	**1211551**	**1341741**	**54210**	**15162**	**17881**
成都市	Chengdu	715978	16683	105545	593750	683941	6411	1826	3378
自贡市	Zigong	33187	3795	6032	23360	27400	1587	489	702
攀枝花市	Panzhihua	23112	1917	3367	17828	18817	1134	372	527
泸州市	Luzhou	62076	4998	10477	46601	51867	1951	611	772
德阳市	Deyang	57495	4570	13619	39306	46715	1951	520	1095
绵阳市	Mianyang	97631	10185	17970	69476	83008	3250	754	1094
广元市	Guangyuan	36204	5882	5817	24505	25349	2023	575	692
遂宁市	Suining	39291	6712	5885	26694	30992	1773	467	746
内江市	Neijiang	33206	5000	4651	23555	24822	2244	460	442
乐山市	Leshan	41012	3488	6500	31024	30453	2564	750	833
南充市	Nanchong	71226	9813	11074	50339	51531	3804	848	1303
眉山市	Meishan	47711	6014	7786	33911	35447	2142	529	742
宜宾市	Yibin	55492	8447	8557	38488	42496	3214	763	809
广安市	Guangan	34622	5219	5807	23596	26559	2061	542	519
达州市	Dazhou	63265	11745	8421	43099	49693	3387	740	690
雅安市	Yaan	27567	2978	5062	19527	20830	1571	595	620
巴中市	Bazhong	32956	6525	4333	22098	20369	2558	538	591
资阳市	Ziyang	25856	3671	4238	17947	17840	1714	329	399
阿坝藏族羌族自治州	Aba	20426	6103	2093	12230	10623	1360	853	584
甘孜藏族自治州	Ganzi	20779	3262	1864	15653	9132	2929	1338	414
凉山彝族自治州	Liangshan	56223	11245	6414	38564	33857	4582	1263	929

注：建筑业企业按照法人单位注册地原则进行统计。
a) Construction enterprises are counted according to the principle of the registered location of legal entities.

1-8 续表 continued

单位：个 (unit)

市(州)	Region	按机构类型分 By Type of Institutions 民办非企业单位 Private Non-enterprise Unit	基金会 Foundation	居委会 Neighborhood Committee	村委会 Village Committee	农民专业合作社 Specialized Farmers' Cooperative	农村集体经济组织 Rural Collective Economic Organization	其他组织机构 Others
全省	**Sichuan**	**20756**	**140**	**7946**	**26663**	**81656**	**24900**	**4260**
成都市	Chengdu	7373	73	1611	1511	7453	1538	863
自贡市	Zigong	586	5	277	696	1262	108	75
攀枝花市	Panzhihua	321	2	107	231	1268	274	59
泸州市	Luzhou	869	6	343	1140	3109	1178	230
德阳市	Deyang	641	4	370	823	3167	2070	139
绵阳市	Mianyang	1228	2	487	1589	4258	1707	254
广元市	Guangyuan	494	2	346	1389	3492	1593	249
遂宁市	Suining	876	2	323	1114	2611	126	261
内江市	Neijiang	683	6	338	952	2246	883	130
乐山市	Leshan	813	6	261	1107	3397	708	120
南充市	Nanchong	1399	6	739	2302	7868	1246	180
眉山市	Meishan	670	2	315	546	3113	4068	137
宜宾市	Yibin	769	3	303	1801	4199	1013	122
广安市	Guangan	662	1	321	1391	2442	10	114
达州市	Dazhou	1171	1	593	1733	3891	1278	88
雅安市	Yaan	469	5	102	567	2488	269	51
巴中市	Bazhong	564	1	487	1306	4952	1463	127
资阳市	Ziyang	501	6	265	963	2885	780	174
阿坝藏族羌族自治州	Aba	94	2	63	1125	5264	185	273
甘孜藏族自治州	Ganzi	28	1	70	2182	3255	942	488
凉山彝族自治州	Liangshan	545	4	225	2195	9036	3461	126

1-9 按地区和控股情况分企业法人单位数(2022年)
Numbers of Corporate Enterprises by Region and the Status of Holdings(2022)

单位：个 (unit)

市(州)	Region	企业单位数 Numbers of Enterprises	国有控股 State-holding	集体控股 Collective-holding	私人控股 Private-holding	港、澳、台商控股 Hong Kong, Macao and Taiwan-holding	外商控股 Foreign-holding	其他 Others
全省	**Sichuan**	**1341741**	**20186**	**12230**	**1300969**	**1687**	**1701**	**4968**
成都市	Chengdu	683941	6304	2657	672029	1166	1228	557
自贡市	Zigong	27400	552	431	25204	14	22	1177
攀枝花市	Panzhihua	18817	440	254	18003	16	14	90
泸州市	Luzhou	51867	1217	1501	48867	28	16	238
德阳市	Deyang	46715	797	594	45117	69	54	84
绵阳市	Mianyang	83008	1230	464	80935	77	54	248
广元市	Guangyuan	25349	574	301	24382	11	16	65
遂宁市	Suining	30992	445	135	30103	30	44	235
内江市	Neijiang	24822	449	279	23650	23	24	397
乐山市	Leshan	30453	550	369	29449	27	22	36
南充市	Nanchong	51531	825	617	49960	39	21	69
眉山市	Meishan	35447	731	333	34194	39	34	116
宜宾市	Yibin	42496	1068	940	40344	29	17	98
广安市	Guangan	26559	532	298	25402	25	22	280
达州市	Dazhou	49693	730	720	47874	21	27	321
雅安市	Yaan	20830	712	384	19257	17	10	450
巴中市	Bazhong	20369	583	411	19314	8	7	46
资阳市	Ziyang	17840	371	252	17042	14	38	123
阿坝藏族羌族自治州	Aba	10623	379	115	9953	6	4	166
甘孜藏族自治州	Ganzi	9132	526	154	8303	4	5	140
凉山彝族自治州	Liangshan	33857	1171	1021	31587	24	22	32

注：建筑业企业按照法人单位注册地原则进行统计。
a) Construction enterprises are counted according to the principle of the registered location of legal entities.

主要统计指标解释

行政区划 指国家对行政区域的划分。根据有关法规规定，我国的行政区域划分如下：(1)全国分为省、自治区、直辖市；(2)省、自治区分为自治州、县、自治县、市；(3)自治州分为县、自治县、市；(4)县、自治县分为乡、民族乡、镇；(5)直辖市和较大的市分为区、县；(6)国家在必要时设立的特别行政区。

平均增长速度 平均增长速度表明社会经济现象在一个较长的时期内逐期平均增长变化的程度，它不能根据各个环比增长速度直接求得，但与平均发展速度之间存在着一定的数量关系：平均增长速度＝平均发展速度－1。

平均发展速度是一种根据环比发展速度计算的序时平均数，由于各时期对比的基础不同，所以计算平均发展速度不能采用一般的序时平均数的计算方法，计算方法分为水平法和累计法。水平法，又称几何平均法，即将环比发展速度按连乘法用几何平均数公式计算。累计法，也称方程法，根据一段时期内各年发展水平总和与基期水平的关系，列出方程式计算平均发展速度。水平法着重考虑最后一年所达到的发展水平；累计法着重考虑整个时期累计发展水平的总量。

本《年鉴》内所列的增长速度，均用“水平法”计算。从某年到某年平均增长速度的年份，均不包括基期年在内。如 1952 年以来的平均增长速度是以 1952 年为基期计算的，则写为 1953—2023 年平均增长速度，其余类推。

国民经济行业分类 自 2017 年年报和 2018 年定期报表开始使用新的《国民经济行业分类》（GB/T4754-2017）。该分类是由国家统计局组织修订，原国家质量监督检验检疫总局和中国国家标准化管理委员会于2017 年 6 月 30 日发布。这次修订是在 2011 年分类标准的基础上，结合我国经济活动特点，参照联合国《全部经济活动的国际标准产业分类》（ISIC/Rev.4）进行的。修订后的《国民经济行业分类》（GB/T4754-2017）共有门类20个，大类97个，中类473个，小类1382个。

Explanatory Notes on Main Statistical Indicators

Divisions of Administrative Areas refers to the division of administrative areas by the State. The relative laws stipulate that 1) the whole country is divided into provinces, autonomous regions and municipalities directly under the Central Government; 2) provinces and autonomous regions are further divided into autonomous prefectures, counties, autonomous counties and cities; 3) autonomous prefectures are further divided into counties, autonomous counties and cities; 4) counties and autonomous counties are further divided into townships, ethnic townships and towns; 5) municipalities directly under the Central Government and large cities are divided into districts and counties; 6) the State shall, when necessary, establish special administrative regions.

Average Annual Growth Rate shows the average growth rate of social and economic development during a longer period. It can not be directly calculated by chain based growth rate. The relation is: Average Annual Growth Rate = Average Speed of Development – 1.

Average speed of development is the time series average of speed which calculated by chain based. Because the reference bases during the different periods are not same, average speed of development can not be calculated by the general method. Level approach and accumulative approach for calculating average speed of development rate are applied. The "level approach", or the method of calculating the geometric average, is derived by the formula of geometric average of the chain-based speeds of development, or comparing the level of the last year of the interval with that of the beginning year; the other is called the "accumulative approach" or the "algebraic average", "equation" method, which is derived by the summation of the actual figure of each year in the interval divided by the figure in the base year. The level approach focuses on the level of the last year, while the accumulative approach emphasizes the aggregate development in the duration.

The average annual growth rates listed in the Yearbook are calculated by the level approach. The base year is not listed in the duration for which average annual growth rates are computed. For instance, the average annual growth rate of the years since 1952 is shown as the average annual growth rate of 1953-2023 without showing the base year 1952.

Industrial Classification of the National Economy The new Industrial Classification of the National Economy (GB/T 4754-2017) is introduced starting from the compilation of 2017 annual statistics and 2018 monthly or quarterly statistics. The revision, based on the 2011 classification, was organized by the National Bureau of Statistics taking into consideration of the characteristics of economic activities in China and the International Standards of the Industrial Classification of All Economic Activities (ISIC/Rev.4) of the United Nations. The new Classification was promulgated by the former National Administration of Quality Supervision, Inspection and Quarantine and the Standardization Administration of the People's Republic of China on June 30, 2017. The revised version of the Industrial Classification of the National Economy (GB/T 4754-2017) is composed of 20 sections, 97 divisions, 473 groups and 1382 classes.

02 国民经济核算

Chapter 2 National Accounts

SICHUAN STATISTICAL YEARBOOK

2-1　地区生产总值

Gross Domestic Product

单位：亿元　　(100 million yuan)

年份 Year	地区生产总值 Gross Domestic Product	第一产业 Primary Industry	第二产业 Secondary Industry	第三产业 Tertiary Industry	农林牧渔业 Agriculture, Forestry, Animal Husbandry and Fishery	工业 Industry	建筑业 Construction
1978	184.61	82.20	65.55	36.86	82.20	59.40	6.15
1980	229.31	101.68	81.05	46.58	101.68	73.18	7.87
1985	421.15	172.90	148.11	100.14	172.90	127.13	20.98
1986	458.23	181.20	160.62	116.41	181.20	138.12	22.50
1987	530.86	202.25	187.88	140.73	202.25	160.49	27.39
1988	659.69	241.95	238.32	179.42	241.95	206.44	31.88
1989	744.98	263.15	263.44	218.39	263.15	231.08	32.36
1990	890.95	321.41	312.64	256.90	321.41	276.08	36.56
1991	1016.31	339.00	376.48	300.83	339.00	331.37	45.11
1992	1177.27	372.04	441.57	363.66	376.24	383.52	62.90
1993	1486.08	449.38	580.38	456.32	454.69	501.36	85.14
1994	2001.41	597.37	782.77	621.27	604.52	676.09	114.92
1995	2443.21	662.46	980.91	799.84	671.18	843.23	147.74
1996	2871.65	770.02	1156.01	945.62	780.27	989.50	178.33
1997	3241.47	880.28	1265.32	1095.87	891.85	1068.55	210.11
1998	3474.09	912.24	1324.01	1237.84	924.65	1090.65	247.66
1999	3649.12	926.03	1349.63	1373.46	939.06	1114.50	250.15
2000	3928.20	945.58	1433.11	1549.51	959.61	1170.63	278.65
2001	4293.49	981.67	1572.01	1739.81	997.00	1270.86	318.82
2002	4725.01	1047.95	1733.38	1943.68	1064.82	1392.09	360.74
2003	5346.20	1128.57	2020.50	2197.13	1147.66	1627.92	414.59
2004	6303.96	1329.07	2439.71	2535.18	1351.58	1990.03	475.63
2005	7195.88	1403.24	2961.19	2831.45	1427.47	2454.28	536.97
2006	8494.68	1613.99	3658.07	3222.62	1638.87	3059.45	633.99
2007	10562.10	1966.53	4607.73	3987.84	1999.83	3896.48	754.25
2008	12756.21	2138.96	5766.49	4850.76	2174.96	4912.40	905.98
2009	14190.60	2160.37	6653.24	5376.99	2194.45	5621.30	1089.57
2010	17224.78	2384.89	8283.21	6556.68	2424.58	7032.89	1317.42
2011	21050.87	2854.62	10014.39	8181.86	2900.43	8457.36	1642.71
2012	23922.41	3142.55	11231.06	9548.80	3198.88	9408.52	1919.92
2013	26518.02	3257.42	12418.94	10841.66	3323.58	10308.99	2217.67
2014	28891.33	3524.74	13082.69	12283.90	3598.67	10703.84	2494.79
2015	30342.01	3660.96	13192.45	13488.60	3745.49	10735.01	2555.50
2016	33138.48	3900.60	13450.13	15787.75	3991.86	10790.93	2757.77
2017	37905.14	4262.51	14569.17	19073.46	4365.27	11437.80	3235.85
2018	42902.10	4427.43	16056.94	22417.73	4544.32	12360.07	3809.77
2019	46363.75	4807.52	17187.92	24368.31	4937.99	13165.91	4150.27
2020	48501.64	5556.86	17505.61	25439.17	5701.23	13401.02	4245.17
2021	54087.98	5662.00	19949.74	28476.24	5818.12	15546.06	4581.01
2022	56610.20	5965.51	20591.44	30053.25	6137.28	16188.73	4557.12
2023	60132.88	6056.64	21306.70	32769.54	6236.20	16705.16	4846.55

注：①本表按当年价格计算；从2013年起，地区生产总值核算执行国家统计局新的《国民经济行业分类》和《三次产业划分规定》(以下有关各表同)；②按照国家统计局统一部署，依据第四次全国经济普查结果修订了1992年以来的GDP历史数据。

a) The data in this table are calculated at current prices; The regional GDP accounting has executed the NBS new "Classification of National Economic Industries" and the "Provisions of Three Industrial Division" since 2013(the same as the following related tables); b) According to the unified deployment of the NBS, the historical GDP data since 1992 have been revised based on the results of the fourth national Economic census.

2-1 续表 continued

单位：亿元 (100 million yuan)

年份 Year	批发和零售业 Wholesale and Retail Trades	交通运输、仓储和邮政业 Transport, Storage and Post	住宿和餐饮业 Hotels and Catering Services	金融业 Financial Intermediation	房地产业 Real Estate	其他 Others	人均地区生产总值（元） Per Capita GDP (yuan)
1978	7.75	6.17	3.02	4.88	2.42	12.62	261
1980	9.68	7.39	3.77	6.71	2.94	16.09	320
1985	24.85	14.31	9.67	11.71	5.93	33.67	570
1986	28.84	17.88	11.21	13.21	6.85	38.42	614
1987	35.09	22.64	13.65	15.98	8.11	45.26	702
1988	47.19	27.80	18.35	19.84	9.92	56.32	861
1989	56.45	33.82	22.04	23.55	11.68	70.85	960
1990	61.29	40.71	24.57	29.79	14.56	85.98	1136
1991	65.94	48.96	27.64	34.09	17.76	106.44	1283
1992	78.45	56.70	31.34	40.68	24.41	123.03	1477
1993	90.29	70.18	39.00	51.13	30.34	163.95	1854
1994	121.26	85.71	54.28	65.01	68.91	210.71	2338
1995	181.21	113.01	70.47	71.31	80.41	264.65	3043
1996	220.19	129.83	85.63	82.13	95.63	310.14	3550
1997	240.78	145.08	93.64	93.19	124.13	374.14	4032
1998	254.51	165.91	99.41	108.45	148.09	434.76	4294
1999	270.84	179.25	109.25	118.32	165.17	502.58	4540
2000	283.26	217.41	120.08	153.05	180.05	565.46	4956
2001	311.95	248.34	133.51	168.86	198.60	645.55	5376
2002	341.12	271.19	151.41	183.13	210.82	749.69	5890
2003	380.53	297.36	167.49	204.35	235.91	870.39	6565
2004	453.41	313.10	193.24	230.35	272.01	1024.61	7751
2005	497.39	355.76	214.82	250.85	296.96	1161.38	8828
2006	575.32	419.97	246.81	284.16	355.52	1280.59	10371
2007	697.05	472.72	294.71	344.75	414.32	1687.99	12963
2008	836.33	472.63	327.03	437.28	539.65	2149.95	15685
2009	1005.62	489.29	393.12	482.55	600.12	2314.58	17387
2010	1197.99	500.87	460.81	606.88	643.27	3040.07	21230
2011	1420.15	545.03	536.34	792.61	723.35	4032.89	26136
2012	1635.88	591.65	588.48	1176.10	832.58	4570.40	29627
2013	1831.37	617.86	645.86	1530.15	918.40	5124.14	32750
2014	2083.19	864.72	706.00	1621.95	1308.04	5510.13	35563
2015	2359.96	941.85	780.26	1878.45	1519.69	5825.80	37150
2016	2760.32	1118.84	852.91	2312.70	1878.64	6674.51	40297
2017	3432.31	1205.90	934.01	2720.81	2602.57	7970.62	45835
2018	3835.52	1401.66	1043.24	2922.37	3118.08	9867.07	51658
2019	4243.77	1473.14	1178.57	3101.67	3269.09	10843.34	55619
2020	4299.46	1359.52	996.27	3320.34	3396.00	11782.63	58009
2021	4924.75	1534.68	1221.35	3552.60	3623.51	13285.90	64610
2022	5255.60	1640.46	1171.58	3779.31	3606.84	14273.29	67610
2023	5683.96	2004.63	1344.27	3997.36	3644.20	15670.55	71835

2-2 地区生产总值指数
Indices of Gross Domestic Product

(上年=100) (preceding year=100)

年份 Year	地区生产总值 Gross Domestic Product	第一产业 Primary Industry	第二产业 Secondary Industry	第三产业 Tertiary Industry	农林牧渔业 Agriculture, Forestry, Animal Husbandry and Fishery	工业 Industry	建筑业 Construction
1978	117.4	113.8	121.2	117.4	113.8	126.0	88.4
1980	109.5	104.0	109.7	118.3	104.0	109.5	111.5
1985	111.9	104.3	118.0	117.1	104.3	117.0	125.0
1986	105.5	101.0	106.5	111.9	101.0	107.0	103.3
1987	108.7	103.0	112.2	112.5	103.0	112.0	113.2
1988	107.5	101.9	113.8	106.2	101.9	116.4	97.0
1989	103.2	102.8	101.9	105.7	102.8	103.5	89.1
1990	109.1	106.9	109.5	111.3	106.9	110.0	105.7
1991	109.1	108.5	106.3	113.4	108.5	104.4	120.6
1992	112.6	104.6	120.5	113.1	104.6	118.9	131.1
1993	112.9	105.0	120.1	113.0	105.1	120.1	118.8
1994	110.6	104.4	117.3	108.2	104.4	118.4	110.1
1995	112.3	105.5	111.5	120.1	105.6	110.7	117.0
1996	111.6	107.3	109.2	118.6	107.4	108.3	115.2
1997	110.5	106.2	111.6	112.8	106.2	111.4	112.7
1998	109.6	104.6	110.8	111.8	104.7	109.8	116.6
1999	106.5	105.0	106.0	108.2	105.0	105.8	106.8
2000	109.0	102.3	108.2	114.6	102.3	108.0	109.2
2001	109.0	105.7	110.2	110.0	105.1	111.6	110.1
2002	110.5	105.6	111.9	112.2	105.6	112.1	110.9
2003	111.0	103.9	116.3	110.0	104.0	117.2	111.8
2004	111.9	106.1	116.0	110.8	106.2	116.6	112.8
2005	112.7	105.4	118.6	110.4	105.4	120.3	109.2
2006	113.5	102.6	117.7	114.6	102.6	121.6	103.9
2007	114.5	104.8	120.9	112.0	104.8	121.6	115.5
2008	111.0	101.0	114.0	111.7	101.0	115.7	103.4
2009	114.5	104.0	116.4	116.2	104.0	115.0	124.0
2010	115.1	104.3	122.8	109.7	104.4	123.5	117.5
2011	115.0	104.4	121.6	110.5	104.5	122.8	116.0
2012	111.7	104.6	115.9	108.3	104.5	115.8	115.2
2013	110.0	103.5	112.0	109.2	103.6	111.3	115.7
2014	108.5	103.8	109.0	109.2	103.9	108.8	109.7
2015	107.9	103.8	107.7	109.4	103.9	107.3	110.1
2016	107.8	103.8	107.6	109.2	104.0	107.5	107.8
2017	108.1	103.8	107.5	109.7	103.9	108.1	105.0
2018	108.0	103.6	107.5	109.5	103.8	108.0	105.4
2019	107.4	102.8	107.4	108.4	103.0	107.8	106.1
2020	103.8	105.1	103.8	103.4	105.2	103.8	103.1
2021	108.2	107.0	107.8	108.8	107.0	110.0	101.3
2022	102.8	104.1	102.0	103.2	104.4	101.4	103.9
2023	106.0	104.0	105.0	107.1	104.0	105.3	106.1

注：本表按可比价格计算。
a) The indices in this table are calculated at comparable prices.

2-2 续表 continued

(上年=100) (preceding year=100)

年份 Year	批发和零售业 Wholesale and Retail Trades	交通运输、仓储和邮政业 Transport, Storage and Post	住宿和餐饮业 Hotels and Catering Services	金融业 Financial Intermediation	房地产业 Real Estate	其他 Others	人均地区生产总值 Per Capita GDP (yuan)
1978							
1980	117.2	115.6	117.2	122.9	117.6	118.8	108.6
1985	120.7	129.7	120.5	107.1	112.6	113.6	111.4
1986	111.7	120.3	111.6	108.7	111.2	108.9	104.6
1987	113.2	117.7	113.2	113.5	110.1	105.7	107.3
1988	112.1	102.4	112.0	101.8	101.9	103.8	106.3
1989	102.4	106.8	102.8	103.1	106.0	111.5	101.8
1990	104.0	112.5	106.8	120.4	113.7	108.1	107.9
1991	105.2	115.3	110.0	109.9	107.4	120.6	108.0
1992	109.9	116.2	104.7	107.6	121.2	114.0	111.9
1993	104.5	114.5	113.0	112.0	129.1	115.4	112.3
1994	107.8	100.2	111.7	109.0	164.2	100.2	103.6
1995	129.8	117.4	112.8	103.6	113.3	126.2	119.7
1996	121.5	112.0	121.5	105.3	120.0	123.2	110.8
1997	105.7	109.0	105.7	109.7	125.5	118.1	111.2
1998	109.3	110.3	109.2	113.2	116.7	112.8	108.9
1999	106.4	103.7	109.9	106.1	113.4	109.5	107.2
2000	107.0	122.7	113.1	129.5	105.5	116.3	110.6
2001	109.3	109.6	110.3	108.3	108.6	109.6	108.2
2002	110.0	109.0	114.1	108.4	105.1	117.5	110.1
2003	111.4	107.3	110.5	109.5	110.1	110.1	109.3
2004	112.4	107.4	111.3	107.9	111.5	111.5	112.0
2005	113.4	108.2	112.3	106.9	107.2	111.4	112.5
2006	113.0	109.5	112.5	110.3	114.2	116.6	113.0
2007	112.5	110.7	108.4	112.8	111.1	113.4	115.1
2008	114.3	105.2	101.1	104.5	105.3	117.9	111.2
2009	126.2	95.5	121.0	129.5	129.6	112.0	114.1
2010	113.5	106.5	110.6	107.7	100.1	111.5	115.8
2011	114.0	106.0	109.2	126.6	106.8	107.1	115.8
2012	111.6	105.8	105.2	118.8	108.5	105.8	111.4
2013	110.2	104.0	104.9	118.3	109.8	107.7	109.7
2014	109.8	106.3	106.2	112.4	112.9	108.3	108.1
2015	108.0	104.8	103.8	112.1	109.9	110.6	107.3
2016	107.6	104.3	106.1	108.3	110.7	110.9	107.1
2017	109.0	104.8	106.8	106.8	109.3	112.1	107.5
2018	107.4	105.9	107.7	100.7	110.4	113.4	107.5
2019	106.5	107.0	108.1	106.1	105.6	110.4	107.0
2020	100.3	99.4	89.3	106.1	102.1	106.4	103.4
2021	111.5	110.7	119.2	103.6	101.8	110.1	108.1
2022	104.6	100.5	95.5	104.0	96.6	105.0	102.8
2023	108.5	112.8	112.2	106.2	99.5	106.9	106.0

2-3 地区生产总值指数
Indices of Gross Domestic Product

(1978年=100) (year of 1978=100)

年份 Year	地区生产总值 Gross Domestic Product	第一产业 Primary Industry	第二产业 Secondary Industry	第三产业 Tertiary Industry	农林牧渔业 Agriculture, Forestry, Animal Husbandry and Fishery	工业 Industry	建筑业 Construction
1978	100.0	100.0	100.0	100.0	100.0	100.0	100.0
1980	120.6	112.3	121.2	133.7	112.3	121.0	123.4
1985	194.0	161.8	202.3	250.7	161.8	193.5	287.2
1986	204.6	163.4	215.4	280.5	163.4	207.1	296.7
1987	222.4	168.3	241.7	315.6	168.3	231.9	335.8
1988	239.1	171.5	275.1	335.2	171.5	270.0	325.7
1989	246.8	176.3	280.3	354.3	176.3	279.4	290.2
1990	269.2	188.5	306.9	394.3	188.5	307.4	306.8
1991	293.7	204.5	326.3	447.1	204.5	320.9	370.0
1992	330.7	213.9	393.1	505.7	213.9	381.5	485.0
1993	373.4	224.6	472.2	571.5	224.8	458.2	576.2
1994	413.0	234.5	553.8	618.3	234.7	542.5	634.4
1995	463.8	247.4	617.5	742.6	247.9	600.6	742.3
1996	517.6	265.5	674.4	880.7	266.2	650.4	855.1
1997	571.9	281.9	752.6	993.5	282.7	724.6	963.7
1998	626.8	294.9	833.9	1110.7	296.0	795.6	1123.7
1999	667.6	309.6	883.9	1201.8	310.8	841.7	1200.1
2000	727.7	316.8	956.4	1377.2	318.0	909.0	1310.5
2001	793.2	334.8	1053.9	1514.9	334.2	1014.5	1442.9
2002	876.4	353.6	1179.3	1699.8	352.9	1137.2	1600.1
2003	972.8	367.3	1371.6	1869.7	367.0	1332.8	1789.0
2004	1088.6	389.8	1591.0	2071.7	389.8	1554.1	2018.0
2005	1226.9	410.8	1887.0	2287.1	410.8	1869.6	2203.6
2006	1392.5	421.5	2220.9	2621.1	421.5	2273.4	2289.5
2007	1594.4	441.7	2685.1	2935.6	441.7	2764.5	2644.4
2008	1769.8	446.1	3061.0	3279.0	446.1	3198.5	2734.3
2009	2026.4	464.0	3563.0	3810.3	464.0	3678.3	3390.6
2010	2332.4	483.9	4375.4	4179.8	484.4	4542.7	3983.9
2011	2682.2	505.2	5320.5	4618.7	506.2	5578.4	4621.4
2012	2996.1	528.5	6166.5	5002.1	529.0	6459.8	5323.8
2013	3295.7	547.0	6906.4	5462.3	548.0	7189.7	6159.6
2014	3575.8	567.7	7528.0	5964.8	569.4	7822.4	6757.1
2015	3858.3	589.3	8107.7	6525.5	591.6	8393.5	7439.6
2016	4159.2	611.7	8723.9	7125.8	615.3	9023.0	8019.9
2017	4496.1	635.0	9378.2	7817.0	639.3	9753.8	8420.9
2018	4855.8	657.8	10081.5	8559.7	663.5	10534.1	8875.6
2019	5215.2	676.2	10827.6	9278.7	683.4	11355.8	9417.0
2020	5413.3	710.7	11239.0	9594.2	719.0	11787.3	9708.9
2021	5857.2	760.5	12115.6	10438.4	769.3	12966.1	9835.2
2022	6023.7	791.7	12358.0	10772.5	803.3	13147.2	10218.1
2023	6383.3	823.3	12975.9	11537.3	835.4	13844.0	10841.4

注：本表按可比价格计算。
a) The indices in this table are calculated at comparable prices.

2-3 续表 continued

(1978年=100) (year of 1978=100)

年份 Year	批发和零售业 Wholesale and Retail Trades	交通运输、仓储和邮政业 Transport, Storage and Post	住宿和餐饮业 Hotels and Catering Services	金融业 Financial Intermediation	房地产业 Real Estate	其他 Others	人均地区生产总值 Per Capita GDP (yuan)
1978	100.0	100.0	100.0	100.0	100.0	100.0	100.0
1980	132.2	126.7	132.2	145.5	128.4	134.7	118.8
1985	295.9	213.9	296.4	221.3	226.2	245.9	185.3
1986	330.5	257.4	330.7	240.6	251.5	267.8	193.9
1987	374.1	302.9	374.4	273.1	276.9	283.0	208.0
1988	419.4	310.2	419.3	278.0	282.1	293.8	221.1
1989	429.5	331.3	431.1	286.6	299.1	327.6	225.1
1990	446.6	372.7	460.4	345.0	340.0	354.1	242.9
1991	469.9	429.7	506.4	379.2	365.2	427.0	262.3
1992	516.4	499.4	530.2	408.0	442.6	486.8	293.5
1993	539.6	571.8	599.1	457.0	571.4	561.8	329.6
1994	581.7	572.9	669.2	498.1	938.3	562.9	341.5
1995	755.1	672.6	754.9	516.0	1063.1	710.4	408.8
1996	917.4	753.3	917.2	543.4	1275.7	875.2	452.9
1997	969.7	821.1	969.5	596.1	1601.0	1033.6	503.7
1998	1059.9	905.7	1058.7	674.8	1868.4	1165.9	548.5
1999	1127.7	939.2	1163.5	716.0	2118.8	1276.7	588.0
2000	1206.6	1152.4	1315.9	927.2	2235.3	1484.8	650.3
2001	1318.9	1263.0	1451.4	1004.1	2427.5	1627.3	703.6
2002	1450.7	1376.7	1656.1	1088.5	2551.3	1912.1	774.7
2003	1616.1	1477.2	1830.0	1191.9	2809.0	2105.3	846.7
2004	1816.5	1586.5	2036.8	1286.0	3132.1	2347.4	948.4
2005	2059.9	1716.6	2287.3	1374.8	3357.6	2615.0	1066.9
2006	2327.7	1879.6	2573.2	1516.4	3834.3	3049.0	1205.6
2007	2618.7	2080.8	2789.4	1710.5	4259.9	3457.6	1387.6
2008	2993.2	2189.0	2820.0	1787.4	4485.7	4076.5	1543.1
2009	3777.4	2090.5	3412.3	2314.7	5813.5	4565.7	1760.6
2010	4287.3	2226.3	3773.9	2493.0	5819.3	5090.8	2038.8
2011	4887.6	2359.9	4121.2	3156.1	6215.0	5452.2	2360.9
2012	5454.5	2496.8	4335.5	3749.4	6743.3	5768.4	2630.1
2013	6010.9	2596.7	4547.9	4435.6	7404.1	6212.6	2885.2
2014	6600.0	2760.3	4829.9	4985.6	8359.3	6728.3	3118.9
2015	7128.0	2892.7	5013.4	5588.8	9186.8	7441.5	3346.6
2016	7669.7	3017.1	5319.2	6052.7	10169.8	8252.6	3584.2
2017	8360.0	3162.0	5680.9	6464.3	11115.6	9251.1	3853.0
2018	8978.6	3348.5	6118.3	6509.5	12271.7	10490.8	4142.0
2019	9562.2	3582.9	6613.9	6906.6	12958.9	11581.8	4431.9
2020	9590.9	3561.4	5906.2	7327.9	13231.0	12323.1	4582.6
2021	10693.8	3942.5	7040.2	7591.7	13469.2	13567.7	4953.8
2022	11187.6	3961.2	6725.3	7896.1	13016.1	14246.1	5092.5
2023	12138.6	4468.2	7545.8	8385.6	12951.0	15229.1	5398.1

2-4 地区生产总值构成
Composition of Gross Domestic Product

单位：% (%)

年份 Year	地区生产总值 Gross Domestic Product	第一产业 Primary Industry	第二产业 Secondary Industry	第三产业 Tertiary Industry
1978	100.0	44.5	35.5	20.0
1980	100.0	44.3	35.3	20.4
1985	100.0	41.1	35.2	23.7
1986	100.0	39.5	35.0	25.5
1987	100.0	38.1	35.4	26.5
1988	100.0	36.7	36.1	27.2
1989	100.0	35.3	35.3	29.4
1990	100.0	36.1	35.1	28.8
1991	100.0	33.4	37.0	29.6
1992	100.0	31.6	37.5	30.9
1993	100.0	30.2	39.1	30.7
1994	100.0	29.8	39.1	31.1
1995	100.0	27.1	40.1	32.8
1996	100.0	26.8	40.3	32.9
1997	100.0	27.2	39.0	33.8
1998	100.0	26.3	38.1	35.6
1999	100.0	25.4	37.0	37.6
2000	100.0	24.1	36.5	39.4
2001	100.0	22.9	36.6	40.5
2002	100.0	22.2	36.7	41.1
2003	100.0	21.1	37.8	41.1
2004	100.0	21.1	38.7	40.2
2005	100.0	19.5	41.2	39.3
2006	100.0	19.0	43.1	37.9
2007	100.0	18.6	43.6	37.8
2008	100.0	16.8	45.2	38.0
2009	100.0	15.2	46.9	37.9
2010	100.0	13.8	48.1	38.1
2011	100.0	13.6	47.6	38.8
2012	100.0	13.1	46.9	40.0
2013	100.0	12.3	46.8	40.9
2014	100.0	12.2	45.3	42.5
2015	100.0	12.1	43.5	44.4
2016	100.0	11.8	40.6	47.6
2017	100.0	11.2	38.4	50.4
2018	100.0	10.3	37.4	52.3
2019	100.0	10.4	37.1	52.5
2020	100.0	11.5	36.1	52.4
2021	100.0	10.5	36.9	52.6
2022	100.0	10.5	36.4	53.1
2023	100.0	10.1	35.4	54.5

注：本表按当年价格计算。
a) The data in this table are calculated at current prices.

2-5 各市(州)按三次产业分地区生产总值(2023年)
Gross Domestic Product by Three Strata of Industry and Region (2023)

单位：亿元 (100 million yuan)

市(州)	Region	地区生产总值 Gross Domestic Product	第一产业 Primary Industry	第二产业 Secondary Industry	第三产业 Tertiary Industry	人均地区生产总值(元) Per Capita GDP (yuan)
全省	**Sichuan**	**60132.88**	**6056.64**	**21306.70**	**32769.54**	**71835**
成都市	Chengdu	22074.72	594.86	6370.87	15108.99	103465
自贡市	Zigong	1750.47	259.77	588.04	902.66	71726
攀枝花市	Panzhihua	1303.80	115.27	717.30	471.23	107133
泸州市	Luzhou	2725.90	281.41	1332.93	1111.56	63913
德阳市	Deyang	3014.41	303.73	1421.68	1289.00	87197
绵阳市	Mianyang	4038.73	393.19	1599.05	2046.49	82347
广元市	Guangyuan	1179.82	215.13	437.46	527.23	52204
遂宁市	Suining	1714.97	221.32	783.11	710.54	62137
内江市	Neijiang	1807.11	297.43	561.74	947.94	58758
乐山市	Leshan	2447.53	308.30	1034.47	1104.76	77699
南充市	Nanchong	2734.76	506.98	949.21	1278.57	49453
眉山市	Meishan	1737.00	243.28	680.40	813.32	58722
宜宾市	Yibin	3806.64	404.18	1888.89	1513.57	82341
广安市	Guangan	1512.51	247.78	460.15	804.58	46798
达州市	Dazhou	2656.69	440.53	896.11	1320.05	49755
雅安市	Yaan	1010.03	173.75	317.28	519.00	70582
巴中市	Bazhong	780.28	195.20	176.58	408.50	29517
资阳市	Ziyang	1019.22	196.64	299.71	522.87	45078
阿坝藏族羌族自治州	Aba	503.19	98.48	122.53	282.18	61067
甘孜藏族自治州	Ganzi	513.35	86.88	147.24	279.23	46478
凉山彝族自治州	Liangshan	2261.11	503.41	779.40	978.30	46159

注：本表按当年价格计算；人均GDP按年平均常住人口计算。

a) The data in this table are calculated at current prices; the per capita GDP are calculated based on the annual average date of resident population.

2-6 各市(州)按三次产业分地区生产总值指数(2023年)
Indices of Gross Domestic Product by Three Strata of Industry and Region(2023)

上年=100 (preceding year=100)

市(州)	Region	地区生产总值 Gross Domestic Product	第一产业 Primary Industry	第二产业 Secondary Industry	第三产业 Tertiary Industry	人均地区生产总值 Per Capita GDP (yuan)
全省	**Sichuan**	**106.0**	**104.0**	**105.0**	**107.1**	**106.0**
成都市	Chengdu	106.0	103.0	103.0	107.5	105.5
自贡市	Zigong	106.2	104.1	105.7	107.2	107.0
攀枝花市	Panzhihua	106.5	104.2	106.3	107.3	106.3
泸州市	Luzhou	105.6	103.9	105.8	105.7	105.5
德阳市	Deyang	106.7	104.1	106.8	107.1	106.7
绵阳市	Mianyang	108.0	103.8	107.7	109.2	107.7
广元市	Guangyuan	106.2	103.8	107.2	106.4	107.0
遂宁市	Suining	106.7	104.0	106.5	107.9	107.3
内江市	Neijiang	107.0	104.3	107.1	108.0	107.7
乐山市	Leshan	106.5	104.2	106.4	107.4	106.6
南充市	Nanchong	105.5	104.1	104.0	107.4	106.0
眉山市	Meishan	106.2	104.2	105.8	107.3	106.3
宜宾市	Yibin	107.5	104.3	107.8	108.0	107.2
广安市	Guangan	106.6	103.9	107.2	107.2	106.9
达州市	Dazhou	106.5	103.4	107.0	107.5	107.0
雅安市	Yaan	105.8	104.1	105.7	106.6	105.9
巴中市	Bazhong	106.0	103.9	110.2	105.0	106.9
资阳市	Ziyang	105.8	103.8	106.0	106.6	106.6
阿坝藏族羌族自治州	Aba	106.8	109.3	104.3	107.0	106.2
甘孜藏族自治州	Ganzi	106.2	104.1	108.9	105.7	106.1
凉山彝族自治州	Liangshan	107.0	104.3	107.1	108.5	106.7

注：本表按可比价格计算。
a) The indices in this table are calculated at comparable prices.

2-7 各市(州)地区生产总值
Gross Domestic Product by Region

单位：亿元 (100 million yuan)

市(州)	Region	2013	2014	2015	2016	2017	2018	2019	2020	2021	2022	2023
全省	**Sichuan**	**26518.02**	**28891.33**	**30342.01**	**33138.48**	**37905.14**	**42902.10**	**46363.75**	**48501.64**	**54087.98**	**56610.20**	**60132.88**
成都市	Chengdu	9450.66	10368.43	10662.31	11874.07	13931.39	15698.94	17010.66	17838.00	19962.31	20789.38	22074.72
自贡市	Zigong	913.37	942.09	970.27	1020.84	1166.17	1314.74	1404.21	1440.03	1595.86	1637.29	1750.47
攀枝花市	Panzhihua	652.33	685.75	712.56	762.93	842.25	941.45	1002.02	1023.82	1150.78	1220.52	1303.80
泸州市	Luzhou	1156.59	1279.12	1369.31	1500.64	1698.91	1895.55	2071.04	2162.63	2432.70	2601.52	2725.90
德阳市	Deyang	1403.84	1465.24	1525.77	1692.82	1907.43	2148.39	2325.74	2383.47	2686.96	2825.10	3014.41
绵阳市	Mianyang	1470.41	1612.08	1743.00	1957.91	2313.57	2613.30	2870.49	3020.54	3404.05	3679.51	4038.73
广元市	Guangyuan	520.25	563.08	614.12	657.27	751.81	880.50	953.20	1008.01	1116.25	1115.09	1179.82
遂宁市	Suining	706.69	809.00	871.36	926.84	1046.43	1230.85	1339.71	1375.63	1519.87	1614.47	1714.97
内江市	Neijiang	915.11	973.86	1018.00	1086.43	1182.11	1318.83	1412.39	1444.49	1605.53	1656.95	1807.11
乐山市	Leshan	1096.93	1195.81	1280.63	1335.40	1481.61	1709.81	1872.60	2001.17	2194.14	2308.81	2447.53
南充市	Nanchong	1283.71	1391.70	1463.40	1592.97	1838.25	2115.73	2302.31	2357.85	2610.62	2616.18	2734.76
眉山市	Meishan	821.09	900.39	958.67	1011.94	1149.22	1269.90	1365.71	1403.00	1556.52	1635.63	1737.00
宜宾市	Yibin	1293.47	1411.37	1470.10	1609.56	1862.19	2349.31	2633.11	2813.34	3196.33	3484.08	3806.64
广安市	Guangan	790.91	838.46	874.39	928.03	1047.67	1157.00	1250.07	1301.57	1417.82	1425.02	1512.51
达州市	Dazhou	1159.16	1272.12	1366.56	1495.49	1697.58	1879.53	2027.51	2117.80	2368.28	2481.96	2656.69
雅安市	Yaan	428.95	475.79	519.02	561.65	608.54	653.34	723.04	754.59	847.56	936.32	1010.03
巴中市	Bazhong	400.22	472.29	507.68	549.91	607.23	704.66	739.87	705.75	737.41	740.89	780.28
资阳市	Ziyang	507.51	537.09	572.76	643.84	688.54	728.63	777.37	807.50	890.50	945.11	1019.22
阿坝藏族羌族自治州	Aba	216.43	237.31	274.99	291.53	318.13	368.66	390.03	410.62	449.63	462.51	503.19
甘孜藏族自治州	Ganzi	185.95	216.42	254.53	265.67	317.31	366.49	388.34	409.94	447.04	471.94	513.35
凉山彝族自治州	Liangshan	1144.43	1243.96	1312.56	1372.73	1448.79	1556.48	1670.21	1733.15	1917.40	2081.36	2261.11

注：本表按当年价格计算。
a) The data in this table are calculated at current prices.

2-8 各市(州)地区生产总值指数
Indices of Gross Domestic Product by Region

上年=100 (preceding year=100)

市(州)	Region	2013	2014	2015	2016	2017	2018	2019	2020	2021	2022	2023
全省	**Sichuan**	**110.0**	**108.5**	**107.9**	**107.8**	**108.1**	**108.0**	**107.4**	**103.8**	**108.2**	**102.8**	**106.0**
成都市	Chengdu	109.9	108.7	107.9	107.8	108.1	108.0	107.8	104.0	108.6	102.8	106.0
自贡市	Zigong	111.1	107.6	108.4	107.7	108.3	108.8	107.6	103.9	108.3	100.5	106.2
攀枝花市	Panzhihua	110.7	109.3	108.1	107.9	107.4	107.5	106.2	103.9	108.3	103.5	106.5
泸州市	Luzhou	111.0	109.9	110.0	109.5	109.1	107.7	108.0	104.2	108.5	104.1	105.6
德阳市	Deyang	109.8	108.7	108.2	108.4	109.0	108.9	107.2	102.5	108.7	103.1	106.7
绵阳市	Mianyang	109.8	108.8	108.6	108.3	109.1	109.0	108.1	104.4	108.7	105.0	108.0
广元市	Guangyuan	110.5	108.9	108.6	108.0	108.1	108.3	107.5	104.2	108.2	100.3	106.2
遂宁市	Suining	110.9	109.2	111.2	109.1	108.4	108.8	108.1	104.3	108.2	104.2	106.7
内江市	Neijiang	110.3	108.8	108.0	107.8	107.1	107.8	107.6	103.9	108.5	101.5	107.0
乐山市	Leshan	110.4	107.0	109.1	108.3	108.2	108.7	107.6	104.1	108.2	103.8	106.5
南充市	Nanchong	110.7	107.2	107.6	107.8	108.6	109.0	107.9	103.8	107.8	101.3	105.5
眉山市	Meishan	110.7	109.0	109.2	108.4	105.3	107.5	107.3	104.2	108.4	103.8	106.2
宜宾市	Yibin	108.1	108.0	108.5	108.2	108.8	109.2	108.8	104.6	108.9	104.5	107.5
广安市	Guangan	110.7	109.2	109.6	107.9	108.2	108.0	107.5	103.6	108.1	100.3	106.6
达州市	Dazhou	110.2	108.4	103.1	107.5	108.3	108.3	107.6	104.1	108.3	103.5	106.5
雅安市	Yaan	103.9	110.0	109.0	108.1	108.0	108.0	108.0	104.4	108.4	104.0	105.8
巴中市	Bazhong	110.7	108.8	108.6	107.8	108.1	108.1	105.8	102.5	103.3	101.3	106.0
资阳市	Ziyang	110.6	108.8	108.8	107.8	107.8	107.7	107.0	104.0	108.1	103.8	105.8
阿坝藏族羌族自治州	Aba	110.2	105.6	107.9	106.2	104.1	104.6	106.1	103.3	107.5	101.3	106.8
甘孜藏族自治州	Ganzi	112.1	104.2	105.1	106.9	109.0	109.3	106.5	103.6	107.0	103.5	106.2
凉山彝族自治州	Liangshan	110.2	108.3	102.8	105.9	105.3	104.1	105.6	103.9	107.2	106.0	107.0

注：本表按可比价格计算。
a) The indices in this table are calculated at comparable prices.

2-9 各市(州)第一产业增加值
Primary Industry by Region

单位：亿元 (100 million yuan)

市(州)	Region	2013	2014	2015	2016	2017	2018	2019	2020	2021	2022	2023
全省	**Sichuan**	**3257.42**	**3524.74**	**3660.96**	**3900.60**	**4262.51**	**4427.43**	**4807.52**	**5556.86**	**5662.00**	**5965.51**	**6056.64**
成都市	Chengdu	343.86	402.92	413.99	492.02	565.18	578.84	612.22	655.20	582.86	588.40	594.86
自贡市	Zigong	118.15	126.50	133.68	145.33	174.70	189.57	202.38	231.36	242.43	253.42	259.77
攀枝花市	Panzhihua	40.39	47.29	52.59	67.23	78.67	86.03	91.69	96.91	103.57	112.27	115.27
泸州市	Luzhou	150.78	167.19	173.76	181.72	192.05	197.30	216.99	256.47	265.08	277.26	281.41
德阳市	Deyang	201.14	202.28	204.38	212.61	219.82	223.48	234.61	272.73	281.34	296.18	303.73
绵阳市	Mianyang	199.01	200.92	202.00	203.16	260.75	266.96	302.46	370.97	377.34	381.46	393.19
广元市	Guangyuan	85.22	95.79	106.82	120.55	137.35	146.59	153.02	186.80	198.64	214.07	215.13
遂宁市	Suining	130.76	136.43	145.38	154.62	163.45	171.08	185.22	218.26	220.81	221.00	221.32
内江市	Neijiang	178.88	187.08	194.91	205.13	216.91	229.18	240.52	269.12	277.07	293.26	297.43
乐山市	Leshan	140.97	150.13	170.34	181.88	204.94	217.86	242.70	290.34	292.00	301.09	308.30
南充市	Nanchong	319.68	338.07	340.84	344.39	355.01	366.56	404.27	460.78	474.85	502.24	506.98
眉山市	Meishan	144.51	156.64	162.05	168.73	183.95	187.54	199.17	222.86	229.80	242.37	243.28
宜宾市	Yibin	198.22	215.39	221.31	232.88	251.99	254.75	277.65	344.57	356.12	396.09	404.18
广安市	Guangan	140.93	159.67	167.06	168.84	183.92	193.94	204.33	235.26	243.51	247.24	247.78
达州市	Dazhou	284.97	300.15	307.15	312.36	313.14	313.63	344.85	393.59	411.60	433.06	440.53
雅安市	Yaan	71.02	81.76	87.64	90.18	101.67	113.84	128.05	151.79	157.90	169.52	173.75
巴中市	Bazhong	82.74	83.85	85.06	89.37	102.09	108.32	124.01	161.82	174.50	192.14	195.20
资阳市	Ziyang	105.83	114.10	119.42	122.31	124.82	127.82	142.07	168.51	173.30	194.09	196.64
阿坝藏族羌族自治州	Aba	28.99	32.44	41.00	47.78	55.93	63.40	67.10	82.07	88.30	92.09	98.48
甘孜藏族自治州	Ganzi	53.65	57.78	57.84	58.25	58.61	58.83	66.52	80.68	79.36	84.28	86.88
凉山彝族自治州	Liangshan	237.73	268.38	273.75	301.25	317.57	331.92	367.68	406.76	431.63	473.97	503.41

注：本表按当年价格计算。
a) The data in this table are calculated at current prices.

2-10 各市(州)第一产业增加值指数
Indices of Primary Industry by Region

上年=100 (preceding year=100)

市(州)	Region	2013	2014	2015	2016	2017	2018	2019	2020	2021	2022	2023
全省	**Sichuan**	**103.5**	**103.8**	**103.8**	**103.8**	**103.8**	**103.6**	**102.8**	**105.1**	**107.0**	**104.1**	**104.0**
成都市	Chengdu	103.4	103.3	103.8	104.0	103.7	103.6	102.5	103.3	104.8	103.8	103.0
自贡市	Zigong	103.7	104.1	103.7	104.0	104.2	103.8	102.9	105.6	107.1	104.4	104.1
攀枝花市	Panzhihua	104.4	104.5	104.0	104.5	104.3	104.0	103.4	105.1	107.6	104.9	104.2
泸州市	Luzhou	104.1	104.1	103.7	103.8	103.9	103.7	102.6	105.6	106.7	104.4	103.9
德阳市	Deyang	103.3	104.1	103.5	101.9	103.8	103.6	102.5	103.6	107.3	104.3	104.1
绵阳市	Mianyang	102.9	103.7	103.4	102.9	104.1	103.9	102.9	105.4	107.5	104.4	103.8
广元市	Guangyuan	103.3	104.1	103.5	104.1	104.2	103.8	103.1	105.8	107.3	104.4	103.8
遂宁市	Suining	103.0	103.6	103.3	103.7	103.6	103.5	102.7	105.3	107.6	104.4	104.0
内江市	Neijiang	103.8	103.7	103.7	104.2	102.9	103.8	102.9	105.8	106.9	104.4	104.3
乐山市	Leshan	103.2	103.8	103.7	103.8	103.9	103.8	102.8	105.8	106.9	104.5	104.2
南充市	Nanchong	103.4	104.2	103.6	103.7	103.8	104.2	102.9	106.2	107.5	104.3	104.1
眉山市	Meishan	103.4	103.9	103.8	103.9	103.8	103.6	103.0	105.7	106.9	104.6	104.2
宜宾市	Yibin	103.4	103.6	103.7	103.6	103.5	103.6	102.9	105.7	107.6	104.3	104.3
广安市	Guangan	103.3	104.0	103.6	102.9	103.4	103.5	102.8	105.6	107.3	104.4	103.9
达州市	Dazhou	103.5	103.7	103.7	104.1	103.7	103.6	102.9	105.5	107.6	104.4	103.4
雅安市	Yaan	102.0	104.5	103.8	103.6	103.9	103.9	103.1	105.8	108.2	104.6	104.1
巴中市	Bazhong	103.1	103.0	103.4	103.7	103.6	103.7	102.6	105.4	107.4	104.2	103.9
资阳市	Ziyang	102.7	103.9	103.0	103.6	103.9	103.6	102.7	105.4	107.4	104.4	103.8
阿坝藏族羌族自治州	Aba	104.4	104.6	103.9	104.8	103.1	103.4	103.1	104.5	106.9	104.4	109.3
甘孜藏族自治州	Ganzi	104.0	104.5	103.8	104.1	104.4	103.5	102.9	104.5	104.8	104.2	104.1
凉山彝族自治州	Liangshan	104.4	104.4	103.9	104.1	103.8	103.8	103.3	104.8	107.0	104.2	104.3

注：本表按可比价格计算。
a) The indices in this table are calculated at comparable prices.

2-11 各市(州)第二产业增加值
Secondary Industry by Region

单位：亿元 (100 million yuan)

市(州)	Region	2013	2014	2015	2016	2017	2018	2019	2020	2021	2022	2023
全省	**Sichuan**	**12418.94**	**13082.69**	**13192.45**	**13450.13**	**14569.17**	**16056.94**	**17187.92**	**17505.61**	**19949.74**	**20591.44**	**21306.70**
成都市	Chengdu	4067.91	4193.64	4210.93	4216.36	4504.73	4834.16	5187.57	5333.93	5989.23	6341.30	6370.87
自贡市	Zigong	452.66	458.45	462.69	472.12	495.86	525.30	558.98	559.47	619.80	561.41	588.04
攀枝花市	Panzhihua	453.16	471.57	475.15	482.91	506.35	522.96	549.76	557.93	631.22	675.69	717.30
泸州市	Luzhou	657.89	725.18	728.47	779.88	856.41	938.00	1023.38	1042.40	1226.49	1284.84	1332.93
德阳市	Deyang	767.09	786.86	789.83	809.96	963.99	1083.27	1133.31	1126.60	1283.90	1356.19	1421.68
绵阳市	Mianyang	742.59	836.29	844.18	878.05	993.66	1090.63	1161.75	1186.89	1404.04	1491.00	1599.05
广元市	Guangyuan	256.29	274.09	282.30	289.08	316.50	359.69	386.68	405.33	459.62	413.82	437.46
遂宁市	Suining	376.84	459.62	480.95	487.66	522.22	562.00	618.31	614.98	701.53	744.49	783.11
内江市	Neijiang	365.10	373.51	375.27	385.41	422.62	445.79	474.70	465.25	531.63	521.78	561.74
乐山市	Leshan	599.33	651.89	655.35	658.50	685.22	740.94	799.33	814.63	923.55	995.95	1034.47
南充市	Nanchong	570.52	613.78	616.67	641.60	709.23	851.20	923.07	916.76	1043.80	933.82	949.21
眉山市	Meishan	411.97	434.44	437.42	447.21	465.78	490.89	526.45	528.02	622.03	652.59	680.40
宜宾市	Yibin	722.18	746.30	754.00	772.30	856.40	1180.98	1324.52	1374.30	1601.44	1742.52	1888.89
广安市	Guangan	336.02	337.96	342.42	349.57	368.55	382.72	414.89	417.78	466.22	433.91	460.15
达州市	Dazhou	491.10	526.55	533.69	548.97	592.60	653.26	720.51	735.05	839.11	842.67	896.11
雅安市	Yaan	195.55	197.94	199.41	200.19	206.46	207.77	227.07	227.44	263.25	294.78	317.28
巴中市	Bazhong	156.31	176.62	177.92	186.03	207.99	238.22	234.38	198.91	201.27	162.90	176.58
资阳市	Ziyang	194.13	199.33	202.76	207.55	216.94	224.95	230.99	228.90	270.71	278.45	299.71
阿坝藏族羌族自治州	Aba	79.32	80.82	81.94	83.08	86.39	91.16	95.26	96.33	109.37	115.47	122.53
甘孜藏族自治州	Ganzi	47.22	52.88	53.50	54.12	75.93	87.32	99.21	104.82	119.38	129.98	147.24
凉山彝族自治州	Liangshan	475.77	484.97	487.59	499.57	515.35	545.72	564.73	575.28	660.73	717.89	779.40

注：本表按当年价格计算。
a) The data in this table are calculated at current prices.

2-12 各市(州)第二产业增加值指数
Indices of Secondary Industry by Region

上年=100 (preceding year=100)

市(州)	Region	2013	2014	2015	2016	2017	2018	2019	2020	2021	2022	2023
全省	**Sichuan**	**112.0**	**109.0**	**107.7**	**107.6**	**107.5**	**107.5**	**107.4**	**103.8**	**107.8**	**102.0**	**105.0**
成都市	Chengdu	111.9	108.6	107.2	106.6	106.7	107.0	106.8	104.3	107.7	105.5	103.0
自贡市	Zigong	112.8	108.0	107.9	108.0	108.0	108.7	108.0	104.9	105.7	96.6	105.7
攀枝花市	Panzhihua	111.6	108.5	108.6	108.2	107.3	107.5	105.8	104.7	106.8	104.0	106.3
泸州市	Luzhou	112.5	111.4	110.0	110.3	109.7	108.5	108.4	103.3	108.6	104.2	105.8
德阳市	Deyang	111.4	109.2	108.5	109.3	109.6	109.3	107.0	101.5	108.0	103.0	106.8
绵阳市	Mianyang	112.3	109.3	108.8	108.4	109.0	109.6	108.0	104.1	108.8	105.9	107.7
广元市	Guangyuan	113.8	109.6	108.8	109.2	108.8	109.6	107.8	104.8	107.3	94.9	107.2
遂宁市	Suining	114.1	110.5	111.5	109.8	108.7	109.1	109.0	104.3	107.6	105.6	106.5
内江市	Neijiang	111.4	109.7	108.3	108.8	107.2	108.5	108.6	104.1	106.7	99.8	107.1
乐山市	Leshan	111.6	106.2	109.9	108.5	108.5	108.4	107.9	103.9	108.6	105.5	106.4
南充市	Nanchong	114.7	107.0	108.3	108.0	109.2	109.9	109.3	102.7	105.9	97.5	104.0
眉山市	Meishan	112.5	111.4	110.6	109.6	103.3	107.2	107.9	103.4	112.7	104.6	105.8
宜宾市	Yibin	108.2	108.1	108.6	109.0	109.1	110.0	109.7	105.2	108.2	105.2	107.8
广安市	Guangan	113.5	111.4	110.8	108.9	108.4	108.6	108.4	103.6	106.6	94.8	107.2
达州市	Dazhou	113.4	109.2	101.1	108.3	107.9	108.3	109.9	105.2	105.4	105.4	107.0
雅安市	Yaan	103.3	112.1	109.9	109.4	107.9	107.6	107.8	104.6	108.4	103.9	105.7
巴中市	Bazhong	115.9	110.0	109.4	109.5	109.7	109.4	102.2	101.8	98.8	96.4	110.2
资阳市	Ziyang	113.4	111.7	109.8	108.5	107.8	107.5	106.9	103.9	108.8	105.1	106.0
阿坝藏族羌族自治州	Aba	114.1	106.5	108.0	105.8	108.7	103.9	104.7	105.3	108.5	100.3	104.3
甘孜藏族自治州	Ganzi	118.8	101.7	104.0	111.3	117.9	116.6	113.9	108.3	107.0	106.0	108.9
凉山彝族自治州	Liangshan	114.4	110.9	100.4	105.5	105.9	100.8	102.5	105.2	108.4	108.6	107.1

注：本表按可比价格计算。
a) The indices in this table are calculated at comparable prices.

2-13 各市(州)第三产业增加值
Tertiary Industry by Region

单位：亿元 (100 million yuan)

市(州)	Region	2013	2014	2015	2016	2017	2018	2019	2020	2021	2022	2023
全省	**Sichuan**	**10841.66**	**12283.90**	**13488.60**	**15787.75**	**19073.46**	**22417.73**	**24368.31**	**25439.17**	**28476.24**	**30053.25**	**32769.54**
成都市	Chengdu	5038.89	5771.87	6037.39	7165.69	8861.48	10285.94	11210.87	11848.87	13390.22	13859.68	15108.99
自贡市	Zigong	342.56	357.14	373.90	403.39	495.61	599.87	642.85	649.20	733.63	822.46	902.66
攀枝花市	Panzhihua	158.78	166.89	184.82	212.79	257.23	332.46	360.57	368.98	416.00	432.56	471.23
泸州市	Luzhou	347.92	386.75	467.08	539.04	650.45	760.25	830.67	863.76	941.13	1039.42	1111.56
德阳市	Deyang	435.61	476.10	531.56	670.25	723.62	841.64	957.82	984.14	1121.72	1172.73	1289.00
绵阳市	Mianyang	528.81	574.87	696.82	876.70	1059.16	1255.71	1406.28	1462.68	1622.66	1807.05	2046.49
广元市	Guangyuan	178.74	193.20	225.00	247.64	297.96	374.22	413.50	415.88	457.98	487.20	527.23
遂宁市	Suining	199.09	212.95	245.03	284.56	360.76	497.77	536.18	542.39	597.53	648.98	710.54
内江市	Neijiang	371.13	413.27	447.82	495.89	542.58	643.86	697.17	710.12	796.83	841.91	947.94
乐山市	Leshan	356.63	393.79	454.94	495.02	591.45	751.01	830.57	896.20	978.58	1011.77	1104.76
南充市	Nanchong	393.51	439.85	505.89	606.98	774.01	897.97	974.97	980.31	1091.97	1180.12	1278.57
眉山市	Meishan	264.61	309.31	359.20	396.00	499.49	591.47	640.09	652.12	704.69	740.67	813.32
宜宾市	Yibin	373.07	449.68	494.79	604.38	753.80	913.58	1030.94	1094.47	1238.77	1345.47	1513.57
广安市	Guangan	313.96	340.83	364.91	409.62	495.20	580.34	630.85	648.53	708.08	743.87	804.58
达州市	Dazhou	383.09	445.42	525.72	634.16	791.84	912.64	962.15	989.16	1117.57	1206.23	1320.05
雅安市	Yaan	162.38	196.09	231.97	271.28	300.41	331.73	367.92	375.36	426.41	472.02	519.00
巴中市	Bazhong	161.17	211.82	244.70	274.51	297.15	358.12	381.48	345.02	361.63	385.85	408.50
资阳市	Ziyang	207.55	223.66	250.58	313.98	346.78	375.86	404.31	410.09	446.49	472.57	522.87
阿坝藏族羌族自治州	Aba	108.12	124.05	152.05	160.67	175.81	214.10	227.67	232.22	251.97	254.95	282.18
甘孜藏族自治州	Ganzi	85.08	105.76	143.19	153.30	182.77	220.34	222.61	224.44	248.31	257.68	279.23
凉山彝族自治州	Liangshan	430.93	490.61	551.22	571.91	615.87	678.84	737.80	751.11	825.03	889.50	978.30

注：本表按当年价格计算。
a) The data in this table are calculated at current prices.

2-14 各市(州)第三产业增加值指数
Indices of Tertiary Industry by Region

上年=100 (preceding year=100)

市(州)	Region	2013	2014	2015	2016	2017	2018	2019	2020	2021	2022	2023
全省	**Sichuan**	**109.2**	**109.2**	**109.4**	**109.2**	**109.7**	**109.5**	**108.4**	**103.4**	**108.8**	**103.2**	**107.1**
成都市	Chengdu	108.3	109.3	109.3	108.9	109.4	109.0	108.7	103.9	109.2	101.5	107.5
自贡市	Zigong	110.3	107.9	110.9	108.6	110.0	110.4	108.5	102.4	111.0	102.4	107.2
攀枝花市	Panzhihua	108.5	112.7	107.2	108.2	108.4	108.5	107.9	101.5	110.7	102.4	107.3
泸州市	Luzhou	111.0	109.1	112.7	110.4	110.0	107.7	109.2	105.2	108.9	104.0	105.7
德阳市	Deyang	109.4	109.7	109.6	109.5	110.1	110.1	108.9	103.5	109.9	103.1	107.1
绵阳市	Mianyang	108.9	109.9	110.2	109.7	110.5	109.6	109.5	104.4	108.9	104.5	109.2
广元市	Guangyuan	110.2	110.3	110.8	108.3	109.1	108.6	108.9	102.8	109.5	103.8	106.4
遂宁市	Suining	109.9	110.0	115.3	111.0	110.3	111.0	109.3	103.9	109.0	102.7	107.9
内江市	Neijiang	111.2	109.3	109.1	108.4	108.7	108.9	108.6	103.1	110.3	101.5	108.0
乐山市	Leshan	110.6	109.7	109.4	109.6	109.3	110.6	108.8	103.9	108.2	102.2	107.4
南充市	Nanchong	110.8	109.8	109.4	110.4	111.0	110.9	109.1	103.8	109.7	103.4	107.4
眉山市	Meishan	111.4	107.2	109.1	109.0	108.5	109.5	108.5	104.5	105.5	102.9	107.3
宜宾市	Yibin	110.4	109.9	110.2	109.1	110.7	110.4	109.8	103.4	110.2	103.9	108.0
广安市	Guangan	110.0	108.1	110.4	109.2	110.0	109.4	108.4	102.9	109.3	102.2	107.2
达州市	Dazhou	110.0	110.2	105.6	108.7	111.1	110.7	107.6	102.5	110.6	101.7	107.5
雅安市	Yaan	105.8	108.5	109.6	108.7	109.7	109.8	109.7	103.8	108.4	103.7	106.6
巴中市	Bazhong	109.9	110.8	110.5	108.0	108.5	108.5	109.4	102.1	104.0	102.6	105.0
资阳市	Ziyang	110.8	106.6	110.2	109.3	109.6	109.6	108.8	103.5	108.0	102.9	106.6
阿坝藏族羌族自治州	Aba	107.8	104.9	109.2	106.8	102.0	105.3	107.6	101.9	107.3	100.6	107.0
甘孜藏族自治州	Ganzi	110.0	106.5	106.7	106.4	107.4	108.4	104.4	100.9	107.7	102.1	105.7
凉山彝族自治州	Liangshan	107.5	106.6	105.7	107.2	105.5	107.0	109.3	102.6	106.3	104.9	108.5

注：本表按可比价格计算。

a) The indices in this table are calculated at comparable prices.

2-15 各市(州)人均地区生产总值
Per Capita GDP by Region

单位：元 (yuan)

市(州)	Region	2013	2014	2015	2016	2017	2018	2019	2020	2021	2022	2023
全省	**Sichuan**	**32750**	**35563**	**37150**	**40297**	**45835**	**51658**	**55619**	**58009**	**64610**	**67610**	**71835**
成都市	Chengdu	57538	61099	60643	65067	73770	80503	84584	86266	94837	97925	103465
自贡市	Zigong	34260	35510	36809	38993	44681	50664	54959	57326	64375	66570	71726
攀枝花市	Panzhihua	53165	55934	58216	62382	68980	77231	82403	84404	94793	100454	107133
泸州市	Luzhou	27656	30741	32869	35832	40383	44918	48903	50885	57132	61054	63913
德阳市	Deyang	39995	41900	43756	48588	54795	61788	67005	68847	77703	81650	87197
绵阳市	Mianyang	31724	34572	37093	41324	48442	54376	59381	62151	69798	75238	82347
广元市	Guangyuan	20986	22797	24883	26795	30990	36749	40355	43337	48638	48972	52204
遂宁市	Suining	22378	25954	28337	30568	35150	42167	46615	48523	54300	58137	62137
内江市	Neijiang	25583	27627	29337	31823	35213	40062	43754	45553	51377	53519	58758
乐山市	Leshan	33940	37125	39858	41640	46315	53633	58942	63188	69501	73249	77699
南充市	Nanchong	20928	22909	24325	26741	31210	36390	40145	41717	46743	47092	49453
眉山市	Meishan	27665	30275	32192	33992	38720	42873	46123	47431	52638	55258	58722
宜宾市	Yibin	29251	31968	33200	36097	41456	51941	57820	61427	69531	75552	82341
广安市	Guangan	24887	26450	27548	29083	32689	35999	38702	40073	43558	43941	46798
达州市	Dazhou	21180	23244	24965	27325	31012	34392	37284	39182	43955	46284	49755
雅安市	Yaan	28483	31656	34694	37847	41341	44688	49796	52366	59105	65386	70582
巴中市	Bazhong	12653	15196	16645	18410	20767	24596	26377	25720	27322	27780	29517
资阳市	Ziyang	20497	21985	23668	26726	28761	30770	33207	34806	38717	41516	45078
阿坝藏族羌族自治州	Aba	24373	26875	31284	33432	36864	43220	46376	49532	54900	56473	61067
甘孜藏族自治州	Ganzi	16813	19550	22951	23848	28432	32869	34891	36931	40347	42807	46478
凉山彝族自治州	Liangshan	25048	27090	28312	29139	30373	32413	34566	35720	39396	42629	46159

注：本表按当年价格计算；人均GDP按年平均常住人口计算。
a) The data in this table are calculated at current prices; the per capita GDP are calculated based on the annual average date of resident population.

2-16 各市(州)人均地区生产总值指数
Indices of Per Capita GDP by Region

上年=100 (preceding year=100)

市(州)	Region	2013	2014	2015	2016	2017	2018	2019	2020	2021	2022	2023
全省	**Sichuan**	**109.7**	**108.1**	**107.3**	**107.1**	**107.5**	**107.5**	**107.0**	**103.4**	**108.1**	**102.8**	**106.0**
成都市	Chengdu	106.4	105.2	104.2	103.8	104.5	104.6	104.5	101.2	106.7	102.0	105.5
自贡市	Zigong	111.1	108.1	109.1	108.4	108.6	109.4	109.3	105.7	109.8	101.3	107.0
攀枝花市	Panzhihua	110.3	109.4	108.3	108.0	107.6	107.7	106.4	104.1	108.2	103.4	106.3
泸州市	Luzhou	111.6	110.5	109.9	108.9	108.6	107.3	107.6	103.8	108.3	104.0	105.5
德阳市	Deyang	111.0	109.1	108.5	108.5	109.1	109.0	107.4	102.7	108.8	103.1	106.7
绵阳市	Mianyang	109.6	108.1	107.8	107.4	108.2	108.3	107.5	103.8	108.3	104.7	107.7
广元市	Guangyuan	110.5	109.3	108.7	108.7	109.3	109.7	109.0	105.8	109.6	101.1	107.0
遂宁市	Suining	112.3	110.6	112.7	110.7	110.4	111.0	109.8	105.7	109.6	105.1	107.3
内江市	Neijiang	111.8	110.4	109.7	109.5	108.9	109.9	109.7	105.8	110.1	102.4	107.7
乐山市	Leshan	110.5	107.4	109.4	108.5	108.5	109.0	108.0	104.5	108.5	104.0	106.6
南充市	Nanchong	111.7	108.3	108.7	108.9	109.8	110.5	109.4	105.3	109.1	101.9	106.0
眉山市	Meishan	110.4	108.8	109.1	108.4	105.7	107.7	107.4	104.3	108.4	103.8	106.3
宜宾市	Yibin	108.6	108.2	108.1	107.5	108.0	108.5	108.1	104.0	108.5	104.2	107.2
广安市	Guangan	111.2	109.5	109.5	107.3	107.7	107.7	106.9	103.0	107.9	100.5	106.9
达州市	Dazhou	110.2	108.4	103.0	107.5	108.2	108.4	108.1	104.8	108.6	103.8	107.0
雅安市	Yaan	104.1	110.2	109.5	109.0	108.9	108.8	108.7	105.2	108.9	104.0	105.9
巴中市	Bazhong	112.5	110.7	110.7	110.1	110.5	110.3	108.0	104.7	105.0	102.4	106.9
资阳市	Ziyang	112.4	110.3	109.9	108.3	108.5	108.9	108.2	104.9	109.0	104.7	106.6
阿坝藏族羌族自治州	Aba	110.7	106.2	108.4	107.1	105.2	105.8	107.6	104.8	108.8	101.3	106.2
甘孜藏族自治州	Ganzi	111.6	104.1	104.9	106.4	108.8	109.4	106.7	103.9	107.2	103.8	106.1
凉山彝族自治州	Liangshan	109.8	107.8	101.9	104.2	104.0	103.4	105.0	103.5	106.9	105.6	106.7

注：本表按可比价格计算。
a) The indices in this table are calculated at comparable prices.

2-17 各市(州)民营经济增加值(2023年)
Civilian-owned Value Added by Region(2023)

单位：亿元 (100 million yuan)

市(州)	Region	民营经济增加值 Civilian-owned Value Added	第一产业 Primary Industry	第二产业 Secondary Industry	第三产业 Tertiary Industry	人均民营经济增加值(元) Per Capita Civilian-owned Value Added (yuan)
全省	**Sichuan**	**32195.15**	**1487.23**	**13819.45**	**16888.47**	**38460**
成都市	Chengdu	10722.13	77.69	3369.04	7275.40	50255
自贡市	Zigong	958.42	53.29	447.36	457.77	39272
攀枝花市	Panzhihua	651.15	22.59	375.60	252.96	53504
泸州市	Luzhou	1517.31	72.29	850.73	594.29	35576
德阳市	Deyang	1711.30	84.79	893.61	732.90	49503
绵阳市	Mianyang	2375.25	44.96	1103.39	1226.90	48430
广元市	Guangyuan	648.46	71.19	305.82	271.45	28693
遂宁市	Suining	1059.80	57.01	596.87	405.92	38399
内江市	Neijiang	1079.97	47.80	482.93	549.24	35115
乐山市	Leshan	1377.17	97.32	728.77	551.08	43720
南充市	Nanchong	1629.27	137.70	778.33	713.24	29462
眉山市	Meishan	982.48	49.18	428.03	505.27	33214
宜宾市	Yibin	2197.48	100.60	1286.67	810.21	47534
广安市	Guangan	854.14	65.79	371.75	416.60	26428
达州市	Dazhou	1614.56	96.60	696.57	821.39	30238
雅安市	Yaan	583.41	30.28	251.71	301.42	40770
巴中市	Bazhong	434.33	67.15	162.09	205.09	16430
资阳市	Ziyang	550.45	44.67	240.63	265.15	24345
阿坝藏族羌族自治州	Aba	221.81	47.32	77.39	97.10	26919
甘孜藏族自治州	Ganzi	194.23	70.88	37.85	85.50	17586
凉山彝族自治州	Liangshan	994.92	155.64	404.26	435.02	20311

注：本表按当年价格计算；人均民营经济增加值年平均人口数按常住人口计算。
a) The data in this table are calculated at current prices; per capita civilian-owned value added are calculated on the annual average resident population.

2-18 各市(州)民营经济增加值指数(2023年)

Indices of Civilian-owned Value Added by Region(2023)

上年=100 (preceding year=100)

市(州)	Region	民营经济增加值 Civilian-owned Value Added	第一产业 Primary Industry	第二产业 Secondary Industry	第三产业 Tertiary Industry	人均民营经济增加值 Per Capita Civilian-owned Value Added
全省	**Sichuan**	**105.6**	**104.0**	**104.7**	**106.6**	**105.6**
成都市	Chengdu	105.5	104.3	102.9	106.8	105.0
自贡市	Zigong	105.1	104.1	110.0	100.9	105.9
攀枝花市	Panzhihua	106.1	105.0	105.6	106.8	105.9
泸州市	Luzhou	104.5	104.1	105.6	103.0	104.4
德阳市	Deyang	107.0	104.8	104.6	110.6	107.1
绵阳市	Mianyang	106.6	102.0	104.4	109.1	106.3
广元市	Guangyuan	105.7	104.2	107.9	103.6	106.5
遂宁市	Suining	107.8	104.5	107.2	109.2	108.4
内江市	Neijiang	106.3	105.3	104.6	108.1	107.1
乐山市	Leshan	106.6	104.4	109.5	102.9	106.7
南充市	Nanchong	104.0	105.2	100.5	108.3	104.5
眉山市	Meishan	104.5	105.7	104.4	104.5	104.6
宜宾市	Yibin	107.5	104.2	110.9	103.0	107.2
广安市	Guangan	105.0	104.8	106.7	103.6	105.4
达州市	Dazhou	106.2	103.2	101.7	110.9	106.6
雅安市	Yaan	104.5	104.1	106.9	102.6	104.6
巴中市	Bazhong	104.9	104.2	107.6	102.9	105.8
资阳市	Ziyang	104.0	103.8	99.3	108.6	104.8
阿坝藏族羌族自治州	Aba	107.1	108.4	105.9	107.3	106.4
甘孜藏族自治州	Ganzi	104.5	102.1	102.2	108.1	104.4
凉山彝族自治州	Liangshan	105.1	100.8	101.4	110.4	104.7

注：本表按可比价格计算。

a) The data in this table are calculated at comparable prices.

主要统计指标解释

国内（地区）生产总值(GDP) 指一个国家（或地区）所有常住单位在一定时期内生产活动的最终成果。国内生产总值有三种表现形态，即价值形态、收入形态和产品形态。从价值形态看，它是所有常住单位在一定时期内生产的全部货物和服务价值与同期投入的全部非固定资产货物和服务价值的差额，即所有常住单位的增加值之和；从收入形态看，它是所有常住单位在一定时期内创造的各项收入之和，包括劳动者报酬、生产税净额、固定资产折旧和营业盈余；从产品形态看，它是所有常住单位在一定时期内最终使用的货物和服务价值与货物和服务净出口价值之和。在实际核算中，国内生产总值有三种计算方法，即生产法、收入法和支出法。三种方法分别从不同的方面反映国内生产总值及其构成。

对于一个地区来说，称为地区生产总值或地区 GDP。

三次产业 三次产业的划分是世界上较为常用的产业结构分类，但各国的划分不尽一致。根据《国民经济行业分类》（GB/T 4754—2017）和《三次产业划分规定》，我国的三次产业划分是：

第一产业是指农、林、牧、渔业（不含农、林、牧、渔专业及辅助性活动）。

第二产业是指采矿业（不含开采专业及辅助性活动），制造业（不含金属制品、机械和设备修理业），电力、热力、燃气及水生产和供应业，建筑业。

第三产业即服务业，是指除第一产业、第二产业以外的其他行业。

民营经济 是具有中国特色的一种经济类型。统计对象包括内地公民、民间机构和内地公民集体拥有所有权、经营权或控制权的营利法人、非营利法人、特别法人、非法人组织和个体经营户。

Explanatory Notes on Main Statistical Indicators

Gross Domestic Product (GDP) refers to the final products produced by all resident units in a country (or in a region) during a certain period of time. Gross domestic product is expressed in three different perspectives, namely value, income, and products respectively. GDP in its value perspective refers to the balance of total value of all goods and services produced by all resident units during a certain period of time, minus the total value of input of goods and services of the nature of non-fixed assets; in other words, it is the sum of the value-added of all resident units. GDP from the perspective of income refers to the sum of all kinds of revenue, including Compensation of Employees, Net Taxes on Production, Depreciation of Fixed Assets, and Operating Surplus. GDP from the perspective of products refers to the value of all goods and services for final demand by all resident units plus the net exports of goods and services during a given period of time. In the practice of national accounting, gross domestic product is calculated from three approaches, namely production approach, income approach and expenditure approach, which reflect gross domestic product and its composition from different angles.

For a region, it is called as Gross Regional Product(GRP) or regional GDP.

Three Strata of Industry Classification of economic activities into three strata of industry is a common practice in the world, although the grouping varies to some extent from country to country. In China, according to Industrial classification for National Economic Activities (GB/T 4754—2017) and Rules on Division of Three Strata of Industries, economic activities are categorized into the following three strata of industry:

Primary industry refers to agriculture, forestry, animal husbandry and fishery industries (not including professional and auxiliary activities of agriculture, forestry, animal husbandry and fishery industries).

Secondary industry refers to mining and quarrying (not including professional and auxiliary activities of mining), manufacturing (not including repair service of metal products, machinery and equipment), production and supply of electricity, heat, gas and water, and construction.

Tertiary industry refers to all other economic activities not included in the primary or secondary industries.

Civilian-owned Economy refers to the economic type with Chinese characteristics.The statistical objects include profit-making legal persons, non-profit legal persons, special legal persons, non legal person organizations and self-employed households with ownership, management or control rights of mainland citizens, non-governmental organizations and profit-making legal persons.

03 人 口
Chapter 3 Population

3-1 年末常住人口、城镇化率、出生率、死亡率和自然增长率
Resident Population(year-end), Urbanization Rate, Birth Rate, Death Rate and Natural Growth Rate of Population

年份 Year	年末常住人口 (万人) Resident Population (year-end)	城镇化率 (%) Urbanization Rate (%)	出生率 (‰) Birth Rate (‰)	死亡率 (‰) Death Rate (‰)	自然增长率 (‰) Natural Growth Rate (‰)
1952			41.0	18.2	22.8
1957			29.2	12.1	17.1
1962			28.0	14.6	13.4
1965			42.4	11.4	31.0
1970			38.7	9.2	29.5
1975			31.2	8.9	22.3
1978			15.1	7.0	8.1
1980			13.0	6.8	6.2
1985			15.4	7.2	8.2
1990			19.1	7.7	11.4
1995			17.1	7.2	9.9
1996			16.6	7.3	9.3
1997			15.7	7.0	8.7
1998			14.6	7.1	7.5
1999			13.8	7.0	6.8
2000	8234.8	26.70	12.1	7.0	5.1
2001	8143.0	27.20	11.2	6.8	4.4
2002	8110.0	28.20	10.4	6.5	3.9
2003	8176.0	30.10	9.2	6.1	3.1
2004	8090.0	31.10	9.1	6.3	2.8
2005	8212.0	33.00	9.7	6.8	2.9
2006	8169.0	34.30	9.2	6.3	2.9
2007	8127.0	35.60	9.2	6.3	2.9
2008	8138.0	37.40	9.5	7.1	2.4
2009	8185.0	38.70	9.1	6.4	2.7
2010	8045.0	40.18	8.9	6.6	2.3
2011	8064.0	41.85	9.8	6.8	3.0
2012	8085.0	43.35	9.9	6.9	3.0
2013	8109.0	44.96	9.9	6.9	3.0
2014	8139.0	46.51	10.2	7.0	3.2
2015	8196.0	48.27	10.3	6.9	3.4
2016	8251.0	50.00	10.5	7.0	3.5
2017	8289.0	51.78	11.3	7.0	4.3
2018	8321.0	53.50	11.1	7.0	4.1
2019	8351.0	55.36	10.7	7.1	3.6
2020	8371.0	56.73	7.60	6.28	1.32
2021	8372.0	57.82	6.85	8.74	-1.89
2022	8374.0	58.35	6.39	9.04	-2.65
2023	8368.0	59.49	6.32	9.44	-3.12

注：①2000年、2010年、2020年为当年人口普查数据推算数，其余年份是依据年度人口变动调查并结合人口普查推算的修订数(以下有关表同)。②本表中出生率、死亡率和自然增长率在1981年及以前均根据公安年报计算，1982年以后按人口变动抽样调查计算。

a) The data of 2000, 2010 and 2020 are estimated by the census data of that year; the data of other years are the revised figures estimated by the annual population change survey and the cunsus (The same as the following related tables). b) Data of birth rate, death rate and natural growth rate in this table before 1981 were taken from the annual reports of the Bureau of Public Security. Since 1982, the data of province have been estimated by the annual population change survey.

3-2 各市(州)年末常住人口、城镇化率、出生率、死亡率、自然增长率和人口密度(2023年)

Resident Population(year-end), Urbanization Rate, Birth rate, Death rate, Natural Growth Rate and Population Density by Region(2023)

市(州)	Region	年末常住人口 (万人) Resident Population (year-end) (10 000 persons)	城镇化率 (%) Urbanization Rate (%)	出生率 (‰) Birth Rate (‰)	死亡率 (‰) Death Rate (‰)	自然增长率 (‰) Natural Growth Rate (‰)	人口密度 (人/平方公里) Population Density (person/sq.km)
全省	**Sichuan**	**8368.0**	**59.49**	**6.32**	**9.44**	**-3.12**	**172**
成都市	Chengdu	2140.3	80.50	7.24	5.35	1.89	1493
自贡市	Zigong	242.9	57.69	4.86	7.96	-3.10	554
攀枝花市	Panzhihua	121.8	70.78	6.81	7.38	-0.57	165
泸州市	Luzhou	426.7	53.16	7.10	8.73	-1.63	349
德阳市	Deyang	345.3	58.77	4.63	9.51	-4.88	584
绵阳市	Mianyang	491.1	56.01	5.70	7.23	-1.53	243
广元市	Guangyuan	224.9	49.57	5.30	8.84	-3.54	138
遂宁市	Suining	274.8	59.78	6.03	6.59	-0.56	516
内江市	Neijiang	306.3	52.57	4.98	5.94	-0.96	569
乐山市	Leshan	314.7	55.79	6.86	7.34	-0.48	247
南充市	Nanchong	551.1	52.83	4.73	6.94	-2.21	442
眉山市	Meishan	295.5	52.81	5.14	9.36	-4.22	414
宜宾市	Yibin	462.8	54.91	7.22	6.65	0.57	349
广安市	Guangan	322.6	46.57	6.31	6.28	0.03	509
达州市	Dazhou	532.4	52.48	5.74	7.28	-1.54	321
雅安市	Yaan	142.9	55.17	7.05	7.67	-0.62	95
巴中市	Bazhong	262.9	48.52	5.55	9.83	-4.28	214
资阳市	Ziyang	225.3	43.86	4.61	9.56	-4.95	392
阿坝藏族羌族自治州	Aba	82.5	43.75	9.45	4.35	5.10	10
甘孜藏族自治州	Ganzi	110.6	32.92	13.15	3.08	10.07	7
凉山彝族自治州	Liangshan	490.6	41.38	15.73	6.12	9.61	81

注：全省年末常住人口、城镇化率、出生率、死亡率、自然增长率数据，由国家统计局核定；市（州）出生率、死亡率、自然增长率数据，由市（州）统计局基于人口普查、年度人口变动调查、公安、卫健、民政等部门数据综合评估确定。

a) The data of resident population, urbanization rate, birth rate, death rate and natural growth rate at the end of the year of the province shall be approved by the National Bureau of Statistics; The data of birth rate, death rate and natural growth rate of the city (prefecture) shall be determined by the municipal (prefecture) statistics bureau based on the comprehensive evaluation of the data from the population census, annual population change survey, and the data from public security, health, civil affairs and other departments.

3-3 各市(州)年末常住人口数
Resident Population(year-end) by Region

单位：万人 (10 000 persons)

市(州)	Region	2013	2014	2015	2016	2017	2018	2019	2020	2021	2022	2023
全省	**Sichuan**	**8109.0**	**8139.0**	**8196.0**	**8251.0**	**8289.0**	**8321.0**	**8351.0**	**8371.0**	**8372.0**	**8374.0**	**8368.0**
成都市	Chengdu	1564.3	1619.8	1685.3	1858.2	1918.8	1981.3	2040.9	2094.7	2119.2	2126.8	2140.3
自贡市	Zigong	266.3	264.3	262.9	260.6	261.3	257.6	253.3	249.0	246.7	245.2	242.9
攀枝花市	Panzhihua	122.7	122.5	122.3	122.2	122.0	121.8	121.3	121.3	121.4	121.6	121.8
泸州市	Luzhou	416.7	415.5	417.7	419.9	421.4	422.6	424.4	425.6	425.9	426.3	426.7
德阳市	Deyang	350.4	348.9	348.5	348.2	347.9	347.4	346.7	345.7	345.9	346.1	345.3
绵阳市	Mianyang	464.3	468.2	471.6	475.9	479.2	481.9	484.9	487.1	488.3	489.8	491.1
广元市	Guangyuan	247.3	246.7	246.8	243.8	241.3	237.9	234.4	230.7	228.3	227.1	224.9
遂宁市	Suining	313.8	309.6	305.4	301.0	294.3	289.4	285.4	281.5	278.2	277.2	274.8
内江市	Neijiang	355.1	349.8	344.2	338.6	332.8	325.6	320.0	314.2	310.4	308.8	306.3
乐山市	Leshan	322.7	321.4	321.1	320.3	319.4	318.2	317.2	316.1	315.1	315.3	314.7
南充市	Nanchong	610.5	604.4	598.7	592.7	585.2	577.6	569.3	561.0	556.2	554.9	551.1
眉山市	Meishan	297.2	297.6	297.9	297.4	296.1	296.2	296.0	295.6	295.9	296.1	295.5
宜宾市	Yibin	441.5	441.5	444.1	447.6	450.8	453.8	456.9	459.1	460.5	461.8	462.8
广安市	Guangan	317.2	316.7	318.0	320.1	320.8	322.0	324.0	325.6	324.8	323.8	322.6
达州市	Dazhou	547.4	547.2	547.6	547.0	547.7	545.3	542.2	538.7	537.0	535.5	532.4
雅安市	Yaan	150.4	150.1	149.1	147.7	146.6	145.7	144.6	143.6	143.1	143.3	142.9
巴中市	Bazhong	313.6	307.9	302.1	295.3	289.4	283.5	277.4	271.4	267.6	265.8	262.9
资阳市	Ziyang	350.8	347.5	347.6	240.3	238.4	235.1	233.0	231.0	228.4	226.9	225.3
阿坝藏族羌族自治州	Aba	88.5	88.1	87.6	86.8	85.8	84.7	83.5	82.3	81.5	82.3	82.5
甘孜藏族自治州	Ganzi	110.7	110.6	111.1	111.7	111.5	111.4	111.2	110.8	110.2	110.3	110.6
凉山彝族自治州	Liangshan	457.6	460.7	466.4	475.7	478.3	482.0	484.4	486.0	487.4	489.1	490.6

3-4 各市(州)常住人口城镇化率
Urbanization Rate of Resident Population by Region

单位：%　　　　(%)

市(州)	Region	2013	2014	2015	2016	2017	2018	2019	2020	2021	2022	2023
全省	**Sichuan**	**44.96**	**46.51**	**48.27**	**50.00**	**51.78**	**53.50**	**55.36**	**56.73**	**57.82**	**58.35**	**59.49**
成都市	Chengdu	69.75	71.36	73.01	74.01	75.29	76.60	78.00	78.77	79.48	79.89	80.50
自贡市	Zigong	44.63	45.98	47.52	48.52	50.39	52.30	54.29	55.40	56.20	56.67	57.69
攀枝花市	Panzhihua	62.94	63.77	65.01	65.78	66.81	67.68	69.13	69.57	69.92	70.23	70.78
泸州市	Luzhou	41.34	42.34	43.71	44.68	46.37	47.64	48.93	50.24	51.36	51.91	53.16
德阳市	Deyang	44.86	46.30	47.91	49.02	50.88	52.58	54.38	55.97	57.07	57.61	58.77
绵阳市	Mianyang	42.57	43.69	44.92	45.90	47.27	48.60	49.71	51.66	53.63	54.29	56.01
广元市	Guangyuan	36.36	37.84	39.36	40.36	42.22	43.82	45.51	47.04	48.06	48.55	49.57
遂宁市	Suining	43.49	45.20	47.09	48.83	50.98	53.51	56.13	57.30	58.21	58.68	59.78
内江市	Neijiang	41.90	42.91	44.02	44.94	46.37	47.77	48.88	50.07	51.08	51.56	52.57
乐山市	Leshan	42.64	43.94	45.69	46.72	48.51	49.95	51.83	53.11	54.07	54.57	55.79
南充市	Nanchong	38.62	40.05	41.81	42.96	44.84	46.75	48.79	50.22	51.22	51.75	52.83
眉山市	Meishan	39.04	40.64	42.42	43.49	45.42	47.08	48.87	50.14	51.11	51.61	52.81
宜宾市	Yibin	40.84	41.89	43.46	44.60	46.37	47.63	49.57	51.39	52.94	53.55	54.91
广安市	Guangan	33.38	34.87	36.41	37.53	39.31	40.94	42.92	44.07	44.86	45.32	46.57
达州市	Dazhou	37.44	39.16	41.12	42.32	44.34	46.31	48.49	49.80	50.83	51.30	52.48
雅安市	Yaan	39.84	41.80	43.78	45.48	47.35	49.35	51.54	52.78	53.55	54.02	55.17
巴中市	Bazhong	34.27	36.00	37.70	38.88	40.67	42.63	45.04	46.16	46.92	47.34	48.52
资阳市	Ziyang	32.97	33.79	34.91	35.61	36.84	38.23	39.88	41.29	42.12	42.66	43.86
阿坝藏族羌族自治州	Aba	33.04	33.88	34.96	35.64	36.67	38.58	40.56	41.49	42.09	42.55	43.75
甘孜藏族自治州	Ganzi	23.23	24.14	25.17	25.90	26.92	28.44	30.10	31.01	31.52	31.92	32.92
凉山彝族自治州	Liangshan	30.11	31.11	32.39	33.00	34.04	34.89	35.96	36.96	38.66	39.46	41.38

3-5 年末户籍总人口数及构成
Total Registered Population and its Composition(year-end)

单位：万人 (10 000 persons)

年份 Year	年末户籍总人口 Total Registered Population (year-end)	按性别分 By Sex		按城乡分 By Residence	
		男 Male	女 Female	城镇人口 Urban Population	乡村人口 Rural Population
1952	4628.5	2357.9	2270.6		
1957	5088.8	2601.0	2487.8	568.0	4520.8
1962	4688.3	2368.9	2319.4	535.9	4152.4
1965	5162.1	2623.3	2538.8	606.4	4555.7
1970	6052.4	3089.0	2963.4	688.9	5363.5
1975	6874.7	3508.2	3366.5	736.6	6138.1
1978	7071.9	3621.5	3450.4	784.2	6287.7
1980	7154.8	3668.3	3486.5	829.6	6325.2
1985	7419.3	3828.9	3590.4	1025.9	6393.4
1990	7892.5	4088.1	3804.4	1101.7	6790.8
1995	8161.2	4238.9	3922.3	1331.8	6829.4
1996	8215.4	4266.6	3948.8	1378.1	6837.3
1997	8264.7	4291.4	3973.3	1420.1	6844.6
1998	8315.7	4317.5	3998.2	1460.3	6855.4
1999	8358.6	4337.7	4020.9	1507.7	6850.9
2000	8407.5	4358.9	4048.6	1565.0	6842.5
2001	8436.6	4375.4	4061.2	1622.1	6814.5
2002	8474.5	4395.3	4079.2	1677.6	6796.9
2003	8529.4	4424.7	4104.7	1795.2	6734.2
2004	8595.3	4460.0	4135.3	1914.3	6681.0
2005	8642.1	4483.6	4158.5	2013.8	6628.3
2006	8722.5	4520.3	4202.2	2070.8	6651.7
2007	8815.2	4566.4	4248.8	2140.0	6675.2
2008	8907.8	4607.7	4300.1	2203.4	6704.4
2009	8984.7	4639.2	4345.5	2286.3	6698.4
2010	9001.3	4640.4	4360.9	2355.2	6646.1
2011	9058.4	4665.6	4392.8	2462.7	6595.7
2012	9097.4	4685.0	4412.4	2512.0	6585.4
2013	9132.6	4700.8	4431.8	2632.4	6500.2
2014	9159.1	4710.4	4448.7	2694.0	6465.1
2015	9102.0	4680.1	4421.9	2785.2	6316.8
2016	9137.0	4696.2	4440.8	2997.5	6139.5
2017	9113.4	4677.8	4435.6	3116.3	5997.1
2018	9121.8	4678.3	4443.5	3271.5	5850.3
2019	9099.5	4665.3	4434.2	3346.8	5752.7
2020	9081.6	4653.7	4427.9	3475.5	5606.1
2021	9094.5	4658.4	4436.1	3496.1	5598.4
2022	9067.5	4640.8	4426.7	3523.9	5543.6
2023	9071.4	4640.3	4431.1	3559.9	5511.5

注：本篇章所列户籍人口资料均由四川省公安厅提供；2014年及以前的城镇人口、乡村人口为非农业人口、农业人口。

a) Data in this table were taken from the annual reports of the Bureau of Sichuan Provincial Public Security; Data of urban population and rural population before 2014 are those of non-agricultural population and agricultural population.

3−6 各市(州)年末户籍总户数及人口数(2023年)

Number of Registered Households and Population by Region(year-end)(2023)

市(州)	Region	年末户籍总户数(万户) Total Registered Households (year-end) (10 000 households)	年末户籍总人口(万人) Total Registered Population (year-end) (10 000 persons)	男性 Male	女性 Female	城镇人口 Urban Population	乡村人口 Rural Population
全省	**Sichuan**	**3163.9**	**9071.4**	**4640.3**	**4431.1**	**3559.9**	**5511.5**
成都市	Chengdu	594.5	1598.2	787.6	810.6	1114.5	483.7
自贡市	Zigong	106.2	312.3	158.5	153.8	113.0	199.3
攀枝花市	Panzhihua	36.8	106.7	53.9	52.7	55.7	51.0
泸州市	Luzhou	159.8	502.2	258.5	243.7	201.9	300.3
德阳市	Deyang	150.9	377.6	191.0	186.6	142.5	235.1
绵阳市	Mianyang	197.6	525.6	268.5	257.1	195.4	330.2
广元市	Guangyuan	111.2	291.2	149.3	142.0	81.5	209.8
遂宁市	Suining	131.7	353.1	182.7	170.4	106.9	246.2
内江市	Neijiang	139.9	396.9	204.3	192.6	111.2	285.7
乐山市	Leshan	125.1	344.9	175.0	169.9	132.9	212.0
南充市	Nanchong	246.2	703.5	367.1	336.4	203.8	499.7
眉山市	Meishan	122.6	338.0	171.0	167.0	132.9	205.1
宜宾市	Yibin	164.1	547.5	283.9	263.6	206.9	340.6
广安市	Guangan	143.7	447.1	234.1	213.1	108.4	338.8
达州市	Dazhou	231.1	639.8	336.1	303.7	234.4	405.4
雅安市	Yaan	54.5	151.1	77.0	74.1	70.2	81.0
巴中市	Bazhong	126.4	356.6	186.4	170.2	103.8	252.8
资阳市	Ziyang	119.2	330.9	172.9	158.0	55.9	275.0
阿坝藏族羌族自治州	Aba	27.8	89.7	45.7	44.0	24.0	65.7
甘孜藏族自治州	Ganzi	26.5	109.8	55.3	54.5	21.5	88.3
凉山彝族自治州	Liangshan	147.9	548.5	281.7	266.8	142.5	406.0

3-7 各市(州)年末户籍人口数
Registered Population(year-end) by Region

单位：万人 (10 000 persons)

市(州)	Region	2013	2014	2015	2016	2017	2018	2019	2020	2021	2022	2023
全省	**Sichuan**	**9132.6**	**9159.1**	**9102.0**	**9137.0**	**9113.4**	**9121.8**	**9099.5**	**9081.6**	**9094.5**	**9067.5**	**9071.4**
成都市	Chengdu	1188.0	1210.7	1228.1	1398.9	1435.3	1478.1	1502.3	1519.7	1556.2	1571.6	1598.2
自贡市	Zigong	329.7	330.0	327.5	327.4	323.9	322.4	320.1	317.8	316.7	313.7	312.3
攀枝花市	Panzhihua	112.0	111.9	110.6	110.5	109.4	108.3	108.4	108.0	107.5	106.9	106.7
泸州市	Luzhou	508.4	508.9	505.7	508.3	509.6	509.7	508.6	508.0	506.7	503.8	502.2
德阳市	Deyang	392.0	392.5	390.0	391.7	387.7	386.8	384.5	382.3	381.5	378.5	377.6
绵阳市	Mianyang	547.4	548.8	545.5	545.2	536.8	536.0	531.4	528.5	527.0	525.7	525.6
广元市	Guangyuan	310.2	310.1	305.3	304.8	302.6	300.5	298.7	297.0	295.2	293.1	291.2
遂宁市	Suining	379.4	380.4	378.8	377.9	369.7	365.4	362.3	359.3	357.6	354.4	353.1
内江市	Neijiang	426.8	426.0	420.4	420.0	415.1	411.8	408.2	405.5	403.0	399.0	396.9
乐山市	Leshan	356.0	355.7	353.8	354.7	351.9	350.5	349.1	348.0	347.2	345.6	344.9
南充市	Nanchong	759.0	759.0	742.3	741.3	732.7	728.7	723.4	719.3	714.8	708.6	703.5
眉山市	Meishan	352.2	353.0	349.1	350.2	345.1	344.4	342.3	341.8	340.5	338.6	338.0
宜宾市	Yibin	550.4	554.3	552.1	555.9	555.4	552.3	551.4	551.0	550.5	548.4	547.5
广安市	Guangan	470.4	471.7	467.4	467.3	464.6	462.2	458.8	455.6	453.2	449.5	447.1
达州市	Dazhou	687.6	688.1	682.8	683.6	671.7	665.8	658.6	652.8	649.1	644.5	639.8
雅安市	Yaan	157.0	157.2	154.9	155.0	153.9	153.3	153.0	152.6	152.2	151.5	151.1
巴中市	Bazhong	390.2	383.1	379.5	375.3	376.2	368.3	365.6	364.1	361.6	359.1	356.6
资阳市	Ziyang	507.3	507.3	503.7	354.5	348.9	346.1	342.2	338.9	336.9	333.2	330.9
阿坝藏族羌族自治州	Aba	92.0	92.2	91.4	92.0	91.5	90.3	90.0	89.7	89.7	89.5	89.7
甘孜藏族自治州	Ganzi	110.2	111.3	109.2	110.1	110.1	110.1	109.7	108.6	109.2	109.3	109.8
凉山彝族自治州	Liangshan	506.4	506.9	503.9	512.4	521.3	530.8	530.9	533.1	538.3	543.0	548.5

3-8 各市(州)年末户籍城镇人口数
Registered Urban Population(year-end) by Region

单位：万人 (10 000 persons)

市(州)	Region	2013	2014	2015	2016	2017	2018	2019	2020	2021	2022	2023
全省	**Sichuan**	**2632.4**	**2694.0**	**2785.2**	**2997.5**	**3116.3**	**3271.5**	**3346.8**	**3475.5**	**3496.1**	**3523.9**	**3559.9**
成都市	Chengdu	728.7	755.8	720.6	784.6	851.1	901.6	940.7	1015.6	1056.4	1081.6	1114.5
自贡市	Zigong	112.5	113.2	126.5	132.1	134.2	135.7	136.4	121.4	113.7	113.0	113.0
攀枝花市	Panzhihua	59.9	59.5	58.9	58.0	57.1	56.5	56.6	57.5	56.3	55.8	55.7
泸州市	Luzhou	152.3	154.0	123.0	192.5	209.1	210.1	212.2	202.3	201.7	201.2	201.9
德阳市	Deyang	117.4	120.6	136.1	121.6	120.5	124.2	126.2	133.9	141.5	141.4	142.5
绵阳市	Mianyang	158.0	163.0	176.8	178.7	179.0	187.3	190.2	193.4	193.2	193.8	195.4
广元市	Guangyuan	72.2	73.5	73.5	68.6	70.9	72.8	75.6	81.3	81.9	81.6	81.5
遂宁市	Suining	97.5	99.2	107.4	98.0	96.4	100.6	103.5	109.6	107.8	107.1	106.9
内江市	Neijiang	96.4	97.4	110.3	115.4	114.5	113.6	112.5	113.8	111.4	111.4	111.2
乐山市	Leshan	118.5	120.4	134.0	122.1	126.5	129.0	132.5	135.8	135.0	132.7	132.9
南充市	Nanchong	176.6	179.1	173.1	207.2	206.6	211.1	210.7	211.6	205.0	204.3	203.8
眉山市	Meishan	98.9	100.6	100.2	111.0	111.3	116.7	119.5	133.7	132.9	132.7	132.9
宜宾市	Yibin	106.2	108.2	118.1	132.3	147.1	196.6	208.8	211.1	206.9	206.6	206.9
广安市	Guangan	90.6	94.1	103.9	107.5	107.7	117.3	116.8	112.0	111.3	108.1	108.4
达州市	Dazhou	139.6	144.2	160.0	204.3	212.0	218.2	222.2	235.9	238.0	235.5	234.4
雅安市	Yaan	42.6	43.6	54.0	65.8	65.9	67.4	67.9	70.7	70.4	70.2	70.2
巴中市	Bazhong	78.1	79.2	89.0	93.8	99.4	99.8	102.2	106.1	104.9	104.4	103.8
资阳市	Ziyang	89.2	90.7	93.4	57.0	56.3	56.9	56.3	64.7	59.2	56.4	55.9
阿坝藏族羌族自治州	Aba	20.5	20.8	31.5	26.3	27.0	25.5	25.3	25.3	24.3	24.1	24.0
甘孜藏族自治州	Ganzi	16.2	16.2	16.3	18.1	19.3	19.2	18.8	18.5	21.6	21.5	21.5
凉山彝族自治州	Liangshan	60.5	60.7	78.6	102.6	104.4	111.4	111.9	121.3	122.7	140.4	142.5

主要统计指标解释

人口数 指一定时点、一定地区范围内有生命的个人总和。

年度统计的年末人口数指每年 12 月 31 日 24 时的人口数。

常住人口 指实际经常居住在某地半年以上的人口。常住人口主要包括：(1) 调查时点居住在本乡、镇、街道，户口也在本乡、镇、街道的人；(2) 调查时点居住在本乡、镇、街道，户口不在本乡、镇、街道，离开户口登记地半年以上的人；(3) 调查时点居住在本乡、镇、街道，尚未办理常住户口的人；(4) 调查时点居住在港澳台或国外，户口在本乡、镇、街道的人。

户籍人口 指不管是否外出和外出时间长短，只要在某地公安户籍管理部门登记了常住户口，则为该地区的户籍人口。户籍人口数据由公安部门统计。

城镇人口和乡村人口 城镇人口是指居住在城镇范围内的全部常住人口；乡村人口是除上述人口以外的全部人口。

城镇化率 城镇化指伴随工业化的发展，非农产业向城镇聚集，农村人口向城镇集中的自然历史过程，是世界各国工业化进程中必然经历的历史阶段。城镇化率是指一个国家（地区）城镇的常住人口占该国家（地区）总人口的比例，是衡量城镇化水平高低，反映城镇化进程的一个重要指标。

出生率（又称粗出生率） 指在一定时期内(通常为一年)一定地区的出生人数与同期内平均人数(或期中人数)之比，用千分率表示。本资料中的出生率指年出生率，其计算公式为：

$$出生率=\frac{年出生人数}{年平均人数}\times 1000‰$$

式中：出生人数指活产婴儿，即胎儿脱离母体时(不管怀孕月数)，有过呼吸或其他生命现象。年平均人数指年初、年底人口数的平均数，也可用年中人口数代替。

死亡率（又称粗死亡率） 指在一定时期内(通常为一年)一定地区的死亡人数与同期内平均人数(或期中人数)之比，用千分率表示。本资料中的死亡率指年死亡率，其计算公式为：

$$死亡率=\frac{年死亡人数}{年平均人数}\times 1000‰$$

人口自然增长率 指在一定时期内(通常为一年)人口自然增加数(出生人数减死亡人数)与该时期内平均人数(或期中人数)之比，用千分率表示。计算公式为：

$$人口自然增长率=\frac{本年出生人数-本年死亡人数}{年平均人数}\times 1000‰$$
$$=人口出生率-人口死亡率$$

Explanatory Notes on Main Statistical Indicators

Total Population refers to the total number of people alive at a certain point of time within a given area.

The annual statistics on total population is taken at midnight, the 31st of December.

Usual Resident Population refers to the population that actually reside in a place, usually longer than half a year. Usual Resident Population mainly includes 1) those who live in their own townships, towns and streets at the time of investigation, and whose household registration is also in their own townships, towns and streets; 2) those who live in their own townships, towns and streets at the time of investigation, and whose household registration is not in their own townships, towns and streets, and who have left the registered place of household registration for more than half a year; 3) those who live in their own townships, towns and streets at the time of investigation, but have not yet processed permanent household registration; 4) Household registration in their own townships, towns and streets, and people living in Hong Kong, Macao, Taiwan or abroad at the time of investigation.

Household Registration Population refers to the population that regardless of whether or not to go out and the length of time, as long as the permanent residence registration is registered in the local public security household registration administration department, it will be the registered residence population in the area. The household registration data are collected by the public security department.

Urban Population and Rural Population Urban population refers to all people residing in cities and towns; while rural population refers to population other than urban population.

Urbanization rate Urbanization refers to the natural historical process in which non-agricultural industries gather in cities and towns and rural population concentrate in cities and towns with the development of industrialization. It is the inevitable historical stage in the process of industrialization in all countries of the world. Urbanization rate refers to the proportion of the permanent population of a country (region) to the total population of the country (region), which is an important index to measure the level of urbanization and reflect the process of urbanization.

Birth Rate or (Crude Birth Rate) refers to the ratio of the number of births to the average population (or mid-period population) during a certain period of time (usually a year), expressed in ‰. Birth rate in the chapter refers to annual birth rate. The following formula is used:

$$\text{Birth Rate} = \frac{\text{Number of Births}}{\text{Annual Average Population}} \times 1000‰$$

Number of births in the formula refers to live births, i.e. when a baby has breathed or showed any vital phenomena regardless of the length of pregnancy.

Annual average population is the average of the number of population at the beginning of the year and that at the end of the year. Sometimes it is substituted by the mid-year population.

Death Rate (or Crude Death Rate) refers to the ratio of the number of deaths to the average population (or mid-period population) during a certain period of time (usually a year), expressed in ‰. Death rate in the chapter refers to annual death rate. The following formula is used:

$$\text{Death Rate} = \frac{\text{Number of Deaths}}{\text{Annual Average Population}} \times 1000‰$$

Natural Growth Rate of Population refers to the ratio of natural increase in population (number of births minus number of deaths) in a certain period of time (usually a year) to the average population (or mid-period population) of the same period, expressed in ‰. The following formula is applied:

$$\begin{aligned}\text{Natural Growth Rate of Population} &= \frac{\text{Number of Births} - \text{Number of Deaths}}{\text{Annual Average Population}} \times 1000‰ \\ &= \text{Birth Rate} - \text{Death Rate}\end{aligned}$$

04 就业和工资

Chapter 4 Employment and Wages

4-1 就业和工资情况
Employment and Wages

(年末数) (year-end)

项目	Item	2013	2014	2015	2016	2017	2018	2019	2020	2021	2022	2023
就业人员合计（万人）	**Total Number of Employed Persons (10 000 persons)**	**4634.00**	**4638.00**	**4652.00**	**4657.00**	**4667.00**	**4690.00**	**4714.00**	**4745.00**	**4727.00**	**4706.00**	**4722.00**
第一产业	Primary Industry	1854.00	1804.00	1758.40	1709.00	1661.50	1618.00	1579.50	1542.00	1506.00	1602.00	1535.00
第二产业	Secondary Industry	1163.00	1155.00	1144.40	1132.00	1120.00	1112.00	1098.00	1098.00	1111.00	1074.00	1100.00
第三产业	Tertiary Industry	1617.00	1679.00	1749.20	1816.00	1885.50	1960.00	2036.50	2105.00	2110.00	2030.00	2087.00
就业人员构成（合计=100）	**Composition of Employed Persons (total=100)**	**100.0**	**100.0**	**100.0**	**100.0**	**100.0**	**100.0**	**100.0**	**100.0**	**100.0**	**100.0**	**100.0**
第一产业	Primary Industry	40.0	38.9	37.8	36.7	35.6	34.5	33.5	32.5	31.9	34.0	32.5
第二产业	Secondary Industry	25.1	24.9	24.6	24.3	24.0	23.7	23.3	23.1	23.5	22.8	23.3
第三产业	Tertiary Industry	34.9	36.2	37.6	39.0	40.4	41.8	43.2	44.4	44.6	43.2	44.2
城镇就业人员（万人）	**Urban Employed Persons (10 000 persons)**	**1828.37**	**1910.49**	**2009.35**	**2108.54**	**2207.38**	**2303.75**	**2406.78**	**2489.00**	**2522.00**	**2508.00**	**2545.00**
#城镇非私营单位就业人员	Urban Employed Persons in Non-private Units	846.24	808.75	795.47	787.53	792.21	780.64	788.94	861.76	871.47	881.43	883.63
#城镇私营单位就业人员	Urban Employed Persons of Private-owned Units	342.10	287.10	307.10	347.40	377.98	423.80	448.68	571.69	558.87	578.30	621.12
乡村就业人员（万人）	**Rural Employed Persons (10 000 persons)**	**2805.63**	**2727.51**	**2642.65**	**2548.46**	**2459.62**	**2386.25**	**2307.22**	**2256.00**	**2205.00**	**2198.00**	**2177.00**
按城乡分就业人员构成（合计=100）	**Composition of Employed Persons by Urban and Rural (Total = 100)**	**100.0**	**100.0**	**100.0**	**100.0**	**100.0**	**100.0**	**100.0**	**100.0**	**100.0**	**100.0**	**100.0**
城镇	Urban	39.5	41.2	43.2	45.3	47.3	49.1	51.1	52.5	53.4	53.3	53.9
乡村	Rural	60.5	58.8	56.8	54.7	52.7	50.9	48.9	47.5	46.6	46.7	46.1
城镇全部单位就业人员工资总额（亿元）	**Total Wages of All Urban Employed Persons (100 million yuan)**	**5287.16**	**5631.68**	**6168.65**	**6612.38**	**7186.52**	**7979.50**	**8806.66**	**10453.20**	**11541.64**	**12330.33**	**13473.68**
城镇全部单位就业人员平均工资（元）	**Average Wage of All Urban Employees (yuan)**	**41795**	**45697**	**50466**	**54425**	**58671**	**64717**	**69267**	**74520**	**81420**	**84912**	**90220**

注：2011-2019年数据根据第七次全国人口普查的结果进行了修订（以下相关表同）。
a) From 2011 to 2019, were revised according to the 7th National Population Census（the same as the following related tables）.

4-2 各市(州)就业人员数
Number of Employed Persons by Region

(年末数)单位：万人　　(year-end)(10 000 persons)

市(州)	Region	2013	2014	2015	2016	2017	2018	2019	2020	2021	2022	2023
全省	**Sichuan**	**4634.00**	**4638.00**	**4652.00**	**4657.00**	**4667.00**	**4690.00**	**4714.00**	**4745.00**	**4727.00**	**4706.00**	**4722.00**
成都市	Chengdu	857.59	885.46	918.65	1006.15	1037.09	1072.31	1107.93	1143.32	1156.12	1159.14	1167.85
自贡市	Zigong	148.60	147.22	145.91	143.59	143.71	141.93	139.56	137.24	135.93	134.37	134.04
攀枝花市	Panzhihua	64.29	64.07	63.81	63.77	63.54	63.56	63.30	63.66	64.69	64.88	65.41
泸州市	Luzhou	230.85	229.77	230.15	230.68	231.08	232.16	233.15	234.54	234.13	233.78	235.15
德阳市	Deyang	215.95	214.40	213.29	213.31	212.78	212.82	212.39	212.81	211.37	210.16	210.60
绵阳市	Mianyang	275.79	276.64	276.71	277.33	278.77	280.52	281.97	283.91	284.03	284.36	286.09
广元市	Guangyuan	141.21	140.62	140.18	138.00	136.34	134.66	132.68	131.28	129.30	127.82	127.50
遂宁市	Suining	187.59	183.83	179.73	176.94	172.71	170.12	167.77	165.32	162.03	160.61	160.15
内江市	Neijiang	217.03	213.03	208.93	204.78	200.94	196.92	193.53	190.96	186.60	183.31	182.75
乐山市	Leshan	183.62	182.56	181.75	180.02	179.19	178.83	178.27	178.40	177.50	176.79	177.39
南充市	Nanchong	360.81	356.60	352.54	346.64	341.17	337.32	334.47	330.48	325.45	322.30	321.04
眉山市	Meishan	177.85	177.37	176.95	175.89	174.83	175.19	175.07	175.42	174.50	173.54	174.12
宜宾市	Yibin	247.68	247.24	247.81	247.97	248.79	250.60	252.01	255.91	258.41	258.75	260.26
广安市	Guangan	168.43	167.85	167.90	169.73	169.78	170.74	171.80	173.63	173.15	171.18	171.49
达州市	Dazhou	309.83	309.17	308.30	307.77	307.62	306.82	306.08	305.72	304.64	303.62	302.83
雅安市	Yaan	84.22	83.91	83.05	83.18	82.41	82.05	81.43	81.30	80.79	80.69	81.38
巴中市	Bazhong	180.63	177.04	174.10	172.00	168.27	165.12	162.57	159.87	155.79	152.92	152.28
资阳市	Ziyang	212.51	210.90	209.54	142.74	141.37	139.65	138.40	137.91	133.41	129.80	129.82
阿坝藏族羌族自治州	Aba	49.12	48.81	48.86	48.97	48.32	47.79	48.61	48.16	45.88	46.07	47.09
甘孜藏族自治州	Ganzi	62.77	62.60	62.66	63.05	62.83	62.89	63.68	63.78	61.61	59.86	60.93
凉山彝族自治州	Liangshan	257.63	258.91	261.18	264.49	265.46	268.00	269.33	271.38	271.67	272.05	273.83

注：因行政区划调整，2016年起，简阳市划入成都市，资阳市数据不再包含简阳市（以下有关表同）。

a) Due to administrative division adjustment，the city of Jianyang has been divided into Chengdu，and the data of Ziyang not contain Jianyang since 2016 (The same as the following related tables).

4-3 按三次产业分就业人员数

Number of Employed Persons by Three Strata of Industry

(年末数) (year-end)

年份 Year	就业人员(万人) Number of Employed Persons (10 000 persons)				构成 Composition in Percentage (合计=100) (total = 100)		
		第一产业 Primary Industry	第二产业 Secondary Industry	第三产业 Tertiary Industry	第一产业 Primary Industry	第二产业 Secondary Industry	第三产业 Tertiary Industry
1952	2027.92	1753.89	89.37	184.66	86.5	4.4	9.1
1957	2258.38	1947.49	108.57	202.32	86.2	4.8	9.0
1962	2101.58	1810.90	117.47	173.21	86.2	5.6	8.2
1965	2267.18	1925.30	163.38	178.50	84.9	7.2	7.9
1970	2737.59	2339.83	210.36	187.40	85.5	7.7	6.8
1975	2998.60	2474.11	271.48	253.01	82.5	9.1	8.4
1978	3087.02	2524.21	279.50	283.31	81.8	9.1	9.1
1980	3259.78	2638.03	309.24	312.51	80.9	9.5	9.6
1985	3742.97	2824.95	491.67	426.35	75.5	13.1	11.4
1990	4265.20	3108.89	578.08	578.23	72.9	13.5	13.6
1995	4619.10	2983.94	752.91	882.25	64.6	16.3	19.1
1996	4627.20	2875.86	772.74	978.60	62.2	16.7	21.1
1997	4641.20	2872.41	780.44	988.35	61.9	16.8	21.3
1998	4651.40	2824.40	786.09	1040.91	60.7	16.9	22.4
1999	4654.30	2747.08	800.54	1106.68	59.0	17.2	23.8
2000	4658.40	2643.35	871.12	1143.93	56.7	18.7	24.6
2001	4664.80	2595.84	867.65	1201.31	55.6	18.6	25.8
2002	4667.60	2517.48	896.18	1253.94	53.9	19.2	26.9
2003	4683.50	2482.80	906.70	1294.00	53.0	19.4	27.6
2004	4691.00	2445.70	916.00	1329.30	52.2	19.5	28.3
2005	4702.00	2421.50	926.30	1354.20	51.5	19.7	28.8
2006	4715.00	2306.90	946.00	1462.10	48.9	20.1	31.0
2007	4731.10	2266.22	1065.71	1399.15	47.9	22.5	29.6
2008	4740.00	2186.18	1108.32	1445.50	46.1	23.4	30.5
2009	4756.62	2144.13	1141.59	1470.90	45.1	24.0	30.9
2010	4677.00	2043.85	1164.57	1468.58	43.7	24.9	31.4
2011	4650.00	1972.00	1167.00	1511.00	42.4	25.1	32.5
2012	4635.00	1905.00	1173.00	1557.00	41.1	25.3	33.6
2013	4634.00	1854.00	1163.00	1617.00	40.0	25.1	34.9
2014	4638.00	1804.00	1155.00	1679.00	38.9	24.9	36.2
2015	4652.00	1758.40	1144.40	1749.20	37.8	24.6	37.6
2016	4657.00	1709.00	1132.00	1816.00	36.7	24.3	39.0
2017	4667.00	1661.50	1120.00	1885.50	35.6	24.0	40.4
2018	4690.00	1618.00	1112.00	1960.00	34.5	23.7	41.8
2019	4714.00	1579.50	1098.00	2036.50	33.5	23.3	43.2
2020	4745.00	1542.00	1098.00	2105.00	32.5	23.1	44.4
2021	4727.00	1506.00	1111.00	2110.00	31.9	23.5	44.6
2022	4706.00	1602.00	1074.00	2030.00	34.0	22.8	43.2
2023	4722.00	1535.00	1100.00	2087.00	32.5	23.3	44.2

4-4 各市(州)按三次产业分就业人员数(2023年)
Number of Employed Persons by Three Strata of Industry and Region(2023)

(年末数) (year-end)

市(州)	Region	就业人员 (万人) Number of Employed Persons (10 000 persons)	第一产业 Primary Industry	第二产业 Secondary Industry	第三产业 Tertiary Industry	构成 Composition in Percentage (合计=100) (total = 100) 第一产业 Primary Industry	第二产业 Secondary Industry	第三产业 Tertiary Industry
全省	**Sichuan**	**4722.00**	**1535.00**	**1100.00**	**2087.00**	**32.5**	**23.3**	**44.2**
成都市	Chengdu	1167.85	153.79	330.74	683.32	13.2	28.3	58.5
自贡市	Zigong	134.04	47.75	34.01	52.28	35.6	25.4	39.0
攀枝花市	Panzhihua	65.41	21.37	13.56	30.48	32.7	20.7	46.6
泸州市	Luzhou	235.15	83.15	67.13	84.87	35.4	28.5	36.1
德阳市	Deyang	210.60	64.36	52.31	93.93	30.6	24.8	44.6
绵阳市	Mianyang	286.09	75.18	85.95	124.96	26.3	30.0	43.7
广元市	Guangyuan	127.50	50.37	23.21	53.92	39.5	18.2	42.3
遂宁市	Suining	160.15	61.37	37.55	61.23	38.3	23.5	38.2
内江市	Neijiang	182.75	49.88	50.55	82.32	27.3	27.7	45.0
乐山市	Leshan	177.39	68.25	32.09	77.05	38.5	18.1	43.4
南充市	Nanchong	321.04	109.60	74.92	136.52	34.1	23.4	42.5
眉山市	Meishan	174.12	68.02	39.17	66.93	39.1	22.5	38.4
宜宾市	Yibin	260.26	108.02	66.59	85.65	41.5	25.6	32.9
广安市	Guangan	171.49	72.50	38.62	60.37	42.3	22.5	35.2
达州市	Dazhou	302.83	125.17	43.67	133.99	41.3	14.4	44.3
雅安市	Yaan	81.38	33.70	13.55	34.13	41.4	16.7	41.9
巴中市	Bazhong	152.28	65.02	31.76	55.50	42.7	20.9	36.4
资阳市	Ziyang	129.82	57.77	21.99	50.06	44.5	16.9	38.6
阿坝藏族羌族自治州	Aba	47.09	24.20	3.10	19.79	51.4	6.6	42.0
甘孜藏族自治州	Ganzi	60.93	42.34	3.94	14.65	69.5	6.5	24.0
凉山彝族自治州	Liangshan	273.83	153.19	35.59	85.05	55.9	13.0	31.1

4-5 按城乡分就业人员数
Number of Employed Persons by Residence in Urban and Rural Areas

(年末数)单位: 万人 (year-end)(10 000 persons)

年份 Year	就业人员合计 Total Number of Employed Persons	城镇就业人员 Urban Employed Persons	#城镇非私营单位就业人员 Employed Persons in Urban Non-private Units	乡村就业人员 Rural Employed Persons
1952	2027.92	196.33	63.56	1831.59
1957	2258.38	227.15	208.22	2031.23
1962	2101.58	243.37	233.16	1858.21
1965	2267.18	296.58	290.53	1970.60
1970	2737.59	341.07	338.68	2396.52
1975	2998.60	395.78	394.26	2602.82
1978	3087.02	465.52	457.92	2621.50
1980	3259.78	511.18	498.31	2748.60
1985	3742.97	639.97	576.12	3103.00
1990	4265.20	800.10	644.21	3465.10
1995	4619.10	1045.80	696.03	3573.30
1996	4627.20	1075.10	692.78	3552.10
1997	4641.20	1103.20	681.56	3538.00
1998	4651.40	1077.90	662.94	3573.50
1999	4654.30	1087.30	547.15	3567.00
2000	4658.40	1093.90	515.45	3564.50
2001	4664.80	1108.60	486.70	3556.20
2002	4667.60	1125.60	481.19	3542.00
2003	4683.50	1166.90	505.68	3516.60
2004	4691.00	1209.20	500.14	3481.80
2005	4702.00	1228.90	512.65	3473.10
2006	4715.00	1262.70	520.56	3452.30
2007	4731.10	1298.40	539.39	3432.70
2008	4740.00	1310.00	550.95	3430.00
2009	4756.62	1345.86	564.38	3410.76
2010	4677.00	1589.97	570.58	3087.03
2011	4650.00	1670.86	614.02	2979.14
2012	4635.00	1746.44	640.89	2888.56
2013	4634.00	1828.37	846.24	2805.63
2014	4638.00	1910.49	808.75	2727.51
2015	4652.00	2009.35	795.47	2642.65
2016	4657.00	2108.54	787.53	2548.46
2017	4667.00	2207.38	792.21	2459.62
2018	4690.00	2303.75	780.64	2386.25
2019	4714.00	2406.78	788.94	2307.22
2020	4745.00	2489.00	861.76	2256.00
2021	4727.00	2522.00	871.47	2205.00
2022	4706.00	2508.00	881.43	2198.00
2023	4722.00	2545.00	883.63	2177.00

4–6 各市(州)按城乡分就业人员数
Number of Urban and Rural Employed Persons by Region

(年末数)单位: 万人 (year-end)(10 000 persons)

市(州)	Region	合计 Total		城镇就业人员 Urban Employed Persons		乡村就业人员 Rural Employed Persons	
		2022	2023	2022	2023	2022	2023
全省	**Sichuan**	**4706.00**	**4722.00**	**2508.00**	**2545.00**	**2198.00**	**2177.00**
成都市	Chengdu	1159.14	1167.85	895.37	907.18	263.77	260.67
自贡市	Zigong	134.37	134.04	64.69	64.74	69.68	69.30
攀枝花市	Panzhihua	64.88	65.41	43.03	43.40	21.85	22.01
泸州市	Luzhou	233.78	235.15	107.30	109.50	126.48	125.65
德阳市	Deyang	210.16	210.60	106.58	107.98	103.58	102.62
绵阳市	Mianyang	284.36	286.09	139.32	143.06	145.04	143.03
广元市	Guangyuan	127.82	127.50	55.51	55.66	72.31	71.84
遂宁市	Suining	160.61	160.15	80.00	80.32	80.61	79.83
内江市	Neijiang	183.31	182.75	85.06	85.56	98.25	97.19
乐山市	Leshan	176.79	177.39	83.53	84.77	93.26	92.62
南充市	Nanchong	322.30	321.04	153.42	154.98	168.88	166.06
眉山市	Meishan	173.54	174.12	79.83	81.08	93.71	93.04
宜宾市	Yibin	258.75	260.26	118.80	121.59	139.95	138.67
广安市	Guangan	171.18	171.49	73.63	74.92	97.55	96.57
达州市	Dazhou	303.62	302.83	138.79	140.62	164.83	162.21
雅安市	Yaan	80.69	81.38	37.08	37.50	43.61	43.88
巴中市	Bazhong	152.92	152.28	60.85	61.26	92.07	91.02
资阳市	Ziyang	129.80	129.82	50.47	51.05	79.33	78.77
阿坝藏族羌族自治州	Aba	46.07	47.09	19.55	20.01	26.52	27.08
甘孜藏族自治州	Ganzi	59.86	60.93	17.94	18.30	41.92	42.63
凉山彝族自治州	Liangshan	272.05	273.83	97.25	101.52	174.80	172.31

4-7 按行业分城镇非私营单位就业人员数
Number of Employed Persons in Urban Non-private Units by Sector

(年末数)单位: 万人 (year-end)(10 000 persons)

年份 Year	合计 Total	农、林、牧、渔业 Agriculture, Forestry, Animal Husbandry and Fishery	采矿业 Mining	制造业 Manufacturing	电力、热力、燃气及水生产和供应业 Production and Supply of Electricity, Heat, Gas and Water	建筑业 Construction	批发和零售业 Wholesale and Retail Trades
2003	505.68	11.27	19.19	119.45	15.62	72.36	20.65
2004	500.14	10.23	18.64	115.98	15.17	72.40	19.74
2005	512.65	9.32	20.51	117.78	15.31	76.67	19.14
2006	520.56	9.05	22.01	118.69	15.05	80.45	17.93
2007	539.39	8.39	23.30	120.37	15.28	90.26	18.61
2008	550.95	7.12	23.19	123.86	15.38	93.79	18.21
2009	564.38	5.13	21.91	123.09	15.42	99.65	17.49
2010	570.58	5.03	20.41	124.20	15.26	99.91	17.13
2011	614.02	4.56	21.31	141.62	16.28	111.80	17.85
2012	640.89	4.03	24.48	144.49	17.63	116.09	18.49
2013	846.24	3.74	23.20	204.58	27.16	177.84	33.23
2014	808.75	3.23	23.51	175.43	26.70	155.56	32.32
2015	795.47	2.90	19.55	159.66	26.14	153.86	30.89
2016	787.53	2.83	18.59	148.33	23.17	151.48	30.51
2017	792.21	2.49	17.02	147.28	22.11	145.52	30.24
2018	780.64	2.14	13.50	127.29	22.39	160.37	27.52
2019	788.94	1.43	12.87	123.82	20.91	151.65	28.13
2020	861.76	2.50	13.63	139.42	23.17	151.42	31.92
2021	871.47	2.20	11.59	144.43	22.99	142.27	34.97
2022	881.43	2.28	11.23	148.72	22.71	132.28	36.76
2023	883.63	1.65	8.50	144.23	21.41	106.83	37.47

4-7 续表 1 continued

(年末数)单位: 万人 (year-end)(10 000 persons)

年份 Year	交通运输、仓储和邮政业 Transport, Storage and Post	住宿和餐饮业 Hotels and Catering Services	信息传输、软件和信息技术服务业 Information Transmission, Software and Information Technology	金融业 Financial Intermediation	房地产业 Real Estate	租赁和商务服务业 Leasing and Business Services
2003	22.52	4.55	4.65	16.12	4.21	3.35
2004	21.94	4.75	5.12	16.22	4.22	3.38
2005	22.79	5.19	5.12	17.18	4.29	6.01
2006	23.03	4.94	5.07	16.37	4.80	5.85
2007	24.09	5.11	5.02	16.85	5.32	5.93
2008	23.22	4.99	5.18	17.94	5.09	6.27
2009	23.75	5.23	5.92	20.38	5.35	6.01
2010	23.06	5.47	6.32	21.31	5.40	5.91
2011	22.59	6.13	6.47	21.45	6.47	6.37
2012	23.56	7.64	5.99	22.97	6.57	5.22
2013	39.38	12.46	15.62	24.12	15.73	12.21
2014	41.33	11.51	16.29	24.22	17.69	12.71
2015	40.71	10.56	18.25	25.87	18.63	14.20
2016	40.43	9.69	18.41	30.39	19.84	15.57
2017	38.91	9.34	20.14	31.70	21.54	16.79
2018	37.39	9.56	19.33	32.40	21.90	18.50
2019	31.99	12.51	20.01	32.70	25.16	25.41
2020	34.57	16.32	23.66	37.86	29.72	28.53
2021	34.43	16.41	25.26	41.76	31.92	30.34
2022	34.65	15.48	26.37	35.53	30.90	36.09
2023	35.88	19.59	27.57	33.14	29.89	41.45

4-7 续表 2 continued

(年末数)单位: 万人 (year-end)(10 000 persons)

年份 Year	科学研究和技术服务业 Scientific Research and Technical Services	水利、环境和公共设施管理业 Management of Water Conservancy, Environment and Public Facilities	居民服务、修理和其他服务业 Services to Households, Repair and Other Services	教育 Education	卫生和社会工作 Health and Social Service	文化、体育和娱乐业 Culture, Sports and Entertainment	公共管理、社会保障和社会组织 Public Management, Social Security and Social Organization
2003	11.04	7.14	2.45	77.84	26.14	5.11	62.02
2004	12.53	7.05	1.31	78.85	25.55	4.51	62.58
2005	11.16	7.17	1.95	79.34	26.36	4.94	62.41
2006	11.49	7.87	1.99	80.70	27.04	4.38	63.85
2007	11.64	8.06	2.05	81.34	27.94	4.30	65.52
2008	12.49	8.27	1.17	81.59	29.24	4.34	69.63
2009	13.13	9.16	1.01	82.12	31.29	4.40	73.95
2010	13.65	9.77	0.95	81.95	32.99	4.44	77.41
2011	14.62	10.10	1.01	85.09	36.59	4.41	79.30
2012	16.20	10.63	1.11	89.40	39.27	4.50	82.64
2013	19.86	12.12	1.70	90.85	42.66	5.92	83.86
2014	21.06	13.16	1.79	94.56	45.14	6.28	86.26
2015	21.01	12.85	1.94	94.80	46.76	6.10	90.79
2016	21.07	12.97	2.22	94.36	48.48	6.08	93.13
2017	21.85	12.69	2.66	96.05	51.44	6.26	98.18
2018	20.36	11.45	1.83	96.14	51.35	5.54	101.68
2019	15.29	9.77	2.75	104.45	57.06	5.47	107.57
2020	20.44	11.02	3.38	114.24	62.18	6.33	111.47
2021	22.51	10.81	3.89	112.92	65.60	6.77	110.41
2022	24.47	11.35	4.58	117.68	69.21	7.35	113.79
2023	27.98	12.20	4.50	123.84	74.49	7.29	125.71

4-8 城镇全部单位就业人员工资总额、平均工资及指数
Total Wage Bill and Average Wage of Urban Employed Persons in all Units and Indices

年份 Year	工资总额(万元) Total Wage Bill (10 000 yuan)	平均工资(元) Average Wage (yuan)	指数(上年为100) Indices (preceding year=100)	
			工资总额 Total Wage Bill	平均工资 Average Wage
1978	263196	590	114.3	106.0
1980	364892	743	121.2	116.3
1985	598403	1062	120.6	116.4
1986	719269	1237	120.2	116.5
1987	802261	1340	111.5	108.3
1988	987813	1598	123.1	119.3
1989	1135724	1796	115.0	112.4
1990	1294823	2011	114.0	112.0
1991	1450034	2194	111.8	109.1
1992	1667894	2458	115.3	112.0
1993	2046047	2984	122.7	121.2
1994	2776839	4064	135.7	136.2
1995	3217827	4703	115.9	115.7
1996	3550444	5218	110.3	111.0
1997	3806429	5626	107.2	107.8
1998	3927403	5939	103.2	105.6
1999	3985709	7249	105.3	110.2
2000	4369495	8323	109.6	114.8
2001	4902582	9934	112.2	119.4
2002	5391189	11183	110.0	112.6
2003	6224989	12320	115.5	110.2
2004	6926273	13887	111.3	112.7
2005	7960325	15638	114.9	112.6
2006	9100898	17612	114.3	112.6
2007	11198309	21081	123.0	119.7
2008	13555288	24725	121.0	117.3
2009	21294971	23572		
2010	25409121	26127	119.3	110.8
2011	31597970	31300	124.4	119.8
2012	37723598	35873	119.4	113.9
2013	52871606	41795	140.2	116.5
2014	56316799	45697	106.5	109.3
2015	61686544	50466	109.5	110.4
2016	66123764	54425	107.2	107.8
2017	71865217	58671	108.7	107.8
2018	79794982	64717	111.0	110.3
2019	88066640	69267	110.4	107.0
2020	104531964	74520	118.7	107.6
2021	115416363	81420	110.4	109.3
2022	123303263	84912	106.8	104.3
2023	134736791	90220	109.3	106.3

注：2009年及以后城镇全部单位包括私营单位（以下相关表同）。
a) Average wage of urban employment in all units includes wage in the private units from 2009(the same as the following related tables).

4–9 各市(州)城镇全部单位就业人员平均工资
Average Wage of Urban Employed Persons in all Units by Region

单位：元 (yuan)

市(州)	Region	2013	2014	2015	2016	2017	2018	2019	2020	2021	2022	2023
全省	**Sichuan**	**41795**	**45697**	**50466**	**54425**	**58671**	**64717**	**69267**	**74520**	**81420**	**84912**	**90220**
成都市	Chengdu	48358	51681	56872	61330	65098	71300	79664	83556	91857	96413	100606
自贡市	Zigong	37081	40162	43157	46595	52339	56040	56719	63896	68484	70532	77846
攀枝花市	Panzhihua	44220	50221	51999	55508	61005	65124	68016	74479	85960	90619	93624
泸州市	Luzhou	37648	41121	44749	47871	52455	58614	61868	68716	72018	74898	82032
德阳市	Deyang	41426	44169	48090	52249	56815	62612	63585	69903	76877	80485	87840
绵阳市	Mianyang	40989	44640	49817	53222	56966	63500	63700	69274	76488	77314	82851
广元市	Guangyuan	37300	41518	46888	51379	54086	58362	63544	64983	72212	74589	79483
遂宁市	Suining	34633	37894	42188	45840	49962	56261	59290	60820	64639	67700	75700
内江市	Neijiang	35479	37695	40617	45234	48790	56574	61517	67573	72690	74484	81230
乐山市	Leshan	37742	41181	45805	49839	53764	58881	62802	68960	76041	79027	85768
南充市	Nanchong	35981	39192	44033	47272	51521	58294	61482	66956	75155	76099	81219
眉山市	Meishan	36595	41161	45379	48293	52410	59325	62444	66866	75226	76313	81543
宜宾市	Yibin	38674	40978	46019	49966	54195	62126	66048	70856	75840	79588	85452
广安市	Guangan	36213	39213	44079	48054	52493	57111	62055	63491	66192	68251	73823
达州市	Dazhou	35292	38271	42446	46281	50756	57940	61582	64810	73377	75703	80524
雅安市	Yaan	35464	39548	42533	46458	48895	53231	62179	67596	71267	74344	78786
巴中市	Bazhong	36825	39205	43080	46849	49341	52317	55288	62210	67730	70610	75855
资阳市	Ziyang	33587	36694	44150	46827	51568	54899	62340	66884	70740	73758	79000
阿坝藏族羌族自治州	Aba	48011	51149	59526	68637	73432	85395	91376	91786	108180	110574	111923
甘孜藏族自治州	Ganzi	47771	53705	63729	69388	74415	79509	82901	88108	103134	107618	115189
凉山彝族自治州	Liangshan	44163	47295	54195	58980	60352	64346	70694	76675	84103	86638	90439

4-10 按行业分城镇全部单位就业人员工资总额
Total Wage Bill of Urban Employed Persons in all Units by Sector

单位：万元 (10 000 yuan)

年份 Year	合计 Total	农、林、牧、渔业 Farming, Forestry, Animal Husbandry and Fishery	采矿业 Mining	制造业 Manufacturing	电力、热力、燃气及水生产和供应业 Production and Supply of Electricity, Heat, Gas and Water	建筑业 Construction	批发和零售业 Wholesale and Retail Trades
1978	263196	7016	22921	91621	5233	23383	26693
1980	364892	8186	28667	126922	8134	32823	37726
1985	598403	12035	46417	219817	8405	48027	28322
1986	719269	14787	57236	258144	10810	58789	65333
1987	802261	15341	59949	297304	12852	67477	71835
1988	987813	17477	70663	371196	16092	81136	90556
1989	1135724	19005	76612	439876	19804	88267	101140
1990	1294823	21185	104553	476728	29408	99025	112974
1991	1450034	23443	112731	547026	29410	115319	123849
1992	1667894	25979	118366	615493	35459	135228	137426
1993	2046047	29031	116455	775305	41259	221791	175633
1994	2776839	38639	171556	956517	55749	262082	220732
1995	3217827	44168	188235	1121615	79256	303939	255632
1996	3550444	50134	211692	1210693	95247	320058	273788
1997	3806429	54280	213126	1249005	119344	349282	279658
1998	3927403	57111	207010	1185340	129699	346700	260947
1999	3985709	63225	171492	1071310	140643	345079	229458
2000	4369495	72727	214016	1108247	155720	360460	217446
2001	4902582	90629	158455	1117906	181767	411914	195433
2002	5391189	95174	195370	1180244	205600	493233	179869
2003	6224989	103745	207903	1357229	240706	627520	212843
2004	6926273	97595	247519	1496103	261516	695040	236843
2005	7960325	95400	340874	1690892	300129	815528	270334
2006	9100898	103637	402290	1958532	328948	997151	284486
2007	11198309	114676	522447	2294500	393339	1257432	309381
2008	13555288	111457	653566	2784093	475273	1603208	384950
2009	21294971	98415	1255861	5130324	576252	3167298	965673
2010	25409121	111552	1506249	6132399	675721	3873904	1176499
2011	31597970	200867	1779562	8103028	844533	4672108	1480791
2012	37723598	243409	2254256	9447049	1003965	5603892	1170441
2013	52871606	239977	2103242	14209605	2106845	8721652	2517380
2014	56316799	225041	2293080	14101830	2159013	9535256	2508880
2015	61686544	235715	2083618	14532969	2267013	10056042	2732732
2016	66123764	259072	1985880	15174238	2171097	10735972	2752547
2017	71865217	263046	2119605	15912709	2159550	10925975	3004453
2018	79794982	258107	2141026	16770293	2392033	13380723	3277549
2019	88066640	140144	1634270	16015084	2415220	16262936	3669478
2020	104531964	375535	1558164	17165088	2799363	18066606	5044369
2021	115416363	301753	1551588	19696206	2985219	18345159	5659536
2022	123303263	365232	1665846	21435417	3066899	17891460	6631836
2023	134736791	283594	1522111	21984595	3059104	17810475	7745095

4-10 续表 1 continued

单位：万元 (10 000 yuan)

年份 Year	交通运输、仓储和邮政业 Transport, Storage and Post	住宿和餐饮业 Hotels and Catering Services	信息传输、软件和信息技术服务业 Information Transmission, Software and IT Services	金融业 Financial Intermediation	房地产业 Real Estate	租赁和商务服务业 Leasing and Business Services
1978	25436	3685		2096	197	
1980	30802	5176		3468	778	
1985	46800	6512	1268	6905	1155	1117
1986	54971	8262	2126	9307	1450	1847
1987	60359	9066	2501	10474	1510	2185
1988	74328	11539	3164	12924	1803	2760
1989	86963	12958	4399	14102	2053	3863
1990	96980	14458	5711	17470	2437	5066
1991	108156	16005	6291	19297	2795	5765
1992	124006	17127	7489	25366	4005	6998
1993	103846	21044	8356	40457	5216	7827
1994	138631	28381	18195	69270	8886	16756
1995	171773	34916	18645	80619	10459	17626
1996	193317	38553	19078	92634	12751	18124
1997	223444	39983	19589	110358	14601	19137
1998	228139	36486	20084	136365	20341	20515
1999	249831	33056	23999	158688	22735	24961
2000	274101	29718	26618	183778	27647	27311
2001	297310	32305	34640	214232	29128	30006
2002	330353	32116	45931	231703	41850	32574
2003	299198	41968	96957	276380	52517	40900
2004	329732	49262	127251	315060	56713	50438
2005	398077	58340	144989	379710	60560	110355
2006	479269	61669	160441	415539	76292	110317
2007	545062	74852	168658	503492	101872	145778
2008	630662	85024	193001	676824	109496	184636
2009	894140	287608	309578	791821	357901	374472
2010	1038718	356303	387007	1007152	430062	468560
2011	1199619	485624	431563	1315866	564549	567142
2012	1482261	1148340	586057	1605422	713886	630263
2013	2538797	1001861	1414378	1864417	1198189	1038280
2014	2735747	1078258	1533657	2065994	1380710	1162998
2015	3013325	1031735	1907386	2267734	1546288	1336259
2016	3130586	1044356	2033157	2654525	1750841	1502037
2017	3345831	1045377	2424533	2974108	1978298	1680327
2018	3702221	1053877	2577192	3182901	2274021	1843401
2019	3708858	1173174	3072712	3271196	2859527	3074756
2020	4298964	1228954	4593751	4182881	3662025	4351300
2021	4625857	1595334	5331464	5378625	4096494	4934683
2022	4790432	1624683	6143707	4725048	4072173	5773461
2023	5306297	2075619	6942153	5378261	4192211	7340620

4-10 续表 2 continued

单位：万元 (10 000 yuan)

年份 Year	科学研究和技术服务业 Scientific Research and Technical Services	水利、环境和公共设施管理业 Management of Water Conservancy, Environment and Public Facilities	居民服务、修理和其他服务业 Services to Households, Repair and Other Services	教育 Education	卫生和社会工作 Health and Social Service	文化、体育和娱乐业 Culture, Sports and Entertainment	公共管理、社会保障和社会组织 Public Management, Social Security and Social Organization
1978	11766	757	307	21420	6069	1042	13554
1980	15088	3021	417	30902	10746	2898	19138
1985	26872	4817	463	51174	17595	3782	36920
1986	29932	5937	589	61038	23114	6009	49588
1987	30870	6985	698	65819	25034	6917	55085
1988	35675	8643	761	84250	30796	8435	65615
1989	39444	11762	815	89940	34583	11037	79101
1990	46459	15061	978	99358	39529	13358	94085
1991	51742	16480	996	107925	43028	13774	106002
1992	64707	19620	783	134970	51266	12593	131013
1993	69586	21830	8053	157693	63269	12508	166888
1994	98468	46332	9316	244518	104740	29282	258789
1995	120187	47932	9687	242074	122049	29689	289326
1996	126915	48639	9804	332534	140925	30614	324991
1997	134609	49533	9840	368133	158473	31191	363001
1998	142113	50345	10137	436783	181650	31955	425980
1999	125873	58322	10817	518933	214225	36587	486655
2000	141697	63432	13251	601173	246975	40099	565261
2001	203335	71987	20125	771304	294859	49890	697637
2002	186623	76808	17648	896710	335438	53535	761243
2003	218656	67579	32828	996203	385244	71653	894960
2004	260908	72086	17409	1100797	425419	76188	1010394
2005	278465	81137	28546	1201121	487875	91225	1126767
2006	341389	100592	32356	1339277	566718	89067	1252926
2007	417854	124712	43016	1720414	710029	101941	1648852
2008	523409	135675	21894	1946943	856137	113486	2065555
2009	665465	180718	123001	2541547	1040967	144975	2388957
2010	783046	207955	171475	2927686	1277654	177429	2699750
2011	1014862	269933	230330	3366310	1713105	239082	3119096
2012	1159404	344307	295883	4013182	2133160	261911	3626511
2013	1614927	466474	357104	4524753	2562136	337687	4053903
2014	1821159	531393	330096	5022372	2940353	429376	4461588
2015	1975685	567042	355036	6075938	3507362	470626	5724040
2016	2104478	618346	417070	6667027	4044483	509211	6568841
2017	2407865	673142	461608	7400464	4676656	582792	7828877
2018	2781473	693098	423722	8111213	5208228	610853	9113053
2019	2316772	772148	559482	9634874	6537772	730778	10217460
2020	4031873	903652	664691	11620154	7480426	823129	11681038
2021	4654030	953836	774139	12591906	8474921	950916	12514698
2022	5202766	1022297	865113	13972366	9572553	1122849	13359124
2023	6051587	1155206	1133423	15454423	11139992	1350283	14811739

4-11 按行业分城镇全部单位就业人员平均工资
Average Wage of Urban Employed Persons in all Units by Sector

单位：元 (yuan)

年份 Year	合计 Total	农、林、牧、渔业 Farming, Forestry, Animal Husbandry and Fishery	采矿业 Mining	制造业 Manufacturing	电力、热力、燃气及水生产和供应业 Production and Supply of Electricity, Heat, Gas and Water	建筑业 Construction	批发和零售业 Wholesale and Retail Trades
1978	590	575	719	577	552	658	509
1980	743	649	914	742	795	834	645
1985	1062	890	1264	1079	1113	1170	883
1986	1237	1119	1520	1211	1337	1364	998
1987	1340	1153	1589	1339	1461	1528	1093
1988	1598	1320	1887	1618	1705	1732	1341
1989	1796	1449	2247	1827	1988	1945	1477
1990	2011	1588	2515	2033	2145	2192	1635
1991	2194	1714	2677	2238	2574	2434	1774
1992	2458	1981	2816	2469	2747	2705	1869
1993	2984	2683	2955	3132	3661	3243	2335
1994	4064	3404	4158	3941	4776	4267	2828
1995	4703	3957	4819	4671	5961	5063	3326
1996	5218	4310	5348	5181	6773	5485	3686
1997	5626	4418	5631	5466	8138	5908	3850
1998	5939	4609	5561	5539	8732	6072	4789
1999	7249	5481	6337	6873	9760	7066	5060
2000	8323	6140	8083	7774	10764	7693	5755
2001	9934	7373	7753	8892	12039	8355	6895
2002	11183	8114	9866	9853	13506	8444	8043
2003	12320	8902	10591	11126	15099	9202	9971
2004	13887	9264	12937	12686	16918	10090	11793
2005	15638	10016	16907	14226	19253	11113	13999
2006	17612	11224	18682	16404	21469	12839	15682
2007	21081	13377	21752	18906	25518	14902	17321
2008	24725	15231	28632	22046	30484	17746	20949
2009	23572	17234	24348	19692	30360	18887	18253
2010	26127	19481	25470	22722	35774	20711	20192
2011	31300	23095	32927	27200	41321	25323	24082
2012	35873	26700	38437	30827	46059	29629	31074
2013	41795	29416	40426	37672	58181	35289	34976
2014	45697	34203	46595	40486	69409	38303	39361
2015	50466	38023	47865	43311	72902	41357	41181
2016	54425	40087	50006	46228	79969	44151	43622
2017	58671	42940	56446	49093	83009	45789	46287
2018	64717	46429	62625	54366	90664	50725	50813
2019	69267	51754	83365	58712	101615	53315	55223
2020	74520	44740	96491	67174	108744	57900	57911
2021	81420	51569	109757	75519	118284	60843	64598
2022	84912	53437	121836	79680	122299	61981	67761
2023	90220	55181	142562	85574	129816	70045	69393

4-11 续表 1 continued

单位：元 (yuan)

年份 Year	交通运输、仓储和邮政业 Transport, Storage and Post	住宿和餐饮业 Hotels and Catering Services	信息传输、软件和信息技术服务业 Information Transmission, Software and IT Services	金融业 Financial Intermediation	房地产业 Real Estate	租赁和商务服务业 Leasing and Business Services
1978	655	501		574	493	
1980	756	637		720	669	
1985	1080	870	1343	1076	974	1005
1986	1268	987	1424	1356	1247	1286
1987	1391	1081	1861	1419	1332	1359
1988	1671	1328	2105	1624	1542	1512
1989	1928	1449	2438	1730	1711	1983
1990	2122	1602	2771	1970	1874	2109
1991	2340	1748	2950	2086	2014	2507
1992	2624	1838	3857	2513	2553	3121
1993	3032	2307	5103	2589	3134	4003
1994	4221	2809	6946	5483	4976	4865
1995	4999	3314	7522	6058	5207	5405
1996	5712	3669	9019	6703	5814	6014
1997	6614	3823	10801	8021	6215	6682
1998	6873	4761	12347	9540	7347	7422
1999	8936	5043	14237	11249	8678	8242
2000	10352	5726	15819	13274	9104	9157
2001	12340	6858	18687	15567	10671	10174
2002	13952	8017	20763	17603	11877	11304
2003	12997	9202	22057	19452	12461	12412
2004	14903	10442	26305	21969	13379	14890
2005	17422	11133	30091	24764	14333	19186
2006	20776	12555	32229	28282	16765	19556
2007	23420	14493	34622	33843	19928	25101
2008	27344	16531	37462	42055	37022	26158
2009	27416	16308	29766	43127	20070	20672
2010	29518	18006	32863	52258	23440	24320
2011	36967	21401	36517	59391	27582	26754
2012	46169	24444	34204	68840	31744	29441
2013	52331	27633	52537	74682	40001	37830
2014	55458	31013	62052	80704	43439	41304
2015	59552	33349	67829	80165	47161	44881
2016	62903	34491	72527	82847	51720	47585
2017	69063	36363	76065	87323	53248	51083
2018	74481	39112	90210	92631	57310	51671
2019	84105	42939	99966	93555	62385	51582
2020	82301	42109	114664	96555	61772	55715
2021	88324	46370	130608	108840	65487	61967
2022	90694	47486	142105	114083	63524	63351
2023	97767	51234	136294	142748	67776	64133

4-11 续表 2 continued

单位：元 (yuan)

年份 Year	科学研究和技术服务业 Scientific Research and Technical Services	水利、环境和公共设施管理业 Management of Water Conservancy, Environment and Public Facilities	居民服务、修理和其他服务业 Services to Households, Repair and Other Services	教育 Education	卫生和社会工作 Health and Social Service	文化、体育和娱乐业 Culture, Sports and Entertainment	公共管理、社会保障和社会组织 Public Management, Social Security and Social Organization
1978	679	590	570	520	541	513	617
1980	872	692	592	678	698	667	773
1985	1275	986	933	1040	998	901	1039
1986	1509	1178	1115	1220	1271	1213	1312
1987	1623	1201	1195	1246	1346	1287	1383
1988	1895	1289	1382	1525	1595	1501	1579
1989	2119	1451	1590	1662	1775	1697	1776
1990	2458	1698	1784	1882	1980	1884	1991
1991	2681	1813	1981	1962	2142	1989	2158
1992	3163	1994	2292	2356	2489	2276	2595
1993	3718	2367	2764	2716	2995	2798	3050
1994	6045	2944	3936	4221	4662	4573	4676
1995	6583	3403	4549	4580	5344	5281	5089
1996	7385	3863	5164	4981	6038	5834	5601
1997	8142	4140	5535	5363	6628	6579	6179
1998	8457	4564	6102	5941	7310	6918	7035
1999	9360	5529	7392	6860	8538	8077	8059
2000	11376	6111	8170	7923	9788	9193	9236
2001	15631	7073	9456	9998	11657	10866	11564
2002	17269	8693	11621	11766	13349	12376	13057
2003	19656	9495	13120	12647	14719	13673	14380
2004	21270	10567	13865	13787	16761	16758	15871
2005	24933	11498	15356	14952	18709	18591	17782
2006	29754	13014	17605	16374	21205	20204	19405
2007	36394	15629	22115	20937	25887	23597	24960
2008	42806	16901	18493	23491	30020	25859	29540
2009	43405	18903	14759	28819	32202	25599	32295
2010	48115	20304	16607	33666	38189	26998	35015
2011	57449	24613	21113	38621	44617	31002	39555
2012	60922	28635	23664	43923	51849	37105	44117
2013	70563	33285	28005	48695	57541	43257	48635
2014	73246	36497	31642	51753	61092	45614	52062
2015	78812	40117	33270	62412	70935	49988	63704
2016	82348	43431	36218	68597	78874	54297	71074
2017	90666	48106	37401	74604	86251	59877	79636
2018	108877	53604	39249	81371	94187	63057	90039
2019	111376	57410	44085	87471	102904	67677	95421
2020	98112	56767	42795	90344	104701	63535	106167
2021	107257	60207	46329	97249	113655	70802	114027
2022	111636	60321	46961	103679	120998	74180	118134
2023	108227	65439	51192	107021	128453	73155	117329

4-12 按登记注册类型和行业分就业人员工资总额(2023年)

Total Wage Bill of Employed Persons by Registered Types and Sector(2023)

单位：万元 (10 000yuan)

项目	Item	城镇全部单位 All Urban Units	城镇非私营单位 Urban Non-Private Units	#国有单位 State-owend Units	#其他内资单位 Other Domestic Units	#港澳台商投资单位 Funds from Hong Kong, Macao,Taiwan	#外商投资单位 Foreign Funded Units	城镇私营单位 Urban Private Units
总计	**Total**	**134736791**	**96250927**	**41308192**	**49982086**	**2342058**	**2618590**	**38485864**
农、林、牧、渔业	Agriculture,Forestry, Animal Husbandry and Fishery	283594	140936	69044	64809	5550	1533	142659
采矿业	Mining	1522111	1363843	3023	1357933		2886	158269
制造业	Manufacturing	21984595	14283221	27027	11604787	1227394	1424013	7701374
电力、热力、燃气及水生产和供应业	Production and Supply of Electricity, Heat, Gas and Water	3059104	2939092	76416	2731665	105053	25958	120012
建筑业	Construction	17810475	8170715	114760	8049203	4551	2202	9639760
批发和零售业	Wholesale and Retail Trades	7745095	3580459	296910	2886937	202417	194196	4164636
交通运输、仓储和邮政业	Transport, Storage and Post	5306297	4237388	246811	3859872	21938	108766	1068909
住宿和餐饮业	Hotels and Catering Services	2075619	1021774	22652	847888	93254	57980	1053845
信息传输、软件和信息技术服务业	Information Transmission, Software and Information Technology Services	6942153	4385712	150794	3386161	420221	428537	2556441
金融业	Financial Intermediation	5378261	5119533	496907	4448472	39938	134216	258728
房地产业	Real Estate	4192211	2537480	25946	2380759	75665	55110	1654732
租赁和商务服务业	Leasing and Business Services	7340620	3210644	274978	2765466	100671	69529	4129976
科学研究和技术服务业	Scientific Research and Technical Services	6051587	4053257	1253540	2666912	27540	105265	1998330
水利、环境和公共设施管理业	Management of Water Conservancy, Environment and Public Facilities	1155206	892016	476428	411343	4076	168	263190
居民服务、修理和其他服务业	Services to Households, Repair and Other Services	1133423	274600	54347	214978	3156	2118	858823
教育	Education	15454423	14240329	13078264	1156918	2203	2944	1214094
卫生和社会工作	Health and Social Service	11139992	10211288	9378929	829362	911	2087	928703
文化、体育和娱乐业	Culture, Sports and Entertainment	1350283	776901	467360	300938	7520	1083	573382
公共管理、社会保障和社会组织	Public Management, Social Security and Social Organization	14811739	14811739	14794056	17684			

注：自2023年起，按照《关于市场主体统计分类的划分规定》（国统字〔2023〕14号）执行新的登记注册统计类别，国有单位包括机关事业单位和全民所有制企业。

a) Implement new registration and statistical categories in accordance with the "Regulations on the Classification of Market Entity Statistics"(Guotongzi〔2023〕No. 14), and state-owend units include government agencies and enterprises owned by the whole people since 2023.

4-13 按登记注册类型和行业分就业人员平均工资(2023年)
Average wage of Employed Persons by Registered Types and Sector(2023)

单位：元 (yuan)

项目	Item	城镇全部单位 All Urban Units	城镇非私营单位 Urban Non-Private Units	#国有单位 State-owend Units	#其他内资单位 Other Domestic Units	#港澳台商投资单位 Funds from Hong Kong, Macao,Taiwan	#外商投资单位 Foreign Funded Units	城镇私营单位 Urban Private Units
总计	**Total**	**90220**	**110160**	**124016**	**101034**	**103341**	**112473**	**62105**
农、林、牧、渔业	Agriculture,Forestry, Animal Husbandry and Fishery	55181	85299	94549	73965	180198	102170	40910
采矿业	Mining	142562	159113	60956	160328		55284	75176
制造业	Manufacturing	85574	99675	79159	101024	88163	100549	67789
电力、热力、燃气及水生产和供应业	Production and Supply of Electricity, Heat, Gas and Water	129816	135500	129715	137033	115342	101240	64031
建筑业	Construction	70045	80698	68979	80878	108866	99620	62996
批发和零售业	Wholesale and Retail Trades	69393	96458	177135	92952	98863	83072	55906
交通运输、仓储和邮政业	Transport, Storage and Post	97767	118242	112871	118240	101379	137813	57971
住宿和餐饮业	Hotels and Catering Services	51234	55068	77517	55760	43052	65111	47994
信息传输、软件和信息技术服务业	Information Transmission, Software and Information Technology Services	136294	160257	148655	146652	346371	209107	108470
金融业	Financial Intermediation	142748	149098	176019	147670	176031	115453	77469
房地产业	Real Estate	67776	85844	83574	84839	126680	93531	51238
租赁和商务服务业	Leasing and Business Services	64133	79693	120651	75026	118624	231967	55682
科学研究和技术服务业	Scientific Research and Technical Services	108227	146232	136112	150384	144020	180513	70868
水利、环境和公共设施管理业	Management of Water Conservancy, Environment and Public Facilities	65439	72529	73412	71138	169846	62222	49155
居民服务、修理和其他服务业	Services to Households, Repair and Other Services	51192	61230	91270	56130	84847	95846	48642
教育	Education	107021	116527	121564	79258	165624	230008	54692
卫生和社会工作	Health and Social Service	128453	138142	144039	94476	88398	130840	72523
文化、体育和娱乐业	Culture, Sports and Entertainment	73155	105808	115588	96638	45273	56856	51585
公共管理、社会保障和社会组织	Public Management, Social Security and Social Organization	117329	117329	117325	120218			

注：自2023年起，按照《关于市场主体统计分类的划分规定》（国统字〔2023〕14号）执行新的登记注册统计类别，国有单位包括机关事业单位和全民所有制企业。

a) Implement new registration and statistical categories in accordance with the "Regulations on the Classification of Market Entity Statistics"(Guotongzi〔2023〕No. 14), and state-owend units include government agencies and enterprises owned by the whole people since 2023.

4–14 各市(州)按登记注册类型分就业人员平均工资及指数(2023年)
Average Wage of Employment in all Units and Related Indices by Region and Registered Types (2023)

市(州)	Region	平均工资(元) Average Wage (yuan)			指数(上年=100) Indices (preceding year=100)		
		城镇全部单位 All Urban Units	城镇非私营单位 Urban Non-Private Units	城镇私营单位 Urban Private Units	城镇全部单位 All Urban Units	城镇非私营单位 Urban Non-Private Units	城镇私营单位 Urban Private Units
全省	**Sichuan**	**90220**	**110160**	**62105**	**106.3**	**108.2**	**105.0**
成都市	Chengdu	100606	125448	67834	104.3	106.8	104.2
自贡市	Zigong	77846	92661	56856	110.4	112.8	104.5
攀枝花市	Panzhihua	93624	109922	58682	103.3	104.0	106.9
泸州市	Luzhou	82032	100398	59325	109.5	113.4	104.1
德阳市	Deyang	87840	105234	66885	109.1	109.6	109.6
绵阳市	Mianyang	82851	102284	59200	107.2	111.1	103.9
广元市	Guangyuan	79483	96938	51102	106.6	106.9	103.1
遂宁市	Suining	75700	89623	56275	111.8	114.0	108.9
内江市	Neijiang	81230	95024	57603	109.1	112.0	104.4
乐山市	Leshan	85768	102579	61660	108.5	109.7	109.5
南充市	Nanchong	81219	104307	56938	106.7	110.0	100.5
眉山市	Meishan	81543	97964	59055	106.9	106.2	102.7
宜宾市	Yibin	85452	103402	59520	107.4	107.5	104.4
广安市	Guangan	73823	95485	51326	108.2	110.2	106.5
达州市	Dazhou	80524	98984	56599	106.4	110.1	104.7
雅安市	Yaan	78786	94094	48771	106.0	108.6	105.6
巴中市	Bazhong	75855	84599	52043	107.4	109.0	104.1
资阳市	Ziyang	79000	90135	51396	107.1	108.3	100.1
阿坝藏族羌族自治州	Aba	111923	122565	54238	101.2	101.0	103.8
甘孜藏族自治州	Ganzi	115189	120885	57505	107.0	107.0	104.0
凉山彝族自治州	Liangshan	90439	102270	54968	104.4	105.3	108.6

4-15 按行业分国有经济单位就业人员平均工资
Average Wage of Employed Persons in State-owned Units by Sector

单位：元 (yuan)

年份 Year	合计 Total	农、林、牧、渔业 Farming, Forestry, Animal Husbandry and Fishery	采矿业 Mining	制造业 Manufacturing	电力、热力、燃气及水生产和供应业 Production and Supply of Electricity, Heat, Gas and Water	建筑业 Construction	批发和零售业 Wholesale and Retail Trades
1978	622	519	722	620	603	703	539
1980	789	674	918	803	826	890	688
1985	1138	941	1268	1174	1334	1157	978
1986	1338	1169	1527	1319	1438	1568	1115
1987	1441	1202	1595	1459	1563	1733	1225
1988	1726	1389	1895	1773	1814	2012	1537
1989	1941	1527	2259	1998	2122	2268	1686
1990	2177	1700	2560	2232	2331	2527	1865
1991	2351	1812	2723	2432	2622	2765	2011
1992	2643	2120	2882	2678	2945	3056	2102
1993	3148	2916	2956	3302	3714	3660	2454
1994	4366	3652	4220	4135	4822	4881	3219
1995	5002	4167	4907	4838	6057	5926	3701
1996	5527	4479	5471	5362	6833	6356	4064
1997	5996	4585	5791	5702	8292	6903	4251
1998	6441	4821	5849	5832	8279	6983	4312
1999	7771	5727	6616	7314	10469	8480	5924
2000	8909	6353	8705	8323	11508	8907	6443
2001	10783	7735	8302	9566	12940	10064	7717
2002	12388	8384	10884	11137	14995	10636	8883
2003	13769	9095	11943	13136	16327	11775	11420
2004	15592	9433	14588	15320	19016	13269	14060
2005	17644	10206	20692	17783	22067	14466	17461
2006	19884	11430	22602	22373	24328	15964	20068
2007	24045	13707	25671	24778	28980	18715	22506
2008	28131	15453	35692	29039	34560	21377	28070
2009	32210	17920	39083	33169	37326	25284	33574
2010	36729	19934	46629	37871	44559	28886	41334
2011	42048	26451	52419	43179	49809	32067	48097
2012	47721	31514	57092	47075	54557	37259	54348
2013	53896	35211	48146	54977	71319	45202	66927
2014	57018	39817	52019	58440	79841	44511	76326
2015	66551	48555	54657	65789	85266	51156	84761
2016	72980	53470	69012	78192	90858	51452	85687
2017	80321	59437	83748	91783	97175	51898	94553
2018	90390	66202	99678	104645	106354	52959	109489
2019	97330	68375	117427	94452	120298	50387	126982
2020	105350	77634	128561	91996	109654	56487	133868
2021	113183	84893	142125	83308	119684	60320	152257
2022	119197	90090	110284	94892	127686	61626	151052
2023	124016	94549	60956	79159	129715	68979	177135

注：自2023年起，按照《关于市场主体统计分类的划分规定》（国统字〔2023〕14号）执行新的登记注册统计类别（下表相同），国有单位包括机关事业单位和全民所有制企业。

a) Implement new registration and statistical categories in accordance with the "Regulations on the Classification of Market Entity Statistics"(Guotongzi〔2023〕No. 14)(the same as the table below), and state-owend units include government agencies and enterprises owned by the whole people since 2023.

4-15 续表 1 continued

单位：元 (yuan)

年份 Year	交通运输、仓储和邮政业 Transport, Storage and Post	住宿和餐饮业 Hotels and Catering Services	信息传输、软件和信息技术服务业 Information Transmission, Software and IT Services	金融业 Financial Intermediation	房地产业 Real Estate	租赁和商务服务业 Leasing and Business Services
1978	682	518		623	493	
1980	836	663		751	679	
1985	1178	954	1512	1185	990	986
1986	1414	996	1866	1460	1268	1258
1987	1536	1209	1975	1496	1353	1342
1988	1853	1506	2413	1726	1546	1533
1989	2126	1642	2858	1805	1712	1664
1990	2336	1827	3177	2071	1885	1832
1991	2557	1983	3843	2179	2030	1973
1992	2878	2085	4620	2668	2585	2450
1993	3402	2396	5431	3943	3060	2900
1994	4815	3149	7872	5872	5023	4761
1995	5648	3544	8655	6505	5254	4980
1996	6376	3971	9310	7156	5896	5539
1997	7499	4148	10044	8670	6374	5988
1998	7974	4201	12786	10271	7620	7158
1999	9889	5719	13899	11788	9076	8526
2000	11410	6222	17001	14403	9344	8778
2001	13557	7487	19123	17012	11334	10643
2002	15109	8485	21247	18860	13793	12952
2003	14151	10123	22463	21309	14740	13934
2004	15914	11879	27235	24320	15980	17189
2005	18255	12883	31395	26744	17285	21531
2006	22484	13976	32947	30830	19248	22195
2007	25031	16883	34077	35986	23745	29596
2008	29519	19452	37033	44898	26987	28529
2009	34183	21450	40649	47335	30409	35599
2010	38996	26240	44039	59311	30448	41002
2011	46270	31380	44616	65572	32826	46130
2012	55021	34732	53353	74670	40669	62383
2013	60511	34048	65885	83191	43221	53195
2014	64722	37800	56396	91670	45943	50290
2015	70884	38894	66465	94957	60356	54238
2016	74242	41792	70389	94466	78518	66785
2017	81897	46576	74081	101667	72999	67908
2018	90779	55743	81873	108929	69739	80763
2019	94593	51404	100248	152377	88737	73839
2020	93561	45163	117077	148806	72841	81209
2021	98497	53358	123060	153332	86387	89757
2022	101641	52079	134725	163961	81463	95044
2023	112871	77517	148655	176019	83574	120651

4-15 续表 2 continued

单位：元 (yuan)

年份 Year	科学研究和技术服务业 Scientific Research and Technical Services	水利、环境和公共设施管理业 Management of Water Conservancy, Environment and Public Facilities	居民服务、修理和其他服务业 Services to Households, Repair and Other Services	教育 Education	卫生和社会工作 Health and Social Service	文化、体育和娱乐业 Culture, Sports and Entertainment	公共管理、社会保障和社会组织 Public Management, Social Security and Social Organization
1978	676	618	593	540	575	622	623
1980	725	633	624	683	754	703	775
1985	1223	1074	1058	1043	1103	1066	1037
1986	1482	1265	1247	1222	1358	1304	1313
1987	1509	1386	1328	1248	1437	1373	1382
1988	1783	1597	1524	1527	1699	1576	1578
1989	1987	1811	1724	1664	1923	1768	1773
1990	2146	2108	1940	1884	2152	1987	1989
1991	2201	2371	2121	1963	2295	2153	2156
1992	2889	2893	2427	2358	2679	2582	2594
1993	3876	3158	3027	2716	3234	3169	3052
1994	5751	4466	4106	4225	5144	5078	4684
1995	6389	4890	4749	4583	5808	5736	5091
1996	7098	5519	5430	4984	6549	6137	5604
1997	8474	5795	5712	5366	7187	6519	6182
1998	10193	6384	6302	5945	8012	7098	7039
1999	11658	7731	7583	6861	9334	8014	8062
2000	14064	8647	8415	7928	10721	9081	9246
2001	16737	9898	9751	9997	12909	11150	11568
2002	18009	10042	11731	11769	14656	12922	13059
2003	19769	9574	14516	12631	16277	13862	14382
2004	21357	10733	16218	13767	18335	17036	15873
2005	25100	11719	17133	14912	20051	18871	17783
2006	29911	13333	19946	16340	22688	17806	19407
2007	36600	16035	25766	20920	27528	23901	24963
2008	43119	17522	22436	23465	31920	26194	29542
2009	48319	19506	28979	29473	34379	28400	33204
2010	54707	20978	30725	34392	40552	32426	35018
2011	64236	25296	38606	39240	47425	37631	39555
2012	67431	29369	38824	44598	55064	44509	44126
2013	74713	32137	42343	49521	60988	48735	48638
2014	77454	35029	44440	52597	65341	52161	52063
2015	80846	41518	47211	63957	76705	60967	63718
2016	85280	44814	60854	70565	86057	67097	71091
2017	95199	49740	64773	77061	94029	76664	79651
2018	117814	55377	66629	84152	102805	84590	90068
2019	111570	67045	72034	92540	112981	95239	95490
2020	115877	65984	75438	102999	117592	93716	106224
2021	123223	70012	85042	110040	126683	103578	114163
2022	128621	73696	84360	117577	135504	110350	118205
2023	136112	73412	91270	121564	144039	115588	117325

主要统计指标解释

就业人员 指年满16周岁，为取得报酬或经营利润，在调查参考周内从事了1个小时（含1小时）以上劳动的人员；或由于在职学习、休假、临时停工等原因在调查参考周内暂时未工作的人员。

单位就业人员 指报告期末最后一日在本单位中工作，并取得工资或其他形式劳动报酬的人员数。该指标为时点指标，不包括最后一日当天及以前已经与单位解除劳动合同关系的人员，是在岗职工、劳务派遣人员及其他就业人员之和。

单位就业人员不包括：(1)离开本单位仍保留劳动关系，并定期领取生活费的人员；(2)在本单位实习的各类在校学生。

在岗职工 指在本单位工作且与本单位签订劳动合同，并由单位支付各项工资和社会保险、住房公积金的人员，以及上述人员中由于学习、病伤、产假等原因暂未工作仍由单位支付工资的人员。在岗职工还包括：

(1) 应订立劳动合同而未订立劳动合同人员；

(2) 处于试用期人员；

(3) 编制外招用的人员，如临时人员；

(4) 派往外单位工作，但工资或其他形式劳动报酬仍由本单位发放的人员（如挂职锻炼、外派工作等情况）。

工资总额 指根据《关于工资总额组成的规定》（1990年1月1日国家统计局发布的一号令）进行修订，本单位在报告期内（季度或年度）直接支付给本单位全部就业人员的劳动报酬总额。包括计时工资、计件工资、奖金、津贴和补贴、加班加点工资、特殊情况下支付的工资。

工资总额是税前工资，包括单位从个人工资中直接为其代扣或代缴的个人所得税、社会保险基金和住房公积金等个人缴纳部分，以及房费、水电费等。

工资总额不论是计入成本的还是不计入成本的，不论是以货币形式支付的还是以实物形式支付的，均应列入工资总额的计算范围。

平均工资 指单位就业人员在一定时期内平均每人所得的工资额。计算公式为：

$$平均工资=\frac{报告期就业人员工资总额}{报告期就业人员平均人数}$$

平均名义工资指数 指报告期就业人员平均工资与基期就业人员平均工资的比率，是反映不同时期就业人员名义工资水平变动情况的相对数。计算公式为：

$$平均名义工资指数=\frac{报告期就业人员平均工资}{基期就业人员平均工资}\times 100\%$$

Explanatory Notes on Main Statistical Indicators

Employed Persons refers to persons, aged 16 and over, who performed some work for compensation or business gains for one hour or more during the reference period of the investigation; or persons who do not work for the reasons of part-time study, on holiday,temporary suspension of work, etc., during the reference period of the investigation.

Persons Employed in Various Units refers to the total number of employees who work at various units and obtain wages or other forms of payment at the end of the reference period. This indicator is a kind of time point index and it equals to the sum of the number of employed staff and workers, labor dispatch personnel and other employed persons.

Employed persons in Various Units do not include:

1) persons who have left their working units while keeping their labor contract (employment relation) unchanged and receiving regular alimony;

2) all kinds of enrolled students who do internship in various units.

Staff and Workers refers to persons who signed labor contracts with working units and working units would pay wages, social insurance and housing funds for them. Persons who have their work posts but are temporarily absent from work for reasons of study or on sick, injury or maternal leave and still receive wages from their working units are also included. Employed staff and workers also include:

1) Persons who should have signed the labor contracts but not;

2) Employees on probation;

3) Employees beyond the staffing quota, for example, temporary employees;

4) Employees who are sent to other working units but still obtain wages or other forms of remuneration from their original units (situations like on-the-job placement, expatriated assignment, etc.).

Total Wages Bill It is revised according to the "Provision of Composition of Total Wages" (Order No.1 by National Bureau of Statistics on January, 1st, 1990), total wage bill refers to the total remuneration payment to all employed persons in various units during the reporting period (by quarter or by year), including hourly-paid wages, piece-rate wages, bonuses, allowance and subsidies, overtime wages and wages paid under special circumstances.

Total wage bill is pre-tax wages, including the personal income tax, social insurance fund, housing provident fund and other personal contributions directly withheld or paid by the unit from the individual's salary, as well as room fees, utilities, etc.

Total wage bill, whether or not included in cost, whether or not paid in money or in kind, shall be included in the calculation of total wage.

Average Wage refers to the average per capita wage during a certain period of time for employed persons. It is calculated as follows:

$$\text{Average Wage} = \frac{\text{Total Wage Bill of Employed Persons at Reference Time}}{\text{Average Number of Persons Employed at Reference Time}}$$

Average Nominal Wage Indices refers to the ratio of average wage of staff and workers in the report period to that in the base period, which reflects the change of nominal wage of staff and workers at the different period. It is calculated as follows:

$$\text{Average Nominal Wage Indices} = \frac{\text{Average Wage of Employed Persons at Reference Time}}{\text{Average Wage of Employeds Persons at Base Time}} \times 100\%$$

05 固定资产投资

Chapter 5 Investment in Fixed Assets

5-1 固定资产投资增长情况(2023年)
Growth Rate of Total Investment in Fixed Assets(2023)

单位：% (%)

指标	Item	比上年增长 Growth Rate Over Preceding Year
固定资产投资	**Investment in Fixed Assets**	**2.4**
#国有及国有控股	State-owned and State Holding Units	13.2
按登记注册类型分	**Grouped by Registration**	
内资	Domestic Funds	2.3
港澳台投资	Units With Funds From Hong Kong, Macao and Taiwan	23.8
外商投资	Foreign Funded Units	1.0
个体经营	Individuals Economy	-29.8
按建设性质分	**Grouped by Character**	
新建	New Construction	1.0
扩建	Expansion	6.1
改建	Reconstruction	6.7
按构成分	**Grouped by Use of Funds**	
建筑安装工程	Construction and Installation	2.8
设备工器具购置	Purchase of Equipment and Instruments	19.1
其他费用	Others	-8.0
按三次产业分	**Grouped by Three Strata of Industry**	
第一产业	Primary Industry	11.6
第二产业	Secondary Industry	21.6
第三产业	Tertiary Industry	-3.4

市(州)	Region	比上年增长 Growth Rate Over Preceding Year
全　省	**Sichuan**	**2.4**
成都市	Chengdu	-19.4
自贡市	Zigong	27.7
攀枝花市	Panzhihua	11.3
泸州市	Luzhou	19.8
德阳市	Deyang	13.2
绵阳市	Mianyang	11.1
广元市	Guangyuan	23.6
遂宁市	Suining	9.6
内江市	Neijiang	13.9
乐山市	Leshan	18.0
南充市	Nanchong	12.7
眉山市	Meishan	10.8
宜宾市	Yibin	-9.9
广安市	Guangan	39.2
达州市	Dazhou	15.3
雅安市	Yaan	7.0
巴中市	Bazhong	55.8
资阳市	Ziyang	6.0
阿坝藏族羌族自治州	Aba	2.2
甘孜藏族自治州	Ganzi	12.9
凉山彝族自治州	Liangshan	-15.4

注：2018年起，计划投资在500万-5000万项目按财务支出法统计，增速按可比口径计算(以下有关表同)。
a) From 2018, planned investment in 5-50 million projects is counted according to the financial expenditure method, and the growth rate is calculated by comparable caliber(the same as the following related tables).

5-2 分行业固定资产投资增长情况(2023年)
Growth Rate of Total Investment in Fixed Assets by Sector(2023)

单位：% (%)

指标	Item	比上年增长 Growth Rate Over Preceding Year
固定资产投资	**Investment in Fixed Assets**	**2.4**
农、林、牧、渔业	Agriculture, Forestry, Animal Husbandry and Fishery	12.2
采矿业	Mining	5.5
制造业	Manufacturing	21.6
电力、热力、燃气及水生产和供应业	Production and Supply of Electricity, Heat, Gas and Water	29.7
建筑业	Construction	-3.0
批发和零售业	Wholesale and Retail Trades	48.5
交通运输、仓储和邮政业	Transport, Storage and Post	1.2
住宿和餐饮业	Hotels and Catering Services	-19.8
信息传输、软件和信息技术服务业	Information Transmission, Software and Information Technology Services	9.4
金融业	Financial Intermediation	-68.3
房地产业	Real Estate	-18.2
租赁和商务服务业	Leasing and Business Services	2.6
科学研究和技术服务业	Scientific Research and Technical Services	27.9
水利、环境和公共设施管理业	Management of Water Conservancy, Environment and Public Facilities	19.9
居民服务、修理和其他服务业	Services to Households, Repair and Other Services	46.9
教育	Education	-0.2
卫生和社会工作	Health and Social Service	-5.5
文化、体育和娱乐业	Culture, Sports and Entertainment	34.2
公共管理、社会保障和社会组织	Public Management, Social Security and Social Organization	-18.2
国际组织	International Organization	

 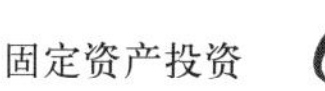 

5-3 分行业按构成分项目固定资产投资增长情况(2023年)
Growth Rate of Item Investment in Fixed Assets by Sector and Composition(2023)

单位：% (%)

指标	Item	合计 Total	建筑安装工程 Construction and Installation	设备工具器具购置 Purchase of Equipment and Instruments	其他费用 Others
投资总额	**Total Investment**	**2.4**	**2.8**	**19.1**	**-8.0**
农、林、牧、渔业	Agriculture, Forestry, Animal Husbandry and Fishery	12.2	13.5	-16.3	-20.7
采矿业	Mining	5.5	8.5	-14.8	15.7
制造业	Manufacturing	21.6	20.8	26.5	8.8
电力、热力、燃气及水生产和供应业	Production and Supply of Electricity, Heat, Gas and Water	29.7	29.8	41.6	15.6
建筑业	Construction	-3.0	53.8	-71.1	-95.8
批发和零售业	Wholesale and Retail Trades	48.5	45.6	156.3	23.8
交通运输、仓储和邮政业	Transport, Storage and Post	1.2	5.1	15.3	-37.6
住宿和餐饮业	Hotels and Catering Services	-19.8	-20.0	-59.7	-5.6
信息传输、软件和信息技术服务业	Information Transmission, Software and Information Technology Services	9.4	6.6	16.5	-35.3
金融业	Financial Intermediation	-68.3	-74.9	56.3	-52.4
房地产业	Real Estate	-18.2	-22.6	-15.7	-5.4
租赁和商务服务业	Leasing and Business Services	2.6	6.6	9.3	-26.3
科学研究和技术服务业	Scientific Research and Technical Services	27.9	35.6	32.1	-29.6
水利、环境和公共设施管理业	Management of Water Conservancy, Environment and Public Facilities	19.9	21.1	-20.7	11.4
居民服务、修理和其他服务业	Services to Households, Repair and Other Services	46.9	63.7	-54.1	-24.2
教育	Education	-0.2	3.9	11.7	-37.5
卫生和社会工作	Health and Social Service	-5.5	-6.0	7.3	-22.8
文化、体育和娱乐业	Culture, Sports and Entertainment	34.2	34.0	0.6	43.7
公共管理、社会保障和社会组织	Public Management, Social Security and Social Organization	-18.2	-15.3	-52.1	-22.9
国际组织	International Organization				

5-4 各市(州)按构成分固定资产投资增长情况(2023年)
Growth Rate of Item Investment in Fixed Assets by Region and Composition(2023)

单位：%　　(%)

市(州)	Region	合计 Total	建筑安装工程 Construction and Installation	设备工具器具购置 Purchase of Equipment and Instruments	其他费用 Others
全省	**Sichuan**	**2.4**	**2.8**	**19.1**	**-8.0**
成都市	Chengdu	-19.4	-26.0	5.5	-11.0
自贡市	Zigong	27.7	40.1	18.0	-48.5
攀枝花市	Panzhihua	11.3	11.2	7.4	20.1
泸州市	Luzhou	19.8	27.3	-14.4	-37.3
德阳市	Deyang	13.2	10.2	40.8	25.7
绵阳市	Mianyang	11.1	15.5	-18.6	16.1
广元市	Guangyuan	23.6	24.0	98.2	-10.0
遂宁市	Suining	9.6	7.8	36.1	12.2
内江市	Neijiang	13.9	14.5	16.3	7.1
乐山市	Leshan	18.0	15.6	49.9	4.2
南充市	Nanchong	12.7	12.3	46.5	12.3
眉山市	Meishan	10.8	1.7	74.3	31.6
宜宾市	Yibin	-9.9	-17.0	69.2	-18.7
广安市	Guangan	39.2	40.9	28.6	23.8
达州市	Dazhou	15.3	16.3	21.9	-3.4
雅安市	Yaan	7.0	5.0	-6.8	43.9
巴中市	Bazhong	55.8	59.9	53.0	16.6
资阳市	Ziyang	6.0	5.0	-3.3	18.2
阿坝藏族羌族自治州	Aba	2.2	-2.5	304.1	-5.7
甘孜藏族自治州	Ganzi	12.9	-2.0	149.5	72.5
凉山彝族自治州	Liangshan	-15.4	-14.2	-22.5	-15.7

5-5 分行业施工和投产项目个数(2023年)
Number of Projects under Construction and Production by Sector(2023)

行业	Sector	施工项目(个) Number of Projects Under Construction (unit)	新开工项目个数(个) Number of Projects Started This Year (unit)	全部建成投产项目(个) Number of Projects Completed and Put into Use (unit)	项目建成投产率(%) Rate of Projects Completed (%)
总计	**Total**	**30616**	**13670**	**11364**	**37.12**
农、林、牧、渔业	Agriculture, Forestry, Animal Husbandry and Fishery	3915	1832	1717	43.86
采矿业	Mining	700	316	274	39.14
制造业	Manufacturing	5516	2492	1871	33.92
电力、热力、燃气及水生产和供应业	Production and Supply of Electricity, Heat, Gas and Water	1993	973	652	32.71
建筑业	Construction	46	21	17	36.96
批发和零售业	Wholesale and Retail Trades	398	187	124	31.16
交通运输、仓储和邮政业	Transport, Storage and Post	4082	1814	1639	40.15
住宿和餐饮业	Hotels and Catering Services	651	347	243	37.33
信息传输、软件和信息技术服务业	Information Transmission, Software and Information Technology Services	286	116	128	44.76
金融业	Financial Intermediation	21	11	4	19.05
房地产业	Real Estate	1099	361	326	29.66
租赁和商务服务业	Leasing and Business Services	724	269	218	30.11
科学研究和技术服务业	Scientific Research and Technical Services	273	129	77	28.21
水利、环境和公共设施管理业	Management of Water Conservancy, Environment and Public Facilities	7222	3294	2731	37.82
居民服务、修理和其他服务业	Services to Households, Repair and Other Services	176	81	59	33.52
教育	Education	1364	558	529	38.78
卫生和社会工作	Health and Social Service	905	323	279	30.83
文化、体育和娱乐业	Culture, Sports and Entertainment	876	384	318	36.30
公共管理、社会保障和社会组织	Public Management, Social Security and Social Organization	369	162	158	42.82
国际组织	International Organization				

5-6 各市(州)施工和投产项目个数(2023年)
Number of Projects under Construction and Production by Region(2023)

市(州)	Region	施工项目(个) Number of Projects under Construction (unit)	新开工项目个数(个) Number of Projects Started This Year (unit)	全部建成投产项目(个) Number of Projects Completed and Put into Use (unit)	项目建成投产率(%) Rate of Projects Completed (%)
全省	**Sichuan**	**30616**	**13670**	**11364**	**37.12**
成都市	Chengdu	3389	1435	671	19.80
自贡市	Zigong	1268	726	238	18.77
攀枝花市	Panzhihua	1828	721	1039	56.84
泸州市	Luzhou	1756	729	659	37.53
德阳市	Deyang	1547	794	623	40.27
绵阳市	Mianyang	2061	994	1051	50.99
广元市	Guangyuan	1299	724	494	38.03
遂宁市	Suining	1657	782	640	38.62
内江市	Neijiang	1341	492	612	45.64
乐山市	Leshan	1038	435	376	36.22
南充市	Nanchong	1791	554	938	52.37
眉山市	Meishan	1147	500	410	35.75
宜宾市	Yibin	1461	696	445	30.46
广安市	Guangan	1211	662	643	53.10
达州市	Dazhou	2163	795	688	31.81
雅安市	Yaan	1140	495	249	21.84
巴中市	Bazhong	787	404	123	15.63
资阳市	Ziyang	409	203	98	23.96
阿坝藏族羌族自治州	Aba	751	334	173	23.04
甘孜藏族自治州	Ganzi	1174	586	606	51.62
凉山彝族自治州	Liangshan	1375	609	588	42.76

注：本表各市(州)数不包括跨区项目。
a) The region data in this table exclude multiregional projects.

5-7 房地产开发主要指标
Major Indicators of Real Estate Development

指标		Item		2019	2020	2021	2022	2023
企业个数	**（个）**	**Number of Enterprises**	**(unit)**	**4350**	**4593**	**4790**	**4755**	**4671**
内资企业		Domestic Invested Enterprises						4612
港澳台投资企业		Enterprises with investment from Hong Kong, Macao and Taiwan						43
外商投资企业		Foreign Invested Enterprises						16
其他		Others						
从业人员数	**（人）**	**Employed Persons**	**(person)**	**162583**	**164291**	**161138**	**141122**	**114305**
内资企业		Domestic Invested Enterprises						112651
港澳台投资企业		Enterprises with investment from Hong Kong, Macao and Taiwan						1028
外商投资企业		Foreign Invested Enterprises						626
其他		Others						
本年土地购置面积	**（万平方米）**	**Area of Land Purchased This Year**	**(10 000 sq.m)**	**1056.69**	**988.00**	**543.63**	**288.32**	
本年完成投资额	**（亿元）**	**Investment Completed This Year**	**(100 million yuan)**	**6573.24**	**7315.31**	**7831.88**	**7215.77**	**5322.02**
#住宅		Residential Buildings		4665.31	5330.14	5767.25	5363.63	4006.34
本年新增固定资产	**（亿元）**	**Newly Increased Fixed Assets This Year**	**(100 million yuan)**	**2054.18**	**2018.09**	**2083.68**	**2032.13**	**2237.21**
资金来源	**（亿元）**	**Sources of Funds**	**(100 million yuan)**	**9349.72**	**10173.17**	**10142.92**	**8293.00**	**7318.99**
国内贷款		Domestic Loans		1118.17	1144.33	960.77	761.65	703.15
利用外资		Foreign Investment		6.55	5.60			
自筹资金		Self-raising Funds		3039.82	3291.37	3174.23	3175.52	2168.92
定金及预收款		Earnest and Money Collected in Advance		3482.52	3874.28	4197.69	2818.42	2891.35
个人按揭贷款		Personal Mortgage Loan		1499.49	1761.00	1748.71	1491.91	1463.71
其他到位资金		Others		203.16	96.58	61.52	45.50	91.86
房屋建筑面积	**（万平方米）**	**Floor Space of Buildings**	**(10 000 sq.m)**					
施工面积		Floor Space of Buildings under Construction		49113.75	50755.54	54248.70	51948.33	47766.63
#住宅		Residential Buildings		32151.96	33706.21	36153.61	34591.64	31904.07
竣工面积		Floor Space of Buildings Completed		4580.04	4545.86	4379.25	4073.40	4371.32
#住宅		Residential Buildings		2940.11	3073.73	2965.13	2735.31	2931.59
本年新开工面积		Floor Space Started This Year		15325.50	13939.74	11493.57	8329.75	5803.82
#住宅		Residential Buildings		10294.70	9631.06	7959.91	5838.46	3898.54
商品房屋销售面积	**（万平方米）**	**Floor Space of Commercial House sold**	**(10 000 sq.m)**	**12978.61**	**13257.75**	**13692.91**	**9321.37**	**8005.48**
#住宅		Residential Buildings		10451.05	10902.37	10912.14	7315.51	6364.98
商品房销售额	**（亿元）**	**Total Sales of Commercial Houses**	**(100 million yuan)**	**9666.73**	**10394.25**	**10796.73**	**7599.51**	**7173.77**
#住宅		Residential Buildings		7869.04	8766.96	9061.34	6488.27	6289.94

注：自2023年起，按照《关于市场主体统计分类的划分规定》（国统字〔2023〕14号）执行新的登记注册统计类别。
a) Implement new registration and statistical categories in accordance with the "Regulations on the Classification of Market Entity Statistics" (Guotongzi〔2023〕No. 14) since 2023.

5-8 各市(州)按登记注册统计类别分房地产开发企业个数(2023年)
Number of Enterprises of Real Estate Development by Ownership and Region(2023)

单位：个 (unit)

市(州)	Region	合计 Total	内资企业 Domestic Invested Enterprises	港澳台投资企业 Enterprises with investment from Hong Kong, Macao and Taiwan	外商投资企业 Foreign Invested Enterprises	其他企业 Others
全省	**Sichuan**	**4671**	**4612**	**43**	**16**	
成都市	Chengdu	1470	1419	37	14	
自贡市	Zigong	84	84			
攀枝花市	Panzhihua	102	102			
泸州市	Luzhou	160	160			
德阳市	Deyang	218	216	2		
绵阳市	Mianyang	409	407	1	1	
广元市	Guangyuan	124	124			
遂宁市	Suining	176	176			
内江市	Neijiang	140	139	1		
乐山市	Leshan	132	132			
南充市	Nanchong	245	245			
眉山市	Meishan	273	272	1		
宜宾市	Yibin	213	213			
广安市	Guangan	158	157		1	
达州市	Dazhou	244	244			
雅安市	Yaan	97	97			
巴中市	Bazhong	135	135			
资阳市	Ziyang	98	98			
阿坝藏族羌族自治州	Aba	18	18			
甘孜藏族自治州	Ganzi	19	18	1		
凉山彝族自治州	Liangshan	156	156			

注：自2023年起，按照《关于市场主体统计分类的划分规定》（国统字〔2023〕14号）执行新的登记注册统计类别。
a) Implement new registration and statistical categories in accordance with the "Regulations on the Classification of Market Entity Statistics" (Guotongzi〔2023〕No. 14) since 2023.

5-9 各市(州)按资质等级分房地产开发企业个数(2023年)

Number of Enterprises of Real Estate Development by Region and Qualification Criteria(2023)

单位：个 (unit)

市(州)	Region	合计 Total	一级 First Grade	二级 Second Grade	三级 Third Grade	四级 Fourth Grade	其他 Others
全省	**Sichuan**	**4671**	**47**	**1799**	**1960**	**35**	**830**
成都市	Chengdu	1470	19	612	646	6	187
自贡市	Zigong	84	5	39	23		17
攀枝花市	Panzhihua	102	2	30	44	2	24
泸州市	Luzhou	160	2	51	69		38
德阳市	Deyang	218	1	71	97	3	46
绵阳市	Mianyang	409		159	211	1	38
广元市	Guangyuan	124		45	70	2	7
遂宁市	Suining	176		55	66		55
内江市	Neijiang	140	1	56	58	2	23
乐山市	Leshan	132	2	56	56	1	17
南充市	Nanchong	245	2	69	46		128
眉山市	Meishan	273	3	112	128	2	28
宜宾市	Yibin	213	3	80	73	2	55
广安市	Guangan	158		74	57	2	25
达州市	Dazhou	244	4	110	113	2	15
雅安市	Yaan	97	1	25	22	5	44
巴中市	Bazhong	135	2	40	50		43
资阳市	Ziyang	98		39	30		29
阿坝藏族羌族自治州	Aba	18		6	7		5
甘孜藏族自治州	Ganzi	19		4	9	4	2
凉山彝族自治州	Liangshan	156		66	85	1	4

5-10 各市(州)按登记注册统计类别分房地产开发企业从业人员数(2023年)
Number of Employees in Enterprises of Real Estate Development by Ownership and Region(2023)

单位：人 (person)

市(州)	Region	合计 Total	内资企业 Domestic Invested Enterprises	港澳台投资企业 Enterprises with investment from Hong Kong, Macao and Taiwan	外商投资企业 Foreign Invested Enterprises	其他企业 Others
全省	**Sichuan**	**114305**	**112651**	**1028**	**626**	
成都市	Chengdu	31724	30319	872	533	
自贡市	Zigong	3510	3510			
攀枝花市	Panzhihua	3077	3077			
泸州市	Luzhou	7072	7072			
德阳市	Deyang	4060	4023	37		
绵阳市	Mianyang	11144	11056	13	75	
广元市	Guangyuan	2769	2769			
遂宁市	Suining	3987	3987			
内江市	Neijiang	4771	4703	68		
乐山市	Leshan	4459	4459			
南充市	Nanchong	4814	4814			
眉山市	Meishan	6206	6184	22		
宜宾市	Yibin	5346	5346			
广安市	Guangan	5239	5221		18	
达州市	Dazhou	6245	6245			
雅安市	Yaan	1471	1471			
巴中市	Bazhong	2318	2318			
资阳市	Ziyang	1942	1942			
阿坝藏族羌族自治州	Aba	214	214			
甘孜藏族自治州	Ganzi	272	256	16		
凉山彝族自治州	Liangshan	3665	3665			

注：自2023年起，按照《关于市场主体统计分类的划分规定》（国统字〔2023〕14号）执行新的登记注册统计类别。
a) Implement new registration and statistical categories in accordance with the "Regulations on the Classification of Market Entity Statistics" (Guotongzi〔2023〕No. 14) since 2023.

5-11 各市(州)按资质等级分房地产开发企业从业人员数(2023年)
Number of Employees in Enterprises of Real Estate Development by Region and Qualification Criteria(2023)

单位：人 (person)

市(州)	Region	合计 Total	一级 First Grade	二级 Second Grade	三级 Third Grade	四级 Fourth Grade	其他 Others
全省	**Sichuan**	**114305**	**3137**	**49694**	**42761**	**399**	**18314**
成都市	Chengdu	31724	1169	15172	11895	40	3448
自贡市	Zigong	3510	497	1510	735		768
攀枝花市	Panzhihua	3077	254	852	1356	14	601
泸州市	Luzhou	7072	30	2788	2208		2046
德阳市	Deyang	4060	61	1347	1825	57	770
绵阳市	Mianyang	11144		4957	5413	1	773
广元市	Guangyuan	2769		1072	1560	8	129
遂宁市	Suining	3987		1601	1363		1023
内江市	Neijiang	4771	7	1604	2566	33	561
乐山市	Leshan	4459	117	1960	2034	35	313
南充市	Nanchong	4814	44	1551	696		2523
眉山市	Meishan	6206	401	2827	2412	15	551
宜宾市	Yibin	5346	427	2046	1498	21	1354
广安市	Guangan	5239		2590	1228	42	1379
达州市	Dazhou	6245	77	3741	2135	23	269
雅安市	Yaan	1471	12	479	408	37	535
巴中市	Bazhong	2318	41	971	708		598
资阳市	Ziyang	1942		815	556		571
阿坝藏族羌族自治州	Aba	214		84	103		27
甘孜藏族自治州	Ganzi	272		83	126	58	5
凉山彝族自治州	Liangshan	3665		1644	1936	15	70

5-12 各市(州)房地产投资完成额
Investment Completed of Real Estate Development by Region

单位：亿元 (100 million yuan)

市(州)	Region	2013	2014	2015	2016	2017	2018	2019	2020	2021	2022	2023
全省	**Sichuan**	**3853.00**	**4380.09**	**4813.03**	**5282.64**	**5149.89**	**5701.09**	**6573.24**	**7315.31**	**7831.88**	**7215.77**	**5322.02**
成都市	Chengdu	2110.27	2220.80	2441.95	2638.89	2487.88	2272.98	2606.84	2845.46	3141.65	3267.92	2446.80
自贡市	Zigong	77.78	101.23	125.81	123.87	122.59	209.31	213.10	218.13	207.47	119.47	55.39
攀枝花市	Panzhihua	51.16	75.20	58.94	55.03	59.96	98.50	102.84	104.00	119.44	110.58	82.44
泸州市	Luzhou	130.92	192.56	196.87	239.20	258.62	318.39	399.04	445.58	391.86	290.97	222.72
德阳市	Deyang	82.66	95.23	115.38	125.78	105.04	149.81	168.05	219.99	259.68	214.12	172.61
绵阳市	Mianyang	169.94	210.74	198.35	205.58	176.65	204.54	264.12	364.28	465.22	434.23	349.91
广元市	Guangyuan	58.67	83.32	86.80	94.63	83.58	84.89	88.04	99.86	125.97	126.71	74.20
遂宁市	Suining	85.99	86.36	111.91	144.56	173.48	172.23	176.05	222.05	229.37	199.22	145.19
内江市	Neijiang	78.64	115.43	123.88	122.81	115.05	155.56	159.70	191.72	204.40	184.70	144.65
乐山市	Leshan	110.19	126.07	152.86	212.02	194.15	194.91	222.20	213.34	201.31	143.61	90.22
南充市	Nanchong	207.91	229.14	213.22	216.64	212.39	310.03	383.26	420.58	473.59	349.30	291.25
眉山市	Meishan	130.31	151.12	195.15	194.29	193.58	257.12	398.75	476.53	523.54	485.20	366.10
宜宾市	Yibin	141.13	171.86	150.42	189.55	228.15	312.04	357.40	369.01	395.90	367.17	233.27
广安市	Guangan	65.25	122.11	184.26	258.22	244.19	238.10	291.17	300.02	277.49	193.43	152.47
达州市	Dazhou	100.53	94.98	82.58	93.28	113.64	156.70	202.29	218.57	270.41	268.82	181.51
雅安市	Yaan	27.02	25.46	27.45	53.94	58.38	85.28	88.15	94.43	91.06	72.68	45.18
巴中市	Bazhong	63.99	88.65	104.49	118.96	136.97	156.99	133.61	137.20	91.78	69.50	52.77
资阳市	Ziyang	136.98	164.77	195.14	150.18	127.89	132.41	144.42	153.29	139.31	114.14	82.34
阿坝藏族羌族自治州	Aba	4.04	4.25	7.80	12.26	4.87	3.10	2.12	4.63	10.05	10.30	6.61
甘孜藏族自治州	Ganzi	1.98	1.71	1.10	1.28	1.51	6.43	5.30	8.86	7.19	7.77	6.42
凉山彝族自治州	Liangshan	17.64	19.11	38.67	31.67	51.32	181.78	166.79	207.77	205.17	185.92	119.98

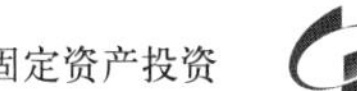

5-13 各市(州)按用途分房地产开发投资完成额(2023年)
Investment Completed of Real Estate Development by Region and Use(2023)

单位：亿元　　　　(100 million yuan)

市(州)	Region	本年完成投资额 Investment Completed in Current Year	住宅 Residential Buildings	办公楼 Office Buildings	商业营业用房 Houses for Business Use	其他 Others
全省	**Sichuan**	**5322.02**	**4006.34**	**188.68**	**421.54**	**705.46**
成都市	Chengdu	2446.80	1718.48	143.29	183.13	401.90
自贡市	Zigong	55.39	38.76	3.73	7.57	5.33
攀枝花市	Panzhihua	82.44	63.52	0.03	6.33	12.56
泸州市	Luzhou	222.72	173.80	4.47	25.02	19.43
德阳市	Deyang	172.61	139.64	5.66	11.70	15.61
绵阳市	Mianyang	349.91	290.85	2.09	17.54	39.43
广元市	Guangyuan	74.20	59.69	0.01	5.87	8.62
遂宁市	Suining	145.19	120.88	3.58	8.12	12.61
内江市	Neijiang	144.65	107.39	1.21	17.22	18.84
乐山市	Leshan	90.22	72.33	0.16	6.38	11.35
南充市	Nanchong	291.25	248.43	0.82	18.16	23.84
眉山市	Meishan	366.10	293.03	12.10	21.30	39.68
宜宾市	Yibin	233.27	171.20	6.94	26.37	28.76
广安市	Guangan	152.47	127.95	0.04	13.88	10.61
达州市	Dazhou	181.51	147.58	0.62	15.46	17.84
雅安市	Yaan	45.18	32.84	1.20	4.62	6.52
巴中市	Bazhong	52.77	47.02	0.08	3.90	1.78
资阳市	Ziyang	82.34	61.39	0.68	9.46	10.80
阿坝藏族羌族自治州	Aba	6.61	4.83	0.16	0.53	1.09
甘孜藏族自治州	Ganzi	6.42	4.81	0.13	1.03	0.46
凉山彝族自治州	Liangshan	119.98	81.93	1.67	17.96	18.42

5-14 各市(州)房地产开发建设房屋建筑面积和造价(2023年)
Floor Space of Buildings and the Cost in Real Estate Development by Region(2023)

市(州)	Region	施工房屋面积(万平方米) Floor Space of Buildings under Construction (10 000 sq.m)	竣工房屋面积(万平方米) Floor Space of Buildings Completed (10 000 sq.m)	房屋建筑面积竣工率(%) Rate of Floor Space of Buildings Completed (%)	竣工房屋价值(万元) Value of Buildings Completed (10 000 yuan)	竣工房屋造价(元/平方米) Cost of Buildings Completed (yuan / sq.m)
全省	**Sichuan**	**47766.63**	**4371.32**	**9.2**	**16657632**	**3811**
成都市	Chengdu	17760.90	1746.16	9.8	7725602	4424
自贡市	Zigong	381.38	49.33	12.9	184065	3731
攀枝花市	Panzhihua	533.14	47.28	8.9	214990	4547
泸州市	Luzhou	1850.76	213.47	11.5	582230	2727
德阳市	Deyang	2223.15	266.18	12.0	729016	2739
绵阳市	Mianyang	2868.79	364.15	12.7	1132893	3111
广元市	Guangyuan	807.33	44.15	5.5	158986	3601
遂宁市	Suining	1623.72	65.95	4.1	193821	2939
内江市	Neijiang	1489.94	80.64	5.4	360084	4465
乐山市	Leshan	1239.32	195.52	15.8	548742	2807
南充市	Nanchong	3945.46	165.37	4.2	523119	3163
眉山市	Meishan	4112.62	163.61	4.0	734736	4491
宜宾市	Yibin	2377.15	546.68	23.0	2298816	4205
广安市	Guangan	1142.60	52.38	4.6	162132	3095
达州市	Dazhou	1714.10	24.49	1.4	91760	3747
雅安市	Yaan	847.40	23.23	2.7	113871	4902
巴中市	Bazhong	886.63	158.29	17.9	429207	2712
资阳市	Ziyang	781.53	20.38	2.6	71230	3495
阿坝藏族羌族自治州	Aba	61.23	2.79	4.6	11730	4204
甘孜藏族自治州	Ganzi	101.68	22.88	22.5	88985	3889
凉山彝族自治州	Liangshan	1017.77	118.42	11.6	301617	2547

5−15 各市(州)商品房销售情况(2023年)
Selling of Commercial Houses by Region(2023)

市(州)	Region	房屋销售面积(万平方米) Floor Space of Commercial Houses (10 000 sq.m)	#住宅 Residential Buildings	#办公楼 Office Buildings	#商业营业用房 Houses for Business Use	房屋销售额(亿元) Total Sale of Commercial Houses (100 million yuan)	#住宅 Residential Buildings	#办公楼 Office Buildings	#商业营业用房 Houses for Business Use
全省	**Sichuan**	**8005.48**	**6364.98**	**191.43**	**480.26**	**7173.77**	**6289.94**	**174.66**	**476.64**
成都市	Chengdu	2203.69	1785.32	120.69	80.31	3819.52	3485.53	122.91	131.08
自贡市	Zigong	231.40	164.45	4.37	29.17	126.31	92.80	2.76	23.13
攀枝花市	Panzhihua	97.94	71.78	1.66	8.08	53.50	42.59	0.94	6.61
泸州市	Luzhou	649.61	516.31	23.02	57.62	385.17	310.73	18.17	46.56
德阳市	Deyang	350.35	243.96	8.02	24.36	191.76	151.23	5.61	20.30
绵阳市	Mianyang	536.34	440.51	2.31	34.66	359.26	309.23	2.00	32.48
广元市	Guangyuan	116.03	98.65	0.22	5.88	67.40	59.71	0.10	5.69
遂宁市	Suining	272.07	248.99	4.14	10.43	163.07	147.10	3.22	10.07
内江市	Neijiang	271.61	181.93	1.68	25.22	137.44	102.03	0.90	22.93
乐山市	Leshan	259.45	222.97		7.37	141.26	128.88		6.00
南充市	Nanchong	670.38	536.57	1.50	19.05	299.39	267.21	0.86	13.73
眉山市	Meishan	701.64	516.84	9.80	44.87	469.62	393.71	7.82	39.99
宜宾市	Yibin	538.36	406.68	7.37	41.45	344.37	281.61	5.04	40.73
广安市	Guangan	216.53	205.98		5.69	116.72	111.55		4.30
达州市	Dazhou	295.38	245.57		29.87	165.20	141.13		19.77
雅安市	Yaan	98.06	71.25	1.14	11.72	55.15	42.61	0.69	9.27
巴中市	Bazhong	149.25	125.14		12.04	67.78	56.60		9.22
资阳市	Ziyang	143.91	129.89	1.31	6.08	74.86	67.81	0.53	5.72
阿坝藏族羌族自治州	Aba	8.33	5.49		1.22	6.41	3.78		1.60
甘孜藏族自治州	Ganzi	9.95	7.44		1.40	6.98	5.38		1.31
凉山彝族自治州	Liangshan	185.19	139.25	4.18	23.79	122.61	88.72	3.12	26.15

5-16 各市(州)商品房期房销售情况(2023年)
Selling of Commercial Houses under Construction by Region(2023)

市(州)	Region	房屋销售面积(万平方米) Floor Space of Commercial Houses (10 000 sq.m)	#住宅 Residential Buildings	#办公楼 Office Buildings	#商业营业用房 Houses for Business Use	房屋销售额(亿元) Total Sale of Commercial Houses (100 million yuan)	#住宅 Residential Buildings	#办公楼 Office Buildings	#商业营业用房 Houses for Business Use
全省	**Sichuan**	**6852.51**	**5722.35**	**159.02**	**339.70**	**6333.76**	**5690.28**	**145.00**	**344.93**
成都市	Chengdu	1787.07	1543.10	96.98	46.12	3340.95	3117.68	98.76	82.20
自贡市	Zigong	192.49	149.82	4.37	22.64	114.53	85.52	2.76	20.21
攀枝花市	Panzhihua	58.75	49.46	0.36	2.82	36.63	32.20	0.30	2.87
泸州市	Luzhou	631.52	500.35	22.74	57.09	376.37	302.81	18.02	46.31
德阳市	Deyang	288.73	227.02	7.85	10.94	165.99	141.24	5.43	10.56
绵阳市	Mianyang	455.74	394.39	1.46	19.44	312.53	280.41	1.27	19.43
广元市	Guangyuan	99.30	87.86	0.22	3.42	58.56	53.46	0.10	3.59
遂宁市	Suining	254.39	232.00	4.14	10.43	155.61	139.73	3.22	10.07
内江市	Neijiang	245.83	171.66	1.59	19.66	124.50	95.33	0.85	18.06
乐山市	Leshan	245.91	214.06		5.33	135.19	124.42		5.01
南充市	Nanchong	602.63	491.28	1.50	16.12	269.30	242.28	0.86	11.29
眉山市	Meishan	558.66	454.92	6.06	21.60	401.06	355.54	5.60	22.64
宜宾市	Yibin	463.40	368.18	6.47	32.44	301.23	253.76	4.41	30.88
广安市	Guangan	184.41	178.49		4.33	102.77	99.06		3.26
达州市	Dazhou	280.36	237.04		26.95	157.29	136.58		17.92
雅安市	Yaan	79.75	65.43	1.14	5.82	46.41	38.73	0.69	5.86
巴中市	Bazhong	132.46	110.81		10.76	60.29	50.42		8.04
资阳市	Ziyang	132.42	120.16	1.31	5.93	69.48	62.70	0.53	5.63
阿坝藏族羌族自治州	Aba	6.89	4.07		1.19	5.59	3.01		1.56
甘孜藏族自治州	Ganzi	7.43	4.96		1.35	5.27	3.72		1.26
凉山彝族自治州	Liangshan	144.39	117.28	2.82	15.33	94.22	71.67	2.21	18.30

5-17 各市(州)商品房现房销售情况(2023年)
Selling of Commercial Houses Completed by Region(2023)

市(州)	Region	房屋销售面积(万平方米) Floor Space of Commercial Houses (10 000 sq.m)	#住宅 Residential Buildings	#办公楼 Office Buildings	#商业营业用房 Houses for Business Use	房屋销售额(亿元) Total Sale of Commercial Houses (100 million yuan)	#住宅 Residential Buildings	#办公楼 Office Buildings	#商业营业用房 Houses for Business Use
全省	**Sichuan**	**1152.96**	**642.63**	**32.41**	**140.57**	**840.01**	**599.67**	**29.66**	**131.71**
成都市	Chengdu	416.62	242.22	23.71	34.19	478.58	367.85	24.15	48.88
自贡市	Zigong	38.91	14.63		6.53	11.77	7.28		2.92
攀枝花市	Panzhihua	39.19	22.33	1.30	5.26	16.87	10.40	0.64	3.75
泸州市	Luzhou	18.09	15.95	0.28	0.53	8.80	7.91	0.15	0.25
德阳市	Deyang	61.62	16.94	0.17	13.42	25.77	9.99	0.18	9.74
绵阳市	Mianyang	80.61	46.12	0.85	15.23	46.73	28.82	0.74	13.05
广元市	Guangyuan	16.73	10.79		2.46	8.84	6.25		2.10
遂宁市	Suining	17.68	16.99			7.46	7.38		
内江市	Neijiang	25.79	10.28	0.09	5.57	12.94	6.71	0.05	4.87
乐山市	Leshan	13.53	8.91		2.04	6.08	4.46		0.99
南充市	Nanchong	67.71	45.29		2.92	30.09	24.92		2.44
眉山市	Meishan	142.98	61.92	3.74	23.27	68.56	38.17	2.22	17.35
宜宾市	Yibin	74.96	38.49	0.90	9.00	43.13	27.85	0.63	9.85
广安市	Guangan	32.13	27.49		1.36	13.95	12.49		1.04
达州市	Dazhou	15.02	8.53		2.92	7.91	4.55		1.85
雅安市	Yaan	18.31	5.82		5.90	8.74	3.88		3.40
巴中市	Bazhong	16.78	14.34		1.28	7.49	6.18		1.18
资阳市	Ziyang	11.50	9.73		0.16	5.38	5.11		0.10
阿坝藏族羌族自治州	Aba	1.45	1.42		0.03	0.82	0.78		0.04
甘孜藏族自治州	Ganzi	2.53	2.48		0.05	1.71	1.66		0.05
凉山彝族自治州	Liangshan	40.80	21.98	1.36	8.46	28.38	17.05	0.91	7.85

5−18　各市(州)商品房待售情况(2023年)
Commercial Houses on Sale by Region(2023)

单位：万平方米　　　　(10 000 sq.m)

市(州)	Region	商品房待售面积 Space of Commercial Houses on Sale	#住宅 Residential Buildings	#办公楼 Office Buildings	#商业营业用房 Houses for Business Use	其中：待售1−3年的面积 Space of Commercial Houses on Sale During 3 Years	#住宅 Residential Buildings	#办公楼 Office Buildings	#商业营业用房 Houses for Business Use
全省	**Sichuan**	**2842.26**	**750.68**	**136.73**	**575.15**	**1065.04**	**255.16**	**59.80**	**219.70**
成都市	Chengdu	1598.54	314.61	121.51	288.57	629.92	112.68	51.86	116.32
自贡市	Zigong	18.78	9.82		3.59	8.90	3.99		3.24
攀枝花市	Panzhihua	114.40	44.62	3.15	32.40	50.44	23.12	2.89	8.92
泸州市	Luzhou	1.25	0.67		0.13	1.10	0.60		0.09
德阳市	Deyang	122.00	29.37	0.04	31.51	34.18	8.78		5.23
绵阳市	Mianyang	204.92	44.14	9.35	63.54	80.59	14.23	4.27	20.74
广元市	Guangyuan	93.21	47.42	0.22	17.51	57.78	28.10	0.22	11.39
遂宁市	Suining	9.31	5.04		0.65	7.60	3.33		0.65
内江市	Neijiang	22.00	3.16	0.02	14.70	7.86	0.91	0.02	4.92
乐山市	Leshan	13.21	4.59	0.01	1.23	2.24			0.80
南充市	Nanchong	91.61	21.23		24.43	11.86	0.56		7.20
眉山市	Meishan	132.52	62.83		23.35	37.06	16.81		6.41
宜宾市	Yibin	81.24	27.01	0.94	10.83	28.52	3.67		5.12
广安市	Guangan	61.29	35.75		10.74	23.50	9.86		8.40
达州市	Dazhou	23.45	4.03	0.01	4.82	5.72	1.53	0.01	1.61
雅安市	Yaan	76.79	10.25	0.53	17.99	25.72	4.33	0.53	5.14
巴中市	Bazhong	70.00	43.46		9.20	14.18	6.06		2.58
资阳市	Ziyang	15.54	7.85		1.28	3.37	2.26		0.33
阿坝藏族羌族自治州	Aba	3.66	3.57		0.02	2.88	2.86		
甘孜藏族自治州	Ganzi	7.29	3.32		2.38	3.49	1.64		0.73
凉山彝族自治州	Liangshan	81.27	27.91	0.94	16.25	28.12	9.86		9.87

主要统计指标解释

固定资产投资（不含农户） 指城镇和农村各种登记注册统计类别的企业、事业、行政单位及城镇个体户进行的计划总投资500万元及以上的建设项目投资和房地产开发投资,包括原口径的城镇固定资产投资加上农村企事业组织项目投资。

实际到位资金 指用于固定资产投资的各种货币资金。包括国家预算资金、国内贷款、利用外资、自筹资金和其他资金。

国家预算资金 国家预算包括一般预算、政府性基金预算、国有资本经营预算和社保基金预算。各类预算中用于固定资产投资的资金全部作为国家预算资金填报,其中一般预算中用于固定资产投资的部分包括基建投资、车购税、灾后恢复重建基金和其他财政投资。各级政府债券也应归入国家预算资金。

国内贷款 指报告期固定资产投资项目单位向银行及非银行金融机构借入用于固定资产投资的各种国内借款,包括银行利用自有资金及吸收存款发放的贷款、上级拨入的国内贷款、国家专项贷款（包括煤代油贷款、劳改煤矿专项贷款等），地方财政专项资金安排的贷款、国内储备贷款、周转贷款等。

利用外资 指报告期收到的境外(包括外国及港澳台地区）资金(包括设备、材料、技术在内)。包括对外借款(外国政府贷款、国际金融组织贷款、出口信贷、外国银行商业贷款、对外发行债券和股票)、外商直接投资、外商其他投资(包括补偿贸易、加工装配由外商提供的设备价款、国际租赁、外商投资收益的再投资资金)。不包括我国自有外汇资金(国家外汇、地方外汇、留成外汇、调剂外汇和国内银行自有资金发放的外汇贷款等)。各类外资按报告期的外汇牌价（中间价）折成人民币计算。

自筹资金 指在报告期内筹集的用于项目建设和购置的资金。包括自有资金、股东投入资金和借入资金，但不包括各类财政性资金、从各类金融机构借入资金和国外资金。

其他资金来源 指在报告期收到的除以上各种资金之外的用于固定资产投资的资金，包括社会集资、个人资金、无偿捐赠的资金及其他单位拨入的资金等。

固定资产投资按国民经济行业分 指根据其从事的社会经济活动性质对各类单位进行的分类。应根据建设项目建成投产后的主要产品种类或主要用途及社会经济活动种类来划分,不能根据项目单位本身的行业类别来划分。如果项目投产后有几种产品，应根据主要产品来确定行业类别。一般情况下，一个建设项目只能属于一种国民经济行业。

固定资产投资按隶属关系分 是按建设单位或企业、事业、行政单位的主管上级机关确定的。

(1)中央　是指中共中央、人大常委会和国务院各部、委、局、总公司以及直属机构直接领导的建设项目和企业、事业、行政单位。这些单位的固定资产投资计划由国务院各部门直接编制和下达，统一组织或委托下级实施。包括有中央垂直管理的部门（如国家统计局各级调查队）和中央直属企业、事业单位（如工商银行、中国电信、中国石油）等。

(2)地方　是由省（自治区、直辖市）、地（区、市、州、盟）、县（区、市、旗）三级政府及业务主管部门直接领导和管理的建设项目、企业、事业、行政单位。地方项目还包括不隶属以上各级政府及主管部门的建设项目和企业、事业单位，如外商投资企业和无主管部门的企业等。

固定资产投资按建设性质分 按整个建设项目情况来确定。建设项目的性质一般分为新建、扩建、改建和技术改造、单纯建造生活设施、迁建、恢复、单纯购置。农户投资不划分建设性质。

(1)新建　指从无到有“平地起家”开始建设的项目。现有企业、事业、行政单位投资的项目一般不属于新建。但如有的单位原有基础很小,经过建设后新增的固定资产价值超过该企业、事业、行政单位原有固定资产价值（原值）三倍以上的，也应作为新建。

(2)扩建　指在厂内或其他地点，为扩大原有产品的生产能力(或效益)或增加新的产品生产能力，而增建的生产车间(或主要工程)、分厂、独立的生产线等项目。行政、事业单位在原单位增建业务性用房(如学校增建教学用房、医院增建门诊部、病房等)也作为扩建。

现有企、事业单位为扩大原有主要产品生产能力或增加新的产品生产能力，增建一个或几个主要生产车间(或主要工程)、分厂，同时进行一些更新改造工程的，也应作为扩建。

(3)改建和技术改造　指现有企业、事业单位对原有设施进行技术改造或更新(包括相应配套的辅助性生产、生活福利设施) 的建设项目。改建项目包括现有企业、事业单位为适应市场变化的需要，而改变企业的主要产品种类(如军工企业转民用产品等) 的建设项目；原有产品生产作业线由于各工序(车间)之间能力不平衡，为填平补齐充分发挥原有生产能力而增建但不增加主要产品生产能力的建设项目。技术改造是指企业、事业单位在现有基础上用先进的技术代替落后的技术，用先进的工艺和装备代替落后的工艺和装备，以改变企业落后的技术经济面貌,实现以内涵为主的扩大再生产，达到提高产品质量、促进产品更新换代、节约能源、降低消耗、扩大生产规模、全面提高社会经济效益的目的。技术改造具体包括以下内容：机器设备和工具的更新改造；生产工艺改革、节约能源和原材料的改造；厂房建筑和公共设施的改造；保护环境进行的“三废”治理改造；劳动条件和生产环境的改造等。

固定资产投资按构成分

(1)建筑工程　指各种房屋、建筑物的建造工程。这部分投资额必须兴工动料，通过施工活动才能实现，是固定资产投资额的重要组成部分。

(2)安装工程　指各种设备、装置的安装工程。

在安装工程中，不包括被安装设备本身价值。

(3)设备工具器具购置　指报告期内购置或自制的，达到固定资产标准的设备、工具、器具的价值。新建单位及扩建单位的新建车间，按照设计或计划要求购置或自制的全部设备、工具、器具，不论是否达到固定资产标准均计入“设备工具器具购置”中。

(4)其他费用　指在固定资产建造和购置过程中发生的，除建筑安装工程和设备、工器具购置投资完成额以外的应当分摊计入固定资产投资的费用，不指经营中财务上的其他费用。

房地产开发投资　指房地产开发企业本年完成的全部用于房屋建设工程、土地开发工程的投资额以及公益性建筑和土地购置费等的投资。

房屋施工面积　指房地产开发企业本年施工的全部房屋建筑面积。包括本年新开工的房屋建筑面积、上年跨入本年继续施工的房屋建筑面积、上年停缓建在本年恢复施工的房屋建筑面积、本年竣工的房屋建筑面积以及本年施工后又停缓建的房屋建筑面积。多层建筑应填各层建筑面积之和。

房屋竣工面积　指房地产开发企业本年按照设计要求已全部完工，达到住人和使用条件，经验收鉴定合格或达到竣工验收标准，可正式移交使用的各栋房屋建筑面积的总和。

商品房销售面积　指房地产开发企业本年出售商品房屋的合同总面积(即双方签署的正式买卖合同中所确定的建筑面积)。

商品房销售额　指房地产开发企业本年出售商品房屋的合同总价款(即双方签署的正式买卖合同中所确定的合同总价)。该指标与商品房销售面积同口径。

Explanatory Notes on Main Statistical Indicators

Investment in Fixed Assets(Excluding Rural Households) refers to the construction project investment and real estate development investment with a total planned investment of 5 million yuan or more by enterprises, public institutions, administrative units and urban self-employed laborers of various registered statistical categories in urban and rural areas, including the original urban fixed assets investment plus the investment in rural enterprises and institutions.

Actual Funds in Place for Investment refers to all kinds of monetary funds used for fixed assets investment.It includes state budget, domestic loans, foreign investment, self-raised funds, and other funds.

Fund from the State Budget State budget consists of general budget, government fund budget, operation budget of state-owned assets and social security fund budget. Funds for investment in fixed assets from various budgets are reported as fund from the state budget, of which, the general budget utilized on fixed assets investment includes investment on infrastructure construction, vehicle purchase tax, post-disaster restoration and reconstruction funds and other financial investment. Government bonds at all levels should also be included.

Domestic Loans refer to loans of various forms borrowed by investing units from banks and non-bank financial institutions during the reference period for the purpose of investment in fixed assets, including loans issued by banks from their self-owned funds and deposit, loans appropriated by higher responsible authorities, special loans by government (including loan for substituting petroleum with coal, special loans for reform-through-labour coal mines), loans arranged by local government from special funds, domestic reserve loan, and revolving loan, etc.

Foreign Investment refers to overseas (including foreign countries, Hongkong, Macao and Taiwan) funds received during the reference period (covering equipment, materials and technology), including foreign borrowings (loans from foreign governments and international financial institutions, export credit, commercial loans from foreign banks, issue of bonds and stocks overseas), foreign direct investment and other foreign investments (Including compensation trade, processing and assembly, equipment price provided by foreign investors, International Lease and Reinvestment funds of foreign investment income). Excluded from this category is capital in foreign exchanges owned by China (foreign exchanges owned by the central and local governments, foreign exchanges retained by enterprises, foreign exchanges by enterprises through the regulating mechanism, loans in foreign exchanges issued by the Bank of China with its own fund, etc.). In calculating the utilization of foreign capital, foreign currencies are converted into Chinese Renminbi applying the exchange rate (central parity rate) at the end of the reference period.

Self-raised Funds refer to funds raised during the reporting period for project construction and purchase, including self owned funds, shareholders' investment funds and borrowed funds, excluded financial funds, funds borrowed from financial institutions and overseas funds.

Other Funds refer to funds for investment in fixed assets received from sources other than those listed above, including funds raised from individuals and through donations, and funds transferred from other units.

Investment in Fixed Assets by Sector refers to the classification of investment by the nature of social economic activities the investing units are engaged in. The classification of construction projects by sector is determined by the major products or the purpose of the projects when they are put into production or use, and by the nature of their social economic activities, instead of being determined by industrial classification of the project enterprises. The project will be classified according to major product if there are several kinds of products yielded. In general, one project can only be classified into one sector.

Investment in Fixed Assets by Jurisdiction of Management refers to the classification of investment by the competent authorities under which investment is made by construction units, enterprises, institutions or administrative units.

1) Central investment refers to the investment in projects or by enterprises, institutions or administrative units which are under the direct leadership and management of the State Council and of the national commissions, ministries, agencies and State-owned large corporations. Various ministries and departments of the State Council prepare and implement plans through unified organization or lower-level commissions, which include departments direct under central government (i.e. survey offices at all level of the National Bureau of Statistics) and enterprises and institutions directly under central government (like the Industrial and Commercial Bank of China, China Telecom and China National Petroleum Corporation).

2) Local investment refers to the investment in projects or by enterprises, institutions or administrative units which are under the direct leadership and management of competent departments and governments at the level of province (autonomous regions and municipalities directly under the Central Government), prefecture（prefectures, cities and leagues）and county (districts, cities and banners). Also included are projects by foreign-invested enterprises and enterprises without competent managing authorities.

Investment in Fixed Assets by Type of Construction Construction projects in general can be classified, by the type of construction, into new construction, expansion, reconstruction and technical transformation, purely construction of living facilities, moving, restoration and purely purchasing. However, investment by type of construction is not applied to investment by rural households.

1) New construction in general refers to construction projects, which start from scratch. The existing projects invested by enterprises, institutions and administrative agencies cannot be classified as new construction. In case the size of the existing unit is quite small, and the value of newly added fixed assets is more than three times of the original value, the expansion will be considered as new construction.

2) Expansion refers to projects of construction of new production workshop, branch factory or independent production line within a factory or in other locations, for the purpose of increasing the production capacity (or improving efficiency) or adding new production capacity. Newly constructed accommodation for the operation of institutions and administrative organizations (such as newly constructed buildings for teaching in schools, buildings for clinics or wards in hospitals, etc.) are also classified as expansion.

Also included in expansion are investments by existing enterprises or institutions in building major production lines or branch factories along with some work on innovation, for the purpose of expanding the production capacity of original products or producing new products.

3) Reconstruction and technical transformation refers to construction projects by existing enterprises or institutions in innovation or technical transformation of the old facilities (including auxiliary production equipment and welfare facilities). Also considered as reconstruction is the construction of new workshops by the existing enterprises or institutions to change the variety of products to meet the market demand (such as the production of civil products by defence industries), or to bring the designed production capacity into full play through a more balanced production process on production lines. Technical transformation refers to replacement of old technology or equipment by new technology or equipment, in order to expand the reproduction through improvement of technology contents in production, to improve product quality, to promote new products, to save energy, to reduce consumption, to expand the production scale and to improve overall social-economic efficiency. Contents of technical transformation include: updating of machinery, equipment and tools; reforming production process by using energy or materials saving technology; construction of factory workshops and transformation of public facilities; treatment transformation of "three wastes" (waste gas, waste water and industrial residue) aiming at environmental protection; improvement of working conditions and environment, etc.

Investment in Fixed Assets by Structure

1) Construction refers to the construction of houses and buildings. This part of investment can only be achieved through construction activities, it is the major component of the total investment in fixed assets.

2) Installation refers to the installation of various kinds of equipment and instruments.

The value of equipment installed itself is not included in the value of installation projects.

3) Purchase of equipment and instruments refers to the total value of equipment, tools, and instruments purchased or self-produced which come up to the cut-off point for fixed assets during the reference period. Equipment, tools and instruments purchased or self-produced for new workshops by newly established or expanded units are categorized as "purchase of equipment and instruments" no matter whether they come up to the cut-off point for fixed assets.

4) Other expenses refer to expenses arising during the construction or purchase of fixed assets other than those expenses on construction, installation and purchase of equipment and instruments. Other financial expenses arising in operation are not included.

Investment in Real Estate Development refers to the investment made by real estate development companies in the construction of housing, development of land, nonprofit buildings and value of land purchased.

Floor Space of Buildings under Construction refers to the total space area of the buildings under construction in the year by real estate development companies. It includes buildings started in the year, continued from the previous year, suspended in earlier years but restarted in the year, completed in the year, and started in the year but suspended in the year as well. The floor space of a multi-storied building should be the sum of floor space of all the stories.

Floor Space of Buildings Completed refers to the total floor space area of each building completed in the year by real estate development enterprises, which meet the requirements as designed, up to the standard for being resided in and put into use, has been checked and accepted by departments concerned as qualified or up to the standard of buildings completed and can be handed over for putting into use.

Floor Space of Commercial Buildings Sold refers to total contracted area of commercial buildings (i.e. area of floor space as designated in the formal contracts signed by both sides) sold by real estate development enterprises in the year.

Sales of Commercial Buildings refers to the total contracted value (i.e. the total contract price as designated in the formal contracts signed by both sides) received from the sales of the buildings by real estate development enterprises in the year. This indicator has the same statistical coverage as the area of commercial buildings sold.

06 能 源
Chapter 6 Energy

SICHUAN STATISTICAL YEARBOOK

6-1 综合能源平衡表
Overall Energy Balance Sheet

单位：万吨标准煤 (10 000 tons SCE)

项目	Item	2018	2019	2020	2021	2022
可供消费的能源总量	**Total Energy Available for Consumption**	**19916.2**	**20790.6**	**21185.9**	**22569.4**	**22545.0**
一次能源生产总量	Primary Energy Output	19172.0	20143.9	20433.1	21565.0	22836.6
外省(区、市)调入量	Imports from Other Provinces	8493.5	8753.1	8889.7	10588.2	10479.5
进口量	Imports					
境内飞机和轮船在境外加油量	The Refill of petroleum by Domestic Airplanes and Ships Abroad	19.3	26.1	11.9	8.3	12.0
本省(区、市)调出量(-)	Exports from Sichuan(-)	7557.7	8121.0	8263.4	9530.6	10665.0
出口量(-)	Exports(-)					
境外飞机和轮船在境内加油量(-)	The Refill of petroleum by Oversea Airplanes and Ships domestically(-)	15.9	15.0	4.6	3.2	2.6
年初年末库存差额	Stock Changes in the Year	-195.0	3.6	119.3	-58.2	-115.4
年初库存量	Stock (year-beginning)	587.7	779.0	761.2	619.9	728.0
年末库存量(-)	Stock (year-end)(-)	782.7	775.4	642.0	678.1	843.3
能源消费总量	**Total Energy Consumption**	**19916.2**	**20790.6**	**21185.9**	**22569.4**	**22545.0**
在总量中：	Consumption by Sector					
1.农、林、牧、渔业	1.Agriculture, Forestry, Animal Husbandry and Fishery	360.7	365.9	369.5	394.7	417.4
2.工业	2.Industry	12053.0	12614.4	12892.7	13740.4	13238.9
3.建筑业	3.Construction	631.0	653.3	643.9	696.6	689.0
4.交通运输、仓储和邮政业	4.Transport, Storage and Post	1813.4	1909.4	1814.7	1898.9	1875.8
5.批发和零售业、住宿和餐饮业	5.Wholesale and Retail Trades, Hotels and Catering Services	891.8	926.1	894.2	976.0	1033.0
6.其他	6.Other	1093.5	1126.9	1200.5	1384.7	1379.2
7.居民生活	7.Household Consumption	3072.7	3194.6	3370.4	3478.1	3911.7
在总量中：	Consumption by Usage					
1.终端消费	1.Final Consumption	19142.7	19995.2	20350.1	21607.8	21717.5
#工业	Industry	11333.4	11876.0	12063.3	12795.2	12429.6
2.加工转换损失量	2.Losses in Processing and Transformation	80.8	101.5	58.7	103.9	-34.5
火力发电	Thermal Power Generation					
供热	Heating	102.3	88.6	81.4	93.8	96.3
洗煤	Coal Washing and Dressing	258.6	288.5	193.3	175.7	122.9
炼焦	Coking	53.9	81.6	62.3	48.2	39.1
炼油	Petroleum Refining	270.9	341.6	367.9	416.0	362.8
制气	Gas Production		12.9	15.4	15.5	17.3
天然气液化	Natural Gas Liquefying	23.5	16.1	18.2	14.6	7.6
煤制品	Coal Products Processing	3.4	2.0	1.0	0.4	6.4
回收能(-)	Recovery of Energy(-)	-631.8	-729.8	-680.9	-660.3	-686.8
3.损失量	3.Other Losses	692.6	693.8	777.2	857.8	862.0
平衡差额	**Balance**					

注：本表按等价值计算。

a) Data in this table are calculated at equal value.

6−2 能源生产量和构成
Total Production of Energy and Composition

单位：万吨标准煤、%　　　　(10 000 tons SCE , %)

项目	Item	2018	2019	2020	2021	2022
一次能源生产量	**Primary Energy Output**					
标准量(当量值)	Standard Volume (Heat Value Equivalent)	12344.3	13135.3	12928.3	13706.4	14666.5
构成(按当量值计算)	Composition (Calculated on the Basic of Heat Value Equivalent)	100.0	100.0	100.0	100.0	100.0
标准量(电力等价值)	Standard Volume (Equal Electricity Value)	19172.0	20143.9	20433.1	21565.0	22836.6
构成(按等价值计算)	Composition (Calculated on the Basic of Equal Electricity Value)	100.0	100.0	100.0	100.0	100.0
原煤	**Coal**					
实物量(万吨)	Physical Volume (10 000 tons)	3736.2	3396.6	2240.3	1952.6	2268.6
标准量(当量值)	Standard Volume (Heat Value Equivalent)	2944.7	2637.2	1744.5	1459.5	1803.2
构成(按当量值计算)	Composition (Calculated on the Basic of Heat Value Equivalent)	23.9	20.1	13.5	10.6	12.3
标准量(电力等价值)	Standard Volume (Equal Electricity Value)	2944.7	2637.2	1744.5	1459.5	1803.2
构成(按等价值计算)	Composition (Calculated on the Basic of Equal Electricity Value)	15.4	13.1	8.5	6.8	7.9
原油	**Crude Oil**					
实物量(万吨)	Physical Volume (10 000 tons)	8.1	8.4	7.9	9.2	11.9
标准量(当量值)	Standard Volume (Heat Value Equivalent)	11.6	12.0	11.2	13.2	17.1
构成(按当量值计算)	Composition (Calculated on the Basic of Heat Value Equivalent)	0.1	0.1	0.1	0.1	0.1
标准量(电力等价值)	Standard Volume (Equal Electricity Value)	11.6	12.0	11.2	13.2	17.1
构成(按等价值计算)	Composition (Calculated on the Basic of Equal Electricity Value)	0.1	0.1	0.1	0.1	0.1
天然气	**Natural Gas**					
实物量(亿立方米)	Physical Volume (100 million cu.m)	369.8	441.4	463.3	522.2	554.1
标准量(当量值)	Standard Volume (Heat Value Equivalent)	4918.7	5870.0	6162.4	6912.2	7306.4
构成(按当量值计算)	Composition (Calculated on the Basic of Heat Value Equivalent)	39.8	44.7	47.7	50.4	49.8
标准量(电力等价值)	Standard Volume (Equal Electricity Value)	4918.7	5870.0	6162.4	6912.2	7306.4
构成(按等价值计算)	Composition (Calculated on the Basic of Equal Electricity Value)	25.7	29.1	30.2	32.1	32.0
一次电力	**Primary Electricity**					
实物量(亿千瓦小时)	Physical Volume (100 million kwh)	3326.2	3415.4	3654.6	3863.5	4051.6
标准量(当量值)	Standard Volume (Heat Value Equivalent)	4087.9	4197.5	4491.5	4748.3	4979.4
构成(按当量值计算)	Composition (Calculated on the Basic of Heat Value Equivalent)	33.1	32.0	34.7	34.6	34.0
标准量(电力等价值)	Standard Volume (Equal Electricity Value)	10915.6	11206.1	11996.3	12606.8	13149.5
构成(按等价值计算)	Composition (Calculated on the Basic of Equal Electricity Value)	56.9	55.6	58.7	58.5	57.6
其他能源	**Other Energy**					
实物量(万吨标准煤)	Physical Volume (10 000 tons SCE)	381.4	418.7	518.6	573.3	560.4
标准量(当量值)	Standard Volume (Heat Value Equivalent)	381.4	418.7	518.6	573.3	560.4
构成(按当量值计算)	Composition (Calculated on the Basic of Heat Value Equivalent)	3.1	3.2	4.0	4.2	3.8
标准量(电力等价值)	Standard Volume (Equal Electricity Value)	381.4	418.7	518.6	573.3	560.4
构成(按等价值计算)	Composition (Calculated on the Basic of Equal Electricity Value)	2.0	2.1	2.5	2.7	2.5

6-3 能源消费量和构成
Total Consumption of Energy and Composition

单位：万吨标准煤、% (10 000 tons SCE , %)

项目	Item	2018	2019	2020	2021	2022
能源消费总量	**Total Energy Consumption**					
标准量(当量值)	Standard Volume(Heat Value Equivalent)	15759.8	16382.2	16355.0	17241.3	17196.1
构成(按当量值计算)	Composition(Calculated on the Basic of Heat Value Equivalent)	100.0	100.0	100.0	100.0	100.0
标准量(电力等价值)	Standard Volume(Equal Electricity Value)	19916.2	20790.6	21185.9	22569.4	22545.0
构成(按等价值计算)	Composition(Calculated on the Basic of Equal Electricity Value)	100.0	100.0	100.0	100.0	100.0
煤品燃料	**Coal Products Fuel**					
标准量(当量值)	Standard Volume(Heat Value Equivalent)	5865.3	5886.1	5728.9	5846.0	5667.4
构成(按当量值计算)	Composition(Calculated on the Basic of Heat Value Equivalent)	37.2	35.9	35.0	33.9	33.0
标准量(电力等价值)	Standard Volume(Equal Electricity Value)	5865.3	5886.1	5728.9	5846.0	5667.4
构成(按等价值计算)	Composition(Calculated on the Basic of Equal Electricity Value)	29.5	28.3	27.0	25.9	25.1
油品燃料	**Oil Fuel**					
标准量(当量值)	Standard Volume(Heat Value Equivalent)	3680.7	3881.8	3729.6	3840.3	3914.0
构成(按当量值计算)	Composition(Calculated on the Basic of Heat Value Equivalent)	23.4	23.7	22.8	22.3	22.8
标准量(电力等价值)	Standard Volume(Equal Electricity Value)	3680.7	3881.8	3729.6	3840.3	3914.0
构成(按等价值计算)	Composition(Calculated on the Basic of Equal Electricity Value)	18.5	18.7	17.6	17.0	17.4
天然气	**Natural Gas**					
标准量(当量值)	Standard Volume(Heat Value Equivalent)	3152.2	3387.7	3486.6	3767.4	3783.8
构成(按当量值计算)	Composition(Calculated on the Basic of Heat Value Equivalent)	20.0	20.7	21.3	21.9	22.0
标准量(电力等价值)	Standard Volume(Equal Electricity Value)	3152.2	3387.7	3486.6	3767.4	3783.8
构成(按等价值计算)	Composition(Calculated on the Basic of Equal Electricity Value)	15.8	16.3	16.5	16.7	16.8
一次电力	**Primary Electricity**					
标准量(当量值)	Standard Volume(Heat Value Equivalent)	4087.9	4197.5	4491.5	4748.3	4979.4
构成(按当量值计算)	Composition(Calculated on the Basic of Heat Value Equivalent)	25.9	25.6	27.5	27.5	29.0
标准量(电力等价值)	Standard Volume(Equal Electricity Value)	10915.6	11206.1	11996.3	12606.8	13149.5
构成(按等价值计算)	Composition(Calculated on the Basic of Equal Electricity Value)	54.8	53.9	56.6	55.9	58.3
电力净调入(+)、调出(-)量	**Net Amount of Electricity Transferred in (+) and out(-)**					
标准量(当量值)	Standard Volume(Heat Value Equivalent)	-1599.4	-1557.3	-1600.3	-1528.9	-1719.4
构成(按当量值计算)	Composition(Calculated on the Basic of Heat Value Equivalent)	-10.1	-9.5	-9.8	-8.9	-10.0
标准量(电力等价值)	Standard Volume(Equal Electricity Value)	-4270.7	-4157.5	-4274.1	-4059.4	-4540.6
构成(按等价值计算)	Composition(Calculated on the Basic of Equal Electricity Value)	-21.4	-20.0	-20.2	-18.0	-20.1
其他能源	**Other Energy**					
标准量(当量值)	Standard Volume(Heat Value Equivalent)	573.1	586.3	518.6	568.2	571.0
构成(按当量值计算)	Composition(Calculated on the Basic of Heat Value Equivalent)	3.6	3.6	3.2	3.3	3.3
标准量(电力等价值)	Standard Volume(Equal Electricity Value)	573.1	586.3	518.6	568.2	571.0
构成(按等价值计算)	Composition(Calculated on the Basic of Equal Electricity Value)	2.9	2.8	2.4	2.5	2.5

6–4 主要能源库存量和周转天数
Stock and Revolving Days of Major Energy

单位：万吨、天 (10 000 tons, day)

项目	Item	2018	2019	2020	2021	2022
煤炭	**Coal**					
年末库存量	Stock (year-end)	608.6	695.1	492.2	600.5	740.5
消费量	Consumption	7495.8	7713.5	7501.6	7796.1	7806.6
库存周转天数	Revolving Days of Stock	29.6	32.9	23.9	28.1	34.6
原煤	**Raw Coal**					
年末库存量	Stock (year-end)	426.1	495.3	367.4	485.2	606.8
消费量	Consumption	8167.4	8320.0	7754.0	7675.8	7622.4
库存周转天数	Revolving Days of Stock	19.0	21.7	17.3	23.1	29.1
洗精煤	**Coal Washed and Dressed**					
年末库存量	Stock (year-end)	140.0	160.8	97.5	76.3	77.3
消费量	Consumption	1580.5	1570.9	1504.7	1511.7	1449.4
库存周转天数	Revolving Days of Stock	32.3	37.4	23.6	18.4	19.5
其他洗煤	**Other Washed Coal**					
年末库存量	Stock (year-end)	37.7	38.5	25.5	37.4	55.4
消费量	Consumption	457.6	367.9	405.0	429.4	560.4
库存周转天数	Revolving Days of Stock	30.0	38.2	23.0	31.8	36.1
焦炭	**Coke**					
年末库存量	Stock (year-end)	32.4	33.1	44.3	43.7	67.1
消费量	Consumption	1165.9	1302.7	1215.7	1188.6	1117.5
库存周转天数	Revolving Days of Stock	10.1	9.3	13.3	13.4	21.9
石油	**Petroleum**					
年末库存量	Stock (year-end)	192.6	142.8	159.4	159.2	157.3
消费量	Consumption	2549.0	2689.1	2584.3	2660.1	2713.4
库存周转天数	Revolving Days of Stock	27.6	19.4	22.5	21.8	21.2
原油	**Crude Oil**					
年末库存量	Stock (year-end)	74.3	49.3	51.8	53.3	49.0
消费量	Consumption	719.8	1010.2	955.2	1024.8	1008.8
库存周转天数	Revolving Days of Stock	37.7	17.8	19.8	19.0	17.7
汽油	**Gasoline**					
年末库存量	Stock (year-end)	72.9	39.4	44.8	38.9	50.0
消费量	Consumption	874.1	917.0	897.2	934.8	985.8
库存周转天数	Revolving Days of Stock	30.4	15.7	18.2	15.2	18.5
煤油	**Kerosene**					
年末库存量	Stock (year-end)	1.4	9.2	9.7	12.6	8.2
消费量	Consumption	209.5	214.2	160.1	169.3	167.5
库存周转天数	Revolving Days of Stock	2.4	15.7	22.2	27.2	17.8
柴油	**Diesel Oil**					
年末库存量	Stock (year-end)	28.4	27.9	36.7	35.5	34.0
消费量	Consumption	902.1	912.9	898.7	925.7	955.2
库存周转天数	Revolving Days of Stock	11.5	11.2	14.9	14.0	13.0
燃料油	**Fuel Oil**					
年末库存量	Stock (year-end)	2.2	2.0	1.2	1.5	1.1
消费量	Consumption	33.3	50.1	40.6	52.4	25.8
库存周转天数	Revolving Days of Stock	24.1	14.3	10.5	10.3	14.8

6-5 能源加工转换情况
Statistics of Energy Conversion

单位：万吨标准煤、% (10 000 tons SCE , %)

项目	Item	2018	2019	2020	2021	2022
合计	**Total**					
投入量	Input	6848.3	7409.9	7053.2	7416.6	7715.1
产出量	Output	5243.4	5578.1	5201.0	5311.6	5460.9
转换损失量	Losses in Conversion	1604.9	1831.7	1852.2	2105.0	2254.2
转换效率	Conversion Efficiency	76.6	75.3	73.7	71.6	70.8
火力发电	**Thermal Power Generation**					
投入量	Input	1426.5	1599.6	1732.0	2175.8	2578.9
产出量	Output	534.2	599.2	648.5	819.5	976.6
转换损失量	Losses in Conversion	892.3	1000.5	1083.5	1356.3	1602.4
转换效率	Conversion Efficiency	37.4	37.5	37.4	37.7	37.9
供热	**Heating**					
投入量	Input	266.6	284.5	342.4	351.1	336.2
产出量	Output	164.2	195.9	260.9	257.3	239.9
转换损失量	Losses in Conversion	102.3	88.6	81.4	93.8	96.3
转换效率	Conversion Efficiency	61.6	68.9	76.2	73.3	71.4
煤炭洗选	**Coal Washing and Dressing**					
投入量	Input	2400.2	2260.0	1767.9	1656.7	1541.7
产出量	Output	2141.7	1971.5	1574.6	1481.1	1418.8
转换损失量	Losses in Conversion	258.6	288.5	193.3	175.7	122.9
转换效率	Conversion Efficiency	89.2	87.2	89.1	89.4	92.0
炼焦	**Coking**					
投入量	Input	1459.1	1476.8	1408.6	1360.5	1300.4
产出量	Output	1405.2	1395.2	1346.3	1312.4	1261.2
转换损失量	Losses in Conversion	53.9	81.6	62.3	48.2	39.1
转换效率	Conversion Efficiency	96.3	94.5	95.6	96.5	97.0
炼油及煤制油	**Petroleum Refineries and Coal-to-liquids**					
投入量	Input	1092.2	1506.2	1485.7	1571.9	1490.5
产出量	Output	821.4	1164.6	1088.7	1171.3	1128.2
转换损失量	Losses in Conversion	270.9	341.6	397.0	400.6	362.3
转换效率	Conversion Efficiency	75.2	77.3	73.3	74.5	75.7

6−6 煤炭平衡表
Coal Balance Sheet

单位：万吨 (10 000 tons)

项目	Item	2018	2019	2020	2021	2022
可供量	**Total Energy Available for Consumption**	**7495.8**	**7713.5**	**7501.6**	**7796.1**	**7806.6**
生产量	Output	3736.2	3396.6	2240.3	1952.6	2268.6
外省(区、市)调入量	Imports from Other Provinces	5504.2	5915.6	6422.6	7036.4	7179.1
进口量	Imports					
本省(区、市)调出量(−)	Exports from Sichuan(-)	1651.4	1512.3	1364.3	1084.5	1501.1
出口量(−)	Exports(-)					
年初年末库存差额	Stock Changes in the Year	-93.3	-86.5	202.9	-108.3	-140.0
年初库存量	Stock (year-beginning)	515.4	608.6	695.1	492.2	600.5
年末库存量(−)	Stock (year-end)(-)	608.6	695.1	492.2	600.5	740.5
消费量	**Total Energy Consumption**	**7495.8**	**7713.5**	**7501.6**	**7796.1**	**7806.6**
在总量中：	Consumption by Sector					
1.农、林、牧、渔业	1.Agriculture, Forestry, Animal Husbandry and Fishery	45.8	46.7	57.8	56.5	59.8
2.工业	2.Industry	7287.9	7555.2	7345.7	7646.3	7649.4
3.建筑业	3.Construction	10.4	10.7	11.5	9.1	9.4
4.交通运输、仓储和邮政业	4.Transport, Storage and Post	4.2	2.3	0.1	0.1	0.1
5.批发和零售业、住宿和餐饮业	5.Wholesale and Retail Trades, Hotels and Catering Services	26.3	15.7	10.2	10.2	9.4
6.其他	6.Other	19.4	10.7	8.6	8.6	8.4
7.居民生活	7.Household Consumption	101.7	72.1	67.8	65.4	70.0
在总量中：	Consumption by Usage					
1.终端消费	1.Final Consumption	3934.8	3573.9	3208.3	3061.0	2487.5
#工业	Industry	3727.0	3415.6	3052.4	2911.2	2330.4
2.中间消费(加工转换)	2.Intermediate Consumption (for processing conversion)	3560.9	4139.5	4293.3	4735.1	5319.0
#火力发电	Thermal Power Generation	1216.4	1691.0	1712.4	2237.8	2840.8
供热	Heating	231.3	292.7	383.6	336.6	358.8
洗选损耗	Losses in Coal Washing and Dressing	496.5	516.8	631.4	648.6	670.0
炼焦	Coking	1619.4	1637.7	1565.1	1511.7	1444.8
炼油及煤制油	Petroleum Refineries and Coal-to-liquids					
制气	Gas Production					
型煤加工损耗	Coal Products Processing Losses	-2.7	1.4	0.8	0.3	4.6
3.损失量	3.Other Losses					
平衡差额	**Balance**					

注：生产量为原煤产量。
a) Data on output refer to the output of raw coal.

6-7 石油平衡表
Petroleum Balance Sheet

单位：万吨 (10 000 tons)

项目	Item	2018	2019	2020	2021	2022
可供量	**Total Energy Available for Consumption**	**2549.0**	**2689.1**	**2584.3**	**2660.1**	**2713.4**
生产量	Output	8.1	8.4	7.9	9.2	11.9
外省(区、市)调入量	Imports from Other Provinces	2620.1	2624.9	2588.1	3262.0	3275.6
进口量	Imports					
境内飞机和轮船在境外加油量	The Refill of petroleum by Domestic Airplanes and Ships Abroad	13.1	17.7	8.1	5.6	8.1
本省(区、市)调出量(-)	Exports from Sichuan(-)		1.5		614.9	582.4
出口量(-)	Exports(-)					
境外飞机和轮船在境内加油量(-)	The Refill of petroleum by Oversea Airplanes and Ships domestically(-)	10.8	10.2	3.2	2.2	1.8
年初年末库存差额	Stock Changes in the Year	-81.6	49.8	-16.7	0.2	1.9
年初库存量	Stock (year-beginning)	111.0	192.6	142.8	159.4	159.2
年末库存量(-)	Stock (year-end)(-)	192.6	142.8	159.4	159.2	157.3
消费量	**Total Energy Consumption**	**2549.0**	**2689.1**	**2584.3**	**2660.1**	**2713.4**
在总量中：	Consumption by Sector					
1.农、林、牧、渔业	1.Agriculture, Forestry, Animal Husbandry and Fishery	99.7	106.5	112.0	110.5	115.0
2.工业	2.Industry	441.2	511.7	500.7	536.3	538.9
3.建筑业	3.Construction	321.9	320.5	321.8	323.0	322.7
4.交通运输、仓储和邮政业	4.Transport, Storage and Post	905.8	946.0	887.9	924.8	922.9
5.批发和零售业、住宿和餐饮业	5.Wholesale and Retail Trades, Hotels and Catering Services	169.9	174.2	152.2	122.0	127.3
6.其他	6.Other	184.9	165.3	140.4	157.8	173.1
7.居民生活	7.Household Consumption	425.7	465.0	469.4	485.7	513.6
在总量中：	Consumption by Usage					
1.终端消费	1.Final Consumption	2321.9	2401.9	2305.1	2355.3	2443.2
#工业	Industry	214.1	224.5	221.5	231.5	268.7
2.中间消费(加工转换)	2.Intermediate Consumption (for processing conversion)	227.1	287.2	279.2	304.7	270.2
火力发电	Thermal Power Generation	3.3	4.0	3.1	2.1	2.0
供热	Heating	16.6	21.0	17.9	16.6	14.6
炼油损耗	Losses in Petroleum Refining	207.2	262.1	258.2	286.0	253.6
制气	Gas Production					
3.损失量	3.Other Losses					
平衡差额	**Balance**					

注：生产量为原油产量。
a) Data on output refer to the output of crude oil.

6-8 天然气平衡表
Natural Gas Balance Sheet

单位：亿立方米 (100 million cu.m)

项目	Item	2018	2019	2020	2021	2022
可供量	**Total Energy Available for Consumption**	**237.0**	**254.4**	**261.8**	**285.4**	**288.9**
生产量	Output	369.8	441.4	463.3	522.2	554.1
外省(区、市)调入量	Imports from Other Provinces			0.4	0.2	0.3
进口量	Imports					
境内飞机和轮船在境外加油量	The Refill of petroleum by Domestic Airplanes and Ships Abroad					
本省(区、市)调出量(-)	Exports from Sichuan(-)	132.8	187.0	202.0	237.1	265.5
出口量(-)	Exports(-)					
境外飞机和轮船在境内加油量(-)	The Refill of petroleum by Oversea Airplanes and Ships domestically(-)					
年初年末库存差额	Stock Changes in the Year			0.1		0.1
年初库存量	Stock (year-beginning)	0.4	0.4	0.4	0.3	0.3
年末库存量(-)	Stock (year-end)(-)	0.4	0.4	0.3	0.3	0.2
消费量	**Total Energy Consumption**	**237.0**	**254.4**	**261.8**	**285.4**	**288.9**
在总量中：	Consumption by Sector					
1.农、林、牧、渔业	1.Agriculture, Forestry, Animal Husbandry and Fishery	1.0	0.7	0.9	1.4	1.4
2.工业	2.Industry	146.3	162.6	169.2	189.5	189.8
3.建筑业	3.Construction	1.0	0.2	0.2	0.3	0.3
4.交通运输、仓储和邮政业	4.Transport, Storage and Post	19.9	19.9	18.8	18.5	18.5
5.批发和零售业、住宿和餐饮业	5.Wholesale and Retail Trades, Hotels and Catering Services	12.6	12.6	11.6	12.1	12.2
6.其他	6.Other	7.5	7.4	6.9	7.4	7.4
7.居民生活	7.Household Consumption	48.8	51.1	54.3	56.2	59.3
在总量中：	Consumption by Usage					
1.终端消费	1.Final Consumption	224.5	239.3	242.1	261.2	261.7
#工业	Industry	137.8	151.8	150.0	166.2	163.6
2.中间消费(加工转换)	2.Intermediate Consumption (for processing conversion)	8.5	10.8	13.7	15.9	17.7
火力发电	Thermal Power Generation	4.0	5.2	4.8	6.6	7.1
供热	Heating	3.2	4.1	3.9	4.7	5.0
制气	Gas Production			3.3	2.9	3.5
天然气液化	Natural Gas Liquefied	1.2	1.6	1.6	1.7	2.0
3.损失量	3.Other Losses	4.0	4.3	6.0	8.4	9.5
平衡差额	**Balance**					

6-9 电力平衡表
Electricity Balance Sheet

单位：亿千瓦小时 (100 million kwh)

项目	Item	2018	2019	2020	2021	2022
可供量	**Total Energy Available for Consumption**	**2459.5**	**2635.8**	**2880.2**	**3286.3**	**3447.1**
生产量	Output	3760.8	3902.9	4182.3	4530.3	4846.2
火电	Thermal Power	434.7	487.5	527.7	666.8	794.6
水电、核电、风电及其它	Hydropower, Nuclear Power and Other Power	3326.2	3415.4	3654.6	3863.5	4051.6
外省(区、市)调入量	Imports from Other Provinces	104.5	116.0	123.0	172.3	159.0
进口量	Imports					
本省(区、市)调出量(-)	Exports from Sichuan(-)	1405.8	1383.1	1425.1	1416.3	1558.1
出口量(-)	Exports(-)					
消费量	**Total Energy Consumption**	**2459.5**	**2635.8**	**2880.2**	**3286.3**	**3447.1**
在总量中：	Consumption by Sector					
1.农、林、牧、渔业	1.Agriculture, Forestry, Animal Husbandry and Fishery	16.5	18.6	22.1	29.8	35.1
2.工业	2.Industry	1527.4	1635.8	1776.9	2032.0	2064.6
3.建筑业	3.Construction	48.9	54.8	56.3	71.9	69.6
4.交通运输、仓储和邮政业	4.Transport, Storage and Post	58.3	64.7	69.3	84.7	81.3
5.批发和零售业、住宿和餐饮业	5.Wholesale and Retail Trades, Hotels and Catering Services	129.9	143.5	148.7	187.9	204.5
6.其他	6.Other	212.2	234.7	270.9	319.2	313.9
7.居民生活	7.Household Consumption	466.4	483.7	536.0	560.7	678.2
在总量中：	Consumption by Usage					
1.终端消费	1.Final Consumption	2264.8	2441.7	2668.0	3059.0	3221.8
#工业	Industry	1332.7	1441.7	1564.7	1804.7	1839.3
2. 输配电损失量	2.Losses in Transmission and Distribution	194.6	194.1	212.2	227.3	225.3
平衡差额	**Balance**					

6-10 各市(州)单位地区生产总值能耗上升或下降(等价值)
Increase or Decrease of Energy Consumption of Gross Regional Product per Unit Area by Region (Equivalent value)

单位：% (%)

市(州)	Region	2012	2013	2014	2015	2016	2017	2018	2019	2020	2021	2022
全省	**Sichuan**	**-7.18**	**-4.92**	**-4.64**	**-7.25**	**-5.00**	**-5.13**	**-4.08**	**-2.76**	**-1.79**	**-1.57**	**-2.92**
成都市	Chengdu	-7.20	-4.72	2.10	-3.89	-2.66	-3.21	-5.79	-1.04	-2.37	-1.20	-3.21
自贡市	Zigong	-7.32	-5.42	-6.55	-10.34	-3.11	-4.50	-5.50	-5.49	-2.16	-3.14	-3.98
攀枝花市	Panzhihua	-5.00	-3.30	-8.43	-10.17	-9.76	-10.26	-7.44	-4.88	-2.15	-2.95	-3.00
泸州市	Luzhou	-6.24	-4.25	-4.00	-6.98	-3.94	-3.61	-3.63	-3.96	-3.21	-3.69	-2.11
德阳市	Deyang	-7.10	-5.05	-2.30	-7.78	-6.22	-8.07	-4.87	-3.08	-0.77	-1.47	-4.07
绵阳市	Mianyang	-7.12	-5.24	-5.75	-9.25	-8.42	-5.61	-3.72	-1.52	-0.53	-0.74	-2.29
广元市	Guangyuan	-5.10	-5.39	-6.69	-3.82	-5.09	-3.74	-4.51	-6.50	25.64	12.11	-7.58
遂宁市	Suining	-7.19	-4.24	-5.83	-9.56	-6.52	-8.00	-8.66	-0.82	-0.17	-0.74	1.06
内江市	Neijiang	-6.47	-3.06	-5.81	-7.95	-4.82	-3.85	-3.09	-5.49	-3.60	-3.69	-3.65
乐山市	Leshan	-7.30	-5.01	-6.59	-8.36	-4.66	-6.51	-4.38	-2.65	-2.52	1.48	5.59
南充市	Nanchong	-4.72	-4.58	-4.22	-5.54	-4.05	-4.73	-5.94	-5.37	-5.07	-3.43	-15.30
眉山市	Meishan	-6.58	-5.13	-6.97	-10.69	-8.91	-4.15	-5.28	-3.07	-0.59	-2.68	-1.64
宜宾市	Yibin	-2.54	-4.19	-5.65	-9.80	-4.21	-5.67	-3.10	-3.90	-2.33	-2.66	-1.24
广安市	Guangan	-7.19	-4.41	-3.87	-7.74	-5.43	-4.15	-3.48	-1.24	-3.72	-4.07	-2.39
达州市	Dazhou	-7.10	-4.68	-6.89	-6.03	-12.04	0.10	-4.31	-4.63	-4.23	-3.60	-3.96
雅安市	Yaan	-6.62	-3.42	-3.15	-6.18	-4.02	-10.10	-2.22	-1.44	-1.07	-1.94	-2.50
巴中市	Bazhong	-2.47	-2.86	-5.14	-1.90	0.36	-5.10	-2.54	-4.45	-1.20	-5.13	0.39
资阳市	Ziyang	-7.19	-4.82	-5.21	-7.92	-5.50	-7.68	-4.12	-5.40	-0.24	-2.04	-2.50
阿坝藏族羌族自治州	Aba	-3.98	-5.29	6.95	-4.80	0.10	-3.60	-6.16	-2.50	-5.32	-0.56	-10.56
甘孜藏族自治州	Ganzi	-2.42	-3.93	-2.55	0.51	0.65	-5.33	-3.69	-1.22	-2.23	-4.39	-9.47
凉山彝族自治州	Liangshan	-6.67	5.52	-6.73	-4.38	0.53	-5.27	0.18	-0.25	-4.31	-3.36	-2.26

注：地区生产总值按可比价格计算。
a) GDP is calculated at comparable prices.

6-11 各市(州)规模以上工业单位增加值能耗上升或下降(当量值)

Increase or Decrease of Energy Consumption of Industrial Value Added per Unit Area by Region(Heat Value Equivalent)

单位：% (%)

市(州)	Region	2012	2013	2014	2015	2016	2017	2018	2019	2020	2021	2022
全省	**Sichuan**	**-12.28**	**-6.78**	**-8.03**	**-12.05**	**-8.44**	**-7.15**	**-7.27**	**-3.32**	**-4.02**	**-2.37**	**-3.37**
成都市	Chengdu	-14.82	-13.25	13.82	-7.79	-7.31	-6.97	-15.43	4.78	-3.40	-1.26	-6.25
自贡市	Zigong	-14.57	-10.81	-27.85	-21.07	-8.33	-8.53	-16.05	-18.63	-10.83	-4.98	-3.38
攀枝花市	Panzhihua	-9.21	-6.23	-12.93	-16.19	-11.68	-11.71	-7.91	-7.48	-3.67	-3.91	-5.95
泸州市	Luzhou	-8.93	-8.90	-6.00	-13.99	-8.59	-5.11	-4.99	-4.68	-2.17	-5.80	-1.98
德阳市	Deyang	-13.78	-10.79	-11.25	-13.78	-13.36	-10.98	-9.49	-5.73	-1.52	-1.63	-4.26
绵阳市	Mianyang	-13.81	-11.62	-7.20	-19.86	-16.56	-6.71	-4.04	0.27	2.67	4.40	9.52
广元市	Guangyuan	-6.12	-8.13	-11.92	-4.74	-9.91	-4.62	-6.99	-9.47	18.33	8.64	5.02
遂宁市	Suining	-11.75	-8.11	-10.93	-16.88	-12.69	-12.08	-18.46	0.06	2.88	-1.90	-8.25
内江市	Neijiang	-12.54	-5.12	-10.49	-14.53	-6.70	-5.33	-4.60	-7.09	-8.57	-6.92	1.50
乐山市	Leshan	-13.38	-8.70	-7.94	-9.22	-5.77	-8.68	-7.47	-4.03	-4.18	-3.17	-3.27
南充市	Nanchong	-9.27	-7.84	-10.81	-7.16	-6.52	-7.51	-7.74	-7.56	-6.86	-3.87	-25.75
眉山市	Meishan	-11.26	-10.45	-11.89	-21.11	-15.15	-6.83	-10.80	-8.43	-4.04	-6.35	-5.61
宜宾市	Yibin	-1.77	-8.52	-9.09	-20.18	-6.44	-11.25	-5.34	-9.76	-5.13	0.00	-2.51
广安市	Guangan	-15.62	-12.27	-6.72	-17.14	-14.27	-7.79	-1.49	1.98	-6.80	-0.36	15.13
达州市	Dazhou	-12.40	-7.81	-11.19	-6.71	-21.79	2.24	-7.44	-5.88	-6.72	-5.37	-3.22
雅安市	Yaan	-14.11	-7.16	-6.06	-9.05	-5.03	-17.64	-4.70	-4.25	-2.58	-4.28	-2.24
巴中市	Bazhong	-6.30	-7.69	-23.43	-1.78	4.12	-23.11	-5.28	-6.28	-10.10	-24.13	1.78
资阳市	Ziyang	-13.95	-9.15	-10.92	-8.42	-11.67	-16.99	-20.28	-17.49	-1.07	9.83	-6.63
阿坝藏族羌族自治州	Aba	-8.26	-14.09	8.76	-5.15	0.21	-3.41	-7.17	-1.17	-8.02	0.93	-8.86
甘孜藏族自治州	Ganzi	-19.00	-6.55	-8.09	2.06	10.37	-23.42	-5.70	-6.42	-9.29	-23.89	-29.52
凉山彝族自治州	Liangshan	-14.10	9.79	-12.81	-1.49	4.14	-5.89	7.22	6.29	-10.05	-6.75	-10.20

注：规模以上工业增加值按可比价格计算。

a) Industrial Value Added above designated size is calculated at comparable prices.

6-12 能源生产和能源消费弹性系数
Elasticity Coefficient of Energy Production and Consumption

项目		Item		2018	2019	2020	2021	2022
能源生产		**Energy Production**						
能源生产比上年增长	(%)	Growth Rate of Primary Energy Production over Preceding Year	(%)	-0.6	5.1	1.4	5.5	5.9
电力生产比上年增长	(%)	Growth Rate of Electricity Production over Preceding Year	(%)	5.4	3.8	7.2	8.3	7.0
地区生产总值比上年增长	(%)	Growth Rate of Gross Regional Product over Preceding Year	(%)	8.0	7.4	3.8	8.2	2.9
能源生产弹性系数		Elasticity Ratio of Energy Production			0.69	0.37	0.68	2.03
电力生产弹性系数		Elasticity Ratio of Electricity Production		0.67	0.51	1.89	1.01	2.41
能源消费		**Energy Consumption**						
能源消费比上年增长	(%)	Growth Rate of Energy Consumption over Preceding Year	(%)	3.6	4.4	1.9	6.5	-0.1
电力消费比上年增长	(%)	Growth Rate of Electricity Consumption over Preceding Year	(%)	11.5	7.2	9.3	14.1	4.9
地区生产总值比上年增长	(%)	Growth Rate of Gross Regional Product over Preceding Year	(%)	8.0	7.4	3.8	8.2	2.9
能源消费弹性系数		Elasticity Ratio of Energy Consumption		0.45	0.59	0.50	0.79	-0.03
电力消费弹性系数		Elasticity Ratio of Electricity Consumption		1.45	0.97	2.45	1.72	1.69

注：地区生产总值增长速度按可比价格计算；能源生产和消费增长速度采用等价值总量计算。
a) Gross regional product growth rate is calculated at constant price; Energy production and consumption growth rate is calculated at total equal value.

主要统计指标解释

一次能源生产总量 指一定时期内，全省一次能源生产量的总和。该指标是观察全省能源生产水平、规模、构成和发展速度的总量指标。包括：原煤、原油、天然气、水电、核能及其他动力能（如风能、地热能等）发电量等，不包括低热值燃料生产量和由一次能源加工转换而成的二次能源产量。

能源消费总量 指一定地域内，国民经济各行业和居民家庭在一定时期内消费的各种能源的总和。包括：原煤、原油、天然气、水能、核能、风能、太阳能、地热能、生物质能等一次能源；一次能源通过加工转换产生的洗煤、焦炭、煤气、电力、热力、成品油等二次能源和同时产生的其他产品；其他化石能源、可再生能源和新能源。其中水能、风能、太阳能、地热能、生物质能等可再生能源，是指人们通过一定技术手段获得的，并作为商品能源使用的部分。在核算过程中，一次能源、二次能源消费不能重复计算。

能源消费总量分为终端能源消费量、能源加工转换损失量和能源损失量三部分。

(1)终端能源消费量：指一定时期内，用于消费（而非用于加工转换产出其他能源）的各种能源之和。

(2)能源加工转换损失量：指一定时期内，全省投入加工转换的各种能源数量之和与产出各种能源产品之和的差额。该指标是观察能源在加工转换过程中损失量变化的指标。

(3)能源损失量：指一定时期内，能源在输送、分配、储存过程中发生的损失和由客观原因造成的各种损失量，不包括各种气体能源放空、放散量。

单位地区生产总值能耗 指一定时期内，一个地区每生产一个单位的地区生产总值所消费的能源。计算公式为：

$$单位地区生产总值能耗=\frac{能源消费总量}{地区生产总值}$$

能源生产弹性系数 是研究能源生产增长速度与国民经济增长速度之间关系的指标。计算公式为：

$$能源生产弹性系数=\frac{能源生产量年平均增长速度}{国民经济年平均增长速度}$$

国民经济年平均增长速度，可根据不同的目的或需要，用国民生产总值、国内（地区）生产总值等指标来计算，本年鉴是采用地区生产总值指标计算。

电力生产弹性系数 是研究电力生产增长速度与国民经济增长速度之间关系的指标。计算公式为：

$$电力生产弹性系数=\frac{电力生产量年平均增长速度}{国民经济年平均增长速度}$$

能源消费弹性系数 反映能源消费增长速度与国民经济增长速度之间关系的指标。计算公式为：

$$能源消费弹性系数=\frac{能源消费量年平均增长速度}{国民经济年平均增长速度}$$

电力消费弹性系数 反映电力消费增长速度与国民经济增长速度之间关系的指标。计算公式为：

$$电力消费弹性系数=\frac{电力消费量年平均增长速度}{国民经济年平均增长速度}$$

Explanatory Notes on Main Statistical Indicators

Total Primary Energy Production refers to the total production of primary energy in a given period of time. It is a comprehensive indicator to show the level, scale, composition and growth of energy production of the country. It includes that of coal, crude oil, natural gas, hydropower and electricity generated by nuclear energy and other means such as wind power and geothermal power, etc. However, it does not include the production of fuels of low calorific value and secondary energy converted from primary energy.

Total Energy Consumption refers to the total consumption of energy of various kinds by the production sectors of the economy and the households in a given period of time. It includes primary energy such as coal, crude oil, natural gas, hydropower, nuclear power, wind power, solar power, geothermal power and bio-energy; the secondary energy and their products which are transformed from the primary energy such as washed coal, coke, coal gas, electricity, heating, and petroleum products; and other kinds of fossil energy, renewable energy and new energy. The renewable energy refers to the part of renewable energy that is attained with some given technical means and used for commercial purposes, including hydropower, wind power, solar power, geothermal power and bio-energy. In the process of accounting, there should be no double or multiple counting between and primary and the secondary accounting. Total energy consumption can be divided into three parts: final energy consumption; loss during the process of energy transformation; and other losses.

1) Final Energy Consumption: It refers to the consumption of various kinds of energy in a given period of time, not involving the energy consumed for transformation.

2) Losses During the Process of Energy Transformation: It refers to the total input of various kinds of energy for transformation, minus the total output of various kinds of energy products in a given period of time. It is an indicator to show the losses that occurs during the process of energy transformation.

3) Other Losses: It refers to the total of the losses of energy during the course of energy transport, distribution and storage and the losses caused by any objective reason in a given period of time. The losses of various kinds of gas due to gas discharges and stocktaking is not included.

Energy Consumption per Unit of GDP refers to the energy consumption per unit of Gross Regional Product in a region in the same reference period. The formula is:

$$\text{Energy Consumption per Unit of GDP} = \frac{\text{Total Energy Consumption}}{\text{Gross Regional Product}}$$

Elasticity Ratio of Energy Production is an indicator to show the relationship between the growth rate of energy production and the growth rate of the national economy. The formula is:

$$\text{Elasticity Ratio of Energy Production} = \frac{\text{Average Annual Growth Rate of Energy Production}}{\text{Average Annual Growth Rate of National Economy}}$$

The average annual growth rate of the national economy can be measured by indicators such as the gross national product or the gross domestic (regional) product, depending on the purposes or needs. The gross regional product has been used in the calculation of the ratio in the Yearbook.

Elasticity Ratio of Electricity Production is an indicator to show the relationship between the growth rate of electricity production and the growth rate of the national economy. The formula is:

$$\text{Elasticity Ratio of Electricity Production} = \frac{\text{Average Annual Growth Rate of Electricity Production}}{\text{Average Annual Growth Rate of National Economy}}$$

Elasticity Ratio of Energy Consumption is an indicator to show the relationship between the growth rate of energy consumption and the growth rate of the national economy. The formula is:

$$\text{Elasticity Ratio of Energy Consumption} = \frac{\text{Average Annual Growth Rate of Energy Consumption}}{\text{Average Annual Growth Rate of National Economy}}$$

Elasticity Ratio of Electricity Consumption is an indicator to show the relationship between the growth rate of electricity consumption and the growth rate of the national economy. The formula is:

$$\text{Elasticity Ratio of Electricity Consumption} = \frac{\text{Average Annual Growth Rate of Electricity Consumption}}{\text{Average Annual Growth Rate of National Economy}}$$

07 / 资源和环境
Chapter 7 Resources and Environment

7-1 主要城市平均气温(2023年)
Monthly Average Temperature of Major Cities(2023)

单位：摄氏度 (℃)

城市	City	1月 Jan.	2月 Feb.	3月 Mar.	4月 Apr.	5月 May	6月 June	7月 July	8月 Aug.	9月 Sept.	10月 Oct.	11月 Nov.	12月 Dec.	年平均 Annual Average
成都市	Chengdu	6.0	9.7	13.7	18.6	21.5	24.5	27.1	26.0	23.3	18.0	13.6	7.7	17.5
自贡市	Zigong	8.4	12.0	16.2	21.5	24.1	25.8	29.1	28.6	25.8	19.7	16.3	10.6	19.8
攀枝花市	Panzhihua	13.5	18.5	22.1	27.1	28.8	26.8	27.5	25.3	25.4	21.7	17.5	15.6	22.5
泸州市	Luzhou	7.8	11.6	15.5	20.7	23.6	24.6	28.0	28.1	25.5	18.9	16.2	10.0	19.2
德阳市	Deyang	6.0	9.6	14.1	19.1	22.3	25.5	27.4	26.5	23.5	18.0	13.7	7.2	17.7
绵阳市	Mianyang	6.9	10.3	14.9	19.9	23.0	25.9	28.2	27.3	24.3	18.5	14.6	8.2	18.5
广元市	Guangyuan	4.9	9.1	13.8	18.0	21.6	24.4	27.5	26.3	22.7	17.0	12.6	6.6	17.0
遂宁市	Suining	6.7	10.3	14.6	19.8	22.9	25.0	28.4	28.1	24.6	18.5	14.3	8.5	18.5
内江市	Neijiang	7.1	11.0	15.2	20.5	23.6	25.4	28.6	28.1	25.1	19.1	15.1	9.4	19.0
乐山市	Leshan	8.1	11.4	15.7	20.7	22.6	25.2	28.4	27.4	24.7	19.1	15.6	10.1	19.1
南充市	Nanchong	6.6	10.0	14.2	19.4	22.2	24.5	28.1	28.2	24.3	18.4	14.4	8.8	18.3
眉山市	Meishan	7.4	10.8	15.0	20.3	22.2	25.3	28.0	27.0	24.2	18.8	15.0	9.2	18.6
宜宾市	Yibin	7.8	11.0	15.1	20.6	22.8	24.1	27.6	27.3	24.7	18.4	15.8	10.1	18.8
广安市	Guangan	6.4	9.8	14.0	19.3	21.8	23.9	28.0	28.4	24.5	18.3	14.3	8.5	18.1
达州市	Dazhou	6.6	9.8	14.3	19.7	21.7	24.4	28.7	29.3	24.9	18.6	14.4	9.1	18.5
雅安市	Yaan	6.9	9.9	14.2	18.9	21.2	24.3	27.3	25.9	23.1	18.0	14.1	8.9	17.7
巴中市	Bazhong	5.5	9.2	13.2	18.1	20.5	23.3	27.2	27.2	22.8	17.0	12.8	7.1	17.0
资阳市	Ziyang	7.4	11.1	15.5	20.6	23.3	25.5	28.5	27.7	25.0	19.0	15.1	9.2	19.0
马尔康市	Maerkang	0.1	5.2	6.8	11.2	13.9	16.5	17.1	17.7	15.1	10.3	4.0	1.0	9.9
康定市	Kangding	-1.7	2.1	5.4	10.0	12.6	13.5	16.8	16.7	14.6	9.2	6.2	1.9	8.9
西昌市	Xichang	9.1	14.9	17.8	22.3	25.1	23.0	24.2	23.2	23.0	18.3	15.0	13.2	19.1

注：气象资料由四川省气象局提供。
a) The meteorological data are provided by the Sichuan Provincial Meteorological Bureau.

7-2 主要城市降水量(2023年)
Monthly Precipitation of Major Cities(2023)

单位：毫米 (millimeters)

城市	City	1月 Jan.	2月 Feb.	3月 Mar.	4月 Apr.	5月 May	6月 June	7月 July	8月 Aug.	9月 Sept.	10月 Oct.	11月 Nov.	12月 Dec.	全年 Annual Total
成都市	Chengdu	0.8	10.2	42.4	68.3	96.2	72.9	305.1	219.4	156.9	48.8	23.7	0.1	1044.8
自贡市	Zigong	0.7	12.1	35.3	39.1	67.1	74.4	248.3	203.5	46.0	88.0	14.3	4.0	832.8
攀枝花市	Panzhihua	0.0	3.0	2.4	0.0	19.7	87.8	81.6	239.7	27.1	47.1	7.1	4.3	519.8
泸州市	Luzhou	10.1	30.5	46.8	52.1	35.8	106.4	146.0	90.7	47.9	130.1	21.3	16.7	734.4
德阳市	Deyang	0.2	12.5	35.6	46.0	52.8	22.8	300.4	75.2	104.6	43.8	18.0	0.1	712.0
绵阳市	Mianyang	0.0	8.3	40.6	38.6	46.7	75.5	226.0	86.1	68.0	44.9	9.6	0.0	644.3
广元市	Guangyuan	0.4	10.0	36.2	70.0	47.7	72.7	247.3	161.9	80.9	44.5	13.2	0.7	785.5
遂宁市	Suining	2.5	18.1	29.9	97.1	22.9	66.6	302.3	180.6	140.0	84.0	47.2	1.3	992.5
内江市	Neijiang	1.8	12.8	21.0	58.1	39.0	53.7	193.4	202.1	63.7	91.3	35.6	6.0	778.5
乐山市	Leshan	0.5	11.4	60.5	74.3	117.6	69.7	137.2	157.2	121.9	70.9	35.4	1.6	858.2
南充市	Nanchong	8.4	15.8	59.0	101.3	68.4	82.5	282.4	214.0	123.5	84.9	46.2	2.0	1088.4
眉山市	Meishan	0.1	6.6	42.3	72.5	65.5	12.7	154.3	130.2	143.2	45.9	15.1	0.3	688.7
宜宾市	Yibin	4.6	15.9	52.7	56.5	76.6	116.6	81.5	86.0	44.5	85.1	18.8	2.5	641.3
广安市	Guangan	11.8	18.5	53.5	77.8	78.2	109.5	197.9	156.1	138.8	98.5	43.8	4.3	988.7
达州市	Dazhou	7.4	24.1	85.8	73.6	256.8	239.3	180.7	148.5	137.2	114.7	36.6	6.5	1311.2
雅安市	Yaan	5.8	22.8	78.8	124.2	109.4	41.3	316.7	448.3	153.2	105.9	62.9	0.9	1470.2
巴中市	Bazhong	2.0	9.1	76.6	102.7	82.2	141.0	106.0	229.5	214.7	66.3	25.4	4.6	1060.1
资阳市	Ziyang	0.2	6.8	17.4	46.4	35.4	27.4	131.4	165.5	26.6	53.2	13.9	0.3	524.5
马尔康市	Maerkang	0.7	15.2	67.9	22.2	97.9	102.0	121.6	150.7	138.5	82.5	7.9	0.1	807.2
康定市	Kangding	0.1	22.8	27.2	45.4	69.5	175.3	108.5	146.5	86.9	86.1	0.6	0.9	769.8
西昌市	Xichang	0.0	2.8	3.0	10.8	12.6	173.4	231.7	338.4	76.0	145.6	9.0	0.0	1003.3

7-3 主要城市平均相对湿度(2023年)
Average Relative Humidity of Major Cities(2023)

单位：% (%)

城市	City	1月 Jan.	2月 Feb.	3月 Mar.	4月 Apr.	5月 May	6月 June	7月 July	8月 Aug.	9月 Sept.	10月 Oct.	11月 Nov.	12月 Dec.	年平均 Annual Average
成都市	Chengdu	75	80	79	72	76	74	76	83	82	85	81	78	78
自贡市	Zigong	69	71	71	61	66	70	70	78	77	85	79	73	73
攀枝花市	Panzhihua	50	38	32	26	34	59	60	76	66	69	63	60	53
泸州市	Luzhou	78	76	78	68	71	79	76	78	77	90	86	84	78
德阳市	Deyang	70	77	73	66	67	65	75	80	81	84	78	78	75
绵阳市	Mianyang	62	69	66	58	61	62	71	75	75	80	70	70	68
广元市	Guangyuan	61	67	61	58	60	69	70	76	79	80	71	71	69
遂宁市	Suining	75	77	74	65	68	73	73	75	78	86	82	81	76
内江市	Neijiang	77	77	76	68	71	74	74	78	78	86	83	79	77
乐山市	Leshan	71	76	73	65	71	71	68	77	79	85	81	75	74
南充市	Nanchong	79	80	79	70	76	80	78	77	81	89	82	81	79
眉山市	Meishan	70	74	73	65	73	70	74	84	85	90	85	79	77
宜宾市	Yibin	76	80	78	66	71	78	75	78	76	85	80	74	76
广安市	Guangan	81	80	80	72	78	81	78	75	80	88	84	85	80
达州市	Dazhou	78	77	76	67	78	82	74	70	75	84	81	82	77
雅安市	Yaan	75	79	75	70	73	67	68	79	82	86	85	77	76
巴中市	Bazhong	71	73	73	66	75	81	72	71	78	84	79	79	75
资阳市	Ziyang	69	71	69	61	66	67	70	78	77	82	78	75	72
马尔康市	Maerkang	42	45	59	50	60	66	74	75	75	74	53	43	60
康定市	Kangding	59	70	72	67	70	79	77	80	81	83	62	58	72
西昌市	Xichang	48	39	40	34	37	62	65	74	66	70	61	53	54

7-4 林业发展情况
Conditions of Development of Forestry

指标		Item		2023
森林资源覆盖率	**(%)**	**Forest Coverage Rate**	**(%)**	
森林面积	(万公顷)	Forest Area	(10 000 hectares)	
森林蓄积量	(亿立方米)	Stock Volume of Forest	(100 million cu.m)	
林业生产情况		**Basic Situation of Forestry Production**		
人工造林面积	(万公顷)	Manual Planting	(10 000 hectares)	2.09
本年新增封山育林面积	(万公顷)	Newly Sealed for Forest Breeding in the Year	(10 000 hectares)	2.12
育苗面积	(万公顷)	Area of Breeding	(10 000 hectares)	0.91
林产品产量		**Output of Forest Products**		
木材产量	(万立方米)	Timber	(10 000 cu.m)	330.99
大径竹产量	(万根)	Large diameter Bamboo	(10 000 sticks)	4636.04
锯材产量	(万立方米)	Sawed Lumber	(10 000 cu.m)	116.63
人造板产量	(万立方米)	Man-made Board	(10 000 cu.m)	477.70
油茶籽产量	(吨)	Tea-oil Seeds	(ton)	18432
笋用竹产量	(吨)	Dried Bamboo Shoot	(ton)	1102634
核桃产量	(吨)	Walnuts	(ton)	697692
森林药材产量	(吨)	Forest Medicinal Materials	(ton)	325454
板栗产量	(吨)	Chestnuts	(ton)	80756
国有林区保护单位个数，国有苗圃、国有林场情况		**State-owned Forestry Protection Units, Nurseries and Centers**		
国有林区保护单位个数	(个)	Number of State-owned Forestry Protection Units	(unit)	90
国有苗圃个数	(个)	Number of State-owned Forestry Nurseries	(unit)	125
国有苗圃经营面积	(公顷)	Working Area of State-owned Forestry Nursery	(hectare)	283
国有林场个数	(个)	Number of State-owned Forestry Centers	(unit)	157
国有林场经营总面积	(万公顷)	Total Operating Area of State-owned Forestry Centers	(10 000 hectares)	269.0
林业草原系统从业人员和劳动报酬		**Employed Persons and Remuneration in Forestry System**		
单位数	(个)	Number of Units	(unit)	1519
#行政事业单位个数	(个)	Number of Administrative Institutions	(unit)	1422
年末人数	(万人)	Staff and Workers year-end	(10 000 persons)	2.72
#行政事业单位人数	(万人)	Number of Employees in Administrative Institutions	(10 000 persons)	1.83
在岗职工年工资总额	(万元)	Total Wages of Fully Employed Staff and Workers	(10 000 yuan)	299461
在岗职工年平均工资	(元)	Average Wage of Fully Employed Staff and Workers	(yuan)	111860

注：本表数据由四川省林业和草原局提供。
1.自2023年起对“大径竹”统计口径进行调整，将5公分以上用于纸浆原料的大径竹归类到小杂竹中统计，故数据与往期不可比。
2.根据国家林草局2022年12月6日下发的《林业草原综合统计调查制度》中，原“竹笋干”变更为“笋用竹”，统计口径随之变化。
a) Data in this table are provided by the bureau of Forestry and Grassland of Sichuan Province; b) Since 2023, the statistical caliber of "large-diameter bamboo" has been adjusted, and large-diameter bamboo over 5 centimeters used as raw materials of pulp has been classified as small miscellaneous bamboo for statistical purposes. Therefore, the data cannot be compared with previous periods; c) According to the "Comprehensive Statistical Survey System for Forestry and Grassland" issued by the National Forestry and Grassland Administration on December 6, 2022, the original "dried bamboo shoots" have been changed to "bamboo used for cultivating shoots", and the statistical caliber has subsequently changed.

7-5 森林火灾情况
Forest Fires

年份 Year	森林火灾次数 (次) Forest Fires (time)	一般火灾 Ordinary Fires	较大火灾 Major Fires	重大火灾 Severe Fires	特大火灾 Especially Severe Fires	火场总面积 (公顷) Total Area of Fires (hectare)	受害森林面积 (公顷) Destructed Forest Area (hectare)	火灾受害率 (‰) Rate of fire victimization (‰)
2000	125	11				850.0	67.0	0.01
2001	248	22				3209.0	385.0	0.03
2002	185	26				1567.0	340.0	0.03
2003	378	76				5919.2	826.8	0.07
2004	169	18				1330.2	176.5	0.02
2005	252	46		4		6818.1	2256.5	0.18
2006	511	48				3109.0	453.1	0.03
2007	458	44				2076.6	455.4	0.04
2008	233	31				4481.0	389.0	0.03
2009	310	247	56	7		5730.9	2577.2	0.02
2010	361	301	58	2		4594.7	1241.5	0.09
2011	309	245	64			3449.5	551.1	0.03
2012	486	394	92			3082.3	815.2	0.05
2013	447	370	77			2673.6	811.2	0.05
2014	442	365	77			4713.1	765.7	0.05
2015	220	183	37			1407.5	303.0	0.02
2016	263	230	33			1206.9	217.2	0.01
2017	171	152	18	1		1610.9	1014.9	0.07
2018	229	201	26	2		3589.5	1540.2	0.10
2019	138	105	31	1	1	2476.5	661.1	0.03
2020	111	88	20	3		5177.6	1452.7	0.08
2021	22	13	9			1736.4	239.2	0.01
2022	15	5	10			481.0	261.9	0.01
2023	10	5	5			447.5	166.3	0.01

注：从2009年起，根据《森林火灾管理条例》规定，森林火灾分类为“一般森林火灾、较大森林火灾、重大森林火灾和特别重大森林火灾”，取消了原“森林火警”指标。根据《全国森林防火规划(2016-2025年)》，自2016年起“火灾损失率”变为“火灾受害率”，但其计算方法不变。

a) According to the "Forest Fire Regulations ",forest fires are classified as "ordinary forest fires, major forest fires, severe forest fires and especially severe fires," and the original "fire alarm" was abolished since 2009. According to the National Forest Fire Prevention Plan (2016-2025), the "rate of fire loss" has changed to the "rate of fire victimization" since 2016, but its calculation method remains unchanged.

7-6 林业有害生物防治情况
Prevention of Forest Biological Disasters

年份 Year	发生面积 (万公顷) Area of Occurrence (10 000 hectares)	防治面积 (万公顷) Area of Prevention (10 000 hectares)	成灾面积 (公顷) Area Covered by Natural Disaster (hectare)	测报准确率 (%) Forecasting Accurate Rate (%)	无公害防治率 (%) Pollution Prevention and Control Rate (%)	种苗产地检疫率 (%) Seeding Origin Quarantine Rate (%)
2000	61.48	57.19	183	94.7	93.0	98.2
2001	62.64	58.58	199	95.2	93.5	98.3
2002	73.93	62.52	390	95.5	84.6	99.7
2003	70.93	66.87	362	95.5	94.3	98.3
2004	71.01	68.02	754	96.5	95.8	96.0
2005	69.45	57.81	1220	90.5	83.3	99.8
2006	76.17	65.62	3065	93.3	81.7	99.8
2007	79.87	58.34	9000	90.8	73.0	99.8
2008	72.81	58.89	287	94.4	68.1	99.8
2009	77.59	61.57	227	93.4	79.4	100.0
2010	71.55	57.33	340	90.7	80.1	100.0
2011	69.87	55.42	513	94.7	93.3	100.0
2012	72.76	62.47	1415	98.4	98.3	99.5
2013	76.60	52.87	728	100.0	98.5	99.9
2014	73.21	52.09	1512	98.6	89.9	96.0
2015	71.60	50.67	3867	97.7	98.5	99.4
2016	69.90	49.90	4001	97.6	97.5	100.0
2017	68.14	45.34	6067	95.5	96.0	100.0
2018	69.13	56.20	4920	98.3	97.8	100.0
2019	68.29	46.99	940	97.6	95.4	100.0
2020	66.76	49.09	1220	98.1	93.6	100.0
2021	62.40	45.40	64473	93.2	96.6	100.0
2022	59.23	46.07	49840	93.0	97.5	100.0
2023	58.67	44.02	40607	98.6	96.2	100.0

注：根据国家林业和草原局规定，从2011年起，将"森林病虫害"改为"林业有害生物""监测率"改为"测报准确率""防治率"改为"无公害防治率""检疫率"改为"种苗产地检疫率"。

a) In accordance with the provisions of Nationa Forestry and Grassland Administration, since 2011, change indicator" forest insect and disease " to "forestry pest control", change indicator "monitoring rate" to "forecast accuracy", change the "prevention rate" to "pollution prevention and control rate", change the "quarantine rate" to "seeding origin quarantine rate".

7-7 主要矿产资源量
Major Mineral Resources

项目		Item		2023
煤炭	(亿吨)	Coal	(100 million tons)	134.72
铁矿	(矿石，亿吨)	Iron	(Ore, 100 million tons)	102.56
锰矿	(矿石，万吨)	Manganese	(Ore, 10 000 tons)	4840.29
钛矿	(钛铁矿TiO_2，万吨)	Titanium	(Ilmenite TiO_2, 10 000 tons)	71265.26
钒矿	(V_2O_5，万吨)	Vanadium	(V_2O_5, 10 000 tons)	1963.62
铜矿	(铜，万吨)	Copper	(Metal, 10 000 tons)	358.81
铅矿	(铅，万吨)	Lead	(Metal, 10 000 tons)	464.78
锌矿	(锌，万吨)	Zinc	(Metal, 10 000 tons)	642.26
镁矿	(矿石，万吨)	Magnesium	(Dolomite Ore, 10 000 tons)	2758.60
金矿	(金，吨)	Gold	(Metal, ton)	492.78
银矿	(银，吨)	Silver	(Metal, ton)	4986.45
锂矿	(Li_2O，万吨)	Lithium	(Li_2O, 10 000 tons)	501.47
石墨	(晶质石墨，万吨)	Graphite Mineral (Crystal)	(Crystalline graphite, 10 000 tons)	5124.65
硫铁矿	(矿石，万吨)	Pyrite Ore	(Ore, 10 000 tons)	174351.64
石棉	(石棉，万吨)	Asbestos	(Asbestos, 10 000 tons)	1500.76
石榴子石	(矿石，万吨)	Garnet	(Ore, 10 000 tons)	1411.99
芒硝（矿石）	(矿石，万吨)	Mirabilite	(Ore, 10 000 tons)	1597729.83
石膏	(矿石，万吨)	Gypsum	(Ore, 10 000 tons)	62855.16
菱镁矿	(矿石，万吨)	Magnesite Ore	(Ore, 10 000 tons)	844.43
熔剂用灰岩	(矿石，亿吨)	Grey Rock Used as Flux	(Ore, 100 million tons)	10.50
水泥用灰岩	(矿石，万吨)	Grey Rock Used as Cement	(Ore, 10 000 tons)	799568.91
冶金用白云岩	(矿石，亿吨)	Dolomite Ore for Metallurgy Use	(Ore, 100 million tons)	1.51
冶金用石英岩	(矿石，万吨)	Quartzite for Metallurgy Use	(Ore, 10 000 tons)	4976.16
玻璃用砂岩	(矿石，万吨)	Sandstone Used as Glass	(Ore, 10 000 tons)	6011.64
水泥配料用砂岩	(矿石，万吨)	Sandstone Used as Cement Burden	(Ore, 10 000 tons)	7179.46
砖瓦用砂岩	(矿石，万立方米)	Sandstone Used as Brick	(Ore, 10 000 cu.m)	1576.35
铸型用砂岩	(矿石，万吨)	Sandstone Used as Casting Mould	(Ore, 10 000 tons)	270.00
玻璃用脉石英	(矿石，万吨)	Quartzite Gangue Used as Glass	(Ore, 10 000 tons)	1919.86
硅藻土	(矿石，万吨)	Diatomaceous Earth	(Ore, 10 000 tons)	1554.79
高岭土	(矿石，万吨)	Kaolin Ore	(Ore, 10 000 tons)	728.04
耐火粘土	(矿石，万吨)	Refractory Clay	(Ore, 10 000 tons)	4251.21
水泥配料用粘土	(矿石，万吨)	Clay Used as Casting Mould	(Ore, 10 000 tons)	4070.84
水泥配料用泥岩	(矿石，万吨)	Mudstone Used as Casting Mould	(Ore, 10 000 tons)	3691.70
化肥用蛇纹岩	(矿石，万吨)	Serpentine Used as Chemistry Fertilizer	(Ore, 10 000 tons)	5963.10
饰面用花岗岩	(矿石，万立方米)	Granite Used for Decorations	(Ore, 10 000 cu.m)	18005.98
霞石正长岩	(矿石，万吨)	Nepheline Syenite	(Ore, 10 000 tons)	1005.18
饰面用大理岩	(矿石，万立方米)	Marble Used for Decorations	(Ore, 10 000 cu.m)	16529.13
盐矿（矿石）	(矿石，万吨)	Sodium Salt NaCl	(Ore, 10 000 tons)	1426887.03
磷矿	(矿石，万吨)	Phosphorus Ore	(Ore, 10 000 tons)	425880.16

注：主要矿产资源量由四川省自然资源厅提供。

a) Data of major mineral resources are provided by the Sichuan Provincial Department of Land and Resources.

7-8 “三废”排放及处理利用情况
Discharge, Treatment and Utilization of Waste Water, Waste Gas and Solid Wastes by Industry

单位：万吨 (10 000 tons)

指标	Item	2020	2021	2022
废水排放总量	Total Wastewater Discharged	425941.23	416689.05	420226.14
工业废水排放量	Industrial Wastewater Discharged	43739.49	42490.98	43956.76
生活污水排放量	Urban Living Wastewater Discharged	381725.63	373738.17	375809.77
集中式治理设施污水排放量	Centralized Management Facilities of Sewage Discharged	476.11	459.90	459.61
化学需氧量(COD)排放量	Total Emission of Chemical Oxygen Demand(COD)	130.46	135.82	126.88
工业废水中COD排放量	COD Emissions from Industrial Wastewater	2.57	1.76	1.47
农业COD排放量	Agricultural COD Emissions	49.07	74.29	72.11
生活污水中COD排放量	COD Emissions in Urban Sewage	78.79	59.73	53.26
集中式治理设施COD排放量	COD Emissions from Centralized Management Facilities	0.02	0.04	0.03
氨氮排放量	Ammonia Nitrogen Emissions	8.02	6.49	5.80
工业废水中氨氮排放量	Ammonia Nitrogen Emissions from Industrial Wastewater	0.13	0.12	0.07
农业氨氮排放量	Agricultural Ammonia Nitrogen Emissions	0.78	1.07	1.09
生活污水中氨氮排放量	Ammonia Nitrogen Emissions from Domestic Sewage	7.10	5.29	4.63
集中式治理设施氨氮排放量	Ammonia Nitrogen Emissions from Centralized Management Facilities		0.01	0.01
二氧化硫(SO_2)排放量	Sulphur Dioxide (SO_2) Emissions	16.31	13.58	12.22
工业SO_2排放量	Industrial SO_2 Emissions	12.50	10.55	9.16
生活SO_2排放量	Urban Living SO_2 Emissions	3.81	3.02	3.06
集中式治理设施SO_2排放量	SO_2 Emissions from Centralized Management Facilities		0.01	
氮氧化物排放量	Nitrogen Oxide Emissions	40.45	34.97	31.07
工业氮氧化物排放量	Industrial Nitrogen Oxide Emissions	16.30	14.60	13.38
生活氮氧化物排放量	Nitrogen Oxide Emissions in Urban Life	2.00	2.14	2.10
机动车氮氧化物排放量	Motor Vehicle Emissions of Nitrogen Oxides	22.12	18.22	15.57
集中式治理设施氮氧化物排放量	Nitrogen Oxide Emissions from Centralized Management Facilities	0.02	0.02	0.02
颗粒物排放量	Smoke and Dust Emissions	22.40	19.21	15.19
工业颗粒物排放量	Industrial Smoke and Dust Emissions	16.12	14.22	10.20
生活颗粒物排放量	Urban Living Smoke and Dust Emissions	5.98	4.80	4.85
机动车颗粒物排放量	Motor Vehicle Emissions of Smoke and Dust	0.30	0.20	0.14
一般工业固体废物产生量	Common Industrial Solid Wastes Generation	14902.59	14435.15	15127.20
一般工业固体废物综合利用量	Common Industrial Solid Wastes Comprehensively Utilized	5656.48	6151.29	6797.50
#综合利用往年贮存量	Previous Storage	288.11	203.04	227.53
一般工业固体废物综合利用率 (%)	Ratio of Common Industrial Solid Wastes Comprehensively Utilized (%)	37.24	42.02	44.27
一般工业固体废物处置量	Common Industrial Solid Wastes Disposed	2562.29	2350.88	2517.36
#处置往年贮存量	Previous Storage	87.08	42.36	78.16
一般工业固体废物处置率 (%)	Ratio of Common Industrial Solid Wastes Disposed (%)	17.09	16.24	16.56
一般工业固体废物贮存量	Ratio of Common Industrial Solid Wastes Previous Storage	7058.00	6178.34	6118.02
一般工业固体废物倾倒丢弃量	Ratio of Common Industrial Solid Wastes Dumping Discard	1.00	0.04	
危险废物产生量	Hazardous Wastes Generation	456.89	482.70	529.49
危险废物利用处置量	Hazardous Wastes Utilized and Disposed	458.56	497.61	534.12
#利用处置往年贮存量	Previous Storage	61.33	33.78	20.90
危险废物利用处置率 (%)	Ratio of Hazardous Wastes Utilized and Disposed (%)	90.23	96.35	97.04
危险废物贮存量	Hazardous Wastes Storage	49.66	44.31	43.30

7-9 环境污染治理投资情况
Investment in Treatment of Environmental Pollution

单位：亿元 (100 million yuan)

指标	Item	2020	2021	2022
环境污染治理投资总额	Total Investment in the Treatment of Environmental Pollution	832.81	795.14	652.63
城市环境基础设施投资	Investment in Urban Environmental Infrastructure	432.25	455.46	529.50
#燃气	Gas Supply	8.96	7.38	24.76
集中供热	Centralized Heating	2.31	2.13	3.16
排水	Drainage Works	220.14	236.76	277.14
园林绿化	Gardening and Greening	174.10	159.10	147.18
市容环境卫生	Environmental Sanitation	26.74	50.09	77.26
工业污染源治理投资	Investment in the Treatment of Industrial Pollution	24.44	8.10	4.21
#治理废水	Waste Water Treatment	1.75	2.55	0.27
治理废气	Waste Gas Treatment	7.57	5.07	2.88
治理固体废物	Solid Wastes Treatment	1.41		
治理噪声	Noise Treatment	0.06	0.07	
治理其他	Others Treatment	13.65	0.41	1.06
完成环保验收项目环保投资	Environmental Investment Projects in the Completion of Environmental Acceptance	376.12	331.58	118.92
环境污染治理投资占GDP比重 (%)	Total Investment in the Treatment of Environmental Pollution as Percent of GDP (%)	1.72	1.47	1.15
工业废气治理设施运行费用	Operating Costs in the Treatment Facilities of Industrial Waste Gas	106.10	60.97	62.79
工业废水治理设施运行费用	Operating Costs in the Treatment Facilities of Industrial Waste Water	47.87	31.42	31.25

注："三废"及环境污染治理资料由四川省生态环境厅提供。
a) The data of waste water, waste gas and solid wastes by industry are provided by the Sichuan Provincial Department of Environmental Protection.

主要统计指标解释

平均气温 气温指空气的温度，我国一般以摄氏度为单位表示。气象观测的温度表是放在离地面约1.5米处通风良好的百叶箱里测量的，因此，通常说的气温指的是离地面1.5米处百叶箱中的温度。计算方法：月平均气温是将全月各日的平均气温相加，除以该月的天数而得；年平均气温是将12个月的月平均气温累加后除以12而得。

平均相对湿度 指空气中实际水气压与当时气温下的饱和水气压之比。其统计方法与气温相同。

降水量 指从天空降落到地面的液态或固态(经融化后)水，未经蒸发、渗透、流失而在地面上积聚的深度。通常以毫米为单位计量。计算方法：月降水量是将全月各日的降水量累加而得。年降水量是将12个月的月降水量累加而得。

日照时数 指太阳实际照射地面的时数，通常以小时为单位表示。其统计方法与降水量相同。

森林面积 包括郁闭度0.2以上的乔木林地面积和竹林面积，国家特别规定的灌木林地面积，农田林网以及村旁、路旁、水旁、宅旁林木的覆盖面积。

森林覆盖率 以行政区域为单位的森林面积占区域土地总面积的百分比。计算公式：

$$森林覆盖率=\frac{森林面积}{土地总面积}\times 100\%$$

活立木总蓄积量 指一定范围土地上全部树木蓄积的总量，包括森林蓄积、疏林蓄积、散生木蓄积和四旁树蓄积。

森林蓄积量 指一定森林面积上存在着的林木树干部分的总材积。

人工造林 指在宜林荒山荒地、宜林沙荒地、无立木林地、疏林地和退耕地等其他宜林地上通过播种、植苗和分植来提高森林植被覆被率的技术措施。

森林火灾次数 指发生在城市市区外的一切森林、林木和林地的火灾次数。按照受害森林面积和伤亡人数，森林火灾分为一般森林火灾、较大森林火灾、重大森林火灾和特别重大森林火灾：(1)一般森林火灾：受害森林面积在1公顷以下或者其他林地起火的，或者死亡1人以上3人以下的，或者重伤1人以上10人以下的；(2)较大森林火灾：受害森林面积在1公顷以上100公顷以下的，或者死亡3人以上10人以下的，或者重伤10人以上50人以下的；(3)重大森林火灾：受害森林面积在100公顷以上1000公顷以下的，或者死亡10人以上30人以下的，或者重伤50人以上100人以下的；(4)特别重大森林火灾：受害森林面积在1000公顷以上的，或者死亡30人以上的，或者重伤100人以上的。本条所称“以上”包括本数，“以下”不包括本数。

林业有害生物 危害森林、林木、荒漠植被、湿地植被等的病虫鼠兔及有害植物。

矿产资源 指由地质作用形成的，具有利用价值的，呈固态、液态、气态的自然资源，是社会生产发展的重要物质基础。目前我国已发现矿种有173种，按其特点和用途，可分为能源矿产（如煤炭、石油、天然气）、金属矿产（如铁矿、锰矿、铜矿、铅矿、铝土矿）、非金属矿产（如磷矿、钾盐、萤石）和水气矿产（如矿泉水、二氧化碳气、氦气）四大类。其中：金属矿产按其物质成份和性质又可分为：黑色金属矿产、有色金属矿产、贵金属矿产、稀有金属矿产、稀土金属矿产、稀散金属矿产六类。

一般工业固体废物产生量 指当年全年调查对象实际产生的一般工业固体废物的量。一般工业固体废物指企业在工业生产过程中产生且不属于危险废物的工业固体废物。

一般工业固体废物综合利用量 指调查年度企业通过回收、加工、循环、交换等方式，从固体废物中提取或者使其转化为可以利用的资源、能源和其他原材料的固体废物量（包括当年利用的往年工业固体废物累计贮存量）。如用作农业肥料、生产建筑材料、筑路、用作充填回填材料等。综合利用量由原产生固体废物的单位统计。

一般工业固体废物处置量 指调查年度企业将工业固体废物焚烧和用其他改变工业固体废物的物理、化学、生物特性的方法，达到减少或者消除其危险成分的活动，或者将工业固体废物最终置于符合环境保护规定要求的填埋场的活动中，所消纳固体废物的量（包括当年处置的往年工业固体废物贮存量）。

一般工业固体废物贮存量 指调查年度企业以综合利用或处置为目的，将固体废物暂时贮存或堆存在专设的贮存设施或专设的集中堆存场所内的量。专设的固体废物贮存场所或贮存设施必须有防扩散、防流失、防渗漏、防止污染大气、水体的措施。

一般工业固体废物倾倒丢弃量 指调查年度企业将所产生的固体废物倾倒或者丢弃到固体废物污染防治设施、场所以外的量。

危险废物产生量 指调查年度调查对象实际产生的危险废物的量，包括利用处置危险废物过程中二次产生的危险废物的量。危险废物指列入国家危险废物名录或者根据国家规定的危险废物鉴别标准和鉴别方法认定的具有危险特性的废物。按《国家危险废物名录》（2016）填报。

危险废物利用处置量 指调查年度调查对象从危险废物中提取物质作为原材料或者燃料的活动中消纳危险废物的量，以及将危险废物焚烧和用其他改变危险废物物理、化学、生物特性的方法，达到减少或者消除其危险成分的活动，或者将危险废物最终置于符合环境保护规定要求的填埋场的活动中，所消纳危险废物的量。包括本单位自行处置利用的本单位产生和接收外单位危险废物量。

危险废物本年末贮存量 指截至调查年度年末，调查对象将危险废物以一定包装方式暂时存放在专设的贮存设施内的量。专设的贮存设施应符合《危险废物贮存污染控制标准》（GB18597-2001）等相关环保法律法规要求，具有防扩散、防流失、防渗漏、防止污染大气和水体措施的设施。包括本单位自行贮存的本单位产生的和接收外单位的危险废物量。

Explanatory Notes on Main Statistical Indicators

Average Temperature refers to the average air temperature on a regular basis, generally expressed in centigrade in China. Thermometers used for meteorological observation are placed in well-ventilated shelters about 1.5 meters above the ground. Therefore, the commonly used temperature refers to the temperature in the shelter 1.5 meters above the ground. The calculation method is as follows:

The summation of daily average temperature of one month divided by the actual days of that month represents the monthly average temperature. The summation of monthly average temperature of a year divided by 12 represents the annual average temperature.

Average Relative Humidity refers to the ratio of actual vapour pressure in the air to the saturation water vapour pressure at the current temperature. The calculation method is the same as that of average temperature.

Precipitation refers to the depth of water in liquid state or solid state (thawed), falling from atmosphere onto the ground without being evaporated, percolating or running off. It is usually expressed in millimeters. The calculation method is as follows: The monthly precipitation is obtained by the sum of daily precipitation of the month. and the annual precipitation is the sum of monthly precipitation of the 12 months of the year.

Sunshine Hours refer to the actual hours of sun irradiating the earth, usually expressed in hours. The calculation method is the same as that of the precipitation.

Forest Area refers to the area of trees and bamboo grow with a canopy density above 0.2 degree, the area of shrubby tree according to regulations of the government, area of land under agroforestry and the area of trees planted by the side of villages, farm houses and along roads and rivers.

Forest Coverage Rate refers to the ratio of forest area to the total land area within the administrative region. The formula is as follows:

$$\text{Forestry coverage rate}=\frac{\text{Area of Afforested Land}}{\text{Area of Total Land}}\times 100\%$$

Total Stock Volume of Living Trees refers to the total stock volume of trees accumulated on a certain area of land, including trees in forest, tress in sparse forest, scattered wood and trees planted by the side of villages, farm houses and along roads and rivers.

Stock Volume of Forest refers to total stock volume of timber of tree trunk in a given forest area.

Manual Planting refers to technical measures of sowing, planting seedlings and divided transplanting on land suitable for afforestation, including barren hills, idle land, sand dunes, non-timber forest land, woodland and "grain for green" land to increase vegetation coverage rate of forests.

Number of Forest Fires refers to the number of wild fires in forests, woods and woodland outside of cities. In light of the area plagued by fires and the number of casualties, forest fires can be categorized into general forest fires, relatively larger fires, serious forest fires and extraordinary serous forest fires: 1) General forest fires: the destructed forest area is less than 1 hectare, or the fire erupts in other woodland, or the number of deaths is no less than 1 but less than 3, or the number of seriously injured persons is no less than 1 but less than 10 persons. 2) Relatively larger forest fires: the destructed forest area is no less than 1 hectare but less than 100 hectares, or the number of deaths is no less than 3 but less than 10, or the number of seriously injured persons is no less than 10 but less than 50 persons. 3) Serious forest fires: the destructed forest area is no less than 100 hectares but less than 1000 hectares, or the number of deaths is no less than 10 but less than 30, or the number of seriously injured persons is no less than 50 but u less than 100 persons. 4) Extraordinary serious forest fires: the destructed forest area is no less than 1000 hectares, or the number of deaths is no less than 30, or the number of seriously injured persons is no less than 100 persons.

Forest Harmful Organisms refer to the diseases, pests, rats and harmful plants that plague forests, wood, desert and wetland vegetation.

Mineral Resources refer to useful minerals, with solid state, liquid state, gaseity, due to the geological process. Minerals are important natural resources, and important material base for economic and social development. At present, there are more than 173 types of minerals discovered in China. They can be categorized into four groups: energy minerals (including coal, oil, and natural gas), metallic minerals (including iron, manganese, copper, lead and bauxite), nonmetallic minerals (including phosphate ore, sylvite and fluorite), and water/gas related minerals (including mineral water, carbon dioxide and helium). Metallic minerals can be further classified as ferrous, non-ferrous, noble metal, rare metal and scattered metal.

Common Industrial Solid Wastes Generated refers to the amount of common industrial solid wastes the surveyed units actual generated over the year. The common industrial solid wastes refers to the industrial solid wastes that are generated during the industrial process and are not hazardous wastes.

Common Industrial Solid Wastes Integrated Use refers to amount of solid wastes from which useable materials can be extracted or converted into usable resources, energy or other materials through reclamation, processing, recycling and exchange (including utilizing in the year the stocks of industrial solid wastes of the previous year) generated by surveyed units over the year of the survey, e.g. being used as agricultural fertilizers, building materials, material for paving road or as backfill material. The information should be measured as the unit of generating wastes.

Common Industrial Solid Wastes Disposed refers to the amount of industrial solid wastes disposed, which covers the amount of previous years, through incineration or other methods to change its physical, chemical and biological properties to reduce or eliminate the hazards or land filled in the sites following the requirements for environmental protection by surveyed units over the year of the survey.

Stock of Common Industrial Solid Wastes refers to the amount of solid wastes placed in special facilities or special sites by enterprises for the purposes of integrated use or disposal over the year of the survey. The sites or facilities should take measures against dispersion, loss, seepage, and air and water contamination.

Common Industrial Solid Wastes Discharged refers to the amount of industrial solid wastes dumped or discharged by producing enterprises to disposal facilities or to other sites over the year of the survey.

Hazardous Wastes Generated refers to the amount of actual hazardous wastes generated by surveyed units over the year of the survey, which is covered secondary generation during the process of disposal and reuse of hazardous wastes. Hazardous waste refers to those listed in the National Hazardous Wastes catalogue or identified as any one of the hazardous properties in light of the national hazardous wastes identification standards and methods. It should be reported following the National Catalogue of Hazardous Wastes (2016 Version).

Hazardous Wastes Reused and Disposed refers to the amount of hazardous wastes that are used to extract materials for raw materials or fuel over the year of the survey, and the amount of hazardous wastes which are incineration or specially disposed using other methods to change its physical, chemical and biological properties and thus to reduce or eliminate the hazards, or placed ultimately in the sites following the requirements for environmental protection over the year of the survey. It includes the hazardous wastes generated by the enterprise itself and received from other enterprises.

Year-end Stock of Hazardous Wastes refers to the amount of hazardous wastes specially packaged and placed in special facilities or special sites by enterprises by the end of the year, which covered stock of surveyed units generated and received from other units. The special stock facilities should meet the requirements set in relevant environment protection laws and regulations such as "Pollution Control Standards for Hazardous Waste Stock" (GB18597-2001) and take measures against dispersion, loss, seepage, and air and water contamination.

08 财政和物价

Chapter 8 Local Government Finance and Price

SICHUAN STATISTICAL YEARBOOK

8-1　地方一般公共预算收入
Local General Public Budget Revenue

单位：万元　　(10 000 yuan)

项目	Item	2018	2019	2020	2021	2022	2023
地方一般公共预算收入合计	**Local General Public Budget Revenue**	**39110092**	**40708260**	**42608928**	**47731545**	**48805453**	**55290870**
税收收入	**Taxes Revenue**	**28197650**	**28887420**	**29671996**	**33348635**	**31514290**	**37008961**
增值税	Value-added Tax	11209546	11263255	11039954	12007099	9204555	14044605
营业税	Business Tax	55405					
企业所得税	Corporate Income Tax	4157932	4724352	5232526	5965298	6043806	6297820
个人所得税	Individual Income Tax	1785881	1262967	1358443	1628893	1733371	1855585
资源税	Resource Tax	525197	633124	735863	830555	891527	923206
城市维护建设税	Urban Maintenance and Construction Tax	1749815	1803428	1813863	2070301	2010116	2132342
房产税	Real Estate Tax	1067767	1118559	1124752	1432857	1527766	1654012
印花税	Stamp Tax	464113	480288	561244	703415	752267	812068
城镇土地使用税	Urban Land Using Tax	816622	791758	780766	928201	1074997	994779
土地增值税	Value-added Tax on Land	2155195	2441022	2443754	2835949	3485503	3439305
车船税	Travel Tax	382152	405684	434717	464688	467643	469876
耕地占用税	Tax on the Occupancy of Cultivated Land	891121	906742	911933	715407	1077316	970922
契税	Tax on Contracts	2809876	2892367	3087980	3584188	3063681	3229173
烟叶税	Tobacco Tax	78483	81629	77102	98910	97398	116178
环境保护税	Environmental Protection Tax	48545	60596	58561	68064	59303	55803
其他收入	Other Incomes		21649	10538	14810	25041	13287
非税收入	**Non-Tax Revenue**	**10912442**	**11820840**	**12936932**	**14382910**	**17291163**	**18281909**
专项收入	Special Revenue	2551749	2445761	2435527	2743118	2597015	2596243
行政事业性收费收入	Income from Administrative Fees	1716961	1612018	1932422	1869101	1908282	1842527
罚没收入	Penalty and Confiscatory Income	843950	1034114	1298239	1869748	2260412	1833021
国有资本经营收入	State-owned Capital Operating Income	279041	615789	654232	811446	957720	665718
国有资源(资产)有偿使用收入	Income from State-owned Assets Compensation	3994898	4442287	4810848	5325535	7591571	9473181
捐赠收入	Donation Income	133357	155756	177580	204231	213793	229136
政府住房基金收入	Government Housing Fund Income	303496	408560	428354	502026	637299	677911
其他收入	Other Incomes	1088990	1106555	1199730	1057705	1125071	964172

注：地方一般公共预算收入和支出情况由四川省财政厅提供。
a) Local general public budget revenue and expenditure are provided by Sichuan Provincial Department of Finance.

8-2　一般公共预算支出
Local General Public Budget Expenditure

单位：万元 (10 000 yuan)

项目	Item	2018	2019	2020	2021	2022	2023
一般公共预算支出合计	**General Public Budget Expenditure**	**97075048**	**103481712**	**111985355**	**112156881**	**119146585**	**127327882**
一般公共服务支出	Expenditure for General Public Services	8970009	9556194	9476220	9768087	10387834	11186642
外交支出	Expenditure for Diplomatic	599	500	255			
国防支出	Expenditure for National Defense	135419	131574	139940	133551	158740	228749
公共安全支出	Expenditure for Public Security	5283495	5256366	5271172	5318948	5620521	6002184
教育支出	Expenditure for Education	14617756	15788811	16861602	17330398	18650412	19491996
科学技术支出	Expenditure for Science and Technology	1479056	1849453	1817009	2731198	2291163	2441212
文化旅游体育与传媒支出	Expenditure for culture, tourism, sports and media	1549093	1964752	2292681	2104725	2021810	2132535
社会保障和就业支出	Expenditure for Social Safety and Employment	16441671	17623003	19986738	21658236	22376244	24400361
卫生健康支出	Expenditure for Health Care and Sanitation	8808866	9432664	10305174	10441444	11709185	12318971
节能环保支出	Expenditure for Energy Conservation and Environment Protection	2269045	2670062	2640163	2185494	2375849	2539035
城乡社区支出	Expenditure for Urban and Rural Community Affairs	6988681	8936367	7111654	6476202	7364226	7750614
农林水支出	Expenditure for Agriculture, Forestry and Water Conservancy	13108851	12884232	13393597	13300961	13593218	14551956
交通运输支出	Expenditure for Transport	6239747	6878330	7927272	7173464	7899840	7088314
资源勘探工业信息等支出	Expenditure for Exploration and Industrial Information, etc	2985761	2216830	2981218	2932452	3636783	4498129
商业服务业等支出	Expenditure for Commerce and Services	775020	573211	658959	661203	743078	1142714
金融支出	Expenditure for Finance	235768	113246	843898	593059	282284	385932
援助其他地区支出	Expenditure for Other Regional Assistance	61714	58672	47865	65205	79621	67044
自然资源海洋气象等支出	Expenditure for Nature Resources, Maritime Meteorology, etc	1083321	731546	871580	826750	1049455	1166040
住房保障支出	Expenditure for Housing Security	3507164	3489816	3814347	3715341	3866464	4314949
粮油物资储备支出	Expenditure for Management of Grain & Oil Reserves	339603	358248	460236	421238	393717	418757
灾害防治及应急管理支出	Expenditure for disaster prevention and emergency management		759504	1687684	1343546	1292016	1536349
债务付息支出	Expenditure for the Principal and Interest of Debts	1491656	1939365	2214628	2276362	2477866	2578976
债务发行费用支出	Expenditure for Issuing Debts	12259	15755	14237	11694	10221	11952
其他支出	Other Expenditures	690494	253211	1167226	687323	866038	1074471

注："卫生健康支出""自然资源海洋气象等支出"在2018年及以前分别是"医疗卫生与计划生育支出""国土海洋气象等支出"；"文化旅游体育与传媒支出""资源勘探工业信息等支出"在2020年及以前分别是"文化体育与传媒支出""资源勘探信息等支出"。

a) "The Expenditure for Health Care and Sanitation", "Expenditure for nature resources, Maritime Meteorology" are respectively "Expenditure for Health Care and Family Planning" and "Expenditure for Land, Maritime Meteorology" in 2018 and before; "The Expenditure for culture, tourism, sports and media", "Expenditure for Exploration and Industrial Information, etc" are respectively "Expenditure for Culture, Sports and Media" and "Expenditure for Exploration and Information" in 2020 and before.

8-3 各市(州)地方一般公共预算收入
Local General Public Budget Revenue by Region

单位：万元 (10 000 yuan)

市(州)	Region	2013	2014	2015	2016	2017	2018	2019	2020	2021	2022	2023
成都市	Chengdu	8985395	10251696	11576393	11754109	12755334	14241550	14829607	15203788	16976341	17224332	19290570
自贡市	Zigong	383331	424059	448256	487574	532240	604091	612455	634540	683865	626797	813829
攀枝花市	Panzhihua	585450	629076	533412	567573	605930	615026	629645	682507	898528	839738	1012291
泸州市	Luzhou	1096014	1159216	1282653	1386632	1460444	1500905	1596417	1700681	1901545	1926139	2123768
德阳市	Deyang	804682	835153	886148	1000653	1061672	1175813	1249635	1320678	1486769	1565365	1836003
绵阳市	Mianyang	904782	1017482	1041308	1076241	1105883	1245419	1311475	1409644	1591990	1596693	2014694
广元市	Guangyuan	304621	347836	408176	405661	439915	476907	484859	526158	593054	613462	681172
遂宁市	Suining	335604	396957	493162	545580	601803	638447	692712	799245	916817	1033696	1136372
内江市	Neijiang	377491	450832	502682	536799	560961	616958	636352	663379	724959	760101	852084
乐山市	Leshan	751097	787878	855322	931001	992170	1099199	1167253	1206182	1319210	1479901	1596042
南充市	Nanchong	655666	765568	850746	943388	1032555	1138963	1232950	1339323	1448719	1048126	1101962
眉山市	Meishan	636067	751991	831491	903008	931612	1031974	1107681	1216203	1378997	1561730	1598391
宜宾市	Yibin	1016000	1056118	1149677	1256843	1388196	1608883	1754916	2000319	2511829	2758097	3139945
广安市	Guangan	386177	459637	567494	642179	712493	800524	856711	860230	935747	953220	1056675
达州市	Dazhou	603088	724120	791548	846636	907078	1010246	1076040	1123309	1333124	1500651	1826600
雅安市	Yaan	229386	273788	303082	321792	348370	400289	430142	484874	593429	655719	787945
巴中市	Bazhong	273501	330371	390502	442945	455280	454580	476651	484045	508021	518366	560663
资阳市	Ziyang	484418	554619	617733	468360	497670	528490	530859	531275	579717	609897	703147
阿坝藏族羌族自治州	Aba	244616	285820	316730	325955	268146	246610	264035	287323	318469	347582	629405
甘孜藏族自治州	Ganzi	221242	275480	314299	322592	273660	300342	341162	401097	461368	478251	546875
凉山彝族自治州	Liangshan	1100148	1123019	1070683	1210336	1345528	1462031	1535931	1603084	1727931	1841770	2047516

8-4 各市(州)一般公共预算支出
Local General Public Budget Expenditure by Region

单位：万元 (10 000 yuan)

市(州)	Region	2013	2014	2015	2016	2017	2018	2019	2020	2021	2022	2023
成都市	Chengdu	11617542	13400433	14684242	15958949	17566621	18374238	20069493	21594765	22376872	24350108	25868282
自贡市	Zigong	1399376	1473005	1733530	1795524	2229037	2422700	2325764	2387153	2403388	2568572	2976729
攀枝花市	Panzhihua	1150583	1211774	1126499	1220322	1370352	1379392	1373279	1598093	1716561	1471293	1758063
泸州市	Luzhou	2501142	2813002	3039880	3371677	3689580	4121544	4430935	4497260	4449876	4587129	4727489
德阳市	Deyang	1899686	1970901	2196393	2271346	2401735	2719508	2881965	3095336	3264015	3502599	3915347
绵阳市	Mianyang	2906401	2946402	3042238	3350412	3650634	4081641	4534296	4446984	4665237	5010834	5775968
广元市	Guangyuan	1772708	1923836	2096211	2305016	2507023	2770144	2590870	2895387	2732265	3027616	3373335
遂宁市	Suining	1441078	1560932	1828440	1999945	2305561	2522120	2680713	2687293	2803315	2857246	3100365
内江市	Neijiang	1589311	1766023	1924370	2002280	2175120	2433876	2720437	2765480	2545471	2585683	3087009
乐山市	Leshan	1936946	2154123	2321550	2570351	2820171	3028632	3171142	3182003	3185028	3151207	3605201
南充市	Nanchong	3097030	3446815	3696431	4271765	4603999	4952197	5551943	5739734	5153605	4931507	5564951
眉山市	Meishan	1726618	1819615	2072222	2166908	2256815	2351578	2593227	2754648	2768778	3107144	3692064
宜宾市	Yibin	2554295	2775160	3078287	3387430	3705395	4160183	4636228	5563088	5638992	6101344	6636884
广安市	Guangan	1625740	1872039	2226191	2443172	2660796	2890322	3043511	3062569	2950356	3240161	3472562
达州市	Dazhou	2559609	2878203	3243334	3590680	3891551	4186791	4199785	4382610	4361838	4826973	5513845
雅安市	Yaan	2610709	3121494	2222395	1515500	1373913	1305375	1456480	1696085	1674875	1851974	2239728
巴中市	Bazhong	1912681	2050667	2460191	2678727	2813892	3138866	3131618	3104203	3146867	3257818	3397788
资阳市	Ziyang	1648956	1886782	2160816	1883649	1803147	1917986	1908888	2033303	2006636	2515201	2552252
阿坝藏族羌族自治州	Aba	1757926	1923022	2152522	2210559	2416638	2950767	3058792	3679485	3099812	3035414	3475468
甘孜藏族自治州	Ganzi	2753253	2888630	3162038	3004766	3433265	4205713	4021741	4538735	4096435	4137602	4441943
凉山彝族自治州	Liangshan	3330204	3658972	4176198	4591525	4798725	6817064	7367767	7077673	6241093	6455348	7442793

8-5　各市(州)地方一般公共预算主要收入项目(2023年)

Major Items of Local General Public Budget Revenue by Region(2023)

单位：万元　　(10 000 yuan)

市(州)	Region	地方一般公共预算收入 Local General Public Budget Revenue	税收收入 Tax Revenue	增值税 Value-added Tax	企业所得税 Corporate Income Tax	个人所得税 Individual Income Tax	资源税 Resources Tax
成都市	Chengdu	19290570	14493789	4376589	2116310	810108	23709
自贡市	Zigong	813829	352899	112369	27058	12397	4966
攀枝花市	Panzhihua	1012291	548682	236994	77939	12733	42667
泸州市	Luzhou	2123768	1271654	439464	285195	40620	20987
德阳市	Deyang	1836003	1094565	426039	151833	49939	22311
绵阳市	Mianyang	2014694	1132422	407434	128782	47121	25439
广元市	Guangyuan	681172	346714	128266	28911	9325	25756
遂宁市	Suining	1136372	612430	185371	94495	17657	55989
内江市	Neijiang	852084	396360	125351	29006	12295	21374
乐山市	Leshan	1596042	864723	324034	186800	39138	34255
南充市	Nanchong	1101962	552173	178104	41591	16892	9446
眉山市	Meishan	1598391	840562	264516	81475	22546	6558
宜宾市	Yibin	3139945	1845733	674789	467829	44037	47388
广安市	Guangan	1056675	477007	143536	44973	8517	9933
达州市	Dazhou	1826600	742313	229182	67394	19262	54714
雅安市	Yaan	787945	448009	229289	50919	11074	9804
巴中市	Bazhong	560663	237931	67923	14434	6383	3215
资阳市	Ziyang	703147	373137	86537	27247	7559	31821
阿坝藏族羌族自治州	Aba	629405	258020	139470	37824	10190	20744
甘孜藏族自治州	Ganzi	546875	342495	159644	39484	14214	22741
凉山彝族自治州	Liangshan	2047516	1250303	558209	181693	29747	89906

8-5 续表 continued

单位：万元 (10 000 yuan)

市(州)	Region	城市维护建设税 Urban Maintenance and Construction Tax	房产税 Housing Property Tax	土地增值税 Increment Tax on Land Value	耕地占用税 Tax on the Occupancy of Cultivated Land	契税 Tax On Contracts	其他各项税收收入 Other Revenue	非税收入 Non-tax Revenue
成都市	Chengdu	1114179	666247	2500724	209938	1714711	961274	4796781
自贡市	Zigong	23466	14147	28442	34199	62732	33123	460930
攀枝花市	Panzhihua	32166	21932	7841	20230	24457	71723	463609
泸州市	Luzhou	122860	40744	71875	44304	106874	98731	852114
德阳市	Deyang	144445	35541	35960	32501	111828	84168	741438
绵阳市	Mianyang	71061	49928	139845	25385	140791	96636	882272
广元市	Guangyuan	23204	11797	13516	35772	38592	31575	334458
遂宁市	Suining	42660	22386	40090	31302	78609	43871	523942
内江市	Neijiang	24075	16960	33250	13837	81408	38804	455724
乐山市	Leshan	54288	23117	44471	10702	80798	67120	731319
南充市	Nanchong	36560	22816	47204	46314	104027	49219	549789
眉山市	Meishan	42048	24590	113213	20027	183267	82322	757829
宜宾市	Yibin	197738	54808	63397	47440	121802	126505	1294212
广安市	Guangan	27250	11011	49041	77742	70753	34251	579668
达州市	Dazhou	37476	18503	130128	26562	103723	55369	1084287
雅安市	Yaan	28029	8346	9735	50277	26034	24502	339936
巴中市	Bazhong	13469	7514	20068	29662	49457	25806	322732
资阳市	Ziyang	16983	10097	48215	61642	58972	24064	330010
阿坝藏族羌族自治州	Aba	10511	7144	6698	7669	7191	10579	371385
甘孜藏族自治州	Ganzi	12903	6611	3713	67521	5946	9718	204380
凉山彝族自治州	Liangshan	55745	26569	31879	77896	57201	141458	797213

8-6 各市(州)一般公共预算主要支出项目(2023年)
Major Items of General Public Budget Expenditure by Region(2023)

单位：万元 (10 000 yuan)

市(州)	Region	一般公共预算支出 General Public Budget Expenditure	一般公共服务 General Public Services	国防 National Defense	公共安全 Public Safe	教育 Education	科学技术 Science Technology	文化旅游体育与传媒 Culture, Tourism, Sports and Media
成都市	Chengdu	25868282	2330795	65468	1478650	4338623	1509243	535085
自贡市	Zigong	2976729	283740	4395	137812	444681	21621	41161
攀枝花市	Panzhihua	1758063	184215	2621	101422	259902	8300	26819
泸州市	Luzhou	4727489	458220	9072	231563	901436	16051	54429
德阳市	Deyang	3915347	496113	5910	191245	489282	41266	127970
绵阳市	Mianyang	5775968	611456	23796	263084	883865	174521	69786
广元市	Guangyuan	3373335	335950	3122	139018	485214	6898	50720
遂宁市	Suining	3100365	318836	3691	130062	475870	33602	39147
内江市	Neijiang	3087009	348856	3781	150420	474399	9912	50950
乐山市	Leshan	3605201	350674	17925	174862	492944	19705	63489
南充市	Nanchong	5564951	550851	6532	251163	1011666	13512	71105
眉山市	Meishan	3692064	490077	4198	177928	499710	17999	43926
宜宾市	Yibin	6636884	520228	33554	269885	1048218	99608	89901
广安市	Guangan	3472562	311003	4089	162641	703202	6828	47336
达州市	Dazhou	5513845	477522	3806	200856	905450	21312	68662
雅安市	Yaan	2239728	266783	1886	113783	257279	14152	40280
巴中市	Bazhong	3397788	327111	1984	121940	591515	11875	51584
资阳市	Ziyang	2552252	217101	4395	101414	509522	27173	28281
阿坝藏族羌族自治州	Aba	3475468	409885	2441	182137	420705	8898	141755
甘孜藏族自治州	Ganzi	4441943	545929	2349	228603	527995	10514	90521
凉山彝族自治州	Liangshan	7442793	652092	5156	293000	1431831	17033	116858

8-6 续表 1 continued

单位：万元 (10 000 yuan)

市(州)	Region	社会保障和就业 Social Safety and Employment	卫生健康 Health Care and Sanitation	节能环保 Energy Conservation and Environment Protection	城乡社区 Urban and Rural Community Affairs	农林水 Agriculture, Forestry and Water Conservancy	交通运输 Transport	资源勘探工业信息等 Exploration and Industrial Information	商业服务业等 Commercial Services
成都市	Chengdu	2556811	2409222	495632	3264680	1372916	722123	1872511	612705
自贡市	Zigong	445940	382916	62846	345944	314018	158713	25309	13658
攀枝花市	Panzhihua	277154	165115	27920	173431	196556	61708	15809	9090
泸州市	Luzhou	623054	634475	111641	286664	649168	183357	86421	29024
德阳市	Deyang	514740	463395	111773	408183	382598	151750	120271	22376
绵阳市	Mianyang	689937	623898	65281	532490	662394	330125	137310	42918
广元市	Guangyuan	459256	413408	104125	89817	608027	233733	57902	11951
遂宁市	Suining	415902	335276	110927	203113	478647	91484	64473	38288
内江市	Neijiang	472266	437171	64572	178431	404343	86904	49414	17945
乐山市	Leshan	498095	396713	67227	239820	532724	222336	170116	18922
南充市	Nanchong	927438	734232	128084	190169	886825	160724	43912	30271
眉山市	Meishan	426236	425005	46805	181403	502419	132493	356078	27411
宜宾市	Yibin	741372	689254	197987	451662	855043	364359	879153	62658
广安市	Guangan	492973	486315	61625	139827	517435	91239	54955	21545
达州市	Dazhou	870301	694684	78666	175770	964881	320607	123622	28582
雅安市	Yaan	256017	257253	96534	146729	262914	202993	35965	13459
巴中市	Bazhong	437887	403278	67967	114792	666613	148562	26912	12760
资阳市	Ziyang	397390	337598	26456	181422	339636	66502	50929	8813
阿坝藏族羌族自治州	Aba	318037	316914	125310	78142	713236	303212	13562	7162
甘孜藏族自治州	Ganzi	384595	339139	143699	121606	940013	602248	18404	11638
凉山彝族自治州	Liangshan	859252	866278	124772	234110	1570320	543222	43958	30499

8-6 续表 2 continued

单位：万元 (10 000 yuan)

市(州)	Region	金融 Finance	援助其他地区 Other Regional Assistance	自然资源海洋气象等 Nature Resources, Maritime Meteorology	住房保障 Housing Security	粮油物资储备 Management of Grain & Oil Reserves	债务付息 Principal and Interest of Debts	债务发行费用支出 Issuing Debts Expenditure	其他 Other
成都市	Chengdu	171505	59205	191143	774539	31977	450187	1828	623434
自贡市	Zigong	5422		28411	151425	7727	68318	348	32324
攀枝花市	Panzhihua	1404		18309	124566	1532	52194	190	49806
泸州市	Luzhou	15054	168	37387	176287	10847	97189	501	115481
德阳市	Deyang	16792	2481	70533	182171	13281	52954	244	50019
绵阳市	Mianyang	21607		72619	218675	22729	104897	716	223864
广元市	Guangyuan	7231	30	25589	165409	15731	84574	471	75159
遂宁市	Suining	4627		28244	171012	8639	70895	363	77267
内江市	Neijiang	5343	2300	27567	108141	7623	109165	524	76982
乐山市	Leshan	2274		66894	133253	8248	78195	389	50396
南充市	Nanchong	2356		41176	295948	12973	129797	607	75610
眉山市	Meishan	6147		120865	106392	10877	75002	344	40749
宜宾市	Yibin	46076		50896	191356	10132	104199	579	-69236
广安市	Guangan	3428	2860	22495	202044	17189	76935	377	46221
达州市	Dazhou	7541		43008	249544	34178	133137	627	111089
雅安市	Yaan	5559		23773	75230	2999	36476	176	129488
巴中市	Bazhong	4440		25878	192223	12216	134259	656	43336
资阳市	Ziyang	1087		36833	104198	8493	85824	365	18820
阿坝藏族羌族自治州	Aba	764		98361	104873	6349	26691	108	196926
甘孜藏族自治州	Ganzi	2774		38145	133661	4273	33761	165	261911
凉山彝族自治州	Liangshan	6321		53036	292221	12177	114675	409	175573

8-7 居民消费价格指数(2023年)
General Consumer Price Index(2023)

(上年=100) (preceding year=100)

项目	Item	居民消费价格指数 General Consumer Price Index		
		全省 Province	城市 Urban Areas	农村 Rural Areas
居民消费价格指数	**General Consumer Price Index**	**100.0**	**100.1**	**99.9**
食品烟酒	Food, Tobacco and Liquor	99.8	99.9	99.8
粮食	Grain	100.7	100.6	100.9
鲜菜	Fresh Vegetables	98.9	98.3	100.3
畜肉	Livestock Meat	91.3	91.4	91.0
水产品	Aquatic Products	97.8	97.6	98.3
蛋	Eggs	102.2	101.5	104.0
鲜果	Fresh Fruits	103.2	103.1	103.6
衣着	Clothing	99.0	99.2	98.5
居住	Residence	100.4	100.2	100.7
生活用品及服务	Daily Necessities and Services	100.0	100.2	99.6
交通通信	Transport and Communications	97.9	97.8	98.0
教育文化娱乐	Education, Culture and Recreation	102.5	102.8	101.7
医疗保健	Health Care	100.6	100.7	100.5
其他用品及服务	Other Articles and Services	102.6	103.0	101.4

8-8 各市(州)城市居民消费价格指数(2023年)
General Consumer Price Index by Region(2023)

(上年=100) (preceding year=100)

市(州)	Region	居民消费价格指数 Consumer Price Index	食品烟酒 Food, Tobacco and Liquor	#粮食 Grain	#鲜菜 Fresh Vegetables	#畜肉 Livestock Meat	#水产品 Aquatic Products	#蛋 Eggs	#鲜果 Fresh Fruits
成都市	Chengdu	100.2	99.9	100.4	97.4	91.1	98.1	100.0	102.0
自贡市	Zigong	100.0	99.6	101.6	98.9	90.3	96.2	102.1	104.1
攀枝花市	Panzhihua	100.9	101.0	99.9	97.4	95.6	97.7	100.5	107.9
泸州市	Luzhou	99.9	100.0	99.9	100.5	94.3	99.5	103.4	98.4
德阳市	Deyang	100.3	99.9	98.9	96.3	88.9	97.2	100.9	110.0
绵阳市	Mianyang	100.0	99.4	100.3	95.0	91.0	94.6	101.3	104.6
广元市	Guangyuan	99.9	100.2	100.7	100.5	89.7	96.4	107.9	106.1
遂宁市	Suining	100.3	100.2	101.4	102.1	89.9	97.0	101.3	104.1
内江市	Neijiang	100.0	98.8	100.3	98.6	88.9	95.1	102.2	107.3
乐山市	Leshan	100.4	100.9	103.1	103.2	91.1	96.9	105.8	103.4
南充市	Nanchong	99.9	99.4	97.3	101.0	92.3	97.3	105.4	103.7
眉山市	Meishan	100.3	100.0	100.2	100.2	91.5	95.5	104.3	103.3
宜宾市	Yibin	99.4	99.1	100.0	98.9	92.9	95.1	101.4	103.0
广安市	Guangan	100.4	100.8	102.4	97.9	94.5	98.3	102.3	113.1
达州市	Dazhou	100.0	99.9	101.8	99.0	89.8	100.5	101.3	102.7
雅安市	Yaan	99.9	100.5	100.2	101.6	90.9	95.7	106.4	107.6
巴中市	Bazhong	99.9	100.3	106.6	97.5	89.6	97.2	102.1	106.7
资阳市	Ziyang	99.9	100.4	100.5	107.1	89.0	101.3	102.0	110.2
阿坝藏族羌族自治州	Aba	100.4	100.3	100.2	101.5	96.9	99.0	99.9	104.6
甘孜藏族自治州	Ganzi	100.4	100.5	100.3	99.9	96.1	100.1	103.8	101.9
凉山彝族自治州	Liangshan	100.0	100.6	102.7	98.4	94.5	97.8	99.6	107.2

8-8 续表 continued

(上年=100) (preceding year=100)

市(州)	Region	衣着 Clothing	居住 Residence	生活用品及服务 Daily Necessities and Services	交通通信 Transport and Communication	教育文化娱乐 Education, Culture and Recreation	医疗保健 Health Care	其他用品及服务 Other Articles and Services
成都市	Chengdu	99.2	100.2	100.6	98.3	102.7	100.5	104.0
自贡市	Zigong	98.4	100.3	100.1	98.0	103.5	101.2	102.5
攀枝花市	Panzhihua	101.5	101.2	100.4	98.2	103.7	100.2	101.5
泸州市	Luzhou	99.5	100.8	99.7	96.2	103.0	99.9	102.0
德阳市	Deyang	99.5	102.2	100.9	98.4	99.6	100.8	104.4
绵阳市	Mianyang	99.3	100.9	100.4	97.5	103.6	100.1	101.4
广元市	Guangyuan	95.0	100.1	100.1	97.9	103.2	101.5	101.1
遂宁市	Suining	99.9	101.0	100.1	98.2	101.4	100.8	102.9
内江市	Neijiang	100.3	101.0	100.3	98.1	101.0	101.2	103.3
乐山市	Leshan	98.8	99.8	100.9	97.5	103.1	101.0	104.4
南充市	Nanchong	100.4	100.0	100.5	97.5	102.4	100.9	101.0
眉山市	Meishan	101.4	100.6	100.4	97.6	102.7	100.3	102.3
宜宾市	Yibin	100.0	99.9	98.0	97.3	100.4	100.9	102.8
广安市	Guangan	101.6	100.1	101.7	94.8	105.6	100.4	100.4
达州市	Dazhou	96.0	98.6	100.3	97.7	105.2	102.6	102.4
雅安市	Yaan	99.8	98.6	100.2	97.6	102.3	100.3	103.9
巴中市	Bazhong	97.8	100.4	99.4	97.4	101.2	100.9	101.0
资阳市	Ziyang	100.7	99.1	100.2	97.6	101.5	99.6	102.1
阿坝藏族羌族自治州	Aba	100.5	100.3	99.6	97.7	103.9	102.1	100.9
甘孜藏族自治州	Ganzi	99.7	100.9	99.3	97.9	102.8	100.3	103.4
凉山彝族自治州	Liangshan	101.4	100.0	99.3	96.5	101.3	99.9	101.7

8-9 农村居民消费价格指数(2023年)
Consumer Price Index in Rural Areas(2023)

(上年=100) (preceding year=100)

项目	Item	温江区 Wenjiang	富顺县 Fushun	叙永县 Xuyong	梓潼县 Zitong	剑阁县 Jiange	威远县 Weiyuan
居民消费价格指数	**Consumer Price Index**	**99.8**	**99.8**	**99.7**	**100.4**	**100.4**	**99.7**
食品烟酒	Food, Tobacco and Liquor	99.8	100.5	99.4	100.0	100.1	99.0
粮食	Grain	96.0	99.9	99.6	98.1	101.4	99.9
鲜菜	Fresh Vegetables	102.4	99.7	100.4	100.8	97.9	102.3
畜肉	Livestock Meat	92.9	91.4	89.8	91.1	93.0	91.8
水产品	Aquatic Products	99.5	95.2	97.7	97.2	97.7	96.6
蛋	Eggs	106.2	102.5	100.2	101.5	94.1	97.2
鲜果	Fresh Fruits	108.9	106.9	108.2	105.4	106.4	100.2
衣着	Clothing	98.7	98.7	94.6	100.0	99.8	99.4
居住	Residence	102.0	99.3	100.1	101.1	101.8	100.4
生活用品及服务	Daily Necessities and Services	99.8	100.0	100.8	99.5	99.9	100.3
交通通信	Transport and Communications	96.5	99.0	98.7	98.8	98.5	98.3
教育文化娱乐	Education, Culture and Recreation	100.4	97.9	103.2	102.5	102.1	100.9
医疗保健	Health Care	101.0	102.3	100.0	100.8	100.0	100.7
其他用品及服务	Other Articles and Services	101.6	101.6	101.8	102.1	102.3	101.4

8-9 续表 continued

(上年=100) (preceding year=100)

项目	Item	峨眉山市 Emeishan	南部县 Nanbu	仁寿县 Renshou	渠县 Quxian	汉源县 Hanyuan	平昌县 Pingchang
居民消费价格指数	**Consumer Price Index**	**99.6**	**99.4**	**99.8**	**99.4**	**100.0**	**100.9**
食品烟酒	Food, Tobacco and Liquor	99.3	98.8	99.1	97.8	100.1	102.6
粮食	Grain	97.6	101.3	97.5	100.3	101.0	107.4
鲜菜	Fresh Vegetables	100.5	96.3	99.0	92.9	97.7	108.3
畜肉	Livestock Meat	91.2	88.4	91.3	87.1	90.9	95.2
水产品	Aquatic Products	97.1	103.2	97.0	98.8	98.3	99.7
蛋	Eggs	100.0	107.5	100.3	110.1	102.2	106.6
鲜果	Fresh Fruits	103.1	101.4	102.5	95.9	107.2	104.4
衣着	Clothing	98.2	98.8	97.2	100.1	99.9	99.3
居住	Residence	101.0	100.4	101.1	99.9	100.0	101.1
生活用品及服务	Daily Necessities and Services	98.6	98.6	100.3	99.9	98.7	98.4
交通通信	Transport and Communications	96.3	97.7	98.4	98.9	97.6	98.1
教育文化娱乐	Education, Culture and Recreation	102.4	102.2	102.4	102.1	101.8	102.3
医疗保健	Health Care	100.5	99.5	100.6	100.1	102.2	100.1
其他用品及服务	Other Articles and Services	102.7	99.3	100.1	101.2	101.5	101.9

8-10 工业生产者出厂价格指数
Producer Price Index for Industrial Products

(上年=100) (preceding year=100)

类别	Item	2005	2010	2015	2017	2018	2019	2020	2021	2022	2023
全部工业品	**Total Industrial Products**	**104.0**	**105.0**	**96.4**	**106.5**	**103.6**	**100.4**	**98.8**	**105.9**	**102.8**	**97.6**
按轻重工业分	**Grouped by Light & Heavy Industry**										
轻工业	Light Industry	101.3	103.3	98.7	102.3	101.6	99.8	100.4	103.6	101.4	98.7
重工业	Heavy Industry	106.2	106.3	95.5	108.3	104.5	100.6	98.0	107.0	103.4	97.1
按类别分	**Grouped by Sector**										
生产资料	Means of Production	105.5	105.7	95.3	108.7	104.6	100.2	97.9	107.3	103.6	97.0
采掘	Mining and Quarrying	114.5	112.6	90.3	116.5	102.3	103.9	101.8	111.6	109.0	100.2
原料	Raw Materials	105.9	109.0	96.4	110.2	105.3	98.0	94.6	112.2	110.0	95.2
加工	Manufacturing	104.0	103.0	95.7	107.4	104.6	100.5	98.4	105.5	101.2	97.1
生活资料	Consumer Goods	100.1	102.8	99.8	100.8	101.1	100.7	101.1	102.3	100.6	99.4
食品	Food	102.2	104.4	100.2	100.9	101.9	102.2	102.9	101.5	100.9	100.1
衣着	Clothing	101.5	101.2	103.5	101.0	103.0	100.9	98.4	97.8	100.3	102.2
一般日用品	Articles for Daily Use	102.0	102.9	98.0	101.5	101.7	100.2	99.0	101.9	102.4	97.6
耐用消费品	Durable Consumer Goods	90.1	94.2	98.1	99.6	97.3	95.6	96.7	106.2	97.6	98.4
按部门分	**Grouped by Industrial Division**										
冶金工业	Metallurgical Industry	105.7	110.6	89.3	123.0	106.7	101.2	99.6	118.3	98.9	94.0
电力工业	Power Industry	104.0	103.1	99.9	98.4	98.1	98.0	96.3	98.4	102.0	100.5
煤炭工业	Coal Industry	122.2	112.1	87.9	133.0	102.0	99.5	96.0	131.7	124.7	90.4
石油工业	Petroleum Industry	104.6	111.0	97.4	105.2	108.7	101.0	90.7	105.8	113.4	99.4
化学工业	Chemical Industry	107.5	105.5	97.5	105.8	105.5	99.1	97.5	110.9	108.9	93.9
机械工业	Machine Building Industry	99.9	100.0	99.1	102.6	101.2	99.4	98.6	102.7	99.9	99.7
建筑材料工业	Building Materials Industry	104.7	99.0	92.8	106.1	110.7	105.6	97.5	103.6	102.8	93.5
森林工业	Timber Industry	100.9	104.7	101.0	100.1	101.4	100.9	99.2	100.7	100.7	100.0
食品工业	Food Industry	102.4	104.4	99.8	100.6	101.9	101.9	102.8	102.4	101.3	99.8
纺织工业	Textile Industry	102.9	115.8	93.5	105.7	105.0	99.2	98.0	106.9	104.4	97.4
缝纫工业	Tailoring Industry	97.1	101.0	104.9	102.7	103.7	99.2	97.9	97.5	100.0	100.5
皮革工业	Leather Industry	105.6	100.7	102.8	100.4	104.9	103.0	99.9	99.2	100.4	105.1
造纸工业	Paper Industry	100.6	102.1	98.8	117.5	106.4	95.0	97.6	106.8	101.5	95.2
文教艺术用品工业	Culture, Education and Art Supply Industry	99.9	102.1	95.0	106.8	104.2	101.2	100.1	101.4	103.2	100.6

8-11 按行业分工业生产者出厂价格指数
Producer Price Index for Industrial Products by Industrial Branch

(上年=100) (preceding year=100)

类别	Item	2023
煤炭开采和洗选业	Mining and Washing of Coal	94.3
石油和天然气开采业	Extraction of Petroleum and Natural Gas	102.3
黑色金属矿采选业	Mining and Processing of Ferrous Metals Ores	101.7
有色金属矿采选业	Mining and Processing of Non-ferrous Metals Ores	98.6
非金属矿采选业	Mining and Processing of Non-metal Ores	102.1
农副食品加工业	Processing of Food from Agricultural Products	100.0
食品制造业	Manufacturing of Foods	100.0
酒、饮料和精制茶制造业	Manufacturing of Alcohol, Beverages and Refined Tea	98.7
烟草制品业	Manufacturing of Tobacco	100.0
纺织业	Manufacturing of Textiles	97.4
纺织服装、服饰业	Manufacturing of Textile Wearing Apparel and Accessories	100.7
皮革、毛皮、羽毛及其制品和制鞋业	Manufacturing of Leather, Fur, Feather and Related Products; Manufacture of Footware	103.4
木材加工和木、竹、藤、棕、草制品业	Processing of Timber, Manufacture of Wood, Bamboo, Rattan, Palm and Straw Products	99.4
家具制造业	Manufacturing of Furniture	100.4
造纸和纸制品业	Manufacturing of Paper and Paper Products	95.2
印刷和记录媒介复制业	Printing and Reproduction of Recorded Media	99.1
文教、工美、体育和娱乐用品制造业	Manufacturing of Articles for Culture, Education, Arts and Crafts, Sport and Entertainment Activities	103.7
石油、煤炭及其他燃料加工业	Processing of Petroleum, Coking and Processing of Nuclear Fuel	88.7
化学原料和化学制品制造业	Manufacturing of Raw Chemical Materials and Chemical Products	90.4
医药制造业	Manufacturing of Medicines	99.3
化学纤维制造业	Manufacturing of Chemical Fibres	96.9
橡胶和塑料制品业	Manufacturing of Rubber and Plastic Products	96.3
非金属矿物制品业	Manufacturing of Non-metallic Mineral Products	93.5
黑色金属冶炼和压延加工业	Smelting and Pressing of Ferrous Metals	90.1
有色金属冶炼和压延加工业	Smelting and Pressing of Non-ferrous Metals	93.4
金属制品业	Manufacturing of Metal Products	98.8
通用设备制造业	Manufacturing of General Purpose Machinery	102.1
专用设备制造业	Manufacturing of Special Purpose Machinery	98.7
汽车制造业	Manufacturing of Automobiles	99.3
铁路、船舶、航空航天和其他运输设备制造业	Manufacturing of Railway, Ship, Aerospace and Other Transport Equipment	99.1
电气机械和器材制造业	Manufacturing of Electrical Machinery and Apparatus	98.0
计算机、通信和其他电子设备制造业	Manufacturing of Computers, Communication and Other Electronic Equipment	99.8
仪器仪表制造业	Manufacturing of Measuring Instruments and Machinery	99.9
其他制造业	Other Manufacturing	104.3
废弃资源综合利用业	Utilization of Waste Resources	87.3
金属制品、机械和设备修理业	Repair Service of Metal Products, Machinery and Equipment	107.3
电力、热力生产和供应业	Production and Supply of Electric Power and Heat Power	100.5
燃气生产和供应业	Production and Supply of Gas	103.8
水的生产和供应业	Production and Supply of Water	100.6

主要统计指标解释

一般公共预算收入 指国家财政参与社会产品分配所取得的收入，是实现国家职能的财力保证。主要包括：

(1)各项税收：包括国内增值税、国内消费税、进口货物增值税、进口消费品消费税、出口货物退增值税、出口消费品退消费税、企业所得税、个人所得税、资源税、城市维护建设税、房产税、印花税、城镇土地使用税、土地增值税、车船税、船舶吨税、车辆购置税、关税、耕地占用税、契税、烟叶税、环境保护税等。

(2)非税收入：包括专项收入、行政事业性收费收入、罚没收入、国有资本经营收入、国有资源（资产）有偿使用收入和其他收入。

财政收入按现行分税制财政体制划分为中央本级收入和地方本级收入。

一般公共预算支出 指国家财政将筹集起来的资金进行分配使用，以满足经济建设和各项事业的需要。主要包括：一般公共服务、外交、国防、公共安全、教育、科学技术、文化旅游体育与传媒、社会保障和就业、卫生健康、节能环保、城乡社区、农林水、交通运输、资源勘探工业信息等、商业服务业等、金融、援助其他地区、自然资源海洋气象等、住房保障、粮油物资储备、灾害防治及应急管理、债务付息、债务发行费用等方面的支出。

财政支出根据政府在经济和社会活动中的不同职权，划分为中央财政支出和地方财政支出。

中央一般公共预算收入和地方一般公共预算收入 属于中央一般公共预算的收入包括关税，进口货物增值税和消费税，出口货物退增值税和消费税，国内消费税，铁道部门、各银行总行、各保险公司总公司等集中缴纳的城市维护建设税，增值税50%部分，纳入共享范围的企业所得税60%部分，未纳入共享范围的中央企业所得税、中央企业上交的利润，个人所得税60%部分，车辆购置税，船舶吨税，证券交易印花税，海洋石油资源税，中央非税收入等。属于地方一般公共预算的收入包括城市维护建设税（不含铁道部门、各银行总行、各保险公司总公司集中缴纳的部分），房产税，城镇土地使用税，土地增值税，车船税，耕地占用税，契税，烟叶税，印花税（不含证券交易印花税），增值税50%部分，纳入共享范围的企业所得税40%部分，个人所得税40%部分，海洋石油资源税以外的其他资源税，地方非税收入等。

中央一般公共预算支出和地方一般公共预算支出 指根据政府在经济和社会活动中的不同职责，划分中央和地方政府的责权，按照政府的责权划分确定的支出。中央一般公共预算支出包括一般公共服务，外交支出，国防支出，公共安全支出，以及中央政府调整国民经济结构、协调地区发展、实施宏观调控的支出等。地方一般公共预算支出包括一般公共服务，公共安全支出，地方统筹的各项社会事业支出等。

居民消费价格指数 指反映一定时期内城乡居民所购买的生活消费品和服务项目价格变动趋势和程度的相对数。

工业生产者出厂价格指数 指反映一定时期内全部工业产品第一次出售时的出厂价格总水平的变动趋势和变动幅度的相对数。

Explanatory Notes on Main Statistical Indicators

General Public Budget Revenue refers to income for the government finance through participating in the distribution of social products. It is the financial guarantee to ensure government functioning. The government revenue includes the following main items:

1) Various tax revenues including domestic value added tax (VAT), domestic consumption tax, VAT from imports, consumption tax from imports, VAT rebate for exports, consumption tax rebate for exports, corporate income tax, individual income tax, resource tax, city maintenance and construction tax, house property tax, stamp tax, urban land use tax, land appreciation tax, tax on vehicles and boat operation, ship tonnage tax, vehicle purchase tax, tariffs, farm land occupation tax, deed tax, and tobacco tax, environment protection tax, etc.

2) Non-tax revenue, including special program receipts, charge income of administrative and institutional units, penalty receipts, operating income from government capital, income from use of state-owned resources (assets) and others non-tax receipts.

Government Revenue at the current decentralized taxation system is divided into the central level revenue and local level revenue.

General Public Budget Expenditure refers to the distribution and use of the funds which the government finance has raised, so as to meet the needs of economic construction and various undertakings. It includes the following main items: expenditure for general public services, expenditure for foreign affairs, expenditure for national defence expenditure for public security, expenditure for education, expenditure for science and technology, expenditure for culture, tourism, sport and media, expenditure for social safety net and employment effort, expenditure for health care, expenditure for energy conservation and environment protection, expenditure for urban and rural community affairs, expenditure for agriculture, forestry and water conservancy, expenditure for transportation, expenditure for resource exploration and industrial information, expenditure for affairs of commerce and services, expenditure for finance, aid to other regions, expenditure for nature resources, ocean and weather, expenditure for housing security, expenditure for grain & oil reserves, expenditure for prevention of disasters and emergency management, interest payment for public debts, expenditure for issuing debts.

General public budget expenditure is divided into general public budget expenditure of central government and general public budget expenditure of local government according to the different functions of the governments played in economic and social activities.

General Public Budget Revenue of the Central Government and the Local Governments The general public budget revenue of the Central Government includes tariff, VAT and consumption tax from imports, VAT and consumption tax rebate for exports, domestic consumption tax, city maintenance and construct tax from the Ministry of Railways, head offices of banks, head offices of insurance company, which are handed over to the government in a centralized way, 50% of the value added tax, 60% the share part of the corporate income tax, unshared part of corporate income tax of the central enterprises, profit handed in by the central enterprises, 60% of individual income tax, vehicle purchase tax, ship tonnage tax, stamp tax on securities transactions, resource tax on the offshore petroleum resources. The general public budget revenue of the local governments includes city maintenance and construct tax (excluding the part of the Ministry of Railways, head offices of banks, head offices of insurance company, which are handed over to the government in a centralized way), house property tax, urban land use tax, land appreciation tax, tax on vehicles and boat operation, farm land occupation tax, deed tax, and tobacco leaf tax, stamp tax (not including stamp tax on security exchange), 50% of the value added tax, 40% the share part of the corporate income tax, 40% of individual income tax, resource tax other than the tax on offshore petroleum resources, local non-tax revenue, etc.

General Public Budget Expenditure of the Central Government and Local Governments according to the different functions of the Central Government and local governments in economic and social activities, the rights of administration are demarcated between those of the Central Government and those of local governments; and the classification of the expenditure between the Central Government and local governments are made on the basis of the classification of the rights administration between them. The general public budget expenditure of the Central Government includes the expenditure for general public services, expenditure for foreign affairs, expenditure for public security, and the general public budget expenditure of the Central Government for adjusting the national economic structure; coordinating the development among different regions; and exercising macroeconomic regulation. The general public budget expenditure of the local governments includes mainly the expenditure for general public services, expenditure for public security, and expenditures for social development which are planed by local governments, etc.

Consumer Price Indices are relative figures reflecting the trend and degree of changes in prices of consumer goods and services purchased by urban and rural households during a given period.

Producer Price Indices for Industrial Products are relative figures reflecting the trend and degree of changes in general ex-factory prices of all manufactured goods for first sale during a given period.

09 人民生活和社会保障

Chapter 9 People's Living Conditions and Social Security

SICHUAN STATISTICAL YEARBOOK

9-1 全体居民人均收支情况

Per Capita Income and Consumption Expenditure of all Residents

单位：元 (yuan)

项目	Item	2017	2018	2019	2020	2021	2022	2023
全体居民人均总收入	**Per Capita Income**	**25785**	**28583**	**31022**	**32919**	**36776**	**38133**	**39406**
可支配收入	Disposable Income	20580	22461	24703	26522	29080	30679	32514
工资性收入	Income of Wages and Salaries	10014	11070	12049	13032	14392	15234	16154
经营净收入	Net Business Income	4264	4558	5058	5289	5758	6045	6433
财产净收入	Net Income from Property	1363	1443	1593	1720	1905	1974	2049
转移净收入	Net Income from Transfer	4940	5389	6003	6482	7024	7427	7878
现金可支配收入	Cash Disposable Income	19208	21028	23068	24715	27072	28677	30873
工资性收入	Income of Wages and Salaries	9954	11000	11958	12928	14257	15103	16017
经营净收入	Net Business Income	3874	4229	4736	4808	5272	5600	6284
财产净收入	Net Income from Property	746	764	845	959	1088	1117	1316
转移净收入	Net Income from Transfer	4633	5034	5530	6020	6456	6858	7256
全体居民人均总支出	**Per Capita Expenditure**	**26197**	**29924**	**32331**	**31650**	**35721**	**35592**	**37182**
消费支出	Consumption Expenditure	16180	17664	19338	19783	21518	22302	23550
食品烟酒	Food,Tobacco and Liquor	5632	5938	6467	7026	7549	7738	7846
衣着	Clothing	1153	1174	1213	1190	1315	1317	1355
居住	Residence	2947	3368	3679	3856	4035	4362	4157
生活用品及服务	Articles for Daily Use and Services	1063	1182	1201	1235	1388	1465	1450
交通通信	Transport and Communications	2200	2399	2576	2465	2807	2806	3300
教育文化娱乐	Education, Cultural and Recreation	1468	1600	1813	1651	1892	2006	2418
医疗保健	Health Care and Medical Services	1320	1569	1935	1908	2072	2105	2435
其他用品及服务	Other Goods and Services	397	435	454	452	459	502	589
现金消费支出	Cash Consumption Expenditure	13346	14574	15923	16223	17768	18490	19800
食品烟酒	Food,Tobacco and Liquor	4910	5296	5820	6299	6806	7025	7112
衣着	Clothing	1150	1173	1213	1190	1315	1316	1354
居住	Residence	1118	1252	1367	1469	1568	1797	1755
生活用品及服务	Articles for Daily Use and Services	1051	1161	1183	1222	1377	1452	1444
交通通信	Transport and Communications	2199	2397	2574	2464	2803	2802	3297
教育文化娱乐	Education, Cultural and Recreation	1467	1597	1813	1650	1891	2006	2416
医疗保健	Health Care and Medical Services	1066	1271	1508	1488	1558	1605	1849
其他商品及服务	Other Goods and Services	385	427	445	442	448	488	573

9-2 居民人均主要食品消费量
Per Capita Consumption of Major Foods of all Residents

单位：公斤 (kg)

项目	Item	全体居民 Whole Households		城镇居民 Urban Households		农村居民 Rural Households	
		2022	2023	2022	2023	2022	2023
粮食	Grain	134.3	126.1	106.2	98.2	161.1	153.6
谷物	Cereal	121.9	114.4	94.3	86.9	148.4	141.4
薯类	Tuber	3.6	3.5	3.3	3.1	3.8	3.8
豆类	Beans	8.8	8.3	8.6	8.2	9.0	8.4
油脂类	Oil and Fats	11.3	11.5	11.3	11.1	11.4	11.9
#植物油	Vegetable Oil	10.2	10.4	10.5	10.3	10.0	10.5
动物油	Animal Oil	1.1	1.1	0.8	0.9	1.4	1.4
蔬菜和菜制品	Vegetables and Related Products	121.6	119.6	125.2	118.1	118.2	121.0
#鲜菜	Fresh Vegetables	118.5	116.4	121.1	114.2	116.0	118.7
肉类	Meat	43.9	49.5	43.9	48.3	43.8	50.7
#猪肉	Pork	38.3	42.4	36.1	38.7	40.4	46.1
牛肉	Beef	1.9	2.6	2.7	3.4	1.1	1.8
羊肉	Mutton	0.5	0.5	0.6	0.6	0.4	0.4
禽类	Poultry	12.6	12.4	12.8	12.9	12.4	11.9
水产品	Aquatic Products	9.8	10.1	11.4	12.0	8.3	8.3
蛋类及蛋制品	Eggs and Related Products	9.8	11.4	10.0	10.4	9.6	12.3
奶及奶制品	Milk and Dairy Products	11.9	12.8	15.4	16.5	8.5	9.2
干鲜瓜果类	Dried and Fresh Melons and Fruits	43.7	46.6	52.1	56.8	35.7	36.6
食糖	Sugar	1.6	1.5	1.2	1.1	1.9	1.9

9−3　居民平均每百户年末耐用消费品拥有量
Number of Main Durable Consumer Goods Owned per 100 Households

单位：平均每百户　　　　(per 100 Households)

项目		Item		全体居民 Whole Households		城镇居民 Urban Households		农村居民 Rural Households	
				2022	2023	2022	2023	2022	2023
家用汽车	（辆）	Automobile	(unit)	32.1	39.3	42.7	49.0	21.8	28.9
摩托车	（辆）	Motorcycle	(unit)	33.7	31.0	17.5	17.5	49.3	45.4
助力车	（辆）	Electric Bicycle	(unit)	41.4	45.1	37.6	44.1	45.1	46.2
洗衣机	（台）	Washing Machine	(set)	100.5	100.7	101.6	101.1	99.4	100.3
电冰箱(柜)	（台）	Refrigerator	(set)	106.1	111.1	103.5	106.2	108.5	116.3
微波炉	（台）	Microwave Oven	(set)	32.4	34.6	51.2	50.9	14.2	17.3
彩色电视机	（台）	Color Television Set	(set)	120.5	113.6	122.4	114.2	118.5	113.0
空调	（台）	Air Conditioner	(set)	132.9	151.2	179.8	197.1	87.5	102.4
热水器	（台）	Water Heater	(set)	93.6	92.2	100.0	97.9	87.4	86.1
洗碗机	（台）	Dishwasher	(set)	1.5	1.5	2.3	2.5	0.7	0.4
排油烟机	（台）	Vacuum Cleaner	(set)	51.2	54.6	79.3	81.7	24.1	25.8
固定电话	（部）	Telephone	(unit)	5.0	5.6	7.6	7.7	2.4	3.5
移动电话	（部）	Mobile Telephone	(unit)	263.6	270.5	259.9	262.0	267.1	279.6
计算机	（台）	Private Computer	(set)	32.7	34.0	50.4	50.0	15.5	17.0
照相机	（台）	Camera	(set)	5.1	4.6	8.7	7.6	1.7	1.3
乐器	（架）	Musical Instrument	(unit)	3.4	3.7	5.8	6.4	1.0	0.8
健身器材	（台）	Health Equipment	(set)	3.3	3.3	5.9	5.3	0.8	1.2
空气净化器	（台）	Air Cleaner	(set)	3.3	3.8	5.7	6.8	0.9	0.7
地面清洁电器	（台）	Ground Cleaning Appliances	(set)	4.8	5.1	8.9	9.0	0.7	1.0

9-4 城镇居民家庭情况
Statistics of Urban Households

项目	Item	2017	2018	2019	2020	2021	2022	2023
平均每户家庭常住人口 （人）	**Average Resident Population per Household (person)**	**3.11**	**2.99**	**2.99**	**2.97**	**3.04**	**3.01**	**2.97**
平均每户就业人口 （人）	**Average Number of Employed Persons per Household (person)**	**1.56**	**2.11**	**2.13**	**2.21**	**2.26**	**2.27**	**1.68**
人均总收入 （元）	**Per Capita Total Income (yuan)**	**36136**	**39854**	**43051**	**45500**	**50228**	**51741**	**52839**
人均可支配收入 （元）	**Per Capita Disposable Income (yuan)**	**30727**	**33216**	**36154**	**38253**	**41444**	**43233**	**45227**
工资性收入	Income of Wages and Salaries	17299	19033	20479	21951	23934	25053	26228
经营净收入	Net Business Income	3586	3900	4393	4334	4799	4999	5250
财产净收入	Net Income from Property	2627	2696	2891	3059	3322	3381	3508
转移净收入	Net Income from Transfer	7215	7587	8391	8910	9389	9801	10240
人均总支出 （元）	**Per Capita Total Expenditure (yuan)**	**33571**	**38626**	**39569**	**39164**	**43887**	**43433**	**45778**
人均消费支出 （元）	**Per Capita Expenditure for Consumption (yuan)**	**21991**	**23484**	**25367**	**25133**	**26971**	**27637**	**29280**
食品烟酒	Food, Tobacco and Liquor	7329	7462	8279	8741	9246	9358	9614
衣着	Clothing	1723	1713	1730	1675	1831	1765	1852
居住	Residence	3906	4470	4742	4951	5158	5558	5370
生活用品及服务	Articles for Daily Use and Services	1404	1562	1525	1600	1724	1806	1870
交通通信	Transport and Communications	3198	3366	3453	3052	3530	3467	4106
教育文化娱乐	Education, Cultural and Recreation	2222	2384	2668	2253	2558	2638	3017
医疗保健	Health Care and Medical Services	1596	1861	2293	2193	2281	2343	2683
其他用品及服务	Other Commodities and Services	612	666	677	668	643	702	769
城镇居民恩格尔系数 （%）	**Engle Coefficient of Urban Households (%)**	**33.3**	**31.8**	**32.6**	**34.8**	**34.3**	**33.9**	**32.8**

9-5 按收入五等份分组的城镇居民人均收入(2023年)
Per Capita Income of Urban Households by Income Quintile (2023)

单位：元 (yuan)

项目	Item	总平均 Average	低收入户 Low Income Households	中低收入户 Lower Middle Income Households	中等收入户 Middle Income Households	中高收入户 Upper Middle Income Households	高收入户 High Income Households
人均总收入	**Per Capita Total Income**	**52839**	**24703**	**34204**	**47011**	**64075**	**118149**
人均可支配收入	**Per Capita Disposable Income**	**45227**	**17372**	**30057**	**41556**	**56998**	**101827**
工资性收入	Income of Wages and Salaries	26228	11054	17461	22988	31697	60420
工资	Wage and Salaries	25006	10929	17052	22097	30132	56287
实物福利	Physical Welfare	193	59	171	188	245	385
其他	Other Incomes	1029	66	238	703	1319	3748
经营净收入	Net Business Income	5250	1043	3553	4797	6006	13989
第一产业	Primary Industry	597	173	682	644	506	1189
第二产业	Secondary Industry	311	84	173	467	186	812
第三产业	Tertiary Industry	4342	787	2698	3686	5314	11988
财产净收入	Net Income from Property	3508	895	1783	2685	3906	10658
利息净收入	Net Interest Income	-33	-158	-69	-12	98	41
红利收入	Bonus Stock Income	945	166	286	493	636	4027
储蓄性保险净收益	Net Income of Savings Insurance	7		1	1	28	10
转让承包土地经营权租金净收入	Net Income of the Transfer of Contracted Land Management Rights	53	52	61	43	25	85
出租房屋财产性收入	Net Income of Rental Housing	1009	205	500	866	1030	3157
转移净收入	Net Income from Transfer	10240	4380	7261	11085	15390	16759

9-6 按收入五等份分组的城镇居民人均消费支出(2023年)
Per Capita Expenditure of Urban Households by Income Quintile (2023)

单位: 元 (yuan)

项目	Item	总平均 Average	低收入户 Low Income Households	中低收入户 Lower Middle Income Households	中等收入户 Middle Income Households	中高收入户 Upper Middle Income Households	高收入户 High Income Households
人均总支出	**Per Capita Total Expenditure**	**45778**	**28136**	**32479**	**39701**	**52325**	**92655**
人均消费支出	**Per Capita Total Living Expenditure for Consumption**	**29280**	**17346**	**22461**	**27859**	**34377**	**53727**
食品烟酒	Food, Tobacco and Liquor	9614	6310	7872	9419	11436	15460
食品	Food	5316	4057	4835	5378	6326	6751
谷物	Cereal	428	364	383	428	473	538
薯类	Tuber	75	71	74	70	85	75
豆类	Beans	60	49	57	64	72	60
食用油	Edible Oil	195	163	206	206	217	193
蔬菜和食用菌	Vegetable and Mushroom	673	502	638	687	828	796
肉类	Meat and Related Products	1524	1206	1447	1566	1784	1783
禽类	Poultry	413	298	397	427	499	504
水产品	Aquatic Products	314	204	284	323	391	432
蛋类	Eggs	154	121	154	147	180	185
奶类	Milk	424	353	335	386	527	593
干鲜瓜果类	Dried and Fresh Melons and Fruits	614	404	494	624	753	940
糖果糕点类	Confectioneries	228	161	184	232	261	351
其他食品	Others	215	160	182	219	256	300
烟酒	Liquor	1000	639	861	924	1151	1687
饮料	Beverages	235	133	156	225	273	476
饮食服务	Catering Services	3064	1481	2019	2893	3686	6546
衣着	Clothing	1852	1045	1374	1788	2186	3498
衣类	Garments	1501	826	1095	1436	1761	2923
鞋类	Shoes	351	218	279	352	425	575
居住	Residence	5370	2902	3831	4890	6360	10920
生活用品及服务	Household Facilities, Articles and Services	1870	927	1292	1744	2347	3787
交通通信	Transportation and Communication	4106	2170	2958	3742	4358	8953
交通	Transportation	3156	1552	2216	2813	3245	7349
通信	Communication	950	618	743	930	1114	1605
教育文化娱乐	Recreation, Education and Cultural Services	3017	2081	2685	2885	3284	4821
教育	Education	2098	1722	2108	1997	2064	2838
文化娱乐	Recreation and Cultural Services	919	359	577	889	1220	1982
医疗保健	Health Care and Medical Services	2683	1589	2012	2726	3431	4448
医疗器具及药品	Medical Equipment and Drugs	697	447	526	680	909	1112
医疗服务	Medical Services	1986	1142	1486	2046	2523	3337
其他商品和服务	Other Commodities and Services	769	322	438	663	974	1840

9-7 各市(州)城镇居民家庭人均收支及住房情况
Per Capita Income and Consumption Expenditure and Housing Conditions of Urban Households by Region

单位：元、平方米 (yuan, sq.m)

市(州)	Region	人均可支配收入 Per Capita Disposable Income		人均消费支出 Per Capita Expenditure for Consumption		#食品烟酒支出 Food, Tobacco and Liquor		人均现住房建筑面积 Per Capita Housing Area	
		2022	2023	2022	2023	2022	2023	2022	2023
全 省	**Sichuan**	**43233**	**45227**	**27637**	**29280**	**9358**	**9614**	**38.2**	**37.7**
成都市	Chengdu	54897	54489	32171	33557	10849	10596	36.1	39.0
自贡市	Zigong	43740	45032	24650	27309	8816	8929	40.0	38.3
攀枝花市	Panzhihua	50009	47803	28223	28705	9096	9218	34.8	35.6
泸州市	Luzhou	45071	45757	29010	29616	10411	10170	41.9	37.9
德阳市	Deyang	44650	46700	27235	29414	9601	10069	41.1	41.0
绵阳市	Mianyang	45131	47187	27394	28972	9536	9460	40.3	36.8
广元市	Guangyuan	40687	40017	25396	24821	8908	8491	44.2	44.0
遂宁市	Suining	42217	41731	26019	27548	9061	8402	44.7	39.3
内江市	Neijiang	43639	44641	26351	27081	9265	9949	37.2	39.9
乐山市	Leshan	44376	45390	28460	29331	9732	10241	40.0	39.7
南充市	Nanchong	41126	40469	24603	24827	8066	8325	42.7	36.7
眉山市	Meishan	43949	45110	26887	27043	9751	9330	38.6	38.2
宜宾市	Yibin	44739	45985	26545	27618	9422	8781	41.3	38.1
广安市	Guangan	43078	42873	26708	26407	9229	8885	37.9	35.4
达州市	Dazhou	41210	40477	25157	25261	9300	8415	41.0	35.9
雅安市	Yaan	42404	41044	24559	25579	8548	8937	43.6	43.3
巴中市	Bazhong	40783	40015	24507	25846	9701	9570	36.1	36.7
资阳市	Ziyang	42419	41729	24240	25125	8493	8325	35.9	36.6
阿坝藏族羌族自治州	Aba	41779	40408	23223	25338	7739	8061	39.3	45.0
甘孜藏族自治州	Ganzi	41277	40152	24991	25707	9080	8977	41.8	48.5
凉山彝族自治州	Liangshan	39357	39042	24227	23694	8469	8220	39.6	40.8

注：由于全省乡镇行政区划和村级建制调整后，各地城乡属性和统计口径发生了较大变化，因此，2022年开展住户调查样本轮换后，2023年全省各市（州）居民收支数据按城乡属性变化后的新口径进行核算，与2022年同期数不可比。

a)After the adjustment of township administrative divisions and village level administrative systems in Sichuan Province, there have been significant changes in the urban-rural attributes and statistical standards in various regions. Therefore, after the sample rotation of household surveys in 2022, the income and expenditure data of residents in various municipalities (autonomous prefectures) in Sichuan in 2023 have been calculated according to the new standards after the changes in urban-rural attributes, which are incomparable to the same period in 2022.

9-8 按收入五等份分组的城镇居民家庭住房情况(2023年)
Housing Conditions of Urban Households by Income Quintile (2023)

项目	Item	总平均 Average	低收入户 Low Income Households	中低收入户 Lower Middle Income Households	中等收入户 Middle Income Households	中高收入户 Upper Middle Income Households	高收入户 High Income Households
人均自有现住房面积 （平方米）	**Per Capita Floor Space of Buildings (sq.m)**	**37.7**	**30.5**	**32.6**	**34.2**	**36.8**	**41.4**
按居住类型划分 (%)	**Grouped by Residential Types (%)**						
普通住宅	Average House	99.5	99.9	99.6	99.8	99.2	99.0
集体宿舍和工棚	Collective Dormitory and Barrack	0.2		0.4	0.1	0.2	0.5
工作地住宿	Workplace Accommodation		0.1				
按居住空间样式划分 (%)	**Grouped by House Patterns (%)**						
单栋楼房	Independent building	19.4	30.9	24.1	18.8	13.0	10.4
单栋平房	Independent bungalow	3.9	9.0	5.1	2.8	1.2	1.1
四居室及以上单元房	Flats With 4 and more Bedrooms	5.4	3.5	3.8	4.7	6.5	8.3
三居室单元房	Flats With 3 Bedrooms	42.6	37.0	42.3	40.6	45.8	47.5
二居室单元房	Flats With 2 Bedrooms	25.2	17.8	22.7	28.6	30.6	26.3
一居室单元房	Flats With 1 Bedroom	3.3	1.4	1.6	4.2	3.0	6.2
筒子楼或连片平房	Tube-shaped Apartment or Continuous Bungalow	0.2	0.2	0.1	0.4		0.1
其他	Others			0.2			
按主要建筑材料划分 (%)	**Grouped by Main Building Materials (%)**						
钢筋混凝土	Reinforced Concrete	67.3	58.5	63.9	65.2	72.3	76.8
砖混材料	Brick Material	30.0	35.3	32.4	33.0	26.9	22.6
砖瓦砖木	Brick and Tile	2.2	5.5	2.8	1.5	0.7	0.6
竹草土坯	Bamboo Grass Adobe		0.1	0.1			
其他	Others	0.4	0.7	0.8	0.3	0.1	
按房屋来源划分 (%)	**Grouped by Source of Housing (%)**						
租赁公房	Public Dwelling House Leased	2.8	1.5	2.8	1.7	2.7	5.2
租赁私房	Private Dwelling House Leased	7.1	6.2	5.5	8.1	7.1	8.3
自建住房	Spontaneous Housing	23.5	38.5	29.2	23.6	14.6	11.4
购买商品房	Commercial Housing Purchased	48.4	36.3	44.8	47.4	53.1	60.3
购买房改住房	Reformd Housing Purchased	2.9	0.9	2.2	2.6	4.8	3.8
购买保障性住房	Affordable Housing Purchased	2.3	1.7	2.0	1.5	4.9	1.6
拆迁安置房	Removal and Resettlement Housing	10.6	12.9	11.5	13.5	10.0	5.0
继承或获赠住房	Inherited or Given Housing	0.4		0.4	0.4		1.2
免费借用房	Free Housing	1.6	1.9	1.4	0.8	1.8	2.3
雇主提供免费住房	Free Housing Provided by Employers	0.4		0.1	0.2	1.0	0.7
其他	Others	0.2	0.1	0.2	0.3		0.3

9-9 农村居民家庭情况
Statistics of Rural Households

项目		Item		2017	2018	2019	2020	2021	2022	2023
平均每户常住人口	(人)	Average Resident Population per Household	(person)	3.07	3.04	3.02	3.01	3.06	3.05	3.20
平均每户整、半劳力	(人)	Average Number of Ablebodied and Semi-ablebodied Laborers per Household	(person)	2.12	2.09	2.08	2.12	2.16	2.15	2.09
平均每个劳动力负担人口(含本人)	(人)	Average Number of Persons Supported by a Laborer (including the laborer himself or herself)	(person)	1.45	1.43	1.45	1.42	1.42	1.43	1.53
人均总收入	**(元)**	**Per Capita Total Income**	**(yuan)**	**17264**	**19016**	**20483**	**21559**	**24258**	**25117**	**26160**
工资性收入		Wages Income		4016	4311	4662	4978	5514	5844	6220
经营性收入		Household Business Income		9167	10153	10777	11036	12560	12539	12947
财产性收入		Property Income		340	414	518	579	655	701	622
转移性收入		Transfer Income		3741	4138	4526	4966	5529	6034	6371
人均可支配收入	**(元)**	**Per Capita Disposable Income**	**(yuan)**	**12227**	**13331**	**14670**	**15929**	**17575**	**18672**	**19978**
工资性收入		Income of Wages and Salaries		4016	4311	4662	4978	5514	5844	6220
经营净收入		Net Business Income		4821	5117	5641	6152	6651	7045	7599
财产净收入		Net Income from Property		323	379	456	510	587	628	609
转移净收入		Net Income from Transfer		3067	3524	3910	4289	4823	5156	5548
人均总支出	**(元)**	**Per Capita Total Expenditure**	**(yuan)**	**20128**	**22538**	**25989**	**24864**	**28122**	**28094**	**28706**
家庭经营费用支出		Expenditure for Household Business		4009	4614	4794	4552	5499	5179	4608
生活消费支出		Expenditure for Consumption		11397	12723	14056	14953	16444	17199	17901
食品烟酒		Food, Tobacco and Liquor		4235	4483	4879	5478	5969	6189	6103
#食品		Food		3139	3225	3481	4018	4238	4164	4044
衣着		Clothing		683	716	760	753	835	888	865
居住		Residence		2157	2500	2748	2866	2991	3218	2961
生活用品及服务		Household Facilities, Articles and Services		782	860	917	905	1075	1139	1036
交通通信		Transportation and Communication		1378	1578	1808	1935	2135	2174	2505
教育文化娱乐		Education, Recreation and Cultural Services		848	934	1065	1107	1273	1401	1828
医疗保健		Medicine and Medical Services		1094	1414	1621	1650	1877	1878	2190
其他商品和服务		Other Commodities and Services		220	238	258	258	289	312	412
恩格尔系数	(%)	Engel's Coefficient	(%)	37.2	35.2	34.7	36.6	36.3	36.0	34.1
人均经营耕地面积	(亩)	Per Capita Area of Cultivated Land under Management	(mu)	1.3	1.5	1.5	1.6	1.6	1.6	1.5
人均经营水面面积	(亩)	Per Capita Water Area under Management	(mu)	0.03	0.02	0.05	0.05	0.06	0.04	0.06
人均自有现住房面积	(平方米)	Per Capita Existing Housing Area	(sq.m)	48.6	47.4	48.0	47.8	46.3	47.0	45.3

9-10 按收入五等份分组的农村居民人均收入和支出情况(2023年)
Per Capita Income and Expenditure of Rural Households by Income Quintile (2023)

单位：元 (yuan)

项目	Item	总平均 Average	低收入户 Low Income Households	中低收入户 Lower Middle Income Households	中等收入户 Middle Income Households	中高收入户 Upper Middle Income Households	高收入户 High Income Households
人均总收入	**Per Capita Total Income**	**26160**	**11326**	**15116**	**20682**	**28005**	**62866**
人均可支配收入	**Per Capita Disposable Income**	**19978**	**7471**	**11729**	**16584**	**22561**	**47164**
工资性收入	Income of Wages and Salaries	6220	2306	3847	5786	9082	11622
经营净收入	Net Business Income	7599	1616	2606	3788	6785	26508
财产净收入	Net Income from Property	609	99	184	290	542	2214
转移净收入	Net Income from Transfer	5548	3450	5092	6719	6152	6820
人均现金收入	**Per Capita Cash Income**	**18669**	**5756**	**10450**	**14801**	**21333**	**46792**
现金工资性收入	Cash Wages Income	6139	2281	3796	5720	8967	11452
现金经营性收入	Cash Household Business Income	6887	208	1704	2723	6237	27141
现金财产性收入	Cash Property Income	609	99	184	290	542	2214
现金转移性收入	Cash Transfer Income	5034	3168	4767	6068	5587	5985
人均总支出	**Per Capita Total Expenditure**	**28706**	**20119**	**20321**	**25972**	**29158**	**52528**
#生产经营费用支出	Expenditure for Production	4608	2884	2449	3007	3680	12229
生活消费支出	Expenditure for Consumption	17901	12828	14417	17188	19760	27496
人均现金支出	**Per Capita Expenditure in Cash**	**24899**	**16725**	**16929**	**21979**	**25094**	**48170**
#生产经营现金费用支出	Expenditure in Cash for Production	4095	2322	1888	2451	3232	11817
现金消费支出	Cash Consumption Expenditure	14607	9996	11586	13750	16144	23550

9-11 各市(州)农村居民家庭人均收支及住房情况

Per Capita Income and Consumption Expenditure and Housing Conditions of Rural Households by Region

单位：元、平方米 (yuan, sq.m)

市(州)	Region	人均可支配收入 Per Capita Disposable Income		人均消费支出 Per Capita Expenditure for Consumption		#食品烟酒支出 Food, Tobacco and Liquor		人均现住房建筑面积 Per Capita Housing Area	
		2022	2023	2022	2023	2022	2023	2022	2023
全 省	**Sichuan**	**18672**	**19978**	**17199**	**17901**	**6189**	**6103**	**47.0**	**45.3**
成都市	Chengdu	30931	30089	21196	21164	7616	7243	49.7	58.1
自贡市	Zigong	21976	20574	17082	15901	6274	5773	54.8	52.5
攀枝花市	Panzhihua	23364	22978	16357	15912	5363	5290	43.3	43.3
泸州市	Luzhou	21348	20016	15852	14846	6168	5616	45.1	44.2
德阳市	Deyang	23192	21899	17416	16281	6183	5679	46.7	55.7
绵阳市	Mianyang	22726	21621	17346	16438	6129	5739	48.0	46.4
广元市	Guangyuan	16881	17192	14059	12713	5061	4516	58.2	59.5
遂宁市	Suining	20986	19959	17101	14863	6639	4950	61.4	50.0
内江市	Neijiang	20996	20099	16237	15625	6408	6131	48.3	54.2
乐山市	Leshan	21339	20367	17344	15200	6004	5638	48.6	47.6
南充市	Nanchong	19469	18960	15502	14694	5524	5327	50.1	57.9
眉山市	Meishan	23099	21689	17731	15613	6631	5625	43.7	42.8
宜宾市	Yibin	21846	20453	17206	15431	6409	5231	50.9	51.1
广安市	Guangan	20964	19812	15899	14445	5634	5038	52.8	53.1
达州市	Dazhou	19906	19435	14646	14397	5519	5207	48.1	50.9
雅安市	Yaan	18794	18501	15798	13294	5617	4791	50.5	51.1
巴中市	Bazhong	16967	17247	14170	14455	5579	5621	56.3	57.6
资阳市	Ziyang	22326	20924	15702	14566	5685	5560	52.4	57.5
阿坝藏族羌族自治州	Aba	18261	18141	13886	13530	4985	4814	48.3	46.5
甘孜藏族自治州	Ganzi	16363	16918	11350	12568	4960	5055	30.8	38.6
凉山彝族自治州	Liangshan	17950	17686	13066	13087	5166	5241	30.9	33.3

注：由于全省乡镇行政区划和村级建制调整后，各地城乡属性和统计口径发生了较大变化，因此，2022年开展住户调查样本轮换后，2023年全省各市（州）居民收支数据按城乡属性变化后的新口径进行核算，与2022年同期数不可比。

a)After the adjustment of township administrative divisions and village level administrative systems in Sichuan Province, there have been significant changes in the urban-rural attributes and statistical standards in various regions. Therefore, after the sample rotation of household surveys in 2022, the income and expenditure data of residents in various municipalities (autonomous prefectures) in Sichuan in 2023 have been calculated according to the new standards after the changes in urban-rural attributes, which are incomparable to the same period in 2022.

9-12 社会保险情况
Social Insurance Indicators

单位：万人、亿元 (10 000 persons, 100 million yuan)

指标	Item	2017	2018	2019	2020	2021	2022	2023
参加城镇职工基本养老保险人数	Participants of Basic Endowment Insurance for Urban Workers	2335.07	2543.71	2700.32	2830.06	3178.54	3327.21	3426.29
参加养老保险职工人数	Number of Workers	1519.03	1662.09	1784.60	1882.57	2201.46	2320.65	2379.16
#执行企业养老保险制度职工人数	Number of Employees Under the Enterprise Endowment Insurance System	1328.06	1469.57	1587.98	1685.06	2000.80	2118.03	2177.39
参加养老保险离退休人数	Number of Retirees	816.04	881.62	915.72	947.49	977.08	1006.56	1047.13
#执行企业养老保险制度人数	Number of Persons Under the Enterprise Endowment Insurance System	720.07	779.68	809.53	839.30	866.85	893.73	929.94
纳入社区管理的人数	Community Management	694.20	753.65	782.38	777.64	792.95	849.46	889.46
企业退休人员社区管理服务率 (%)	Rate of Enterprise Retirees in Socialized Management (%)	96.5	96.7	96.7	92.7	91.5	95.1	95.7
城镇职工基本养老保险费征缴收入总额	Total Income of Basic Endowment Insurance for Urban Workers	2569.64	2081.00	1880.53	1612.68	2283.11	2526.47	2827.10
参加失业保险人数	Participants of Unemployment Insurance	776.68	875.10	953.54	1047.03	1128.93	1179.02	1191.32
城镇失业人员领取失业保险金人数	Number of Persons Drawing Unemployment Insurance	39.81	39.74	22.57	23.12	24.58	29.11	20.94
失业保险费征缴收入总额	Total Revenue of Unemployment Insurance	121.28	93.61	85.60	40.93	68.55	76.57	85.52
参加城镇职工基本医疗保险人数	Participants of Basic Medical Insurance for Urban Workers	1531.30	1667.67	1778.05	1875.93	1945.80	1967.20	1999.33
#退休人员	Retirees	458.34	481.41	498.70	511.68	510.38	532.78	559.10
参加补充医疗保险人数	Participants of Supplementary Medical Insurance	1362.70	1510.65	1736.36	1800.05	1904.27	1903.70	1956.07
列入公务员医疗补助范围人数	Persons in Civil Servant Medical Benefits Coverage	165.70	172.62	181.97	185.95	182.94	184.94	176.19
城镇职工基本医疗保险费征缴收入总额	Total Revenue of Basic Medical Insurance of Urban Workers	634.79	649.41	692.45	751.29	921.10	1047.22	1110.33
参加城乡居民基本医疗保险人数	Participants of Basic Medical Insurance for Urban and Rural Residents	6642.09	6969.48	6838.80	6715.75	6640.43	6426.69	6133.50
参加工伤保险人数	Participants of Work-related Injury Insurance	876.04	1012.59	1177.14	1320.08	1472.06	1544.80	1584.76
享受工伤保险待遇人数	Persons Enjoying Work-related Injury Insurance Treatment	7.69	8.18	8.61	7.86	8.92	8.83	9.96
工伤保险费征缴收入总额	Total Revenue of Work Injury Insurance	31.29	40.80	36.55	21.63	43.35	48.67	49.98
参加生育保险人数	Participants of Maternity Insurance	776.34	878.18	954.94	1129.05	1201.73	1216.76	1218.88
享受生育保险待遇人(次)数	Persons(Times) Enjoying Maternity Insurance Treatment	34.34	34.12	36.79	35.45	33.17	43.70	60.67
生育保险费征缴收入总额	Total Revenue of Maternity Insurance	20.44	31.96	36.69				

注：①社会保险和离退休资料由四川省人力资源和社会保障厅及四川省医疗保障局提供；②失业保险从2020年开始不包含失地农民数据；因生育保险和职工基本医保合并实施，故生育保险从2020年开始不再单独统计(以下有关表同)；③从2020年起，城镇职工基本医疗保险征缴收入总额含生育保险征缴收入总额。

a) Data of provincial social insurance and retirement are provided by Department of Human Resources and Social Security of Sichuan province and Sichuan provincial Medical Security Bureau; b)Unemployment insurance does not include the data of landless farmers from 2020; Since maternity insurance and basic medical insurance for employees are implemented together, maternity insurance will not be counted separately from 2020(the same as the following related tables); c) the total revenue of basic medical insurance of urban workers includes the total revenue of maternity Insurance from 2020.

9-13 各类社会保险参保人数
Number of Social Insurance Participants

(年末数)单位：万人　　(year-end)(10 000 persons)

年份 Year	城镇职工基本养老保险（未包括离退休人员） Basic Endowment Insurance for Urban Worker (excluding Retired and Resigned Persons)	失业保险 Unemployment Insurance	基本医疗保险 Basic Medical Insurance	#城乡居民医疗保险 Medical Insurance for Urban and Rural Residents	工伤保险 Work-related Injury Insurance	生育保险 Maternity Insurance
1995	294.5	365.0			196.5	99.8
2000	508.5	470.2			201.1	188.2
2005	556.0	358.3	649.6		285.3	215.7
2010	861.9	469.8	2063.1	1011.2	583.8	484.2
2011	998.8	544.6	2254.8	1079.3	650.8	601.7
2012	1073.7	585.5	2389.1	1143.0	689.4	654.4
2013	1124.1	613.5	2491.0	1204.0	690.1	689.1
2014	1191.6	635.8	2581.5	1247.1	709.7	730.4
2015	1250.1	661.0	2655.7	1272.1	753.2	670.3
2016	1379.8	702.0	5662.8	4217.2	799.1	713.1
2017	1519.0	776.7	8173.4	6642.1	876.0	776.3
2018	1662.1	875.1	8637.2	6969.5	1012.6	878.2
2019	1784.6	953.5	8616.9	6838.8	1177.1	954.9
2020	1882.6	1047.0	8591.7	6715.7	1320.1	1129.1
2021	2201.5	1128.9	8586.2	6640.4	1472.1	1201.7
2022	2320.7	1179.0	8393.9	6426.7	1544.8	1216.8
2023	2379.2	1191.3	8132.8	6133.5	1584.8	1218.9

注：2021年及以前年份，城镇职工基本养老保险参保人数实际口径为职工养老保险人数（未包括离退休人员）。
a)In 2021 and prior years, the number of Basic Endowment Insurance for Urban Worker is based on the number of Endowment Insurance for Urban Worker (excluding retirees).

9-14 各类社会保险基金征缴情况
Collection of Social Insurance Funds

单位：亿元、%　　(100 million yuan, %)

年份 Year	城镇职工基本养老保险 Basic Endowment Insurance for Urban Worker		失业保险 Unemployment Insurance	城镇职工基本医疗保险 Basic Medical Insurance of Urban Workers		工伤保险 Work-related Injury Insurance		生育保险 Maternity Insurance	
	保险费收入 Revenue of Insurance	征缴率 Rate of Collection	保险费收入 Revenue of Insurance	保险费收入 Revenue of Insurance	征缴率 Rate of Collection	保险费收入 Revenue of Insurance	征缴率 Rate of Collection	保险费收入 Revenue of Insurance	征缴率 Rate of Collection
1995	27.3	85.3	1.1				96.2		97.2
2000	61.5	92.8	5.5			1.8	56.7	1.0	66.7
2005	189.9	96.8	11.0	49.0	98.4	4.1	93.1	1.5	94.2
2010	670.9	97.9	40.0	182.5	97.4	12.1	96.2	4.9	97.8
2011	870.3	98.0	59.2	223.4	98.6	16.6	96.0	8.5	97.0
2012	901.4	98.0	68.2	258.8	98.8	21.2	95.8	11.1	97.0
2013	1101.4	98.2	77.7	305.7	99.2	25.4	97.2	13.4	98.8
2014	1217.7	97.6	100.7	363.8	98.7	28.1	96.5	15.8	98.4
2015	1251.9	97.1	94.9	414.1	98.5	29.3	93.6	17.1	97.4
2016	1902.1	93.9	84.7	479.7	98.1	27.0	93.7	15.7	97.6
2017	2569.6	98.1	121.3	634.8		31.3	95.7	20.4	98.8
2018	2081.0	98.5	93.6	649.4	99.3	40.8	96.0	32.0	99.0
2019	1880.5	98.4	85.6	692.5	99.5	36.5	96.5	36.7	99.0
2020	1612.7	73.6	40.9	751.3	99.2	21.6	46.4		
2021	2283.1	98.5	68.6	921.1	98.5	43.4	96.4		
2022	2526.5	96.9	76.6	1047.2	97.0	48.7	93.7		
2023	2827.1	97.0	85.5	1110.3	98.5	50.0	96.0		

注：养老保险参保人数，2003年及以前年份未包括机关事业单位数据；2020年各类社会保险因国家及我省减免政策，征缴率有一定幅度下降。工伤保险征缴率不包含项目参保收入。

a) The contributors of basic pension insurance exclude contributors of government agencies and institutions in 2003 and before; and in 2020, due to the national and provincial reduction and exemption policies, the collection rate of various social insurances will decrease to a certain extent. The collection rate of work-related injury insurance does not include project participation income.

9-15 各市(州)社会保险参保人数(2023年)
Number of Social Insurance Participants by Region(2023)

(年末数)单位：万人 (year-end)(10 000 persons)

市(州)	Region	城镇职工基本养老保险 Basic Endowment Insurance for Urban Workers	失业保险 Unemployment Insurance	基本医疗保险 Basic Medical Insurance	工伤保险 Work-related Injury Insurance	生育保险 Maternity Insurance
全省	**Sichuan**	**3426.29**	**1191.32**	**8132.84**	**1584.76**	**1218.88**
成都市	Chengdu	1433.33	675.21	1813.93	773.74	666.44
自贡市	Zigong	91.54	18.87	256.06	26.78	19.77
攀枝花市	Panzhihua	57.72	17.93	107.69	26.65	18.49
泸州市	Luzhou	126.73	36.83	439.24	56.28	37.94
德阳市	Deyang	148.17	46.09	333.69	65.46	47.63
绵阳市	Mianyang	179.18	53.01	454.49	64.40	54.67
广元市	Guangyuan	68.35	18.15	247.85	23.75	19.51
遂宁市	Suining	93.88	21.42	266.29	30.67	22.84
内江市	Neijiang	98.49	21.07	328.64	30.58	21.93
乐山市	Leshan	139.27	30.77	303.28	46.59	34.10
南充市	Nanchong	138.25	29.35	565.19	55.53	33.36
眉山市	Meishan	102.73	29.21	290.53	57.77	31.15
宜宾市	Yibin	128.40	40.13	463.72	77.92	46.49
广安市	Guangan	84.00	20.02	361.87	29.02	21.56
达州市	Dazhou	121.91	21.29	521.91	36.26	24.96
雅安市	Yaan	55.70	14.67	139.61	27.49	16.05
巴中市	Bazhong	59.02	14.48	293.11	18.45	14.39
资阳市	Ziyang	57.57	13.20	251.69	24.23	14.72
阿坝藏族羌族自治州	Aba	22.93	8.70	81.66	13.89	10.93
甘孜藏族自治州	Ganzi	19.90	8.76	102.28	20.46	11.39
凉山彝族自治州	Liangshan	67.74	26.99	473.78	45.72	30.18
省本级	Provincial level	131.48	25.18	36.34	33.13	20.39

9-16 各市(州)社会保险基金征缴情况(2023年)
Collection of Social Insurance Funds by Region(2023)

单位：亿元 (100 million yuan)

市(州)	Region	城镇职工养老保险 Basic Endowment Insurance for Urban Workers		失业保险 Unemployment Insurance	城镇职工基本医疗保险 Basic Medical Insurance of Urban Workers		工伤保险 Work-related Injury Insurance	
		保险费收入 Revenue of Insurance	征缴率(%) Rate of Collection(%)	保险费收入 Revenue of Insurance	保险费收入 Revenue of Insurance	征缴率(%) Rate of Collection(%)	保险费收入 Revenue of Insurance	征缴率(%) Rate of Collection(%)
全省	**Sichuan**	**2827.10**	**96.98**	**85.52**	**1110.33**	**98.45**	**49.98**	**95.96**
成都市	Chengdu	1250.97	97.77	46.72	580.21	98.26	15.32	96.95
自贡市	Zigong	51.52	95.71	1.38	22.09	98.10	1.16	95.88
攀枝花市	Panzhihua	48.92	96.54	1.49	24.03	98.95	1.82	97.51
泸州市	Luzhou	88.16	97.33	2.46	34.65	98.09	1.53	96.44
德阳市	Deyang	101.76	98.50	2.97	38.88	99.23	1.96	97.53
绵阳市	Mianyang	122.10	96.02	3.70	51.65	97.68	1.69	94.26
广元市	Guangyuan	49.95	96.04	1.32	16.88	99.50	1.24	95.46
遂宁市	Suining	54.58	96.65	1.35	19.20	98.91	0.95	95.38
内江市	Neijiang	56.95	94.11	1.46	25.01	99.19	1.73	87.45
乐山市	Leshan	92.74	97.64	2.03	27.79	99.17	2.50	96.05
南充市	Nanchong	89.51	93.80	2.01	33.49	96.95	1.88	91.37
眉山市	Meishan	66.85	98.08	1.81	22.67	99.70	1.45	97.37
宜宾市	Yibin	104.23	97.81	2.90	39.15	99.35	4.22	97.53
广安市	Guangan	57.06	97.20	1.39	15.90	99.42	1.27	97.85
达州市	Dazhou	72.13	84.82	1.52	22.92	98.53	2.10	87.56
雅安市	Yaan	38.80	97.76	0.97	14.21	99.27	1.21	96.59
巴中市	Bazhong	41.60	89.63	1.05	12.28	100.00	0.92	86.93
资阳市	Ziyang	36.71	95.80	0.93	16.74	99.12	0.59	94.22
阿坝藏族羌族自治州	Aba	27.87	99.10	0.85	13.03	100.00	0.74	98.77
甘孜藏族自治州	Ganzi	28.87	97.44	0.82	9.34	99.38	0.68	97.75
凉山彝族自治州	Liangshan	71.77	99.04	2.05	30.68	97.95	2.30	98.95
省本级	Provincial level	274.05	97.66	4.34	39.51	98.11	2.72	99.48

9-17 城市居民最低生活保障情况
Basic Statistics on Residents under Basic Provision Protection in Urban Area

单位：户、人、万元 (household, person, 10 000 yuan)

年份 Year	最低生活保障家庭数 Number of Households Receiving Minimum Living Allowances	最低生活保障人数 Number of Persons Receiving Minimum Living Allowances	#在职人员 Employed	#老年人 Elderly	城市低保资金 Funds for Urban Residents under Basic Provision Protection
2005	806737	1586126	11426	14744	112183
2010	1014429	1869694	25472	255385	403601
2011	1033800	1893114	13334	285339	455812
2012	1032332	1863842	15552	301762	428390
2013	1027660	1835734	17825	314598	507682
2014	989346	1734415	19440	325042	468792
2015	925095	1563548	16519	311675	490012
2016	819361	1344965	14622	301757	484439
2017	702040	1184095	13415	240296	431683
2018	568251	937070	11449	181309	387269
2019	466511	768376	8014	145757	307327
2020	429112	677479	4956	116075	313477
2021	387684	588657	596	101183	245657
2022	353953	521488	398	97650	241961
2023	348853	514327	552	106447	232394

9-18 农村居民最低生活保障和救济情况
Basic Statistics on Residents under Basic Provision Protection and Receiving Almsgiving in Rural Area

单位：户、人、万元 (household, person, 10 000 yuan)

年份 Year	最低生活保障家庭数 Number of Households Receiving Minimum Living Allowances	最低生活保障人数 Number of Persons Receiving Minimum Living Allowances	#老年人 Elderly	#未成年人 Minors	#残疾人 Disabled	农村特困人员救助供养人数 Number of Rural Poor Personnel Relief Support	农村低保资金 Funds for Rural Residents under Basic Provision Protection
2005	296176	647007					8035
2010	2005227	3944748	1609275	434813	339357	211323	310207
2011	2221734	4251001	1737689	464960	356790	234494	437368
2012	2360143	4344818	1825940	463760	361101	257064	411568
2013	2501780	4394553	1878508	479749	366885	510267	559692
2014	2513702	4253319	1861781	455977	361682	504771	531594
2015	2482609	4054741	1832063	410835	667113	494722	590045
2016	2243946	3566780	1646309	358976	592631	485843	705993
2017	2180895	3663099	1608418	407129	549868	459085	728896
2018	1968055	3399154	1467388	388574	489133	445371	748958
2019	1962933	3537479	1466388	481134	473344	437035	817362
2020	2089249	3732812	1527145	540560	502293	428030	1084342
2021	2073623	3595635	1485896	514842	564593	417791	977180
2022	2027404	3426310	1466825	475569	569548	404893	1049126
2023	2096645	3582205	1586563	489411	592581	400573	1108803

9−19 各市(州)城市居民最低生活保障和救济情况(2023年)
Basic Statistics on Residents under Basic Provision Protection and Receiving Almsgiving in Urban Area by Region(2023)

市(州)	Region	最低生活保障家庭数(户) Number of Households Receiving Minimum Living Allowances (household)	最低生活保障人数(人) Number of Persons Receiving Minimum Living Allowances (person)	#在职人员 Employed	#老年人 Elderly	#登记失业 Registered Unemployed	#无就业条件 Lack of Employment Conditions	城市低保资金(万元) Funds for Urban Residents under Basic Provision Protection (10 000 yuan)
全省	**Sichuan**	**348853**	**514327**	**552**	**106447**	**41264**	**224546**	**232394**
成都市	Chengdu	18077	21811	158	2549	2027	12839	21565
自贡市	Zigong	28826	40961	29	7055	1835	17628	17199
攀枝花市	Panzhihua	3908	5112	12	712	1174	2201	4695
泸州市	Luzhou	12012	16433	1	3784	400	8985	9003
德阳市	Deyang	14798	20920	18	5628	1327	10801	7796
绵阳市	Mianyang	20478	30749	18	6583	1619	7869	14875
广元市	Guangyuan	31056	55007	4	9450	5244	24986	15131
遂宁市	Suining	9652	12677	23	2981	429	6510	6042
内江市	Neijiang	16396	23200	110	3174	5860	8348	11177
乐山市	Leshan	13997	18001	10	3764	1664	9189	11048
南充市	Nanchong	56861	86587	16	24401	5645	30529	28937
眉山市	Meishan	6905	8720		2101	114	1349	3717
宜宾市	Yibin	13603	18380	33	4975	1034	8269	12343
广安市	Guangan	27731	44469	1	8030	4715	20394	16174
达州市	Dazhou	28862	38452	2	8986	442	23612	17723
雅安市	Yaan	2764	3437	13	827	168	1240	1698
巴中市	Bazhong	13085	22770		4481	3491	9079	8094
资阳市	Ziyang	4546	5749	7	1308	103	3028	2935
阿坝藏族羌族自治州	Aba	6270	9452	20	1808	799	2392	4746
甘孜藏族自治州	Ganzi	5213	7329	75	883	912	3243	3929
凉山彝族自治州	Liangshan	13813	24111	2	2967	2262	12055	13567

注：城乡居民低保和救济资料由四川省民政厅提供；城市低保资金全省合计中含省本级数据。

a) Data of urban and rural residents under basic provision protection and relief materials are provided by Sichuan Provincial Civil Affairs Department; Data of funds for urban residents under basic provision protection include provincial data.

9-20 各市(州)农村居民最低生活保障和救济情况(2023年)
Basic Statistics on Residents under Basic Provision Protection and Receiving Almsgiving in Rural Area by Region(2023)

市(州)	Region	最低生活保障家庭数(户) Number of Households Receiving Minimum Living Allowances (household)	最低生活保障人数(人) Number of Persons Receiving Minimum Living Allowances (person)				农村特困人员救助供养人数(人) Number of Rural Poor Personnel Relief Support (person)	农村低保资金(万元) Funds for Rural Residents under Basic Provision Protection (10 000 yuan)
				#老年人 Elderly	#未成年人 Minors	#残疾人 Disabled		
全省	**Sichuan**	**2096645**	**3582205**	**1586563**	**489411**	**592581**	**400573**	**1108803**
成都市	Chengdu	46296	72417	21113	9266	22718	29137	55742
自贡市	Zigong	81930	123713	61578	11330	21821	17908	31653
攀枝花市	Panzhihua	8053	16345	4982	3421	3197	2417	8626
泸州市	Luzhou	108216	190916	73437	34234	44166	25137	61095
德阳市	Deyang	69525	115502	64703	9061	25335	18384	27460
绵阳市	Mianyang	67692	103379	51829	8255	27416	21228	39640
广元市	Guangyuan	116997	188579	102564	12150	26737	10090	44813
遂宁市	Suining	80356	103012	55550	8059	29817	20347	33168
内江市	Neijiang	62184	101146	41277	13548	22258	31392	30951
乐山市	Leshan	52454	103022	35419	16080	24492	12503	40255
南充市	Nanchong	326731	508197	313803	32670	73525	48277	110893
眉山市	Meishan	68788	85538	43130	4896	13144	17536	27595
宜宾市	Yibin	68690	142391	47149	30373	32486	21695	58504
广安市	Guangan	108813	192426	89873	20524	33404	26084	44408
达州市	Dazhou	259211	356148	209013	25238	50826	34771	102508
雅安市	Yaan	25358	37108	13743	3927	9358	5191	13229
巴中市	Bazhong	151230	288370	154331	29123	48429	11847	61061
资阳市	Ziyang	86476	114985	60368	10583	28792	20499	41109
阿坝藏族羌族自治州	Aba	33090	66199	14478	9932	6734	5108	23375
甘孜藏族自治州	Ganzi	51900	146308	19035	41577	8065	7182	52156
凉山彝族自治州	Liangshan	222655	526504	109188	155164	39861	13840	200564

注：农村低保资金全省合计中含省本级数据。
a) Funds for rural residents under basic provision protection include provincial funds.

主要统计指标解释

城乡一体化住户调查 从2012年四季度起，国家统计局对分别进行的城乡住户调查实施了一体化改革，规范了城乡划分范围，统一了城乡居民收入指标名称、分类和统计标准，建立了城乡统一的一体化住户调查，并据此采集全国居民有关数据。

居民可支配收入 指居民可用于最终消费支出和储蓄的总和，即居民可用于自由支配的收入。既包括现金收入，也包括实物收入。按照收入的来源，可支配收入包含四项，分别为：工资性收入、经营净收入、财产净收入和转移净收入。

工资性收入 指就业人员通过各种途径得到的全部劳动报酬和各种福利，包括受雇于单位或个人、从事各种自由职业、兼职和零星劳动得到的全部劳动报酬和福利。

经营净收入 指住户或住户成员从事生产经营活动所获得的净收入，是全部经营收入中扣除经营费用、生产性固定资产折旧和生产税之后得到的净收入。计算公式为：

经营净收入=经营收入-经营费用-生产性固定资产折旧-生产税

财产净收入 指住户或住户成员将其所拥有的金融资产、住房等非金融资产和自然资源交由其他机构单位、住户或个人支配而获得的回报并扣除相关的费用之后得到的净收入。财产净收入包括利息净收入、红利收入、储蓄性保险净收益、转让承包土地经营权租金净收入、出租房屋净收入、出租其他资产净收入和自有住房折算净租金等。财产净收入不包括转让资产所有权的溢价所得。

转移净收入 计算公式为：转移净收入=转移性收入-转移性支出

转移性收入 指国家、单位、社会团体对住户的各种经常性转移支付和住户之间的经常性收入转移。包括养老金或退休金、社会救济和补助、政策性生产补贴、政策性生活补贴、经常性捐赠和赔偿、报销医疗费、住户之间的赡养收入，本住户非常住成员寄回带回的收入等。转移性收入不包括住户之间的实物馈赠。

转移性支出 指调查户对国家、单位、住户或个人的经常性或义务性转移支付。包括缴纳的税款、各项社会保障支出、赡养支出、经常性捐赠和赔偿支出以及其他经常转移支出等。

居民消费支出 指居民用于满足家庭日常生活消费需要的全部支出，既包括现金消费支出，也包括实物消费支出。消费支出可划分为食品烟酒、衣着、居住、生活用品及服务、交通通信、教育文化娱乐、医疗保健以及其他用品及服务八大类。

食品烟酒支出 指用于各种食品和烟草、酒类的支出。

衣着支出 指与居民穿着有关的支出，包括服装、服装材料、鞋类、其他衣类及配件、衣着相关加工服务的支出。

居住支出 指与居住有关的支出，包括房租、水、电、燃料、物业管理等方面的支出，也包括自有住房折算租金。

生活用品及服务支出 指家庭及个人的各类生活品及家庭服务。包括家具及室内装饰品、家用器具、家用纺织品、家庭日用杂品、个人用品和家庭服务。

交通通信支出 指用于交通和通信工具及相关的各种服务费、维修费和车辆保险等支出。

教育文化娱乐支出 指用于教育、文化和娱乐方面的支出。

医疗保健支出 指用于医疗和保健的药品、用品和服务的总费用。包括医疗器具及药品，以及医疗服务。

其他用品及服务支出 指无法直接归入上述各类支出的其他用品与服务支出。

恩格尔系数 指食物支出金额占总支出金额的比重。

$$\text{恩格尔系数}=\frac{\text{食物支出金额}}{\text{总支出金额}}\times 100\%$$

城镇职工基本养老保险

1．参保职工人数 指报告期末参加城镇职工基本养老保险并在社保经办机构已建立缴费记录档案的职工人数，包括中断缴费但未终止养老保险关系的职工人数，不包括只登记未建立缴费记录档案的人数。

2．离退休人员人数 指报告期末参加城镇职工基本养老保险并由养老保险基金支付养老金的离休、退休和退职人员的人数。

3．基金收入 指根据国家有关规定，由纳入职工基本养老保险范围的缴费单位和个人按国家规定的缴费基数和缴费比例缴纳的养老保险费，以及通过其他方式取得的形成基金来源的收入。包括单位和职工个人缴纳的基本养老保险费、基本养老保险基金利息收入、委托投资收益、上级补助收入、下级上解收入、转移收入、财政补贴和其他收入。

基本医疗保险

1．参保人数 指报告期末参加职工基本医疗保险和城乡居民基本医疗保险人员的合计。

2．基金收入（含生育保险） 基本医疗保险基金收入包括职工基本医疗保险基金收入（含生育保险）和城乡居民基本医疗保险基金收入。职工基本医疗保险基金收入（含生育保险）包括基本医疗保险待遇收入（含生育保险）、利息收入、财政补贴收入、其他收入、待转保险费收入、待转利息收入、转移收入。城乡居民基本医疗保险基金收入包括基本医疗保险费收入、利息收入、财政补贴收入、其他收入。

失业保险

1．参保人数 指报告期末城镇企业、事业单位职工参加失业保险的人数及按地方规定参加失业保险的其他人员人数之和，不包括领取失业保险金人数。

2．基金收入　指报告期内筹集的失业保险基金的总额，包括失业保险费收入、利息收入、财政补贴收入、其他收入、转移收入。

工伤保险

1．参保人数　指报告期末参加工伤保险的职工人数和有雇工的个体工商户的雇工数。

2．享受工伤保险待遇人数　指年报告期内由工伤基金支付，享受工伤医疗、伤残、工亡待遇的总人数。不进行重复计算。

3．基金收入　指根据国家有关规定，由参加工伤保险的单位按国家规定的缴费基数和缴费比例缴纳及难以直接按照工资总额计算缴纳工伤保险费的部分行业企业按规定方式缴纳的工伤保险费，以及依法通过其他形式取得的形成基金来源的款项。包括：工伤保险费收入、利息收入、上级补助收入、下级上解收入、其他收入。

Explanatory Notes on Main Statistical Indicators

Integrated Urban and Rural Household Survey Data from 1978 to 2012 are estimated based on the historical data of Urban Household Survey and Rural Household Survey according to the comparable definition and coverage of main income and consumption indicators of Household Survey on Income and Expenditure and Living Conditions.

Disposable Income of Residents refers to the income of residents for purpose of final expenditure and savings. It includes income both in cash and in kind. By sources of income, disposable income includes four categories: income from wages and salaries, net business income, net income from properties and net income from transfer.

Income from Wages and Salaries refers to remuneration and benefits of all kinds of employed persons, including those employed by other units or individuals, freelance workers, part-time jobs, and sporadic workers.

Net Business Income refers to net income earned by households and their members engaged in production and business activities. It refers to the net income of operating revenue minus operating costs, depreciation of productive fixed assets, and production tax. The formula is:

Net business income = operating revenue-operating costs -depreciation of productive fixed assets-production tax

Net Income from Properties refers to the net income received as returns by households or members through lending of their financial assets, non-financial assets such as housing, to other institutions, households or individuals, minus relevant costs. Net income from properties includes net income of interest, bonus income, net income of saving insurance, net income from transferring management right of contract land, income from lending of housing, income from lending other assets, net converted rents of self-owned housing. Net income from properties do not include premium of transferring ownership of assets.

Net Income from Transfer The formula is:

Net income from transfer = income from transfer - expenditure from transfer

Income from Transfer refers to the regular transfer received from governments, institutions, social organizations to households and between households. It includes old-age and retirement pension, regular donation and compensation, reimbursement of medical fees, supporting income between households, income from non-resident members of households, etc. Income from transfer do not include gifts in kinds between households.

Expenditure from Transfer refers to regular or obligatory transfer paid to government, institutions, households or individuals. It includes tax payment, expenditure on all kinds of social security, supporting expenditure, regular donation, compensation payment and other regular transfer expenditure.

Consumption Expenditure of Residents refers to all expenditure of residents for living expenditure to satisfy family daily living. It includes expenditure in cash and in kind. It includes eight categories: food, tobacco and liquor; clothing and footwear; housing; household equipment, furnishings and services; transport and communications; education, culture and recreation; health care and medical services, and miscellaneous goods and services.

Food, Tobacco and Liquor Expenditure refers to expenditure for food, tobacco and liquor of all kinds.

Clothing Expenditure refers to expenditure related to clothing, including clothes, clothing materials, footwear, other clothing and accessories, processing services related to clothing.

Residence Expenditure refers to expenditure related to housing, including rents, water, electricity, fuel, property management, as well as imputed rent on owner-occupied dwellings.

Household Facilities, Articles and Services Expenditure refers to expenditure of households and individuals on equipment, furnishings and articles for living purpose and on household services. It includes furniture and interior decoration, home appliances, home textiles, household miscellaneous daily articles, personal articles, and household services.

Transport and Communications Expenditure refers to expenditure on transport and communication and related services, maintenance and repairs, and vehicle insurance.

Education, Cultural and Recreational Activities Expenditure refers to expenditure on educational, cultural and recreational activities.

Health Care and Medical Services Expenditure refers to expenditure on drugs, supplies and services of medical and health care. It includes medical appliances and drugs, and medical services.

Miscellaneous Goods and Services Expenditure refers to expenditure on all other articles and services that can not classified into the above categories.

Engel Coefficient refers to the percentage of expenditure on food to the total consumption, using the following formula:

$$\text{Engel Coefficient} = \frac{\text{Expenditure on Food}}{\text{Total Consumption Expenditure}} \times 100\%$$

Basic Endowment Insurance for Urban Workers

1.Number of workers covered refers to staff and workers participating in the basic endowment insurance for urban workers at the end of the reference period, who have already had payment records in social security management agencies, including those who have interrupt payment without terminating the insurance programme. Those who have registered in the programme but with no payment records are not included.

2.Number of retirees covered refers to the number of retirees participating in the basic endowment insurance for

urban workers and the pension paid by the pension insurance fund by the end of the reference period.

3. Revenue refers to payments made by employers and employees participating in the basic endowment insurance for urban workers in accordance with the basis and proportion stipulated in state regulations, and income from other sources that become the source of endowment insurance fund, including the premium paid by employers and staff and workers, interest income, entrusted investment income, subsidies from higher level agencies, income as transfer from subordinate agencies, transferred income, government financial subsidies and other income.

Basic Medical Insurance

1.Participants refers to the total number of people who participate in the basic medical insurance for workers and basic medical insurance for urban and rural residents at the end of the reference period.

2.Revenue (birth insurance included) refers to basic medical insurance fund income for employees (including birth insurance) and basic medical insurance fund income for urban and rural residents. The basic medical insurance fund income of employees (including birth insurance) includes basic medical insurance premium income (including birth insurance), interest income, financial subsidy income, other income, insurance premium income to be transferred, interest income to be transferred and transfer income.

Unemployment Insurance

1.Participants refers to the number of staff and workers in urban enterprises or institutions who have participated in the unemployment insurance, and other people who have participated according to local regulations at the end of the reference period, excluding the number of people receiving unemployment insurance benefits.

2.Revenue refers to the total unemployment insurance funds raised in the reference period, including unemployment insurance premium, interest income, financial subsidies, other revenue, and transferred revenue.

Work-related Injury Insurance

1.Participants refers to staff and workers who have participated in the work-related injury insurance and employees who work as self-employed and have participated in the work-related injury insurance at the end of the reference period.

2.Number of beneficiaries refers to number of people who are paid by the work-related injury fund and enjoy the medical treatment, disability and death benefits during the annual report period. No double calculation is performed.

3.Revenue refers to payments made by employers participating in the work-related injury insurance programme in accordance with the basis and proportion stipulated in state regulations, and payment by enterprises of some industries where it is difficult to estimate the injury insurance premium directly according to the total wage bill in accordance with stipulated way, and revenue from other sources according to law that become source of work-related injury insurance fund, including revenue of injury insurance, interest income, subsidies from higher level agencies, revenue as transfer from subordinate agencies, and other revenues.

10 城市发展
Chapter 10 Urban Development

SICHUAN STATISTICAL YEARBOOK

10-1 城市设施水平(2023年)
Level of Public Facilities in Cities(2023)

城市	City	供水普及率(%) Water Coverage Rate (%)	燃气普及率(%) Gas Coverage Rate (%)	人均城市道路面积(平方米) Per Capita Area of Roads (sq.m)	污水处理率(%) Wastewater Treatment Rate (%)	人均公园绿地面积(平方米) Per Capita Public Recreational Green Space (sq.m)	建成区绿化覆盖率(%) Green Covered Area as Percentage of Built Districts (%)	生活垃圾处理率(%) Household Garbage Treatment Rate (%)
全省	**Sichuan**	**99.01**	**97.96**	**19.88**	**96.73**	**14.59**	**44.16**	**100.00**
成都市	Chengdu	98.87	98.32	17.80	95.80	11.76	45.11	100.00
简阳市	Jianyang	100.00	100.00	22.43	95.11	16.19	44.60	100.00
都江堰市	Dujiangyan	98.90	97.54	22.65	94.05	16.25	46.55	100.00
彭州市	Pengzhou	100.00	100.00	15.93	97.81	15.36	45.77	100.00
邛崃市	Qionglai	100.00	94.72	23.58	98.00	26.50	46.59	100.00
崇州市	Chongzhou	100.00	99.67	25.34	95.40	13.50	46.06	100.00
自贡市	Zigong	96.01	98.37	23.09	97.01	18.44	44.81	100.00
攀枝花市	Panzhihua	100.00	90.96	27.58	98.28	20.99	43.91	100.00
泸州市	Luzhou	98.47	98.08	22.30	96.82	14.96	43.93	100.00
德阳市	Deyang	99.89	99.98	26.41	98.14	16.33	45.62	100.00
广汉市	Guanghan	100.00	100.00	22.06	98.21	14.65	49.96	100.00
什邡市	Shifang	99.40	100.00	19.96	97.02	16.38	44.21	100.00
绵竹市	Mianzhu	99.87	99.80	27.03	96.15	15.12	41.24	100.00
绵阳市	Mianyang	99.89	99.57	21.11	98.11	14.75	42.49	100.00
江油市	Jiangyou	100.00	100.00	21.79	96.93	16.58	45.01	100.00
广元市	Guangyuan	99.98	99.91	19.53	97.58	18.00	42.15	100.00
遂宁市	Suining	100.00	99.86	27.13	98.23	14.68	43.34	100.00
射洪市	Shehong	100.00	99.64	17.49	98.08	12.41	44.37	100.00
内江市	Neijiang	100.00	100.00	21.17	97.52	17.74	40.17	100.00
隆昌市	Longchang	100.00	100.00	23.80	99.17	13.90	43.72	100.00
乐山市	Leshan	99.38	97.80	20.30	96.87	18.08	43.45	100.00
峨眉山市	Emeishan	98.75	99.10	29.18	95.37	18.18	43.90	100.00
南充市	Nanchong	100.00	99.36	19.23	98.12	17.68	47.42	100.00
阆中市	Langzhong	100.00	100.00	17.93	95.19	17.03	46.05	100.00
眉山市	Meishan	99.97	98.22	20.23	98.24	15.63	45.18	100.00
宜宾市	Yibin	98.05	98.67	17.71	97.11	22.05	41.69	100.00
广安市	Guangan	97.55	97.22	25.34	99.63	17.21	42.43	100.00
华蓥市	Huaying	95.89	99.14	21.02	99.52	15.17	39.23	100.00
达州市	Dazhou	99.56	99.90	15.41	95.67	16.62	44.12	100.00
万源市	Wanyuan	99.88	99.88	9.79	99.00	23.56	44.30	100.00
雅安市	Yaan	98.57	98.22	44.30	98.42	17.60	40.35	100.00
巴中市	Bazhong	100.00	100.00	21.56	98.18	19.39	45.01	100.00
资阳市	Ziyang	100.00	100.00	27.15	98.03	15.80	43.03	100.00
马尔康市	Maerkang	99.70	86.36	11.98	99.85	13.64	39.01	100.00
康定市	Kangding	100.00	89.68	16.99	98.15	19.78	42.59	100.00
会理市	Huili	99.86	74.48	25.10	83.60	18.74	39.05	100.00
西昌市	Xichang	95.98	68.50	14.73	95.08	13.64	43.93	100.00

10-2 城市供水情况(2023年)
Basic Statistics on Water Supply in Cities(2023)

城市	City	供水综合生产能力(万立方米/日) Production Capacity of Tap Water Supply (10 000 cu.m / day)	供水管道长度(公里) Length of Water Supply Pipelines (km)	供水总量(万立方米) Total Volume of Water Supply (10 000 cu.m)	#居民家庭用水 Water for Residential Use	用水人口(万人) Number of Residents with Access to Tap Water (10 000 persons)	人均日生活用水量(升) Per Capita Daily Consumption of Tap Water for Residential Use (liter)
全省	**Sichuan**	**1357.11**	**57125.92**	**355124.66**	**180178.45**	**3018.96**	**211.64**
成都市	Chengdu	575.26	22574.17	174539.38	84991.29	1415.27	233.61
简阳市	Jianyang	16.00	330.01	2836.84	1443.85	31.34	143.79
都江堰市	Dujiangyan	23.90	516.89	4001.33	1607.18	26.16	198.47
彭州市	Pengzhou	18.00	1103.45	2481.00	1205.00	27.36	148.76
邛崃市	Qionglai	10.00	336.07	2223.59	882.09	24.45	113.08
崇州市	Chongzhou	8.00	360.00	2395.00	1096.00	18.10	222.96
自贡市	Zigong	39.20	4572.02	7579.64	4565.99	99.08	126.26
攀枝花市	Panzhihua	49.90	1646.33	10599.18	2993.28	49.13	262.26
泸州市	Luzhou	59.25	3614.85	12663.99	7541.10	118.18	207.26
德阳市	Deyang	70.75	1779.49	16483.62	7796.77	124.63	198.87
广汉市	Guanghan	10.00	465.96	3108.88	1763.35	27.47	220.60
什邡市	Shifang	8.00	425.00	2783.10	988.08	16.43	219.99
绵竹市	Mianzhu	7.50	148.30	2400.60	763.70	15.01	171.76
绵阳市	Mianyang	82.10	6328.48	20273.74	11381.57	177.27	214.54
江油市	Jiangyou	16.00	990.01	3356.66	1971.21	30.03	183.68
广元市	Guangyuan	24.50	932.33	5768.48	3224.36	55.94	172.39
遂宁市	Suining	58.60	1574.65	11596.97	5300.03	91.77	194.65
射洪市	Shehong	6.00	210.00	1920.22	1314.07	30.23	128.65
内江市	Neijiang	28.83	1822.49	9318.59	5467.70	85.00	204.23
隆昌市	Longchang	7.20	804.02	2511.30	1327.85	20.02	181.72
乐山市	Leshan	49.68	2822.68	12967.19	6529.67	96.12	206.00
峨眉山市	Emeishan	13.68	263.80	3126.00	1622.00	19.72	297.66
南充市	Nanchong	69.50	1509.00	18743.73	10553.08	156.37	209.74
阆中市	Langzhong	14.50	329.00	3672.48	1736.95	28.37	175.66
眉山市	Meishan	35.50	902.61	7361.82	4147.02	60.64	228.66
宜宾市	Yibin	65.00	1445.38	11722.08	5691.39	119.98	161.79
广安市	Guangan	23.90	1138.00	5685.90	3332.32	58.94	200.68
华蓥市	Huaying	2.90	301.00	1005.95	629.38	11.20	163.09
达州市	Dazhou	34.00	1175.21	7829.86	4145.00	120.55	104.37
万源市	Wanyuan	4.00	138.21	760.00	515.00	8.00	181.51
雅安市	Yaan	20.50	699.55	4547.20	1324.00	25.54	201.83
巴中市	Bazhong	17.94	668.00	5371.00	4377.00	58.32	225.84
资阳市	Ziyang	19.00	691.40	4344.71	2245.38	38.43	200.42
马尔康市	Maerkang	2.60	58.00	422.00	280.00	3.00	522.13
康定市	Kangding	1.30	117.75	362.00	276.00	3.60	223.48
会理市	Huili	4.80	289.79	622.68	380.50	7.20	163.81
西昌市	Xichang	25.00	763.74	6320.90	3635.00	54.00	199.04

10-3 城市燃气情况(2023年)
Basic Statistics on Gas Supply in Cities(2023)

城市	City	天然气销售量(万立方米) Total Volume of Gas Sales (10 000 cu.m)	#居民家庭 Volume of Residential Use	天然气用气人口(万人) Population with Access to Gas (10 000 persons)	液化石油气销售量(吨) Total Volume of LPG Sales (tons)	#居民家庭 Volume of Residential Use	液化石油气用气人口(万人) Population with Access to LPG (10 000 persons)
全省	**Sichuan**	**1061339.77**	**486628.68**	**2873.50**	**220641.98**	**90771.79**	**99.54**
成都市	Chengdu	488541.70	243309.96	1363.93	153586.16	55626.84	45.34
简阳市	Jianyang	9313.22	4252.66	32.99	671.00	466.00	0.24
都江堰市	Dujiangyan	9347.02	4653.66	25.44	245.87	102.03	0.36
彭州市	Pengzhou	9511.00	8422.00	24.26	960.00	890.00	3.20
邛崃市	Qionglai	9683.58	5057.27	22.74	924.00	389.00	0.42
崇州市	Chongzhou	20161.95	6613.39	16.60	6685.48	2082.25	1.44
自贡市	Zigong	27623.23	20993.13	101.22	1300.00	1300.00	0.30
攀枝花市	Panzhihua	18237.56	1573.46	23.88	2125.14	1481.98	3.57
泸州市	Luzhou	59956.60	18716.00	115.61	966.50	893.70	2.11
德阳市	Deyang	94442.70	24624.89	118.98	10842.56	3977.91	5.76
广汉市	Guanghan	16032.00	4375.97	25.34	6124.30	1666.34	2.13
什邡市	Shifang	11804.00	5901.00	15.53	563.00	489.00	1.00
绵竹市	Mianzhu	13486.00	4813.00	14.84	720.00	680.00	0.16
绵阳市	Mianyang	88731.52	33763.93	175.25	3648.97	2828.97	1.44
江油市	Jiangyou	12367.30	8392.30	29.76	970.00	663.00	0.27
广元市	Guangyuan	18782.48	7514.96	55.09	746.70	687.00	0.81
遂宁市	Suining	50720.51	13609.42	91.22	880.00	67.00	0.42
射洪市	Shehong	5898.00	5310.00	30.12			
内江市	Neijiang	20368.66	10146.17	84.45	9354.43	1098.68	0.55
隆昌市	Longchang	3485.04	2078.17	19.72	207.07	44.83	0.30
乐山市	Leshan	34414.16	15483.39	93.09	6869.26	2496.98	1.50
峨眉山市	Emeishan	6604.58	3982.65	19.64	1663.00	98.56	0.15
南充市	Nanchong	37176.65	24593.98	153.00	5950.00	4250.00	2.37
阆中市	Langzhong	5842.20	5257.98	28.00	1150.00	600.00	0.37
眉山市	Meishan	16360.56	8232.10	59.10	240.23	77.00	0.48
宜宾市	Yibin	39761.05	18180.37	118.15	3673.05	3170.05	2.59
广安市	Guangan	13185.90	10977.39	57.94	1354.32	1016.08	0.80
华蓥市	Huaying	2549.00	1850.00	11.23	851.68	533.44	0.35
达州市	Dazhou	15683.22	12483.79	119.86	1180.30	1180.30	1.10
万源市	Wanyuan	1132.87	877.29	7.00	670.00	670.00	1.00
雅安市	Yaan	7886.41	6620.92	25.24	2053.41	881.00	0.21
巴中市	Bazhong	12983.32	9581.53	56.34	1975.00	1975.00	1.98
资阳市	Ziyang	13490.22	4783.26	36.73	307.00	132.00	1.70
马尔康市	Maerkang	87.00	83.00	1.30	710.00	710.00	1.55
康定市	Kangding	30.00	26.30	0.57	1405.00	1276.30	3.60
会理市	Huili	102.48	79.73	3.42	820.95	505.00	1.95
西昌市	Xichang	2773.84	1251.00	19.13	10653.00	5140.00	19.41

10-4 城市道路和桥梁情况(2023年)
Basic Statistics on City Roads and Bridges(2023)

城市	City	道路长度(公里) Length of Paved Roads (km)	#建成区 Built Districts	道路面积(万平方米) Area of Paved Roads (10 000 sq.m)	#人行道面积 Area of Sidewalk	桥梁数(座) Number of Bridges (unit)	道路照明灯盏数(盏) Number of lamps for Road Lighting (unit)
全省	**Sichuan**	**30358.50**	**27959.83**	**60684.00**	**15305.83**	**4373**	**2212567**
成都市	Chengdu	12098.01	10599.17	25507.88	5839.18	2631	698395
简阳市	Jianyang	364.85	343.35	745.37	247.65	32	25326
都江堰市	Dujiangyan	326.81	326.81	599.17	210.17	105	28654
彭州市	Pengzhou	238.47	238.47	437.42	142.01	8	14354
邛崃市	Qionglai	218.15	218.15	576.52	218.81	4	23083
崇州市	Chongzhou	221.75	221.75	458.72	164.64	9	72531
自贡市	Zigong	1703.93	1532.44	2382.58	378.11	139	59076
攀枝花市	Panzhihua	1018.80	939.39	1355.00	358.96	106	40008
泸州市	Luzhou	1267.81	1267.81	2676.52	792.86	97	113674
德阳市	Deyang	1395.04	1315.31	3294.94	913.79	130	161078
广汉市	Guanghan	296.11	296.11	606.11	146.54	19	25490
什邡市	Shifang	130.36	130.36	329.88	84.05	36	17699
绵竹市	Mianzhu	183.59	118.00	406.20	171.20	22	25920
绵阳市	Mianyang	1760.29	1760.29	3746.63	1120.76	227	186908
江油市	Jiangyou	253.00	253.00	654.26	287.24	28	33443
广元市	Guangyuan	599.92	599.92	1092.73	323.26	192	48188
遂宁市	Suining	1056.53	959.69	2489.88	517.10	121	54115
射洪市	Shehong	270.80	202.30	528.65	93.61	19	14785
内江市	Neijiang	969.54	961.82	1799.14	525.90	64	80478
隆昌市	Longchang	231.20	231.20	476.47	131.49	23	4997
乐山市	Leshan	1007.87	923.55	1963.22	433.05	101	109292
峨眉山市	Emeishan	186.20	185.00	582.72	162.42	21	37240
南充市	Nanchong	1317.80	1296.80	3007.73	909.96	90	96413
阆中市	Langzhong	218.80	197.80	508.73	157.96	25	28563
眉山市	Meishan	589.97	575.17	1226.85	285.51	65	101254
宜宾市	Yibin	1288.60	1243.98	2166.68	677.23	89	106839
广安市	Guangan	758.47	695.04	1530.97	442.60	41	45852
华蓥市	Huaying	144.06	142.53	245.54	52.33	22	10921
达州市	Dazhou	1167.19	1126.45	1866.40	624.84	45	52630
万源市	Wanyuan	73.17	73.17	78.40	33.10	8	4020
雅安市	Yaan	462.95	432.51	1147.91	284.85	62	42305
巴中市	Bazhong	721.33	680.80	1257.48	345.49	39	21281
资阳市	Ziyang	551.79	469.53	1043.20	275.40	74	40613
马尔康市	Maerkang	39.80	30.50	39.52	8.12	19	1050
康定市	Kangding	98.60	68.10	79.00	29.50	16	2180
会理市	Huili	99.00	96.30	180.95	50.88	16	9958
西昌市	Xichang	385.26	385.26	828.79	168.48	9	140980

10-5 城市绿地和园林情况(2023年)
Basic Statistics on Parks and Green Areas in Cities(2023)

城市	City	绿化覆盖面积(公顷) Areas Covered by Green Land (hectare)	#建成区 Built Districts	绿地面积(公顷) Green Area (hectare)	#建成区 Built Districts	公园绿地面积(公顷) Public Green Area (hectare)	公园个数(个) Number of Parks (unit)	公园面积(公顷) Area of Parks (hectare)
全省	**Sichuan**	**164524.76**	**150057.64**	**145164.96**	**133083.44**	**44545.55**	**1064**	**28176.16**
成都市	Chengdu	56083.23	54985.11	48354.54	47382.60	16855.27	274	7895.53
简阳市	Jianyang	2801.26	1895.50	2325.51	1530.10	538.03	16	734.48
都江堰市	Dujiangyan	1888.53	1888.53	1689.80	1689.80	429.70	4	126.30
彭州市	Pengzhou	1347.39	1347.39	1140.39	1140.39	421.84	8	114.79
邛崃市	Qionglai	1293.37	1101.01	1187.37	1010.84	648.01	13	639.00
崇州市	Chongzhou	1074.57	1074.57	993.44	993.44	244.39	8	230.42
自贡市	Zigong	6042.99	5914.99	5297.00	5189.00	1902.59	24	657.54
攀枝花市	Panzhihua	3682.13	3682.13	3451.06	3451.06	1031.01	24	819.93
泸州市	Luzhou	8281.48	7649.48	7852.93	6606.82	1794.97	47	1001.16
德阳市	Deyang	8053.90	8041.10	6848.41	6843.21	2036.94	58	795.94
广汉市	Guanghan	2115.21	2113.31	1692.85	1687.85	402.34	9	116.00
什邡市	Shifang	803.74	803.74	729.75	729.75	270.79	5	66.26
绵竹市	Mianzhu	778.00	767.10	707.81	707.61	227.20	7	39.10
绵阳市	Mianyang	9806.62	9796.02	8963.50	8911.37	2617.84	29	1645.47
江油市	Jiangyou	1585.96	1575.36	1395.33	1343.20	497.80	6	191.00
广元市	Guangyuan	4339.42	3049.67	4142.15	2842.15	1006.98	37	821.91
遂宁市	Suining	8085.12	5325.33	7677.00	4911.11	1346.79	48	1119.45
射洪市	Shehong	1369.33	1369.33	1229.27	1229.27	375.25	10	329.54
内江市	Neijiang	5914.29	5213.77	4911.19	4772.34	1507.78	41	830.49
隆昌市	Longchang	1268.11	1149.90	1095.91	1018.41	278.28	9	75.20
乐山市	Leshan	9374.66	4601.52	8588.29	4243.71	1748.75	57	1236.03
峨眉山市	Emeishan	1101.00	1101.00	1019.00	1019.00	363.00	14	210.00
南充市	Nanchong	11115.00	9916.00	8941.00	8537.00	2764.00	37	2632.00
阆中市	Langzhong	1860.00	1569.00	1690.00	1427.00	483.00	9	355.00
眉山市	Meishan	3474.27	3227.74	3059.09	2835.83	948.08	24	521.79
宜宾市	Yibin	8022.63	7906.63	7169.68	7091.59	2698.37	103	1725.27
广安市	Guangan	3839.79	3753.98	3430.89	3418.33	1039.87	62	1050.96
华蓥市	Huaying	651.80	635.94	611.01	598.45	177.13	8	211.40
达州市	Dazhou	6307.31	6206.31	6194.40	5948.19	2012.70	77	2344.41
万源市	Wanyuan	720.31	720.31	660.40	660.40	188.70	3	604.41
雅安市	Yaan	3099.62	2168.75	2151.48	2017.02	456.10	36	670.67
巴中市	Bazhong	2907.19	2907.19	2815.26	2815.26	1130.89	24	1110.82
资阳市	Ziyang	2375.00	2375.00	2229.76	2229.76	607.14	13	430.79
马尔康市	Maerkang	393.20	205.20	199.00	199.00	45.00	2	44.00
康定市	Kangding	230.01	230.01	203.00	203.00	92.00	4	18.00
会理市	Huili	533.00	533.00	478.29	478.29	135.11	3	47.00
西昌市	Xichang	2563.90	2368.71	2207.04	2156.80	767.37	40	757.00

10-6 城市排水和污水处理情况(2023年)
Basic Statistics on City Drainage and Sewage Treatment(2023)

城市	City	排水管道长度(公里) Length of Drain Pipes (km)	#污水管道 Wastewater Pipes	#雨水管道 Rainwater Pipes	污水排放量(万立方米) Volume of Sewage Discharged (10 000 cu.m)	污水处理厂(座) Wastewater Treatment Plants (unit)	污水处理厂处理量(万立方米) Volume of Wastewater Treatment Plants (10 000 cu.m)
全省	**Sichuan**	**51451.46**	**24261.70**	**24602.18**	**326794.73**	**188**	**303350.48**
成都市	Chengdu	21838.47	10261.40	11333.04	165280.95	69	149300.29
简阳市	Jianyang	552.00	237.00	246.00	2497.37	2	2375.18
都江堰市	Dujiangyan	572.40	238.95	314.20	4760.20	2	4476.98
彭州市	Pengzhou	512.56	218.30	294.26	2516.00	2	2461.00
邛崃市	Qionglai	400.00	200.00	180.00	2231.61	4	2186.98
崇州市	Chongzhou	301.06	153.36	136.51	1680.58	1	1603.28
自贡市	Zigong	1978.40	515.99	1043.34	7268.00	6	6788.47
攀枝花市	Panzhihua	1196.54	868.05	287.31	7868.29	9	4945.48
泸州市	Luzhou	2048.13	1078.60	967.30	10480.19	5	10076.05
德阳市	Deyang	3047.15	1318.30	1665.18	16619.39	9	16233.19
广汉市	Guanghan	565.60	278.45	270.35	3046.12	2	2991.50
什邡市	Shifang	367.07	149.44	215.29	2257.14	1	2189.99
绵竹市	Mianzhu	495.00	250.00	215.00	1610.34	1	1548.35
绵阳市	Mianyang	3655.79	1774.56	1881.23	21600.53	11	21192.61
江油市	Jiangyou	491.32	245.66	245.66	3934.77	2	3814.00
广元市	Guangyuan	1082.32	617.58	428.74	6015.42	4	5870.11
遂宁市	Suining	1967.36	1047.89	858.17	12155.16	8	11439.94
射洪市	Shehong	497.65	235.27	234.53	2976.48	2	2919.33
内江市	Neijiang	1681.24	691.61	655.66	8467.70	9	8252.30
隆昌市	Longchang	266.24	78.73	100.69	1986.27	1	1964.42
乐山市	Leshan	1547.58	766.54	638.55	9315.43	8	9023.66
峨眉山市	Emeishan	410.00	330.00	78.00	3014.54	1	2874.97
南充市	Nanchong	2418.00	1198.00	1073.00	17053.00	9	16733.16
阆中市	Langzhong	438.00	180.00	153.00	3492.00	2	3324.00
眉山市	Meishan	953.42	336.21	513.21	6554.76	5	6439.35
宜宾市	Yibin	1875.84	863.44	750.54	9134.88	9	8870.73
广安市	Guangan	1167.32	677.50	460.82	5412.74	8	5392.91
华蓥市	Huaying	322.90	170.00	136.40	1211.32	3	1205.49
达州市	Dazhou	1655.01	796.55	572.00	6101.58	2	5837.64
万源市	Wanyuan	182.11	41.55	57.00	704.68	1	697.64
雅安市	Yaan	641.00	288.55	258.45	2912.00	3	2866.00
巴中市	Bazhong	940.00	427.00	507.00	4884.04	4	4795.17
资阳市	Ziyang	1012.54	456.21	533.83	3604.00	4	3533.00
马尔康市	Maerkang	37.63	25.63	12.00	687.00	2	686.00
康定市	Kangding	58.70	37.39	9.11	325.00	1	319.00
会理市	Huili	167.80	89.20	43.70	440.41	1	368.19
西昌市	Xichang	481.22	125.50	110.00	4614.26	2	4387.23

10-7 城市市容环境卫生情况(2023年)
Basic Statistics on City Sanitation (2023)

城市	City	道路清扫保洁面积(万平方米) Clean Area of Road (10 000 sq.m)	生活垃圾清运量(万吨) Volume of Household Garbage Treatment (10 000 tons)	生活垃圾无害化处理厂(场)(座) Domestic Garbage Harmless Treatment Plants (unit)	生活垃圾无害化处理量(万吨) Volume of Domestic Garbage Harmless Treatment (10 000 tons)	公共厕所(座) Number of Public Lavatories (unit)	市容环卫专用车辆设备总数(辆) Number of Vehicles for Environmental Sanitation (unit)
全省	**Sichuan**	**62088.64**	**1322.33**	**52**	**1321.75**	**9998**	**16148**
成都市	Chengdu	28548.80	653.78	14	653.20	3120	9260
简阳市	Jianyang	520.00	17.29	1	17.29	82	185
都江堰市	Dujiangyan	579.00	11.20	1	11.20	121	150
彭州市	Pengzhou	466.00	21.42		21.42	164	70
邛崃市	Qionglai	411.00	15.81		15.81	101	309
崇州市	Chongzhcu	566.00	21.83		21.24	73	172
自贡市	Zigong	2396.00	37.90	1	37.90	557	607
攀枝花市	Panzhihua	1316.04	22.43	2	22.43	414	239
泸州市	Luzhou	2660.00	43.66	1	43.66	316	436
德阳市	Deyang	2951.00	69.23	2	69.23	289	964
广汉市	Guanghan	841.00	19.52		19.52	63	77
什邡市	Shifang	307.00	9.82		9.82	60	261
绵竹市	Mianzhu	318.00	11.25		11.25	30	43
绵阳市	Mianyang	3555.00	79.89	3	79.89	523	393
江油市	Jiangyou	670.00	17.77	1	17.77	74	78
广元市	Guangyuan	958.00	23.84	4	23.84	350	211
遂宁市	Suining	2105.00	34.27	3	34.27	332	393
射洪市	Shehong	493.00	10.99	2	10.99	91	115
内江市	Neijiang	1592.20	42.75	3	42.75	503	376
隆昌市	Longchang	454.20	11.97		11.97	41	82
乐山市	Leshan	1755.00	46.49	4	46.49	287	374
峨眉山市	Emeishan	308.00	12.34	1	12.34	55	40
南充市	Nanchong	3039.00	57.43	3	57.43	690	412
阆中市	Langzhong	700.00	12.00	1	12.00	200	66
眉山市	Meishan	1484.60	21.35	2	21.35	164	258
宜宾市	Yibin	2221.02	42.32		42.32	458	798
广安市	Guangan	1963.51	27.51		27.51	223	278
华蓥市	Huaying	319.00	4.67		4.67	43	61
达州市	Dazhou	1607.67	36.08	1	36.08	704	347
万源市	Wanyuan	80.00	3.40		3.40	85	68
雅安市	Yaan	736.00	14.61	1	14.61	299	123
巴中市	Bazhong	1253.80	19.56	1	19.56	279	275
资阳市	Ziyang	960.00	15.89		15.89	170	114
马尔康市	Maerkang	110.00	2.81	2	2.81	19	32
康定市	Kangding	79.00	2.97	1	2.97	15	27
会理市	Huili	87.00	3.16	1	3.16	37	36
西昌市	Xichang	710.00	24.40	3	24.40	249	195

主要统计指标解释

供水综合生产能力　指按供水设施取水、净化、送水、出厂输水干管等环节设计能力计算的综合生产能力。计算时，以四个环节中最薄弱的环节为主确定能力。

供水管道长度　指从送水泵至各类用户引入管之间所有市政管道的长度。不包括新安装尚未使用、水厂内以及用户建筑物内的管道。

城市供水总量　指报告期供水企业(单位)供出的全部水量。包括有效供水量和漏损水量。

生活用水　包括公共服务用水和居民家庭用水。公共服务用水指为城区社会公共生活服务的用水。包括行政事业单位、部队营区和公共设施服务、批发零售业、住宿餐饮业以及社会服务业等单位的用水。居民家庭用水指城市范围内所有居民家庭的日常生活用水。包括城市居民、农民家庭、公共供水站用水。

供水普及率　指报告期末城区用水人口数与城市人口总数的比率。计算公式：

$$供水普及率=\frac{城区用水人口（含暂住人口）}{城区人口+城区暂住人口}\times 100\%$$

城市供气总量　指报告期燃气企业(单位)向用户供应的燃气数量。包括销售量和损失量。

燃气普及率　指报告期末城区使用燃气的城市人口数与城市人口总数的比率。其中燃气包括人工煤气、天然气、液化石油气三种。计算公式为：

$$燃气普及率=\frac{城区用气人口（含暂住人口）}{城区人口+城区暂住人口}\times 100\%$$

道路长度　指道路长度和与道路相通的桥梁、隧道的长度，按车行道中心线计算。

城市桥梁　指为跨越天然或人工障碍物而修建的构筑物。包括跨河桥、立交桥、人行天桥以及人行地下通道等。

城市排水管道长度　指所有市政排水总管、干管、支管、检查井及连接井进出口等长度之和。

城市绿地面积　指报告期末用作园林和绿化的各种绿地面积。包括公园绿地、防护绿地、广场用地、附属绿地和位于建成区范围内的区域绿地面积。

公园绿地　指向公众开放、以游憩为主要功能，兼具生态、景观、文教和应急避险等功能，有一定游憩和服务设施的绿地。

市容环卫专用车辆设备　指用于环境卫生作业、监察的专用车辆和设备，包括用于道路清扫、冲洗、洒水、除雪、垃圾粪便清运、市容监察以及与其配套使用的车辆和设备。

Explanatory Notes on Main Statistical Indicators

Production Capacity of Water Supply refers to the designed overall production capacity of water facilities, covering the four segments of water collection, purification, conveyance, and outflow through trunk pipelines. The capacity is determined mainly on the weakest of the above-mentioned four segments.

Length of Water Supply Pipelines refers to the total length of all municipal pipelines between the water pumps and the user service pipes, excluding pipelines newly installed but not in use yet, pipelines in the water factories, and pipelines in the users' buildings.

Total Volume of Urban Water Supply refers to the total volume of water supplied by water-works (units) during the reference period, including both the effective water supply and loss during the water supply.

Consumption of Water for Daily Use includes consumption of water for public service use and consumption of water for household use. Consumption of water for public service use refers to water consumption for public service in the urban areas, including water consumption of administrative institutions, military barracks, public facilities, wholesale and retail, accommodation and catering industries and social service industry, etc. Consumption of water for household use refers to consumption of water for daily life of all households in cities, including households of urban residents and farmers, and public water supply stations.

Coverage Rate of Urban Population with Access to Water Supply refers to the ratio of the urban population with access to tap water to the total urban population at the end of reference period. The formula is:

$$\text{Coverage rate of urban population with access to water supply} = \frac{\text{Urban population with access to tap water}}{\text{Urban population}} \times 100\%$$

Volume of Gas Supply refers to the total volume of gas provided to users by gas-producing enterprises (units) during the reporting period, including the volume sold and the volume lost.

Coverage Rate of Urban Population with Access to Gas refers to the ratio of the urban population with access to gas to the total urban population at the end of the reference period. Gas here includes gaswork gas, natural gas and liquefied petroleum gas. The formula is:

$$\text{Coverage rate of urban population with access to Gas} = \frac{\text{Urban population with access to gas}}{\text{Urban population}} \times 100\%$$

Length of Paved Roads refers to the length of roads with paved surface, including bridges and tunnels connected with roads. Length of the roads is measured by the central lines.

Urban Bridges refer to bridges built to cross over natural or man-made barriers, including bridges over rivers, overpasses for traffic and for pedestrians, underpasses for pedestrians, etc.

Length of Urban Sewage Pipes refers to the total length of municipal general drainage, trunks, branch and inspection wells, connection wells, inlets and outlets, etc.

Urban Green Area refers to the total area occupied for gardening and greening at the end of the reference period, including public recreational green space, protection green land, land for squares, green land attached to institutions, and area of regional green space within the built-up area.

Public Recreational Green Space refers to green areas open to the public for amusement and rest with the facilities of amusement, rest and services. Its function also includes improving ecology, beautifying landscape, education and preventing and reducing disaster.

Vehicles and Facilities Dedicated to Urban Cleanliness and Environmental Sanitation refer to vehicles and facilities dedicated for use in the operation, management and monitoring of environmental hygiene work. They include vehicles for road cleaning, washing, showering, ice removal, disposal of garbage and human wastes, cleanliness monitoring and related activities.

11 民族自治地方概况

Chapter 11 Survey of Ethnic Minority Autonomous Areas

 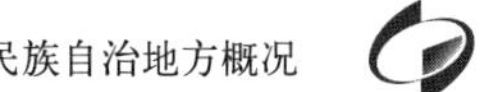

11-1 民族自治地方年末户籍总人口和就业人员
Registered Population and Employment in Minority Nationality Autonomous Areas

单位:万人 (10 000 persons)

年份 Year	年末户籍总人口 Registered Population (year-end)	就业人员 Number of Employed Persons	第一产业 Primary Industry	第二产业 Secondary Industry	第三产业 Tertiary Industry
1978	471.36	216.92			
1980	484.10	229.08			
1985	514.65	261.61			
1990	549.03	296.09			
1995	573.91	346.98	258.93	33.48	54.57
1996	578.54	345.07	257.30	32.25	55.52
1997	584.60	342.22	270.79	20.91	50.52
1998	589.96	343.89	271.25	20.25	52.39
1999	594.89	345.32	273.52	19.75	52.05
2000	606.11	351.99	278.93	18.65	54.41
2001	610.93	354.43	279.69	16.49	58.25
2002	616.81	356.25	280.90	16.77	58.58
2003	639.71	373.91	284.69	22.62	66.60
2004	649.17	387.38	281.85	22.98	82.55
2005	653.76	378.56	280.80	24.96	72.80
2006	663.73	385.37	279.63	25.98	79.76
2007	681.72	397.43	283.94	30.96	82.53
2008	698.87	409.69	285.42	33.37	90.90
2009	723.42	448.49	287.57	49.53	111.39
2010	734.16	439.29	289.21	46.12	103.96
2011	746.67	444.08	280.01	47.47	116.60
2012	759.54	459.83	290.33	45.31	124.19
2013	769.56	460.11	289.26	44.81	126.04
2014	771.62	466.41	286.09	44.43	135.89
2015	764.80	442.19	276.12	45.64	120.43
2016	775.06	440.54	263.77	52.34	124.43
2017	783.22	441.08	258.69	54.62	127.77
2018	791.49	405.91	233.18	45.15	127.58
2019	790.90	408.45	229.38	45.35	133.72
2020	791.76	409.99	229.18	46.16	134.65
2021	797.75	406.17	224.07	47.52	134.58
2022	802.45	405.05	235.99	45.63	123.43
2023	808.65	409.16	231.23	47.95	129.98

注：2018年以后就业人员数据依据第七次全国人口普查进行了修订。
a) The number of employed persons were revised according to the 7th National Population Censu from 2018.

11-2 民族自治地方主要统计指标(2023年)

指标		Item	
年末常住人口	(万人)	Resident Population (year-end)	(10 000 persons)
城镇人口	(万人)	Urban Population	(10 000 persons)
乡村人口	(万人)	Rural Population	(10 000 persons)
城镇化率	(%)	Urbanization Rate	(%)
就业人员	(万人)	Number of Employed Persons	(10 000 persons)
第一产业	(万人)	Primary Industry	(10 000 persons)
第二产业	(万人)	Secondary Industry	(10 000 persons)
第三产业	(万人)	Tertiary Industry	(10 000 persons)
地区生产总值(当年价)	(亿元)	Gross Regional Product (at current prices)	(100 million yuan)
第一产业增加值	(亿元)	Value-added of Primary Industry	(100 million yuan)
第二产业增加值	(亿元)	Value-added of Secondary Industry	(100 million yuan)
第三产业增加值	(亿元)	Value-added of Tertiary Industry	(100 million yuan)
人均地区生产总值(当年价)	(元)	Per Capita Gross Regional Product (at current prices)	(yuan)
耕地灌溉面积	(万公顷)	Irrigated Areas of Cultivated Land	(10 000 hectare)
农林牧渔业总产值(当年价)	(亿元)	Gross Output Value of Farming, Forestry, Animal Husbandry and Fishery (at current prices)	(100 million yuan)
规模以上工业企业营业收入	(亿元)	Revenue from Industrial Enterprises above Designated Size	(100 million yuan)
规模以上工业企业利润总额	(亿元)	Total Profits from Industrial Enterprises above Designated Size	(100 million yuan)
境内公路总里程	(公里)	Total Length of Highway	(km)
#等级公路	(公里)	Expressway and Class I to IV Highways	(km)
公路旅客周转量	(万人公里)	Passenger-Kilometers of Highways	(10 000 passenger-km)
公路货物周转量	(万吨公里)	Freight Ton-Kilometers of Highways	(10 000 ton-km)

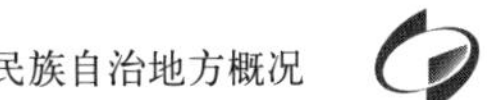

Main Statistical Indicators of Minority Nationality Autonomous Areas(2023)

合计 Total	阿坝州 Aba	甘孜州 Ganzi	凉山州 Liangshan	北川县 Beichuan	峨边县 Ebian	马边县 Mabian
732.7	82.5	110.6	490.6	18.0	12.0	19.0
295.4	36.1	36.4	203.0	7.1	4.9	7.9
437.2	46.4	74.2	287.6	10.8	7.1	11.1
40.32	43.75	32.92	41.38	39.64	41.00	41.48
409.16	47.09	60.93	273.83	9.80	6.65	10.86
231.23	24.20	42.34	153.19	3.31	2.83	5.36
47.95	3.10	3.94	35.59	2.32	1.37	1.63
129.98	19.79	14.65	85.05	4.17	2.45	3.87
3517.98	503.19	513.35	2261.11	106.55	69.04	64.73
728.42	98.48	86.88	503.41	15.72	9.73	14.19
1133.99	122.53	147.24	779.40	26.35	33.05	25.42
1655.56	282.18	279.24	978.29	64.49	26.26	25.11
48081	61067	46478	46159	59445	57296	34069
28.15	3.14	4.39	19.46	0.24	0.38	0.54
1191.65	172.01	130.84	817.95	32.31	16.00	22.54
1967.12	266.69	186.92	1320.17	66.15	79.02	48.17
264.04	17.96	13.82	204.84	4.79	9.30	13.33
85347	15863	33201	29911	3004	1557	1810
83098	15345	32730	28769	2901	1555	1798
340639	83452	86218	157599	10874	1947	550
2069595	486022	244780	1245708	49073	3679	40333

11-2 续表

指标		Item	
全社会固定资产投资增长情况	(%)	The Growth of Total Investment in Fixed Assets	(%)
建筑业总产值	(亿元)	Gross Output Value of Construction	(100 million yuan)
社会消费品零售总额	(亿元)	Total Retail Sales of Consumer Goods	(100 million yuan)
出口总额	(亿元)	Total Exports	(100 million yuan)
城镇居民人均可支配收入	(元)	Per Capita Disposable Income of Urban Households	(yuan)
农村居民人均可支配收入	(元)	Per Capita Disposable Income of Rural Households	(yuan)
参加城镇职工基本养老保险人数	(万人)	Persons of Urban Workers in Basic Endowment Pension Insurance	(10 000 persons)
参加基本医疗保险人数	(万人)	Persons in Basic Medical Insurance	(10 000 persons)
地方一般公共预算收入	(亿元)	Local General Public Budget Revenue	(100 million yuan)
#税收收入	(亿元)	Taxes Revenue	(100 million yuan)
一般公共预算支出	(亿元)	General Public Budget Expenditure	(100 million yuan)
年末金融机构人民币各项存款余额	(亿元)	Deposits of Financial Institutions	(100 million yuan)
住户存款余额	(亿元)	Balance of Household Savings	(100 million yuan)
年末金融机构人民币各项贷款余额	(亿元)	Loans of Financial Institutions	(100 million yuan)
小学在校学生人数	(人)	Students in Primary Schools	(person)
普通中学在校学生人数	(人)	Students in Regular Secondary Schools	(person)
中等职业教育学校在校学生数	(人)	Students in Secondary Vocational Schools	(person)
卫生机构数	(个)	Number of Medical and Health Institutions	(unit)
卫生机构床位数	(张)	Beds in Medical and Health Institutions	(unit)
卫生技术人员数	(人)	Medical Technical Personnel in Medical and Health Institutions	(person)
#执业(助理)医师	(人)	Practicing Doctors (Assistants)	(person)

continued

合计 Total	阿坝州 Aba	甘孜州 Ganzi	凉山州 Liangshan	北川县 Beichuan	峨边县 Ebian	马边县 Mabian
8.0	8.2	10.4	6.4	17.5	23.1	-0.3
484.25	66.47	50.11	337.93	21.07	4.50	4.17
1236.34	117.30	143.52	872.55	42.27	30.11	30.59
30.52	3.29	2.56	20.27	0.47	3.03	0.90
39489	40408	40152	39042	39762	40816	41657
17659	18141	16918	17686	20254	17256	17600
123.29	22.93	19.90	67.74	8.60	1.80	2.31
705.73	81.66	102.28	473.78	20.12	10.84	17.05
341.39	62.94	54.69	204.75	6.81	5.29	6.91
197.90	25.80	34.25	125.03	3.75	3.02	6.05
1607.67	347.55	444.19	744.28	23.48	20.26	27.90
5293.47	819.86	943.25	3145.94	179.02	99.06	106.34
3249.77	434.01	409.39	2114.69	137.74	76.12	77.83
3453.50	545.53	581.32	1988.85	172.73	93.23	71.84
827804	62702	115852	606531	8957	11663	22099
498881	41879	65549	364033	9357	5851	12212
48815	2690	6670	30790	6377	1037	1251
8489	1531	2494	3939	243	123	159
48343	5832	7180	32071	1856	582	822
58284	7775	7948	39143	1587	696	1135
22834	2822	2579	16378	509	240	306

11-3 民族自治地方地区生产总值
Gross Regional Product in Minority Nationality Autonomous Areas

单位：亿元 (100 million yuan)

年份 Year	地区生产总值 Gross Regional Product	第一产业 Primary Industry	第二产业 Secondary Industry	第三产业 Tertiary Industry	人均地区生产总值(元) Per Capita GDP (yuan)
1978	14.08	6.46	4.73	2.89	292
1980	16.71	7.66	5.72	3.33	337
1985	28.56	13.46	8.61	6.48	541
1990	57.56	24.90	16.48	16.18	1026
1995	149.89	49.99	47.93	51.97	2558
2000	230.87	79.94	61.93	88.99	3733
2005	447.86	120.05	140.37	187.44	6690
2006	539.90	148.54	180.77	210.59	8057
2007	675.06	183.15	229.38	262.53	10039
2008	788.44	184.00	290.01	314.43	11713
2009	884.24	189.39	346.27	348.58	12990
2010	1084.83	222.59	440.36	421.88	15615
2011	1336.36	293.51	515.66	527.19	18961
2012	1489.70	329.13	566.28	594.30	21095
2013	1640.29	337.67	647.40	655.22	23188
2014	1798.59	376.57	667.39	754.63	25357
2015	1951.56	391.94	672.34	887.29	27360
2016	2047.97	427.44	686.86	933.68	28424
2017	2217.82	456.02	730.97	1030.84	30570
2018	2445.54	479.08	778.79	1187.66	33634
2019	2624.53	529.54	823.64	1271.34	36046
2020	2746.16	606.24	827.97	1311.95	37727
2021	3006.76	636.44	950.16	1420.16	41322
2022	3236.79	687.59	1055.82	1493.38	44379
2023	3517.98	728.42	1134.00	1655.56	48081

11-4 民族自治地方地区生产总值指数
Indices of Gross Regional Product in Minority Nationality Autonomous Areas

(1978年=100) (year of 1978=100)

年份 Year	地区生产总值 Gross Regional Product	第一产业 Primary Industry	第二产业 Secondary Industry	第三产业 Tertiary Industry	人均地区生产总值 Per Capita GDP
1978	100.0	100.0	100.0	100.0	100.0
1980	114.1	109.7	116.4	121.8	111.2
1985	162.9	156.8	148.0	206.8	149.0
1990	208.4	176.5	196.3	315.9	179.4
1995	331.1	243.4	341.1	547.5	272.9
2000	500.7	350.9	477.0	954.5	391.1
2005	855.8	449.4	1134.4	1554.5	617.6
2006	973.1	464.1	1355.2	1804.2	701.5
2007	1113.7	492.7	1647.2	2051.6	800.1
2008	1181.0	487.3	1723.6	2277.0	847.6
2009	1380.3	511.3	2070.5	2733.0	979.6
2010	1593.6	533.6	2617.8	3047.7	1108.1
2011	1831.5	557.7	3236.2	3393.3	1255.3
2012	2043.8	583.2	3763.3	3719.9	1398.1
2013	2254.1	608.3	4311.3	4012.8	1539.3
2014	2422.8	634.8	4709.6	4277.9	1650.1
2015	2519.5	659.6	4812.1	4554.3	1706.3
2016	2677.0	686.8	5116.1	4879.6	1794.9
2017	2830.3	713.0	5486.3	5143.8	1884.6
2018	2974.0	739.4	5663.2	5507.6	1975.9
2019	3150.6	762.7	5910.7	5961.0	2090.3
2020	3270.7	798.9	6212.0	6112.3	2170.7
2021	3509.5	852.5	6715.1	6540.2	2329.1
2022	3678.0	888.3	7191.9	6775.6	2501.3
2023	3931.8	931.8	7709.7	7297.4	2668.8

11−5 民族自治地方耕地面积和农业生产条件
Cultivated Land Areas and Production Conditions of Agriculture in Minority Nationality Autonomous Areas

年份 Year	耕地面积 (万公顷) Cultivated Areas (10 000 hectares)	耕地灌溉面积 (万公顷) Irrigated Areas of Cultivated Land (10 000 hectares)	化肥施用量 (折纯、万吨) Consumption of Chemical Fertilizers (10 000 tons)	农业机械总动力 (万千瓦) Total Agricultural Machinery Power (10 000 kw)
1978	51.52	15.47	3.44	27.11
1980	51.84	16.17	3.12	37.21
1985	50.32	15.96	3.34	53.88
1990	50.00	15.32	4.75	78.58
1995	50.97	15.90	6.83	109.30
1996	51.45	16.06	7.53	112.00
1997	51.56	15.21	9.77	119.00
1998	51.12	15.73	10.64	134.00
1999	50.74	15.24	11.12	135.00
2000	48.39	16.13	11.82	137.00
2001	49.47	16.36	11.63	142.00
2002	46.14	16.28	10.41	154.00
2003	45.32	16.24	11.14	162.00
2004	47.91	16.19	11.70	173.00
2005	49.47	16.63	12.59	201.00
2006	49.97	16.62	13.43	173.00
2007	51.25	17.31	14.38	250.00
2008	52.06	17.59	15.25	287.00
2009	52.96	18.34	16.52	333.00
2010	53.37	18.60	16.72	370.00
2011	53.35	19.33	17.29	415.95
2012	53.53	19.89	17.83	439.04
2013	53.81	21.19	16.66	480.58
2014	53.93	20.60	17.14	502.76
2015	79.94	21.54	17.17	529.51
2016	82.77	22.44	17.32	541.75
2017	82.77	23.12	17.14	556.45
2018	82.73	25.79	16.89	552.54
2019	75.42	26.38	16.01	564.12
2020	75.12	28.74	15.11	569.72
2021	75.13	27.58	14.99	577.38
2022	75.16	28.01	14.85	585.52
2023	72.50	28.15	14.72	608.11

11-6 民族自治地方邮电主营业务收入、社会消费品零售总额和医疗卫生情况

Revenue from Principal Business of Postal and Telecommunication, Total Retail Sales of Consumer Goods, Public Health in Minority Nationality Autonomous Areas

年份 Year	邮电主营业务收入 (万元) Revenue from Principal Business of Post and Telecommunication (10 000 yuan)	社会消费品零售总额 (亿元) Total Retail Sales of Consumer Goods (100 million yuan)	医疗卫生机构床位数 (张) Beds in Medical and Health Institutions (unit)	医院、卫生院技术人员数 (人) Medical Technical Personnel (person)	#执业(助理)医师 Practicing Doctors (Assistants)
1978	1248	4.76	14225	15058	7303
1980	1290	6.00	14471	17699	9102
1985	1719	10.70	14938	19438	10203
1990	3108	19.96	15588	18481	10155
1995	8807	39.13	15688	18957	10037
1996	12028	43.89	14923	18189	9768
1997	16285	48.52	15348	19066	10414
1998	23483	51.68	15113	18441	10080
1999	29025	55.46	15313	18554	10841
2000	41608	59.81	16475	14807	7889
2001	56484	67.92	14263	22337	8867
2002	67374	76.99	13901	16180	8159
2003	90594	90.85	15097	16345	8450
2004	111646	110.65	16538	15005	7860
2005	130946	142.96	14647	19535	8686
2006	154313	167.00	15635	14384	8124
2007	176723	197.36	15898	16127	10045
2008	202155	224.72	16737	15516	8518
2009	234607	273.67	18363	17615	8807
2010	265913	337.04	19791	24848	7485
2011	302272	396.36	21448	29648	9433
2012	345136	459.12	24607	24655	7571
2013	376606	521.83	25908	22862	10069
2014	411888	624.82	31360	30263	10934
2015	416006	691.78	33443	33505	11542
2016	454941	766.81	35376	35935	11744
2017	490039	849.26	38725	38417	11768
2018	488177	889.00	40314	40712	12282
2019	402995	1004.57	41504	43717	13406
2020	549863	966.91	43378	45681	14798
2021	563731	1089.28	43720	48797	15923
2022	637542	1109.92	47224	50889	16295
2023	705875	1236.34	48343	58284	22834

注：2023年邮电主营业务收入未包含北川羌族自治县数据。
a)The main business income of postal and telecommunications in 2023 does not include data from Beichuan Qiang Autonomous County.

11-7 民族自治地方住户存款余额和各类学校在校学生人数
Balance of Household Savings and Number of Student Enrollment by Type of Schools in Minority Nationality Autonomous Areas

年份 Year	住户 存款余额 (亿元) Balance of Household Savings (100 million yuan)	普通高等院校 在校学生人数 (人) Number of Students in Regular Institutions of Higher Education (person)	中等职业学校 在校学生人数 (人) Number of Students in Specialized Secondary Schools (person)	普通中学 在校学生人数 (人) Number of Students in Regular Secondary Schools (person)	小学 在校学生人数 (人) Number of Students in Primary Schools (person)
1978	0.72	970	11756	184900	673479
1980	1.25	1231	10343	162751	605404
1985	4.39	2826	7570	126389	521659
1990	17.68	4225	10173	133208	493900
1995	51.71	6144	14497	121232	578205
1996	65.19	6467	15381	126736	605960
1997	73.15	7355	16954	129029	632731
1998	84.23	7805	18232	128916	656367
1999	95.75	9688	19573	133369	657565
2000	107.26	10725	14731	145534	640229
2001	126.98	15229	13825	164038	659357
2002	147.91	17350	11203	186065	692423
2003	175.68	20829	15942	221096	731794
2004	202.39	24488	11486	243812	756318
2005	232.37	27857	13963	283307	780372
2006	268.91	27025	19998	323742	829904
2007	299.03	25132	25977	337781	824988
2008	381.04	25092	33575	345560	811499
2009	481.67	26371	35221	360138	794927
2010	584.83	27494	39672	373524	781008
2011	712.78	28546	36839	380705	772207
2012	860.16	29673	39278	378296	766925
2013	1006.81	30728	46084	360158	740478
2014	1111.63	30953	42572	363107	744127
2015	1019.18	32013	41922	360638	759084
2016	1420.57	33530	41003	368252	783445
2017	1581.13	36580	43264	384941	803467
2018	1781.55	41394	44326	408067	823914
2019	2011.40	45697	44314	447308	840814
2020	2305.60	42876	47101	490464	852981
2021	2565.70	51260	54283	473254	853884
2022	2918.48	51245	54517	480450	841955
2023	3453.50	56793	48815	498881	827804

注：2014年及以前，“住户存款余额”为“城乡居民储蓄存款余额”。
a) Household saving was known as saving deposit of residents before 2014.

12 县（市、区）概况

Chapter 12 Survey of County(City, District)

12-1 各县(市、区)年末常住人口及城镇化率(2023年)
Resident Population and Proportion Registered by Counties (City, Districts)(2023)

单位：万人 (10 000 persons)

县(市、区)	Counties (City,Districts)	常住人口 Resident Population	城镇人口 Urban Population	乡村人口 Rural Population	城镇化率(%) Proportion (%)
成都市	**Chengdu**				
锦江区	Jinjiang	91.9	91.9		100.00
青羊区	Qingyang	97.3	97.3		100.00
金牛区	Jinniu	128.8	128.8		100.00
武侯区	Wuhou	191.0	191.0		100.00
成华区	Chenghua	141.2	141.2		100.00
龙泉驿区	Longquanyi	137.8	128.9	8.9	93.55
青白江区	Qingbaijiang	51.0	39.8	11.2	78.03
新都区	Xindu	159.3	126.1	33.2	79.15
温江区	Wenjiang	101.1	80.1	21.1	79.18
双流区	Shuangliu	279.4	226.4	53.0	81.03
郫都区	Pidu	169.7	135.5	34.2	79.83
新津区	Xinjin	37.5	26.6	10.9	70.99
金堂县	Jintang	81.2	46.2	35.0	56.89
大邑县	Dayi	50.8	25.4	25.4	50.00
蒲江县	Pujiang	25.6	12.8	12.8	50.03
都江堰市	Dujiangyan	71.5	46.5	25.0	65.02
彭州市	Pengzhou	78.1	44.2	33.9	56.59
邛崃市	Qionglai	59.8	33.8	26.0	56.48
崇州市	Chongzhou	74.2	42.0	32.2	56.58
简阳市	Jianyang	113.1	58.5	54.6	51.75
自贡市	**Zigong**				
自流井区	Ziliujing	47.8	45.0	2.8	94.21
贡井区	Gongjing	21.4	12.3	9.1	57.34
大安区	Daan	28.3	15.8	12.5	55.93
沿滩区	Yantan	29.0	14.7	14.3	50.85
荣县	Rongxian	45.4	20.7	24.7	45.61
富顺县	Fushun	71.0	31.6	39.4	44.44
攀枝花市	**Panzhihua**				
东区	Dongqu	41.3	40.9	0.4	99.06
西区	Xiqu	12.9	12.3	0.6	95.30
仁和区	Renhe	26.8	16.1	10.7	60.10
米易县	Miyi	22.8	10.6	12.2	46.69
盐边县	Yanbian	18.0	6.2	11.8	34.45
泸州市	**Luzhou**				
江阳区	Jiangyang	76.6	59.3	17.3	77.42
纳溪区	Naxi	36.0	18.5	17.5	51.27
龙马潭区	Longmatan	48.3	39.0	9.3	80.74
泸县	Luxian	76.4	33.9	42.5	44.32
合江县	Hejiang	69.0	31.1	37.9	45.02
叙永县	Xuyong	55.2	21.3	33.9	38.66
古蔺县	Gulin	65.2	23.8	41.4	36.47

12-1 续表 1 continued

单位：万人 (10 000 persons)

县(市、区)	Counties (City,Districts)	常住人口 Resident Population	城镇人口 Urban Population	乡村人口 Rural Population	城镇化率(%) Proportion (%)
德阳市	**Deyang**				
旌阳区	Jingyang	83.1	62.8	20.3	75.56
罗江区	Luojiang	20.8	11.4	9.4	54.93
中江县	Zhongjiang	94.5	42.1	52.4	44.52
广汉市	Guanghan	62.7	38.6	24.1	61.50
什邡市	Shifang	40.5	23.6	16.9	58.18
绵竹市	Mianzhu	43.7	24.5	19.2	56.14
绵阳市	**Mianyang**				
涪城区	Fucheng	133.6	112.4	21.1	84.17
游仙区	Youxian	57.0	35.9	21.1	63.02
安州区	Anzhou	38.4	18.2	20.3	47.24
三台县	Santai	94.4	30.9	63.4	32.79
盐亭县	Yanting	36.2	14.8	21.5	40.76
梓潼县	Zitong	27.8	10.0	17.8	35.94
北川县	Beichuan	18.0	7.1	10.8	39.64
平武县	Pingwu	12.5	3.9	8.6	30.98
江油市	Jiangyou	73.3	41.9	31.4	57.16
广元市	**Guangyuan**				
利州区	Lizhou	64.1	49.3	14.8	76.94
昭化区	Zhaohua	12.8	4.6	8.2	35.99
朝天区	Chaotian	12.2	4.1	8.0	33.91
旺苍县	Wangcang	31.8	14.5	17.2	45.77
青川县	Qingchuan	14.7	5.5	9.2	37.48
剑阁县	Jiange	39.6	15.7	23.8	39.70
苍溪县	Cangxi	49.8	17.7	32.2	35.45
遂宁市	**Suining**				
船山区	Chuanshan	84.3	70.6	13.7	83.71
安居区	Anju	41.3	14.5	26.8	35.07
蓬溪县	Pengxi	40.9	17.0	23.9	41.63
大英县	Daying	37.3	17.6	19.7	47.13
射洪市	Shehong	71.0	44.6	26.4	62.85
内江市	**Neijiang**				
内江市中区	Neijiang Downtown	41.5	27.1	14.4	65.26
东兴区	Dongxing	75.1	43.2	31.9	57.51
威远县	Weiyuan	52.3	27.9	24.4	53.29
资中县	Zizhong	82.9	35.1	47.8	42.33
隆昌市	Longchang	54.5	27.8	26.7	50.98
乐山市	**Leshan**				
乐山市中区	Leshan Downtown	83.9	63.7	20.2	75.96
沙湾区	Shawan	14.0	7.0	7.0	49.89
五通桥区	Wutongqiao	23.5	13.1	10.4	55.55

12-1 续表 2 continued

单位：万人 (10 000 persons)

县(市、区)	Counties (City,Districts)	常住人口 Resident Population	城镇人口 Urban Population	乡村人口 Rural Population	城镇化率(%) Proportion (%)
金口河区	Jinkouhe	3.8	1.6	2.2	43.16
犍为县	Qianwei	41.1	18.0	23.1	43.68
井研县	Jingyan	27.4	12.0	15.4	43.64
夹江县	Jiajiang	29.9	14.9	15.0	49.67
沐川县	Muchuan	18.6	6.9	11.7	37.33
峨边县	Ebian	12.0	4.9	7.1	41.00
马边县	Mabian	19.0	7.9	11.1	41.48
峨眉山市	Emeishan	41.5	25.6	15.9	61.66
南充市	**Nanchong**				
顺庆区	Shunqing	83.0	71.0	12.0	85.49
高坪区	Gaoping	56.1	30.3	25.8	54.03
嘉陵区	Jialing	52.2	26.8	25.4	51.32
南部县	Nanbu	80.1	37.8	42.3	47.17
营山县	Yingshan	61.0	28.2	32.8	46.25
蓬安县	Pengan	45.2	18.1	27.1	40.11
仪陇县	Yilong	71.3	29.7	41.6	41.70
西充县	Xichong	41.1	18.4	22.7	44.72
阆中市	Langzhong	61.1	30.9	30.2	50.51
眉山市	**Meishan**				
东坡区	Dongpo	90.9	57.3	33.6	63.01
彭山区	Pengshan	33.0	19.9	13.1	60.37
仁寿县	Renshou	110.6	49.8	60.8	45.04
洪雅县	Hongya	29.5	14.1	15.4	47.80
丹棱县	Danling	14.8	6.7	8.1	45.47
青神县	Qingshen	16.7	8.3	8.5	49.38
宜宾市	**Yibin**				
翠屏区	Cuiping	92.3	72.5	19.8	78.54
南溪区	Nanxi	33.3	19.8	13.5	59.32
叙州区	Xuzhou	95.6	49.6	46.0	51.85
江安县	Jiangan	42.6	21.3	21.3	50.07
长宁县	Changning	33.0	17.1	15.9	51.87
高县	Gaoxian	37.6	16.9	20.7	45.03
珙县	Gongxian	33.1	18.0	15.1	54.29
筠连县	Junlian	32.8	14.1	18.7	43.06
兴文县	Xingwen	38.1	16.5	21.6	43.18
屏山县	Pingshan	24.4	8.4	16.0	34.36
广安市	**Guangan**				
广安区	Guanganqu	74.2	40.5	33.7	54.62
前锋区	Qianfeng	22.9	9.4	13.5	40.94
岳池县	Yuechi	73.7	32.4	41.2	44.03
武胜县	Wusheng	55.0	22.1	32.9	40.19

12-1 续表 3 continued

单位：万人 (10 000 persons)

县(市、区)	Counties (City,Districts)	常住人口 Resident Population	城镇人口 Urban Population	乡村人口 Rural Population	城镇化率(%) Proportion (%)
邻水县	Linshui	70.1	31.1	39.0	44.34
华蓥市	Huaying	26.7	14.7	12.0	54.95
达州市	**Dazhou**				
通川区	Tongchuan	91.1	69.4	21.7	76.18
达川区	Dachuan	93.5	47.9	45.6	51.22
宣汉县	Xuanhan	94.7	44.6	50.1	47.10
开江县	Kaijiang	40.8	18.7	22.1	45.74
大竹县	Dazhu	83.0	40.0	43.0	48.19
渠县	Quxian	89.2	40.6	48.6	45.51
万源市	Wanyuan	40.1	18.2	21.9	45.47
雅安市	**Yaan**				
雨城区	Yucheng	36.9	24.3	12.6	65.81
名山区	Mingshan	25.3	11.7	13.6	46.28
荥经县	Yingjing	13.0	6.9	6.1	53.31
汉源县	Hanyuan	28.4	12.8	15.6	44.90
石棉县	Shimian	11.4	8.7	2.7	76.48
天全县	Tianquan	13.1	6.6	6.5	50.01
芦山县	Lushan	10.0	5.6	4.4	56.42
宝兴县	Baoxing	4.8	2.2	2.6	45.20
巴中市	**Bazhong**				
巴州区	Bazhou	71.1	48.4	22.7	68.07
恩阳区	Enyang	33.4	13.3	20.0	40.00
通江县	Tongjiang	50.2	20.8	29.4	41.49
南江县	Nanjiang	44.9	18.2	26.7	40.53
平昌县	Pingchang	63.3	26.8	36.5	42.29
资阳市	**Ziyang**				
雁江区	Yanjiang	85.3	47.7	37.6	55.94
安岳县	Anyue	92.9	31.0	61.9	33.35
乐至县	Lezhi	47.1	20.2	26.9	42.81
阿坝州	**Aba**				
马尔康市	Maerkang	6.0	3.4	2.7	55.98
汶川县	Wenchuan	8.3	4.6	3.8	54.74
理县	Lixian	3.6	1.5	2.1	40.95
茂县	Maoxian	9.5	5.0	4.5	52.68
松潘县	Songpan	6.7	2.6	4.2	38.13
九寨沟县	Jiuzhaigou	6.7	3.8	2.9	56.69
金川县	Jinchuan	5.7	2.1	3.6	36.36
小金县	Xiaojin	6.4	2.6	3.8	40.63
黑水县	Heishui	4.3	1.8	2.5	41.86
壤塘县	Rangtang	4.6	1.3	3.3	27.91

12-1 续表 4 continued

单位：万人 (10 000 persons)

县(市、区)	Counties (City,Districts)	常住人口 Resident Population	城镇人口 Urban Population	乡村人口 Rural Population	城镇化率(%) Proportion (%)
阿坝县	Abaxian	8.1	2.7	5.5	32.96
若尔盖县	Ruoergai	7.8	2.8	5.0	35.48
红原县	Hongyuan	4.8	2.2	2.6	44.98
甘孜州	**Ganzi**				
康定市	Kangding	13.0	7.3	5.7	56.28
泸定县	Luding	8.6	4.2	4.3	49.36
丹巴县	Danba	5.1	1.7	3.4	33.14
九龙县	Jiulong	5.4	1.5	3.9	28.65
雅江县	Yajiang	5.2	1.6	3.6	30.98
道孚县	Daofu	5.2	1.3	3.9	24.04
炉霍县	Luhuo	4.7	1.4	3.3	29.09
甘孜县	Ganzixian	7.4	2.3	5.1	31.57
新龙县	Xinlong	4.5	0.9	3.6	20.22
德格县	Dege	8.8	2.6	6.2	29.45
白玉县	Baiyu	5.9	1.5	4.5	24.62
石渠县	Shiqu	10.1	1.7	8.3	17.20
色达县	Seda	6.2	1.7	4.5	26.94
理塘县	Litang	6.7	2.8	4.0	41.10
巴塘县	Batang	5.0	1.5	3.5	29.52
乡城县	Xiangcheng	3.1	1.0	2.1	31.15
稻城县	Daocheng	3.4	0.9	2.5	25.59
得荣县	Derong	2.4	0.6	1.8	27.08
凉山州	**Liangshan**				
西昌市	Xichang	97.0	68.4	28.6	70.48
会理市	Huili	39.3	18.5	20.8	47.18
木里县	Muli	12.5	3.1	9.4	24.67
盐源县	Yanyuan	34.4	12.0	22.4	34.77
德昌县	Dechang	21.8	10.0	11.8	46.08
会东县	Huidong	34.6	15.2	19.4	43.95
宁南县	Ningnan	18.4	8.0	10.4	43.29
普格县	Puge	18.3	3.8	14.5	20.56
布拖县	Butuo	18.9	4.9	14.0	26.11
金阳县	Jinyang	17.1	5.1	12.0	29.71
昭觉县	Zhaojue	25.7	6.9	18.8	26.98
喜德县	Xide	16.1	5.1	11.0	31.45
冕宁县	Mianning	36.6	14.9	21.7	40.66
越西县	Yuexi	30.5	11.1	19.4	36.32
甘洛县	Ganluo	20.8	5.3	15.5	25.39
美姑县	Meigu	24.2	4.4	19.8	18.27
雷波县	Leibo	24.4	6.4	18.0	26.21

12−2 各县(市、区)地区生产总值(2023年)
Gross Regional Product by Counties (City, Districts)(2023)

县(市、区)	Counties (City,Districts)	地区生产总值(万元) Gross Regional Product (10 000 yuan)	第一产业 Primary Industry	第二产业 Secondary Industry	第三产业 Tertiary Industry	人均地区生产总值(元) Per Capita Gross Regional Product (yuan)
成都市	**Chengdu**					
锦江区	Jinjiang	14461970	2952	2196546	12262472	157727
青羊区	Qingyang	15895350	202	2091254	13803894	163844
金牛区	Jinniu	16012073	1280	2830856	13179937	124516
武侯区	Wuhou	38999597	292	5022375	33976930	205142
成华区	Chenghua	14436923	28	5087917	9348978	102571
龙泉驿区	Longquanyi	15025376	217711	8801854	6005811	109622
青白江区	Qingbaijiang	6840977	168065	1877939	4794973	134691
新都区	Xindu	10861045	259056	3225906	7376083	68520
温江区	Wenjiang	7288916	223529	2425913	4639474	72534
双流区	Shuangliu	20506726	325343	5079245	15102138	73934
郫都区	Pidu	14289394	262505	7542360	6484529	84385
新津区	Xinjin	5026626	193952	2128611	2704063	134240
金堂县	Jintang	6503071	819803	2494171	3189097	80523
大邑县	Dayi	3443541	337710	1325995	1779836	67660
蒲江县	Pujiang	2144611	294355	712110	1138146	83529
都江堰市	Dujiangyan	5067957	404054	1395985	3267918	70881
彭州市	Pengzhou	6606916	658757	3619741	2328418	84655
邛崃市	Qionglai	4252163	543007	1712644	1996512	70917
崇州市	Chongzhou	5014032	453534	2513676	2046822	67565
简阳市	Jianyang	8069892	782446	1623575	5663871	71198
自贡市	**Zigong**					
自流井区	Ziliujing	4572318	87332	1051146	3433840	95555
贡井区	Gongjing	1657727	280377	592545	784805	76747
大安区	Daan	2018228	264987	765966	987275	70815
沿滩区	Yantan	2676731	284791	1382394	1009546	91826
荣县	Rongxian	2731501	875080	727694	1128727	59770
富顺县	Fushun	3848178	805111	1360686	1682381	54010
攀枝花市	**Panzhihua**					
东区	Dongqu	5710216	24560	3226362	2459294	138262
西区	Xiqu	945972	28142	659339	258491	73331
仁和区	Renhe	2717443	365274	1483363	868806	101587
米易县	Miyi	1968485	416808	841624	710053	86337
盐边县	Yanbian	1695917	317952	962325	415640	94480
泸州市	**Luzhou**					
江阳区	Jiangyang	8126499	320546	4317755	3488198	106229
纳溪区	Naxi	2483179	339930	1212323	930926	69169
龙马潭区	Longmatan	4482767	150600	2345472	1986695	92907
泸县	Luxian	4646282	728362	2386235	1531685	60775
合江县	Hejiang	3191062	514793	1395443	1280826	46247
叙永县	Xuyong	1849835	387001	620246	842588	33512
古蔺县	Gulin	2479376	372824	1051798	1054754	38027

12-2 续表 1 continued

县(市、区)	Counties (City,Districts)	地区生产总值(万元) Gross Regional Product (10 000 yuan)	第一产业 Primary Industry	第二产业 Secondary Industry	第三产业 Tertiary Industry	人均地区生产总值(元) Per Capita Gross Regional Product (yuan)
德阳市	**Deyang**					
旌阳区	Jingyang	9208018	460680	4184274	4563064	110940
罗江区	Luojiang	1815146	274336	974819	565991	87057
中江县	Zhongjiang	4661418	1027196	1763052	1871170	49223
广汉市	Guanghan	5364740	460943	2657519	2246278	85562
什邡市	Shifang	4708907	424553	2333301	1951053	115840
绵竹市	Mianzhu	4385821	389555	2303845	1692421	100133
绵阳市	**Mianyang**					
涪城区	Fucheng	14436525	320412	6688802	7427311	108615
游仙区	Youxian	5128186	416877	1610658	3100651	90110
安州区	Anzhou	2624608	368512	1145352	1110744	68340
三台县	Santai	5305522	1048315	1734064	2523143	56191
盐亭县	Yanting	2301541	472526	628475	1200540	63368
梓潼县	Zitong	2071886	387350	624478	1060058	74636
北川县	Beichuan	1065543	157182	263501	644860	59445
平武县	Pingwu	764319	123340	282571	358408	60829
江油市	Jiangyou	6689143	637375	3012576	3039192	91344
广元市	**Guangyuan**					
利州区	Lizhou	4070943	187660	1799674	2083609	64276
昭化区	Zhaohua	817527	225152	302694	289681	63448
朝天区	Chaotian	851948	166542	387137	298269	69604
旺苍县	Wangcang	1642053	326709	710202	605142	51483
青川县	Qingchuan	608222	145988	165282	296952	40848
剑阁县	Jiange	1688462	512686	447783	727993	41567
苍溪县	Cangxi	2119055	586534	561797	970724	42250
遂宁市	**Suining**					
船山区	Chuanshan	4744785	244847	1828904	2671034	56351
安居区	Anju	2550070	468441	1283802	797827	61226
蓬溪县	Pengxi	2089989	343529	847383	899077	50605
大英县	Daying	1959622	328822	716761	914039	52118
射洪市	Shehong	6010537	827543	3359602	1823392	84358
内江市	**Neijiang**					
内江市中区	Neijiang Downtown	3355495	356725	1050378	1948392	80564
东兴区	Dongxing	3162796	592698	567245	2002853	41975
威远县	Weiyuan	4506359	565572	1943351	1997436	85754
资中县	Zizhong	3383105	943774	907203	1532128	40638
隆昌市	Longchang	3663299	515511	1149215	1998573	66910
乐山市	**Leshan**					
乐山市中区	Leshan Downtown	4807733	372852	1251100	3183781	57543
沙湾区	Shawan	2264066	211768	1438203	614095	161143
五通桥区	Wutongqiao	4017174	299894	2835464	881816	170581

12-2 续表 2 continued

县(市、区)	Counties (City,Districts)	地区生产总值(万元) Gross Regional Product (10 000 yuan)	第一产业 Primary Industry	第二产业 Secondary Industry	第三产业 Tertiary Industry	人均地区生产总值(元) Per Capita Gross Regional Product (yuan)
金口河区	Jinkouhe	384672	53158	185990	145524	101229
犍为县	Qianwei	2854988	534230	1150875	1169883	69212
井研县	Jingyan	1489828	397508	440975	651345	54077
夹江县	Jiajiang	2357005	377298	1066113	913594	78567
沐川县	Muchuan	934044	233216	318244	382584	50083
峨边县	Ebian	690411	97341	330479	262591	57296
马边县	Mabian	647311	141949	254245	251117	34069
峨眉山市	Emeishan	4028037	363833	1072996	2591208	96944
南充市	**Nanchong**					
顺庆区	Shunqing	5228373	336023	1658085	3234265	62955
高坪区	Gaoping	2405971	454336	836404	1115231	42773
嘉陵区	Jialing	2422518	506951	999483	916084	46275
南部县	Nanbu	4720952	904526	2087487	1728939	58682
营山县	Yingshan	2699827	537525	892668	1269634	44079
蓬安县	Pengan	2102560	498488	691796	912276	46312
仪陇县	Yilong	2707100	683024	882044	1142032	37782
西充县	Xichong	2123388	502092	596215	1025081	51476
阆中市	Langzhong	2936863	646828	847926	1442109	47871
眉山市	**Meishan**					
东坡区	Dongpo	6110856	659287	2492064	2959505	67259
彭山区	Pengshan	2200173	194655	1065036	940482	66642
仁寿县	Renshou	5431851	1037398	1947528	2446925	49033
洪雅县	Hongya	1603334	239475	486631	877228	54286
丹棱县	Danling	910802	163767	341171	405864	61272
青神县	Qingshen	1112934	138198	471595	503141	66444
宜宾市	**Yibin**					
翠屏区	Cuiping	15124594	507838	9763209	4853547	164756
南溪区	Nanxi	2371362	392026	1009961	969375	71319
叙州区	Xuzhou	6403285	634639	2943796	2824850	67156
江安县	Jiangan	2355355	421266	854090	1079999	55096
长宁县	Changning	2195566	402919	806458	986189	66432
高县	Gaoxian	2159691	363381	796631	999679	57210
珙县	Gongxian	2167370	327884	863610	975876	65678
筠连县	Junlian	2006982	359393	751818	895771	61095
兴文县	Xingwen	2087077	348990	695500	1042587	54851
屏山县	Pingshan	1195069	283430	403822	507817	48878
广安市	**Guangan**					
广安区	Guanganqu	2733539	405341	381488	1946710	36816
前锋区	Qianfeng	1635281	181543	839284	614454	71194
岳池县	Yuechi	3155871	673048	837848	1644975	42742
武胜县	Wusheng	2833638	476773	856352	1500513	51363

12−2 续表 3 continued

县(市、区)	Counties (City,Districts)	地区生产总值(万元) Gross Regional Product (10 000 yuan)	第一产业 Primary Industry	第二产业 Secondary Industry	第三产业 Tertiary Industry	人均地区生产总值(元) Per Capita Gross Regional Product (yuan)
邻水县	Linshui	2825813	578033	821856	1425924	40227
华蓥市	Huaying	1940927	163051	864702	913174	72610
达州市	**Dazhou**					
通川区	Tongchuan	4120535	294275	1148860	2677400	45221
达川区	Dachuan	3400633	520806	966455	1913372	36271
宣汉县	Xuanhan	7011186	1066741	3520520	2423925	73934
开江县	Kaijiang	1668304	428807	351716	887781	40755
大竹县	Dazhu	4513595	741544	1546227	2225824	54211
渠县	Quxian	4200597	921922	1043287	2235388	46743
万源市	Wanyuan	1652047	431158	384062	836827	41111
雅安市	**Yaan**					
雨城区	Yucheng	2808429	359188	792232	1657009	76109
名山区	Mingshan	1350464	335595	445046	569823	53273
荥经县	Yingjing	909879	161880	243705	504294	69723
汉源县	Hanyuan	1552906	309881	474750	768275	54584
石棉县	Shimian	1355919	187364	477300	691255	118940
天全县	Tianquan	930843	157786	295228	477829	70787
芦山县	Lushan	683025	141338	224693	316994	68303
宝兴县	Baoxing	508861	84499	219815	204547	106013
巴中市	**Bazhong**					
巴州区	Bazhou	2332769	411100	482976	1438693	32737
恩阳区	Enyang	935621	286499	186573	462549	27836
通江县	Tongjiang	1345193	415840	291396	637957	26646
南江县	Nanjiang	1386617	377874	347967	660776	30654
平昌县	Pingchang	1802591	460654	456869	885068	28270
资阳市	**Ziyang**					
雁江区	Yanjiang	4403116	640843	1496260	2266013	51529
安岳县	Anyue	3359295	900012	754838	1704445	36063
乐至县	Lezhi	2429827	425546	745964	1258317	51154
阿坝州	**Aba**					
马尔康市	Maerkang	706232	48965	225380	431887	117509
汶川县	Wenchuan	915473	129296	408900	377277	109967
理县	Lixian	348897	44024	97935	206938	97051
茂县	Maoxian	555294	133158	198107	224029	58421
松潘县	Songpan	318554	69205	30403	218946	47333
九寨沟县	Jiuzhaigou	370986	29598	50261	291127	55871
金川县	Jinchuan	253504	49839	26657	177008	44358
小金县	Xiaojin	299315	59255	51933	188127	46805
黑水县	Heishui	313179	50009	86444	176726	72832
壤塘县	Rangtang	155015	43723	6400	104892	34182

12−2 续表 4 continued

县(市、区)	Counties (City,Districts)	地区生产总值(万元) Gross Regional Product (10 000 yuan)	第一产业 Primary Industry	第二产业 Secondary Industry	第三产业 Tertiary Industry	人均地区生产总值(元) Per Capita Gross Regional Product (yuan)
阿坝县	Abaxian	236449	82270	13971	140208	29137
若尔盖县	Ruoergai	341202	151360	14385	175457	43913
红原县	Hongyuan	217820	94139	14553	109128	45712
甘孜州	**Ganzi**					
康定市	Kangding	1253270	66787	504540	681943	97190
泸定县	Luding	354577	70348	86385	197844	41544
丹巴县	Danba	263847	45070	76222	142555	52299
九龙县	Jiulong	367928	48191	178404	141333	68261
雅江县	Yajiang	396553	32923	235673	127957	76114
道孚县	Daofu	160021	35536	16018	108467	30393
炉霍县	Luhuo	157487	35086	26627	95774	33651
甘孜县	Ganzixian	224694	51779	34512	138403	30675
新龙县	Xinlong	150842	38218	10732	101892	33821
德格县	Dege	200652	65642	10019	124991	22763
白玉县	Baiyu	219958	45281	56521	118156	37376
石渠县	Shiqu	230408	52399	22262	155747	22790
色达县	Seda	179950	65817	11228	102905	28473
理塘县	Litang	262135	89943	27567	144625	38921
巴塘县	Batang	238704	45811	63352	129541	48223
乡城县	Xiangcheng	197063	30132	74031	92900	64717
稻城县	Daocheng	155521	27026	12572	115923	46494
得荣县	Derong	119921	22789	25732	71400	49148
凉山州	**Liangshan**					
西昌市	Xichang	7510603	643140	3262823	3604640	77597
会理市	Huili	2404358	753079	729435	921844	61250
木里县	Muli	668931	125244	314395	229292	53686
盐源县	Yanyuan	1737125	651930	576879	508316	50564
德昌县	Dechang	1001166	245752	301832	453582	45978
会东县	Huidong	1927513	646621	593108	687784	55789
宁南县	Ningnan	1000175	328551	329752	341872	54343
普格县	Puge	401982	112495	77419	212068	22020
布拖县	Butuo	454940	164364	79376	211200	24135
金阳县	Jinyang	550865	121739	180077	249049	32252
昭觉县	Zhaojue	545590	173583	67782	304225	21283
喜德县	Xide	408287	109862	59865	238560	25391
冕宁县	Mianning	1440140	379433	512967	547740	39397
越西县	Yuexi	698824	186820	96962	415042	22924
甘洛县	Ganluo	562771	110261	187474	265036	27076
美姑县	Meigu	454952	120834	59185	274933	18827
雷波县	Leibo	842845	160383	364707	317755	34621

12-3 各县(市、区)地区生产总值指数(2023年)
Indices of Gross Regional Product by Counties (City, Districts)(2023)

上年=100 (preceding year=100)

县(市、区)	Counties (City,Districts)	地区生产总值 Gross Regional Product	第一产业 Primary Industry	第二产业 Secondary Industry	第三产业 Tertiary Industry	人均地区生产总值 Per Capita Gross Regional Product
成都市	**Chengdu**					
锦江区	Jinjiang	106.0	50.9	102.4	106.7	105.4
青羊区	Qingyang	106.1	60.8	100.8	107.0	105.4
金牛区	Jinniu	106.2	101.1	103.4	106.9	105.9
武侯区	Wuhou	106.3	104.8	102.5	107.0	105.5
成华区	Chenghua	106.2	7.7	104.4	107.1	105.6
龙泉驿区	Longquanyi	106.1	102.1	106.0	106.6	105.3
青白江区	Qingbaijiang	105.4	103.2	101.0	107.4	104.5
新都区	Xindu	106.0	103.1	102.9	107.6	105.3
温江区	Wenjiang	105.5	102.5	100.3	108.8	104.3
双流区	Shuangliu	107.4	102.0	104.2	108.8	106.0
郫都区	Pidu	105.1	102.6	102.5	108.7	104.7
新津区	Xinjin	105.3	102.9	105.3	105.6	105.0
金堂县	Jintang	108.1	103.8	108.5	109.1	107.8
大邑县	Dayi	105.5	103.7	102.9	108.3	106.0
蒲江县	Pujiang	105.4	102.6	104.9	106.5	106.0
都江堰市	Dujiangyan	105.2	103.4	99.3	108.8	105.3
彭州市	Pengzhou	103.1	103.2	100.6	107.1	103.4
邛崃市	Qionglai	106.2	103.6	105.4	107.8	106.7
崇州市	Chongzhou	105.6	103.6	104.5	107.5	105.8
简阳市	Jianyang	110.4	102.4	103.0	115.2	110.7
自贡市	**Zigong**					
自流井区	Ziliujing	106.6	104.0	105.6	107.0	106.9
贡井区	Gongjing	106.2	104.0	105.5	107.5	108.1
大安区	Daan	106.3	104.1	105.2	107.9	107.6
沿滩区	Yantan	105.8	104.0	105.5	106.8	106.5
荣县	Rongxian	105.6	104.1	105.7	106.8	106.6
富顺县	Fushun	106.4	104.1	106.5	107.4	106.9
攀枝花市	**Panzhihua**					
东区	Dongqu	106.7	103.8	107.2	106.1	106.5
西区	Xiqu	104.5	103.9	103.9	106.1	104.5
仁和区	Renhe	106.5	104.2	105.2	109.9	106.3
米易县	Miyi	106.8	104.2	107.0	108.1	106.5
盐边县	Yanbian	106.5	104.1	106.3	109.0	106.2
泸州市	**Luzhou**					
江阳区	Jiangyang	105.6	104.2	108.9	102.1	105.3
纳溪区	Naxi	106.5	103.8	106.3	108.0	106.1
龙马潭区	Longmatan	106.6	103.8	105.3	108.6	106.4
泸县	Luxian	100.5	103.7	96.9	105.0	100.6
合江县	Hejiang	106.5	103.5	107.2	107.1	106.4
叙永县	Xuyong	108.1	104.0	111.3	108.0	108.1
古蔺县	Gulin	110.0	104.6	114.2	108.5	109.9

12-3 续表 1 continued

上年=100 (preceding year=100)

县(市、区)	Counties (City,Districts)	地区生产总值 Gross Regional Product	第一产业 Primary Industry	第二产业 Secondary Industry	第三产业 Tertiary Industry	人均地区生产总值 Per Capita Gross Regional Product
德阳市	**Deyang**					
旌阳区	Jingyang	106.2	104.1	106.5	106.1	106.0
罗江区	Luojiang	106.0	104.2	105.6	107.6	106.2
中江县	Zhongjiang	106.1	104.1	105.8	107.6	106.2
广汉市	Guanghan	106.0	104.0	105.5	107.0	105.9
什邡市	Shifang	108.1	104.5	108.0	109.0	108.5
绵竹市	Mianzhu	108.0	104.4	109.3	107.2	108.3
绵阳市	**Mianyang**					
涪城区	Fucheng	109.7	103.4	110.5	109.4	108.7
游仙区	Youxian	105.7	103.6	102.4	108.2	105.4
安州区	Anzhou	108.3	104.1	108.8	109.6	108.1
三台县	Santai	108.0	103.7	109.2	109.3	108.0
盐亭县	Yanting	108.1	103.9	111.0	108.8	108.5
梓潼县	Zitong	108.0	103.9	108.3	109.9	108.0
北川县	Beichuan	108.2	103.8	109.8	108.8	108.0
平武县	Pingwu	108.0	103.7	109.0	109.0	109.0
江油市	Jiangyou	105.7	103.7	102.3	109.8	105.6
广元市	**Guangyuan**					
利州区	Lizhou	106.5	103.9	107.7	105.8	105.3
昭化区	Zhaohua	106.0	104.0	107.0	106.4	107.3
朝天区	Chaotian	106.7	103.8	107.6	107.1	107.8
旺苍县	Wangcang	107.0	104.2	109.5	105.7	107.7
青川县	Qingchuan	105.6	103.8	107.1	105.6	107.3
剑阁县	Jiange	105.8	103.9	106.5	106.8	108.9
苍溪县	Cangxi	105.3	103.3	103.6	107.5	106.3
遂宁市	**Suining**					
船山区	Chuanshan	106.5	103.7	105.1	107.9	106.2
安居区	Anju	107.0	104.3	107.7	107.9	108.1
蓬溪县	Pengxi	106.2	104.1	105.3	108.0	107.6
大英县	Daying	106.0	104.1	104.5	108.1	107.1
射洪市	Shehong	108.1	103.7	109.9	107.8	109.0
内江市	**Neijiang**					
内江市中区	Neijiang Downtown	106.7	104.1	105.6	107.8	107.6
东兴区	Dongxing	107.0	104.3	108.5	107.5	107.5
威远县	Weiyuan	107.0	104.2	106.6	108.3	107.7
资中县	Zizhong	107.3	104.5	109.0	108.2	108.0
隆昌市	Longchang	107.2	104.1	107.2	108.1	107.8
乐山市	**Leshan**					
乐山市中区	Leshan Downtown	105.4	102.9	105.5	105.8	104.9
沙湾区	Shawan	106.6	106.7	106.8	106.3	107.4
五通桥区	Wutongqiao	110.6	102.9	113.5	105.0	109.9

12-3 续表 2 continued

上年=100 (preceding year=100)

县(市、区)	Counties (City,Districts)	地区生产总值 Gross Regional Product	第一产业 Primary Industry	第二产业 Secondary Industry	第三产业 Tertiary Industry	人均地区生产总值 Per Capita Gross Regional Product
金口河区	Jinkouhe	104.3	103.1	102.8	107.0	104.3
犍为县	Qianwei	107.4	104.7	107.4	108.9	108.0
井研县	Jingyan	105.2	102.8	107.2	105.7	106.0
夹江县	Jiajiang	101.5	105.6	96.4	106.1	102.1
沐川县	Muchuan	105.6	104.5	106.4	105.8	106.2
峨边县	Ebian	106.9	103.6	107.3	107.9	107.4
马边县	Mabian	107.2	105.2	110.6	105.4	107.0
峨眉山市	Emeishan	106.9	104.5	98.7	111.2	107.1
南充市	**Nanchong**					
顺庆区	Shunqing	107.0	104.0	106.6	107.5	107.1
高坪区	Gaoping	108.0	104.1	110.2	107.7	108.3
嘉陵区	Jialing	107.3	103.8	109.3	107.1	107.8
南部县	Nanbu	101.0	104.2	94.9	107.4	101.5
营山县	Yingshan	108.1	103.7	111.2	108.0	108.6
蓬安县	Pengan	106.2	103.8	106.7	107.2	106.9
仪陇县	Yilong	107.2	104.4	109.9	107.0	107.7
西充县	Xichong	103.8	104.3	98.7	107.1	104.4
阆中市	Langzhong	106.3	103.9	106.6	107.3	106.9
眉山市	**Meishan**					
东坡区	Dongpo	107.1	104.2	107.0	107.8	106.9
彭山区	Pengshan	105.2	104.3	106.1	104.3	105.0
仁寿县	Renshou	104.8	104.1	101.7	107.9	105.1
洪雅县	Hongya	107.6	104.4	109.7	107.5	107.8
丹棱县	Danling	108.6	104.5	111.2	108.3	108.8
青神县	Qingshen	107.0	104.0	108.9	106.2	107.3
宜宾市	**Yibin**					
翠屏区	Cuiping	109.2	103.5	109.9	108.4	108.0
南溪区	Nanxi	106.0	104.7	105.3	107.4	106.6
叙州区	Xuzhou	106.1	104.5	104.8	108.0	105.5
江安县	Jiangan	105.9	104.2	104.7	107.6	106.2
长宁县	Changning	107.2	104.5	108.1	107.7	107.2
高县	Gaoxian	105.9	104.0	105.8	106.8	106.6
珙县	Gongxian	105.6	103.6	104.5	107.3	104.9
筠连县	Junlian	107.8	104.4	109.5	108.2	108.1
兴文县	Xingwen	107.3	104.6	106.5	108.8	107.0
屏山县	Pingshan	107.6	104.8	108.2	109.0	107.4
广安市	**Guangan**					
广安区	Guanganqu	106.3	103.8	106.1	106.9	106.5
前锋区	Qianfeng	106.8	103.4	107.7	106.9	107.4
岳池县	Yuechi	108.0	104.1	110.0	108.6	108.4
武胜县	Wusheng	106.3	104.0	106.1	107.3	106.6

12-3 续表 3 continued

上年=100 (preceding year=100)

县(市、区)	Counties (City,Districts)	地区生产总值 Gross Regional Product	第一产业 Primary Industry	第二产业 Secondary Industry	第三产业 Tertiary Industry	人均地区生产总值 Per Capita Gross Regional Product
邻水县	Linshui	106.1	103.9	106.8	106.6	106.4
华蓥市	Huaying	106.1	103.5	106.2	106.5	106.5
达州市	**Dazhou**					
通川区	Tongchuan	107.0	103.3	106.5	107.7	106.9
达川区	Dachuan	104.6	103.7	100.8	107.1	105.0
宣汉县	Xuanhan	107.5	103.2	109.3	107.3	107.8
开江县	Kaijiang	104.8	103.2	102.3	106.8	105.4
大竹县	Dazhu	106.8	103.4	107.2	107.8	107.3
渠县	Quxian	107.0	103.5	108.3	108.0	108.0
万源市	Wanyuan	106.2	103.6	108.0	107.1	106.7
雅安市	**Yaan**					
雨城区	Yucheng	106.7	103.7	109.1	106.4	106.7
名山区	Mingshan	105.3	103.8	105.3	106.4	105.5
荥经县	Yingjing	104.0	104.4	99.0	106.7	104.4
汉源县	Hanyuan	106.0	104.6	106.2	106.5	106.2
石棉县	Shimian	105.5	104.3	104.0	106.9	105.5
天全县	Tianquan	106.1	104.0	105.5	107.3	106.1
芦山县	Lushan	105.3	104.1	104.5	106.6	104.8
宝兴县	Baoxing	106.9	104.1	108.0	107.2	106.9
巴中市	**Bazhong**					
巴州区	Bazhou	106.0	103.9	110.8	105.0	106.3
恩阳区	Enyang	106.3	104.0	112.0	105.2	107.3
通江县	Tongjiang	106.1	103.9	111.0	105.0	107.2
南江县	Nanjiang	107.3	104.0	112.9	106.0	108.5
平昌县	Pingchang	104.8	103.7	106.3	104.5	106.1
资阳市	**Ziyang**					
雁江区	Yanjiang	105.7	103.7	105.0	106.8	106.1
安岳县	Anyue	105.7	103.8	106.9	106.3	106.4
乐至县	Lezhi	106.2	103.9	107.2	106.5	107.8
阿坝州	**Aba**					
马尔康市	Maerkang	105.8	107.8	102.1	107.4	103.0
汶川县	Wenchuan	106.9	107.4	106.3	107.2	106.0
理县	Lixian	105.6	105.5	105.0	105.8	105.7
茂县	Maoxian	106.8	107.4	107.2	106.1	106.2
松潘县	Songpan	107.0	111.1	104.4	106.1	106.7
九寨沟县	Jiuzhaigou	109.2	108.5	100.7	110.9	108.8
金川县	Jinchuan	106.6	105.3	106.5	107.1	106.4
小金县	Xiaojin	106.7	111.2	99.0	107.5	106.7
黑水县	Heishui	104.4	105.9	100.5	105.9	104.4
壤塘县	Rangtang	106.8	111.1	96.2	105.6	106.2

12-3 续表 4 continued

上年=100 (preceding year=100)

县(市、区)	Counties (City,Districts)	地区生产总值 Gross Regional Product	第一产业 Primary Industry	第二产业 Secondary Industry	第三产业 Tertiary Industry	人均地区生产总值 Per Capita Gross Regional Product
阿坝县	Abaxian	108.4	112.4	101.0	107.0	107.6
若尔盖县	Ruoergai	108.0	111.5	97.2	105.4	107.4
红原县	Hongyuan	108.5	112.4	105.7	105.3	107.6
甘孜州	**Ganzi**					
康定市	Kangding	105.6	104.3	105.7	105.6	104.5
泸定县	Luding	104.0	104.4	102.0	104.9	102.9
丹巴县	Danba	103.2	104.2	98.1	105.7	102.5
九龙县	Jiulong	106.0	104.4	105.5	107.3	104.9
雅江县	Yajiang	119.5	104.1	138.2	103.9	118.0
道孚县	Daofu	104.7	104.2	101.7	105.3	105.7
炉霍县	Luhuo	105.6	104.3	109.8	105.1	105.5
甘孜县	Ganzixian	106.0	104.1	107.8	106.3	104.7
新龙县	Xinlong	106.1	103.5	104.8	107.3	106.7
德格县	Dege	105.9	104.1	99.6	107.4	105.7
白玉县	Baiyu	105.8	104.1	103.0	107.4	105.5
石渠县	Shiqu	103.7	104.1	95.9	104.8	104.9
色达县	Seda	103.5	103.1	98.4	104.5	105.2
理塘县	Litang	103.6	104.1	93.1	105.5	103.3
巴塘县	Batang	109.7	104.0	147.7	104.3	110.0
乡城县	Xiangcheng	111.4	104.2	122.1	107.0	112.3
稻城县	Daocheng	105.9	104.2	104.1	106.6	104.4
得荣县	Derong	102.1	104.3	92.3	105.3	104.2
凉山州	**Liangshan**					
西昌市	Xichang	108.7	104.4	108.7	109.7	108.3
会理市	Huili	106.4	104.4	105.2	108.8	106.1
木里县	Muli	103.7	104.3	102.8	104.6	103.3
盐源县	Yanyuan	105.5	104.3	105.0	107.6	105.2
德昌县	Dechang	108.9	104.2	113.0	109.5	108.6
会东县	Huidong	107.9	104.3	109.3	110.3	107.6
宁南县	Ningnan	108.4	104.2	112.8	108.3	108.4
普格县	Puge	104.8	104.0	108.5	103.9	104.3
布拖县	Butuo	104.6	104.2	109.4	103.1	104.0
金阳县	Jinyang	105.9	104.2	105.6	107.1	105.6
昭觉县	Zhaojue	104.4	104.2	103.2	104.8	103.8
喜德县	Xide	105.3	104.1	103.8	106.3	104.6
冕宁县	Mianning	106.5	104.1	106.4	108.3	106.4
越西县	Yuexi	106.1	104.2	98.6	109.0	105.9
甘洛县	Ganluo	106.9	104.2	102.5	111.4	106.7
美姑县	Meigu	105.5	103.9	99.9	107.9	105.3
雷波县	Leibo	103.2	104.3	101.3	104.7	102.5

12-4 各县(市、区)民营经济增加值(2023年)
Added Value of Civilian-owned Economy by Counties (City, Districts)(2023)

县(市、区)	Counties (City,Districts)	民营经济增加值(万元) Added Value of Civilian-owned Economy (10 000 yuan)	第一产业 Primary Industry	第二产业 Secondary Industry	第三产业 Tertiary Industry	人均民营经济增加值(元) Per Capita Added Value of Civilian-owned Economy (yuan)
成都市	**Chengdu**					
锦江区	Jinjiang	6894496		176609	6717887	75194
青羊区	Qingyang	6209927		784144	5425783	64010
金牛区	Jinniu	7095013		1144248	5950765	55173
武侯区	Wuhou	20212182		3064761	17147421	106318
成华区	Chenghua	4505597		226264	4279333	32011
龙泉驿区	Longquanyi	6409807	34491	3621899	2753417	46765
青白江区	Qingbaijiang	3204288	27986	1077454	2098848	63089
新都区	Xindu	6103943	39703	2438702	3625538	38508
温江区	Wenjiang	4179739	32761	1583100	2563878	41594
双流区	Shuangliu	10937943	21977	3470021	7445945	39435
郫都区	Pidu	8395336	33502	4855172	3506662	49578
新津区	Xinjin	3244488	24205	1632804	1587479	86647
金堂县	Jintang	4252156	107117	2306852	1838187	52652
大邑县	Dayi	1758577	52568	1018835	687174	34553
蒲江县	Pujiang	1213345	37269	585873	590203	47258
都江堰市	Dujiangyan	2815525	58489	804577	1952459	39378
彭州市	Pengzhou	2319996	74255	1157654	1088087	29726
邛崃市	Qionglai	2419615	74389	1236387	1108839	40354
崇州市	Chongzhou	2444976	59061	1441609	944306	32947
简阳市	Jianyang	2604359	99120	1075183	1430056	22977
自贡市	**Zigong**					
自流井区	Ziliujing	2021112	26669	642251	1352192	42238
贡井区	Gongjing	995567	38726	476651	480190	46091
大安区	Daan	1229616	50012	627946	551658	43144
沿滩区	Yantan	1583638	61481	936759	585398	54327
荣县	Rongxian	1634326	233971	696306	704049	35762
富顺县	Fushun	2119986	122043	1093715	904228	29754
攀枝花市	**Panzhihua**					
东区	Dongqu	2382227	11949	1166987	1203291	57681
西区	Xiqu	485465	9593	338315	137557	37633
仁和区	Renhe	1802799	76594	1194141	532064	67394
米易县	Miyi	1113433	56674	627325	429434	48835
盐边县	Yanbian	727562	71135	429243	227184	40533
泸州市	**Luzhou**					
江阳区	Jiangyang	4146522	49114	2445854	1651554	54203
纳溪区	Naxi	1406375	79382	819176	507817	39175
龙马潭区	Longmatan	2478747	35884	1270220	1172643	51373
泸县	Luxian	2835915	196972	1723724	915219	37095
合江县	Hejiang	1932369	146939	1072903	712527	28005
叙永县	Xuyong	1032197	102202	472979	457016	18699
古蔺县	Gulin	1340954	112448	702446	526060	20567

12-4 续表 1 continued

县(市、区)	Counties (City,Districts)	民营经济增加值（万元）Added Value of Civilian-owned Economy (10 000 yuan)	第一产业 Primary Industry	第二产业 Secondary Industry	第三产业 Tertiary Industry	人均民营经济增加值（元）Per Capita Added Value of Civilian-owned Economy (yuan)
德阳市	**Deyang**					
旌阳区	Jingyang	4111672	105869	1690332	2315471	49538
罗江区	Luojiang	1198043	73134	779859	345050	57460
中江县	Zhongjiang	3096523	314850	1592935	1188738	32698
广汉市	Guanghan	3652545	191107	2018869	1442569	58254
什邡市	Shifang	2182887	50529	1040303	1092055	53700
绵竹市	Mianzhu	2871345	112431	1813774	945140	65556
绵阳市	**Mianyang**					
涪城区	Fucheng	8404689	34864	4315858	4053967	63234
游仙区	Youxian	2981238	44538	985127	1951573	52385
安州区	Anzhou	1603520	49584	846382	707554	41753
三台县	Santai	3128094	116147	1487622	1524325	33130
盐亭县	Yanting	1342949	51421	522709	768819	36975
梓潼县	Zitong	1211933	42153	509143	660637	43658
北川县	Beichuan	643411	19125	239938	384348	35895
平武县	Pingwu	466346	16105	232439	217802	37115
江油市	Jiangyou	3970274	75660	1894640	1999974	54216
广元市	**Guangyuan**					
利州区	Lizhou	2239147	49623	1156236	1033288	35354
昭化区	Zhaohua	445146	86790	213506	144850	34548
朝天区	Chaotian	460234	48335	252846	159053	37601
旺苍县	Wangcang	920776	105440	513594	301742	28869
青川县	Qingchuan	328151	43043	126782	158326	22038
剑阁县	Jiange	928089	183230	387590	357269	22848
苍溪县	Cangxi	1163039	195413	407599	560027	23189
遂宁市	**Suining**					
船山区	Chuanshan	3009225	39616	1412355	1557254	35739
安居区	Anju	1350713	170496	697179	483038	32430
蓬溪县	Pengxi	1273416	100334	688016	485066	30833
大英县	Daying	1243629	86606	615129	541894	33075
射洪市	Shehong	3721047	173049	2556047	991951	52225
内江市	**Neijiang**					
内江市中区	Neijiang Downtown	1905420	29728	717299	1158393	45748
东兴区	Dongxing	1751852	88810	489546	1173496	23250
威远县	Weiyuan	2771963	44174	1616481	1111308	52749
资中县	Zizhong	2103320	262924	893755	946641	25265
隆昌市	Longchang	2267147	52354	1112265	1102528	41409
乐山市	**Leshan**					
乐山市中区	Leshan Downtown	2355032	118377	794282	1442373	28187
沙湾区	Shawan	872390	66761	483149	322480	62092
五通桥区	Wutongqiao	3076083	92652	2527448	455983	130619

12-4 续表 2 continued

县(市、区)	Counties (City,Districts)	民营经济增加值(万元) Added Value of Civilian-owned Economy (10 000 yuan)	第一产业 Primary Industry	第二产业 Secondary Industry	第三产业 Tertiary Industry	人均民营经济增加值(元) Per Capita Added Value of Civilian-owned Economy (yuan)
金口河区	Jinkouhe	229323	17026	145343	66954	60348
犍为县	Qianwei	1655362	171117	929533	554712	40130
井研县	Jingyan	861968	127575	424888	309505	31287
夹江县	Jiajiang	1435716	118682	864370	452664	47857
沐川县	Muchuan	445832	73454	182513	189865	23905
峨边县	Ebian	317836	28004	152763	137069	26376
马边县	Mabian	293467	43206	123997	126264	15446
峨眉山市	Emeishan	2228731	116319	659364	1453048	53640
南充市	**Nanchong**					
顺庆区	Shunqing	3103040	85474	1348523	1669043	37364
高坪区	Gaoping	1420726	117105	741606	562015	25257
嘉陵区	Jialing	1414974	135905	857785	421284	27029
南部县	Nanbu	2863258	246399	1545557	1071302	35591
营山县	Yingshan	1598550	156910	722736	718904	26099
蓬安县	Pengan	1237357	132777	576933	527647	27255
仪陇县	Yilong	1617736	191577	742491	683668	22578
西充县	Xichong	1242378	130468	539380	572530	30118
阆中市	Langzhong	1794706	180392	708259	906055	29254
眉山市	**Meishan**					
东坡区	Dongpo	3301874	91371	1604634	1605869	36342
彭山区	Pengshan	1256999	28349	561461	667189	38074
仁寿县	Renshou	3125316	239518	1333565	1552233	28212
洪雅县	Hongya	958106	55387	309383	593336	32440
丹棱县	Danling	534556	39196	215832	279528	35961
青神县	Qingshen	647901	38000	255386	354515	38681
宜宾市	**Yibin**					
翠屏区	Cuiping	7805047	123968	5149252	2531827	85022
南溪区	Nanxi	1550940	98476	897947	554517	46645
叙州区	Xuzhou	3816944	158430	2285661	1372853	40031
江安县	Jiangan	1500261	104618	782280	613363	35094
长宁县	Changning	1451834	101431	757761	592642	43928
高县	Gaoxian	1316488	89161	697033	530294	34874
珙县	Gongxian	1245444	80570	656349	508525	37741
筠连县	Junlian	1234295	91811	661477	481007	37574
兴文县	Xingwen	1324626	87567	613556	623503	34813
屏山县	Pingshan	728884	69998	365338	293548	29811
广安市	**Guangan**					
广安区	Guanganqu	1480449	160474	319563	1000412	19939
前锋区	Qianfeng	842946	24211	500928	317807	36699
岳池县	Yuechi	1864327	160690	836928	866709	25250
武胜县	Wusheng	1628587	159795	691026	777766	29520

12-4 续表 3 continued

县(市、区)	Counties (City,Districts)	民营经济增加值(万元) Added Value of Civilian-owned Economy (10 000 yuan)	第一产业 Primary Industry	第二产业 Secondary Industry	第三产业 Tertiary Industry	人均民营经济增加值(元) Per Capita Added Value of Civilian-owned Economy (yuan)
邻水县	Linshui	1623742	116211	725511	782020	23115
华蓥市	Huaying	1101324	36524	643560	421240	41200
达州市	**Dazhou**					
通川区	Tongchuan	2701312	67951	956265	1677096	29646
达川区	Dachuan	2194023	122300	895899	1175824	23402
宣汉县	Xuanhan	3708236	199438	2304743	1204055	39104
开江县	Kaijiang	1002317	87218	314189	600910	24486
大竹县	Dazhu	2809551	165398	1303917	1340236	33744
渠县	Quxian	2741334	228595	887386	1625353	30505
万源市	Wanyuan	988782	95150	303291	590341	24606
雅安市	**Yaan**					
雨城区	Yucheng	1421803	56607	535963	829233	38531
名山区	Mingshan	791939	55486	378016	358437	31240
荥经县	Yingjing	628588	31215	231363	366010	48168
汉源县	Hanyuan	841745	50010	334832	456903	29587
石棉县	Shimian	792463	32658	377375	382430	69514
天全县	Tianquan	629166	32501	266123	330542	47845
芦山县	Lushan	415457	29636	205157	180664	41546
宝兴县	Baoxing	312978	14728	188274	109976	65204
巴中市	**Bazhong**					
巴州区	Bazhou	1315388	145221	438501	731666	18460
恩阳区	Enyang	516133	97630	166997	251506	15356
通江县	Tongjiang	751741	140873	262892	347976	14891
南江县	Nanjiang	747195	127048	322519	297628	16518
平昌县	Pingchang	1012827	160750	429941	422136	15884
资阳市	**Ziyang**					
雁江区	Yanjiang	2432629	156060	1227101	1049468	28468
安岳县	Anyue	1504493	174382	575737	754374	16151
乐至县	Lezhi	1567382	116209	603441	847732	32998
阿坝州	**Aba**					
马尔康市	Maerkang	302262	21620	161009	119633	50293
汶川县	Wenchuan	430505	63637	218148	148720	51712
理县	Lixian	139322	19896	60143	59283	38754
茂县	Maoxian	219502	43711	91699	84092	23093
松潘县	Songpan	120660	31535	20797	68328	17929
九寨沟县	Jiuzhaigou	174718	17004	40888	116826	26313
金川县	Jinchuan	112470	24057	19303	69110	19680
小金县	Xiaojin	136244	26945	40519	68780	21305
黑水县	Heishui	152425	26893	80264	45268	35448
壤塘县	Rangtang	57996	22089	4524	31383	12789

12-4 续表 4 continued

县(市、区)	Counties (City,Districts)	民营经济增加值(万元) Added Value of Civilian-owned Economy (10 000 yuan)	第一产业 Primary Industry	第二产业 Secondary Industry	第三产业 Tertiary Industry	人均民营经济增加值(元) Per Capita Added Value of Civilian-owned Economy (yuan)
阿坝县	Abaxian	104946	36947	13190	54809	12932
若尔盖县	Ruoergai	164390	88286	11907	64197	21157
红原县	Hongyuan	102675	50617	11532	40526	21548
甘孜州	**Ganzi**					
康定市	Kangding	423231	64415	80203	278613	32821
泸定县	Luding	168915	42559	25397	100959	19791
丹巴县	Danba	100134	36941	11251	51942	19848
九龙县	Jiulong	93605	36048	26502	31055	17366
雅江县	Yajiang	94349	29150	25551	39648	18109
道孚县	Daofu	60219	28520	7996	23703	11438
炉霍县	Luhuo	62695	30677	13997	18021	13396
甘孜县	Ganzixian	122539	51217	29940	41382	16729
新龙县	Xinlong	68007	32711	9414	25882	15248
德格县	Dege	83523	52116	7257	24150	9475
白玉县	Baiyu	83542	39846	22575	21121	14196
石渠县	Shiqu	110521	51953	21331	37237	10932
色达县	Seda	71439	46297	9293	15849	11304
理塘县	Litang	117516	58032	22568	36916	17449
巴塘县	Batang	103185	42974	29951	30260	20845
乡城县	Xiangcheng	64148	25289	12513	26346	21067
稻城县	Daocheng	69649	21168	11375	37106	20822
得荣县	Derong	45114	18840	11336	14938	18489
凉山州	**Liangshan**					
西昌市	Xichang	4064847	193707	2156865	1714275	41997
会理市	Huili	1124144	243633	395166	485345	28637
木里县	Muli	165376	36098	50893	78385	13273
盐源县	Yanyuan	567028	199656	125554	241818	16505
德昌县	Dechang	502532	73551	220948	208033	23078
会东县	Huidong	773296	206830	191480	374986	22382
宁南县	Ningnan	367082	100675	129554	136853	19945
普格县	Puge	129468	33121	31232	65115	7092
布拖县	Butuo	140718	47874	25313	67531	7465
金阳县	Jinyang	163330	39039	37929	86362	9563
昭觉县	Zhaojue	162712	56800	21099	84813	6347
喜德县	Xide	141130	32648	41970	66512	8777
冕宁县	Mianning	594487	114540	221593	258354	16263
越西县	Yuexi	309766	57428	63978	188360	10161
甘洛县	Ganluo	251670	35063	121714	94893	12108
美姑县	Meigu	136143	36415	22547	77181	5634
雷波县	Leibo	355501	49346	184729	121426	14603

12−5 各县(市、区)民营经济增加值指数(2023年)
Indices of Civilian-owned Economy Added Value by Counties (City, Districts)(2023)

上年=100 (preceding year=100)

县(市、区)	Counties (City,Districts)	民营经济增加值 Added Value of Civilian-owned Economy	第一产业 Primary Industry	第二产业 Secondary Industry	第三产业 Tertiary Industry	人均民营经济增加值 Per Capita Added Value of Civilian-owned Economy
成都市	**Chengdu**					
锦江区	Jinjiang	110.2		90.2	110.8	109.5
青羊区	Qingyang	106.5		100.3	107.4	105.8
金牛区	Jinniu	100.8		100.6	100.8	100.5
武侯区	Wuhou	105.1		101.0	101.1	104.3
成华区	Chenghua	99.9		76.6	101.6	99.4
龙泉驿区	Longquanyi	110.8	79.3	114.6	106.7	109.9
青白江区	Qingbaijiang	107.3	111.9	96.3	114.0	106.3
新都区	Xindu	104.1	114.5	104.5	103.7	103.4
温江区	Wenjiang	99.0	96.2	92.7	103.9	98.0
双流区	Shuangliu	102.0	63.2	91.2	108.1	100.7
郫都区	Pidu	110.0	97.7	109.8	110.6	109.6
新津区	Xinjin	109.1	105.0	101.2	118.6	108.8
金堂县	Jintang	112.1	120.1	113.6	109.6	111.8
大邑县	Dayi	104.7	111.9	103.6	105.6	105.2
蒲江县	Pujiang	103.8	113.8	100.6	106.6	104.4
都江堰市	Dujiangyan	104.5	109.4	101.4	105.6	104.6
彭州市	Pengzhou	106.5	102.0	106.5	106.9	106.8
邛崃市	Qionglai	108.2	107.9	106.7	110.1	108.7
崇州市	Chongzhou	100.7	113.2	101.0	99.3	100.9
简阳市	Jianyang	108.1	101.9	104.1	112.0	108.4
自贡市	**Zigong**					
自流井区	Ziliujing	105.0	104.0	110.6	102.8	105.3
贡井区	Gongjing	105.0	104.0	110.7	100.0	106.9
大安区	Daan	105.4	104.1	109.2	101.5	106.7
沿滩区	Yantan	105.2	104.0	108.9	99.6	105.9
荣县	Rongxian	105.0	104.1	105.7	104.6	106.0
富顺县	Fushun	105.2	104.1	114.0	96.3	105.7
攀枝花市	**Panzhihua**					
东区	Dongqu	104.9	104.7	105.4	104.4	104.7
西区	Xiqu	107.0	104.8	107.6	105.5	107.0
仁和区	Renhe	106.3	105.0	104.8	109.9	106.1
米易县	Miyi	106.5	105.1	104.6	109.2	106.2
盐边县	Yanbian	108.7	105.0	108.7	110.0	108.3
泸州市	**Luzhou**					
江阳区	Jiangyang	103.8	104.2	108.6	97.5	103.6
纳溪区	Naxi	105.6	104.0	106.6	104.3	105.2
龙马潭区	Longmatan	105.2	104.0	103.2	107.5	105.0
泸县	Luxian	100.1	103.9	98.7	102.0	100.2
合江县	Hejiang	106.5	103.7	108.6	103.8	106.4
叙永县	Xuyong	107.7	104.1	109.2	107.0	107.7
古蔺县	Gulin	109.5	104.8	112.1	107.5	109.4

12−5 续表 1 continued

上年=100 (preceding year=100)

县(市、区)	Counties (City,Districts)	民营经济增加值 Added Value of Civilian-owned Economy	第一产业 Primary Industry	第二产业 Secondary Industry	第三产业 Tertiary Industry	人均民营经济增加值 Per Capita Added Value of Civilian-owned Economy
德阳市	**Deyang**					
旌阳区	Jingyang	106.5	105.2	102.0	110.0	106.3
罗江区	Luojiang	106.9	106.1	105.5	110.5	107.2
中江县	Zhongjiang	106.8	104.1	104.2	111.8	107.0
广汉市	Guanghan	106.0	104.9	100.8	114.3	105.9
什邡市	Shifang	108.8	105.2	108.2	109.6	109.2
绵竹市	Mianzhu	108.3	105.2	109.7	106.1	108.7
绵阳市	**Mianyang**					
涪城区	Fucheng	108.3	101.7	106.0	111.1	107.3
游仙区	Youxian	104.4	101.9	101.9	106.0	104.0
安州区	Anzhou	107.0	102.4	103.5	112.4	106.8
三台县	Santai	106.7	102.0	105.8	108.0	106.7
盐亭县	Yanting	106.8	102.2	109.6	105.2	107.1
梓潼县	Zitong	106.7	102.2	104.8	108.9	106.7
北川县	Beichuan	106.9	102.1	107.7	106.7	106.7
平武县	Pingwu	106.7	102.0	105.3	108.6	107.7
江油市	Jiangyou	104.4	101.9	99.1	110.0	104.2
广元市	**Guangyuan**					
利州区	Lizhou	105.8	104.4	108.5	102.9	104.6
昭化区	Zhaohua	104.9	104.4	106.6	102.7	106.2
朝天区	Chaotian	105.1	104.2	106.9	102.5	106.2
旺苍县	Wangcang	106.6	104.6	110.4	101.2	107.4
青川县	Qingchuan	105.4	104.2	109.3	102.8	107.2
剑阁县	Jiange	104.9	104.3	105.5	104.7	108.0
苍溪县	Cangxi	106.0	103.7	106.1	106.7	107.0
遂宁市	**Suining**					
船山区	Chuanshan	107.7	105.0	105.5	110.1	107.4
安居区	Anju	107.9	104.2	109.3	107.7	109.1
蓬溪县	Pengxi	107.2	105.3	107.0	108.1	108.7
大英县	Daying	107.3	104.7	104.4	111.8	108.5
射洪市	Shehong	108.1	104.1	108.6	107.6	108.9
内江市	**Neijiang**					
内江市中区	Neijiang Downtown	106.2	108.3	107.4	105.4	107.1
东兴区	Dongxing	106.7	106.7	106.0	107.0	107.2
威远县	Weiyuan	106.1	103.4	97.3	122.9	106.8
资中县	Zizhong	106.3	104.9	106.6	106.6	107.1
隆昌市	Longchang	106.5	105.3	112.7	100.9	107.2
乐山市	**Leshan**					
乐山市中区	Leshan Downtown	104.0	106.4	111.4	100.2	103.5
沙湾区	Shawan	105.9	110.6	107.7	102.3	106.7
五通桥区	Wutcngqiao	112.3	106.1	115.7	97.5	111.6

12-5 续表 2 continued

上年=100 (preceding year=100)

县(市、区)	Counties (City,Districts)	民营经济增加值 Added Value of Civilian-owned Economy	第一产业 Primary Industry	第二产业 Secondary Industry	第三产业 Tertiary Industry	人均民营经济增加值 Per Capita Added Value of Civilian-owned Economy
金口河区	Jinkouhe	103.6	106.5	105.1	99.7	103.6
犍为县	Qianwei	107.3	108.3	110.0	102.7	107.8
井研县	Jingyan	105.2	106.3	109.7	99.3	106.0
夹江县	Jiajiang	100.9	109.3	99.4	101.3	101.4
沐川县	Muchuan	104.7	108.1	109.0	99.7	105.3
峨边县	Ebian	107.0	107.0	111.1	102.8	107.5
马边县	Mabian	107.4	109.1	114.8	100.6	107.2
峨眉山市	Emeishan	106.6	108.1	102.9	108.3	106.8
南充市	**Nanchong**					
顺庆区	Shunqing	102.7	104.7	98.5	106.6	102.9
高坪区	Gaoping	105.5	103.7	107.2	103.7	105.9
嘉陵区	Jialing	107.1	104.9	108.2	105.8	107.6
南部县	Nanbu	100.2	111.9	89.4	118.2	100.7
营山县	Yingshan	106.4	106.3	104.9	108.2	107.0
蓬安县	Pengan	106.3	102.6	105.7	108.1	107.0
仪陇县	Yilong	106.1	100.2	107.9	105.9	106.7
西充县	Xichong	102.5	102.8	97.0	109.0	103.1
阆中市	Langzhong	104.4	105.4	102.2	106.4	105.0
眉山市	**Meishan**					
东坡区	Dongpo	104.2	105.9	107.7	100.7	104.0
彭山区	Pengshan	102.8	105.8	103.3	102.1	102.6
仁寿县	Renshou	103.4	105.5	99.8	106.4	103.6
洪雅县	Hongya	108.6	105.8	108.7	108.9	108.8
丹棱县	Danling	107.6	106.3	100.6	113.9	107.8
青神县	Qingshen	106.6	105.4	109.9	104.5	106.9
宜宾市	**Yibin**					
翠屏区	Cuiping	108.1	102.2	111.9	101.4	106.9
南溪区	Nanxi	107.6	103.9	113.6	99.2	108.2
叙州区	Xuzhou	108.3	106.6	112.1	101.8	107.7
江安县	Jiangan	105.8	103.0	107.6	104.3	106.2
长宁县	Changning	107.5	104.2	108.1	107.3	107.5
高县	Gaoxian	105.7	101.8	106.4	105.5	106.4
珙县	Gongxian	105.5	103.5	108.4	103.0	104.8
筠连县	Junlian	107.9	107.2	111.5	104.2	108.2
兴文县	Xingwen	107.7	103.1	109.8	107.0	107.4
屏山县	Pingshan	107.5	106.2	110.1	104.4	107.3
广安市	**Guangan**					
广安区	Guanganqu	104.0	104.6	111.2	102.0	104.2
前锋区	Qianfeng	101.3	103.7	99.3	104.3	101.9
岳池县	Yuechi	108.0	103.6	110.2	106.9	108.4
武胜县	Wusheng	105.3	105.5	107.9	102.9	105.6

12-5 续表 3 continued

上年=100 (preceding year=100)

县(市、区)	Counties (City,Districts)	民营经济增加值 Added Value of Civilian-owned Economy	第一产业 Primary Industry	第二产业 Secondary Industry	第三产业 Tertiary Industry	人均民营经济增加值 Per Capita Added Value of Civilian-owned Economy
邻水县	Linshui	104.4	104.6	106.2	102.7	104.7
华蓥市	Huaying	105.1	104.8	106.4	103.1	105.6
达州市	**Dazhou**					
通川区	Tongchuan	106.5	101.9	99.8	111.1	106.4
达川区	Dachuan	104.4	102.9	98.7	109.5	104.8
宣汉县	Xuanhan	106.8	103.0	104.9	111.2	107.1
开江县	Kaijiang	104.3	103.0	96.9	109.4	104.9
大竹县	Dazhu	106.7	103.9	101.4	113.1	107.2
渠县	Quxian	106.7	103.4	101.3	111.0	107.8
万源市	Wanyuan	106.2	103.5	102.9	108.3	106.7
雅安市	**Yaan**					
雨城区	Yucheng	105.1	105.0	112.0	101.5	105.1
名山区	Mingshan	104.4	103.6	104.8	104.1	104.6
荥经县	Yingjing	102.9	103.6	103.1	102.8	103.3
汉源县	Hanyuan	104.3	103.2	106.6	102.7	104.5
石棉县	Shimian	104.7	104.1	107.3	102.7	104.7
天全县	Tianquan	104.5	104.3	105.5	103.7	104.5
芦山县	Lushan	104.3	104.4	105.3	103.2	103.8
宝兴县	Baoxing	105.4	104.4	108.0	101.7	105.4
巴中市	**Bazhong**					
巴州区	Bazhou	105.0	104.2	108.4	103.0	105.2
恩阳区	Enyang	106.1	104.3	108.8	104.9	107.1
通江县	Tongjiang	105.1	104.2	108.0	103.1	106.3
南江县	Nanjiang	105.7	104.3	109.6	102.3	106.9
平昌县	Pingchang	103.4	104.0	104.7	101.8	104.7
资阳市	**Ziyang**					
雁江区	Yanjiang	104.1	103.5	98.8	110.8	104.5
安岳县	Anyue	103.7	104.0	104.1	103.4	104.3
乐至县	Lezhi	104.3	103.9	96.2	111.0	105.8
阿坝州	**Aba**					
马尔康市	Maerkang	106.7	106.7	106.7	106.7	103.9
汶川县	Wenchuan	107.4	106.4	107.3	108.1	106.6
理县	Lixian	105.9	104.5	106.0	106.4	106.0
茂县	Maoxian	106.9	106.3	109.2	105.0	106.3
松潘县	Songpan	107.7	110.0	102.3	108.3	107.4
九寨沟县	Jiuzhaigou	108.5	107.3	102.4	110.6	108.1
金川县	Jinchuan	106.5	104.3	108.5	106.9	106.3
小金县	Xiaojin	107.1	110.2	100.9	109.5	107.1
黑水县	Heishui	104.0	104.9	103.3	104.5	104.0
壤塘县	Rangtang	106.4	110.0	93.7	105.7	105.8

12-5 续表 4 continued

上年=100 (preceding year=100)

县(市、区)	Counties (City,Districts)	民营经济增加值 Added Value of Civilian-owned Economy	第一产业 Primary Industry	第二产业 Secondary Industry	第三产业 Tertiary Industry	人均民营经济增加值 Per Capita Added Value of Civilian-owned Economy
阿坝县	Abaxian	108.5	111.4	107.9	106.5	107.6
若尔盖县	Ruoergai	107.9	110.5	97.0	106.1	107.3
红原县	Hongyuan	108.6	111.5	107.7	105.2	107.7
甘孜州	**Ganzi**					
康定市	Kangding	105.3	100.1	105.4	106.7	104.2
泸定县	Luding	105.2	104.5	73.1	116.9	104.1
丹巴县	Danba	103.0	101.7	113.4	101.8	102.3
九龙县	Jiulong	104.4	102.0	94.5	120.6	103.3
雅江县	Yajiang	108.5	101.9	131.9	104.6	107.2
道孚县	Daofu	102.6	102.0	98.4	105.4	103.5
炉霍县	Luhuo	104.3	102.0	111.7	104.5	104.2
甘孜县	Ganzixian	105.9	102.3	109.2	109.1	104.6
新龙县	Xinlong	104.1	102.0	108.7	105.3	104.7
德格县	Dege	102.4	101.9	102.8	103.3	102.2
白玉县	Baiyu	104.6	102.0	107.1	108.4	104.3
石渠县	Shiqu	103.1	103.6	100.9	103.7	104.3
色达县	Seda	103.1	102.0	103.0	107.1	104.8
理塘县	Litang	105.3	101.9	101.2	114.0	105.0
巴塘县	Batang	104.6	102.0	107.9	107.2	104.8
乡城县	Xiangcheng	104.3	102.0	95.7	111.4	105.2
稻城县	Daocheng	102.7	101.9	105.4	102.4	101.2
得荣县	Derong	103.2	101.8	100.6	108.1	105.3
凉山州	**Liangshan**					
西昌市	Xichang	107.1	100.5	102.3	114.5	106.7
会理市	Huili	105.2	103.2	101.6	109.1	104.9
木里县	Muli	101.0	97.4	104.5	100.3	100.6
盐源县	Yanyuan	107.5	100.2	112.9	111.1	107.2
德昌县	Dechang	103.1	99.5	104.1	103.7	102.8
会东县	Huidong	106.7	103.3	98.5	113.4	106.3
宁南县	Ningnan	100.4	101.2	98.5	101.5	100.4
普格县	Puge	107.1	100.1	119.8	106.0	106.6
布拖县	Butuo	100.1	96.7	98.2	103.4	99.6
金阳县	Jinyang	107.2	101.3	106.9	110.3	106.9
昭觉县	Zhaojue	104.8	101.8	106.3	106.4	104.2
喜德县	Xide	101.5	94.8	104.0	104.3	100.9
冕宁县	Mianning	100.5	99.1	95.0	106.9	100.3
越西县	Yuexi	102.7	99.8	87.5	110.2	102.6
甘洛县	Ganluo	104.2	101.8	100.8	109.7	104.0
美姑县	Meigu	100.8	102.2	86.7	105.0	100.6
雷波县	Leibo	100.2	98.2	97.5	105.7	99.6

12-6 各县(市、区)固定资产投资和建筑业情况(2023年)
Investment in Fixed Assets and Construction by Counties (City, Districts)(2023)

县(市、区)	Counties (City,Districts)	全社会固定资产投资比上年增长 (%) Growth Rate of Total Investment Over Preceding Year(%)	房地产开发投资额 (万元) Real Estate Investment (10 000 yuan)	建筑企业单位数 (个) Number of Construction Enterprises (unit)	建筑业总产值 (亿元) Gross Output Value of Construction (100 million yuan)
成都市	**Chengdu**				
锦江区	Jinjiang	16.4	1489687	194	799.25
青羊区	Qingyang	8.5	1243840	237	960.64
金牛区	Jinniu	17.9	1907227	350	2027.14
武侯区	Wuhou	6.4	1753659	580	1969.71
成华区	Chenghua	5.3	2077034	153	378.66
龙泉驿区	Longquanyi	-8.9	1799328	90	106.03
青白江区	Qingbaijiang	1.6	654754	25	109.07
新都区	Xindu	5.0	1343620	53	99.26
温江区	Wenjiang	-9.6	991788	58	115.81
双流区	Shuangliu	9.0	6966176	152	538.46
郫都区	Pidu	19.4	801908	44	366.53
新津区	Xinjin	-11.0	770585	61	41.35
金堂县	Jintang	-6.5	220918	63	43.55
大邑县	Dayi	-1.1	221884	54	21.34
蒲江县	Pujiang	1.4	40895	23	9.99
都江堰市	Dujiangyan	-20.6	526339	57	125.06
彭州市	Pengzhou	-2.5	436869	38	32.00
邛崃市	Qionglai	-0.6	173287	57	24.94
崇州市	Chongzhou	-11.9	294408	56	42.63
简阳市	Jianyang	7.9	753798	89	145.86
自贡市	**Zigong**				
自流井区	Ziliujing	-8.2	199776	49	123.24
贡井区	Gongjing	3.4	27140	11	10.15
大安区	Daan	3.6	158081	34	37.35
沿滩区	Yantan	15.0	46306	39	51.25
荣县	Rongxian	3.7	20499	22	35.68
富顺县	Fushun	4.0	102092	75	94.09
攀枝花市	**Panzhihua**				
东区	Dongqu	5.8	134690	62	296.99
西区	Xiqu	6.0	1210	11	9.86
仁和区	Renhe	6.3	388252	34	23.20
米易县	Miyi	6.1	275665	17	9.94
盐边县	Yanbian	6.2	24543	12	4.25
泸州市	**Luzhou**				
江阳区	Jiangyang	0.2	1043544	116	278.94
纳溪区	Naxi	5.1	109592	45	65.84
龙马潭区	Longmatan	5.4	585289	103	264.16
泸县	Luxian	0.5	64003	166	347.07
合江县	Hejiang	5.3	197863	97	177.68
叙永县	Xuyong	5.1	130081	40	52.81

12-6 续表 1 continued

县(市、区)	Counties (City,Districts)	全社会固定资产投资比上年增长 (%) Growth Rate of Total Investment Over Preceding Year(%)	房地产开发投资额 (万元) Real Estate Investment (10 000 yuan)	建筑企业单位数 (个) Number of Construction Enterprises (unit)	建筑业总产值 (亿元) Gross Output Value of Construction (100 million yuan)
古蔺县	Gulin	6.9	96800	47	41.89
德阳市	**Deyang**				
旌阳区	Jingyang	6.8	837683	160	244.26
罗江区	Luojiang	5.1	88872	19	26.69
中江县	Zhongjiang	7.4	163396	68	37.79
广汉市	Guanghan	5.1	278303	77	129.22
什邡市	Shifang	7.2	202403	33	40.74
绵竹市	Mianzhu	0.6	155465	51	44.63
绵阳市	**Mianyang**				
涪城区	Fucheng	6.3	1771795	503	486.67
游仙区	Youxian	-4.5	423822	152	72.84
安州区	Anzhou	16.6	335349	62	51.78
三台县	Santai	13.6	376514	51	65.33
盐亭县	Yanting	18.9	67586	50	48.36
梓潼县	Zitong	16.5	84023	47	38.04
北川县	Beichuan	17.5	49038	36	21.07
平武县	Pingwu	36.5	9532	25	11.83
江油市	Jiangyou	3.2	381394	67	81.08
广元市	**Guangyuan**				
利州区	Lizhou	13.9	470468	195	116.71
昭化区	Zhaohua	1.5	8112	51	20.46
朝天区	Chaotian	-4.3	34742	20	25.91
旺苍县	Wangcang	5.7	95832	30	34.15
青川县	Qingchuan	-5.9	36224	19	8.11
剑阁县	Jiange	1.7	42160	43	24.68
苍溪县	Cangxi	-7.2	54455	30	46.94
遂宁市	**Suining**				
船山区	Chuanshan	6.3	997515	215	233.29
安居区	Anju	6.4	79885	32	32.00
蓬溪县	Pengxi	6.4	106330	37	71.96
大英县	Daying	6.3	73599	54	86.06
射洪市	Shehong	6.8	194609	39	91.39
内江市	**Neijiang**				
内江市中区	Neijiang Downtown	7.4	313498	37	46.96
东兴区	Dongxing	6.0	450535	50	94.44
威远县	Weiyuan	7.3	212959	24	60.21
资中县	Zizhong	8.4	193112	35	40.63
隆昌市	Longchang	7.8	276432	32	98.14
乐山市	**Leshan**				
乐山市中区	Leshan Downtown	16.4	352158	161	172.89
沙湾区	Shawan	-39.2	4292	7	8.91

12-6 续表 2 continued

县(市、区)	Counties (City,Districts)	全社会固定资产投资比上年增长 (%) Growth Rate of Total Investment Over Preceding Year(%)	房地产开发投资额 (万元) Real Estate Investment (10 000 yuan)	建筑企业单位数 (个) Number of Construction Enterprises (unit)	建筑业总产值 (亿元) Gross Output Value of Construction (100 million yuan)
五通桥区	Wutongqiao	41.2	39155	10	11.84
金口河区	Jinkouhe	0.2	8297		
犍为县	Qianwei	12.2	48213	21	33.13
井研县	Jingyan	6.1	50839	11	31.95
夹江县	Jiajiang	-28.9	112534	23	22.19
沐川县	Muchuan	-24.4	11829	13	7.65
峨边县	Ebian	23.1	11253	8	4.50
马边县	Mabian	-0.3	19798	10	4.17
峨眉山市	Emeishan	9.8	243862	30	32.03
南充市	**Nanchong**				
顺庆区	Shunqing	16.6	231226	151	218.25
高坪区	Gaoping	18.7	529894	92	109.34
嘉陵区	Jialing	19.2	582817	80	103.29
南部县	Nanbu	-26.6	379678	89	293.23
营山县	Yingshan	20.9	401327	46	138.93
蓬安县	Pengan	6.3	232800	52	70.44
仪陇县	Yilong	10.1	360646	93	269.51
西充县	Xichong	-48.6	99920	26	87.55
阆中市	Langzhong	17.3	94164	57	195.20
眉山市	**Meishan**				
东坡区	Dongpo	5.1	726094	158	260.60
彭山区	Pengshan	42.8	674822	46	28.29
仁寿县	Renshou	-2.2	1964770	137	175.19
洪雅县	Hongya	0.3	171657	31	27.30
丹棱县	Danling	9.2	47451	19	19.53
青神县	Qingshen	13.0	76255	17	34.72
宜宾市	**Yibin**				
翠屏区	Cuiping	8.0	1228550	213	369.46
南溪区	Nanxi	1.1	113696	63	38.74
叙州区	Xuzhou	10.3	360944	211	149.41
江安县	Jiangan	-4.5	66485	43	65.63
长宁县	Changning	-5.7	104358	33	64.14
高县	Gaoxian	-11.2	83732	55	34.78
珙县	Gongxian	-13.3	36789	37	32.83
筠连县	Junlian	-10.7	64037	46	31.43
兴文县	Xingwen	7.8	113810	76	30.17
屏山县	Pingshan	9.5	160257	70	24.40
广安市	**Guangan**				
广安区	Guanganqu	-12.7	583496	118	82.13
前锋区	Qianfeng	15.5	124864	33	24.59
岳池县	Yuechi	9.2	240360	54	98.76

12-6 续表 3 continued

县(市、区)	Counties (City,Districts)	全社会固定资产投资比上年增长(%) Growth Rate of Total Investment Over Preceding Year(%)	房地产开发投资额(万元) Real Estate Investment (10 000 yuan)	建筑企业单位数(个) Number of Construction Enterprises (unit)	建筑业总产值(亿元) Gross Output Value of Construction (100 million yuan)
武胜县	Wusheng	4.3	216754	33	62.8700
邻水县	Linshui	3.8	297974	44	83.2500
华蓥市	Huaying	4.2	61294	59	97.1000
达州市	**Dazhou**				
通川区	Tongchuan	5.7	791518	137	139.89
达川区	Dachuan	10.4	258294	73	102.05
宣汉县	Xuanhan	8.6	169759	48	49.98
开江县	Kaijiang	4.0	80693	24	14.48
大竹县	Dazhu	5.9	322686	51	14.54
渠县	Quxian	6.7	146197	54	43.19
万源市	Wanyuan	5.9	45904	22	15.10
雅安市	**Yaan**				
雨城区	Yucheng	7.3	154263	49	35.80
名山区	Mingshan	9.7	137409	36	17.2800
荥经县	Yingjing	-3.0	31891	15	12.7200
汉源县	Hanyuan	6.3	55837	21	8.2600
石棉县	Shimian	11.5	58641	10	7.10
天全县	Tianquan	-15.6	11568	14	7.16
芦山县	Lushan	7.6	2214	13	9.01
宝兴县	Baoxing	6.2		5	2.22
巴中市	**Bazhong**				
巴州区	Bazhou	1.1	251849	105	54.72
恩阳区	Enyang	2.2	53911	38	31.19
通江县	Tongjiang	2.1	26104	44	19.54
南江县	Nanjiang	1.3	85121	32	28.00
平昌县	Pingchang	0.6	110709	43	17.85
资阳市	**Ziyang**				
雁江区	Yanjiang	2.6	506576	65	73.3201
安岳县	Anyue	2.5	183625	36	27.2505
乐至县	Lezhi	2.1	133168	27	22.45
阿坝州	**Aba**				
马尔康市	Maerkang	23.1	28498	18	5.20
汶川县	Wenchuan	12.0	5501	46	20.59
理县	Lixian	2.3	6300	26	6.88
茂县	Maoxian	4.5	5891	20	10.53
松潘县	Songpan	25.0	14086	15	3.38
九寨沟县	Jiuzhaigou	3.0	5788	20	4.51
金川县	Jinchuan	21.6		8	0.86
小金县	Xiaojin	8.0		15	5.58
黑水县	Heishui	47.0		12	3.4072
壤塘县	Rangtang	12.5		11	1.6974

12-6 续表 4 continued

县(市、区)	Counties (City,Districts)	全社会固定资产投资比上年增长 (%) Growth Rate of Total Investment Over Preceding Year(%)	房地产开发投资额 (万元) Real Estate Investment (10 000 yuan)	建筑企业单位数 (个) Number of Construction Enterprises (unit)	建筑业总产值 (亿元) Gross Output Value of Construction (100 million yuan)
阿坝县	Abaxian	8.0		5	1.6912
若尔盖县	Ruoergai	7.6		7	1.9995
红原县	Hongyuan	9.0		4	0.1411
甘孜州	**Ganzi**				
康定市	Kangding	167.5	39742	37	19.62
泸定县	Luding	25.7	3356	11	2.62
丹巴县	Danba	2.3	14029	3	1.59
九龙县	Jiulong	16.8			
雅江县	Yajiang	36.0	7034	5	0.54
道孚县	Daofu	0.5			
炉霍县	Luhuo	-16.6		3	0.22
甘孜县	Ganzixian	15.7		4	1.95
新龙县	Xinlong	6.6		4	3.33
德格县	Dege	-20.4		3	0.79
白玉县	Baiyu	5.9		4	1.43
石渠县	Shiqu	9.0	40	6	2.35
色达县	Seda	-2.1		8	2.29
理塘县	Litang	3.8			
巴塘县	Batang	-6.8			
乡城县	Xiangcheng	-70.8			
稻城县	Daocheng	2.4			
得荣县	Derong	20.1		5	4.38
凉山州	**Liangshan**				
西昌市	Xichang	3.1	455400	123	240.80
会理市	Huili	-5.8	116410	21	14.72
木里县	Muli	4.9	19571	15	1.44
盐源县	Yanyuan	43.7	43743	20	6.57
德昌县	Dechang	5.0	130360	24	17.56
会东县	Huidong	18.8	76898	12	5.72
宁南县	Ningnan	2.1	44810	19	3.46
普格县	Puge	41.9	16387	19	2.82
布拖县	Butuo	-7.2	25000	12	2.36
金阳县	Jinyang	-1.9	26062	14	4.28
昭觉县	Zhaojue	8.6	40929	21	2.16
喜德县	Xide	12.5	20635	34	7.27
冕宁县	Mianning	-2.9	83683	38	10.38
越西县	Yuexi	1.8	7737	27	5.85
甘洛县	Ganluo	4.8	39332	23	4.30
美姑县	Meigu	1.9	32892	13	2.12
雷波县	Leibo	32.7	19919	12	6.12

12－7 各县(市、区)农村经济情况(2023年)

Basic Statistics on Agriculture of Counties(City, Districts)(2023)

县(市、区)	Counties (City,Districts)	2022年末实有耕地面积(公顷) Cultivated Land Area (year-end 2022) (hectare)	耕地灌溉面积(公顷) Irrigated Area of Cultivated Land (hectare)	农林牧渔业增加值(万元) Gross Output Value of Farming, Forestry, Animal Husbandry and Fishery (10 000 yuan)	农用化肥施用量(折纯量)(吨) Consumption of Chemical Fertilizers (ton)
成都市	**Chengdu**				
锦江区	Jinjiang	447	423	2952	8
青羊区	Qingyang	487	499	202	2
金牛区	Jinniu	920	888	1280	19
武侯区	Wuhou	200	1078	292	2
成华区	Chenghua	1280	1283	28	
龙泉驿区	Longquanyi	5580	4334	238487	3051
青白江区	Qingbaijiang	12787	8739	180633	3794
新都区	Xindu	18147	18145	275409	8353
温江区	Wenjiang	2093	2018	227318	2632
双流区	Shuangliu	9473	21981	336890	5510
郫都区	Pidu	9793	10202	275925	11861
新津区	Xinjin	9347	9772	200291	5455
金堂县	Jintang	45287	37250	876234	20471
大邑县	Dayi	21673	17630	347834	5676
蒲江县	Pujiang	1233	1124	300425	3696
都江堰市	Dujiangyan	10020	10830	437635	9742
彭州市	Pengzhou	35200	36012	668913	16973
邛崃市	Qionglai	22467	19954	560289	14921
崇州市	Chongzhou	20893	20130	471811	11586
简阳市	Jianyang	86853	56053	806910	26014
自贡市	**Zigong**				
自流井区	Ziliujing	4500	4100	90417	2564
贡井区	Gongjing	17593	12770	285690	10338
大安区	Daan	18920	16406	267627	8533
沿滩区	Yantan	21727	11536	287986	15694
荣县	Rongxian	58620	40607	882689	17977
富顺县	Fushun	59007	31850	820445	24108
攀枝花市	**Panzhihua**				
东区	Dongqu	133	330	25528	198
西区	Xiqu	533	1030	29009	195
仁和区	Renhe	9913	10010	368889	8282
米易县	Miyi	20480	20060	419999	4251
盐边县	Yanbian	25127	14470	321602	7923
泸州市	**Luzhou**				
江阳区	Jiangyang	23240	11753	337611	11467
纳溪区	Naxi	30233	16213	345827	8392
龙马潭区	Longmatan	9720	8573	154690	4658
泸县	Luxian	73127	42270	740750	29326
合江县	Hejiang	55673	33973	529121	10378

注：①年末实有耕地面积指标，由四川省自然资源厅提供；成都高新区、天府新区数据未分拆至对应县区，分别为762.2公顷、1187.5公顷。②耕地灌溉面积由四川省水利厅提供，因两部门统计口径不同，部分县耕地灌溉面积大于年末实有耕地面积。

a) The year-end cultivated land area is provided by Bureau of Land and Resources of Sichuan Province; The data of Chengdu Hi tech Zone and Tianfu New Area are not divided into corresponding counties and districts, which are 762.2 hectares and 1187.5 hectares respectively. b) The irrigated land area is provided by Si-chuan Provincial Water Resources Department. Due to the two sector statistics caliber is different, the irrigated land area of some counties is greater than the year-end cultivated land area.

12-7 续表 1 continued

县(市、区)	Counties (City,Districts)	2022年末实有耕地面积(公顷) Cultivated Land Area (year-end 2022) (hectare)	耕地灌溉面积(公顷) Irrigated Area of Cultivated Land (hectare)	农林牧渔业增加值(万元) Gross Output Value of Farming, Forestry, Animal Husbandry and Fishery (10 000 yuan)	农用化肥施用量(折纯量)(吨) Consumption of Chemical Fertilizers (ton)
叙永县	Xuyong	60733	25290	394597	16200
古蔺县	Gulin	71847	26600	381667	12629
德阳市	**Deyang**				
旌阳区	Jingyang	27180	23380	489669	15274
罗江区	Luojiang	18960	13340	287794	14819
中江县	Zhongjiang	94980	55340	1052984	63304
广汉市	Guanghan	28453	25720	491287	24000
什邡市	Shifang	20660	19260	441066	21655
绵竹市	Mianzhu	30580	23430	426104	22191
绵阳市	**Mianyang**				
涪城区	Fucheng	11727	11030	335098	11964
游仙区	Youxian	33393	24960	435230	17534
安州区	Anzhou	30673	24490	385081	14725
三台县	Santai	102753	72930	1095695	42832
盐亭县	Yanting	53267	23700	494492	38135
梓潼县	Zitong	46040	22790	403606	15931
北川县	Beichuan	7393	2350	162789	6128
平武县	Pingwu	15100	2990	127583	6044
江油市	Jiangyou	55000	37300	659093	25325
广元市	**Guangyuan**				
利州区	Lizhou	16533	5790	206591	5771
昭化区	Zhaohua	30453	12580	232679	11628
朝天区	Chaotian	22833	5156	170154	6325
旺苍县	Wangcang	36427	9600	334632	9714
青川县	Qingchuan	20040	6300	149517	3550
剑阁县	Jiange	84973	35830	523790	27269
苍溪县	Cangxi	63780	25750	596907	22368
遂宁市	**Suining**				
船山区	Chuanshan	18767	12969	256149	9350
安居区	Anju	55367	40600	492671	28601
蓬溪县	Pengxi	43620	24740	358485	31259
大英县	Daying	29740	22220	341217	19524
射洪市	Shehong	53480	37248	850512	25597
内江市	**Neijiang**				
内江市市中区	Neijiang Downtown	15967	12200	374191	5614
东兴区	Dongxing	50893	21153	602200	25498
威远县	Weiyuan	43820	32600	574753	14680
资中县	Zizhong	74520	40653	958237	35643
隆昌市	Longchang	39093	29220	538134	8814
乐山市	**Leshan**				
乐山市市中区	Leshan Downtown	16787	15290	377570	7285
沙湾区	Shawan	8153	5200	215115	3980

12-7 续表 2 continued

县(市、区)	Counties (City,Districts)	2022年末实有耕地面积(公顷) Cultivated Land Area (year-end 2022) (hectare)	耕地灌溉面积(公顷) Irrigated Area of Cultivated Land (hectare)	农林牧渔业增加值(万元) Gross Output Value of Farming, Forestry, Animal Husbandry and Fishery (10 000 yuan)	农用化肥施用量(折纯量)(吨) Consumption of Chemical Fertilizers (ton)
五通桥区	Wutongqiao	11700	10490	307305	4493
金口河区	Jinkouhe	2540	930	53621	312
犍为县	Qianwei	35793	23080	538867	10707
井研县	Jingyan	23320	33190	400605	12955
夹江县	Jiajiang	14393	18800	383636	15101
沐川县	Muchuan	9873	9610	237000	6583
峨边县	Ebian	7253	3770	102670	1879
马边县	Mabian	15747	5430	146373	6850
峨眉山市	Emeishan	16140	18860	367298	6083
南充市	**Nanchong**				
顺庆区	Shunqing	18407	11416	339455	12363
高坪区	Gaoping	30640	16060	458927	13800
嘉陵区	Jialing	45093	28200	513911	24485
南部县	Nanbu	82640	47680	939227	16358
营山县	Yingshan	56800	19740	542250	29551
蓬安县	Pengan	49347	23270	511126	29034
仪陇县	Yilong	62040	50540	694800	24485
西充县	Xichong	37667	29340	507989	11523
阆中市	Langzhong	67500	25400	657223	27327
眉山市	**Meishan**				
东坡区	Dongpo	28367	47880	674744	30776
彭山区	Pengshan	8520	18940	201401	10193
仁寿县	Renshou	80493	73330	1070030	52012
洪雅县	Hongya	13313	15080	243195	6938
丹棱县	Danling	3920	9390	166222	3593
青神县	Qingshen	8227	7430	140522	2986
宜宾市	**Yibin**				
翠屏区	Cuiping	53273	24746	517175	11319
南溪区	Nanxi	25693	16100	402532	5664
叙州区	Xuzhou	76673	29782	654989	15651
江安县	Jiangan	34520	19494	427550	4324
长宁县	Changning	23987	20482	413548	4544
高县	Gaoxian	39973	26210	373879	7488
珙县	Gongxian	27633	14110	335747	6889
筠连县	Junlian	26107	19650	365129	4067
兴文县	Xingwen	33093	16850	354523	4924
屏山县	Pingshan	17660	16680	288745	5989
广安市	**Guangan**				
广安区	Guanganqu	43627	24190	416325	20571
前锋区	Qianfeng	15407	7710	187169	10152
岳池县	Yuechi	70147	28580	687842	17155
武胜县	Wusheng	41513	27547	491111	12770

12-7 续表 3 continued

县(市、区)	Counties (City,Districts)	2022年末实有耕地面积(公顷) Cultivated Land Area (year-end 2022) (hectare)	耕地灌溉面积(公顷) Irrigated Area of Cultivated Land (hectare)	农林牧渔业增加值(万元) Gross Output Value of Farming, Forestry, Animal Husbandry and Fishery (10 000 yuan)	农用化肥施用量(折纯量)(吨) Consumption of Chemical Fertilizers (ton)
邻水县	Linshui	61153	22370	592915	21303
华蓥市	Huaying	10620	6040	167509	7902
达州市	**Dazhou**				
通川区	Tongchuan	23320	12950	302628	5651
达川区	Dachuan	80920	26800	549272	22299
宣汉县	Xuanhan	88127	47007	1093337	37820
开江县	Kaijiang	33400	23080	444751	15857
大竹县	Dazhu	78427	31270	766292	39567
渠县	Quxian	84167	43180	943157	32608
万源市	Wanyuan	42313	21473	444025	22022
雅安市	**Yaan**				
雨城区	Yucheng	5993	6640	364905	3544
名山区	Mingshan	5280	12450	342251	9114
荥经县	Yingjing	2607	4500	164577	3663
汉源县	Hanyuan	11067	14100	315147	13012
石棉县	Shimian	1493	3950	190397	1920
天全县	Tianquan	7533	7520	160540	4920
芦山县	Lushan	4020	4220	143523	4444
宝兴县	Baoxing	2487	550	85926	2333
巴中市	**Bazhong**				
巴州区	Bazhou	44367	14410	420043	21915
恩阳区	Enyang	40780	15510	296221	11453
通江县	Tongjiang	67420	20330	427271	21992
南江县	Nanjiang	52740	15570	387726	22122
平昌县	Pingchang	56433	30310	472924	26815
资阳市	**Ziyang**				
雁江区	Yanjiang	74187	43543	679306	19481
安岳县	Anyue	94267	46090	962915	24969
乐至县	Lezhi	65633	26240	452866	14990
阿坝州	**Aba**				
马尔康市	Maerkang	6027	1510	51660	138
汶川县	Wenchuan	1447	1570	132494	1557
理县	Lixian	1860	2250	46553	549
茂县	Maoxian	3953	6630	136504	2165
松潘县	Songpan	10700	890	72726	968
九寨沟县	Jiuzhaigou	5373	1300	33177	969
金川县	Jinchuan	5407	4072	52797	1591
小金县	Xiaojin	8480	4540	61900	764
黑水县	Heishui	6260	2230	54428	463
壤塘县	Rangtang	3093	490	46538	129

12-7 续表 4 continued

县(市、区)	Counties (City,Districts)	2022年末实有耕地面积（公顷）Cultivated Land Area (year-end 2022) (hectare)	耕地灌溉面积(公顷) Irrigated Area of Cultivated Land (hectare)	农林牧渔业增加值(万元) Gross Output Value of Farming, Forestry, Animal Husbandry and Fishery (10 000 yuan)	农用化肥施用量(折纯量)(吨) Consumption of Chemical Fertilizers (ton)
阿坝县	Abaxian	9033	4530	84367	45
若尔盖县	Ruoergai	4007	1210	155500	30
红原县	Hongyuan	187	128	96414	62
甘孜州	**Ganzi**				
康定市	Kangding	7320	1440	68832	162
泸定县	Luding	4007	4470	70964	622
丹巴县	Danba	4400	3690	46460	276
九龙县	Jiulong	3693	2400	48470	392
雅江县	Yajiang	3073	1030	33560	34
道孚县	Daofu	7300	3810	35732	201
炉霍县	Luhuo	6167	1000	35396	27
甘孜县	Ganzixian	11853	3110	52776	141
新龙县	Xinlong	3767	2430	38584	40
德格县	Dege	4880	2760	66236	103
白玉县	Baiyu	5773	1930	45545	30
石渠县	Shiqu	4180	2820	52692	47
色达县	Seda	1133	900	66209	26
理塘县	Litang	4880	1120	90775	34
巴塘县	Batang	4553	4210	46384	190
乡城县	Xiangcheng	2880	2380	30362	189
稻城县	Daocheng	3980	3060	27355	28
得荣县	Derong	3273	1360	23282	233
凉山州	**Liangshan**				
西昌市	Xichang	46727	44610	663711	10446
会理市	Huili	65800	24320	766923	16072
木里县	Muli	17927	4150	131935	1094
盐源县	Yanyuan	52227	19600	667331	7948
德昌县	Dechang	17180	12760	254984	8200
会东县	Huidong	58087	17910	658145	20786
宁南县	Ningnan	23680	13850	333276	7014
普格县	Puge	31853	5600	117597	4028
布拖县	Butuo	29007	2120	166418	1811
金阳县	Jinyang	16627	2850	123953	2392
昭觉县	Zhaojue	44407	4110	174605	3927
喜德县	Xide	29693	3215	110298	2662
冕宁县	Mianning	34840	20950	391093	9360
越西县	Yuexi	27753	7330	190472	7499
甘洛县	Ganluo	19740	5090	110973	9729
美姑县	Meigu	34347	1950	123385	5050
雷波县	Leibo	20053	4130	160745	2550

12-7 续表 5 continued

县(市、区)	Counties (City,Districts)	粮食 播种面积(公顷) Total Sown Area (hectares)	粮食 产量(吨) Output of Grain (ton)	油料产量(吨) Yield of Oil Bearing Crops (ton)	#花生 Peanut	#油菜籽 Rapeseeds	蔬菜及食用菌产量(吨) Output of Vegetables and Edible Fungus (ton)
成都市	**Chengdu**						
锦江区	Jinjiang			11		11	64
青羊区	Qingyang			9		9	606
金牛区	Jinniu			6		6	4174
武侯区	Wuhou						529
成华区	Chenghua						100
龙泉驿区	Longquanyi	3126	15209	2053	214	1839	154346
青白江区	Qingbaijiang	11367	65683	11687	2133	9554	241686
新都区	Xindu	19865	141330	12907	513	12394	371354
温江区	Wenjiang	1482	10758	659		659	59196
双流区	Shuangliu	17888	114837	15630	3432	12198	468535
郫都区	Pidu	8393	57433	4141	31	3560	691066
新津区	Xinjin	9249	64593	6050	383	5667	233067
金堂县	Jintang	49688	267992	53745	20141	33603	1047550
大邑县	Dayi	26592	170372	9921	11	9910	249971
蒲江县	Pujiang	7263	37865	825	36	789	124815
都江堰市	Dujiangyan	13524	98233	14750		14750	308368
彭州市	Pengzhou	37894	256349	14172	1447	12725	1289690
邛崃市	Qionglai	38447	248377	15717	241	15476	348928
崇州市	Chongzhou	31915	226895	13940		13940	390714
简阳市	Jianyang	108517	543461	77467	12574	64893	544090
自贡市	**Zigong**						
自流井区	Ziliujing	5871	30957	7864	654	7210	117429
贡井区	Gongjing	23732	120170	29529	6508	23021	396051
大安区	Daan	21537	113434	29667	9408	20198	330724
沿滩区	Yantan	27290	165480	26869	6270	20541	344577
荣县	Rongxian	70840	442514	44639	10452	34187	916711
富顺县	Fushun	88853	560816	53538	6896	46215	657158
攀枝花市	**Panzhihua**						
东区	Dongqu	143	832	48	48		9188
西区	Xiqu	350	2055	34	34		13141
仁和区	Renhe	8060	44028	1127	882	245	341918
米易县	Miyi	18023	116551	1306	171	1135	556358
盐边县	Yanbian	19208	97766	1933	148	1785	169904
泸州市	**Luzhou**						
江阳区	Jiangyang	32440	206838	10590	1141	9449	563054
纳溪区	Naxi	45825	282181	11297	584	10642	291489
龙马潭区	Longmatan	11327	69089	2905	257	2637	152096
泸县	Luxian	85379	552835	52415	5423	46689	712246
合江县	Hejiang	81211	520281	14480	2176	12304	523165
叙永县	Xuyong	74753	365555	13050	2482	10534	414782
古蔺县	Gulin	74559	356400	28157	1493	26472	531469

12-7 续表 6 continued

县(市、区)	Counties (City,Districts)	粮食 播种面积(公顷) Total Sown Area (hectares)	粮食 产量(吨) Output of Grain (ton)	油料产量(吨) Yield of Oil Bearing Crops (ton)	#花生 Peanut	#油菜籽 Rapeseeds	蔬菜及食用菌产量(吨) Output of Vegetables and Edible Fungus (ton)
德阳市	**Deyang**						
旌阳区	Jingyang	35181	241036	38026	6166	31860	433190
罗江区	Luojiang	18760	137994	48191	2986	45205	178043
中江县	Zhongjiang	145400	826312	147683	36336	111347	529503
广汉市	Guanghan	44068	323766	30715	1973	28742	585627
什邡市	Shifang	26472	199076	11492	997	10495	633658
绵竹市	Mianzhu	44918	289286	21816	1201	20605	412416
绵阳市	**Mianyang**						
涪城区	Fucheng	14163	88168	24047	3707	20340	438091
游仙区	Youxian	39434	245530	56928	6983	49945	225894
安州区	Anzhou	38716	265215	56858	2034	54824	221144
三台县	Santai	120782	675181	176552	38620	137902	403234
盐亭县	Yanting	53499	300064	65380	20789	44548	173655
梓潼县	Zitong	51599	300115	75663	18655	56978	270249
北川县	Beichuan	19297	88235	10714	616	10098	89040
平武县	Pingwu	25475	103793	5863	447	5402	40942
江油市	Jiangyou	46253	292790	66883	6206	60673	461139
广元市	**Guangyuan**						
利州区	Lizhou	18854	81494	13024	3403	9621	456325
昭化区	Zhaohua	25437	129136	34687	3500	31000	438195
朝天区	Chaotian	29067	122308	13527	3476	10031	1002912
旺苍县	Wangcang	44635	238571	27090	3840	23000	273780
青川县	Qingchuan	30600	129677	22196	3010	17374	152798
剑阁县	Jiange	90871	470642	119546	28419	91126	440346
苍溪县	Cangxi	80431	446405	77972	21614	56358	436390
遂宁市	**Suining**						
船山区	Chuanshan	24089	125664	19113	3655	15359	281512
安居区	Anju	78015	411059	53444	9013	44345	341092
蓬溪县	Pengxi	60115	332847	38869	12567	26251	363420
大英县	Daying	39979	212277	37605	2924	34620	138246
射洪市	Shehong	75220	397355	68947	16387	52560	247884
内江市	**Neijiang**						
内江市市中区	Neijiang Downtown	22703	119004	17408	4718	12690	276852
东兴区	Dongxing	68487	375614	47267	11775	35492	1009023
威远县	Weiyuan	63523	342810	45142	6517	38625	1160275
资中县	Zizhong	108960	573539	56809	15995	40814	891597
隆昌市	Longchang	51149	332359	27486	3713	23773	546031
乐山市	**Leshan**						
乐山市市中区	Leshan Downtown	16347	108795	12670	2494	10176	351313
沙湾区	Shawan	9920	52590	3046	392	2654	91137
五通桥区	Wutongqiao	12987	81699	4114	709	3405	153788

12−7 续表 7 continued

县(市、区)	Counties (City,Districts)	粮食 播种面积(公顷) Total Sown Area (hectares)	粮食 产量(吨) Output of Grain (ton)	油料产量(吨) Yield of Oil Bearing Crops (ton)	#花生 Peanut	#油菜籽 Rapeseeds	蔬菜及食用菌产量(吨) Output of Vegetables and Edible Fungus (ton)
金口河区	Jinkouhe	5280	20745	277	151	126	12355
犍为县	Qianwei	43927	279297	13725	4071	9654	277289
井研县	Jingyan	44033	244997	13009	918	12091	127050
夹江县	Jiajiang	16733	114035	15950	1006	14944	144124
沐川县	Muchuan	20593	103102	8865	994	7871	122311
峨边县	Ebian	12733	51000	3572	338	3234	35759
马边县	Mabian	23327	95907	4194	686	3508	27016
峨眉山市	Emeishan	18601	102021	14209	307	13902	225120
南充市	**Nanchong**						
顺庆区	Shunqing	26359	149341	22848	7342	15506	383430
高坪区	Gaoping	36762	212044	34494	7129	27365	558795
嘉陵区	Jialing	67257	361116	47074	13301	33773	262223
南部县	Nanbu	98174	530084	108104	36264	71840	828969
营山县	Yingshan	69800	405983	67667	18280	49168	451589
蓬安县	Pengan	54867	316563	63998	17389	46512	421090
仪陇县	Yilong	77133	443631	92441	18537	73577	485536
西充县	Xichong	56661	322923	52489	9469	42776	571778
阆中市	Langzhong	85005	452449	63484	13034	50360	540615
眉山市	**Meishan**						
东坡区	Dongpo	38647	305221	45018	2789	42188	765134
彭山区	Pengshan	12800	97462	12452	714	11738	50388
仁寿县	Renshou	116917	649671	58736	6074	52576	540488
洪雅县	Hongya	14613	104701	12688	99	12574	84957
丹棱县	Danling	7927	54633	8675	277	8384	32116
青神县	Qingshen	9433	65112	8193	1019	7174	81103
宜宾市	**Yibin**						
翠屏区	Cuiping	53610	349160	29394	16120	13190	464027
南溪区	Nanxi	28844	194636	16847	4850	11097	767821
叙州区	Xuzhou	100225	573920	66702	28344	38148	259729
江安县	Jiangan	41085	276995	21934	2302	19005	348530
长宁县	Changning	33616	214322	24804	3610	21168	199586
高县	Gaoxian	46003	266643	19058	8118	10940	222573
珙县	Gongxian	36183	194329	18736	7210	10226	347295
筠连县	Junlian	34731	181284	8290	2222	6016	162359
兴文县	Xingwen	40648	248689	13106	3528	9444	484865
屏山县	Pingshan	17265	95147	13101	1195	11866	117693
广安市	**Guangan**						
广安区	Guanganqu	55027	334304	33059	6017	27036	503355
前锋区	Qianfeng	16613	109540	13002	2214	10477	291465
岳池县	Yuechi	73808	494114	36172	5408	30678	880285
武胜县	Wusheng	51567	330160	26695	4312	22039	420613

12-7 续表 8 continued

县(市、区)	Counties (City,Districts)	粮食 播种面积(公顷) Total Sown Area (hectares)	粮食 产量(吨) Output of Grain (ton)	油料产量(吨) Yield of Oil Bearing Crops (ton)	#花生 Peanut	#油菜籽 Rapeseeds	蔬菜及食用菌产量(吨) Output of Vegetables and Edible Fungus (ton)
邻水县	Linshui	77993	464021	39758	12256	27102	688329
华蓥市	Huaying	18080	104492	4789	643	4045	165695
达州市	**Dazhou**						
通川区	Tongchuan	32469	187527	25109	2929	21850	368410
达川区	Dachuan	90269	549241	71740	5055	66667	578707
宣汉县	Xuanhan	99068	603280	103159	10821	90058	574588
开江县	Kaijiang	53176	309448	50880	10266	40614	447744
大竹县	Dazhu	113668	622786	61048	8812	52236	599930
渠县	Quxian	120335	664946	90638	30675	59947	666813
万源市	Wanyuan	61602	328631	42093	8482	32970	186980
雅安市	**Yaan**						
雨城区	Yucheng	9880	49376	1695		1695	254540
名山区	Mingshan	10973	68464	4186		4186	58797
荥经县	Yingjing	6227	36187	3166	95	3070	47185
汉源县	Hanyuan	20053	95226	739	208	520	240658
石棉县	Shimian	4660	21736	1286	280	1006	75581
天全县	Tianquan	8181	44684	2565		2565	69414
芦山县	Lushan	4953	27020	2103	153	1950	56428
宝兴县	Baoxing	5540	23743	280		280	22829
巴中市	**Bazhong**						
巴州区	Bazhou	60879	345634	36956	4742	32198	360858
恩阳区	Enyang	61225	349051	40746	6746	33911	476477
通江县	Tongjiang	82101	471754	50981	4528	46446	331362
南江县	Nanjiang	70127	397841	43391	2541	40532	376061
平昌县	Pingchang	69164	397147	75908	5978	69720	323203
资阳市	**Ziyang**						
雁江区	Yanjiang	107733	520634	90350	19000	71350	676170
安岳县	Anyue	143067	743981	119304	17376	101928	938931
乐至县	Lezhi	83673	413400	87002	13102	73900	272860
阿坝州	**Aba**						
马尔康市	Maerkang	3934	9789	45		45	35727
汶川县	Wenchuan	3010	11482	539		539	47507
理县	Lixian	1587	7381	15		15	106598
茂县	Maoxian	6767	25922	739		709	252798
松潘县	Songpan	4210	13569	466		466	91048
九寨沟县	Jiuzhaigou	2953	11302	376		374	18539
金川县	Jinchuan	5735	22630	494		494	44646
小金县	Xiaojin	6346	21354	987		987	81724
黑水县	Heishui	6095	18231				45814
壤塘县	Rangtang	2137	4401	377		377	4259

12−7 续表 9 continued

县(市、区)	Counties (City,Districts)	粮食 播种面积(公顷) Total Sown Area (hectares)	粮食 产量(吨) Output of Grain (ton)	油料产量(吨) Yield of Oil Bearing Crops (ton)	#花生 Peanut	#油菜籽 Rapeseeds	蔬菜及食用菌产量(吨) Output of Vegetables and Edible Fungus (ton)
阿坝县	Abaxian	4737	12653	1400		1400	10821
若尔盖县	Ruoergai	2205	6280	1050		1050	13640
红原县	Hongyuan						12563
甘孜州	**Ganzi**						
康定市	Kangding	5104	17178	72		72	38417
泸定县	Luding	3658	11898	1836	70	1757	109237
丹巴县	Danba	3008	10852	1106		1106	27100
九龙县	Jiulong	4381	20615	400		400	49302
雅江县	Yajiang	2644	9975	11		11	22663
道孚县	Daofu	4960	14408	2603		2603	18403
炉霍县	Luhuo	3703	10322	3606		3606	14802
甘孜县	Ganzixian	11116	35429	2502		2502	28033
新龙县	Xinlong	3323	10472	960		960	12191
德格县	Dege	3573	10306				15503
白玉县	Baiyu	3403	10594	709		709	7765
石渠县	Shiqu	2655	7130	528		528	5922
色达县	Seda	880	2266	51		51	2425
理塘县	Litang	3446	12756	1400		1400	67923
巴塘县	Batang	4109	16035	441		441	11638
乡城县	Xiangcheng	2648	9844	402		402	19000
稻城县	Daocheng	2789	9640	1102		1102	6479
得荣县	Derong	3414	13347	362	62	300	10541
凉山州	**Liangshan**						
西昌市	Xichang	41460	247913	2340	132	2208	639421
会理市	Huili	68324	354578	3250	700	2453	544932
木里县	Muli	17642	72795	166		166	54796
盐源县	Yanyuan	50701	239392	762	74	230	197308
德昌县	Dechang	18397	104893	987	86	900	311076
会东县	Huidong	56407	261825	15172	1755	12920	636025
宁南县	Ningnan	24940	107577	1130	1007	123	485825
普格县	Puge	18439	81553	419	18	401	48428
布拖县	Butuo	26488	109279	121	121		36283
金阳县	Jinyang	16420	72886	227	227		74089
昭觉县	Zhaojue	27200	115009	608		608	59874
喜德县	Xide	20194	83090	248		248	25373
冕宁县	Mianning	44554	227089	3852	155	3605	452447
越西县	Yuexi	32236	139261	6549		6482	126373
甘洛县	Ganluo	25403	114638	1435	45	1373	72163
美姑县	Meigu	24775	100733	56	11	45	26654
雷波县	Leibo	19944	94007	1664	333	1330	75582

12-7 续表 10 continued

县(市、区)	Counties (City,Districts)	茶叶产量(吨) Yield of Tea (ton)	水果产量(吨) Output of Fruits (ton)	肉猪出栏头数(头) Slaughtered Fattened Hogs (head)	猪年末存栏头数(头) Hogs at the Year-end (head)	肉牛出栏头数(头) Slaughtered Fattened Cattle and Buffaloes (head)	羊出栏只数(只) Slaughtered Fattened Sheep and Goats (head)	家禽出栏只数(只) Slaughtered Poultry (head)
成都市	**Chengdu**							
锦江区	Jinjiang		18					
青羊区	Qingyang							
金牛区	Jinniu							
武侯区	Wuhou							
成华区	Chenghua							
龙泉驿区	Longquanyi		162871	10138	5287	38	1636	196174
青白江区	Qingbaijiang		49420	29943	22297	754	3694	665335
新都区	Xindu		37214	25607	7069	1281	2259	3529128
温江区	Wenjiang		394	4131	1896	11	282	96307
双流区	Shuangliu		218391	33006	24663	192	7769	1781993
郫都区	Pidu		2613	3868	1886			97871
新津区	Xinjin		49789	135610	59920	400	4431	6575709
金堂县	Jintang		291690	604369	350025	15061	211930	8379528
大邑县	Dayi	153	43408	511964	305652	3051	21198	8294820
蒲江县	Pujiang	8594	484682	402209	249015	402	5204	3544402
都江堰市	Dujiangyan	2357	65675	210813	99682	2729	2776	5472509
彭州市	Pengzhou	20	50193	414093	240143	5087	8481	5809008
邛崃市	Qionglai	11487	206875	752180	426076	3328	30768	7151345
崇州市	Chongzhou	396	26367	495344	291749	5606	9577	6613651
简阳市	Jianyang		219643	718346	397543	1487	409006	6739591
自贡市	**Zigong**							
自流井区	Ziliujing		13474	59983	31094	668	10300	1079655
贡井区	Gongjing		48343	186223	91738	900	67396	3351141
大安区	Daan		16085	165644	72965	8027	77902	12455757
沿滩区	Yantan		55354	169102	73122	877	50106	2959430
荣县	Rongxian	17900	249596	701325	397449	7250	336353	7164564
富顺县	Fushun	118	166141	643095	375734	11084	455815	8896435
攀枝花市	**Panzhihua**							
东区	Dongqu		23746	14459	5545	158	2796	888747
西区	Xiqu		8915	14362	7437	263	4674	610325
仁和区	Renhe		248367	178737	100029	9345	137164	1531779
米易县	Miyi		208166	168643	116270	16303	151780	633059
盐边县	Yanbian	103	191105	248105	161494	11194	222321	981828
泸州市	**Luzhou**							
江阳区	Jiangyang		31167	278233	151089	964	36800	2632400
纳溪区	Naxi	17506	38576	565893	322262	1387	29501	4373800
龙马潭区	Longmatan		14517	105619	58610	495	17165	4744500
泸县	Luxian	1410	101964	1031258	562178	2957	86635	15874500
合江县	Hejiang	730	88300	827606	467416	4593	186900	9220000
叙永县	Xuyong	1611	48718	726492	397121	29452	39240	1699500
古蔺县	Gulin	1746	26805	686701	375576	39916	150460	1197300

12−7 续表 11 continued

县(市、区)	Counties (City,Districts)	茶叶产量 (吨) Yield of Tea (ton)	水果产量 (吨) Output of Fruits (ton)	肉猪出栏头数 (头) Slaughtered Fattened Hogs (head)	猪年末存栏头数 (头) Hogs at the Year-end (head)	肉牛出栏头数 (头) Slaughtered Fattened Cattle and Buffaloes (head)	羊出栏只数 (只) Slaughtered Fattened Sheep and Goats (head)	家禽出栏只数 (只) Slaughtered Poultry (head)
德阳市	**Deyang**							
旌阳区	Jingyang		34069	366078	205283	7730	11429	20211895
罗江区	Luojiang		74577	402440	216777	3360	7981	5670229
中江县	Zhongjiang		68278	1178498	604076	38648	176797	22621547
广汉市	Guanghan	2	45894	233408	119742	12800	7499	11788845
什邡市	Shifang	95	22514	228119	118679	3183	19659	5197100
绵竹市	Mianzhu	325	49855	454463	245414	4941	6901	5987710
绵阳市	**Mianyang**							
涪城区	Fucheng		27889	99711	60155	2735	3340	7409412
游仙区	Youxian		32185	202904	124840	7773	29253	7209378
安州区	Anzhou	462	34938	189013	122761	7113	15114	9822656
三台县	Santai		96290	1188029	676713	36683	130888	15219392
盐亭县	Yanting		57593	581263	377743	24004	279523	9028688
梓潼县	Zitong		107871	604721	375193	16554	244300	7954761
北川县	Beichuan	1010	6453	222380	141310	7802	131549	1527589
平武县	Pingwu	2669	3603	122134	76296	8734	46954	799539
江油市	Jiangyou	49	116066	643123	389308	15289	68686	12045861
广元市	**Guangyuan**							
利州区	Lizhou	6	33735	205224	154780	10618	42679	2823304
昭化区	Zhaohua		23078	650666	388935	10235	74397	4317237
朝天区	Chaotian		7840	190779	137810	10450	88892	3554286
旺苍县	Wangcang	8260	35550	590032	340498	16920	127012	3879547
青川县	Qingchuan	10500	19451	190235	134040	14566	93858	3580016
剑阁县	Jiange	8	86611	1010011	563980	19472	190171	11108535
苍溪县	Cangxi		293888	1070015	571653	26508	109040	8297030
遂宁市	**Suining**							
船山区	Chuanshan	6	30296	582640	353195	4070	47202	2624143
安居区	Anju		36824	947128	461917	3780	46954	5078028
蓬溪县	Pengxi	33	46723	725984	430822	9218	143201	4274011
大英县	Daying		20191	589819	325661	4030	43184	4394993
射洪市	Shehong		22473	961454	490692	16807	111820	10261661
内江市	**Neijiang**							
内江市市中区	Neijiang Downtown		16344	266957	102679	1674	19922	2155826
东兴区	Dongxing		61536	643650	334220	6553	133908	7275614
威远县	Weiyuan	2837	101997	531023	287245	3038	236077	5026721
资中县	Zizhong	151	371175	771456	394900	10271	188808	8336540
隆昌市	Longchang	490	61116	436415	255100	1584	37047	9810300
乐山市	**Leshan**							
乐山市市中区	Leshan Downtown	682	30095	337693	175488	1636	9415	7988441
沙湾区	Shawan	290	7517	116741	71180	1316	8109	2778124
五通桥区	Wutongqiao	2102	38332	146941	92002	1171	6974	4371840

12-7 续表 12 continued

县(市、区)	Counties (City,Districts)	茶叶产量(吨) Yield of Tea (ton)	水果产量(吨) Output of Fruits (ton)	肉猪出栏头数(头) Slaughtered Fattened Hogs (head)	猪年末存栏头数(头) Hogs at the Year-end (head)	肉牛出栏头数(头) Slaughtered Fattened Cattle and Buffaloes (head)	羊出栏只数(只) Slaughtered Fattened Sheep and Goats (head)	家禽出栏只数(只) Slaughtered Poultry (head)
金口河区	Jinkouhe	145	1267	41844	26964	1498	5870	189501
犍为县	Qianwei	8131	75475	573061	316857	8072	60316	10425781
井研县	Jingyan	244	45372	687072	378627	896	65372	5592446
夹江县	Jiajiang	12227	13218	213350	134626	1926	3016	5700430
沐川县	Muchuan	9067	19533	206312	135169	1114	39462	1462238
峨边县	Ebian	327	1036	166361	103006	8080	25700	1067371
马边县	Mabian	12028	5788	144805	102046	6632	120578	658223
峨眉山市	Emeishan	12115	35943	183856	107379	2786	12808	3815545
南充市	**Nanchong**							
顺庆区	Shunqing		26672	279284	158572	6835	156202	5925196
高坪区	Gaoping		187299	588175	360134	4253	124662	6806596
嘉陵区	Jialing		61199	666863	389592	7543	307552	7418900
南部县	Nanbu		165569	878400	544008	15928	291184	10861863
营山县	Yingshan	16	56548	811273	520845	24014	389351	9170896
蓬安县	Pengan		139308	615676	357247	13740	179672	6535191
仪陇县	Yilong		40651	852321	597956	38108	224332	10175030
西充县	Xichong		93908	690602	395196	6774	100613	6386900
阆中市	Langzhong	24	122134	799600	464631	24558	188533	8170928
眉山市	**Meishan**							
东坡区	Dongpo	686	249938	529328	315892	2704	43709	12704070
彭山区	Pengshan	21	93968	130962	89560	1038	21747	3612010
仁寿县	Renshou	17	836547	1082824	641887	6657	303119	13890834
洪雅县	Hongya	22183	10301	191092	112550	12420	39011	3314260
丹棱县	Danling	3944	250045	169021	103638	658	18472	2255140
青神县	Qingshen	785	95190	172822	99430	4468	11870	3759530
宜宾市	**Yibin**							
翠屏区	Cuiping	8548	113679	518229	307166	6542	27055	4352119
南溪区	Nanxi	321	126872	406896	225577	3429	55012	7613698
叙州区	Xuzhou	9502	103205	844408	495067	7735	74942	8607719
江安县	Jiangan	1806	254944	570156	319137	3857	65312	5572832
长宁县	Changning	2150	99579	512996	318183	7339	12737	6803086
高县	Gaoxian	23904	19540	486375	278116	13171	31435	4849346
珙县	Gongxian	11400	9100	534735	314186	16584	12987	2371699
筠连县	Junlian	22442	31431	508365	323191	63173	9810	2738425
兴文县	Xingwen	1315	12657	557888	340748	27923	18514	5110988
屏山县	Pingshan	24405	198491	295666	148438	5052	165703	1559681
广安市	**Guangan**							
广安区	Guanganqu		18323	792162	481563	4422	36325	6183695
前锋区	Qianfeng	57	9520	174383	91046	1803	49053	1911194
岳池县	Yuechi		81783	867828	519550	5608	29192	8510651
武胜县	Wusheng	16	62823	919797	518040	5086	50986	7760312

12-7 续表 13 continued

县(市、区)	Counties (City,Districts)	茶叶产量(吨) Yield of Tea (ton)	水果产量(吨) Output of Fruits (ton)	肉猪出栏头数(头) Slaughtered Fattened Hogs (head)	猪年末存栏头数(头) Hogs at the Year-end (head)	肉牛出栏头数(头) Slaughtered Fattened Cattle and Buffaloes (head)	羊出栏只数(只) Slaughtered Fattened Sheep and Goats (head)	家禽出栏只数(只) Slaughtered Poultry (head)
邻水县	Linshui	411	150557	852745	511271	8709	60954	7704728
华蓥市	Huaying	120	21077	235451	133953	2084	26369	2174194
达州市	**Dazhou**							
通川区	Tongchuan	86	78281	365000	233751	19426	57085	3839276
达川区	Dachuan	251	98002	848962	459709	68387	178002	12357267
宣汉县	Xuanhan	5217	109846	819906	457729	108350	268415	9484906
开江县	Kaijiang	459	30686	402108	242198	14811	129001	12206115
大竹县	Dazhu	691	59433	803444	453097	47294	259441	16970409
渠县	Quxian	301	242044	964664	467984	59725	197280	16355492
万源市	Wanyuan	8319	15112	396629	242136	46136	156616	4770250
雅安市	**Yaan**							
雨城区	Yucheng	39169	15888	203780	95856	4852	38979	1885515
名山区	Mingshan	60510	8200	594503	431469	693	28728	1786543
荥经县	Yingjing	4520	5290	71310	45539	5830	15274	334463
汉源县	Hanyuan	20	525026	202927	110130	15600	59215	499905
石棉县	Shimian	57	125888	73037	41808	8812	41650	481530
天全县	Tianquan	4374	3724	101965	63100	3541	11407	1349525
芦山县	Lushan	1310	2129	86635	51602	2835	6900	1038739
宝兴县	Baoxing	881	1919	54511	30665	15791	23404	69855
巴中市	**Bazhong**							
巴州区	Bazhou	116	29253	570581	341460	23974	61794	1967501
恩阳区	Enyang	71	47720	533816	315311	22165	51507	1976011
通江县	Tongjiang	1901	25470	834063	457952	53758	170072	2447588
南江县	Nanjiang	3320	35689	725227	420777	40698	473221	2732323
平昌县	Pingchang	9464	19532	851886	458387	57068	51601	2813331
资阳市	**Ziyang**							
雁江区	Yanjiang		359641	943415	576963	2955	340312	8165000
安岳县	Anyue		595093	1142392	658591	14789	337540	10520848
乐至县	Lezhi		54998	822180	457615	2047	631183	5359032
阿坝州	**Aba**							
马尔康市	Maerkang		824	19200	23841	39117	3027	74542
汶川县	Wenchuan	43	106394	96286	96091	4370	6715	150767
理县	Lixian		14528	25000	24445	10195	5770	65597
茂县	Maoxian		139650	68200	34053	6191	13409	69679
松潘县	Songpan		2507	19000	31780	47372	36358	43900
九寨沟县	Jiuzhaigou		7822	28000	23633	19082	7043	73425
金川县	Jinchuan	1	21007	45000	49562	14797	9236	135801
小金县	Xiaojin		84679	29000	23157	19292	19279	22521
黑水县	Heishui		8358	62200	17565	13102	5709	89245
壤塘县	Rangtang					40471	21211	

12−7 续表 14 continued

县(市、区)	Counties (City,Districts)	茶叶产量 (吨) Yield of Tea (ton)	水果产量 (吨) Output of Fruits (ton)	肉猪出栏头数 (头) Slaughtered Fattened Hogs (head)	猪年末存栏头数 (头) Hogs at the Year-end (head)	肉牛出栏头数 (头) Slaughtered Fattened Cattle and Buffaloes (head)	羊出栏只数 (只) Slaughtered Fattened Sheep and Goats (head)	家禽出栏只数 (只) Slaughtered Poultry (head)
阿坝县	Abaxian			281	653	109697	20281	
若尔盖县	Ruoergai		1	19000	12472	181262	244546	
红原县	Hongyuan			106	11	135052	1241	
甘孜州	**Ganzi**							
康定市	Kangding		5953	22756	11372	31112	3382	25014
泸定县	Luding	2	6167	53975	38680	3521	10585	60801
丹巴县	Danba		1745	37097	25053	11093	9200	15551
九龙县	Jiulong	84	2059	39498	30086	15236	40569	58162
雅江县	Yajiang		430	8030	7354	14934	13471	2702
道孚县	Daofu		681	3913	2054	25819	3938	
炉霍县	Luhuo		70	538	177	36304	13242	
甘孜县	Ganzixian			92		39341	6575	
新龙县	Xinlong		210			28509	8685	
德格县	Dege			243	227	68500	25724	
白玉县	Baiyu		35	1112	515	31871	34513	200
石渠县	Shiqu		16	11	25	55624	32072	
色达县	Seda			219	263	62313	49521	
理塘县	Litang		113	1135	1312	55473	13147	3020
巴塘县	Batang		1811	11019	5306	26427	6387	10567
乡城县	Xiangcheng		7425	20246	11431	13091	3355	13381
稻城县	Daocheng		370	15553	20470	16605	2925	13479
得荣县	Derong		2679	16991	22939	10008	5702	32013
凉山州	**Liangshan**							
西昌市	Xichang		175797	346389	201418	21152	172032	4847776
会理市	Huili		907786	899803	536503	34100	498737	3045938
木里县	Muli		13509	122833	99037	46347	214384	397075
盐源县	Yanyuan		657274	400051	286395	36370	403516	3479467
德昌县	Dechang		192842	281802	148017	13402	136472	1168949
会东县	Huidong	12	262295	563307	391906	47692	697851	1439376
宁南县	Ningnan	40	27313	295240	154640	22000	163651	689843
普格县	Puge		4651	113011	64587	9891	136769	365209
布拖县	Butuo		383	170047	82488	19995	225461	365368
金阳县	Jinyang		5714	134373	71703	10832	155671	534818
昭觉县	Zhaojue		10121	206184	110041	28630	360460	457507
喜德县	Xide		16294	276300	164126	9585	138869	783662
冕宁县	Mianning		94233	406522	257585	27555	205051	1008767
越西县	Yuexi		37635	249257	98875	15853	175698	579372
甘洛县	Ganluo	10	8417	177873	88804	22200	158417	664671
美姑县	Meigu		8177	211064	128893	25181	249367	1080170
雷波县	Leibo	861	24766	158828	84239	7784	135039	442985

12-8 各县(市、区)规模以上工业经济情况(2023年)
Basic Statistics on Industrial Enterprises above Designated Size by Counties (City, Districts)(2023)

县(市、区)	Counties (City,Districts)	工业企业单位数 (个) Number of Industrial Enterprises (unit)	工业增加值增速 (%) Growth Rate of Industrial Value Added (%)	营业收入 (万元) Business Revenue (10 000 yuan)	利润总额 (万元) Total Profits (10 000 yuan)
成都市	**Chengdu**				
锦江区	Jinjiang	9	2.5	363345	37970
青羊区	Qingyang	36	3.3	9374395	510835
金牛区	Jinniu	60	7.4	1825702	195016
武侯区	Wuhou	225	6.0	25160562	2060566
成华区	Chenghua	46	7.1	11141442	936758
龙泉驿区	Longquanyi	425	8.6	24499357	2173329
青白江区	Qingbaijiang	278	-3.4	5232071	149550
新都区	Xindu	360	6.2	7290678	559140
温江区	Wenjiang	283	-4.5	4665788	399772
双流区	Shuangliu	510	1.4	16264832	427103
郫都区	Pidu	555	-1.2	43657794	1659132
新津区	Xinjin	223	6.7	5624724	207447
金堂县	Jintang	228	21.0	8496022	411638
大邑县	Dayi	214	2.0	3529520	108823
蒲江县	Pujiang	126	10.9	997945	59794
都江堰市	Dujiangyan	154	-6.3	2341200	125270
彭州市	Pengzhou	248	-3.3	9367655	488524
邛崃市	Qionglai	192	8.3	3717996	123689
崇州市	Chongzhou	274	7.1	6336306	191876
简阳市	Jianyang	153	10.7	2049957	110528
自贡市	**Zigong**				
自流井区	Ziliujing	37	8.9	1951453	112000
贡井区	Gongjing	96	8.7	283461	24149
大安区	Daan	69	8.2	843484	62114
沿滩区	Yantan	192	8.8	1703011	165124
荣县	Rongxian	100	8.6	577574	53919
富顺县	Fushun	93	8.8	677655	60462
攀枝花市	**Panzhihua**				
东区	Dongqu	93	8.6	11412150	551380
西区	Xiqu	87	5.3	1129483	71448
仁和区	Renhe	170	6.5	3600851	395019
米易县	Miyi	82	8.6	2301787	443825
盐边县	Yanbian	78	8.9	2341410	606110
泸州市	**Luzhou**				
江阳区	Jiangyang	211	8.4	5649810	2131460
纳溪区	Naxi	125	1.1	2125004	290288
龙马潭区	Longmatan	157	-3.0	4160501	486662
泸县	Luxian	191	-17.3	1916517	265997
合江县	Hejiang	105	1.3	2099365	246349
叙永县	Xuyong	62	8.1	684603	61783

12-8 续表 1 continued

县(市、区)	Counties (City,Districts)	工业企业单位数 (个) Number of Industrial Enterprises (unit)	工业增加值增速 (%) Growth Rate of Industrial Value Added (%)	营业收入 (万元) Business Revenue (10 000 yuan)	利润总额 (万元) Total Profits (10 000 yuan)
古蔺县	Gulin	98	11.9	2288006	570099
德阳市	**Deyang**				
旌阳区	Jingyang	353	7.5	11509440	677703
罗江区	Luojiang	165	6.8	4479817	147163
中江县	Zhongjiang	156	5.5	3436878	473691
广汉市	Guanghan	403	5.5	9266988	969220
什邡市	Shifang	271	10.3	5677242	548799
绵竹市	Mianzhu	176	11.2	6922760	1059478
绵阳市	**Mianyang**				
涪城区	Fucheng	422	19.8	22429152	881793
游仙区	Youxian	193	-6.8	4085466	398407
安州区	Anzhou	159	7.4	4166432	278657
三台县	Santai	146	5.3	2294222	253930
盐亭县	Yanting	52	17.2	448065	40848
梓潼县	Zitong	60	1.2	854691	54995
北川县	Beichuan	80	13.0	661462	47941
平武县	Pingwu	52	4.9	425485	34339
江油市	Jiangyou	243	-4.1	5798897	355606
广元市	**Guangyuan**				
利州区	Lizhou	211	9.4	4930474	433903
昭化区	Zhaohua	62	8.8	360103	6109
朝天区	Chaotian	43	9.6	481249	44086
旺苍县	Wangcang	82	10.0	562646	27105
青川县	Qingchuan	54	7.5	299040	18895
剑阁县	Jiange	64	9.7	270626	15604
苍溪县	Cangxi	68	7.2	449055	100622
遂宁市	**Suining**				
船山区	Chuanshan	253	7.6	5370384	374169
安居区	Anju	69	7.6	2588661	261072
蓬溪县	Pengxi	87	7.3	1702270	89597
大英县	Daying	93	7.2	744439	39500
射洪市	Shehong	140	15.8	5607363	1284404
内江市	**Neijiang**				
内江市中区	Neijiang Downtown	154	9.0	1805564	175334
东兴区	Dongxing	86	18.0	842528	73721
威远县	Weiyuan	132	8.1	5933172	219428
资中县	Zizhong	115	10.6	1182714	177114
隆昌市	Longchang	156	10.6	2193758	298143
乐山市	**Leshan**				
乐山市中区	Leshan Downtown	116	-0.8	1797017	125118
沙湾区	Shawan	59	9.5	2437690	345104

12-8 续表 2 continued

县(市、区)	Counties (City,Districts)	工业企业单位数 (个) Number of Industrial Enterprises (unit)	工业增加值增速 (%) Growth Rate of Industrial Value Added (%)	营业收入 (万元) Business Revenue (10 000 yuan)	利润总额 (万元) Total Profits (10 000 yuan)
五通桥区	Wutongqiao	80	21.2	7974835	4039295
金口河区	Jinkouhe	11	-1.0	366787	277092
犍为县	Qianwei	80	8.0	1136792	151278
井研县	Jingyan	62	1.0	398679	18142
夹江县	Jiajiang	132	-11.6	1963927	168051
沐川县	Muchuan	30	5.6	393361	55534
峨边县	Ebian	39	6.6	790234	93011
马边县	Mabian	28	7.3	481740	133355
峨眉山市	Emeishan	98	-10.7	2859739	487832
南充市	**Nanchong**				
顺庆区	Shunqing	99	7.6	1896451	195524
高坪区	Gaoping	99	8.3	1559558	97799
嘉陵区	Jialing	128	8.2	2565768	135142
南部县	Nanbu	163	-20.1	949219	93086
营山县	Yingshan	110	7.8	1332823	72188
蓬安县	Pengan	82	14.3	430400	35339
仪陇县	Yilong	81	12.3	350383	28182
西充县	Xichong	111	1.5	1147647	97654
阆中市	Langzhong	99	7.5	1070736	69232
眉山市	**Meishan**				
东坡区	Dongpo	313	9.6	8157654	536261
彭山区	Pengshan	201	11.9	3761687	148996
仁寿县	Renshou	228	2.4	3174760	246068
洪雅县	Hongya	68	16.7	638974	39623
丹棱县	Danling	68	20.1	671950	31283
青神县	Qingshen	63	16.4	792509	38187
宜宾市	**Yibin**				
翠屏区	Cuiping	219	14.3	330566289	53213771
南溪区	Nanxi	104	13.6	12254519	21673
叙州区	Xuzhou	118	4.9	65933518	1428235
江安县	Jiangan	82	6.8	18527862	2185127
长宁县	Changning	96	12.3	5137313	485131
高县	Gaoxian	82	8.2	10698044	236733
珙县	Gongxian	63	4.1	15589345	-261217
筠连县	Junlian	75	20.3	8637551	1363915
兴文县	Xingwen	87	6.7	3985219	251569
屏山县	Pingshan	76	2.1	9992319	-58956
广安市	**Guangan**				
广安区	Guanganqu	31	14.9	237120	24173
前锋区	Qianfeng	167	8.9	2872524	192070
岳池县	Yuechi	89	16.0	426063	53576

12-8 续表 3 continued

县(市、区)	Counties (City,Districts)	工业企业单位数 (个) Number of Industrial Enterprises (unit)	工业增加值增速 (%) Growth Rate of Industrial Value Added (%)	营业收入 (万元) Business Revenue (10 000 yuan)	利润总额 (万元) Total Profits (10 000 yuan)
武胜县	Wusheng	108	5.9	1173839	116227
邻水县	Linshui	144	3.7	1912553	152427
华蓥市	Huaying	92	8.8	1149098	161095
达州市	**Dazhou**				
通川区	Tongchuan	117	8.9	1039726	43345
达川区	Dachuan	228	7.3	5134781	139491
宣汉县	Xuanhan	151	13.5	3211455	507692
开江县	Kaijiang	109	-27.1	227722	14465
大竹县	Dazhu	195	3.6	1067357	91101
渠县	Quxian	181	3.8	1152201	108351
万源市	Wanyuan	72	8.9	365632	27564
雅安市	**Yaan**				
雨城区	Yucheng	48	23.2	1649647	133082
名山区	Mingshan	101	3.5	1539787	57878
荥经县	Yingjing	41	-24.9	294562	5806
汉源县	Hanyuan	43	2.0	1152046	95600
石棉县	Shimian	60	6.1	1260042	137988
天全县	Tianquan	41	8.1	710819	21377
芦山县	Lushan	57	5.7	588601	52294
宝兴县	Baoxing	32	18.9	1389187	62829
巴中市	**Bazhong**				
巴州区	Bazhou	114	7.2	487369	31892
恩阳区	Enyang	46	13.5	169694	1878
通江县	Tongjiang	54	8.8	116374	5292
南江县	Nanjiang	74	8.2	257151	15107
平昌县	Pingchang	83	2.0	361415	10498
资阳市	**Ziyang**				
雁江区	Yanjiang	165	2.4	1848770	9494
安岳县	Anyue	88	3.7	378678	40529
乐至县	Lezhi	88	8.1	298191	10034
阿坝州	**Aba**				
马尔康市	Maerkang	6	12.7	64675	11535
汶川县	Wenchuan	42	4.3	1100077	68665
理县	Lixian	14	8.0	170183	4846
茂县	Maoxian	24	6.3	806671	15563
松潘县	Songpan	9	3.2	41382	5385
九寨沟县	Jiuzhaigou	5	5.6	56851	1245
金川县	Jinchuan	6	15.1	153117	54591
小金县	Xiaojin	11	-3.8	61296	424
黑水县	Heishui	10	0.8	93849	10041
壤塘县	Rangtang				

12−8 续表 4 continued

县(市、区)	Counties (City,Districts)	工业企业单位数 (个) Number of Industrial Enterprises (unit)	工业增加值增速 (%) Growth Rate of Industrial Value Added (%)	营业收入 (万元) Business Revenue (10 000 yuan)	利润总额 (万元) Total Profits (10 000 yuan)
阿坝县	Abaxian	6	8.4	30369	4597
若尔盖县	Ruoergai	6	-15.1	29144	3734
红原县	Hongyuan	13	1.7	55455	-391
甘孜州	**Ganzi**				
康定市	Kangding	20	7.5	775065	156654
泸定县	Luding	10	-1.5	109149	5344
丹巴县	Danba	9	-29.4	79666	-15062
九龙县	Jiulong	11	1.7	190917	51018
雅江县	Yajiang				
道孚县	Daofu				
炉霍县	Luhuo				
甘孜县	Ganzixian	4	0.8	15586	1886
新龙县	Xinlong				
德格县	Dege				
白玉县	Baiyu				
石渠县	Shiqu				
色达县	Seda				
理塘县	Litang	5	-46.0	26377	745
巴塘县	Batang				
乡城县	Xiangcheng	9	21.7	95175	-328
稻城县	Daocheng				
得荣县	Derong				
凉山州	**Liangshan**				
西昌市	Xichang	106	14.8	6680856	988507
会理市	Huili	47	7.8	1357406	140727
木里县	Muli	9	4.8	285699	30518
盐源县	Yanyuan	30	5.2	304841	70947
德昌县	Dechang	34	24.2	675422	45517
会东县	Huidong	29	15.7	417293	88451
宁南县	Ningnan	18	23.8	1409051	329686
普格县	Puge	7	7.7	165557	38215
布拖县	Butuo	7	19.8	51505	16197
金阳县	Jinyang	6	6.1	35465	6491
昭觉县	Zhaojue	8	2.6	112025	24504
喜德县	Xide	13	5.5	111005	16608
冕宁县	Mianning	33	14.6	757674	112940
越西县	Yuexi	11	0.1	80408	8842
甘洛县	Ganluo	19	1.5	210489	27616
美姑县	Meigu	8	0.2	122236	37165
雷波县	Leibo	15	1.7	424799	65449

12-9 各县(市、区)财政和贸易情况(2023年)
Basic Statistics on Finance and Trade by Counties (City, Districts)(2023)

县(市、区)	Counties (City,Districts)	地方一般公共预算收入（万元） Local General Public Budget Revenue (10 000 yuan)	一般公共预算支出（万元） General Public Budget Expenditure (10 000 yuan)	社会消费品零售总额（万元） Total Retail Sales of Consumer Goods (10 000 yuan)	出口总额（万美元） Total Exports (USD 10 000)
成都市	**Chengdu**				
锦江区	Jinjiang	1009009	747077	14448550	109775
青羊区	Qingyang	1144215	755370	11221367	69682
金牛区	Jinniu	1006913	906676	10633995	279837
武侯区	Wuhou	4169480	4555549	20803802	1201855
成华区	Chenghua	872516	861589	6628605	234630
龙泉驿区	Longquanyi	854715	1256578	2947678	240863
青白江区	Qingbaijiang	491197	875738	1719392	482448
新都区	Xindu	705681	950368	3838029	85275
温江区	Wenjiang	557259	815525	1898492	87432
双流区	Shuangliu	2286528	2995918	7577908	589459
郫都区	Pidu	617650	805330	3436123	2544560
新津区	Xinjin	371355	585506	1152731	38780
金堂县	Jintang	447565	753659	1526809	112261
大邑县	Dayi	219859	469214	1015511	12585
蒲江县	Pujiang	155702	292547	503141	13904
都江堰市	Dujiangyan	403100	623911	1872761	10060
彭州市	Pengzhou	419628	673194	1389309	15415
邛崃市	Qionglai	365857	628166	1330436	28451
崇州市	Chongzhou	328632	594461	1500659	13828
简阳市	Jianyang	520305	1343606	4571390	23236
自贡市	**Zigong**				
自流井区	Ziliujing	90201	172730	2041608	16464
贡井区	Gongjing	39575	223752	1012048	34
大安区	Daan	57037	193674	803367	26648
沿滩区	Yantan	70191	255065	708259	1404
荣县	Rongxian	88274	418596	1195528	1146
富顺县	Fushun	154036	559603	1706328	241
攀枝花市	**Panzhihua**				
东区	Dongqu	95464	197583	1448883	32289
西区	Xiqu	28533	93848	254232	3004
仁和区	Renhe	83795	199238	695532	9973
米易县	Miyi	165934	267173	581487	9285
盐边县	Yanbian	302122	263821	178489	3669
泸州市	**Luzhou**				
江阳区	Jiangyang	286363	512208	4892913	49736
纳溪区	Naxi	148011	327829	1257037	13738
龙马潭区	Longmatan	189188	322109	2455480	22952
泸县	Luxian	137892	569499	1620063	5403
合江县	Hejiang	122300	489888	1340186	2961
叙永县	Xuyong	121699	459900	703828	2648

12-9 续表 1 continued

县(市、区)	Counties (City,Districts)	地方一般公共预算收入（万元） Local General Public Budget Revenue (10 000 yuan)	一般公共预算支出（万元） General Public Budget Expenditure (10 000 yuan)	社会消费品零售总额（万元） Total Retail Sales of Consumer Goods (10 000 yuan)	出口总额（万美元） Total Exports (USD 10 000)
古蔺县	Gulin	300667	637027	892116	1963
德阳市	**Deyang**				
旌阳区	Jingyang	210683	432889	3138638	40673
罗江区	Luojiang	94162	207702	464156	17268
中江县	Zhongjiang	132576	662584	2474951	13503
广汉市	Guanghan	325706	519460	2441062	43621
什邡市	Shifang	279812	446843	1350589	38442
绵竹市	Mianzhu	330184	538138	1271312	68546
绵阳市	**Mianyang**				
涪城区	Fucheng	713748	1099701	7450754	244404
游仙区	Youxian	168587	503623	1845431	11005
安州区	Anzhou	140296	345775	1173241	15266
三台县	Santai	162803	743511	2684913	5131
盐亭县	Yanting	60863	407352	1182123	2489
梓潼县	Zitong	53430	301519	733689	1196
北川县	Beichuan	68137	234824	422662	658
平武县	Pingwu	36679	209708	283699	65
江油市	Jiangyou	360736	624724	2447111	7311
广元市	**Guangyuan**				
利州区	Lizhou	95204	361395	1891482	1210
昭化区	Zhaohua	40029	278866	331476	58
朝天区	Chaotian	37384	218588	273269	155
旺苍县	Wangcang	62080	394561	618849	297
青川县	Qingchuan	57107	282568	295114	403
剑阁县	Jiange	60631	459323	721619	612
苍溪县	Cangxi	100143	529668	887985	103
遂宁市	**Suining**				
船山区	Chuanshan	276166	680655	2338919	63806
安居区	Anju	125716	439110	637595	1437
蓬溪县	Pengxi	81275	427541	611824	1658
大英县	Daying	100169	315887	636490	1861
射洪市	Shehong	330338	652015	2014748	977
内江市	**Neijiang**				
内江市中区	Neijiang Downtown	61832	269809	1767073	68114
东兴区	Dongxing	111735	382217	1349759	31713
威远县	Weiyuan	150815	441903	1273887	15328
资中县	Zizhong	120698	539818	1142650	8256
隆昌市	Longchang	120246	422727	1505015	15830
乐山市	**Leshan**				
乐山市中区	Leshan Downtown	109040	284729	2983959	1343
沙湾区	Shawan	107963	181611	486962	438

12-9 续表 2 continued

县(市、区)	Counties (City,Districts)	地方一般公共预算收入（万元）Local General Public Budget Revenue (10 000 yuan)	一般公共预算支出（万元）General Public Budget Expenditure (10 000 yuan)	社会消费品零售总额（万元）Total Retail Sales of Consumer Goods (10 000 yuan)	出口总额（万美元）Total Exports (USD 10 000)
五通桥区	Wutongqiao	210524	329358	979394	60260
金口河区	Jinkouhe	36098	101448	89112	
犍为县	Qianwei	130226	327167	997448	1119
井研县	Jingyan	38419	236710	672088	3953
夹江县	Jiajiang	127064	270801	977598	502
沐川县	Muchuan	48086	177542	380415	2032
峨边县	Ebian	52882	202603	301145	
马边县	Mabian	69134	279027	305908	652
峨眉山市	Emeishan	231648	396500	1769689	3669
南充市	**Nanchong**				
顺庆区	Shunqing	158178	504346	4583707	26769
高坪区	Gaoping	78700	398169	1884312	48072
嘉陵区	Jialing	88380	408756	1184597	60162
南部县	Nanbu	100897	549778	2376644	36287
营山县	Yingshan	91758	548600	1454566	350
蓬安县	Pengan	71726	415224	1232144	5507
仪陇县	Yilong	86292	667537	1354409	2161
西充县	Xichong	71914	420091	1027002	998
阆中市	Langzhong	105523	527322	1433692	9
眉山市	**Meishan**				
东坡区	Dongpo	303646	655536	2290800	21656
彭山区	Pengshan	248218	491534	866914	2282
仁寿县	Renshou	509990	1176713	2218864	35673
洪雅县	Hongya	129332	311661	514957	4759
丹棱县	Danling	56438	169409	259909	2598
青神县	Qingshen	70285	192363	300648	2128
宜宾市	**Yibin**				
翠屏区	Cuiping	372043	706138	3261047	242561
南溪区	Nanxi	167573	434356	948809	2157
叙州区	Xuzhou	226389	707187	2499088	21775
江安县	Jiangan	158234	329281	1088778	44042
长宁县	Changning	78354	267454	1147613	1010
高县	Gaoxian	103509	331187	820205	298
珙县	Gongxian	185536	381076	873948	10
筠连县	Junlian	121020	334748	645580	141
兴文县	Xingwen	151943	397177	799842	396
屏山县	Pingshan	146082	301742	365769	4602
广安市	**Guangan**				
广安区	Guanganqu	120622	537355	1968855	1328
前锋区	Qianfeng	76070	246951	520544	31701
岳池县	Yuechi	179955	625157	1376746	5320

12-9 续表 3 continued

县(市、区)	Counties (City,Districts)	地方一般公共预算收入（万元）Local General Public Budget Revenue (10 000 yuan)	一般公共预算支出（万元）General Public Budget Expenditure (10 000 yuan)	社会消费品零售总额（万元）Total Retail Sales of Consumer Goods (10 000 yuan)	出口总额（万美元）Total Exports (USD 10 000)
武胜县	Wusheng	126123	440012	1017724	4585
邻水县	Linshui	167549	543361	1401805	8441
华蓥市	Huaying	123928	290144	555103	8450
达州市	**Dazhou**				
通川区	Tongchuan	196786	406285	2863809	8675
达川区	Dachuan	192787	580225	2467964	91287
宣汉县	Xuanhan	430333	905434	2298583	14498
开江县	Kaijiang	74340	396294	1044659	7394
大竹县	Dazhu	244406	683331	2281809	8085
渠县	Quxian	232767	809676	2639474	10134
万源市	Wanyuan	84123	432754	1030831	3100
雅安市	**Yaan**				
雨城区	Yucheng	76869	258902	1023122	666
名山区	Mingshan	57438	193177	468235	30485
荥经县	Yingjing	80111	201429	327088	148
汉源县	Hanyuan	125864	217220	506064	815
石棉县	Shimian	102038	253047	327236	
天全县	Tianquan	47130	189978	310178	1213
芦山县	Lushan	36277	144947	277476	1412
宝兴县	Baoxing	86476	166212	119418	363
巴中市	**Bazhong**				
巴州区	Bazhou	92666	525352	1773649	5039
恩阳区	Enyang	66326	405703	574570	3847
通江县	Tongjiang	55928	590203	950766	1289
南江县	Nanjiang	86222	523931	944800	1240
平昌县	Pingchang	92432	593391	1177883	2317
资阳市	**Ziyang**				
雁江区	Yanjiang	201401	533075	1741347	42293
安岳县	Anyue	150119	644765	1908010	9519
乐至县	Lezhi	86579	406402	1059249	4588
阿坝州	**Aba**				
马尔康市	Maerkang	173411	250775	114169	
汶川县	Wenchuan	55504	233116	170759	3316
理县	Lixian	10401	134864	74353	
茂县	Maoxian	24077	194253	136451	
松潘县	Songpan	12244	186671	77685	7
九寨沟县	Jiuzhaigou	18863	183973	130566	
金川县	Jinchuan	60552	198903	75220	
小金县	Xiaojin	12492	175380	83175	67
黑水县	Heishui	9972	154234	52452	
壤塘县	Rangtang	4012	179658	38968	

12-9 续表 4 continued

县(市、区)	Counties (City,Districts)	地方一般公共预算收入（万元） Local General Public Budget Revenue (10 000 yuan)	一般公共预算支出（万元） General Public Budget Expenditure (10 000 yuan)	社会消费品零售总额（万元） Total Retail Sales of Consumer Goods (10 000 yuan)	出口总额（万美元） Total Exports (USD 10 000)
阿坝县	Abaxian	17059	278625	76338	
若尔盖县	Ruoergai	10556	268061	86589	
红原县	Hongyuan	13581	245979	56238	
甘孜州	**Ganzi**				
康定市	Kangding	82597	280559	298674	29
泸定县	Luding	41228	258131	230480	208
丹巴县	Danba	24850	150667	84768	
九龙县	Jiulong	32113	189351	49652	5522
雅江县	Yajiang	29796	168025	60147	282
道孚县	Daofu	21317	170787	38347	
炉霍县	Luhuo	7150	159246	54998	512
甘孜县	Ganzixian	8177	210927	107996	48
新龙县	Xinlong	5213	158817	26193	
德格县	Dege	10050	182152	40846	466
白玉县	Baiyu	23876	171785	49341	
石渠县	Shiqu	7085	241762	59728	
色达县	Seda	6676	234200	39202	744
理塘县	Litang	14871	204624	102300	12734
巴塘县	Batang	23859	146335	77902	
乡城县	Xiangcheng	10490	119586	44394	2267
稻城县	Daocheng	11217	143500	49020	
得荣县	Derong	6770	119198	21221	
凉山州	**Liangshan**				
西昌市	Xichang	651215	890222	3802024	18182
会理市	Huili	132021	395552	989835	135
木里县	Muli	75531	284801	109538	
盐源县	Yanyuan	127626	423442	367937	59
德昌县	Dechang	74634	246261	415936	627
会东县	Huidong	126856	344384	752358	44
宁南县	Ningnan	70073	223530	349917	48
普格县	Puge	20092	267866	136766	4885
布拖县	Butuo	20482	300412	77299	
金阳县	Jinyang	41043	309978	107255	
昭觉县	Zhaojue	20046	375347	116552	
喜德县	Xide	15963	261982	121614	
冕宁县	Mianning	121336	357766	694991	71
越西县	Yuexi	33651	359890	231478	68
甘洛县	Ganluo	33364	278056	165199	
美姑县	Meigu	15317	353028	93692	41
雷波县	Leibo	120155	386812	193132	

12-10 各县(市、区)教育情况(2023年)
Basic Statistics on Education of Counties (City, Districts)(2023)

县(市、区)	Counties (City,Districts)	小学学校数(个) Number of Primary Schools (unit)	小学在校学生(人) Students Enrollment of Primary Schools (person)	小学专任教师(人) Full-time Teachers in Primary Schools (person)	普通中学学校数(个) Number of Regular Secondary Schools (unit)	普通中学在校学生(人) Students Enrollment of Regular Secondary Schools (person)	普通中学专任教师(人) Full-time Teachers in Regular Secondary Schools (person)
成都市	**Chengdu**						
锦江区	Jinjiang	38	67026	4361	19	34077	3122
青羊区	Qingyang	33	80416	4461	19	40507	3503
金牛区	Jinniu	49	80328	4379	30	48438	3823
武侯区	Wuhou	85	154126	9624	62	80305	7211
成华区	Chenghua	28	74769	4473	27	34434	2921
龙泉驿区	Longquanyi	40	80709	4816	33	41471	3439
青白江区	Qingbaijiang	17	28679	1576	15	20441	1628
新都区	Xindu	36	97834	5317	45	50357	3842
温江区	Wenjiang	17	67237	3833	25	39483	3243
双流区	Shuangliu	62	148092	9066	67	75279	6850
郫都区	Pidu	24	75835	4204	43	37585	3149
新津区	Xinjin	17	21589	1325	17	15606	1363
金堂县	Jintang	32	44666	2454	26	37595	2657
大邑县	Dayi	14	27405	1568	19	20778	1654
蒲江县	Pujiang	12	13308	854	10	9634	832
都江堰市	Dujiangyan	25	38553	2592	24	28953	2411
彭州市	Pengzhou	23	42044	2510	30	28227	2597
邛崃市	Qionglai	35	32037	1775	25	25232	1948
崇州市	Chongzhou	28	35927	2090	18	24966	2006
简阳市	Jianyang	32	59557	3786	89	62874	5129
自贡市	**Zigong**						
自流井区	Ziliujing	17	33363	1888	15	26562	1828
贡井区	Gongjing	14	10435	762	12	8670	638
大安区	Daan	10	13008	940	14	11867	908
沿滩区	Yantan	12	15580	1046	15	10438	775
荣县	Rongxian	27	22480	1608	23	22666	1786
富顺县	Fushun	22	49076	3134	53	47948	3755
攀枝花市	**Panzhihua**						
东区	Dongqu	10	22019	1166	19	21619	1713
西区	Xiqu	4	5577	500	7	6916	633
仁和区	Renhe	16	13309	930	12	12168	1051
米易县	Miyi	13	16134	1005	9	11308	983
盐边县	Yanbian	12	11244	846	5	7110	670
泸州市	**Luzhou**						
江阳区	Jiangyang	20	53646	2642	26	50061	3537
纳溪区	Naxi	15	19078	1283	15	20576	1648
龙马潭区	Longmatan	14	31321	1671	20	25185	1868
泸县	Luxian	27	40324	3112	54	53478	4213
合江县	Hejiang	57	41165	2686	21	46189	3346
叙永县	Xuyong	29	43177	2539	37	36274	2651

12-10 续表 1 continued

县(市、区)	Counties (City,Districts)	小学学校数(个) Number of Primary Schools (unit)	小学在校学生(人) Students Enrollment of Primary Schools (person)	小学专任教师(人) Full-time Teachers in Primary Schools (person)	普通中学学校数(个) Number of Regular Secondary Schools (unit)	普通中学在校学生(人) Students Enrollment of Regular Secondary Schools (person)	普通中学专任教师(人) Full-time Teachers in Regular Secondary Schools (person)
古蔺县	Gulin	32	65137	3601	35	48316	3398
德阳市	**Deyang**						
旌阳区	Jingyang	36	51790	3000	21	39361	3017
罗江区	Luojiang	17	9623	624	8	9206	710
中江县	Zhongjiang	82	49364	3516	52	48738	3950
广汉市	Guanghan	22	30313	1842	20	19364	1807
什邡市	Shifang	18	18328	1291	16	14560	1298
绵竹市	Mianzhu	26	18744	1253	11	13504	1118
绵阳市	**Mianyang**						
涪城区	Fucheng	44	92285	4538	44	93629	6670
游仙区	Youxian	30	37013	2047	20	37705	2478
安州区	Anzhou	21	21714	1312	11	16425	1226
三台县	Santai	83	53084	3569	35	45062	3993
盐亭县	Yanting	38	15480	1260	17	14452	1335
梓潼县	Zitong	23	14443	1020	9	11853	858
北川县	Beichuan	13	8957	721	5	9357	744
平武县	Pingwu	38	4945	519	7	4774	460
江油市	Jiangyou	41	38012	2250	18	30770	2231
广元市	**Guangyuan**						
利州区	Lizhou	37	49559	2784	29	41213	3098
昭化区	Zhaohua	27	4615	712	11	4512	480
朝天区	Chaotian	19	4892	641	9	4745	491
旺苍县	Wangcang	36	16524	1608	20	15775	1450
青川县	Qingchuan	26	6195	977	8	7014	715
剑阁县	Jiange	58	24350	2242	20	23589	1915
苍溪县	Cangxi	50	25358	2344	42	30100	2510
遂宁市	**Suining**						
船山区	Chuanshan	39	65554	3694	33	49381	3496
安居区	Anju	34	23302	1875	25	23003	2019
蓬溪县	Pengxi	16	21749	1691	30	18923	1633
大英县	Daying	29	25513	1645	21	20125	1504
射洪市	Shehong	45	39317	2752	28	33476	2751
内江市	**Neijiang**						
内江市中区	Neijiang Downtown	27	27688	1819	22	23429	1754
东兴区	Dongxing	36	43379	2627	33	37854	2788
威远县	Weiyuan	34	27616	2287	30	27809	2375
资中县	Zizhong	56	44072	2620	49	44291	3392
隆昌市	Longchang	47	33359	2251	28	34494	2301
乐山市	**Leshan**						
乐山市中区	Leshan Downtown	29	50247	2959	33	33446	2993
沙湾区	Shawan	13	6169	528	8	5196	498

12-10 续表 2 continued

县(市、区)	Counties (City,Districts)	小学学校数(个) Number of Primary Schools (unit)	小学在校学生(人) Students Enrollment of Primary Schools (person)	小学专任教师(人) Full-time Teachers in Primary Schools (person)	普通中学学校数(个) Number of Regular Secondary Schools (unit)	普通中学在校学生(人) Students Enrollment of Regular Secondary Schools (person)	普通中学专任教师(人) Full-time Teachers in Regular Secondary Schools (person)
五通桥区	Wutongqiao	16	9859	722	13	8715	845
金口河区	Jinkouhe	9	2472	217	1	1477	118
犍为县	Qianwei	26	22376	1419	21	20273	1679
井研县	Jingyan	20	12071	999	23	11414	1130
夹江县	Jiajiang	16	15053	958	15	9637	825
沐川县	Muchuan	10	12374	863	13	9686	780
峨边县	Ebian	17	11663	772	11	5851	471
马边县	Mabian	29	22099	1334	10	12212	853
峨眉山市	Emeishan	18	22411	1343	11	16747	1377
南充市	**Nanchong**						
顺庆区	Shunqing	39	51766	3092	24	45523	3479
高坪区	Gaoping	32	36237	2271	31	32044	2323
嘉陵区	Jialing	28	32483	2435	38	24519	2227
南部县	Nanbu	33	45861	3674	67	43361	3680
营山县	Yingshan	26	38678	2595	63	35768	2742
蓬安县	Pengan	28	23672	1982	30	22388	1893
仪陇县	Yilong	44	45694	3461	49	39067	3499
西充县	Xichong	22	20434	1962	10	16998	1476
阆中市	Langzhong	19	31929	2404	60	28398	2593
眉山市	**Meishan**						
东坡区	Dongpo	48	58323	3531	38	39961	3308
彭山区	Pengshan	15	16325	933	11	9977	710
仁寿县	Renshou	63	67137	4955	82	59327	5555
洪雅县	Hongya	22	17992	1046	8	10589	817
丹棱县	Danling	12	8398	561	5	4930	440
青神县	Qingshen	14	7533	503	4	5122	455
宜宾市	**Yibin**						
翠屏区	Cuiping	30	59515	3642	56	60142	4800
南溪区	Nanxi	17	23565	1551	18	22504	1664
叙州区	Xuzhou	62	64559	3792	48	50652	4060
江安县	Jiangan	34	30214	1922	23	24735	1738
长宁县	Changning	16	24872	1373	20	19764	1420
高县	Gaoxian	54	27940	1750	20	22783	1717
珙县	Gongxian	24	26620	1563	12	19398	1374
筠连县	Junlian	11	30257	1849	29	23863	1784
兴文县	Xingwen	27	29903	2000	23	26128	2104
屏山县	Pingshan	11	20586	1339	18	15900	1229
广安市	**Guangan**						
广安区	Guanganqu	24	50360	3077	55	50674	4391
前锋区	Qianfeng	14	14356	1099	14	11581	1057
岳池县	Yuechi	35	47339	3476	69	38946	3698

12−10 续表 3 continued

县(市、区)	Counties (City,Districts)	小学学校数（个）Number of Primary Schools (unit)	小学在校学生（人）Students Enrollment of Primary Schools (person)	小学专任教师（人）Full-time Teachers in Primary Schools (person)	普通中学学校数（个）Number of Regular Secondary Schools (unit)	普通中学在校学生（人）Students Enrollment of Regular Secondary Schools (person)	普通中学专任教师（人）Full-time Teachers in Regular Secondary Schools (person)
武胜县	Wusheng	37	33722	2606	37	28996	2710
邻水县	Linshui	29	51253	3218	48	43627	3847
华蓥市	Huaying	14	19415	1254	22	15115	1253
达州市	**Dazhou**						
通川区	Tongchuan	26	49703	3107	36	41756	3137
达川区	Dachuan	43	49077	4014	79	60696	4834
宣汉县	Xuanhan	52	76627	5222	68	70358	5072
开江县	Kaijiang	27	28082	1922	25	25739	1919
大竹县	Dazhu	37	51263	3654	46	51992	3959
渠县	Quxian	39	45678	4567	62	44596	4196
万源市	Wanyuan	34	29648	2211	38	27187	2033
雅安市	**Yaan**						
雨城区	Yucheng	21	23201	1495	18	17901	1616
名山区	Mingshan	20	14510	914	15	11732	971
荥经县	Yingjing	11	7282	579	4	4470	398
汉源县	Hanyuan	25	17965	1207	8	13173	1018
石棉县	Shimian	16	8967	631	4	5978	431
天全县	Tianquan	14	7507	662	5	6593	617
芦山县	Lushan	14	5876	509	4	3882	403
宝兴县	Baoxing	4	2473	310	4	1449	196
巴中市	**Bazhong**						
巴州区	Bazhou	23	59658	4164	52	45465	4340
恩阳区	Enyang	20	17459	1472	36	15499	1639
通江县	Tongjiang	54	33552	3205	29	28873	2893
南江县	Nanjiang	50	29740	2432	34	26092	2328
平昌县	Pingchang	26	43069	3981	61	37112	3865
资阳市	**Ziyang**						
雁江区	Yanjiang	58	54789	3121	63	52483	3922
安岳县	Anyue	44	58735	3811	90	65495	4908
乐至县	Lezhi	41	23426	1890	40	26305	2126
阿坝州	**Aba**						
马尔康市	Maerkang	12	3945	390	4	3665	390
汶川县	Wenchuan	11	4703	610	6	6275	637
理县	Lixian	6	1871	310	2	1192	205
茂县	Maoxian	9	6316	557	4	4580	505
松潘县	Songpan	13	4415	512	8	2264	265
九寨沟县	Jiuzhaigou	14	4334	393	2	2973	319
金川县	Jinchuan	19	3277	419	4	2093	326
小金县	Xiaojin	18	3555	467	4	2883	359
黑水县	Heishui	10	1686	320	2	1068	156
壤塘县	Rangtang	10	6393	425	4	2369	175

12−10 续表 4 continued

县(市、区)	Counties (City,Districts)	小学学校数(个) Number of Primary Schools (unit)	小学在校学生(人) Students Enrollment of Primary Schools (person)	小学专任教师(人) Full-time Teachers in Primary Schools (person)	普通中学学校数(个) Number of Regular Secondary Schools (unit)	普通中学在校学生(人) Students Enrollment of Regular Secondary Schools (person)	普通中学专任教师(人) Full-time Teachers in Regular Secondary Schools (person)
阿坝县	Abaxian	26	9041	708	2	3534	337
若尔盖县	Ruoergai	23	7256	603	7	5530	479
红原县	Hongyuan	12	5910	484	2	3453	269
甘孜州	**Ganzi**						
康定市	Kangding	18	8827	582	7	8465	674
泸定县	Luding	11	5773	468	7	7921	643
丹巴县	Danba	13	2761	380	4	2570	301
九龙县	Jiulong	8	4906	358	4	4486	335
雅江县	Yajiang	15	3773	327	2	2658	174
道孚县	Daofu	18	5170	327	2	2443	177
炉霍县	Luhuo	12	6444	398	3	3238	228
甘孜县	Ganzixian	26	7974	554	4	5075	405
新龙县	Xinlong	18	5999	387	1	1993	112
德格县	Dege	23	11197	671	2	5047	231
白玉县	Baiyu	18	7146	366	1	2437	127
石渠县	Shiqu	25	16028	828	3	4739	282
色达县	Seda	18	8225	445	2	3628	230
理塘县	Litang	27	9422	615	3	3720	268
巴塘县	Batang	19	5509	452	2	4201	313
乡城县	Xiangcheng	6	2184	241	1	1034	106
稻城县	Daocheng	8	2536	253	2	1174	118
得荣县	Derong	10	1978	259	2	720	86
凉山州	**Liangshan**						
西昌市	Xichang	110	99421	4125	36	62123	4055
木里县	Muli	39	27574	1609	13	19490	1390
盐源县	Yanyuan	33	11192	822	3	7956	574
德昌县	Dechang	50	32691	1764	12	25640	1573
会理县	Huili	22	22442	1148	5	16569	1089
会东县	Huidong	31	27389	1664	10	24238	1789
宁南县	Ningnan	33	18257	957	4	12903	864
普格县	Puge	36	35058	1722	5	17062	1132
布拖县	Butuo	36	34697	1653	3	17088	1031
金阳县	Jinyang	35	30417	1526	10	14886	852
昭觉县	Zhaojue	37	53729	2365	8	22925	1270
喜德县	Xide	34	25132	1393	8	16424	1008
冕宁县	Mianning	45	42967	2022	13	25850	1482
越西县	Yuexi	51	47208	2198	10	27753	1255
甘洛县	Ganluo	31	25687	1369	10	15570	895
美姑县	Meigu	40	38923	2020	6	17418	1137
雷波县	Leibo	48	33747	1677	12	20138	1393

13 农 业

Chapter 13 Agriculture

13-1 农林牧渔业总产值

Gross Output Value of Farming, Forestry, Animal Husbandry and Fishery

单位：亿元 (100 million yuan)

年份 Year	农林牧渔业总产值 Total	#第一产业 Primary Industry	农业 Farming	林业 Forestry	牧业 Animal Husbandry	渔业 Fishery
1980	136.92	136.92	98.07	4.21	34.07	0.57
1985	234.82	234.82	161.14	13.09	58.74	1.85
1990	484.31	484.31	301.46	18.51	157.04	7.30
1991	513.43	513.43	317.43	19.43	168.41	8.16
1992	565.62	565.62	344.52	22.23	189.41	9.46
1993	660.69	660.69	389.21	24.90	234.30	12.28
1994	930.80	930.80	521.00	28.48	365.33	15.99
1995	1113.96	1113.96	645.17	34.32	413.84	20.63
1996	1274.32	1274.32	750.07	38.58	461.32	24.35
1997	1395.43	1395.43	798.22	41.31	527.60	28.30
1998	1455.19	1455.19	823.72	45.87	554.15	31.45
1999	1444.86	1444.86	792.80	45.34	572.63	34.09
2000	1483.52	1483.52	785.37	49.13	611.76	37.26
2001	1534.89	1534.90	769.95	50.85	673.10	41.00
2002	1651.53	1651.53	807.43	54.60	743.91	45.59
2003	1784.49	1749.64	804.70	59.26	832.34	53.34
2004	2252.30	2213.72	987.70	62.70	1097.60	65.80
2005	2457.46	2415.81	1037.20	69.94	1230.18	78.49
2006	2602.10	2556.40	1075.08	76.75	1317.41	87.16
2007	3377.00	3317.00	1317.00	106.42	1807.58	86.00
2008	3903.00	3816.00	1608.00	153.21	1980.79	104.00
2009	3689.81	3634.35	1815.98	102.60	1596.72	119.05
2010	4081.81	4007.21	2059.33	160.06	1658.00	129.83
2011	4932.73	4850.72	2454.26	203.29	2046.00	147.16
2012	5433.12	5340.03	2764.90	234.34	2177.02	163.77
2013	5620.27	5510.97	2886.48	249.02	2197.97	177.49
2014	5888.09	5765.79	3068.61	268.54	2236.29	192.35
2015	6377.84	6237.43	3315.51	297.26	2414.15	210.52
2016	6816.92	6656.50	3701.64	329.31	2405.54	220.01
2017	6955.55	6785.64	4004.20	346.80	2199.72	234.92
2018	7195.65	7006.47	4153.71	358.74	2246.08	247.94
2019	7889.35	7678.61	4395.04	372.21	2647.88	263.47
2020	9216.40	8983.05	4701.88	379.82	3613.81	287.54
2021	9383.32	9131.01	5089.48	408.44	3305.28	327.82
2022	9859.75	9591.75	5528.76	438.22	3281.67	343.11
2023	9977.76	9698.18	5821.66	481.80	3035.62	359.09

注：①本表按当年价格计算；②从2013年起，农业核算执行国家统计局新的《国民经济行业分类》和《三次产业划分规定》。

a) Data of this year are calculated at current prices; b) Since 2013, agricultural accounting has been based on the "Industrial Classification for National Economic Activities" and "Rules of Clarification of Three Industries" which were newly promulgated by National Statistical Bureau.

13-2 农林牧渔业总产值指数
Indices of Gross Output Value of Farming, Forestry, Animal Husbandry and Fishery

(1952年=100) (1952=100)

年份 Year	农林牧渔业总产值 Total	#农业 Farming	#林业 Forestry	#牧业 Animal Husbandry	#渔业 Fishery
1980	242.2	201.9	373.4	482.6	400.0
1985	332.7	251.1	933.0	756.5	1272.4
1990	409.4	290.8	742.2	1104.3	2386.2
1991	427.6	300.5	742.9	1179.3	2589.7
1992	445.7	308.2	800.4	1255.7	2831.0
1993	450.2	299.4	812.4	1341.1	3210.3
1994	465.3	297.1	859.6	1461.1	3586.2
1995	504.9	321.2	932.6	1584.8	4369.0
1996	533.3	338.0	1004.6	1674.3	4893.1
1997	559.4	351.8	1031.2	1772.2	5481.2
1998	584.5	361.4	1061.6	1889.9	6126.0
1999	605.8	368.7	1048.3	1997.8	6855.0
2000	636.0	379.2	1080.7	2144.1	7717.7
2001	651.3	369.0	1083.2	2318.2	8521.1
2002	695.3	387.3	1145.4	2512.5	9551.7
2003	738.5	394.6	1257.0	2744.7	11309.2
2004	790.9	410.8	1303.5	3019.2	12756.8
2005	842.4	421.6	1422.0	3304.8	14382.0
2006	873.7	416.7	1525.5	3540.1	15689.3
2007	904.1	436.3	1604.8	3610.9	16944.4
2008	933.9	447.6	1652.9	3744.5	17961.1
2009	973.5	468.3	1743.8	3886.8	18889.8
2010	1017.3	492.2	1841.5	4022.8	19807.8
2011	1064.1	520.7	2020.1	4127.4	21134.9
2012	1112.0	545.2	2187.8	4284.2	22572.1
2013	1149.8	564.8	2378.1	4395.6	23926.4
2014	1195.8	586.8	2501.8	4567.0	25218.4
2015	1250.8	618.5	2772.2	4684.6	27502.1
2016	1300.4	648.6	2911.6	4782.4	28857.6
2017	1349.9	682.3	3067.9	4839.6	30371.1
2018	1402.5	713.7	3120.1	4955.7	31859.3
2019	1439.0	752.9	3185.6	4787.2	33165.5
2020	1517.7	787.2	3278.4	5133.7	34815.1
2021	1633.7	826.9	3458.6	5740.3	36758.4
2022	1706.1	863.0	3686.8	5978.1	38426.7
2023	1774.3	905.3	4051.8	6073.7	40232.8

注：本表按可比价格计算；2003年起按新口径计算；2004年起指数按可比价格缩减法计算。

a) Data in this table are calculated at comparable prices; Since 2003, calculation has been based on the new range; Data have been calculated at comparable prices by deflation approach since 2004.

13-3 各市(州)按产业分农林牧渔业总产值(2023年)
Gross Output Value of Farming, Forestry, Animal Husbandry and Fishery by Industry and Region(2023)

单位：亿元 (100 million yuan)

市(州)	Region	农林牧渔业总产值 Total	#第一产业 Primary Industry	农业 Farming	林业 Forestry	牧业 Animal Husbandry	渔业 Fishery
全省	**Sichuan**	**9977.76**	**9698.18**	**5821.66**	**481.80**	**3035.62**	**359.09**
成都市	Chengdu	957.76	918.26	664.12	15.78	207.62	30.75
自贡市	Zigong	417.15	411.16	235.18	31.35	126.81	17.81
攀枝花市	Panzhihua	176.31	174.36	136.32	3.13	32.15	2.77
泸州市	Luzhou	470.21	459.20	260.91	25.84	151.20	21.25
德阳市	Deyang	508.41	485.35	302.50	14.29	152.42	16.14
绵阳市	Mianyang	656.24	629.30	327.01	49.61	223.32	29.36
广元市	Guangyuan	386.02	376.83	199.51	19.63	146.22	11.46
遂宁市	Suining	365.98	352.96	193.00	14.65	133.37	11.94
内江市	Neijiang	462.93	451.22	277.00	20.01	126.19	28.03
乐山市	Leshan	458.81	451.49	239.16	35.29	149.35	27.69
南充市	Nanchong	835.83	821.59	500.13	25.36	269.93	26.17
眉山市	Meishan	411.82	401.36	263.63	9.79	101.86	26.09
宜宾市	Yibin	657.15	642.32	366.14	52.58	195.19	28.41
广安市	Guangan	401.29	391.10	231.06	15.38	129.89	14.76
达州市	Dazhou	707.75	687.02	416.00	38.14	208.62	24.27
雅安市	Yaan	270.27	265.39	184.83	22.13	53.73	4.70
巴中市	Bazhong	350.38	341.81	197.22	12.15	115.63	16.82
资阳市	Ziyang	362.66	339.99	194.73	18.56	110.88	15.82
阿坝藏族羌族自治州	Aba	172.01	165.78	62.01	13.25	90.50	0.02
甘孜藏族自治州	Ganzi	130.84	129.13	56.51	6.65	65.97	
凉山彝族自治州	Liangshan	817.95	802.54	514.67	38.25	244.80	4.83

注：本表按当年价格计算。
a) Data in this table are calculated at current prices.

13-4 各市(州)按产业分农林牧渔业总产值指数(2023年)
Indices of Gross Output Value of Farming, Forestry, Animal Husbandry and Fishery by Industry and Region(2023)

(上年=100) (preceding year=100)

市(州)	Region	农林牧渔业总产值 Total	#第一产业 Primary Industry	农业 Farming	林业 Forestry	牧业 Animal Husbandry	渔业 Fishery
全省	**Sichuan**	**104.0**	**104.0**	**104.9**	**109.9**	**101.6**	**104.7**
成都市	Chengdu	103.0	103.0	104.8	93.3	99.0	101.5
自贡市	Zigong	104.0	104.0	104.8	108.2	101.8	104.3
攀枝花市	Panzhihua	104.2	104.1	105.1	107.2	100.5	100.6
泸州市	Luzhou	104.0	103.9	104.2	111.3	102.0	106.3
德阳市	Deyang	104.1	104.2	105.4	112.4	101.5	103.0
绵阳市	Mianyang	103.6	103.6	104.9	112.8	100.1	103.8
广元市	Guangyuan	103.8	103.8	105.9	108.8	101.0	102.7
遂宁市	Suining	103.8	103.8	105.2	107.0	101.3	107.6
内江市	Neijiang	104.3	104.2	104.9	107.0	102.7	103.7
乐山市	Leshan	104.2	104.2	106.2	109.2	100.6	103.6
南充市	Nanchong	104.1	104.1	105.7	112.4	100.5	106.3
眉山市	Meishan	104.2	104.2	105.3	108.8	101.5	102.9
宜宾市	Yibin	104.3	104.3	104.9	109.6	101.2	112.2
广安市	Guangan	103.9	103.9	104.8	114.3	101.2	104.6
达州市	Dazhou	103.4	103.4	103.9	118.7	100.5	103.2
雅安市	Yaan	104.1	104.1	104.5	110.1	100.7	106.0
巴中市	Bazhong	104.0	103.9	104.2	108.7	102.9	105.7
资阳市	Ziyang	103.6	103.7	103.4	115.2	102.5	104.2
阿坝藏族羌族自治州	Aba	110.7	110.9	103.4	114.1	115.8	56.8
甘孜藏族自治州	Ganzi	104.1	104.1	105.9	141.9	101.3	100.0
凉山彝族自治州	Liangshan	104.3	104.2	106.2	103.2	100.9	106.0

13-5 各市(州)农林牧渔业总产值
Gross Output Value of Farming, Forestry, Animal Husbandry and Fishery by Region

单位：亿元 (100 million yuan)

市(州)	Region	2013	2014	2015	2016	2017	2018	2019	2020	2021	2022	2023
全省	**Sichuan**	**5620.27**	**5888.09**	**6377.84**	**6816.92**	**6955.55**	**7195.65**	**7889.35**	**9216.40**	**9383.32**	**9859.75**	**9977.76**
成都市	Chengdu	716.33	751.65	815.34	880.76	916.15	951.44	1003.34	1071.95	942.61	950.42	957.76
自贡市	Zigong	229.41	240.62	260.64	279.23	286.01	294.54	324.23	374.81	392.93	408.86	417.15
攀枝花市	Panzhihua	101.72	105.37	114.46	123.79	124.78	126.71	140.12	148.85	159.55	172.32	176.31
泸州市	Luzhou	251.22	263.07	284.90	304.10	309.86	319.49	357.18	430.29	444.85	464.15	470.21
德阳市	Deyang	291.34	305.08	330.57	352.98	359.25	372.01	406.33	460.31	475.22	498.12	508.41
绵阳市	Mianyang	350.58	367.95	397.50	424.55	432.71	448.99	504.47	631.15	641.28	648.31	656.24
广元市	Guangyuan	198.05	206.88	224.06	237.75	240.10	247.95	272.04	336.57	358.79	385.38	386.02
遂宁市	Suining	212.40	222.42	240.91	257.27	262.12	271.14	309.98	363.11	367.17	367.16	365.98
内江市	Neijiang	271.41	284.81	308.53	330.34	338.59	350.00	377.32	422.97	434.91	457.77	462.93
乐山市	Leshan	287.23	300.15	325.18	344.35	347.42	358.00	385.96	436.64	437.85	449.81	458.81
南充市	Nanchong	486.95	509.08	550.15	585.90	591.37	611.18	656.03	763.92	787.46	830.81	835.83
眉山市	Meishan	235.84	247.89	268.48	288.70	297.85	308.39	333.19	380.42	391.90	411.78	411.82
宜宾市	Yibin	321.47	336.84	365.01	389.72	397.20	410.69	450.84	563.75	583.42	646.22	657.15
广安市	Guangan	242.29	253.45	274.44	292.43	297.10	307.20	331.68	384.44	397.07	401.87	401.29
达州市	Dazhou	390.73	410.50	444.04	475.32	485.84	503.67	551.43	636.04	665.26	698.09	707.75
雅安市	Yaan	127.42	134.05	145.20	157.17	162.91	169.11	193.40	237.62	247.28	264.62	270.27
巴中市	Bazhong	147.73	154.42	167.27	177.40	179.29	185.32	214.36	291.16	314.88	345.55	350.38
资阳市	Ziyang	179.48	188.58	204.91	219.51	224.09	233.87	261.79	318.20	324.60	359.48	362.66
阿坝藏族羌族自治州	Aba	82.32	85.58	93.07	97.00	97.51	100.51	115.06	142.21	153.20	159.24	172.01
甘孜藏族自治州	Ganzi	76.19	78.88	85.33	86.87	87.11	89.65	100.36	123.29	120.52	127.46	130.84
凉山彝族自治州	Liangshan	420.15	440.81	477.86	511.77	518.27	535.81	600.23	698.72	742.56	812.32	817.95

注：本表按当年价格计算。
a) Data in this table are calculated at current prices.

13-6 各市(州)农林牧渔业总产值指数
Indices of Gross Output Value of Farming, Forestry, Animal Husbandry and Fishery by Region

(上年=100) (preceding year=100)

市(州)	Region	2013	2014	2015	2016	2017	2018	2019	2020	2021	2022	2023
全省	**Sichuan**	**103.4**	**104.0**	**104.6**	**104.0**	**103.8**	**103.9**	**102.6**	**105.5**	**107.6**	**104.4**	**104.0**
成都市	Chengdu	103.5	103.7	104.3	103.9	103.8	103.4	102.1	103.3	105.0	103.6	103.0
自贡市	Zigong	103.9	104.2	104.4	104.0	104.2	103.7	102.6	105.9	107.9	104.5	104.0
攀枝花市	Panzhihua	104.6	104.7	104.4	104.7	104.4	104.2	103.1	105.6	108.6	105.1	104.2
泸州市	Luzhou	104.4	104.2	104.4	103.8	103.8	103.6	102.7	105.9	107.5	104.6	104.0
德阳市	Deyang	103.7	104.2	104.4	103.9	103.6	103.7	102.1	103.7	108.1	104.3	104.1
绵阳市	Mianyang	103.6	105.5	104.5	104.0	104.0	103.8	102.7	106.0	108.2	104.6	103.6
广元市	Guangyuan	103.8	104.5	104.5	103.0	104.2	103.7	102.8	106.2	108.2	104.6	103.8
遂宁市	Suining	103.1	104.1	104.2	103.8	103.5	103.6	103.4	105.6	108.5	104.6	103.8
内江市	Neijiang	104.1	103.9	104.4	103.8	102.9	103.6	103.1	106.2	107.6	104.3	104.3
乐山市	Leshan	103.6	104.1	104.4	104.0	103.7	103.9	103.0	105.6	107.6	104.7	104.2
南充市	Nanchong	103.7	104.4	104.4	104.1	103.8	103.8	103.4	106.8	108.4	104.4	104.1
眉山市	Meishan	103.7	104.0	104.5	103.9	103.9	103.7	102.6	106.1	107.6	104.8	104.2
宜宾市	Yibin	103.7	103.8	104.4	103.5	103.3	103.6	102.8	106.0	108.7	104.5	104.3
广安市	Guangan	103.5	104.2	104.1	102.5	103.4	103.6	102.9	105.9	108.1	104.5	103.9
达州市	Dazhou	103.8	103.9	104.4	103.9	103.9	103.7	103.3	105.7	108.5	104.6	103.4
雅安市	Yaan	102.1	104.6	104.4	103.7	104.0	103.8	103.3	106.2	109.3	104.8	104.1
巴中市	Bazhong	103.4	103.8	104.2	103.7	103.7	103.8	102.5	105.8	108.2	104.4	104.0
资阳市	Ziyang	103.6	104.0	104.5	104.2	103.8	103.8	103.1	106.3	107.9	104.5	103.6
阿坝藏族羌族自治州	Aba	105.0	104.9	105.3	103.9	103.3	103.9	103.7	104.8	107.5	104.5	110.7
甘孜藏族自治州	Ganzi	104.1	104.8	104.6	105.1	104.6	103.6	104.1	104.5	105.0	104.3	104.1
凉山彝族自治州	Liangshan	104.9	104.7	104.6	103.7	103.9	103.7	104.4	105.5	107.8	104.4	104.3

13-7 各市(州)农林牧渔业增加值及指数(2023年)

Added Value and Indices of Farming, Forestry, Animal Husbandry and Fishery by Region(2023)

市(州)	Region	农林牧渔业增加值(亿元) Added Value of Farming, Forestry, Animal Husbandry and Fishery (100 million yuan)	#第一产业 Primary Industry	农林牧渔业增加值指数(上年=100) Indices of Added Value of Farming, Forestry, Animal Husbandry and Fishery (preceding year=100)	#第一产业 Primary Industry
全省	**Sichuan**	**6236.20**	**6056.64**	**104.0**	**104.0**
成都市	Chengdu	620.98	594.86	103.0	103.0
自贡市	Zigong	263.49	259.77	104.1	104.1
攀枝花市	Panzhihua	116.50	115.27	104.2	104.2
泸州市	Luzhou	288.43	281.41	104.0	103.9
德阳市	Deyang	318.89	303.73	104.1	104.1
绵阳市	Mianyang	409.87	393.19	103.7	103.8
广元市	Guangyuan	221.43	215.13	103.8	103.8
遂宁市	Suining	229.90	221.32	104.0	104.0
内江市	Neijiang	304.75	297.43	104.3	104.3
乐山市	Leshan	313.01	308.30	104.2	104.2
南充市	Nanchong	516.49	506.98	104.1	104.1
眉山市	Meishan	249.61	243.28	104.2	104.2
宜宾市	Yibin	413.38	404.18	104.3	104.3
广安市	Guangan	254.29	247.78	103.9	103.9
达州市	Dazhou	454.35	440.53	103.4	103.4
雅安市	Yaan	176.73	173.75	104.1	104.1
巴中市	Bazhong	200.42	195.20	104.0	103.9
资阳市	Ziyang	209.51	196.64	103.6	103.8
阿坝藏族羌族自治州	Aba	102.51	98.48	109.2	109.3
甘孜藏族自治州	Ganzi	87.96	86.88	104.1	104.1
凉山彝族自治州	Liangshan	514.58	503.41	104.3	104.3

注：本表绝对值按当年价格计算，指数按可比价格计算。
a) The absolute value in this table are calculated at current prices, and the indices are calculated at the comparable prices.

13-8 主要农业机械拥有量
Number of Major Agricultural Machinery

(年底数) (year-end)

年份 Year	农业机械总动力(万千瓦) Total Power of Agricultural Machinery (10 000 kw)	农用大中型拖拉机 Large and Medium Agricultural Tractors		农用小型拖拉机 Small Agricultural Tractors		脱粒机(万台) Thresher (10 000 units)	谷物联合收割机(台) grain combine harvester (unit)
		数量(台) Number (unit)	动力(万千瓦) Capacity (10 000 kw)	数量(万台) Number (10 000 units)	动力(万千瓦) Capacity (10 000 kw)		
1978	350.21	14571	42.52	5.22	45.91		
1980	500.34	19233	52.59	8.37	74.19	9.04	51
1985	700.42	18496	51.67	11.53	109.74	4.47	32
1986	772.77	18469	51.55	13.10	127.54	4.04	36
1987	828.98	17939	50.57	14.56	145.39	3.80	31
1988	887.72	16900	48.36	15.69	160.88	3.78	38
1989	918.92	15064	43.51	15.90	163.74	4.09	52
1990	956.00	12788	37.64	15.51	161.06	5.05	127
1991	1007.23	10553	31.62	15.17	159.81	5.86	147
1992	1035.60	8662	25.81	14.75	156.59	6.72	210
1993	1066.35	7545	23.28	14.47	154.38	7.76	321
1994	1165.11	6625	21.17	14.16	152.45	11.80	368
1995	1209.73	5632	18.05	13.78	149.09	12.81	428
1996	1263.26	4997	16.13	13.81	149.98	13.67	738
1997	1348.21	6644	18.16	13.84	151.56	19.19	1450
1998	1468.33	10144	23.48	13.98	155.43	27.62	2150
1999	1606.90	14833	37.58	14.26	159.14	33.31	2681
2000	1680.11	29645	74.59	13.29	149.22	38.25	3258
2001	1735.10	33606	86.87	13.06	148.74	40.44	3587
2002	1803.68	42156	108.21	13.09	150.99	45.82	4100
2003	1891.06	46882	128.02	12.25	141.09	45.60	4719
2004	2006.78	51585	143.82	12.59	151.29	55.70	5400
2005	2181.70	12728	35.18	12.48	155.94	69.87	5830
2006	2344.87	15936	40.74	12.83	161.15	72.61	6831
2007	2523.05	20151	49.81	13.35	171.61	80.00	7621
2008	2687.55	55488	122.75	11.43	143.11	96.14	8501
2009	2952.66	77809	179.10	11.84	147.96	103.28	9958
2010	3155.14	91112	206.02	12.03	147.37	107.62	12005
2011	3426.10	107484	246.51	12.47	147.99	115.90	14086
2012	3694.03	115036	267.45	12.55	141.66	126.60	18499
2013	3953.09	121753	291.65	11.91	134.40	135.20	22498
2014	4160.12	126104	307.48	11.36	127.07	160.60	26115
2015	4404.55	132242	331.40	10.45	115.52	172.80	29433
2016	4267.32	134754	339.74	10.06	109.29	173.12	34731
2017	4420.30	134088	348.24	9.69	104.40	169.65	36021
2018	4603.88	74614	247.22	15.34	220.01	168.82	37278
2019	4682.30	74408	257.32	15.00	216.91	170.15	37430
2020	4754.00	76077	271.42	14.82	215.29	171.20	38211
2021	4833.88	76673	279.94	14.42	209.37	172.88	39256
2022	4923.33	78159	296.84	13.58	199.39	170.83	40687
2023	5027.19	76925	303.90	12.47	186.71	171.79	41690

注：①农业机械数据由四川省农业农村厅提供；②自2016年起农业机械总动力不包括农用运输车数据；③自2018年大中小型拖拉机统计口径调整；④2017年及以前谷物联合收割机为联合收割机数据；⑤2022年原“机动脱粒机”变更为“脱粒机”。

a) Data of agricultural machinery are provided by Bureau of Agricultural and Rural of Sichuan Province; b)Since 2016, total power of agricultural machinery does not include power of agricultural transporters; c)The statistical caliber of large, medium and small tractors has been adjusted since 2018; d)Data of grain combine harvesters ware data of combine harvesters in 2017 and before; e)The indicator "Power-driven Thresher" was changed to "Thresher" since 2022.

13-9 各市(州)主要农业机械拥有量(2023年)
Number of Major Agricultural Machinery by Region(2023)

(年底数) (year-end)

市(州)	Region	农业机械总动力(万千瓦) Total Power of Agricultural Machinery (10 000 kw)	农用大中型拖拉机 Large and Medium Agricultural Tractors		农用小型拖拉机 Small Agricultural Tractors		脱粒机(万台) Thresher (10 000 units)	谷物联合收割机(台) grain combine harvester (unit)
			数量(台) Number (unit)	动力(万千瓦) Capacity (10 000 kw)	数量(台) Number (unit)	动力(万千瓦) Capacity (10 000 kw)		
全省	**Sichuan**	**5027.19**	**76925**	**303.90**	**124723**	**186.71**	**171.79**	**41690**
成都市	Chengdu	428.53	9532	49.77	15106	20.10	8.57	2505
自贡市	Zigong	130.34	79	0.38	97	0.19	10.93	372
攀枝花市	Panzhihua	73.39	1976	6.56	3187	4.03	0.96	115
泸州市	Luzhou	251.70	110	0.53	2		7.21	823
德阳市	Deyang	202.31	9066	41.28	10133	18.65	2.92	4896
绵阳市	Mianyang	374.70	13103	52.15	11410	14.10	8.61	7634
广元市	Guangyuan	311.88	5127	16.98	3480	3.60	13.69	9471
遂宁市	Suining	146.05	2298	12.55	594	1.23	7.66	1125
内江市	Neijiang	259.17	161	0.76	268	0.41	3.68	1051
乐山市	Leshan	290.55	680	3.52	1632	1.91	5.88	850
南充市	Nanchong	340.36	2363	10.04	1059	1.49	13.32	3223
眉山市	Meishan	227.48	2869	12.94	3282	4.54	12.34	1025
宜宾市	Yibin	287.68	208	0.60	496	0.58	15.93	963
广安市	Guangan	270.63	463	2.68	224	0.34	12.72	508
达州市	Dazhou	308.25	530	2.15	768	0.92	15.12	1477
雅安市	Yaan	168.02	269	0.79	1824	2.60	1.60	60
巴中市	Bazhong	200.84	759	3.25	435	0.74	7.86	1569
资阳市	Ziyang	194.97	345	1.29	1150	1.29	16.38	1675
阿坝藏族羌族自治州	Aba	71.79	4756	14.61	13910	20.82	0.69	33
甘孜藏族自治州	Ganzi	106.37	7361	19.82	27321	45.37	1.23	649
凉山彝族自治州	Liangshan	382.18	14870	51.25	28345	43.80	4.50	1666

13-10 农用化肥施用量
Consumption of Chemical Fertilizers in Rural Area

年份 Year	农用化肥施用量(折纯)(万吨) Consumption of Chemical Fertilizers (10 000 tons)	氮肥 Nitrogenous Fertilizer	磷肥 Phosphate Fertilizer	钾肥 Potash Fertilizer	复合肥 Compound Fertilizer
1952	0.4	0.4			
1957	1.0	0.7	0.3		
1962	4.0	3.0	1.0		
1965	11.3	8.4	2.8	0.1	
1970	11.5	8.5	2.8	0.2	
1975	23.0	17.1	5.6	0.3	
1978	62.5	46.4	15.7	0.4	
1980	80.4	52.6	24.0	1.0	1.1
1985	103.1	82.6	16.4	1.7	2.1
1990	143.9	101.4	28.2	2.6	11.7
1995	182.9	111.0	37.4	7.0	27.3
1996	192.8	117.8	38.4	7.4	29.2
1997	201.3	121.3	40.0	8.4	31.6
1998	205.3	123.7	40.3	8.8	32.5
1999	210.3	124.2	40.4	9.3	36.4
2000	212.6	123.0	42.0	10.0	37.5
2001	212.0	121.8	41.9	10.4	37.9
2002	209.6	118.5	42.3	11.0	37.8
2003	208.4	117.5	41.9	11.6	37.4
2004	214.7	120.2	42.9	12.2	39.3
2005	220.9	121.8	45.1	12.9	40.6
2006	228.2	124.7	46.6	13.7	43.0
2007	238.2	127.9	48.0	14.8	46.6
2008	242.8	128.6	48.9	15.8	48.0
2009	248.0	130.7	49.7	16.4	50.3
2010	248.0	129.6	49.2	16.4	51.1
2011	251.2	128.8	50.6	17.3	53.2
2012	252.8	127.9	50.7	17.5	55.0
2013	251.1	126.1	50.3	17.7	55.0
2014	252.1	125.7	49.9	17.7	56.9
2015	252.1	124.7	49.6	17.8	57.7
2016	249.0	121.9	48.9	17.9	60.2
2017	242.0	117.0	47.1	17.6	60.2
2018	235.2	112.1	45.4	17.4	60.3
2019	222.8	103.5	41.4	15.8	62.1
2020	210.8	90.7	38.0	15.1	67.0
2021	207.2	81.8	34.8	14.9	75.6
2022	204.4	76.4	32.1	14.3	81.5
2023	202.2	74.5	31.4	14.0	82.3

13-11 各市(州)农用化肥施用量(2023年)
Consumption of Chemical Fertilizers in Rural Area by Region(2023)

市(州)	Region	农用化肥施用量(折纯)(万吨) Consumption of Chemical Fertilizers (10 000 tons)	氮肥 Nitrogenous Fertilizer	磷肥 Phosphate Fertilizer	钾肥 Potash Fertilizer	复合肥 Compound Fertilizer
全省	**Sichuan**	**202.16**	**74.47**	**31.37**	**13.99**	**82.33**
成都市	Chengdu	14.98	4.69	2.59	1.52	6.17
自贡市	Zigong	7.92	3.25	1.89	0.96	1.81
攀枝花市	Panzhihua	2.08	0.75	0.24	0.22	0.88
泸州市	Luzhou	9.31	3.92	1.62	0.63	3.14
德阳市	Deyang	16.12	3.80	1.28	0.66	10.38
绵阳市	Mianyang	17.86	5.81	3.81	1.05	7.19
广元市	Guangyuan	8.66	2.54	1.12	0.52	4.49
遂宁市	Suining	11.43	4.65	1.94	0.73	4.10
内江市	Neijiang	9.02	3.72	1.40	0.40	3.51
乐山市	Leshan	7.62	3.42	0.94	0.34	2.92
南充市	Nanchong	18.89	4.95	2.68	0.87	10.39
眉山市	Meishan	10.65	3.07	1.23	1.27	5.09
宜宾市	Yibin	7.09	2.55	1.16	0.63	2.74
广安市	Guangan	8.99	5.32	1.83	0.61	1.22
达州市	Dazhou	17.58	9.89	2.84	1.14	3.72
雅安市	Yaan	4.29	1.93	0.51	0.51	1.35
巴中市	Bazhong	10.43	3.71	1.70	0.87	4.15
资阳市	Ziyang	5.94	1.26	0.40	0.25	4.04
阿坝藏族羌族自治州	Aba	0.94	0.34	0.19	0.06	0.35
甘孜藏族自治州	Ganzi	0.28	0.13	0.03	0.01	0.12
凉山彝族自治州	Liangshan	12.06	4.76	1.96	0.76	4.58

13-12 耕地面积、机耕面积、耕地灌溉面积和农作物总播种面积
Cultivated Area, Area Ploughed by Tractors, Irrigated Area of Cultivated Land and Total Sown Area of Farm Crops

单位：万公顷 (10 000 hectares)

年份 Year	年末实有耕地面积 Cultivated Area (year-end)	机耕面积 Area Ploughed by Tractors	耕地灌溉面积 Irrigated Area of Cultivated Land	农作物总播种面积 Total Sown Area	#粮食 Grain Crops
1952	547.85		53.70	827.66	686.30
1957	569.13	0.40	86.40	968.20	784.90
1962	510.07	2.60	106.90	805.65	676.70
1965	518.96	2.60	120.90	789.59	622.50
1970	510.66	4.60	139.30	819.65	674.80
1975	497.21	45.30	175.00	903.94	728.90
1978	490.91	86.50	198.90	885.91	744.10
1980	487.16	67.90	211.40	861.90	746.10
1985	474.12	51.70	215.40	855.80	663.60
1990	464.71	59.20	222.60	905.00	698.50
1995	456.04	71.60	230.10	930.24	705.50
1996	454.31	70.10	232.50	940.08	713.80
1997	451.99	84.40	235.62	949.75	721.10
1998	449.49	85.60	239.06	971.44	733.80
1999	445.47	98.30	242.79	971.77	729.70
2000	434.61	93.70	246.90	960.91	685.40
2001	428.44	95.05	248.70	949.17	662.69
2002	405.99	95.40	250.10	934.41	642.50
2003	390.37	98.10	250.30	908.50	608.80
2004	390.44	98.80	250.30	924.44	633.33
2005	390.60	107.50	249.50	941.69	650.16
2006	391.66	115.04	248.70	953.08	644.90
2007	394.59	121.10	250.00	925.24	643.46
2008	395.95	182.20	250.70	929.47	640.88
2009	397.61	196.53	252.40	915.78	621.30
2010	401.07	219.02	255.30	915.87	619.51
2011	398.34	275.50	260.10	921.54	619.67
2012	399.15	330.28	256.60	931.96	625.56
2013	399.38	409.47	261.65	937.17	626.99
2014	673.42	459.79	266.63	937.77	624.96
2015	673.61	485.51	273.51	945.11	628.61
2016	673.29	508.10	281.36	949.38	629.13
2017	672.59	531.93	287.31	957.51	629.20
2018	672.28	514.23	293.25	961.54	626.56
2019	522.72	563.67	295.41	969.30	627.93
2020	518.17	587.77	299.22	984.99	631.26
2021	519.55	669.99	296.29	999.99	635.77
2022	520.99	749.37	297.57	1022.74	646.35
2023		796.01	299.42	1026.44	640.40

注：①自2014年起耕地面积数据由四川省自然资源厅提供；2019年、2020年为第三次全国国土调查后定案数；②机耕面积由四川省农业农村厅提供；③耕地灌溉面积由四川省水利厅提供；④根据第三次全国农业普查结果对2007年至2017年农作物播种面积(种植)和产量数据进行了修订(以下有关各表同)。

a) Since 2014, data of cultivated area have been provided by Bureau of Natural Resources of Sichuan Province; and the data of 2019 and 2020 are calculated on the third national land survey; b) Data of area ploughed by tractors are provided by Bureau of Sichuan Agricultural and Rural of Sichuan Province; c)Data of Irrigated area of cultivated land are provided by Bureau of Water Conservancy of Sichuan Province; d) Data of total sown area and yield since 2007 to 2017 were revised according to the results of the Third National Agricultural Census(the same as the following related tables).

13−13 各市(州)耕地面积、耕地灌溉面积和农作物总播种面积(2023年) Cultivated Area, Irrigated Area of Cultivated Land and Total Sown Area of Farm Crops by Region(2023)

单位：千公顷 (1 000 hectares)

市(州)	Region	2022年末实有耕地面积 Actual Cultivated Area (year-end 2022)	耕地灌溉面积 Irrigated Area of Cultivated Land	农作物总播种面积 Total Sown Area	#粮食 Grain Crops
全省	**Sichuan**	**5209.87**	**2994.20**	**10264.42**	**6403.97**
成都市	Chengdu	326.65	278.35	699.29	385.21
自贡市	Zigong	180.37	117.27	400.72	238.12
攀枝花市	Panzhihua	56.19	45.90	75.93	45.78
泸州市	Luzhou	324.57	164.67	574.12	405.49
德阳市	Deyang	220.81	160.47	507.12	314.80
绵阳市	Mianyang	355.35	222.54	694.65	409.22
广元市	Guangyuan	275.03	101.01	544.47	319.89
遂宁市	Suining	200.97	137.78	404.94	277.42
内江市	Neijiang	224.29	135.83	510.39	314.82
乐山市	Leshan	161.71	144.65	362.04	224.48
南充市	Nanchong	450.13	251.65	978.43	572.02
眉山市	Meishan	142.85	172.05	333.37	200.34
宜宾市	Yibin	358.62	204.10	652.21	432.21
广安市	Guangan	242.47	116.44	447.41	293.09
达州市	Dazhou	430.67	205.76	884.77	570.59
雅安市	Yaan	40.47	53.93	122.08	70.47
巴中市	Bazhong	261.75	96.13	558.45	343.50
资阳市	Ziyang	234.09	115.87	536.27	334.47
阿坝藏族羌族自治州	Aba	65.83	31.35	81.87	49.72
甘孜藏族自治州	Ganzi	87.11	43.92	106.43	68.82
凉山彝族自治州	Liangshan	569.93	194.55	789.45	533.52

13-14 各市(州)农作物总播种面积
Sown Areas of Farm Crops by Region

单位：千公顷 (1 000 hectares)

市(州)	Region	2013	2014	2015	2016	2017	2018	2019	2020	2021	2022	2023
全省	**Sichuan**	**9371.69**	**9377.69**	**9451.06**	**9493.82**	**9575.05**	**9615.39**	**9692.99**	**9849.91**	**9999.92**	**10227.37**	**10264.42**
成都市	Chengdu	778.72	753.26	740.23	728.48	730.99	739.32	733.32	728.87	730.58	736.09	699.29
自贡市	Zigong	323.93	332.52	342.53	352.49	362.65	366.41	372.03	377.94	386.32	398.03	400.72
攀枝花市	Panzhihua	67.51	67.97	69.17	70.81	70.21	71.41	72.26	72.88	73.99	75.38	75.93
泸州市	Luzhou	525.98	524.46	527.03	528.62	541.29	540.67	541.96	550.21	556.15	568.45	574.12
德阳市	Deyang	480.07	479.35	478.52	476.48	477.25	476.72	477.92	483.58	491.83	504.45	507.12
绵阳市	Mianyang	662.10	660.19	662.20	659.14	660.18	661.96	666.89	674.53	677.43	696.18	694.65
广元市	Guangyuan	469.32	477.02	486.49	493.08	495.44	498.60	502.89	513.49	522.55	535.96	544.47
遂宁市	Suining	398.75	396.66	395.03	387.62	387.71	387.00	388.50	395.42	402.58	412.08	404.94
内江市	Neijiang	438.82	444.06	455.93	464.66	476.73	478.15	481.38	486.83	493.12	503.80	510.39
乐山市	Leshan	327.13	328.80	331.75	335.87	338.55	340.79	344.11	356.04	363.58	371.42	362.04
南充市	Nanchong	886.29	883.35	883.86	882.12	885.32	888.87	897.66	924.70	945.69	965.51	978.43
眉山市	Meishan	320.88	316.82	314.31	310.51	313.40	314.55	318.08	319.91	323.49	330.06	333.37
宜宾市	Yibin	529.10	545.34	566.72	585.37	589.39	591.97	598.45	613.69	628.90	642.14	652.21
广安市	Guangan	400.44	400.29	402.54	405.29	406.71	406.27	410.20	416.77	427.20	438.23	447.41
达州市	Dazhou	794.62	795.59	802.54	807.23	809.52	810.29	815.92	836.67	856.76	879.14	884.77
雅安市	Yaan	118.32	117.46	115.90	115.74	115.61	115.97	116.78	117.51	119.15	121.37	122.08
巴中市	Bazhong	477.44	480.73	485.96	489.17	500.52	508.33	514.72	531.67	540.89	552.04	558.45
资阳市	Ziyang	522.21	518.18	516.99	513.65	516.39	517.27	521.96	521.18	522.61	531.62	536.27
阿坝藏族羌族自治州	Aba	68.28	66.89	68.35	69.76	69.77	74.09	75.41	76.96	77.84	80.05	81.87
甘孜藏族自治州	Ganzi	80.26	79.22	80.61	81.95	85.69	88.90	91.49	93.34	94.37	102.20	106.43
凉山彝族自治州	Liangshan	701.50	709.52	724.41	735.81	741.76	737.86	751.06	757.71	764.88	783.19	789.45

13-15 农作物播种面积和产量

Sown Areas of Farm Crops and Output of Major Farm Products

单位：万公顷、万吨 (10 000 hectares, 10 000 tons)

年份 Year	粮食 Grain Crops		#谷物 Cereal		#稻谷 Rice		#小麦 Wheat		#玉米 Corn	
	播种面积 Sown Area	产量 Yield	播种面积 Sown Area	产量 Yield	播种面积 Sown Area	产量 Yield	播种面积 Sown Area	产量 Yield	播种面积 Sown Area	产量 Yield
1952	686.3	1170.1			253.1	769.2	79.4	65.3	93.4	91.8
1957	784.9	1531.0			280.6	939.6	104.6	123.5	103.9	157.5
1962	676.7	1054.7			203.1	572.8	114.5	94.7	81.3	95.1
1965	622.5	1489.4			241.0	869.2	93.5	113.1	84.4	150.7
1970	674.8	1756.1			233.7	937.7	107.3	187.6	95.4	196.4
1975	728.9	1976.8			264.8	1035.4	139.8	248.8	104.2	248.6
1978	744.1	2381.8			226.9	1086.4	165.4	368.6	117.1	360.6
1980	746.1	2599.7			225.5	1207.4	182.6	410.2	124.5	457.3
1985	663.6	2875.1			230.8	1463.3	151.6	506.7	107.2	418.7
1990	698.5	3269.2			230.0	1700.8	168.0	570.9	119.9	486.1
1995	705.5	3395.3	544.1	2887.8	220.3	1657.8	178.0	682.4	120.2	471.6
1996	713.8	3483.1	552.4	2986.2	221.8	1705.7	181.0	656.9	124.7	548.6
1997	721.1	3554.4	557.9	3076.1	219.6	1700.2	182.4	687.3	129.0	605.7
1998	733.8	3626.3	566.4	3096.7	216.8	1685.3	186.5	673.2	136.5	659.4
1999	729.7	3668.4	561.3	3115.7	217.6	1724.4	181.8	620.9	135.9	693.7
2000	685.4	3568.5	520.2	2996.7	212.4	1692.5	160.5	614.3	123.5	616.6
2001	662.7	3056.5	496.4	2530.0	203.7	1452.4	150.3	517.8	120.1	493.1
2002	642.5	3275.2	481.0	2714.3	202.0	1540.0	142.5	526.5	114.5	578.2
2003	608.8	3183.3	452.3	2625.3	193.0	1498.2	128.6	488.3	110.1	572.7
2004	633.3	3326.5	461.0	2709.8	197.1	1525.4	128.3	501.5	115.6	620.4
2005	650.2	3409.2	473.0	2769.5	199.5	1526.9	136.0	543.1	118.5	641.8
2006	644.9	2859.8	475.8	2371.1	204.9	1337.2	123.5	426.7	129.0	551.7
2007	643.5	3032.7	481.3	2541.4	202.4	1411.6	125.7	432.5	136.9	651.2
2008	640.9	3111.0	474.0	2597.7	201.2	1480.1	117.2	398.7	140.2	674.8
2009	621.3	3120.4	470.6	2604.3	199.1	1493.3	111.1	366.2	145.5	701.0
2010	619.5	3182.8	468.1	2633.0	196.7	1484.1	105.1	355.9	152.1	750.7
2011	619.7	3249.5	465.3	2675.6	194.3	1478.1	99.8	346.4	157.4	810.3
2012	625.6	3271.3	462.5	2689.4	193.0	1484.0	93.4	331.5	163.0	833.6
2013	627.0	3336.1	459.6	2754.3	190.5	1483.4	87.9	311.0	168.6	920.1
2014	625.0	3324.6	456.8	2734.7	189.2	1450.5	81.4	298.0	173.9	946.7
2015	628.6	3394.6	456.0	2779.6	187.9	1465.2	74.7	284.5	181.7	992.3
2016	629.1	3469.9	453.8	2822.1	187.4	1467.3	68.4	259.6	186.6	1058.0
2017	629.2	3488.9	450.8	2831.8	187.5	1473.7	65.3	251.6	186.4	1068.0
2018	626.6	3493.7	448.0	2830.9	187.4	1478.6	63.5	247.3	185.6	1066.3
2019	627.9	3498.5	445.9	2825.4	187.0	1469.8	61.1	246.2	184.4	1062.2
2020	631.3	3527.4	444.4	2836.9	186.6	1475.3	59.7	246.7	183.9	1065.0
2021	635.8	3582.1	446.3	2879.4	187.5	1493.4	58.3	245.4	184.9	1084.7
2022	646.3	3510.5	447.8	2814.7	187.4	1462.3	58.9	249.7	185.5	1046.2
2023	640.4	3593.8	447.3	2904.2	184.5	1480.8	59.3	265.9	186.6	1097.2

注：2007年至2017年所有农作物的播种面积和产量均依据第三次全国农业普查结果进行了修订(以下有关各表同)。

a) Data of sown area and yield of all crops in 2007 to 2017 were approved according to the results of the third national agricultural census(the same as the following related tables).

13-15 续表 1 continued

单位：万公顷、万吨 (10 000 hectares, 10 000 tons)

年份 Year	#豆类 Soybeans		#薯类 Tubers		油料 Oil-bearing Crops		#花生 Peanut		#油菜籽 Rapeseeds	
	播种面积 Sown Area	产量 Yield	播种面积 Sown Area	产量 Yield	播种面积 Sown Area	产量 Yield	播种面积 Sown Area	产量 Yield	播种面积 Sown Area	产量 Yield
1952	105.9	76.1	108.9	138.8	34.3	25.2	7.6	8.4	25.8	16.5
1957	114.9	96.5	125.3	220.5	40.3	35.1	9.8	11.4	29.5	23.4
1962	90.7	64.1	121.9	217.4	27.5	14.8	7.3	6.2	19.0	8.3
1965	92.7	93.3	102.5	214.1	38.8	35.4	10.2	10.7	27.1	24.3
1970	83.9	107.6	103.9	260.2	32.0	34.5	6.9	9.1	23.9	24.5
1975	70.8	86.9	105.3	289.8	36.2	39.9	7.3	10.8	28.2	28.7
1978	60.0	79.9	134.3	412.1	41.3	52.8	7.4	12.4	30.3	38.1
1980	55.0	77.3	117.1	349.4	47.0	68.4	8.4	11.8	39.5	56.4
1985	39.9	71.0	99.4	325.2	84.2	133.1	13.5	23.6	70.1	109.0
1990	34.3	63.4	113.6	279.6	79.7	133.5	12.6	23.7	66.9	109.5
1995	38.4	74.0	122.9	433.4	84.6	145.1	15.3	25.9	68.8	118.7
1996	37.9	74.8	123.5	422.1	82.2	133.2	15.2	28.1	66.4	104.6
1997	38.6	77.8	124.6	400.6	79.9	134.2	15.4	28.8	64.0	104.8
1998	38.9	76.9	128.5	452.7	83.6	146.4	16.6	33.3	66.4	112.6
1999	40.2	78.9	128.2	473.8	89.1	151.6	19.3	41.2	69.0	109.5
2000	44.5	98.0	120.7	473.8	102.6	193.0	24.0	54.3	77.7	137.5
2001	47.9	97.1	118.3	429.5	104.9	181.0	25.8	45.8	78.0	133.7
2002	48.1	107.1	113.4	453.8	104.9	201.5	26.4	55.4	77.3	144.8
2003	49.0	111.9	107.5	446.2	108.7	217.1	27.0	59.9	80.6	155.9
2004	50.7	119.2	121.7	497.5	108.9	226.3	26.3	59.8	81.4	165.0
2005	52.0	122.9	125.2	516.8	109.4	232.3	26.4	62.0	81.7	168.7
2006	45.2	91.6	123.9	397.1	107.0	217.3	26.1	47.1	79.7	169.0
2007	45.8	103.4	116.4	388.0	118.2	253.6	26.1	54.5	89.9	195.1
2008	45.4	101.8	121.5	411.5	126.7	276.2	25.9	58.0	98.9	213.9
2009	43.0	99.0	107.7	417.1	132.0	288.5	25.9	58.8	104.4	225.5
2010	43.0	98.0	108.4	451.9	133.7	296.1	26.1	59.9	106.0	232.0
2011	43.8	101.7	110.6	472.3	135.2	306.7	25.8	60.6	107.8	242.0
2012	44.4	103.9	118.6	478.0	136.9	315.9	25.6	60.7	109.8	251.1
2013	45.4	103.5	122.1	478.2	139.0	320.2	25.6	62.2	112.0	253.7
2014	45.8	106.1	122.3	483.8	141.4	332.0	25.7	63.1	114.4	264.8
2015	46.6	107.0	126.0	507.9	143.0	339.6	25.8	64.1	116.0	271.7
2016	49.6	113.0	125.7	534.8	144.0	346.2	26.0	64.8	116.7	277.0
2017	51.8	119.2	126.6	537.9	147.9	357.9	26.1	66.0	120.6	288.0
2018	52.5	121.5	126.1	541.4	149.1	362.5	26.3	67.7	121.8	292.2
2019	56.0	129.9	126.0	543.2	149.5	367.4	26.5	68.4	122.3	296.4
2020	59.9	138.8	126.9	551.7	158.4	392.9	28.3	73.8	129.2	317.2
2021	61.5	143.5	127.9	559.2	165.2	416.6	29.0	76.2	135.4	338.7
2022	69.6	145.4	128.9	550.5	168.9	433.8	29.5	78.5	138.7	354.1
2023	72.5	163.1	120.6	526.5	172.9	438.6	30.6	82.7	141.4	354.4

13-15 续表 2 continued

单位：万公顷、万吨 (10 000 hectares, 10 000 tons)

年份 Year	棉花 Cotton		甘蔗 Sugarcane		生麻 Bast Fiber		烟叶(未加工) Tobacco		#烤烟 Fluecured Tobacco	
	播种面积 Sown Area	产量 Yield	播种面积 Sown Area	产量 Yield	播种面积 Sown Area	产量 Yield	播种面积 Sown Area	产量 Yield	播种面积 Sown Area	产量 Yield
1952	22.50	4.00	3.00	115.30	0.10		4.17	4.25	2.08	2.04
1957	30.70	6.60	3.84	164.40		0.10	4.00	4.38	1.97	2.12
1962	21.00	2.60	1.41	28.30			1.63	1.14	0.38	0.41
1965	26.50	10.60	3.61	133.25	0.20	0.10	3.25	3.45	0.75	1.29
1970	25.70	12.70	3.35	107.61	0.60	0.20	2.13	2.32	0.47	0.48
1975	25.70	12.30	4.50	139.63	0.80	0.80	3.65	3.98	1.07	1.49
1978	25.60	14.40	4.65	154.11	1.90	5.90	5.20	6.94	1.83	2.58
1980	24.60	9.40	3.70	141.77	2.40	10.30	4.19	5.73	1.35	1.81
1985	12.60	11.30	4.62	233.98	6.80	12.40	6.83	10.68	2.90	3.87
1990	12.30	11.50	4.24	218.15	4.20	8.20	8.35	13.26	4.91	4.32
1995	13.97	11.18	3.25	170.73	4.53	6.57	5.87	7.77	3.11	3.50
1996	15.31	12.29	3.11	164.16	4.38	6.49	6.97	12.93	3.90	7.48
1997	13.92	10.73	3.09	155.66	3.97	5.39	10.02	18.56	6.88	12.33
1998	13.96	10.16	2.96	161.48	3.11	4.28	7.24	10.67	4.62	5.89
1999	9.41	7.59	2.92	161.04	2.71	3.94	7.38	11.86	4.89	6.94
2000	7.01	5.89	3.06	166.68	2.56	4.02	8.22	15.61	5.46	9.37
2001	6.64	2.98	3.06	155.67	2.48	3.94	7.03	12.17	4.23	6.55
2002	3.30	2.36	3.19	171.21	2.99	4.47	7.01	14.09	4.68	8.85
2003	3.12	2.54	3.19	170.53	3.18	5.02	6.66	13.42	4.43	8.23
2004	3.58	3.31	2.88	146.10	3.50	6.09	6.64	14.41	4.59	9.38
2005	2.78	2.47	2.67	132.89	3.70	6.85	7.95	18.17	5.88	13.23
2006	2.45	1.57	2.64	124.61	4.00	6.58	8.88	20.01	6.86	15.39
2007	1.08	0.85	2.08	109.29	2.34	4.06	7.86	16.35	6.95	14.44
2008	0.94	0.80	1.87	98.53	2.28	3.97	9.34	18.84	8.50	17.07
2009	0.83	0.75	1.58	78.60	2.21	3.85	10.43	21.63	9.58	19.52
2010	0.82	0.72	1.56	78.13	2.08	3.75	9.12	20.24	8.17	18.01
2011	0.78	0.71	1.30	62.72	1.98	3.57	10.00	20.90	9.08	18.79
2012	0.71	0.64	1.13	48.77	1.85	3.35	10.48	23.11	9.62	21.28
2013	0.66	0.62	1.06	44.69	1.82	3.29	10.33	22.15	9.63	20.02
2014	0.64	0.60	1.02	43.29	1.76	3.20	8.94	19.97	8.31	17.94
2015	0.49	0.48	0.99	41.79	1.72	3.13	8.78	19.79	8.05	18.03
2016	0.45	0.50	0.91	35.56	1.69	3.05	8.87	19.52	8.34	18.02
2017	0.44	0.40	0.91	34.74	1.68	3.03	8.63	18.05	8.13	16.56
2018	0.40	0.40	0.93	36.18	1.70	3.10	7.65	16.25	6.77	13.97
2019	0.29	0.28	0.96	37.18	1.72	3.17	7.46	16.04	6.52	13.70
2020	0.23	0.22	0.97	37.84	1.81	3.06	7.36	16.15	6.85	14.62
2021	0.21	0.20	0.96	38.61	1.83	3.26	7.26	16.13	6.75	14.68
2022	0.03	0.03	0.96	38.44	1.89	3.36	7.58	16.09	7.08	14.64
2023	0.02	0.01	0.96	39.23	1.94	3.53	7.97	17.27	7.44	15.69

注：1994年及以前年份“生麻”统计口径为“黄红麻”。

a) Bast fiber includes only jute and ambary hemp before 1995.

13-15 续表 3 continued

单位：万公顷、万吨 (10 000 hectares, 10 000 tons)

年份 Year	蔬菜及食用菌 Vegetables and Edible Fungus		蚕茧产量 Yield of Silkworm Cocoons	茶叶产量 Yield of Tea	水果产量 Total Fruits Yield					水产品产量 Yield of Aquatic Products
	播种面积 Sown Area	产量 Yield				#园林水果 Garden Fruits	#苹果 Apples	#柑橘 Citrus	#梨 Pears	
1952			0.98	0.79	10.30	10.30		0.40		0.81
1957			0.94	1.21	10.80	10.80		3.60		1.11
1962			0.77	0.70	8.60	8.60		1.80		1.10
1965			0.97	0.90	11.70	11.70		3.40		1.56
1970			1.84	1.01	7.90	7.90		2.40		1.66
1975			2.55	1.31	15.20	15.20		4.50		3.01
1978			3.66	1.90	17.80	17.80		5.90		3.06
1980			6.60	1.98	27.50	27.50	4.00	9.90	5.10	3.69
1985			7.39	3.71	57.00	57.00	4.60	37.70	6.30	9.27
1990			10.00	4.00	92.00	92.00	6.10	62.40	9.10	16.83
1995			15.16	4.35	155.76	155.76	12.26	93.33	17.26	29.86
1996			9.46	4.39	168.48	168.48	13.47	101.01	18.17	33.26
1997			8.53	4.52	185.13	185.13	16.12	106.89	20.04	37.20
1998	68.34	1888.41	9.28	5.09	273.95	212.92	17.74	117.84	24.97	42.29
1999	71.74	1942.15	8.10	5.29	297.25	234.53	18.68	116.22	27.27	46.57
2000	85.86	2312.56	8.73	5.45	321.63	252.57	20.23	132.75	34.45	51.31
2001	96.90	2440.79	9.22	5.84	361.93	272.90	19.40	149.77	39.48	57.13
2002	103.52	2684.94	9.30	6.28	425.93	306.69	20.69	166.18	46.97	64.84
2003	100.62	2639.60	9.29	7.21	464.93	348.21	22.54	186.16	54.77	76.40
2004	97.06	2623.87	9.74	8.65	494.83	385.45	24.05	198.78	62.03	86.15
2005	99.15	2714.29	9.80	9.79	527.16	415.76	24.29	213.74	68.46	98.25
2006	118.19	2971.23	9.83	11.29	535.32	423.81	24.80	205.78	74.60	81.30
2007	105.16	2863.99	10.68	13.73	580.05	469.18	29.54	229.79	76.89	91.05
2008	105.68	2927.13	10.19	14.22	625.17	513.59	38.62	255.43	78.00	95.20
2009	107.96	3087.00	10.15	15.74	679.12	564.81	40.61	275.23	80.11	100.13
2010	110.52	3206.45	10.33	17.20	707.74	594.08	42.61	289.97	82.44	105.06
2011	114.81	3403.84	10.27	18.97	752.94	637.13	44.45	315.36	85.36	112.15
2012	118.23	3569.18	10.26	21.03	791.42	676.84	47.50	334.53	88.42	116.83
2013	121.09	3705.10	9.99	21.97	822.03	709.84	51.11	340.85	90.36	123.64
2014	124.20	3838.35	9.82	23.47	862.87	747.06	57.53	357.60	90.26	130.00
2015	127.05	3988.38	9.55	24.61	912.14	793.65	60.68	375.82	90.97	135.97
2016	129.57	4118.12	8.95	26.51	960.05	838.67	61.85	397.91	92.84	142.16
2017	132.43	4252.27	9.08	27.78	1007.88	883.23	65.22	415.68	91.72	150.74
2018	136.92	4438.02	9.22	30.07	1080.67	948.39	72.55	432.98	94.75	153.48
2019	141.30	4639.13	9.65	32.54	1136.70	1000.76	76.51	457.73	94.28	157.69
2020	144.40	4813.39	10.00	34.42	1221.30	1083.62	80.75	488.96	95.56	160.41
2021	148.04	5039.09	9.73	37.48	1290.90	1153.37	87.24	522.28	95.96	166.49
2022	154.23	5198.70	10.14	39.28	1380.50	1238.38	90.75	563.21	98.89	172.15
2023	158.28	5417.87	10.38	42.46	1490.35	1341.76	102.15	614.99	93.28	178.86

注：①1997年及以前年份的水果产量为园林水果产量；②水产品产量数据由四川省水产局提供。
a) Total fruits yield in 1997 and before was known as garden fruits yield; b) Data of aquatic products output were provided by Sichuan Fisheries Bureau.

13-16 各市(州)粮食作物播种面积和产量(2023年)

Sown Areas of Farm Crops and Output of Major Farm Products by Region(2023)

单位：千公顷、万吨 (1 000 hectares, 10 000 tons)

市(州)	Region	粮食 Grain Crops		谷物 Cereal		#稻谷 Rice		豆类 Soybeans		薯类 Tubers	
		播种面积 Sown Area	产量 Yield	播种面积 Sown Area	产量 Yield	播种面积 Sown Area	产量 Yield	播种面积 Sown Area	产量 Yield	播种面积 Sown Area	产量 Yield
全省	**Sichuan**	**6404.0**	**3593.8**	**4473.2**	**2904.2**	**1845.2**	**1480.8**	**725.0**	**163.1**	**1205.8**	**526.5**
成都市	Chengdu	385.2	231.9	283.2	195.9	145.0	118.2	45.2	10.6	56.9	25.4
自贡市	Zigong	238.1	143.3	136.7	107.4	80.2	74.4	57.7	15.3	43.8	20.7
攀枝花市	Panzhihua	45.8	26.1	37.6	23.7	8.3	7.0	4.9	1.0	3.3	1.4
泸州市	Luzhou	405.5	235.3	275.9	187.8	133.4	109.9	33.4	7.6	96.2	39.9
德阳市	Deyang	314.8	201.7	260.7	182.6	118.7	100.7	27.6	7.2	26.6	12.0
绵阳市	Mianyang	409.2	235.9	350.0	215.9	117.3	92.3	28.6	6.8	30.6	13.1
广元市	Guangyuan	319.9	161.8	241.5	138.4	63.5	49.3	44.4	9.1	34.0	14.4
遂宁市	Suining	277.4	147.9	207.2	124.1	56.7	45.8	31.9	6.6	38.3	17.2
内江市	Neijiang	314.8	174.3	183.3	128.1	80.4	66.4	58.6	13.0	72.9	33.1
乐山市	Leshan	224.5	125.4	155.9	102.8	83.4	65.2	29.5	6.3	39.0	16.4
南充市	Nanchong	572.0	319.4	425.3	264.7	150.5	119.8	50.0	12.4	96.7	42.4
眉山市	Meishan	200.3	127.7	155.1	113.3	96.9	79.8	23.7	5.1	21.5	9.2
宜宾市	Yibin	432.2	259.5	298.1	209.2	151.5	124.7	44.1	11.1	90.0	39.3
广安市	Guangan	293.1	183.7	210.6	155.9	132.3	107.0	30.9	5.9	51.6	21.9
达州市	Dazhou	570.6	326.6	346.9	247.2	191.1	144.0	68.7	14.3	154.9	65.0
雅安市	Yaan	70.5	36.6	50.7	30.7	16.1	11.9	6.7	1.1	13.1	4.9
巴中市	Bazhong	343.5	196.1	238.3	155.2	94.8	70.1	27.6	6.3	77.6	34.6
资阳市	Ziyang	334.5	167.8	189.3	120.7	68.8	51.7	73.2	15.9	72.0	31.3
阿坝藏族羌族自治州	Aba	49.7	16.5	27.1	8.8			6.0	1.2	16.6	6.4
甘孜藏族自治州	Ganzi	68.8	23.3	54.2	17.8			3.9	0.9	10.7	4.6
凉山彝族自治州	Liangshan	533.5	252.7	345.6	173.8	56.2	42.5	28.5	5.5	159.5	73.3

13-17 各市(州)粮食总产量
Total Grain Output by Region

单位：万吨 (10 000 tons)

市(州)	Region	2013	2014	2015	2016	2017	2018	2019	2020	2021	2022	2023
全省	**Sichuan**	**3336.1**	**3324.6**	**3394.6**	**3469.9**	**3488.9**	**3493.7**	**3498.5**	**3527.4**	**3582.1**	**3510.5**	**3593.8**
成都市	Chengdu	247.8	237.1	232.9	230.7	231.9	230.3	225.9	227.9	230.6	227.0	231.9
自贡市	Zigong	126.9	127.6	132.0	136.4	137.8	138.3	138.7	140.8	143.0	140.3	143.3
攀枝花市	Panzhihua	22.3	22.6	23.8	25.4	25.4	25.4	25.7	25.9	26.3	26.0	26.1
泸州市	Luzhou	221.9	222.2	224.6	229.4	229.2	229.7	229.1	231.6	235.6	230.2	235.3
德阳市	Deyang	188.2	187.4	189.6	193.9	195.2	194.9	195.3	196.4	199.4	196.1	201.7
绵阳市	Mianyang	221.1	221.7	225.7	229.0	230.6	229.7	230.5	231.1	235.2	230.8	235.9
广元市	Guangyuan	146.1	148.6	153.7	156.9	157.1	156.4	157.7	159.4	161.3	158.2	161.8
遂宁市	Suining	142.4	140.4	140.9	141.0	142.0	142.3	142.4	144.3	146.8	144.6	147.9
内江市	Neijiang	155.4	155.8	162.2	168.7	170.4	170.8	170.7	172.2	174.6	169.4	174.3
乐山市	Leshan	114.8	114.3	116.9	120.4	121.6	122.1	122.2	123.5	125.7	122.6	125.4
南充市	Nanchong	300.9	298.6	302.3	304.6	306.4	307.1	307.8	311.6	317.1	312.4	319.4
眉山市	Meishan	126.9	122.9	122.8	122.3	123.4	123.8	125.0	125.9	127.5	125.4	127.7
宜宾市	Yibin	220.9	227.5	239.7	252.2	252.8	253.3	253.0	255.3	259.8	251.4	259.5
广安市	Guangan	170.0	169.2	173.4	178.2	179.3	179.9	180.0	181.1	183.7	179.7	183.7
达州市	Dazhou	304.4	302.5	310.7	316.1	316.6	317.1	317.8	319.4	324.2	319.6	326.6
雅安市	Yaan	35.4	34.6	34.5	35.5	35.8	35.8	35.9	36.2	36.7	36.4	36.6
巴中市	Bazhong	180.5	179.8	184.2	188.1	189.4	190.5	191.0	192.8	195.8	191.9	196.1
资阳市	Ziyang	161.9	160.3	163.2	164.7	165.4	166.1	166.1	166.1	168.1	162.0	167.8
阿坝藏族羌族自治州	Aba	14.3	14.4	14.6	15.3	15.5	15.5	15.8	16.0	16.4	16.3	16.5
甘孜藏族自治州	Ganzi	21.8	21.6	22.1	22.4	22.5	22.6	22.7	23.1	23.3	23.1	23.3
凉山彝族自治州	Liangshan	212.1	215.7	224.7	238.5	240.6	242.0	245.2	247.0	250.8	247.2	252.7

13-18 各市(州)经济作物播种面积和产量(2023年)
Sown Areas and Output of Economic Crops by Region(2023)

单位：公顷、吨 (hectare, ton)

市(州)	Region	棉花 Cotton		油料 Oil bearing Crops		#花生 Peanut		#油菜籽 Rapeseeds		生麻 Bast Fiber	
		播种面积 Sown Area	产量 Yield	播种面积 Sown Area	产量 Yield	播种面积 Sown Area	产量 Yield	播种面积 Sown Area	产量 Yield	播种面积 Sown Area	产量 Yield
全省	**Sichuan**	**152**	**138**	**1728936**	**4386411**	**305974**	**827142**	**1413850**	**3543901**	**19438**	**35322**
成都市	Chengdu			102144	253690	14140	41156	87357	211983		
自贡市	Zigong			81124	192106	14980	40188	65900	151372		
攀枝花市	Panzhihua			2896	4448	797	1283	2099	3165		
泸州市	Luzhou			61606	132894	6395	13556	53999	118727		
德阳市	Deyang	18	14	101440	297923	15594	49659	85842	248254		
绵阳市	Mianyang	4	4	181608	538888	25982	98057	155532	440710		
广元市	Guangyuan			119013	308042	17158	67262	100828	238510		
遂宁市	Suining	130	120	77839	217978	16921	44546	60640	173135		
内江市	Neijiang			89780	194112	20300	42718	69480	151394	46	52
乐山市	Leshan			50034	93631	5554	12066	44480	81565		
南充市	Nanchong			196083	552599	57139	140745	138246	410877	26	90
眉山市	Meishan			63762	145762	3653	10972	60037	134634	1	3
宜宾市	Yibin			105276	231972	29270	77499	74287	151100	47	84
广安市	Guangan			66269	153475	12266	30850	53711	121377	36	85
达州市	Dazhou			171089	444667	34020	77040	135589	364342	19253	34985
雅安市	Yaan			8475	16020	245	736	8223	15272		
巴中市	Bazhong			109839	247982	10344	24535	99027	222807	6	5
资阳市	Ziyang			110426	296656	19025	49478	91401	247178		
阿坝藏族羌族自治州	Aba			4246	6489			4229	6457		
甘孜藏族自治州	Ganzi			7662	18091	68	132	7588	17950		
凉山彝族自治州	Liangshan			18325	38986	2124	4664	15356	33092	24	18

13-18 续表 1 continued

单位：公顷、吨 (hectare, ton)

市(州)	Region	糖料 Sugar Crops		#甘蔗 Sugarcane		烟叶(未加工烟草) Tobacco (unmanufactured)		中草药材 Medicinal Herbs	蔬菜及食用菌 Vegetables and Edible Fungus	
		播种面积 Sown Area	产量 Yield	播种面积 Sown Area	产量 Yield	播种面积 Sown Area	产量 Yield	播种面积 Sown Area	播种面积 Sown Area	产量 Yield
全省	**Sichuan**	**9620**	**392723**	**9610**	**392307**	**79664**	**172747**	**168635**	**1582831**	**54178707**
成都市	Chengdu	172	7623	172	7623	85	335	14602	183073	6528848
自贡市	Zigong	1049	34454	1049	34454			1675	73235	2762650
攀枝花市	Panzhihua	207	25559	207	25559	4641	10241	974	18898	1090510
泸州市	Luzhou	1331	77700	1331	77700	4943	8964	6163	85650	3188301
德阳市	Deyang	138	6440	138	6440	1018	4509	10424	73118	2772437
绵阳市	Mianyang	69	2514	69	2514			13610	77609	2323388
广元市	Guangyuan	65	764	63	650	2583	4660	14010	82228	3202746
遂宁市	Suining	153	6055	144	5753			2628	39544	1372154
内江市	Neijiang	566	21157	566	21157	1	3	2092	91525	3883778
乐山市	Leshan	483	17044	483	17044	700	1200	16016	59073	1567262
南充市	Nanchong	908	24855	908	24855	61	277	11920	176429	4504025
眉山市	Meishan	300	12228	300	12228	65	141	2699	52122	1554186
宜宾市	Yibin	978	29698	978	29698	5362	12598	5615	93907	3374478
广安市	Guangan	245	6834	245	6834	15	40	2623	76745	2949742
达州市	Dazhou	921	24018	921	24018	1246	3321	11046	101036	3423172
雅安市	Yaan	1	12	1	12			8287	33376	825432
巴中市	Bazhong	840	20692	840	20692	166	465	23014	73364	1867961
资阳市	Ziyang	506	18025	506	18025	36	62	1784	66191	1887961
阿坝藏族羌族自治州	Aba							5206	19372	765683
甘孜藏族自治州	Ganzi							4090	15188	467344
凉山彝族自治州	Liangshan	688	57051	688	57051	58743	125932	10157	91146	3866649

13-18 续表 2 continued

单位：吨 (ton)

市(州)	Region	蚕茧产量 Yield of Silkworm Cocoons	茶叶产量 Yield of Tea	水果产量 Yield of Fruits	#园林水果 Yield of Garden Fruits	苹果 Apples	柑橘 Citrus	梨 Pears	其他 Other Fruits	水产品产量 Yield of Aquatic Products
全省	**Sichuan**	**103802**	**424554**	**14903525**	**13417593**	**1021472**	**6149924**	**932756**	**5313441**	**1788643**
成都市	Chengdu	54	23007	1909243	1724427	2716	872257	76705	772749	153023
自贡市	Zigong	2461	18018	548993	484060		418564	16836	48660	95638
攀枝花市	Panzhihua	3355	103	680299	642563	233	4434	30035	607861	13489
泸州市	Luzhou	979	23003	350047	325120	680	134809	10899	178732	111483
德阳市	Deyang	3094	422	295187	192472	1707	75693	42907	72165	73566
绵阳市	Mianyang	9615	4190	482888	329146	1452	121753	32406	173535	134810
广元市	Guangyuan	738	18774	500153	481178	9917	53008	166421	251832	62747
遂宁市	Suining	475	39	156507	112704	478	63137	16716	32373	59046
内江市	Neijiang	2245	3478	612168	569228		470249	16477	82502	141635
乐山市	Leshan	407	57358	273576	253912	9	158637	7535	87732	139310
南充市	Nanchong	13685	40	893288	746208	542	623151	45796	76719	133178
眉山市	Meishan	164	27636	1535989	1499580	38	1115272	73490	310780	149577
宜宾市	Yibin	31515	105793	969498	876004		462593	91577	321834	127232
广安市	Guangan	2026	604	344083	233266		193548	14364	25354	76789
达州市	Dazhou		15324	633404	492234	3439	332470	28795	127530	119866
雅安市	Yaan	5	110841	688064	679140	177652	115701	121139	264648	12558
巴中市	Bazhong	561	14872	157664	126898	3081	50012	16879	56926	77854
资阳市	Ziyang	4887		1009732	857924		815246	9614	33064	82488
阿坝藏族羌族自治州	Aba		44	385771	384642	101796		16302	266545	24
甘孜藏族自治州	Ganzi		86	29765	28704	14640	1404	2256	10404	1
凉山彝族自治州	Liangshan	27535	923	2447207	2378182	703092	67986	95607	1511497	24329

13–19 各市(州)油料产量
Output of Oil-bearing Crops by Region

单位：万吨 (10 000 tons)

市(州)	Region	2013	2014	2015	2016	2017	2018	2019	2020	2021	2022	2023
全省	**Sichuan**	**320.2**	**332.0**	**339.6**	**346.2**	**357.9**	**362.5**	**367.4**	**392.9**	**416.6**	**433.8**	**438.6**
成都市	Chengdu	34.2	35.3	35.1	35.5	36.9	37.3	35.4	34.6	34.7	34.0	25.4
自贡市	Zigong	10.9	11.9	12.6	13.4	15.0	15.4	15.9	16.8	17.9	19.0	19.2
攀枝花市	Panzhihua	0.4	0.4	0.4	0.4	0.4	0.4	0.4	0.4	0.4	0.4	0.4
泸州市	Luzhou	6.7	7.1	7.4	7.7	10.2	10.1	10.1	11.6	12.1	13.0	13.3
德阳市	Deyang	24.2	24.5	24.7	24.7	24.7	24.8	24.6	26.1	28.1	29.4	29.8
绵阳市	Mianyang	39.6	40.9	42.2	42.5	43.0	43.6	44.5	46.8	49.6	53.2	53.9
广元市	Guangyuan	22.6	23.3	24.1	24.5	25.0	25.4	26.0	27.2	28.4	28.9	30.8
遂宁市	Suining	18.0	18.8	19.2	19.4	19.5	19.6	20.1	21.3	22.7	23.6	21.8
内江市	Neijiang	13.8	14.5	14.9	15.5	16.9	17.0	17.3	17.8	18.5	18.9	19.4
乐山市	Leshan	7.1	7.8	8.0	8.2	8.2	8.2	8.2	9.5	10.4	10.9	9.4
南充市	Nanchong	36.4	37.5	38.0	38.6	39.3	40.0	41.0	46.4	49.9	50.7	55.3
眉山市	Meishan	10.7	11.1	11.6	12.0	12.1	12.4	12.7	12.5	13.0	13.9	14.6
宜宾市	Yibin	12.5	13.3	14.0	14.8	15.4	15.6	15.6	17.7	19.5	20.9	23.2
广安市	Guangan	9.7	9.9	10.1	10.3	10.4	10.6	10.9	11.7	12.6	13.5	15.3
达州市	Dazhou	31.5	32.3	32.9	33.8	34.5	35.1	35.7	38.9	41.9	43.7	44.5
雅安市	Yaan	1.5	1.6	1.5	1.5	1.5	1.5	1.5	1.5	1.5	1.5	1.6
巴中市	Bazhong	14.7	14.9	15.4	15.8	16.1	16.4	16.8	20.0	21.7	22.6	24.8
资阳市	Ziyang	21.0	22.3	22.9	23.6	24.5	24.2	25.1	26.5	28.0	29.9	29.7
阿坝藏族羌族自治州	Aba	0.3	0.3	0.3	0.4	0.4	0.5	0.5	0.5	0.6	0.6	0.6
甘孜藏族自治州	Ganzi	0.7	0.7	0.7	0.8	0.9	1.3	1.7	1.8	1.8	1.8	1.8
凉山彝族自治州	Liangshan	3.8	3.6	3.7	2.9	3.1	3.2	3.3	3.3	3.3	3.5	3.9

13-20 牲畜饲养情况

Number of Livestock

单位：万头、万只 (10 000 heads)

年份 Year	肉猪出栏头数 Slaughtered Fattened Hogs	猪年末头数 Hogs (year-end)	肉牛出栏头数 Slaughtered Beef Cattle	大牲畜年末头数 Large Livestock (year-end)	#牛 Cattle and Buffaloes	#马 Horses	肉羊出栏只数 Slaughtered Sheep	羊年末只数 Sheep and Goats (year-end)	家禽出栏只数 Slaughtered Poultry	家禽年末只数 Poultry (year-end)
1952	393.00	943.00		500.00	474.00	23.00		262.00		
1957	733.00	1754.00		556.00	527.00	25.00		438.00		
1962	276.00	982.00		508.00	488.00	17.00		482.00		
1965	1130.00	1804.00		615.00	591.00	20.00		578.00		
1970	1195.00	2244.00		726.00	698.00	23.00		682.00		
1975	1314.00	2988.00		769.00	737.00	27.00		800.00		
1978	1614.00	3243.00		781.00	745.00	30.00		861.00		
1980	2264.00	3823.00	48.70	809.00	773.00	32.00	372.00	923.00		
1985	3223.00	4370.00	45.10	855.00	808.00	41.00	283.90	786.00		
1990	4507.00	4842.00	70.20	936.00	876.00	51.00	247.80	833.00		
1995	5844.00	5284.00	143.15	1035.00	963.00	60.00	424.74	1000.00	46318.62	
1996	6068.00	5277.00	159.05	1049.00	976.00	61.00	552.39	1095.00	43202.82	
1997	6234.00	5280.00	179.34	1073.00	996.00	64.00	687.07	1178.00	49744.21	
1998	6402.00	5271.00	194.88	1092.00	1012.00	67.00	843.72	1282.00	55430.69	
1999	6439.00	5204.00	194.86	1113.00	1030.00	69.00	1012.42	1383.00	63782.96	28891.80
2000	6594.37	5229.23	220.92	1132.90	1046.66	71.29	1249.43	1516.93	72291.88	32724.80
2001	6778.21	5222.78	244.99	1151.99	1062.27	74.59	1459.61	1633.31	79915.99	34113.57
2002	7090.89	5339.69	276.01	1176.87	1082.81	78.09	1704.59	1745.54	89018.51	37987.85
2003	7490.28	5484.17	310.05	1208.73	1110.88	81.47	1984.24	1898.97	97886.23	41537.17
2004	8103.34	5717.31	337.87	1234.09	1131.51	84.79	2314.33	2040.89	107208.79	44949.57
2005	8817.32	5970.69	366.80	1253.75	1146.92	88.45	2546.22	2140.25	119283.77	47810.85
2006	6905.58	5100.24	248.91	1096.15	985.67	91.10	1477.57	1629.32	47508.00	41309.25
2007	6014.61	5127.39	246.98	1098.40	981.31	95.18	1543.02	1659.05	51370.10	43215.29
2008	6429.19	5143.91	249.42	1044.86	930.06	94.07	1558.69	1617.71	53933.92	39804.47
2009	6914.93	4906.95	240.98	1050.93	933.46	96.45	1576.80	1572.10	54565.33	39897.82
2010	7174.95	4917.49	242.47	1054.06	934.70	97.54	1609.48	1467.39	56423.74	39745.36
2011	7000.41	4705.02	235.32	1051.34	935.37	94.58	1550.84	1424.63	57942.73	37714.54
2012	7170.70	4718.45	238.25	965.31	857.24	87.19	1562.70	1390.85	61999.60	36245.82
2013	7314.10	4507.69	242.04	958.80	858.67	80.38	1583.60	1362.79	63774.70	36052.58
2014	7445.00	4510.22	251.61	966.88	869.88	77.29	1632.70	1369.74	64667.60	37353.45
2015	7236.54	4288.39	263.34	953.72	857.80	76.22	1698.00	1352.31	66154.91	39869.79
2016	6907.82	4078.80	268.58	922.38	831.18	74.75	1739.19	1296.03	68489.75	38754.07
2017	6579.10	4376.64	267.26	947.18	853.19	75.46	1780.38	1599.26	65259.81	36619.20
2018	6638.34	4258.47	276.19	925.15	824.30	74.31	1740.89	1462.90	66070.96	38440.70
2019	4852.61	2870.70	291.66	944.52	851.65	75.59	1780.20	1504.08	78756.59	43949.43
2020	5614.36	3875.44	296.44	969.50	880.27	73.39	1792.10	1524.78	77444.49	43406.23
2021	6314.88	4255.14	293.14	917.56	830.51	70.60	1766.16	1511.69	77467.32	45682.62
2022	6548.45	4158.55	306.04	943.91	868.72	60.04	1792.65	1529.85	78087.06	45473.74
2023	6662.68	3854.98	316.36	921.13	848.50	58.42	1767.33	1381.98	76511.89	43472.61

注：2007年至2017年牲畜饲养及畜禽产品产量数据根据第三次全国农业普查结果进行了修订(以下有关各表同)。

a) Data of livestock raising and livestock production in 2007 to 2017 were revised according to the results of the Third National Agricultural Census (the same as the following related tables).

13-21 各市(州)牲畜饲养情况(2023年)
Number of Livestock by Region(2023)

单位：万头、万只 (10 000 heads)

市(州)	Region	肉猪出栏头数 Slaughtered Fattened Hogs	猪年末头数 Hogs (year-end)	肉牛出栏头数 Slaughtered Beef Cattle	大牲畜年末头数 Large Animals (year-end)	#牛 Cattle and Buffaloes	#马 Horses	肉羊出栏只数 Slaughtered Sheep	羊年末只数 Sheep and Goats (year-end)	家禽出栏只数 Slaughtered Poultry	家禽年末只数 Poultry (year-end)
全省	**Sichuan**	**6662.68**	**3854.98**	**316.36**	**921.13**	**848.50**	**58.42**	**1767.33**	**1381.98**	**76511.89**	**43472.61**
成都市	Chengdu	435.16	248.29	3.94	6.92	6.90	0.01	71.90	32.89	6494.74	2941.00
自贡市	Zigong	192.54	104.21	2.88	4.99	4.99		99.79	46.30	3590.70	2000.86
攀枝花市	Panzhihua	62.43	39.08	3.73	9.24	8.67	0.24	51.87	46.72	464.57	345.39
泸州市	Luzhou	422.18	233.43	7.98	19.31	19.01	0.22	54.67	37.00	3974.20	2793.93
德阳市	Deyang	286.30	151.00	7.07	12.66	12.66		23.03	17.34	7147.73	3043.45
绵阳市	Mianyang	385.33	234.43	12.67	26.93	26.52	0.40	94.96	62.86	7101.73	3578.41
广元市	Guangyuan	390.70	229.17	10.88	26.38	26.36	0.02	72.60	50.50	3756.00	2703.53
遂宁市	Suining	380.70	206.23	3.79	8.16	8.16		39.24	25.52	2663.28	1729.03
内江市	Neijiang	264.95	137.41	2.31	4.52	4.50	0.02	61.58	41.98	3260.50	1885.56
乐山市	Leshan	281.80	164.33	3.51	6.38	6.21	0.17	35.76	26.11	4404.99	2578.09
南充市	Nanchong	618.22	378.82	14.18	31.07	30.75	0.31	196.21	142.38	7145.15	4596.83
眉山市	Meishan	227.60	136.30	2.79	5.77	5.77		43.79	30.63	3953.58	1914.13
宜宾市	Yibin	523.57	306.98	15.48	32.13	31.71	0.42	47.35	33.98	4957.96	2830.72
广安市	Guangan	384.24	225.54	2.77	8.17	8.15	0.02	25.29	16.64	3424.48	2152.99
达州市	Dazhou	460.07	255.66	36.41	62.45	62.02	0.32	124.58	80.14	7598.37	3626.39
雅安市	Yaan	138.87	87.02	5.80	9.81	9.00	0.74	22.56	14.10	744.61	644.23
巴中市	Bazhong	351.56	199.39	19.77	42.38	42.38		80.82	74.19	1193.68	860.22
资阳市	Ziyang	290.80	169.32	1.98	4.11	3.97	0.14	130.90	65.72	2404.49	1620.31
阿坝藏族羌族自治州	Aba	41.13	33.73	64.00	222.46	212.54	9.82	39.38	56.17	72.55	48.96
甘孜藏族自治州	Ganzi	23.24	17.73	54.58	229.48	207.05	20.69	28.30	27.19	23.49	28.02
凉山彝族自治州	Liangshan	501.29	296.93	39.86	147.81	111.19	24.87	422.74	453.62	2135.10	1550.56

13-22 各市(州)猪年末头数
Number of Hogs by Region at Year-end

单位：万头 (10 000 heads)

市(州)	Region	2013	2014	2015	2016	2017	2018	2019	2020	2021	2022	2023
全省	**Sichuan**	**4507.69**	**4510.22**	**4288.39**	**4078.80**	**4376.64**	**4259.22**	**2870.70**	**3875.44**	**4255.14**	**4158.55**	**3854.98**
成都市	Chengdu	488.81	482.23	442.37	377.67	402.32	367.62	158.25	260.00	278.80	274.03	248.29
自贡市	Zigong	139.17	136.01	121.95	101.67	108.11	105.66	74.24	109.54	116.29	111.96	104.21
攀枝花市	Panzhihua	41.30	41.97	41.31	40.64	41.48	41.12	29.99	38.59	42.06	41.99	39.08
泸州市	Luzhou	243.31	250.21	240.98	234.21	261.39	248.98	203.02	245.59	266.75	259.15	233.43
德阳市	Deyang	214.90	214.52	192.97	177.05	194.11	187.80	97.35	153.20	163.36	160.12	151.00
绵阳市	Mianyang	243.00	240.43	222.51	218.63	232.68	231.71	175.57	227.09	253.36	249.75	234.43
广元市	Guangyuan	230.64	229.09	222.01	219.56	241.62	238.54	189.27	235.09	255.73	251.47	229.17
遂宁市	Suining	230.85	237.21	224.88	209.19	239.39	228.68	145.48	209.34	225.29	219.45	206.23
内江市	Neijiang	187.11	188.21	171.45	149.88	160.94	157.63	88.74	143.19	153.24	148.68	137.41
乐山市	Leshan	220.63	204.79	202.73	184.84	197.91	192.92	92.49	152.89	174.81	180.68	164.33
南充市	Nanchong	369.35	375.20	355.00	365.17	386.66	380.14	285.34	380.33	414.72	403.90	378.82
眉山市	Meishan	176.09	179.74	173.22	154.94	165.23	161.32	94.92	139.12	149.97	146.53	136.30
宜宾市	Yibin	291.12	311.47	302.16	280.42	315.92	321.78	265.36	318.39	337.80	327.69	306.98
广安市	Guangan	269.12	266.61	254.98	221.40	242.20	235.50	171.77	208.57	245.07	242.31	225.54
达州市	Dazhou	292.29	287.13	278.66	276.75	286.05	281.29	196.16	255.02	283.22	274.66	255.66
雅安市	Yaan	80.36	87.23	86.03	83.92	87.15	83.91	60.61	78.19	96.98	94.54	87.02
巴中市	Bazhong	218.38	210.53	202.81	217.68	227.12	218.86	148.37	205.79	217.28	213.16	199.39
资阳市	Ziyang	201.97	196.90	192.17	180.74	200.30	193.89	106.05	160.00	185.51	182.95	169.32
阿坝藏族羌族自治州	Aba	26.06	27.50	27.42	27.04	26.88	27.48	26.54	35.59	39.11	36.97	33.73
甘孜藏族自治州	Ganzi	16.70	16.91	16.86	17.46	17.45	17.87	17.08	18.79	20.00	19.47	17.73
凉山彝族自治州	Liangshan	326.52	326.32	315.90	339.95	341.71	336.53	244.19	301.09	335.79	319.10	296.93

13−23 各市(州)大牲畜年末头数
Number of Large Livestock by Region at Year-end

单位：万头 (10 000 heads)

市(州)	Region	2013	2014	2015	2016	2017	2018	2019	2020	2021	2022	2023
全省	**Sichuan**	**958.80**	**966.88**	**953.72**	**922.38**	**947.18**	**916.28**	**944.52**	**969.50**	**917.56**	**943.91**	**921.13**
成都市	Chengdu	11.23	11.65	11.68	7.98	7.87	7.33	7.18	7.53	6.61	6.98	6.92
自贡市	Zigong	5.95	6.40	5.80	3.85	4.75	4.66	4.83	5.74	5.75	5.09	4.99
攀枝花市	Panzhihua	9.64	9.60	9.67	9.41	10.23	9.22	9.48	9.53	9.26	9.38	9.24
泸州市	Luzhou	24.71	22.79	19.36	17.16	18.59	18.82	19.10	19.92	18.58	19.56	19.31
德阳市	Deyang	14.15	13.92	13.72	10.72	11.31	11.09	11.40	12.21	12.62	12.90	12.66
绵阳市	Mianyang	28.11	29.04	22.99	21.22	23.48	23.10	23.70	24.61	26.56	27.50	26.93
广元市	Guangyuan	20.36	20.04	20.06	20.07	20.44	20.51	21.97	25.13	24.84	26.72	26.38
遂宁市	Suining	8.41	7.92	7.07	6.30	6.43	6.47	6.90	7.18	8.03	8.24	8.16
内江市	Neijiang	5.02	5.10	3.65	2.94	3.20	3.26	3.44	4.70	4.67	4.60	4.52
乐山市	Leshan	8.79	7.98	6.55	5.63	6.05	6.19	6.01	6.61	6.32	6.49	6.38
南充市	Nanchong	28.29	29.18	26.12	25.10	25.42	25.71	26.49	30.46	30.67	31.77	31.07
眉山市	Meishan	8.06	7.50	5.63	4.50	4.77	4.80	4.89	5.45	5.62	5.92	5.77
宜宾市	Yibin	23.87	23.95	22.81	22.02	24.72	24.89	27.70	32.86	31.50	32.96	32.13
广安市	Guangan	8.23	8.01	5.61	4.75	4.92	4.85	5.05	7.03	7.96	8.39	8.17
达州市	Dazhou	61.68	62.26	58.25	53.73	55.73	56.34	58.29	59.66	60.77	64.31	62.45
雅安市	Yaan	14.07	14.05	13.98	13.03	13.66	13.55	13.73	13.15	11.91	11.65	9.81
巴中市	Bazhong	37.85	40.43	37.73	36.87	35.98	36.96	38.35	38.02	40.08	43.03	42.38
资阳市	Ziyang	4.19	3.81	3.45	3.16	3.34	3.45	3.54	3.73	3.94	4.17	4.11
阿坝藏族羌族自治州	Aba	226.73	234.42	236.15	244.24	248.22	226.36	239.03	242.14	219.13	227.46	222.46
甘孜藏族自治州	Ganzi	252.96	254.31	258.23	259.61	263.35	253.92	256.26	258.26	235.33	235.30	229.48
凉山彝族自治州	Liangshan	156.48	154.51	155.22	150.10	154.72	154.80	157.31	155.59	147.41	151.47	147.81

13-24 畜产品产量
Output of Livestock Products

年份 Year	肉类总产量 (万吨) Output of Meat (10 000 tons)	#猪肉 Pork	#牛肉 Beef	#羊肉 Mutton	#禽肉 Poultry	#兔肉 Rabbit	禽蛋产量 (万吨) Output of Poultry Eggs (10 000 tons)	奶类产量 (万吨) Output of Milk (10 000 tons)	蜂蜜产量 (吨) Output of Honey (ton)	绵羊毛产量 (吨) Output of Sheep Wool (ton)
1952	17.10	15.60								
1957	35.20	33.40								
1962	8.00	6.90								
1965	52.20	49.80								
1970	52.80	51.50								
1975	59.60	57.30								
1978	78.00	76.00						5.77		
1980	125.40	119.80	3.56	3.69				11.00		2602
1985	208.40	202.50	4.09	3.15				19.00	11584	2392
1990	301.00	292.30	6.86	3.74			35.00	22.00	14763	2729
1995	472.96	391.87	15.51	6.29	67.90		60.00	24.00	17922	3265
1996	501.64	408.71	17.07	8.09	63.35		67.00	24.00	18541	3269
1997	531.57	424.39	19.30	10.04	72.75		74.00	26.00	19403	3434
1998	568.11	447.10	21.33	12.74	81.35		80.00	27.00	21414	3760
1999	605.40	464.03	22.87	15.74	95.92		89.00	27.00	22829	3963
2000	641.25	478.59	25.27	19.19	109.68		99.70	28.92	22681	4108
2001	680.41	495.42	28.37	22.85	121.95	10.09	108.76	33.34	26567	4288
2002	735.84	522.19	33.01	27.88	139.02	11.98	121.11	39.32	29396	4800
2003	795.26	554.39	37.32	32.59	154.57	14.30	133.61	45.84	32944	5059
2004	870.62	601.37	41.55	38.53	170.44	16.77	145.21	53.00	32613	5375
2005	955.87	657.07	45.19	42.74	189.77	19.13	157.17	59.03	34704	5801
2006	622.67	481.42	28.34	21.36	68.07	21.39	140.69	62.71	38863	6047
2007	565.47	407.70	27.58	23.88	78.82	25.26	145.20	65.60	42753	6513
2008	587.53	434.46	27.69	24.06	80.76	18.92	142.96	68.93	43354	6548
2009	627.36	472.38	27.82	24.31	81.49	19.81	143.97	68.88	47370	6824
2010	651.53	492.25	27.94	24.80	84.11	20.74	144.81	71.25	46037	6892
2011	644.99	484.73	27.11	23.90	86.73	20.83	145.02	72.36	49890	6940
2012	663.16	496.40	27.24	24.00	93.00	20.81	146.40	72.12	52683	7098
2013	682.31	510.80	28.44	24.50	95.60	21.22	145.20	71.09	51107	5854
2014	704.10	527.20	30.15	25.30	97.40	22.30	145.30	71.30	53933	5939
2015	694.33	512.42	31.53	26.32	99.69	22.61	146.65	67.49	55862	6038
2016	680.36	492.32	32.44	26.78	103.10	23.98	149.68	62.77	55815	6046
2017	653.82	472.23	33.31	27.24	99.05	20.23	144.50	63.79	57668	5840
2018	664.74	481.20	34.47	26.31	100.59	20.43	148.80	64.27	54287	5475
2019	559.53	353.45	36.43	27.08	119.70	21.15	161.70	66.77	55253	5519
2020	597.94	394.79	37.02	27.27	115.92	21.22	167.93	68.09	62658	4644
2021	664.01	460.49	36.86	27.08	115.98	21.99	169.24	68.31	62663	4505
2022	685.72	478.00	38.58	27.43	117.15	22.86	175.50	70.83	64900	4301
2023	697.09	489.70	39.07	27.06	115.02	24.07	183.11	72.06	66615	4488

13-25 各市(州)畜产品产量(2023年)
Output of Livestock Products by Region(2023)

市(州)	Region	肉类总产量(万吨) Output of Meat (10 000 tons)	#猪肉 Pork	#牛肉 Beef	#羊肉 Mutton	#禽肉 Poultry	#兔肉 Rabbit
全省	**Sichuan**	**697.09**	**489.70**	**39.07**	**27.06**	**115.02**	**24.07**
成都市	Chengdu	46.03	32.12	0.51	1.04	10.36	1.91
自贡市	Zigong	26.55	14.13	0.39	1.47	5.29	5.24
攀枝花市	Panzhihua	6.61	4.57	0.47	0.80	0.73	0.02
泸州市	Luzhou	40.01	30.90	1.01	0.86	5.90	1.33
德阳市	Deyang	36.12	21.08	0.91	0.36	11.39	2.33
绵阳市	Mianyang	43.42	28.24	1.62	1.40	10.87	1.21
广元市	Guangyuan	37.58	28.60	1.37	1.09	5.48	1.02
遂宁市	Suining	33.98	27.77	0.48	0.58	4.34	0.77
内江市	Neijiang	27.18	19.36	0.30	0.89	4.81	1.81
乐山市	Leshan	29.97	20.51	0.47	0.56	6.72	1.20
南充市	Nanchong	62.85	45.41	1.76	3.07	9.80	2.25
眉山市	Meishan	24.34	16.63	0.35	0.65	5.81	0.70
宜宾市	Yibin	50.00	38.33	2.05	0.67	7.24	1.71
广安市	Guangan	34.27	28.08	0.37	0.34	4.69	0.73
达州市	Dazhou	52.54	33.93	4.65	1.96	11.42	0.50
雅安市	Yaan	12.77	10.21	0.71	0.30	1.37	0.17
巴中市	Bazhong	31.77	25.87	2.43	1.13	1.77	0.52
资阳市	Ziyang	28.00	21.44	0.27	1.95	3.68	0.51
阿坝藏族羌族自治州	Aba	10.97	2.96	7.22	0.67	0.11	
甘孜藏族自治州	Ganzi	8.99	1.66	6.81	0.48	0.04	
凉山彝族自治州	Liangshan	53.16	37.89	4.92	6.77	3.19	0.14

13-25 续表 continued

市(州)	Region	奶类 (万吨) Milk (10 000 tons)	出栏家禽 (万只) Slaughtered Poultry (10 000 heads)	出栏肉兔 (万只) Slaughtered Rabbit (10 000 heads)	禽蛋 (吨) Poultry Eggs (ton)	蜂蜜 (吨) Honey (ton)	蚕茧 (吨) Silkworm Cocoons (ton)
全省	**Sichuan**	**72.06**	**76511.89**	**17971.71**	**1811151**	**66615**	**103802**
成都市	Chengdu	8.33	6494.74	1209.82	187957	8314	54
自贡市	Zigong	1.83	3590.70	4509.02	67830	1181	2461
攀枝花市	Panzhihua	0.02	464.57	11.57	11943	109	3355
泸州市	Luzhou	0.17	3974.20	1041.47	52563	3701	979
德阳市	Deyang	1.19	7147.73	1741.90	132733	5825	3094
绵阳市	Mianyang	1.68	7101.73	848.12	170299	6892	9615
广元市	Guangyuan		3756.00	505.53	57854	2130	738
遂宁市	Suining	0.05	2663.28	642.24	98137	2306	475
内江市	Neijiang	1.16	3260.50	1418.84	54000	1086	2245
乐山市	Leshan	0.07	4404.99	846.88	164239	845	407
南充市	Nanchong	2.39	7145.15	1669.74	258352	1758	13683
眉山市	Meishan	16.07	3953.58	438.88	64937	13942	164
宜宾市	Yibin	0.32	4957.96	1173.22	54701	2149	31515
广安市	Guangan	0.27	3424.48	509.46	84880	650	2026
达州市	Dazhou	2.33	7598.37	364.45	122170	8326	
雅安市	Yaan	2.42	744.61	133.90	26600	738	5
巴中市	Bazhong		1193.68	406.27	74687	1120	561
资阳市	Ziyang	1.70	2404.49	398.90	93173	1064	4887
阿坝藏族羌族自治州	Aba	16.00	72.55	2.52	1981	1018	
甘孜藏族自治州	Ganzi	11.31	23.49	0.45	733	233	
凉山彝族自治州	Liangshan	4.77	2135.10	98.56	31382	3229	27535

13-26 各市(州)肉类总产量
Output of Meat by Region

单位：万吨 (10 000 tons)

市(州)	Region	2013	2014	2015	2016	2017	2018	2019	2020	2021	2022	2023
全省	**Sichuan**	**682.31**	**704.10**	**694.33**	**680.36**	**653.82**	**664.74**	**559.53**	**597.94**	**664.01**	**685.72**	**697.09**
成都市	Chengdu	78.23	78.68	75.00	68.15	62.03	59.36	43.72	44.14	45.19	45.45	46.03
自贡市	Zigong	24.37	24.99	24.30	23.37	21.61	22.30	20.30	22.18	24.70	25.83	26.55
攀枝花市	Panzhihua	5.27	5.55	5.80	5.61	5.68	5.86	5.19	5.65	6.22	6.50	6.61
泸州市	Luzhou	34.79	36.62	36.55	37.06	36.40	37.21	32.70	34.54	38.68	39.57	40.01
德阳市	Deyang	37.18	36.95	36.45	35.59	34.14	34.56	29.12	31.11	34.43	35.63	36.12
绵阳市	Mianyang	41.40	41.55	40.68	38.95	37.79	38.97	35.63	38.35	41.40	43.37	43.42
广元市	Guangyuan	30.90	32.13	32.22	32.50	31.54	32.56	28.79	31.20	35.43	36.73	37.58
遂宁市	Suining	32.36	33.54	33.00	33.38	31.68	32.34	26.77	28.79	32.19	33.35	33.98
内江市	Neijiang	27.62	28.37	27.28	26.26	24.22	24.84	19.98	22.35	25.50	26.53	27.18
乐山市	Leshan	30.62	30.55	30.83	30.24	28.39	28.85	22.52	25.45	27.87	28.94	29.97
南充市	Nanchong	58.34	60.91	59.96	60.34	57.25	58.38	48.44	54.46	60.95	62.31	62.85
眉山市	Meishan	26.01	27.31	27.05	25.43	24.18	24.70	19.66	20.44	22.85	24.10	24.34
宜宾市	Yibin	42.11	45.25	44.37	44.17	44.95	46.05	41.29	42.56	48.29	49.51	50.00
广安市	Guangan	36.09	37.41	36.88	35.02	32.51	33.09	24.94	28.76	33.04	33.90	34.27
达州市	Dazhou	47.25	47.74	46.86	46.41	44.73	46.01	42.03	44.16	50.03	51.91	52.54
雅安市	Yaan	11.66	13.16	13.08	11.61	11.45	11.69	10.30	10.94	12.16	12.58	12.77
巴中市	Bazhong	30.12	30.85	30.52	30.24	30.13	30.89	24.38	26.26	29.85	31.21	31.77
资阳市	Ziyang	29.27	29.77	29.00	28.63	27.29	27.10	19.96	23.12	26.47	27.51	28.00
阿坝藏族羌族自治州	Aba	8.04	9.18	9.96	10.35	10.32	10.80	10.81	10.74	10.68	10.90	10.97
甘孜藏族自治州	Ganzi	6.64	7.40	7.99	8.98	9.00	9.21	9.11	9.22	8.69	8.91	8.99
凉山彝族自治州	Liangshan	44.02	46.18	46.53	48.18	48.53	49.37	43.94	43.96	49.42	50.98	53.16

13−27 林产品产量及造林面积

Output of Major Forest Products and Areas under Afforestation

年份 Year	林产品产量 (吨) Output of Major Forest Products (ton)			造林面积 (万公顷) Area under Afforestation (10 000 hectares)
	油茶籽 Tea-oil Seeds	核桃(干重) Walnut (dry weight)	笋用竹 Fresh Bamboo Shoots	
1952	5643	2933	279	2.13
1957	15276	8703	604	10.18
1962	2793	3075	2046	12.72
1965	2223	1750	604	11.57
1970	1141	4162	976	15.41
1975	3288	5474	1022	21.59
1978	8439	9060	906	20.05
1980	5282	9468	1119	20.29
1985	2242	7222	1437	47.44
1990	1878	15655	2946	26.50
1995	4047	22928	5378	25.00
1996	2922	24819	6146	25.60
1997	3903	22059	5593	28.15
1998	6479	28711	6100	38.51
1999	4273	23842	7886	40.46
2000	4372	32095	8914	48.91
2001	4278	32744	9925	51.66
2002	10228	70534	23722	69.46
2003	11854	77004	28250	72.32
2004	4037	56731	40696	37.01
2005	2464	59272	62190	24.19
2006	3578	61112	48895	10.49
2007	10272	76721	40434	33.23
2008	3358	91170	62826	57.46
2009	3426	123683	51349	48.78
2010	4360	126109	78952	38.22
2011	4649	176710	128841	25.19
2012	4180	211944	42292	11.22
2013	5361	245876	87855	12.62
2014	13718	293750	109554	9.82
2015	20708	458435	138195	31.82
2016	17254	451486	135266	56.85
2017	20852	537474	122376	65.84
2018	23119	573685	72900	43.68
2019	19792	563233	104802	40.04
2020	25059	605797	107357	34.39
2021	28402	888524	103501	24.37
2022	15594	680284	149593	18.60
2023	18432	697692	1102634	12.31

注：本表数据由四川省林业和草原局提供；根据部门制度变更，自2023年起原“竹笋干”变更为“笋用竹”，统计口径随之变化，故数据与往期不可比。

a) Data in this table are provided by the bureau of Forestry and Grassland of Sichuan Province; b)According to the departmental system change, the original "dried bamboo shoots" have been changed to "fresh bamboo shoots", and the statistical caliber has also changed accordingly since 2023.Therefore, the data cannot be compared with previous periods.

13-28 受灾面积和绝收面积
Areas Covered by Natural Disaster and Total Crop Failure

单位:万公顷 (10 000 hectares)

年份 Year	受灾面积 Area Covered by Natural Disaster	绝收面积 Area of Total Crop Failure	水灾 Flood		旱灾 Drought	
			受灾面积 Area Covered	绝收面积 Total Crop Failure	受灾面积 Area Covered	绝收面积 Total Crop Failure
1952	53.8	30.1	7.6	4.2	46.2	25.9
1957	28.8	16.3	2.6	1.5	25.0	14.2
1962	193.6	109.9	22.0	10.2	157.1	94.2
1965	80.6	45.5	11.1	6.3	55.9	37.9
1975	110.0	62.1	13.8	7.5	92.7	51.4
1978	302.7	273.5	7.0	4.0	273.4	185.8
1980	201.5	112.9	51.8	26.9	83.0	42.3
1985	299.3	168.2	30.5	18.4	137.5	83.3
1990	322.8	169.4	63.7	33.0	181.5	93.2
1995	288.1	185.7	89.3	51.7	163.0	92.8
1996	393.2	221.9	56.3	31.8	174.3	103.5
1997	311.5	174.9	47.2	22.3	194.9	117.5
1998	316.3	172.7	141.6	81.9	141.6	71.2
1999	297.3	163.3	81.6	45.3	117.2	63.7
2000	432.0	251.3	82.3	42.2	309.3	186.0
2001	444.9	299.9	93.5	59.0	325.4	224.5
2002	241.9	135.3	92.8	59.8	90.3	44.7
2003	259.2	203.2	94.2	78.6	124.1	95.8
2004	149.0	22.9	70.1	70.0	30.4	4.0
2005	294.3	119.8	87.6	46.4	31.7	15.7
2006	156.6	21.6	79.2	10.1	40.2	2.6
2007	260.1	22.0	89.8	11.0	138.1	8.2
2008	141.2	6.7	20.6	1.6	10.7	0.3
2009	245.9	46.9	110.5	20.3	128.8	26.4
2010	232.4	85.1	150.8	42.3	62.8	38.4
2011	206.3	112.1	72.4	37.8	98.7	56.3
2012	201.2	119.3	113.4	58.9	97.5	63.2
2013	244.2	125.8	88.2	51.2	135.4	63.1
2014	92.8	48.4	29.2	17.1	58.3	28.2
2015	40.9	22.2	25.6	12.7	9.6	5.4
2016	41.0	25.2	17.8	10.9	8.7	5.9
2017	18.6	11.9	13.7	8.7	3.2	2.2
2018	49.3	6.5	35.7	5.6	9.9	0.8
2019	32.4	3.3	23.8	3.1	7.9	0.1
2020	63.3	7.6	36.0	5.7	24.9	1.6
2021	26.6	4.2	24.4	3.9	0.1	
2022	61.1	8.9	5.5	0.9	52.3	5.4
2023	22.8	1.6	9.7	0.8	12.7	0.8

注：本表由四川省民政厅提供。2004年及以前绝收面积为成灾面积。

a) Data in this table are provided by Civil Affairs Department of Sichuan Province. Data of total crop failure were area affected in 2004 and before.

主要统计指标解释

农林牧渔业总产值 指以货币表现的农、林、牧、渔业全部产品和对农林牧渔业生产活动进行的各种支持性服务活动的价值总量，它反映一定时期内农林牧渔业生产总规模和总成果。农林牧渔业总产值采用“产品法”进行计算，通常是按农、林、牧、渔业产品及其副产品的产量分别乘以各自单位产品价格求得；少数生产周期较长，当年没有产品或产品产量不易统计的，则采用间接方法匡算其产值；然后将四业产品产值及农林牧渔专业及辅助性活动产值相加即为农林牧渔业总产值。

粮食产量 指日历年度内生产的全部粮食数量。按收获季节包括夏收粮食、早稻和秋收粮食，按作物品种包括谷物、豆类和薯类。其产量计算方法：谷物按脱粒后的原粮计算，豆类按去豆荚后的干豆计算；薯类(包括甘薯和马铃薯，不包括芋头和木薯)1964 年以前按每 4 公斤鲜薯折 1 公斤粮食计算，从 1964 年开始改为按每 5 公斤鲜薯折 1 公斤粮食计算；城市郊区作为蔬菜的薯类(如马铃薯等)按鲜品计算，并且不作粮食统计。

棉花产量 指全社会棉花的产量。包括春播棉和夏播棉。产量按皮棉计算。不包括木棉。

油料产量 指全部油料作物的生产量。包括花生、油菜籽、芝麻、向日葵籽、胡麻籽(亚麻籽)和其他油料。不包括大豆、木本油料和野生油料。花生以带壳干花生计算。

水产品产量 指渔业（捕捞和养殖）生产活动的最终有效成果，包括全部海水和淡水鱼类、甲壳类（虾、蟹）、贝类、头足类、藻类和其他类渔业产品的最终产量。

猪、牛、羊、禽肉产量 指当年出栏并已屠宰、除去头蹄下水后带骨肉(即胴体重)的重量。

期初(末)畜禽存栏头(只)数 指报告期初(末)饲养的大牲畜、猪、羊、家禽等畜禽的数量。数据上报方式及数据调整情况同猪、牛、羊、禽肉产量。

耕地 指利用地表耕作层种植农作物为主，每年种植一季及以上（含以一年一季以上的耕种方式种植多年生作物）的土地，包括熟地，新开发、复垦、整理地，休闲地（含轮歇地、休耕地）；以及间有零星果树、桑树或其他树木的耕地；包括南方宽度<1.0 米，北方宽度<2.0 米固定的沟、渠、路和地坎(埂)；包括直接利用地表耕作层种植的温室、大棚、地膜等保温、保湿设施用地。

农作物播种面积 指日历年度内收获农作物在全部土地（耕地或非耕地）上的播种或移植面积。凡是本年内收获的农作物，无论是本年还是上年播种，都算为播种面积，但不包括本年播种，下年收获的农作物面积。

耕地灌溉面积 指具有一定的水源，地块比较平整，灌溉工程或设备已经配套，在一般年景下能够进行正常灌溉的耕地面积。在一般情况下，耕地灌溉面积应等于灌溉工程或设备已经配套，能够进行正常灌溉的水田和水浇地面积之和。它是反映我国农田水利建设的重要指标。

农用化肥施用量 指本年内实际用于农业生产的化肥数量，包括氮肥、磷肥、钾肥和复合肥。化肥施用量要求按折纯量计算数量。折纯量是指把氮肥、磷肥、钾肥分别按含氮、含五氧化二磷、含氧化钾的百分之百成份进行折算后的数量。复合肥按其所含主要成分折算。公式为：

折纯量=实物量×某种化肥有效成份含量的百分比

农业机械总动力 指全部农业机械动力的额定功率之和。农业机械是指用于种植业、畜牧业、渔业、农产品初加工、农用运输和农田基本建设等活动的机械及设备。农机总动力按使用能源不同分为以下四部分：

(1)柴油发动机动力：指全部柴油发动机额定功率之和；

(2)汽油发动机动力：指全部汽油发动机额定功率之和；

(3)电动机动力：指全部电动机（含潜水电泵的电动机）额定功率之和；

(4)其他机械动力：指采用柴油、汽油、电力之外的其他能源，如水力、风力、煤炭、太阳能等动力机械功率之和。

Explanatory Notes on Main Statistical Indicators

Gross Output Value of Agriculture, Forestry, Animal Husbandry and Fishery refers to the total value of products (expressed in monetary terms) of agriculture, forestry, animal husbandry and fishery, and total value of services in support of agriculture, forestry, animal husbandry and fishery activities. It reflects the total scale and results of agricultural production during a given period. Gross output value of agriculture is calculated by product method, and is obtained by multiplying the output of each product or by-product by its price, resulting in the output value of each single item. For a small number of products, annual output of which is not available or difficult to get due to the long production process involved, the output value is estimated through an indirect approach. The sum of output values of all products of agriculture, forestry, animal husbandry and fishery and professional and auxiliary activities of agriculture, forestry, animal husbandry and fishery is then equal to the gross output value of agriculture.

Grain Output refers to the total output of grains produced within a calendar year. It includes summer crops, early rice and autumn crops by harvest seasons; and covers cereals, beans and tubers by type of crops. Output of cereals cover husked grain only. Output of beans refers to dry beans without pods. The output of tubers (sweet potatoes and potatoes, not including taros and cassava) are converted with the ratio of 4:1, i.e. 4 kilograms of fresh tubers were equivalent to 1 kilogram of grain before 1964. Since 1964 the ratio has been changed to 5:1. Tubers consumed as vegetables (such as potatoes) in cities and suburbs are calculated as fresh vegetables and their output is not included in the output of grain.

Cotton Output refers to cotton production in the whole country including cotton planted in spring and in summer. Output is measured as the weight of ginned cotton. Ceiba is not included.

Output of Oil-bearing Crops refers to the total production of oil-bearing crops of various kinds, including peanuts, rapeseeds, sesame, sunflower seeds, flax seeds, and other oil-bearing crops. Soybeans, oil-bearing woody plants, and wild oil-bearing crops are not included.

Output of Aquatic Products refers to final output actually yielded from fishing production (fishery and breeding), including all output of marine and freshwater fish, crustaceans (shrimps, crabs), shellfish, cephalopod, seaweed and other fishery products. Data on output of aquatic products are reported by fishery agencies level by level.

Output of Pork, Beef, Mutton and Poultry refers to the meat of slaughtered hogs, cattle, sheep and goats with head, feet, and offal taken away.

Number of Livestock or Poultry in Stock at Beginning/End of Period refers to the total number of large animals, pigs, sheep, fowls, etc. raised at the beginning/end of the reference period. Data reporting system and data adjustment are the same as that in the output of pork, beef, mutton and poultry.

Arable Land refers to the area of land mainly for the regular cultivation of farm crops (including vegetables), with some fruit trees, mulberry trees and others, covers cultivated land, newly-developed land, reclaimed land, consolidated land, fallow, beach land that can guarantee one harvest per year on average. It also covers fixed ditch, canal, road and sill (ridge) with width less than 1 meter in the South and 2 meters in the North, lands planted temporarily with herbs, grass, flowers and nursery stocks, and other cultivated land with temporary change of use.

Sown Area of Crops refers to area of all land (cultivated or non-cultivated area) sown or transplanted with crops that are harvested within the calendar year. All crops harvested within the year are counted as sown area, regardless of being sown in this year or the previous year. Crops sown this year but will be harvested in the coming year are excluded.

Irrigated Area of Cultivated Land refers to area of land that are effectively irrigated, i.e. relatively level land, where there are water sources or complete sets of irrigation facilities to lift and move adequate water for irrigation purpose under normal conditions. Under normal situations, irrigated area of cultivated land is the sum of watered fields and irrigated fields where irrigation systems or equipment have been installed for regular irrigation purpose. It is an important indicator to reflect the farmland water conservancy construction in China.

Consumption of Chemical Fertilizers in Agriculture refers to the quantity of chemical fertilizers applied in agriculture in the year, including nitrogenous fertilizer, phosphate fertilizer, potash fertilizer, and compound fertilizer. The consumption of chemical fertilizers is calculated in terms of volume of effective components by means of converting the gross weight of the respective fertilizers into weight containing effective component (e.g. nitrogen content in nitrogenous fertilizer, phosphorous pentoxide contents in phosphate fertilizer, and potassium oxide contents in potash fertilizer). Compound fertilizer is converted in regard to its major components. The formula is:

Volume of effective component = physical quantity × effective component of certain chemical fertilizer (%)

Total Power of Farm Machinery refers to the total rated capacity of all agricultural machinery. Agricultural machinery refers to the machines and equipment which are used for activities of farming, animal husbandry, fishery, primary processing of agricultural products, agricultural transport and infrastructure construction of farmland. Total power of agricultural machinery is classified into 4 groups according to the energy used:

1) Diesel engine power refers to the total rated capacity of all diesel engines.

2) Gasoline engine power refers to the total rated capacity of all gasoline engines.

3) Electric motor power refers to the total rated capacity of all electric motors (include submersible pump motors).

4) Other mechanical powers refer to the total mechanical capacity of the sources of energy besides diesel, gasoline and motor power, such as hydro power, wind power, coal and sola energy.

14 工 业
Chapter 14 Industry

14-1 规模以上工业企业情况(2023年)
Information of Industrial Enterprises above Designated Size(2023)

分类	Item	企业单位数(个) Number of Enterprises (unit)	资产总计(亿元) Total Assets (100 million yuan)	营业收入(亿元) Business Revenue (100 million yuan)	利润总额(亿元) Total Profits (100 million yuan)	平均用工人数(万人) Annual Average Employees (10 000 persons)
总计	**Total**	**18557**	**74351.86**	**50393.25**	**4607.14**	**304.40**
按轻重工业分	**Grouped by Light &Heavy Industries**					
轻工业	Light Industry	6399	16192.51	12393.50	1555.44	96.72
重工业	Heavy Industry	12158	58159.35	37999.74	3051.70	207.68
按企业规模分	**Grouped by Size of Enterprises**					
大型企业	Large-sized Enterprises	309	31480.23	24202.29	2325.28	108.40
中型企业	Medium-sized Enterprises	1296	15755.26	9816.76	1019.74	67.08
小型企业	Small-sized Enterprises	16952	27116.37	16374.20	1262.13	128.92
按登记注册类型分	**Grouped by Status of Registration**					
内资企业	Domestic Funded Enterprises	17974	68246.54	43713.18	4244.62	272.89
国有企业	State-owned Enterprises	21	206.38	77.55	3.62	0.78
集体企业	Collective-owned Enterprises	26	10.34	11.94	1.03	0.19
股份合作企业	Cooperative Share-holding Enterprises	31	59.14	41.72	2.49	0.44
联营企业	Joint-owned Enterprises	3	21.64	0.63	-1.39	0.04
有限责任公司	Limited Liability Corporations	16650	58288.89	38226.47	3253.39	238.47
国有独资企业	State Sole-proprietorship Enterprises	138	3606.34	1822.73	168.91	6.2
其他有限责任公司	Others	4187	42160.38	23717.25	2083.64	115.26
股份有限公司	Share-holding Corporations Limited	588	9385.34	5015.71	953.3	29.37
私营企业	Private Enterprises	13296	15204.49	14311.06	1172.22	130.49
私营独资企业	Private Sole-proprietorship Enterprises	563	230.43	263.07	25.06	2.97
私营合伙企业	Private Partnership Enterprises	92	44.39	76.1	7.11	0.64
私营有限责任公司	Private Limited Liability Corporations	12325	12522.17	12686.49	1000.84	117.01
私营股份有限公司	Private Share-holding Corporations Ltd.	316	2407.5	1285.41	139.21	9.87
其他企业	Others					
港、澳、台商投资企业	Enterprises with Investment from Hong Kong, Macao and Taiwan	243	3387.68	3641.79	133.03	15.22
合资经营企业(港或澳、台资)	Joint-venture Enterprises	223	2782.75	3408.76	106.24	13.72
合作经营企业(港或澳、台资)	Cooperative Enterprises	16	555.29	224.08	25.71	1.41
港、澳、台商独资企业	Sole-proprietorship Enterprises from Hong Kong,Macao and Taiwan	4	49.63	8.95	1.08	0.08
港、澳、台商股份有限公司	Share-holding Corporations Ltd. from Hong Kong,Macao and Taiwan					
外商投资企业	Foreign Invested Enterprises	330	2468.20	2976.43	224.69	16.05
外商投资有限责任公司	Foreign Invested Corporations Ltd.	305	2259.67	2847.79	218.09	15.43
外商投资股份有限公司	Foreign Invested Share-holding Corporations Ltd.	9	53.42	27.66	5.22	0.33
外商投资合伙企业	Foreign Invested Partnership Enterprises	8	125.62	66.20	0.57	0.16
其他外商投资企业	Other Foreign Invested Enterprises	8	29.49	34.77	0.81	0.13

14-2 规模以上工业企业主要指标

Main Indicators of Industrial Enterprises above Designated Size

单位：亿元 (100 million yuan)

年份 Year	企业单位数 (个) Number of Enterprises (unit)	资产总计 Total Assets	流动资产合计 Total Current Assets	固定资产原价 Original Value of Fixed Assets	负债合计 Total Liabilities	流动负债合计 Total Current Liabilities	所有者权益合计 Owners' Equities
1998	4980	3901.41	1697.45	2333.82	2533.99	1674.19	1367.42
1999	4538	4468.41	1753.12	2915.58	2845.91	1701.77	1622.50
2000	4394	4586.11	1845.51	2917.04	2955.77	1773.71	1630.26
2001	4572	4862.54	1980.49	3115.87	3054.15	1919.52	1808.39
2002	4908	5245.63	2130.16	3204.04	3239.96	2054.99	2005.67
2003	5448	6024.49	2476.34	3658.81	3696.53	2418.37	2326.96
2004	7413	6817.78	2874.36	4346.45	4306.81	2970.85	2510.36
2005	7959	7908.62	3309.89	4845.07	4934.81	3354.28	2966.06
2006	8995	9182.08	3890.88	5289.43	5588.76	3766.54	3589.27
2007	10709	11690.21	4971.06	6769.68	6956.94	4792.47	4733.27
2008	13725	15589.47	6458.42	8042.60	9241.79	6228.80	6347.68
2009	13267	17986.99	7447.84	10073.14	10832.20	7126.69	7077.73
2010	13706	22564.76	9321.70	13695.10	13889.83	9502.58	8571.93
2011	12085	26113.61	11248.78	15442.86	15991.15	11119.10	10049.11
2012	12719	30362.89	13344.68	17035.75	18721.46	12768.70	11471.16
2013	12998	36239.56	14841.33	20574.50	22204.87	13935.65	13491.64
2014	13267	38359.92	15900.10	23620.98	23413.64	15559.93	14703.51
2015	13525	40401.38	16015.98	24412.86	24238.90	15127.72	16075.60
2016	13819	41514.58	17075.54	28317.19	24234.79	15879.88	17167.51
2017	13904	43253.61	18472.38	27148.14	25120.16	16893.84	18033.84
2018	13915	46015.75	19818.22	28047.89	26150.93	18315.72	19864.82
2019	14599	49024.52	21243.58	30205.16	27487.81	18530.34	21422.76
2020	15280	53091.09	23297.90	33055.92	29718.74	21045.67	23266.90
2021	16453	61644.05	28393.70	36807.92	34786.30	24224.68	26805.66
2022	17523	68314.26	32134.38	39772.38	38943.57	26926.02	29370.65
2023	18557	74351.86	34100.93	43320.38	41696.84	28111.30	32653.12

14-2 续表 continued

单位：亿元 (100 million yuan)

年份 Year	营业收入 Business Revenue	营业成本 Business Cost	销售费用 Selling Expenses	管理费用 Management Expenses	财务费用 Financial Expenses	利润总额 Total Profits	平均用工人数(万人) Annual Average Employees (10 000 persons)
1998						39.70	252.79
1999						26.42	230.03
2000			108.44	176.02	83.66	71.32	208.00
2001			122.97	186.07	85.31	84.77	195.97
2002			142.26	201.11	87.73	122.60	191.62
2003			171.10	248.74	89.92	153.08	201.62
2004	4633.36	3766.65	193.15	331.01	94.23	188.51	209.77
2005	6008.12	4900.53	232.70	339.09	99.44	326.65	219.00
2006	7711.35	6296.60	273.72	403.63	125.36	448.07	233.53
2007	10611.52	8572.00	351.30	539.95	162.84	700.05	257.46
2008	14286.43	11748.93	454.09	720.06	237.69	844.56	297.54
2009	17486.41	14400.22	535.53	845.01	216.60	1123.48	311.38
2010	23062.82	19003.96	699.15	1215.96	292.99	1661.85	351.67
2011	29887.91	24721.71	823.18	1334.58	403.76	2197.84	380.48
2012	31427.16	25755.76	906.74	1385.65	506.12	2333.76	391.44
2013	35686.14	29660.84	1006.62	1498.64	569.61	2328.99	385.05
2014	38063.87	31963.29	1102.91	1494.21	696.40	2237.00	374.10
2015	38645.91	32514.83	1157.77	1592.69	690.41	2171.26	354.47
2016	41529.25	34935.31	1296.99	1674.17	616.15	2339.82	335.48
2017	41631.26	34660.03	1313.40	1718.32	565.54	2824.26	318.97
2018	41833.78	34465.16	1368.80	1736.90	558.25	3055.93	299.18
2019	44125.23	36335.94	1496.08	1551.78	540.01	3036.89	298.86
2020	46565.30	38367.50	1460.51	1540.55	516.41	3386.38	302.16
2021	54215.01	44305.55	1576.03	1764.43	519.18	4546.72	310.15
2022	50413.61	40961.84	1309.87	1647.40	455.03	4602.33	301.90
2023	50393.25	40861.66	1313.69	1623.39	421.76	4607.14	304.40

注：2017年及以前营业收入、营业成本分别为主营业务收入、主营业务成本；2018年及以前平均用工人数为全部从业人员年平均人数(以下有关各表同)。

a) Business revenue and business cost before 2017 are revenue of principal business and cost of principal business respectively; Annual average employees before 2018 is annual average employed persons. (The same as the following related tables)

14-3　按行业分规模以上工业企业主要指标(2023年)

单位：亿元

行业	Sector	企业单位数(个) Number of Enterprises (unit)
总计	**Total**	**18557**
煤炭开采和洗选业	Mining and Washing of Coal	225
石油和天然气开采业	Extraction of Petroleum and Natural Gas	24
黑色金属矿采选业	Mining and Processing of Ferrous Metal Ores	125
有色金属矿采选业	Mining and Processing of Non-Ferrous Metal Ores	112
非金属矿采选业	Mining and Processing of Non-metal Ores	461
开采专业及辅助性活动	Professional and Support Activities for Mining	7
其他采矿业	Mining of Other Ores	
农副食品加工业	Processing of Food from Agricultural Products	1412
食品制造业	Manufacture of Foods	591
酒、饮料和精制茶制造业	Manufacture of Liquor, Beverages and Refined Tea	685
烟草制品业	Manufacture of Tobacco	
纺织业	Manufacture of Textile	324
纺织服装、服饰业	Manufacture of Textile, Wearing Apparel and Accessories	172
皮革、毛皮、羽毛及其制品和制鞋业	Manufacture of Leather, Fur, Feather and Related Products and Footwear	149
木材加工和木、竹、藤、棕、草制品业	Processing of Timber, Manufacture of Wood, Bamboo, Rattan, Palm and Straw Products	298
家具制造业	Manufacture of Furniture	308
造纸和纸制品业	Manufacture of Paper and Paper Products	324
印刷和记录媒介复制业	Printing and Reproduction of Recording Media	307
文教、工美、体育和娱乐用品制造业	Manufacture of Articles for Culture, Education, Arts and Crafts, Sport and Entertainment Activities	78
石油、煤炭及其他燃料加工业	Processing of Petroleum, Coal and Other Fuel	80
化学原料和化学制品制造业	Manufacture of Raw Chemical Materials and Chemical Products	1000
医药制造业	Manufacture of Medicines	564
化学纤维制造业	Manufacture of Chemical Fibers	39
橡胶和塑料制品业	Manufacture of Rubber and Plastics Products	728
非金属矿物制品业	Manufacture of Non-metallic Mineral Products	2926
黑色金属冶炼和压延加工业	Smelting and Pressing of Ferrous Metals	200
有色金属冶炼和压延加工业	Smelting and Pressing of Non-ferrous Metals	356
金属制品业	Manufacture of Metal Products	1091
通用设备制造业	Manufacture of General Purpose Machinery	973
专用设备制造业	Manufacture of Special Purpose Machinery	724
汽车制造业	Manufacture of Automobiles	669
铁路、船舶、航空航天和其他运输设备制造业	Manufacture of Railway, Ship, Aerospace and Other Transport Equipment	268
电气机械和器材制造业	Manufacture of Electrical Machinery and Apparatus	846
计算机、通信和其他电子设备制造业	Manufacture of Computers, Communication and Other Electronic Equipment	956
仪器仪表制造业	Manufacture of Measuring Instruments and Machinery	164
其他制造业	Other Manufactures	30
废弃资源综合利用业	Utilization of Waste Resources	151
金属制品、机械和设备修理业	Repair Service of Metal Products, Machinery and Equipment	26
电力、热力生产和供应业	Production and Supply of Electric Power and Heat Power	484
燃气生产和供应业	Production and Supply of Gas	361
水的生产和供应业	Production and Supply of Water	316

注：根据《中华人民共和国统计法》规定，可推断单户企业的相关统计数据不予公布(以下有关各表同)。

Main Indicators of Industrial Enterprises above Designated Size by Industrial Sector(2023)

(100 million yuan)

资产总计 Total Assets	流动资产合计 Total Current Assets	固定资产原价 Original Value of Fixed Assets	负债合计 Total Liabilities	流动负债合计 Total Current Liabilities	所有者权益 Owners' Equities
74351.86	**34100.93**	**43320.38**	**41696.84**	**28111.30**	**32653.12**
588.49	241.08	376.27	435.66	331.65	152.83
2836.76	577.82	3421.24	1156.21	537.27	1680.55
525.55	185.61	276.92	270.39	228.67	255.17
544.52	207.81	204.49	276.74	217.59	267.78
1454.48	664.06	273.77	706.41	395.63	748.06
424.70	169.70	562.99	151.83	127.71	272.87
1342.78	779.42	558.66	754.84	577.67	588.61
893.26	471.85	442.59	390.31	319.85	502.96
6018.89	3389.02	1366.42	2699.25	2328.17	3319.64
484.59	210.75	263.98	286.08	193.01	198.51
105.17	61.35	50.59	48.22	38.70	56.95
137.62	62.76	43.15	74.68	56.15	62.94
180.64	86.24	108.33	106.75	69.57	73.88
291.65	136.20	159.56	161.51	136.34	130.14
448.63	207.97	319.19	252.98	205.35	195.65
323.83	185.90	184.28	135.59	104.89	188.24
74.40	61.50	18.76	52.13	48.37	22.27
718.40	296.71	585.22	354.63	269.58	363.77
4200.60	2096.41	2008.34	1941.55	1371.36	2259.05
2269.65	1277.73	697.24	854.50	671.90	1415.15
498.53	201.68	202.14	370.76	229.93	127.77
696.66	369.51	330.85	322.09	247.68	374.57
6116.53	3195.42	2850.70	3252.13	2369.13	2864.40
2495.08	852.66	2385.12	1507.34	1165.27	987.74
1065.14	597.48	445.90	611.34	467.02	453.85
1425.62	820.72	681.84	880.02	690.51	545.51
2050.55	1444.94	651.84	1230.19	1046.10	820.36
1791.86	1192.72	607.95	962.75	786.91	829.10
2336.07	1510.94	1102.57	1531.08	1166.37	804.99
2575.44	2019.97	573.25	1798.29	1591.99	777.15
3766.77	2006.52	1449.18	2315.36	1668.12	1451.40
8394.15	5263.82	3814.90	4872.89	4009.44	3521.27
333.27	235.60	83.38	160.56	141.30	172.71
282.85	124.06	238.26	194.50	73.21	88.36
217.10	134.56	82.21	138.87	117.23	78.23
195.12	120.91	40.76	92.06	67.48	103.06
11878.71	1077.72	14207.25	7971.29	2808.94	3904.91
936.14	363.08	467.13	469.11	359.72	467.03
3140.15	980.72	1067.17	1775.95	746.56	1364.20

a) According to the provisions of the statistics law, the relevant statistical data which can infer a single enterprise will not be published (The same as the following related tables).

14−3 续表

单位：亿元

行业	Sector	营业收入 Business Revenue
总计	**Total**	**50393.25**
煤炭开采和洗选业	Mining and Washing of Coal	252.40
石油和天然气开采业	Extraction of Petroleum and Natural Gas	1113.12
黑色金属矿采选业	Mining and Processing of Ferrous Metal Ores	340.26
有色金属矿采选业	Mining and Processing of Non-Ferrous Metal Ores	292.67
非金属矿采选业	Mining and Processing of Non-metal Ores	345.19
开采专业及辅助性活动	Professional and Support Activities for Mining	384.90
其他采矿业	Mining of Other Ores	
农副食品加工业	Processing of Food from Agricultural Products	1901.14
食品制造业	Manufacture of Foods	898.43
酒、饮料和精制茶制造业	Manufacture of Liquor, Beverages and Refined Tea	3432.97
烟草制品业	Manufacture of Tobacco	
纺织业	Manufacture of Textile	398.05
纺织服装、服饰业	Manufacture of Textile, Wearing Apparel and Accessories	116.68
皮革、毛皮、羽毛及其制品和制鞋业	Manufacture of Leather, Fur, Feather and Related Products and Footwear	115.47
木材加工和木、竹、藤、棕、草制品业	Processing of Timber, Manufacture of Wood, Bamboo, Rattan, Palm and Straw Products	152.18
家具制造业	Manufacture of Furniture	286.60
造纸和纸制品业	Manufacture of Paper and Paper Products	455.12
印刷和记录媒介复制业	Printing and Reproduction of Recording Media	281.74
文教、工美、体育和娱乐用品制造业	Manufacture of Articles for Culture, Education, Arts and Crafts, Sport and Entertainment Activities	94.87
石油、煤炭及其他燃料加工业	Processing of Petroleum, Coal and Other Fuel	975.66
化学原料和化学制品制造业	Manufacture of Raw Chemical Materials and Chemical Products	3329.10
医药制造业	Manufacture of Medicines	1192.61
化学纤维制造业	Manufacture of Chemical Fibers	467.78
橡胶和塑料制品业	Manufacture of Rubber and Plastics Products	705.60
非金属矿物制品业	Manufacture of Non-metallic Mineral Products	3857.04
黑色金属冶炼和压延加工业	Smelting and Pressing of Ferrous Metals	2695.54
有色金属冶炼和压延加工业	Smelting and Pressing of Non-ferrous Metals	1585.75
金属制品业	Manufacture of Metal Products	1447.04
通用设备制造业	Manufacture of General Purpose Machinery	1347.16
专用设备制造业	Manufacture of Special Purpose Machinery	1059.18
汽车制造业	Manufacture of Automobiles	2316.47
铁路、船舶、航空航天和其他运输设备制造业	Manufacture of Railway, Ship, Aerospace and Other Transport Equipment	1392.33
电气机械和器材制造业	Manufacture of Electrical Machinery and Apparatus	3112.14
计算机、通信和其他电子设备制造业	Manufacture of Computers, Communication and Other Electronic Equipment	8537.38
仪器仪表制造业	Manufacture of Measuring Instruments and Machinery	271.59
其他制造业	Other Manufactures	102.92
废弃资源综合利用业	Utilization of Waste Resources	273.06
金属制品、机械和设备修理业	Repair Service of Metal Products, Machinery and Equipment	112.64
电力、热力生产和供应业	Production and Supply of Electric Power and Heat Power	3251.34
燃气生产和供应业	Production and Supply of Gas	715.09
水的生产和供应业	Production and Supply of Water	334.60

continued

(100 million yuan)

营业成本 Business Cost	销售费用 Selling Expenses	管理费用 Management Expenses	财务费用 Financial Expenses	利润总额 Total Profits	平均用工人数 (万人) Annual Average Employees (10 000 persons)
40861.66	**1313.69**	**1623.39**	**421.76**	**4607.14**	**304.40**
194.82	5.74	18.97	2.47	17.14	5.74
711.73	1.42	95.94	12.19	185.73	3.10
254.70	8.33	14.35	2.09	46.15	1.49
183.12	1.32	15.46	2.27	78.92	1.63
248.84	14.06	20.15	9.96	39.92	2.81
356.87	0.08	4.94	-0.84	8.22	2.06
1672.18	48.99	46.63	10.71	103.98	11.46
687.36	64.09	37.77	3.86	94.10	9.65
1868.76	274.44	133.75	-7.18	847.43	16.66
346.59	6.15	11.27	5.40	23.57	4.71
92.45	4.84	7.84	0.86	8.83	2.28
97.26	2.08	6.55	1.67	7.35	3.11
130.58	3.78	6.50	1.59	8.99	1.90
226.17	14.51	21.22	1.68	17.81	6.09
382.56	13.06	15.36	4.00	32.97	4.21
227.12	7.60	17.10	0.98	23.55	3.68
81.76	5.59	2.52	0.32	3.92	0.64
831.72	6.16	16.95	0.03	42.41	1.50
2687.36	55.94	109.30	14.00	598.74	16.86
663.11	210.18	66.79	9.67	192.63	12.10
444.82	4.95	6.66	10.05	1.69	1.57
578.30	24.73	28.23	4.66	53.33	7.18
3074.05	102.85	143.25	29.94	432.66	28.34
2402.70	14.65	37.10	18.10	99.28	8.56
1428.23	8.61	24.56	6.79	106.07	5.58
1228.78	31.07	61.14	12.46	67.69	13.05
1077.33	36.91	67.58	6.07	108.25	11.78
838.75	39.76	59.55	5.88	70.81	9.93
1984.72	20.01	63.40	9.40	169.90	12.54
1211.89	18.42	57.04	-10.35	75.87	7.70
2668.10	100.21	90.47	7.66	159.75	17.25
7802.45	108.21	150.18	22.04	275.22	43.35
200.30	11.92	13.30	0.59	29.80	2.12
81.03	0.66	8.79	0.60	8.95	0.90
239.99	2.48	6.99	1.06	20.05	1.21
98.36	1.87	4.45	0.56	5.84	0.59
2596.98	2.99	54.98	202.09	365.49	14.14
585.69	21.67	31.38	2.83	75.55	2.97
228.99	7.44	27.02	17.96	56.80	3.48

14−4 各市(州)规模以上工业企业资产总计
Total Assets of Industrial Enterprises above Designated Size by Region

单位：亿元 (100 million yuan)

市(州)	Region	2013	2014	2015	2016	2017	2018	2019	2020	2021	2022	2023
全省	**Sichuan**	**36239.56**	**38359.92**	**40401.38**	**41514.58**	**43253.61**	**46015.75**	**49024.52**	**53091.09**	**61644.05**	**68314.26**	**74351.86**
成都市	Chengdu	12606.49	10627.48	10952.40	11382.46	12110.16	13667.82	18289.55	19749.56	22318.68	24602.24	24961.70
自贡市	Zigong	1067.68	1099.62	1040.01	1051.47	975.54	925.92	979.10	1033.96	1106.18	1040.03	1199.96
攀枝花市	Panzhihua	2099.09	2129.96	2273.42	2200.59	2331.22	2254.88	2621.66	2752.13	2428.81	2701.91	2919.10
泸州市	Luzhou	1117.77	1056.03	1059.23	1130.09	1222.20	1371.83	1705.95	2035.81	2490.27	2896.69	3405.23
德阳市	Deyang	2356.22	2424.44	2330.88	2534.85	2527.93	2743.65	2671.15	2855.69	3193.20	3790.25	4145.23
绵阳市	Mianyang	2163.59	2313.05	2364.58	2540.05	2738.11	2981.22	3557.30	3906.80	4408.59	4848.70	5521.02
广元市	Guangyuan	496.47	604.53	692.97	696.75	752.25	834.79	873.59	942.79	965.33	968.43	996.58
遂宁市	Suining	585.87	697.87	724.94	821.21	936.07	983.49	874.01	1101.34	1249.39	1513.29	1858.36
内江市	Neijiang	974.72	933.72	911.94	889.86	754.99	809.90	857.28	902.20	1066.93	1143.34	1669.69
乐山市	Leshan	1706.68	1785.78	1871.47	1999.56	2003.05	2043.26	2000.77	2392.37	2732.68	3321.63	3599.18
南充市	Nanchong	1159.52	1225.44	1337.25	1502.81	1392.33	1470.59	1624.74	1716.92	1928.63	1843.85	1907.76
眉山市	Meishan	818.45	828.49	869.67	908.61	896.13	884.35	1077.32	1279.84	1590.18	2085.14	2590.71
宜宾市	Yibin	2759.05	2149.60	2678.36	2531.87	2797.60	3154.26	3655.61	3839.31	5308.07	6027.82	7463.36
广安市	Guangan	512.28	614.99	644.00	669.21	678.88	750.47	807.90	884.51	968.85	917.35	940.18
达州市	Dazhou	960.79	925.43	1445.50	1031.77	1038.74	1253.36	1275.37	1343.49	1499.49	1616.31	1588.68
雅安市	Yaan	948.93	952.92	1179.27	1207.52	1264.89	1246.73	1271.80	1311.92	1402.67	1605.38	1773.70
巴中市	Bazhong	120.81	173.64	201.35	219.96	239.51	280.13	265.12	283.32	272.35	224.24	284.59
资阳市	Ziyang	817.91	887.33	598.63	501.57	511.65	439.97	363.01	388.16	411.39	432.99	471.61
阿坝藏族羌族自治州	Aba	503.39	534.05	568.78	592.66	606.66	583.51	608.67	629.03	650.58	681.00	722.22
甘孜藏族自治州	Ganzi	354.88	372.28	764.21	826.89	1081.35	1113.35	1121.51	1155.01	1627.46	1809.90	1991.17
凉山彝族自治州	Liangshan	2108.97	2376.50	2924.62	2464.44	2517.03	2506.49	2523.10	2586.93	4024.34	4243.75	4341.85

14-5 各市(州)规模以上工业企业营业收入

Business Revenue of Industrial Enterprises above Designated Size by Region

单位：亿元 (100 million yuan)

市(州)	Region	2013	2014	2015	2016	2017	2018	2019	2020	2021	2022	2023
全省	**Sichuan**	**35686.14**	**38063.87**	**38645.91**	**41529.25**	**41631.26**	**41833.78**	**44125.23**	**46565.30**	**54215.01**	**50413.61**	**50393.25**
成都市	Chengdu	10783.98	10234.61	10726.37	11864.26	12488.88	11468.00	13995.13	14966.49	17419.24	19042.38	19193.73
自贡市	Zigong	1513.11	1605.30	1664.04	1735.65	1521.51	1326.01	1138.21	1216.14	1191.52	522.72	603.66
攀枝花市	Panzhihua	1627.64	1581.22	1495.90	1554.08	1737.10	1758.57	1871.12	1953.47	2293.25	2019.00	2078.57
泸州市	Luzhou	1404.23	1365.02	1447.72	1604.04	1610.82	1788.32	2056.13	2207.15	2618.43	2252.19	1892.38
德阳市	Deyang	2406.47	2658.70	2826.05	3267.50	3321.28	3543.72	3392.71	3336.03	4066.59	3847.25	4129.31
绵阳市	Mianyang	1979.56	2115.45	2307.29	2450.81	2737.43	2731.11	3015.57	3230.57	3757.31	3905.68	4116.39
广元市	Guangyuan	618.27	688.20	732.28	815.11	885.28	1003.78	1144.09	1250.14	1546.39	698.19	735.32
遂宁市	Suining	1176.50	1297.66	1179.87	1305.63	1487.89	1361.68	1254.17	1297.20	1483.21	1669.24	1601.31
内江市	Neijiang	1652.69	1632.91	1618.27	1733.46	1050.46	1014.60	1145.31	1250.62	1503.02	1119.23	1195.77
乐山市	Leshan	1512.64	1576.94	1525.24	1702.21	1355.22	1492.49	1551.13	1566.37	2043.82	2278.68	2060.08
南充市	Nanchong	1834.82	1940.42	2181.35	2460.74	2320.04	2659.38	2942.87	2892.87	3272.56	1243.34	1130.30
眉山市	Meishan	1010.21	1183.61	1318.39	1480.72	1210.35	1389.71	1537.57	1682.79	2025.26	1801.68	1719.75
宜宾市	Yibin	1860.20	1927.34	2078.77	2253.25	2562.54	2692.85	3108.90	3555.43	4267.35	4555.38	4915.65
广安市	Guangan	1136.35	1244.59	1383.33	1561.45	1566.76	1605.99	1758.57	1821.34	1727.84	780.02	777.12
达州市	Dazhou	1077.39	1129.35	1365.55	945.07	1079.05	1271.29	1442.79	1545.81	1965.82	1743.83	1219.89
雅安市	Yaan	378.16	409.16	417.10	462.93	481.82	536.12	597.99	596.63	769.19	869.81	858.47
巴中市	Bazhong	363.08	452.11	512.12	568.32	587.79	585.09	591.98	604.45	356.87	120.05	139.20
资阳市	Ziyang	1911.51	1980.42	1169.82	997.99	840.78	562.96	371.28	362.83	404.46	242.40	252.56
阿坝藏族羌族自治州	Aba	138.87	169.20	186.26	201.42	172.96	177.08	182.96	181.75	231.64	271.03	266.69
甘孜藏族自治州	Ganzi	68.80	55.79	54.63	59.88	87.26	104.25	118.30	127.64	135.29	167.40	186.92
凉山彝族自治州	Liangshan	1231.64	1222.13	1074.56	1062.30	866.93	891.52	908.46	919.60	1135.97	1264.09	1320.17

14–6 各市(州)规模以上工业企业利润总额

Total Profits of Industrial Enterprises above Designated Size by Region

单位：亿元 (100 million yuan)

市(州)	Region	2013	2014	2015	2016	2017	2018	2019	2020	2021	2022	2023
全省	**Sichuan**	**2328.99**	**2237.00**	**2171.26**	**2339.82**	**2824.26**	**3055.93**	**3036.89**	**3386.38**	**4546.72**	**4602.33**	**4607.14**
成都市	Chengdu	672.15	718.76	510.98	845.01	994.19	675.83	761.62	950.74	1087.50	1205.01	1093.68
自贡市	Zigong	77.93	75.61	76.08	71.50	76.21	65.50	61.00	72.06	74.78	32.67	47.78
攀枝花市	Panzhihua	60.29	45.57	19.44	-111.60	89.04	151.03	131.45	145.61	225.75	197.21	206.78
泸州市	Luzhou	122.36	87.65	103.42	119.93	118.17	171.72	222.88	245.26	377.17	393.17	405.26
德阳市	Deyang	152.77	84.67	180.57	235.64	250.10	304.40	204.88	196.01	271.55	338.85	387.61
绵阳市	Mianyang	99.15	102.60	101.00	125.16	141.94	120.67	139.66	151.81	178.58	168.52	234.65
广元市	Guangyuan	31.71	31.81	35.67	43.00	59.23	82.13	87.94	95.14	133.57	52.32	64.63
遂宁市	Suining	86.60	76.99	69.01	78.72	115.81	138.31	99.64	108.83	136.77	228.93	204.87
内江市	Neijiang	95.61	75.22	71.98	67.01	33.64	63.75	49.64	47.14	112.50	71.66	94.37
乐山市	Leshan	78.79	44.70	63.59	81.11	84.09	174.36	136.00	115.32	319.88	520.96	589.38
南充市	Nanchong	123.22	133.49	156.58	176.71	165.75	195.70	221.28	209.68	249.53	86.76	82.41
眉山市	Meishan	67.99	70.81	80.76	92.73	73.46	73.53	78.09	90.32	120.54	118.31	104.04
宜宾市	Yibin	221.60	177.25	207.92	198.08	247.48	372.78	434.47	497.01	580.36	646.73	622.74
广安市	Guangan	60.83	54.64	52.24	65.56	67.11	70.91	93.87	93.51	141.50	71.11	69.96
达州市	Dazhou	89.47	95.78	120.99	13.99	51.10	105.70	99.74	132.13	204.92	149.21	93.20
雅安市	Yaan	31.03	30.67	32.24	30.36	29.63	32.84	41.84	47.17	64.18	99.61	56.69
巴中市	Bazhong	9.58	13.84	16.95	20.19	22.53	31.54	25.82	29.11	18.16	11.98	6.47
资阳市	Ziyang	161.28	141.95	83.47	56.85	45.70	29.94	17.87	13.62	10.04	-2.66	6.01
阿坝藏族羌族自治州	Aba	-0.28	7.55	7.88	9.66	6.54	10.10	10.67	14.47	31.36	18.43	17.96
甘孜藏族自治州	Ganzi	12.95	6.74	6.60	2.16	7.47	4.22	13.45	18.51	10.87	8.41	13.82
凉山彝族自治州	Liangshan	73.95	96.86	97.39	77.46	94.64	113.85	105.09	112.94	197.22	185.14	204.84

14-7 各市(州)规模以上工业企业主要指标(2023年)
Main Indicators of Industrial Enterprises above Designated Size by Region(2023)

单位：亿元 (100 million yuan)

市(州)	Region	企业单位数(个) Number of Enterprises (unit)	资产总计 Total Assets	流动资产合计 Total Current Assets	应收账款 Accounts Receivables	存货 Inventory	固定资产原价 Original Value of Fixed Assets
全省	**Sichuan**	**18557**	**74351.86**	**34100.93**	**8828.77**	**6977.34**	**43320.38**
成都市	Chengdu	4599	24961.70	13481.73	4149.59	2780.22	14228.27
自贡市	Zigong	587	1199.96	667.29	180.00	116.75	411.23
攀枝花市	Panzhihua	510	2919.10	954.82	186.32	121.63	1818.79
泸州市	Luzhou	949	3405.23	1663.83	230.49	535.71	1503.80
德阳市	Deyang	1524	4145.23	2741.72	586.92	574.17	1477.95
绵阳市	Mianyang	1407	5521.02	2710.54	779.52	586.61	2830.51
广元市	Guangyuan	584	996.58	318.97	105.63	48.79	757.06
遂宁市	Suining	642	1858.36	960.29	156.48	234.75	793.93
内江市	Neijiang	643	1669.69	602.63	143.33	91.49	1834.13
乐山市	Leshan	734	3599.18	1336.47	226.97	316.38	2247.47
南充市	Nanchong	972	1907.76	789.03	184.97	126.59	1010.50
眉山市	Meishan	941	2590.71	1167.59	320.75	263.16	1379.49
宜宾市	Yibin	1007	7463.36	3683.31	591.17	642.20	2406.33
广安市	Guangan	631	940.18	399.11	122.88	71.64	596.87
达州市	Dazhou	1053	1588.68	723.21	381.33	66.59	1389.84
雅安市	Yaan	423	1773.70	577.71	98.21	193.32	1406.23
巴中市	Bazhong	371	284.59	117.04	36.36	20.55	143.85
资阳市	Ziyang	341	471.61	241.03	65.68	55.83	206.84
阿坝藏族羌族自治州	Aba	154	722.22	177.76	56.05	25.72	650.59
甘孜藏族自治州	Ganzi	85	1991.17	135.08	47.19	5.11	2090.40
凉山彝族自治州	Liangshan	400	4341.85	651.77	178.92	100.12	4136.31

14-7 续表1 continued

单位：亿元 (100 million yuan)

市(州)	Region	负债合计 Total Liabilities	流动负债合计 Total Current Liabilities	所有者权益合计 Owners' Equities	营业收入 Business Revenue	营业成本 Business Cost
全省	**Sichuan**	**41696.84**	**28111.30**	**32653.12**	**50393.25**	**40861.66**
成都市	Chengdu	13529.87	10869.62	11432.37	19193.73	16139.98
自贡市	Zigong	675.88	524.02	524.08	603.66	485.15
攀枝花市	Panzhihua	1797.00	1290.90	1122.10	2078.57	1652.30
泸州市	Luzhou	1717.41	1052.25	1687.82	1892.38	1143.14
德阳市	Deyang	2396.67	1920.20	1748.56	4129.31	3243.42
绵阳市	Mianyang	3332.56	2264.15	2188.46	4116.39	3506.10
广元市	Guangyuan	515.28	247.21	481.30	735.32	608.21
遂宁市	Suining	931.74	573.79	926.61	1601.31	1264.98
内江市	Neijiang	1059.31	679.63	610.38	1195.77	1023.86
乐山市	Leshan	1586.03	938.19	2013.15	2060.08	1540.78
南充市	Nanchong	996.25	569.34	909.00	1130.30	937.55
眉山市	Meishan	1520.15	966.55	1070.56	1719.75	1473.50
宜宾市	Yibin	4065.55	3236.48	3397.81	4915.65	3837.06
广安市	Guangan	452.91	319.53	487.26	777.12	644.26
达州市	Dazhou	722.29	353.07	866.39	1219.89	998.70
雅安市	Yaan	1096.70	520.19	677.05	858.47	739.94
巴中市	Bazhong	164.50	97.84	120.09	139.20	116.39
资阳市	Ziyang	294.57	233.01	177.06	252.56	209.36
阿坝藏族羌族自治州	Aba	473.80	225.63	248.42	266.69	214.83
甘孜藏族自治州	Ganzi	1537.93	313.68	447.11	186.92	122.17
凉山彝族自治州	Liangshan	2830.44	916.00	1517.55	1320.17	959.99

14-7 续表2 continued

单位：亿元 (100 million yuan)

市(州)	Region	销售费用 Selling Expenses	管理费用 Management Expenses	财务费用 Financial Expenses	利润总额 Total Profits	平均用工人数(万人) Annual Average Employees (10 000 persons)
全省	**Sichuan**	**1313.69**	**1623.39**	**421.76**	**4607.14**	**304.40**
成都市	Chengdu	489.64	624.19	75.31	1093.68	108.81
自贡市	Zigong	20.15	32.81	6.49	47.78	5.54
攀枝花市	Panzhihua	18.99	60.73	20.03	206.78	10.13
泸州市	Luzhou	110.31	89.98	17.93	405.26	14.28
德阳市	Deyang	150.94	157.02	13.96	387.61	24.83
绵阳市	Mianyang	115.75	119.01	27.49	234.65	28.60
广元市	Guangyuan	13.46	23.54	11.10	64.63	4.15
遂宁市	Suining	31.48	39.23	11.39	204.87	10.15
内江市	Neijiang	22.00	29.37	7.97	94.37	8.83
乐山市	Leshan	30.73	69.01	24.05	589.38	12.25
南充市	Nanchong	30.95	44.04	15.95	82.41	9.68
眉山市	Meishan	46.05	58.13	13.14	104.04	14.67
宜宾市	Yibin	152.01	111.44	8.94	622.74	20.38
广安市	Guangan	14.86	30.88	6.47	69.96	6.87
达州市	Dazhou	21.74	36.19	7.88	93.20	8.66
雅安市	Yaan	12.13	21.68	18.80	56.69	4.36
巴中市	Bazhong	4.98	8.09	2.36	6.47	1.77
资阳市	Ziyang	7.34	16.46	3.97	6.01	3.15
阿坝藏族羌族自治州	Aba	4.66	10.37	11.59	17.96	1.44
甘孜藏族自治州	Ganzi	0.70	5.72	40.38	13.82	0.89
凉山彝族自治州	Liangshan	14.79	35.50	76.54	204.84	4.97

注：2017年及以前营业收入、营业成本分别为主营业务收入、主营业务成本(以下有关各表同)。
a) Business revenue and business cost before 2017 are revenue of principal business and cost of principal business respectively(The same as the following related tables).

14-8 国有控股工业企业主要指标
Main Indicators of State-holding Industrial Enterprises

单位：亿元 (100 million yuan)

年份 Year	企业单位数 (个) Number of Enterprises (unit)	资产总计 Total Assets	流动资产合计 Total Current Assets	固定资产原价 Original Value of Fixed Assets	负债合计 Total Liabilities	流动负债合计 Total Current Liabilities	所有者权益合计 Owners' Equities
1998	2372	3080.34	1314.34	1923.21	1994.47	1252.47	1085.87
1999	2065	3548.38	1328.96	2442.68	2258.93	1244.29	1289.45
2000	1699	3522.23	1347.30	2383.24	2299.29	1260.77	1222.86
2001	1485	3616.84	1392.49	2506.88	2315.25	1348.07	1301.58
2002	1324	3709.04	1409.16	2442.48	2347.13	1358.96	1361.91
2003	1065	3846.39	1455.26	2627.61	2450.16	1470.03	1396.23
2004	1057	3801.84	1405.99	2896.33	2529.36	1566.75	1271.88
2005	928	4473.03	1683.30	3260.59	2877.77	1795.29	1587.51
2006	933	5109.55	1943.60	3428.41	3232.76	1952.59	1872.75
2007	878	6325.71	2448.14	4366.82	4019.44	2453.22	2306.27
2008	1006	8515.93	3098.43	4606.00	5401.06	3214.03	3114.87
2009	971	9499.46	3572.94	5401.57	6137.14	3674.12	3347.13
2010	921	11429.22	4134.86	6655.41	7641.93	4772.31	3777.87
2011	851	13189.13	4918.31	7338.88	8752.85	5711.90	4414.98
2012	888	14797.73	5412.38	8398.72	9864.31	5976.14	4906.05
2013	914	17343.43	5635.05	9389.16	11568.57	6094.28	5486.79
2014	929	19021.19	6100.45	12137.96	12496.96	7169.81	6520.19
2015	978	20092.37	5901.10	13221.06	13318.05	6951.52	6762.66
2016	977	20086.48	6469.21	15716.10	13128.84	7461.16	6958.39
2017	970	20947.40	6869.82	15983.97	13195.98	7615.47	7738.08
2018	1004	22278.06	7504.19	15718.23	13336.17	7724.40	8941.89
2019	1109	24172.99	8050.19	17953.23	13875.07	7825.25	10296.89
2020	1239	25529.03	8592.40	19066.54	14477.10	8729.91	11027.28
2021	1422	31402.73	11558.18	22403.74	18411.72	11082.30	12939.23
2022	1555	34958.92	13279.20	24839.34	20732.31	12670.51	14226.61
2023	1674	38648.74	14667.32	26232.40	22716.49	13551.44	15929.74

14-8 续表 continued

单位：亿元 (100 million yuan)

年份 Year	营业收入 Business Revenue	营业成本 Business Cost	销售费用 Selling Expenses	管理费用 Management Expenses	财务费用 Financial Expenses	利润总额 Total Profits	平均用工人数（万人） Annual Average Employees (10 000 persons)
1998						23.27	179.70
1999						6.76	159.84
2000			59.06	127.13	59.91	37.79	132.09
2001			63.59	127.69	62.90	45.04	117.57
2002			66.96	130.07	62.50	63.32	101.76
2003			70.76	149.22	58.32	67.58	93.67
2004	1925.02	1507.99	56.97	158.71	49.84	97.70	79.11
2005	2506.44	1969.58	87.39	176.68	47.14	166.71	80.00
2006	3135.60	2471.32	100.48	201.13	66.56	216.68	82.44
2007	3926.09	3096.90	115.92	252.67	83.51	305.85	83.86
2008	4765.38	3874.58	130.93	317.73	117.20	198.13	87.08
2009	5296.72	4221.47	160.93	332.65	94.77	295.09	88.01
2010	6424.93	5132.85	180.37	385.65	116.79	478.18	90.16
2011	7895.50	6308.18	210.08	436.12	162.69	538.74	93.40
2012	8689.36	6962.15	227.66	470.30	210.67	589.29	97.05
2013	9545.34	7714.20	250.77	535.89	245.77	506.85	98.20
2014	9989.33	8099.70	257.91	495.14	339.84	484.94	97.64
2015	9746.25	7882.09	234.73	475.71	342.38	565.95	89.41
2016	9757.21	7872.16	276.22	494.39	294.98	460.69	81.97
2017	10299.10	8263.04	282.30	515.03	267.65	713.81	76.11
2018	11264.73	8933.78	297.10	559.24	264.73	880.23	73.01
2019	12039.49	9461.49	344.08	458.08	253.27	960.43	71.42
2020	12728.92	9991.57	311.25	456.92	238.89	1143.21	70.92
2021	15502.59	12077.79	351.00	534.54	258.58	1498.59	74.06
2022	17702.19	14004.84	332.56	595.03	272.64	1561.79	75.51
2023	18163.37	14272.01	336.99	586.95	241.77	1741.55	75.35

14-9 按行业分国有控股工业企业主要指标(2023年)

单位：亿元

行业	Sector	企业单位数(个) Number of Enterprises (unit)
总计	**Total**	**1674**
煤炭开采和洗选业	Mining and Washing of Coal	15
石油和天然气开采业	Extraction of Petroleum and Natural Gas	18
黑色金属矿采选业	Mining and Processing of Ferrous Metal Ores	11
有色金属矿采选业	Mining and Processing of Non-Ferrous Metal Ores	14
非金属矿采选业	Mining and Processing of Non-metal Ores	84
开采专业及辅助性活动	Professional and Support Activities for Mining	
其他采矿业	Mining of Other Ores	
农副食品加工业	Processing of Food from Agricultural Products	39
食品制造业	Manufacture of Foods	13
酒、饮料和精制茶制造业	Manufacture of Liquor, Beverages and Refined Tea	29
烟草制品业	Manufacture of Tobacco	
纺织业	Manufacture of Textile	18
纺织服装、服饰业	Manufacture of Textile, Wearing Apparel and Accessories	10
皮革、毛皮、羽毛及其制品和制鞋业	Manufacture of Leather, Fur, Feather and Related Products and Footwear	
木材加工和木、竹、藤、棕、草制品业	Processing of Timber, Manufacture of Wood, Bamboo, Rattan, Palm and Straw Products	6
家具制造业	Manufacture of Furniture	
造纸和纸制品业	Manufacture of Paper and Paper Products	6
印刷和记录媒介复制业	Printing and Reproduction of Recording Media	11
文教、工美、体育和娱乐用品制造业	Manufacture of Articles for Culture, Education, Arts and Crafts, Sport and Entertainment Activities	
石油、煤炭及其他燃料加工业	Processing of Petroleum, Coal and Other Fuel	6
化学原料和化学制品制造业	Manufacture of Raw Chemical Materials and Chemical Products	74
医药制造业	Manufacture of Medicines	37
化学纤维制造业	Manufacture of Chemical Fibers	8
橡胶和塑料制品业	Manufacture of Rubber and Plastics Products	11
非金属矿物制品业	Manufacture of Non-metallic Mineral Products	218
黑色金属冶炼和压延加工业	Smelting and Pressing of Ferrous Metals	10
有色金属冶炼和压延加工业	Smelting and Pressing of Non-ferrous Metals	28
金属制品业	Manufacture of Metal Products	35
通用设备制造业	Manufacture of General Purpose Machinery	39
专用设备制造业	Manufacture of Special Purpose Machinery	39
汽车制造业	Manufacture of Automobiles	49
铁路、船舶、航空航天和其他运输设备制造业	Manufacture of Railway, Ship, Aerospace and Other Transport Equipment	43
电气机械和器材制造业	Manufacture of Electrical Machinery and Apparatus	46
计算机、通信和其他电子设备制造业	Manufacture of Computers, Communication and Other Electronic Equipment	105
仪器仪表制造业	Manufacture of Measuring Instruments and Machinery	15
其他制造业	Other Manufactures	5
废弃资源综合利用业	Utilization of Waste Resources	9
金属制品、机械和设备修理业	Repair Service of Metal Products, Machinery and Equipment	7
电力、热力生产和供应业	Production and Supply of Electric Power and Heat Power	302
燃气生产和供应业	Production and Supply of Gas	112
水的生产和供应业	Production and Supply of Water	195

Main Indicators of State-holding Industrial Enterprises by Industrial Sector(2023)

(100 million yuan)

资产总计 Total Assets	流动资产合计 Total Current Assets	固定资产原价 Original Value of Fixed Assets	负债合计 Total Liabilities	流动负债合计 Total Current Liabilities	所有者权益 Owners' Equities
38648.74	**14667.32**	**26232.40**	**22716.49**	**13551.44**	**15929.74**
340.29	138.97	225.82	270.31	217.51	69.98
2831.31	575.81	3417.72	1152.14	533.92	1679.16
214.30	34.99	128.86	105.73	90.91	108.57
187.94	59.51	78.27	73.82	53.53	114.12
1083.54	505.91	74.64	489.03	235.68	594.51
91.04	54.96	19.31	53.01	26.04	38.03
46.33	22.36	24.68	32.46	21.76	13.87
3845.82	2119.47	490.44	1654.84	1464.95	2190.98
91.22	34.42	34.78	27.16	16.93	64.07
25.99	17.79	13.02	12.83	11.17	13.15
14.49	4.46	7.79	8.40	3.47	6.09
43.18	20.80	31.16	33.69	28.38	9.48
67.40	45.43	48.75	17.61	14.34	49.80
500.16	182.82	440.69	200.16	145.97	300.00
1278.75	569.96	696.21	647.84	437.94	630.92
259.23	101.58	89.60	70.72	49.51	188.52
407.57	166.48	136.67	304.49	182.63	103.08
37.55	19.73	29.96	18.31	13.10	19.24
1784.15	1018.77	597.45	1127.96	733.71	656.19
1435.96	357.51	974.61	831.61	636.15	604.35
274.71	118.52	162.08	155.15	93.35	119.56
238.62	139.73	113.32	155.31	112.01	83.31
777.36	623.26	135.71	533.60	486.01	243.76
569.50	403.01	158.24	342.83	284.18	226.67
898.80	596.20	459.60	654.94	468.76	243.86
2082.66	1707.45	375.32	1556.93	1422.31	525.73
894.90	614.60	154.67	610.36	501.45	284.54
3267.39	1829.29	1666.98	2002.89	1456.63	1264.50
122.48	95.49	17.07	66.00	59.48	56.48
270.50	116.90	232.59	188.12	67.40	82.38
24.09	15.48	7.34	14.60	11.11	9.48
117.36	92.44	28.97	66.77	57.32	50.59
10978.82	876.69	13325.05	7406.07	2620.69	3570.24
372.48	171.21	198.22	188.37	144.25	184.11
2438.17	808.27	956.74	1344.17	575.71	1094.00

14−9 续表

单位：亿元

行业	Sector	营业收入 Business Revenue
总计	**Total**	**18163.37**
煤炭开采和洗选业	Mining and Washing of Coal	108.76
石油和天然气开采业	Extraction of Petroleum and Natural Gas	1110.19
黑色金属矿采选业	Mining and Processing of Ferrous Metal Ores	74.62
有色金属矿采选业	Mining and Processing of Non-Ferrous Metal Ores	95.55
非金属矿采选业	Mining and Processing of Non-metal Ores	117.95
开采专业及辅助性活动	Professional and Support Activities for Mining	
其他采矿业	Mining of Other Ores	
农副食品加工业	Processing of Food from Agricultural Products	60.79
食品制造业	Manufacture of Foods	29.03
酒、饮料和精制茶制造业	Manufacture of Liquor, Beverages and Refined Tea	2144.50
烟草制品业	Manufacture of Tobacco	
纺织业	Manufacture of Textile	34.64
纺织服装、服饰业	Manufacture of Textile, Wearing Apparel and Accessories	28.44
皮革、毛皮、羽毛及其制品和制鞋业	Manufacture of Leather, Fur, Feather and Related Products and Footwear	
木材加工和木、竹、藤、棕、草制品业	Processing of Timber, Manufacture of Wood, Bamboo, Rattan, Palm and Straw Products	8.12
家具制造业	Manufacture of Furniture	
造纸和纸制品业	Manufacture of Paper and Paper Products	36.87
印刷和记录媒介复制业	Printing and Reproduction of Recording Media	37.74
文教、工美、体育和娱乐用品制造业	Manufacture of Articles for Culture, Education, Arts and Crafts, Sport and Entertainment Activities	
石油、煤炭及其他燃料加工业	Processing of Petroleum, Coal and Other Fuel	781.22
化学原料和化学制品制造业	Manufacture of Raw Chemical Materials and Chemical Products	812.30
医药制造业	Manufacture of Medicines	108.32
化学纤维制造业	Manufacture of Chemical Fibers	409.76
橡胶和塑料制品业	Manufacture of Rubber and Plastics Products	43.73
非金属矿物制品业	Manufacture of Non-metallic Mineral Products	575.54
黑色金属冶炼和压延加工业	Smelting and Pressing of Ferrous Metals	1046.10
有色金属冶炼和压延加工业	Smelting and Pressing of Non-ferrous Metals	332.20
金属制品业	Manufacture of Metal Products	166.44
通用设备制造业	Manufacture of General Purpose Machinery	359.18
专用设备制造业	Manufacture of Special Purpose Machinery	240.64
汽车制造业	Manufacture of Automobiles	943.53
铁路、船舶、航空航天和其他运输设备制造业	Manufacture of Railway, Ship, Aerospace and Other Transport Equipment	1124.12
电气机械和器材制造业	Manufacture of Electrical Machinery and Apparatus	499.92
计算机、通信和其他电子设备制造业	Manufacture of Computers, Communication and Other Electronic Equipment	2021.90
仪器仪表制造业	Manufacture of Measuring Instruments and Machinery	89.45
其他制造业	Other Manufactures	87.40
废弃资源综合利用业	Utilization of Waste Resources	16.42
金属制品、机械和设备修理业	Repair Service of Metal Products, Machinery and Equipment	97.33
电力、热力生产和供应业	Production and Supply of Electric Power and Heat Power	3067.42
燃气生产和供应业	Production and Supply of Gas	357.74
水的生产和供应业	Production and Supply of Water	223.47

continued

(100 million yuan)

营业成本 Business Cost	销售费用 Selling Expenses	管理费用 Management Expenses	财务费用 Financial Expenses	利润总额 Total Profits	平均用工人数 (万人) Annual Average Employees (10 000 persons)
14272.01	**336.99**	**586.95**	**241.77**	**1741.55**	**75.35**
76.20	1.45	8.40	1.78	10.15	2.98
709.44	1.42	95.77	12.17	185.36	3.05
50.61	0.95	5.36	0.65	13.65	0.44
59.01	0.26	5.83	0.73	24.70	0.48
89.88	3.09	6.29	7.14	7.13	0.59
54.15	0.87	1.71	0.33	2.99	0.25
24.10	1.36	1.84	0.63	0.16	0.40
1187.57	130.93	54.21	-15.34	603.01	5.77
31.17	0.32	1.25	0.56	1.20	0.40
22.86	0.53	3.48	0.05	1.39	0.28
7.52	0.12	0.26	0.29	0.29	0.05
34.38	0.41	1.25	0.62	0.13	0.22
28.78	0.17	4.84	-1.09	4.76	0.33
661.24	3.48	9.35	-0.43	34.41	0.83
691.47	9.76	32.80	3.62	59.76	4.35
60.43	17.43	5.46	-0.02	19.77	1.06
394.50	2.42	4.65	8.66	1.01	1.05
37.04	1.68	2.40	0.07	1.41	0.37
477.91	10.76	20.33	10.51	44.41	2.96
922.53	4.03	15.45	10.91	27.24	4.05
295.50	0.84	6.03	1.22	19.51	0.93
147.37	2.18	5.89	1.38	4.49	1.02
297.56	6.27	20.25	-2.52	25.96	1.60
194.79	5.55	13.95	0.50	12.32	1.64
783.98	-2.21	18.76	1.66	110.26	3.08
1012.47	10.41	39.65	-12.43	45.12	4.19
424.67	15.52	24.69	-0.40	7.36	2.56
1776.08	73.38	58.94	13.67	11.61	9.34
71.94	2.91	3.67	0.10	7.30	0.54
68.72	0.20	8.02	0.55	7.49	0.67
15.26	0.25	0.54	0.22	-0.04	0.10
87.72	1.38	2.56		5.09	0.36
2487.07	2.23	47.22	184.72	322.89	13.09
302.16	10.19	14.30	1.28	30.72	1.24
152.29	6.58	18.44	13.03	36.83	2.59

14-10 各市(州)国有控股工业企业主要指标(2023年)
Main Indicators of State-holding Industrial Enterprises by Region(2023)

单位：亿元 (100 million yuan)

市(州)	Region	企业单位数(个) Number of Enterprises (unit)	资产总计 Total Assets	流动资产合计 Total Current Assets	固定资产原价 Original Value of Fixed Assets	负债合计 Total Liabilities	流动负债合计 Total Current Liabilities	所有者权益合计 Owners' Equities
全省	**Sichuan**	**1674**	**38648.74**	**14667.32**	**26232.40**	**22716.49**	**13551.44**	**15929.74**
成都市	Chengdu	434	12665.68	5444.24	10164.50	7090.87	5222.46	5574.81
自贡市	Zigong	34	601.62	311.85	214.78	285.82	227.96	315.81
攀枝花市	Panzhihua	42	1928.92	498.34	1293.42	1214.81	844.06	714.12
泸州市	Luzhou	80	1578.13	771.15	650.37	793.65	425.74	784.48
德阳市	Deyang	77	1565.74	1113.57	450.56	1084.81	892.92	480.93
绵阳市	Mianyang	124	2826.63	1547.72	1401.95	1867.99	1323.24	958.64
广元市	Guangyuan	66	578.64	124.74	518.36	326.50	98.81	252.14
遂宁市	Suining	32	540.53	233.44	164.36	249.21	100.87	291.33
内江市	Neijiang	36	507.51	132.07	228.26	357.52	184.58	149.99
乐山市	Leshan	64	976.04	232.03	641.26	572.60	188.47	403.44
南充市	Nanchong	76	640.36	187.46	266.30	336.10	156.38	301.74
眉山市	Meishan	66	931.77	421.21	433.55	542.70	308.14	389.07
宜宾市	Yibin	106	4846.37	2289.31	1469.76	2458.68	2020.67	2387.69
广安市	Guangan	46	334.62	118.49	261.41	151.11	83.90	183.51
达州市	Dazhou	55	736.35	374.93	707.74	307.98	83.33	428.37
雅安市	Yaan	62	1078.15	206.54	1081.11	678.93	226.83	399.22
巴中市	Bazhong	45	115.67	36.85	61.85	74.00	36.22	41.67
资阳市	Ziyang	22	175.77	82.10	44.41	116.05	69.87	59.72
阿坝藏族羌族自治州	Aba	45	463.84	54.05	474.59	325.81	120.72	138.03
甘孜藏族自治州	Ganzi	40	1750.73	77.36	1885.38	1373.52	271.42	371.08
凉山彝族自治州	Liangshan	122	3805.65	409.83	3818.48	2507.84	664.87	1303.95

14-10 续表 continued

单位：亿元 (100 million yuan)

市(州)	Region	营业收入 Business Revenue	营业成本 Business Cost	销售费用 Selling Expenses	管理费用 Management Expenses	财务费用 Financial Expenses	利润总额 Total Profits	平均用工人数(万人) Annual Average Employees (10 000 persons)
全省	**Sichuan**	**18163.37**	**14272.01**	**336.99**	**586.95**	**241.77**	**1741.55**	**75.35**
成都市	Chengdu	7578.26	6204.76	80.43	257.40	31.80	472.58	29.27
自贡市	Zigong	254.03	210.71	7.57	13.52	-0.51	18.81	1.17
攀枝花市	Panzhihua	1010.76	816.98	2.96	24.54	14.58	81.09	5.07
泸州市	Luzhou	593.56	263.91	47.90	32.80	1.97	209.12	2.45
德阳市	Deyang	815.70	676.75	20.17	38.82	-0.83	43.56	3.72
绵阳市	Mianyang	1975.72	1708.32	60.50	51.47	17.16	63.07	9.59
广元市	Guangyuan	199.30	154.49	3.81	8.63	8.34	19.38	1.02
遂宁市	Suining	155.07	118.30	1.65	5.76	2.74	26.89	0.95
内江市	Neijiang	107.38	88.44	1.42	3.20	2.32	11.44	0.56
乐山市	Leshan	265.58	206.16	2.76	12.93	12.09	26.17	1.54
南充市	Nanchong	191.27	165.36	4.44	9.22	6.39	3.75	1.22
眉山市	Meishan	275.48	248.14	2.20	9.43	5.28	12.09	1.96
宜宾市	Yibin	2686.13	1896.10	86.19	67.25	3.62	465.40	8.73
广安市	Guangan	148.94	123.40	1.36	4.98	2.52	16.53	0.93
达州市	Dazhou	325.99	243.39	2.45	11.86	3.21	49.49	1.71
雅安市	Yaan	220.15	169.59	4.04	5.98	12.93	22.09	1.07
巴中市	Bazhong	28.46	22.46	1.18	1.79	1.05	2.14	0.32
资阳市	Ziyang	62.76	52.21	1.50	2.44	0.84	3.95	0.44
阿坝藏族羌族自治州	Aba	98.36	73.99	1.02	2.73	8.75	9.69	0.46
甘孜藏族自治州	Ganzi	148.30	103.23	0.14	2.52	34.85	4.76	0.62
凉山彝族自治州	Liangshan	1022.19	725.33	3.31	19.64	72.67	179.54	2.57

14-11 大中型工业企业主要指标
Main Indicators of Large and Medium-Sized Industrial Enterprises

单位：亿元 (100 million yuan)

年份 Year	企业单位数 (个) Number of Enterprises (unit)	资产总计 Total Assets	流动资产合计 Total Current Assets	固定资产原价 Original Value of Fixed Assets	负债合计 Total Liabilities	流动负债合计 Total Current Liabilities	所有者权益合计 Owners' Equities
1998	870	2938.50	1300.17	1778.60	1854.56	1179.64	1083.94
1999	836	3574.60	1379.53	2398.73	2225.70	1241.21	1348.91
2000	783	3607.02	1421.73	2374.75	2305.85	1285.79	1301.09
2001	884	3918.90	1572.97	2574.24	2438.89	1466.63	1480.01
2002	972	4231.06	1690.32	2641.97	2593.73	1585.30	1637.34
2003	843	4707.48	1943.03	2910.60	2886.08	1874.30	1821.40
2004	909	4879.50	2088.53	3314.60	3112.58	958.57	1766.31
2005	984	5689.02	2452.25	3700.42	3565.22	2464.06	2116.05
2006	1050	6557.26	2823.62	3821.43	3986.70	2762.09	2566.51
2007	1228	8427.97	3666.10	4949.00	5031.63	3496.33	3396.35
2008	1423	10881.79	4556.76	5376.74	6566.77	4462.80	4315.03
2009	1603	12490.71	5346.84	6630.78	7638.68	5156.30	4812.08
2010	1989	15940.79	6874.81	9124.91	9956.92	6872.76	5935.53
2011	2790	19695.11	8621.32	11471.96	12187.05	8752.14	7446.71
2012	2769	21074.33	9714.15	11876.04	13376.19	9429.04	7651.59
2013	2635	26044.06	10838.81	14662.95	15808.26	10227.38	9811.84
2014	2521	26729.05	11240.43	16652.47	16336.70	11425.02	10347.35
2015	2386	26696.01	10992.73	15942.04	16178.16	10825.60	10516.84
2016	2260	27213.60	11722.69	19123.53	15622.92	10906.63	11590.68
2017	2100	28652.69	12821.14	18183.64	16348.27	11891.39	12304.42
2018	1897	30521.68	13762.87	17968.88	17055.01	12771.35	13466.67
2019	1820	31697.52	14309.59	19705.79	17403.74	12453.36	14293.66
2020	1784	33614.38	15065.67	21546.67	18479.68	13912.16	15134.32
2021	1833	38484.15	18856.17	23276.19	21051.75	16637.42	17432.40
2022	1738	40452.25	19335.65	24661.86	22170.32	16692.30	18281.93
2023	1605	47235.49	22057.73	28391.52	25922.46	18561.63	21313.03

14-11 续表 continued

单位：亿元 (100 million yuan)

年份 Year	营业收入 Business Revenue	营业成本 Business Cost	销售费用 Selling Expenses	管理费用 Management Expenses	财务费用 Financial Expenses	利润总额 Total Profits	平均用工人数（万人） Annual Average Employees (10 000 persons)
1998						46.47	160.77
1999						26.68	149.23
2000			74.82	127.11	62.28	57.64	126.57
2001			88.78	139.58	67.83	71.57	119.39
2002			107.39	150.95	70.37	99.72	115.18
2003			126.20	189.75	69.50	122.44	125.64
2004	3068.51	2437.99	131.77	242.95	65.04	154.96	119.10
2005	3934.89	3138.94	161.13	243.65	67.43	245.57	128.00
2006	4941.02	3962.09	184.95	276.91	84.80	332.77	134.79
2007	6511.90	5171.48	231.11	366.06	106.81	496.14	146.44
2008	8262.77	6761.45	279.92	466.74	145.15	483.25	159.86
2009	9964.93	8093.80	333.12	533.54	126.03	668.87	175.95
2010	13854.97	11240.86	452.96	792.20	181.28	1069.06	211.98
2011	19862.11	16271.38	573.44	950.07	266.26	1510.47	271.53
2012	19928.38	16161.68	609.47	934.30	313.17	1585.57	276.54
2013	23506.70	19418.54	680.47	1040.34	359.40	1567.71	267.16
2014	24438.81	20434.41	723.44	989.94	423.11	1447.05	255.76
2015	22900.94	19188.78	718.71	1019.95	398.78	1208.28	237.07
2016	24920.35	20798.76	821.51	1059.12	334.84	1406.09	218.68
2017	24613.39	20169.60	803.30	1059.00	304.29	1888.99	203.70
2018	24430.19	19898.82	824.37	1054.46	283.28	1893.77	185.49
2019	25764.43	20929.21	910.38	860.04	272.01	1943.20	177.95
2020	27069.62	22064.24	886.97	833.19	240.58	2120.99	176.79
2021	32859.02	26567.47	969.82	975.30	213.80	3053.47	179.01
2022	32697.80	26338.60	841.50	930.83	175.27	3264.36	170.63
2023	34019.05	27545.99	864.00	933.48	176.88	3345.01	175.48

14-12 按行业分大中型工业企业主要指标(2023年)

单位：亿元

行业	Sector	企业单位数(个) Number of Enterprises (unit)
总计	**Total**	**1605**
煤炭开采和洗选业	Mining and Washing of Coal	41
石油和天然气开采业	Extraction of Petroleum and Natural Gas	6
黑色金属矿采选业	Mining and Processing of Ferrous Metal Ores	14
有色金属矿采选业	Mining and Processing of Non-Ferrous Metal Ores	11
非金属矿采选业	Mining and Processing of Non-metal Ores	9
开采专业及辅助性活动	Professional and Support Activities for Mining	
其他采矿业	Mining of Other Ores	
农副食品加工业	Processing of Food from Agricultural Products	49
食品制造业	Manufacture of Foods	68
酒、饮料和精制茶制造业	Manufacture of Liquor, Beverages and Refined Tea	47
烟草制品业	Manufacture of Tobacco	
纺织业	Manufacture of Textile	34
纺织服装、服饰业	Manufacture of Textile, Wearing Apparel and Accessories	14
皮革、毛皮、羽毛及其制品和制鞋业	Manufacture of Leather, Fur, Feather and Related Products and Footwear	27
木材加工和木、竹、藤、棕、草制品业	Processing of Timber, Manufacture of Wood, Bamboo, Rattan, Palm and Straw Products	8
家具制造业	Manufacture of Furniture	21
造纸和纸制品业	Manufacture of Paper and Paper Products	30
印刷和记录媒介复制业	Printing and Reproduction of Recording Media	19
文教、工美、体育和娱乐用品制造业	Manufacture of Articles for Culture, Education, Arts and Crafts, Sport and Entertainment Activities	4
石油、煤炭及其他燃料加工业	Processing of Petroleum, Coal and Other Fuel	11
化学原料和化学制品制造业	Manufacture of Raw Chemical Materials and Chemical Products	109
医药制造业	Manufacture of Medicines	87
化学纤维制造业	Manufacture of Chemical Fibers	9
橡胶和塑料制品业	Manufacture of Rubber and Plastics Products	33
非金属矿物制品业	Manufacture of Non-metallic Mineral Products	149
黑色金属冶炼和压延加工业	Smelting and Pressing of Ferrous Metals	30
有色金属冶炼和压延加工业	Smelting and Pressing of Non-ferrous Metals	36
金属制品业	Manufacture of Metal Products	65
通用设备制造业	Manufacture of General Purpose Machinery	68
专用设备制造业	Manufacture of Special Purpose Machinery	63
汽车制造业	Manufacture of Automobiles	85
铁路、船舶、航空航天和其他运输设备制造业	Manufacture of Railway, Ship, Aerospace and Other Transport Equipment	50
电气机械和器材制造业	Manufacture of Electrical Machinery and Apparatus	95
计算机、通信和其他电子设备制造业	Manufacture of Computers, Communication and Other Electronic Equipment	205
仪器仪表制造业	Manufacture of Measuring Instruments and Machinery	15
其他制造业	Other Manufactures	4
废弃资源综合利用业	Utilization of Waste Resources	4
金属制品、机械和设备修理业	Repair Service of Metal Products, Machinery and Equipment	6
电力、热力生产和供应业	Production and Supply of Electric Power and Heat Power	47
燃气生产和供应业	Production and Supply of Gas	12
水的生产和供应业	Production and Supply of Water	16

Main Indicators of Large and Medium-sized Industrial Enterprises by Industrial Sector(2023)

(100 million yuan)

资产总计 Total Assets	流动资产合计 Total Current Assets	固定资产原价 Original Value of Fixed Assets	负债合计 Total Liabilities	流动负债合计 Total Current Liabilities	所有者权益 Owners' Equities
47235.49	**22057.73**	**28391.52**	**25922.46**	**18561.63**	**21313.03**
435.19	168.95	287.43	329.56	262.00	105.63
2162.78	466.67	2782.25	771.22	382.03	1391.56
332.96	90.49	188.66	135.54	113.54	197.42
275.41	74.90	102.80	103.65	87.52	171.76
241.06	105.36	40.66	137.05	43.77	104.01
364.19	218.64	105.03	193.42	166.76	170.77
521.92	294.20	236.98	199.25	173.34	322.67
5277.22	3058.25	1004.43	2293.02	2011.11	2984.20
246.83	100.20	124.25	141.13	84.96	105.70
41.26	26.48	15.21	20.29	16.40	20.97
87.52	34.17	19.75	42.08	30.44	45.44
44.69	13.04	36.07	27.29	12.24	17.40
145.71	60.07	92.51	83.15	74.38	62.56
246.91	104.68	196.12	132.05	114.71	114.86
109.09	73.41	73.35	26.86	19.36	82.24
35.23	33.15	4.66	27.21	26.69	8.03
604.07	233.84	534.93	292.47	222.87	311.60
2809.24	1344.43	1330.22	1189.40	848.64	1619.84
1619.40	917.75	412.21	530.10	406.30	1089.30
464.01	186.44	166.68	343.99	206.73	120.03
254.82	117.11	106.00	105.93	73.16	148.89
2260.10	1019.84	1314.17	999.76	735.61	1260.33
2321.37	749.83	2280.38	1381.16	1056.49	940.20
542.76	278.74	264.33	312.80	231.30	229.96
590.38	356.66	299.64	386.95	288.17	203.43
1232.40	918.78	334.98	785.42	679.82	446.98
1014.10	658.30	348.20	535.73	442.18	478.37
1702.91	1094.11	819.69	1131.80	845.30	571.11
2225.07	1795.60	483.29	1609.96	1443.93	615.11
2988.71	1504.34	1169.53	1897.12	1343.54	1091.59
7230.19	4548.67	3400.20	4278.73	3525.57	2951.46
165.10	116.29	44.69	78.12	69.81	86.97
270.68	117.30	232.54	188.42	67.75	82.26
35.49	25.61	8.47	19.43	15.68	16.06
122.16	95.54	31.30	67.53	58.47	54.62
6417.21	402.01	8414.58	4225.16	1830.28	2192.05
171.24	77.26	95.91	88.42	73.31	82.82
952.26	213.90	318.85	546.68	226.82	405.58

14−12 续表

单位：亿元

行业	Sector	营业收入 Business Revenue
总计	**Total**	**34019.05**
煤炭开采和洗选业	Mining and Washing of Coal	173.01
石油和天然气开采业	Extraction of Petroleum and Natural Gas	991.86
黑色金属矿采选业	Mining and Processing of Ferrous Metal Ores	150.25
有色金属矿采选业	Mining and Processing of Non-Ferrous Metal Ores	133.37
非金属矿采选业	Mining and Processing of Non-metal Ores	42.57
开采专业及辅助性活动	Professional and Support Activities for Mining	
其他采矿业	Mining of Other Ores	
农副食品加工业	Processing of Food from Agricultural Products	490.24
食品制造业	Manufacture of Foods	520.81
酒、饮料和精制茶制造业	Manufacture of Liquor, Beverages and Refined Tea	2973.25
烟草制品业	Manufacture of Tobacco	
纺织业	Manufacture of Textile	192.11
纺织服装、服饰业	Manufacture of Textile, Wearing Apparel and Accessories	49.91
皮革、毛皮、羽毛及其制品和制鞋业	Manufacture of Leather, Fur, Feather and Related Products and Footwear	62.49
木材加工和木、竹、藤、棕、草制品业	Processing of Timber, Manufacture of Wood, Bamboo, Rattan, Palm and Straw Products	27.84
家具制造业	Manufacture of Furniture	171.31
造纸和纸制品业	Manufacture of Paper and Paper Products	218.95
印刷和记录媒介复制业	Printing and Reproduction of Recording Media	86.32
文教、工美、体育和娱乐用品制造业	Manufacture of Articles for Culture, Education, Arts and Crafts, Sport and Entertainment Activities	47.61
石油、煤炭及其他燃料加工业	Processing of Petroleum, Coal and Other Fuel	868.98
化学原料和化学制品制造业	Manufacture of Raw Chemical Materials and Chemical Products	2216.66
医药制造业	Manufacture of Medicines	757.85
化学纤维制造业	Manufacture of Chemical Fibers	432.10
橡胶和塑料制品业	Manufacture of Rubber and Plastics Products	196.86
非金属矿物制品业	Manufacture of Non-metallic Mineral Products	1580.03
黑色金属冶炼和压延加工业	Smelting and Pressing of Ferrous Metals	2353.10
有色金属冶炼和压延加工业	Smelting and Pressing of Non-ferrous Metals	652.61
金属制品业	Manufacture of Metal Products	618.24
通用设备制造业	Manufacture of General Purpose Machinery	653.58
专用设备制造业	Manufacture of Special Purpose Machinery	504.08
汽车制造业	Manufacture of Automobiles	1705.44
铁路、船舶、航空航天和其他运输设备制造业	Manufacture of Railway, Ship, Aerospace and Other Transport Equipment	1184.69
电气机械和器材制造业	Manufacture of Electrical Machinery and Apparatus	2379.36
计算机、通信和其他电子设备制造业	Manufacture of Computers, Communication and Other Electronic Equipment	7685.12
仪器仪表制造业	Manufacture of Measuring Instruments and Machinery	158.98
其他制造业	Other Manufactures	89.26
废弃资源综合利用业	Utilization of Waste Resources	23.29
金属制品、机械和设备修理业	Repair Service of Metal Products, Machinery and Equipment	99.36
电力、热力生产和供应业	Production and Supply of Electric Power and Heat Power	2481.36
燃气生产和供应业	Production and Supply of Gas	98.95
水的生产和供应业	Production and Supply of Water	138.54

continued

(100 million yuan)

营业成本 Business Cost	销售费用 Selling Expenses	管理费用 Management Expenses	财务费用 Financial Expenses	利润总额 Total Profits	平均用工人数 (万人) Annual Average Employees (10 000 persons)
27545.99	**864.00**	**933.48**	**176.88**	**3345.01**	**175.48**
129.13	2.79	13.27	2.07	13.79	4.40
619.17	1.40	86.92	7.76	172.67	2.95
101.07	2.81	8.81	1.25	28.50	0.76
74.87	0.28	5.84	0.52	48.20	0.73
25.30	2.00	2.74	2.16	8.81	0.41
414.01	16.76	10.15	2.23	44.31	3.16
389.45	44.23	18.11	0.83	63.55	5.02
1557.61	255.89	113.33	-11.99	785.49	12.23
168.52	2.58	4.29	2.90	11.67	2.05
39.21	2.84	2.42	0.29	3.77	0.82
53.07	0.91	3.59	1.21	4.02	1.87
25.19	0.43	0.62	0.34	1.54	0.28
133.12	8.27	13.63	0.64	12.70	3.84
181.33	7.43	6.49	2.26	17.65	1.74
66.15	2.13	6.81	-0.82	10.48	1.23
39.15	4.35	0.93	0.22	2.66	0.13
741.15	3.92	11.44	-0.24	38.74	1.11
1774.41	25.64	62.03	6.15	517.83	9.89
365.07	164.30	40.08	6.22	149.54	7.34
413.15	3.65	5.05	9.44	1.68	1.31
155.74	10.01	7.06	1.12	17.20	2.18
1204.70	24.89	45.84	5.48	265.10	9.89
2088.08	10.02	30.38	16.64	92.29	7.13
578.06	3.33	10.79	4.97	51.94	2.79
527.00	12.21	26.25	5.27	22.16	5.43
536.94	16.66	30.01	0.72	49.27	4.25
404.17	17.19	26.53	2.40	30.88	4.21
1463.59	7.78	35.55	3.32	141.86	7.11
1043.92	13.74	44.93	-13.17	63.43	5.63
2050.04	81.40	59.45	2.34	123.46	11.50
7105.18	89.51	109.63	17.57	222.30	36.45
121.55	6.19	5.07	0.12	19.58	0.86
70.18	0.32	8.09	0.56	7.69	0.73
19.67	0.03	1.56	0.22	1.00	0.34
88.62	1.54	2.90	0.07	5.47	0.40
2119.96	1.80	35.06	95.05	212.46	11.08
77.77	6.31	5.69	-0.08	12.03	0.66
93.44	2.61	11.27	4.21	27.06	1.08

14-13 各市(州)大中型工业企业主要指标(2023年)
Main Indicators of Large and Medium-Sized Industrial Enterprises by Region(2023)

单位：亿元 (100 million yuan)

市(州)	Region	企业单位数(个) Number of Enterprises (unit)	资产总计 Total Assets	流动资产合计 Total Current Assets	固定资产原价 Original Value of Fixed Assets	负债合计 Total Liabilities	流动负债合计 Total Current Liabilities	所有者权益合计 Owners' Equities
全省	**Sichuan**	**1605**	**47235.49**	**22057.73**	**28391.52**	**25922.46**	**18561.63**	**21313.03**
成都市	Chengdu	553	17824.18	8939.15	12333.56	9529.79	7775.30	8294.39
自贡市	Zigong	24	632.60	395.91	152.14	411.77	311.22	220.84
攀枝花市	Panzhihua	39	2171.87	652.10	1358.42	1314.45	971.56	857.42
泸州市	Luzhou	79	2007.92	1148.36	844.66	973.12	664.22	1034.80
德阳市	Deyang	124	2772.89	1941.62	845.78	1623.74	1362.55	1149.15
绵阳市	Mianyang	136	3978.06	2014.12	1842.06	2463.47	1706.83	1514.60
广元市	Guangyuan	22	250.61	116.90	150.20	115.42	99.29	135.18
遂宁市	Suining	62	1074.80	590.18	460.81	533.86	328.92	540.94
内江市	Neijiang	48	709.17	315.66	1216.11	482.45	338.95	226.72
乐山市	Leshan	88	2501.61	917.62	1426.65	905.60	569.31	1596.00
南充市	Nanchong	51	498.13	214.96	320.23	294.28	171.98	203.85
眉山市	Meishan	102	1302.41	512.05	766.27	767.73	488.78	534.69
宜宾市	Yibin	111	6157.49	3084.01	1559.87	3264.91	2641.69	2892.58
广安市	Guangan	35	372.41	155.59	318.97	164.15	122.44	208.26
达州市	Dazhou	39	884.58	464.06	863.54	353.15	163.60	531.43
雅安市	Yaan	27	386.62	210.53	187.96	201.70	148.91	184.92
巴中市	Bazhong	6	24.22	6.70	20.73	11.39	6.93	12.84
资阳市	Ziyang	20	142.63	75.21	84.90	91.67	86.55	50.97
阿坝藏族羌族自治州	Aba	7	80.06	44.42	64.49	24.42	23.52	55.65
甘孜藏族自治州	Ganzi	4	751.10	33.27	709.07	609.34	119.48	135.62
凉山彝族自治州	Liangshan	28	2712.12	225.32	2865.09	1786.07	459.60	932.19

14-13 续表 continued

单位：亿元 (100 million yuan)

市(州)	Region	营业收入 Business Revenue	营业成本 Business Cost	销售费用 Selling Expenses	管理费用 Management Expenses	财务费用 Financial Expenses	利润总额 Total Profits	平均用工人数（万人） Annual Average Employees (10 000 persons)
全省	**Sichuan**	**34019.05**	**27545.99**	**864.00**	**933.48**	**176.88**	**3345.01**	**175.48**
成都市	Chengdu	14833.95	12539.49	331.72	397.63	38.76	880.52	72.57
自贡市	Zigong	283.68	235.44	4.53	13.80	2.31	22.16	1.75
攀枝花市	Panzhihua	1506.51	1199.53	9.27	45.16	13.09	144.86	7.67
泸州市	Luzhou	1070.50	552.34	86.79	53.90	3.11	294.48	7.60
德阳市	Deyang	2212.59	1688.51	106.93	91.47	3.27	219.30	12.33
绵阳市	Mianyang	2768.59	2382.98	78.74	72.20	12.24	129.64	16.05
广元市	Guangyuan	269.38	221.65	2.22	6.62	1.69	26.85	1.13
遂宁市	Suining	1085.11	823.75	20.92	22.49	6.53	171.10	5.94
内江市	Neijiang	707.46	628.09	8.91	11.89	3.14	43.12	4.16
乐山市	Leshan	1382.16	1007.57	18.83	44.61	9.77	505.35	7.22
南充市	Nanchong	328.67	279.92	8.83	10.79	3.22	19.99	3.25
眉山市	Meishan	954.23	824.62	22.65	25.15	4.58	62.32	7.71
宜宾市	Yibin	4211.49	3239.72	138.81	81.90	1.00	585.11	15.16
广安市	Guangan	249.93	208.94	2.04	6.94	1.25	26.50	2.48
达州市	Dazhou	685.93	543.61	7.32	16.26	1.81	65.99	3.69
雅安市	Yaan	337.42	305.11	5.09	7.84	2.07	14.86	1.78
巴中市	Bazhong	19.20	16.01	0.49	1.30	0.26	1.26	0.25
资阳市	Ziyang	83.74	72.61	2.29	4.24	2.00	-2.25	1.48
阿坝藏族羌族自治州	Aba	94.91	88.99	0.65	2.00	0.53	0.74	0.47
甘孜藏族自治州	Ganzi	57.67	52.12	0.07	0.87	12.13	-7.26	0.36
凉山彝族自治州	Liangshan	875.92	634.98	6.89	16.41	54.12	140.38	2.42

14-14 按行业分规模以上工业企业主要经济效益指标(2023年)
Main Indicators on Economic Benefits of Industrial Enterprises above Designated Size by Industrial Sector(2023)

单位：%　　(%)

行业	Sector	资产负债率 Ratio of Debts to Assets	总资产贡献率 Ratio of Profits, Taxes and Interests to Average Assets	工业成本费用利润率 Ratio of Profits to Industrial Costs
总计	**Total**	**56.08**	**9.70**	**10.22**
煤炭开采和洗选业	Mining and Washing of Coal	74.03	6.02	7.61
石油和天然气开采业	Extraction of Petroleum and Natural Gas	40.76	10.46	21.98
黑色金属矿采选业	Mining and Processing of Ferrous Metal Ores	51.45	12.63	16.33
有色金属矿采选业	Mining and Processing of Non-Ferrous Metal Ores	50.82	19.07	38.10
非金属矿采选业	Mining and Processing of Non-metal Ores	48.57	4.75	13.56
开采专业及辅助性活动	Professional and Support Activities for Mining	35.75	4.21	2.20
其他采矿业	Mining of Other Ores			
农副食品加工业	Processing of Food from Agricultural Products	56.21	10.10	5.80
食品制造业	Manufacture of Foods	43.69	14.46	11.73
酒、饮料和精制茶制造业	Manufacture of Liquor, Beverages and Refined Tea	44.85	22.05	36.99
烟草制品业	Manufacture of Tobacco	44.60	107.66	24.72
纺织业	Manufacture of Textile	59.03	7.26	6.28
纺织服装、服饰业	Manufacture of Textile, Wearing Apparel and Accessories	45.85	11.60	8.22
皮革、毛皮、羽毛及其制品和制鞋业	Manufacture of Leather, Fur, Feather and Related Products and Footwear	54.27	9.26	6.76
木材加工和木、竹、藤、棕、草制品业	Processing of Timber, Manufacture of Wood, Bamboo, Rattan, Palm and Straw Products	59.10	8.19	6.26
家具制造业	Manufacture of Furniture	55.38	9.89	6.66
造纸和纸制品业	Manufacture of Paper and Paper Products	56.39	10.96	7.82
印刷和记录媒介复制业	Printing and Reproduction of Recording Media	41.87	10.46	9.15
文教、工美、体育和娱乐用品制造业	Manufacture of Articles for Culture, Education, Arts and Crafts, Sport and Entertainment Activities	70.07	7.12	4.33
石油、煤炭及其他燃料加工业	Processing of Petroleum, Coal and Other Fuel	49.36	20.35	4.94
化学原料和化学制品制造业	Manufacture of Raw Chemical Materials and Chemical Products	46.22	16.78	20.44
医药制造业	Manufacture of Medicines	37.65	11.73	19.06
化学纤维制造业	Manufacture of Chemical Fibers	74.37	3.22	0.36
橡胶和塑料制品业	Manufacture of Rubber and Plastics Products	46.23	10.93	8.23
非金属矿物制品业	Manufacture of Non-metallic Mineral Products	53.17	9.62	12.69
黑色金属冶炼和压延加工业	Smelting and Pressing of Ferrous Metals	60.41	6.85	3.94
有色金属冶炼和压延加工业	Smelting and Pressing of Non-ferrous Metals	57.40	14.63	7.11
金属制品业	Manufacture of Metal Products	61.73	7.97	4.98
通用设备制造业	Manufacture of General Purpose Machinery	59.99	7.67	8.80
专用设备制造业	Manufacture of Special Purpose Machinery	53.73	6.13	7.21
汽车制造业	Manufacture of Automobiles	65.54	11.53	8.07
铁路、船舶、航空航天和其他运输设备制造业	Manufacture of Railway, Ship, Aerospace and Other Transport Equipment	69.82	3.58	5.78
电气机械和器材制造业	Manufacture of Electrical Machinery and Apparatus	61.47	6.41	5.45
计算机、通信和其他电子设备制造业	Manufacture of Computers, Communication and Other Electronic Equipment	58.05	4.81	3.32
仪器仪表制造业	Manufacture of Measuring Instruments and Machinery	48.18	11.15	12.55
其他制造业	Other Manufactures	68.76	4.63	9.51
废弃资源综合利用业	Utilization of Waste Resources	63.97	16.43	7.94
金属制品、机械和设备修理业	Repair Service of Metal Products, Machinery and Equipment	47.18	4.35	5.44
电力、热力生产和供应业	Production and Supply of Electric Power and Heat Power	67.11	6.23	12.76
燃气生产和供应业	Production and Supply of Gas	50.11	9.89	11.75
水的生产和供应业	Production and Supply of Water	56.56	2.83	20.13

14-15 按行业分国有控股工业企业主要经济效益指标(2023年)
Main Indicators on Economic Benefits of State-holding Industrial Enterprises by Industrial Sector(2023)

单位：% (%)

行业	Sector	资产负债率 Ratio of Debts to Assets	总资产贡献率 Ratio of Profits, Taxes and Interests to Average Assets	工业成本费用利润率 Ratio of Profits to Industrial Costs
总计	**Total**	**58.78**	**8.30**	**11.05**
煤炭开采和洗选业	Mining and Washing of Coal	79.44	6.56	11.19
石油和天然气开采业	Extraction of Petroleum and Natural Gas	40.69	10.46	22.00
黑色金属矿采选业	Mining and Processing of Ferrous Metal Ores	49.34	9.43	23.15
有色金属矿采选业	Mining and Processing of Non-Ferrous Metal Ores	39.28	17.71	36.51
非金属矿采选业	Mining and Processing of Non-metal Ores	45.13	1.77	6.67
开采专业及辅助性活动	Professional and Support Activities for Mining	34.81	4.23	2.12
其他采矿业	Mining of Other Ores			
农副食品加工业	Processing of Food from Agricultural Products	58.22	4.58	5.18
食品制造业	Manufacture of Foods	70.06	4.45	0.57
酒、饮料和精制茶制造业	Manufacture of Liquor, Beverages and Refined Tea	43.03	23.12	44.10
烟草制品业	Manufacture of Tobacco	44.60	107.66	24.72
纺织业	Manufacture of Textile	29.77	2.54	3.56
纺织服装、服饰业	Manufacture of Textile, Wearing Apparel and Accessories	49.39	8.50	5.11
皮革、毛皮、羽毛及其制品和制鞋业	Manufacture of Leather, Fur, Feather and Related Products and Footwear			
木材加工和木、竹、藤、棕、草制品业	Processing of Timber, Manufacture of Wood, Bamboo, Rattan, Palm and Straw Products	57.99	4.35	3.52
家具制造业	Manufacture of Furniture	97.21	-9.38	-17.78
造纸和纸制品业	Manufacture of Paper and Paper Products	78.04	1.55	0.35
印刷和记录媒介复制业	Printing and Reproduction of Recording Media	26.12	9.17	14.18
文教、工美、体育和娱乐用品制造业	Manufacture of Articles for Culture, Education, Arts and Crafts, Sport and Entertainment Activities	77.90	7.80	5.56
石油、煤炭及其他燃料加工业	Processing of Petroleum, Coal and Other Fuel	40.02	25.88	5.09
化学原料和化学制品制造业	Manufacture of Raw Chemical Materials and Chemical Products	50.66	6.33	7.87
医药制造业	Manufacture of Medicines	27.28	9.69	22.81
化学纤维制造业	Manufacture of Chemical Fibers	74.71	3.10	0.24
橡胶和塑料制品业	Manufacture of Rubber and Plastics Products	48.76	6.68	3.34
非金属矿物制品业	Manufacture of Non-metallic Mineral Products	63.22	4.05	8.36
黑色金属冶炼和压延加工业	Smelting and Pressing of Ferrous Metals	57.91	3.68	2.79
有色金属冶炼和压延加工业	Smelting and Pressing of Non-ferrous Metals	56.48	9.78	6.27
金属制品业	Manufacture of Metal Products	65.09	3.99	2.78
通用设备制造业	Manufacture of General Purpose Machinery	68.64	4.32	7.69
专用设备制造业	Manufacture of Special Purpose Machinery	60.20	3.81	5.46
汽车制造业	Manufacture of Automobiles	72.87	18.52	13.61
铁路、船舶、航空航天和其他运输设备制造业	Manufacture of Railway, Ship, Aerospace and Other Transport Equipment	74.76	2.27	4.20
电气机械和器材制造业	Manufacture of Electrical Machinery and Apparatus	68.20	2.92	1.51
计算机、通信和其他电子设备制造业	Manufacture of Computers, Communication and Other Electronic Equipment	61.30	2.22	0.58
仪器仪表制造业	Manufacture of Measuring Instruments and Machinery	53.89	6.48	8.87
其他制造业	Other Manufactures	69.55	4.09	9.33
废弃资源综合利用业	Utilization of Waste Resources	60.62	4.77	-0.24
金属制品、机械和设备修理业	Repair Service of Metal Products, Machinery and Equipment	56.89	5.45	5.47
电力、热力生产和供应业	Production and Supply of Electric Power and Heat Power	67.46	6.09	11.83
燃气生产和供应业	Production and Supply of Gas	50.57	10.32	9.35
水的生产和供应业	Production and Supply of Water	55.13	2.52	19.30

14-16 按行业分大中型工业企业主要经济效益指标(2023年)

Main Indicators on Economic Benefits of Large and Medium-sized Industrial Enterprises by Industrial Sector(2023)

单位：%　　(%)

行业	Sector	资产负债率 Ratio of Debts to Assets	总资产贡献率 Ratio of Profits, Taxes and Interests to Average Assets	工业成本费用利润率 Ratio of Profits to Industrial Costs
总计	**Total**	**54.88**	**10.95**	**11.10**
煤炭开采和洗选业	Mining and Washing of Coal	75.73	6.69	9.18
石油和天然气开采业	Extraction of Petroleum and Natural Gas	35.66	12.25	23.37
黑色金属矿采选业	Mining and Processing of Ferrous Metal Ores	40.71	12.32	24.40
有色金属矿采选业	Mining and Processing of Non-Ferrous Metal Ores	37.63	22.18	55.92
非金属矿采选业	Mining and Processing of Non-metal Ores	56.85	5.17	27.26
开采专业及辅助性活动	Professional and Support Activities for Mining	34.30	3.34	1.26
其他采矿业	Mining of Other Ores			
农副食品加工业	Processing of Food from Agricultural Products	53.11	15.30	9.88
食品制造业	Manufacture of Foods	38.18	16.36	13.89
酒、饮料和精制茶制造业	Manufacture of Liquor, Beverages and Refined Tea	43.45	23.00	40.66
烟草制品业	Manufacture of Tobacco	46.77	115.09	23.89
纺织业	Manufacture of Textile	57.18	6.92	6.40
纺织服装、服饰业	Manufacture of Textile, Wearing Apparel and Accessories	49.18	12.77	8.27
皮革、毛皮、羽毛及其制品和制鞋业	Manufacture of Leather, Fur, Feather and Related Products and Footwear	48.08	8.84	6.78
木材加工和木、竹、藤、棕、草制品业	Processing of Timber, Manufacture of Wood, Bamboo, Rattan, Palm and Straw Products	61.07	6.53	5.77
家具制造业	Manufacture of Furniture	57.07	13.31	8.04
造纸和纸制品业	Manufacture of Paper and Paper Products	53.48	10.54	8.75
印刷和记录媒介复制业	Printing and Reproduction of Recording Media	24.62	12.29	13.78
文教、工美、体育和娱乐用品制造业	Manufacture of Articles for Culture, Education, Arts and Crafts, Sport and Entertainment Activities	77.21	8.69	5.94
石油、煤炭及其他燃料加工业	Processing of Petroleum, Coal and Other Fuel	48.42	22.58	5.10
化学原料和化学制品制造业	Manufacture of Raw Chemical Materials and Chemical Products	42.34	20.79	27.09
医药制造业	Manufacture of Medicines	32.73	12.47	24.06
化学纤维制造业	Manufacture of Chemical Fibers	74.13	3.15	0.39
橡胶和塑料制品业	Manufacture of Rubber and Plastics Products	41.57	9.47	9.57
非金属矿物制品业	Manufacture of Non-metallic Mineral Products	44.24	14.61	20.12
黑色金属冶炼和压延加工业	Smelting and Pressing of Ferrous Metals	59.50	6.79	4.21
有色金属冶炼和压延加工业	Smelting and Pressing of Non-ferrous Metals	57.63	12.90	8.51
金属制品业	Manufacture of Metal Products	65.54	7.03	3.80
通用设备制造业	Manufacture of General Purpose Machinery	63.73	5.64	8.11
专用设备制造业	Manufacture of Special Purpose Machinery	52.83	4.90	6.57
汽车制造业	Manufacture of Automobiles	66.46	13.06	9.28
铁路、船舶、航空航天和其他运输设备制造业	Manufacture of Railway, Ship, Aerospace and Other Transport Equipment	72.36	3.19	5.68
电气机械和器材制造业	Manufacture of Electrical Machinery and Apparatus	63.48	6.14	5.51
计算机、通信和其他电子设备制造业	Manufacture of Computers, Communication and Other Electronic Equipment	59.18	4.53	2.97
仪器仪表制造业	Manufacture of Measuring Instruments and Machinery	47.32	13.08	14.15
其他制造业	Other Manufactures	69.61	4.19	9.38
废弃资源综合利用业	Utilization of Waste Resources	54.76	5.86	4.52
金属制品、机械和设备修理业	Repair Service of Metal Products, Machinery and Equipment	55.29	5.74	5.78
电力、热力生产和供应业	Production and Supply of Electric Power and Heat Power	65.84	6.49	9.41
燃气生产和供应业	Production and Supply of Gas	51.63	8.39	13.34
水的生产和供应业	Production and Supply of Water	57.41	3.80	24.23

14-17 各市(州)规模以上工业企业主要经济效益指标(2023年)
Main Indicators on Economic Benefits of Industrial Enterprises above Designated Size by Region(2023)

单位：% (%)

市(州)	Region	资产负债率 Ratio of Debts to Assets	总资产贡献率 Ratio of Profits, Taxes and Interests to Average Assets	工业成本费用利润率 Ratio of Profits to Industrial Costs
全省	**Sichuan**	**56.08**	**9.70**	**10.22**
成都市	Chengdu	54.20	8.22	6.18
自贡市	Zigong	56.33	5.97	8.53
攀枝花市	Panzhihua	61.56	9.95	11.56
泸州市	Luzhou	50.43	17.82	29.13
德阳市	Deyang	57.82	13.93	10.68
绵阳市	Mianyang	60.36	6.75	6.07
广元市	Guangyuan	51.70	10.19	9.73
遂宁市	Suining	50.14	14.32	14.96
内江市	Neijiang	63.44	7.78	8.58
乐山市	Leshan	44.07	19.28	34.56
南充市	Nanchong	52.22	6.47	7.88
眉山市	Meishan	58.68	6.06	6.42
宜宾市	Yibin	54.47	12.30	14.98
广安市	Guangan	48.17	10.04	9.92
达州市	Dazhou	45.46	8.90	8.60
雅安市	Yaan	61.83	6.71	7.07
巴中市	Bazhong	57.80	4.16	4.81
资阳市	Ziyang	62.46	3.58	2.49
阿坝藏族羌族自治州	Aba	65.60	5.75	7.37
甘孜藏族自治州	Ganzi	77.24	3.67	8.16
凉山彝族自治州	Liangshan	65.19	8.22	18.64

14−18 各市(州)国有控股工业企业主要经济效益指标(2023年)
Main Indicators on Economic Benefits of State-holding Industrial Enterprises by Region(2023)

单位：%　　(%)

市(州)	Region	资产负债率 Ratio of Debts to Assets	总资产贡献率 Ratio of Profits, Taxes and Interests to Average Assets	工业成本费用利润率 Ratio of Profits to Industrial Costs
全省	**Sichuan**	**58.78**	**8.30**	**11.05**
成都市	Chengdu	55.98	8.79	7.04
自贡市	Zigong	47.51	3.93	7.87
攀枝花市	Panzhihua	62.98	6.44	9.20
泸州市	Luzhou	50.29	18.76	58.76
德阳市	Deyang	69.28	4.39	5.70
绵阳市	Mianyang	66.09	4.68	3.32
广元市	Guangyuan	56.43	6.33	10.95
遂宁市	Suining	46.10	6.47	20.79
内江市	Neijiang	70.45	3.20	11.84
乐山市	Leshan	58.67	5.19	11.02
南充市	Nanchong	52.49	2.33	1.99
眉山市	Meishan	58.24	2.91	4.46
宜宾市	Yibin	50.73	14.74	22.46
广安市	Guangan	45.16	7.73	12.37
达州市	Dazhou	41.83	10.03	18.58
雅安市	Yaan	62.97	4.77	11.29
巴中市	Bazhong	63.98	3.65	7.96
资阳市	Ziyang	66.02	3.48	6.77
阿坝藏族羌族自治州	Aba	70.24	5.32	11.18
甘孜藏族自治州	Ganzi	78.45	3.11	3.38
凉山彝族自治州	Liangshan	65.90	8.24	21.63

14-19 各市(州)大中型工业企业主要经济效益指标(2023年)
Main Indicators on Economic Benefits of Large and Medium-sized Industrial Enterprises by Region(2023)

单位：% (%)

市(州)	Region	资产负债率 Ratio of Debts to Assets	总资产贡献率 Ratio of Profits, Taxes and Interests to Average Assets	工业成本费用利润率 Ratio of Profits to Industrial Costs
全省	**Sichuan**	**54.88**	**10.95**	**11.10**
成都市	Chengdu	53.47	9.39	6.49
自贡市	Zigong	65.09	5.04	8.37
攀枝花市	Panzhihua	60.52	9.45	11.13
泸州市	Luzhou	48.46	21.42	41.18
德阳市	Deyang	58.56	12.33	11.33
绵阳市	Mianyang	61.93	5.44	4.93
广元市	Guangyuan	46.06	15.63	11.30
遂宁市	Suining	49.67	19.99	19.25
内江市	Neijiang	68.03	8.86	6.49
乐山市	Leshan	36.20	22.85	45.33
南充市	Nanchong	59.08	6.58	6.48
眉山市	Meishan	58.95	6.77	6.96
宜宾市	Yibin	53.02	13.70	16.71
广安市	Guangan	44.08	9.73	11.86
达州市	Dazhou	39.92	10.99	11.35
雅安市	Yaan	52.17	6.84	4.59
巴中市	Bazhong	47.01	9.83	6.89
资阳市	Ziyang	64.27	1.16	-2.69
阿坝藏族羌族自治州	Aba	30.50	5.28	0.79
甘孜藏族自治州	Ganzi	81.13	0.98	-11.13
凉山彝族自治州	Liangshan	65.85	9.11	19.45

14-20 规模以上工业企业主要产品产量
Output of Major Products of Industrial Enterprises above Designated Size

产品名称		Item		2005	2010	2015	2020	2021	2022	2023
化学纤维	(万吨)	Chemical Fiber	(10 000 tons)	26.56	51.22	118.10	79.00	77.40	69.70	62.74
纱	(万吨)	Yarn	(10 000 tons)	25.48	70.81	118.00	60.80	73.50	70.80	56.97
布	(亿米)	Cloth	(100 million m)	7.07	14.90	18.50	14.60	13.70	12.16	10.27
蚕丝及交织机织物	(万米)	Silk and Woven Fabric	(10 000 m)	11330	23042	17247	17906	15680	10802	6049
服装	(万件)	Garments	(10 000 pcs)	2764	9933	18780	19298	24700	19969	12015
机制纸及纸板	(万吨)	Machine-made Paper and Paperboard	(10 000 tons)	110.59	342.86	189.80	365.80	389.00	347.66	365.33
合成洗涤剂	(万吨)	Synthetic Detergents	(10 000 tons)	52.51	76.66	151.40	104.20	108.10	109.10	121.88
原电池及原电池组(非扣式)	(亿只)	Primary Battery and Primary Battery Pack (non-button type)	(100 million pieces)	0.58	3.80	7.50	21.20	25.20	23.00	16.14
原盐	(万吨)	Salt	(10 000 tons)	412.11	763.18	325.00	512.70	532.90	475.27	432.33
卷烟	(亿支)	Cigarettes	(100 million pieces)	685.05	914.24	945.80	895.20	910.80	911.58	913.92
乳制品	(万吨)	Dairy Products	(10 000 tons)	15.04	58.00	104.90	116.00	113.70	105.20	72.37
白酒(商品量)	(万千升)	Liquor	(10 000 kiloliter)	57.83	229.80	370.90	367.60	364.10	348.10	140.11
啤酒	(万千升)	Beer	(10 000 kiloliter)	126.22	158.30	221.00	218.00	249.90	260.30	268.71
软饮料	(万千升)	Soft Drink	(10 000 kiloliter)	120.41	495.91	1311.90	2002.20	1832.20	1582.10	1322.88
食用植物油	(万吨)	Vegetable Oil	(10 000 tons)	40.83	117.73	205.10	244.70	215.20	221.10	285.79
配、混合饲料	(万吨)	Mingled Feedstuff	(10 000 tons)	449.94	701.16	1201.40	1577.80	1221.60	2157.70	1501.45
中成药	(万吨)	Traditional Chinese Medicir	(10 000 tons)	9.83	29.81	53.60	27.50	33.60	33.90	20.89
化学原料药	(万吨)	Chemical Medicine	(10 000 tons)	5.40	2.67	22.50	6.80	30.80	9.90	12.68
塑料制品	(万吨)	Plastics Goods	(10 000 tons)	47.17	254.29	415.50	446.80	415.40	361.10	241.81
家用电冰箱	(万台)	Household Refrigerators	(10 000 units)	23.00	81.22	73.60	111.10	124.20	115.21	140.02
房间空气调节器	(万台)	Air Conditioner	(10 000 units)	145.23	119.49	142.80	210.80	229.00	386.42	526.24
彩色电视机	(万台)	Color Television Sets	(10 000 units)	781.61	1208.90	1055.70	970.10	1286.60	1543.68	1918.26
原油	(万吨)	Crude Oil	(10 000 tons)	13.92	15.12	15.43	7.86	9.22	11.94	19.65
柴油	(万吨)	Diesel Oil	(10 000 tons)	49.23	83.30	340.91	216.84	206.16	234.53	184.95

14-20 续表 continued

产品名称		Item		2005	2010	2015	2020	2021	2022	2023
汽油	(万吨)	Gasoline	(10 000 tons)	28.16	57.76	217.44	232.30	260.67	213.88	183.41
天然气	(亿立方米)	Natural Gas	(100 million cu.m)	135.24	234.16	266.21	452.41	522.21	554.06	594.80
发电量	(亿千瓦小时)	Electricity	(100 million kwh)	958.03	1683.82	2969.54	3980.83	4329.50	4633.68	4712.56
#水电	(亿千瓦小时)	Hydropower	(100 million kwh)	616.99	1103.37	2508.44	3349.15	3531.40	3681.28	3583.35
焦炭	(万吨)	Coke	(10 000 tons)	827.94	1157.09	1304.37	1074.23	1058.58	1038.83	977.61
生铁	(万吨)	Pig Iron	(10 000 tons)	1060.50	1593.81	1747.40	2136.80	2092.00	2036.41	1984.78
粗钢	(万吨)	Crude Steel	(10 000 tons)	1094.45	1580.99	2110.40	2792.60	2782.90	2787.34	2688.79
成品钢材	(万吨)	Rolled Steel Products	(10 000 tons)	1172.72	1976.55	2702.50	3437.20	3496.20	3583.01	4224.90
铁合金	(万吨)	Ferroalloy	(10 000 tons)	106.62	238.89	211.60	86.10	109.60	103.20	88.05
水泥	(万吨)	Cement	(10 000 tons)	4194.74	13227.55	14040.60	14495.80	14147.10	13070.02	12379.41
平板玻璃	(万重量箱)	Plate Glass	(10 000 wt. Cases)	1304.94	4275.94	4073.60	5885.70	6040.60	6145.77	6546.00
硫酸	(万吨)	Sulfuric Acid	(10 000 tons)	324.85	388.22	642.50	513.00	505.50	541.95	499.08
浓硝酸	(万吨)	Concentrated Nitric Acid	(10 000 tons)	5.43	8.43	5.40	6.70	8.20	7.50	7.57
碳酸钠(纯碱)	(万吨)	Soda Ash	(10 000 tons)	106.51	169.78	106.90	128.90	119.50	123.14	128.54
氢氧化钠(烧碱)	(万吨)	Caustic Soda	(10 000 tons)	75.49	106.93	97.30	120.40	130.90	135.94	155.77
合成氨	(万吨)	Synthetic Ammonia	(10 000 tons)	374.47	403.34	388.40	321.60	330.40	351.60	336.15
农用氮、磷、钾化学肥料总计	(折纯)(万吨)	Chemical Fertilizers	(10 000 tons)	428.82	510.12	497.10	349.60	335.70	381.85	286.73
#氮肥	(万吨)	Nitrogen Fertilizers	(10 000 tons)	337.60	414.76	307.90	228.90	234.10	274.90	228.15
化学农药	(万吨)	Chemical Pesticide	(10 000 tons)	3.88	12.81	17.80	27.60	30.80	28.69	32.98
电石(折合量)	(万吨)	Calcium carbide	(10 000 tons)	65.76	75.98	68.30	49.40	50.80	46.80	48.62
初级形态塑料	(万吨)	Primary Form of Plastics	(10 000 tons)	61.52	104.37	208.40	284.00	267.90	241.86	236.35
轮胎外胎	(万条)	Tyres	(10 000 pcs)	615.33	1558.12	3449.80	4777.70	6162.20	6424.80	7715.34
发电设备(500千瓦及以上)	(万千瓦)	Power Generating Equipment (each above 500kw)	(10000 kw)	2327.64	3781.54	2905.90	2654.10	3718.90	3701.95	4512.41
变压器	(万千伏安)	Transformer	(10 000 kva)	846.77	1151.61	1896.80	2001.80	2056.60	1520.10	2559.42
金属切削机床	(万台)	Metal-cutting Machine Tools	(10 000 units)	0.79	0.73	0.60	0.80	1.00	0.96	0.36
汽车	(万辆)	Motor Vehicles	(10 000 units)	5.66	10.29	105.10	71.30	72.70	72.48	97.20

主要统计指标解释

工业 指从事自然资源的开采，对采掘品和农产品进行加工和再加工的物质生产部门。具体包括：(1)对自然资源的开采，如采矿、晒盐等(但不包括禽兽捕猎和水产捕捞)；(2)对农副产品的加工、再加工，如粮油加工、食品加工、缫丝、纺织、制革等；(3)对采掘品的加工、再加工，如炼铁、炼钢、化工生产、石油加工、机器制造、木材加工等，以及电力、燃气及水的生产和供应等；(4)对工业品的修理、翻新，如机器设备的修理等。

工业统计调查单位为工业法人单位。

工业法人单位 指从事工业生产经营活动的法人单位。工业法人单位应同时具备以下条件：①依法成立，有自己的名称、组织机构和场所，能够独立承担民事责任；②独立拥有（或授权）使用资产，承担负债，有权与其他单位签订合同；③具有包括资产负债表在内的帐户，或者能够根据需要编制帐户。

本篇资料中规模以上工业企业的统计范围：1998至2006年为全部国有和年主营业务收入500万元及以上的非国有工业法人单位；2007至2010年为年主营业务收入500万元及以上工业法人单位；从2011年开始，为年主营业务收入2000万元及以上的工业法人单位。

国有控股企业 即原来的国有及国有控股企业，根据企业实收资本中国有经济成分的出资人的实际投资情况，或国有经济成分的出资人对企业资产的实际控制、支配程度进行分类。以下情况为国有控股：(1)在企业的全部实收资本中，国有经济成分的出资人拥有的实收资本（股本）所占企业全部实收资本（股本）的比例大于50%的国有绝对控股。(2)在企业的全部实收资本中，国有经济成分的出资人拥有的实收资本（股本）所占比例虽未大于50%，但相对大于其他任何一方经济成分的出资人所占比例的国有相对控股；或者虽不大于其他经济成分，但根据协议规定拥有企业实际控制权的国有协议控股。(3)投资双方各占50%，且未明确由谁绝对控股的企业，若其中一方为国有经济成分的，一律按国有控股处理。

轻工业 指主要提供生活消费品和制作手工工具的工业。按其所使用的原料不同，可分为两大类：(1)以农产品为原料的轻工业，是指直接或间接以农产品为基本原料的轻工业。主要包括食品制造、饮料制造、烟草加工、纺织、缝纫、皮革和毛皮制作、造纸以及印刷等工业；(2)以非农产品为原料的轻工业，是指以工业品为原料的轻工业。主要包括文教体育用品、化学药品制造、合成纤维制造、日用化学制品、日用玻璃制品、日用金属制品、手工工具制造、医疗器械制造、文化和办公用机械制造等工业。

重工业 指为国民经济各部门提供物质技术基础的主要生产资料的工业。按其生产性质和产品用途，可以分为下列三类：(1)采掘(伐)工业，是指对自然资源的开采，包括石油开采、煤炭开采、金属矿开采、非金属矿开采等工业；(2)原材料工业，指向国民经济各部门提供基本材料、动力和燃料的工业。包括金属冶炼及加工、炼焦及焦炭、化学、化工原料、水泥、人造板以及电力、石油和煤炭加工等工业；(3)加工工业，是指对工业原材料进行再加工制造的工业。包括装备国民经济各部门的机械设备制造工业、金属结构、水泥制品等工业，以及为农业提供的生产资料如化肥、农药等工业。

根据上述划分原则，修理业中以重工业产品为修理作业对象的划为重工业，反之划为轻工业。

资产总计 指企业过去的交易或者事项形成的、由企业拥有或者控制的、预期会给企业带来经济利益的资源。包括企业拥有的土地、办公楼、厂房、机器、运输工具、存货等实物资产和现金、存款、应收账款和预付账款等金融资产。资产一般按流动性分为流动资产和非流动资产。其中流动资产可分为货币资金、交易性金融资产、应收票据、应收账款、预付款项、其他应收款、存货等；非流动资产可分为长期股权投资、固定资产、无形资产及其他非流动资产等。来源于会计“资产负债表”中“资产总计”项目的期末余额数。

流动资产合计 资产满足以下条件之一应归为流动资产：(1)预计在一个正常营业周期中变现、出售或耗用，主要包括存货、应收账款等；(2)主要为交易目的而持有；(3)预计在资产负债表日起一年内（含一年）变现；(4)自资产负债日起一年内，交换其他资产或清偿负债的能力不受限制的现金或现金等价物。包括货币资金、应收票据、应收账款、存货等项目。来源于会计“资产负债表”中“流动资产合计”项目的期末余额数。

固定资产原价 指固定资产的成本，包括企业在购置、自行建造、安装、改建、扩建、技术改造某项固定资产时所发生的全部支出总额。根据会计“固定资产”科目的期末借方余额填报。

负债合计 指企业过去的交易或者事项形成的，预期会导致经济利益流出企业的现时义务。包括银行贷款、借款、应付账款、应付职工工资、应付职工福利费、应交税金等企业负有偿还责任的债务。负债一般按偿还期长短分为流动负债和非流动负债。来源于会计“资产负债表”中“负债合计”项目的期末余额数。

所有者权益 指企业资产扣除负债后由所有者享有的剩余权益。公司的所有者权益又称股东权益。包括实收资本、资本公积、盈余公积、未分配利润等。根据会计“资产负债表”中“所有者权益合计”项目的期末余额数填报。

营业收入 指企业从事销售商品、提供劳务和让渡资产使用权等生产经营活动形成的经济利益流入。营业收入包

括“主营业务收入”和“其他业务收入”。来源于会计“利润表”中“营业收入”项目的本年累计数。

营业成本 指企业从事销售商品、提供劳务和让渡资产使用权等生产经营活动发生的实际成本。包括企业（单位）在报告期内从事销售商品、提供劳务等日常活动发生的各种耗费。包括“主营业务成本”和“其他业务成本”。来源于会计“利润表”中“营业成本”项目的本年累计数。

销售费用 指企业在销售商品和材料、提供劳务的过程中发生的各种费用，包括保险费、包装费、展览费和广告费、商品维修费、预计产品质量保证损失、运输费、装卸费等以及为销售本企业商品而专设的销售机构（含销售网点、售后服务网点等）的职工薪酬、业务费、折旧费等经营费用。

管理费用 指企业为组织和管理企业生产经营所发生的费用，包括企业在筹建期间内发生的开办费、董事会和行政管理部门在企业经营管理中发生的，或者应当由企业统一负担的公司经费等。来源于会计“利润表”中“管理费用”项目的本年累计数。

财务费用 指企业为筹集生产经营所需资金等而发生的筹资费用，包括企业生产经营期间发生的利息支出（减利息收入）、汇兑损失（减汇兑收益）以及相关的手续费等。来源于会计“利润表”中“财务费用”项目的本年累计数。

利润总额 指企业在一定会计期间的经营成果，是生产经营过程中各种收入扣除各种耗费后的盈余，反映企业在报告期内实现的盈亏总额。来源于会计“利润表”中“利润总额”项目的本年累计数。

平均用工人数 指报告期企业平均实际拥有的、参与本企业生产经营活动的人员数。

总资产贡献率 反映企业全部资产的获利能力，是企业经营业绩和管理水平的集中体现，是评价和考核企业盈利能力的核心指标。计算公式为：

$$总资产贡献率=\frac{利润总额+税金总额+利息净支出}{平均资产总额}\times 100\%$$

公式中：税金总额为主营业务税金及附加与应交增值税之和；平均资产总额为期初期末资产之和的算术平均值。

资产负债率 该指标既反映企业经营风险的大小，也反映企业利用债权人提供的资金从事经营活动的能力。计算公式为：

$$资产负债率=\frac{负债总额}{资产总额}\times 100\%$$

成本费用利润率 反映企业投入的生产成本及费用的经济效益，同时也反映企业降低成本所取得的经济效益。计算公式为：

$$成本费用利润率=\frac{利润总额}{成本费用总额}\times 100\%$$

公式中：成本费用总额为主营业务成本、销售费用、管理费用、财务费用之和。

Explanatory Notes on Main Statistical Indicators

Industry refers to the material production sector which is engaged in the extraction of natural resources and processing and reprocessing of minerals and agricultural products, including (1) extraction of natural resources, such as mining, salt production (but not including hunting and fishing); (2) processing and reprocessing of farm and sideline produces, such as grain and oil processing, food processing, silk reeling, spinning and weaving and leather making; (3) processing and reprocessing of mineral products, such as steel making, iron smelting, chemicals manufacturing, petroleum processing, machine building, timber processing, and production and supply of electricity, gas and water; (4) repairing and renovating of industrial products such as the machinery.

In industrial surveys, the units of enquiry are industria corporate units.

Industrial corporate units refer to corporate units engaging in industrial production and operation activities, which meet the following requirements: (1) They are established legally, having their own names, organizations, location, and are able to take civil liability independently; (2) They possess (or are authorized to use) assets independently, assume liabilities and are entitled to sign contracts with other units; (3) They have accounts including the balance sheets or can compile the accounts according to the need.

The scopes of industrial enterprises above designated size were: all State-owned industrial enterprises and the non-State-owned industrial enterprises with revenue from principal business over 5 million yuan from 1998 to 2006; all industrial enterprises with revenue from principal business over 5 million yuan from 2007 to 2010; and all industrial enterprises with revenue from principal business above 20 million yuan since 2011.

State-holding Enterprises cover the original state-owned enterprises and state-holding enterprises. They are classified according to the actual investment made by the contributor of state-owned part in the paid-in capital of the enterprises, or the degree of control or dominance of the contributor on the assets of the enterprises. The following cases are regarded as state holding: (1) Absolute state-holding in which the contributor of state-owned parts possess more than 50% of all the paid-in capital (stocks) of the enterprises; (2) Relative state-holding in which the contributor of state-owned parts possess no more than 50% of the paid-in capital (stocks) of the enterprises, but more than that of any other contributors; or Agreed state-holding in which the contributor of state-owned parts possess no more than other contributors but have actual control over the enterprises according to agreements; (3) In the case both contributors possess 50% and it is not clear which one is in absolute holding position, the enterprise is regarded as state-holding enterprise if one of the contributor has state-owned elements.

Light Industry refers to the industry that produces consumer goods and hand tools. It consists of two categories, depending on the materials used: (1) Industries using farm products as raw materials. These are branches of light industry which directly or indirectly use farm products as basic raw materials, including the manufacture of food and beverages, tobacco processing, textile, clothing, fur and leather manufacturing, paper making, printing, etc; (2) Industries using non farm products as raw materials. These are branches of light industry which use manufactured goods as raw materials, including the manufacture of cultural, educational articles and sports goods, chemicals, synthetic fiber, chemical products for daily use, glass products for daily use, metal products for daily use, hand tools, medical apparatus and instruments, and the manufacture of cultural and clerical machinery.

Heavy Industry refers to the industry, which produces capital goods, and provides various sectors of the national economy with necessary material and technical basis. It consists of the following three branches according to the purpose of production or the use of products: (1)Mining, quarrying and logging industry refers to the industry that extracts natural resources, including extraction of petroleum, coal, metal and non-metal ores and logging; (2) Raw materials industry refers to the industry that provides various sectors of the national economy with raw materials, fuels and power. It includes smelting and processing of metals, coking and coke chemistry, chemical materials and building materials such as cement, plywood, and power, petroleum refining and coal dressing; (3) Manufacturing industry refers to the industry that processes raw materials. It includes machine-building industry, which equips sectors of the national economy, industries of metal structure and cement products, industries producing means of agricultural production, such as chemical fertilizers and pesticides.

According to the above principle of classification, the repairing trades which are engaged primarily in repairing products of heavy industry are classified into heavy industry while these engaged in repairing products of light industry are classified into light industry.

Total Assets refer to all resources that are owned or controlled by enterprises through previous trades or transactions, with expectation of making economic profits to enterprises. Included are all assets owned by enterprises such as land, office buildings, factories, machines, vehicles, inventories and other physical assets as well as cash, deposits, accounts receivable, prepayments and other financial assets. Classified by the degree of liquidity, total assets include current assets and non-current assets. Current assets can be classified into monetary capital, trading financial assets, notes receivable, accounts receivable, advanced payments, other receivables and inventories. Non-current assets can be divided into long-term equity investment, fixed assets, intangible assets and other non-current assets. Data on this indicator can be obtained from the year-end figures of total assets in the Balance Sheet of accounting records.

Current Assets refer to the assets that meet one of the

following requirements: (1) expected to be cashed, sold or used in a normal operation cycle, mainly including inventory and accounts receivable; (2) owned for transaction purpose mainly; (3) expected to be cashed within one year (including one year) from the day of the Balance Sheet; (4) unlimited cash or cash equivalents that can be exchanged with other assets or capable of settling debts during one year since the day of the Balance Sheet. Included are monetary capital, notes receivable, accounts receivable and inventories. Data on this indicator can be obtained from the year-end figures of total current assets in the Balance Sheet of accounting records.

Original Value of Fixed Assets refer to the cost of fixed assets, or the total expenditure of an enterprise spent on certain fixed assets, through purchase, construction, installation, transformation, expansion or technical upgrading. It is reported according to the year-end debit balance of fixed assets of accounting records.

Total Liabilities refer to payable liabilities of enterprises that are accumulated from earlier transactions with expectation of leaking out of economic profits. Included are debts that enterprises are responsible for repaying such as bank loans, borrowings, accounts payable, wages payable, employee benefits payable, taxes payable, etc. In terms of payment, it can be divided into liquid liabilities and long-term liabilities. Data on this indicator can be obtained from the year-end figures of total liabilities in the Balance Sheet of accounting records.

Total Owner's Equity refers to the residual ownership of enterprise investors by deducting total liabilities from the total assets, including the paid-in capital, accumulation of capital, operating surplus and non-distributed profits. Data can be obtained from the year-end figures of total equity in the Balance Sheet of accounting records.

Business Revenue refers to the inflow of economic benefits through production and operation activities of enterprises, such as selling commodities, providing labor services and transferring the right to use of assets. Business revenue includes "revenue from principal business" and " revenue from other business". It comes from current year's cumulative report of "business revenue" items from the "income statement".

Business Cost refers to the actual costs incurred by the enterprises in such production and operation activities as selling commodities, providing labor services and transferring the right to use of assets. It includes various expenditures incurred by enterprises (units) in their daily activities of selling goods and providing labour services during the reporting period. It includes "cost of principal business" and "cost of other business". It comes from current year's cumulative report of "operating cost" items from the "income statement".

Selling Expense refer to the cost during the sale of goods and materials, providing labour services, including insurance, packing, exhibition fees and advertising fees, merchandise maintenance costs, expected product quality guarantee loss, transportation fees, handling fees, and operating expenses for the sales of the company's products, such as employee compensation, business expenses, depreciation costs for dedicated sales offices (including sales outlets, after-sales service outlets, etc.).

Management Expenses refer to the expenses for the organization and management of enterprise operation, including the start-up costs during the construction of enterprises, funds occurred during enterprises operation by board of directors and executive management in the enterprise management, and other costs to be paid by enterprises. It comes from current year's cumulative amount of management cost in income statement.

Financial Expenses refer to cost of fund-raising for enterprises to raise funds for production and operation, including interest payments (a reduction in interest income), exchange loss (less exchange gains) and related fees during the period of production. It comes from current year's cumulative amount of financial expenses in income statement.

Total Profits refer to the operational results in a certain accounting period, and it is the balance of various incomes minus various spending in the course of operation, reflecting the total profits and losses of enterprises in reference period. Data are obtained from current year's cumulative amount of total profits in the profit statement of the accounting record of enterprise.

Annual Average Employees refer to the number of persons engaged in the production and operation activities of enterprises in the reporting period, which are actually employed by the enterprises.

Ratio of Profits, Taxes and Interests to Average Assets reflects the profit-making capability of all assets of the enterprise and is a key indicator manifesting the performance and management and evaluating the profit-making potential of the enterprise. It is calculated as follows:

$$\text{Ratio of profits, taxes and interests to average as sets} = \frac{\text{total profits+total taxes+net interest payment}}{\text{average assets}} \times 100\%$$

In the above formula, total taxes is the sum of tax and extra charges from principal business and value-added tax payable; and average assets is the arithmetic mean of the sum of beginning assets and ending assets.

Ratio of Debts to Assets reflects both the operation risk and the capability of the enterprise in making use of the capital from the creditors. It is calculated as follows:

$$\text{Ratio of debts to assets} = \frac{\text{total debts}}{\text{total assets}} \times 100\%$$

Ratio of Profits to Total Industrial Costs refers to the ratio of profits realized in a given period to the total costs in the same period, which reflects the economic efficiency of input cost and is calculated as follows:

$$\text{Ratio of profits to total industrial cost} = \frac{\text{total profits}}{\text{total costs}} \times 100\%$$

Total costs in the above formula are the sum of cost of principal business, marketing cost, management cost and financial cost.

15 建筑业
Chapter 15 Construction

SICHUAN STATISTICAL YEARBOOK

15-1 建筑业企业个数、产值、人数及竣工面积

Number of Enterprises, Gross Output Value, Number of Employed Persons and Floor Space of Buildings Completed of Construction

年份 Year	企业个数 (个) Number of Enterprises (unit)	总产值 (亿元) Gross Output Value (100 million yuan)	就业人员数 (万人) Number of Employed Persons (10 000 persons)	竣工房屋建筑面积 (万平方米) Floor Space of Buildings Completed (10 000 sq.m)
1952	41	0.63	3.54	20.21
1957	87	2.82	14.61	136.38
1962	133	1.58	12.14	48.01
1965	187	7.82	28.93	218.01
1970	222	9.16	43.12	238.60
1975	252	10.36	43.05	272.03
1978	276	13.17	42.38	556.56
1980	325	13.36	39.03	501.02
1985	555	31.85	49.45	835.24
1990	756	67.11	60.21	1060.60
1995	1144	279.10	89.70	2081.00
1996	2725	468.66	160.50	4537.00
1997	2779	520.64	154.24	5638.48
1998	3028	597.76	159.20	5017.25
1999	3050	649.52	160.13	5429.28
2000	3305	713.81	158.10	5839.32
2001	3125	822.87	171.85	7029.93
2002	3475	1078.25	200.42	8491.14
2003	3498	1235.04	212.68	8784.56
2004	4183	1321.22	173.84	8837.99
2005	4073	1480.88	181.80	8692.18
2006	3924	1768.87	188.50	9177.55
2007	3887	2130.17	204.71	9630.60
2008	4559	2624.96	235.78	9797.98
2009	4386	3374.06	265.24	11393.53
2010	4334	4200.86	335.53	12086.29
2011	4318	5305.89	249.46	13663.11
2012	4283	6292.67	230.23	15768.08
2013	4271	7277.41	262.65	18211.86
2014	3965	8148.52	241.79	19544.25
2015	3952	8847.59	244.23	20666.78
2016	4333	10044.16	291.82	20977.99
2017	5191	11996.22	377.99	22598.10
2018	5860	13752.27	382.56	24876.82
2019	6043	14668.15	351.62	20355.93
2020	7405	15612.70	395.12	22572.79
2021	8453	17351.19	364.57	23250.76
2022	9214	17845.61	341.05	22389.91
2023	10055	17272.54	341.73	18709.60

注：2003年建筑业统计数据仅包括当年有工作量的建筑业企业，2004年建筑业统计数据是普查数据。

a) The data of construction enterprises of 2003 only include the enterprises which had taken in 2003.The data of 2004 was obtained from surveys.

15-2 按登记注册统计类别分建筑业企业主要指标（2023年）

指标		Item		合计 Total Enterprises
建筑业企业个数	（个）	Number of Construction Enterprises	（unit）	10055
从业人员平均人数	（万人）	Average Number of Persons Employed	(10 000 persons)	422.67
自有固定资产原价	（万元）	Fixed Assets Owned (original value)	(10 000 yuan)	14092180
自有固定资产净价	（万元）	Fixed Assets Owned (net value)	(10 000 yuan)	8118758
自有机械设备净值	（万元）	Machinery and Equipment Owned (net value)	(10 000 yuan)	1483575
自有机械设备台数	（台）	Number of Machinery and Equipment Owned	(set)	174552
自有机械设备总功率	（万千瓦）	Total Power of Machinery and Equipment Owned	(10 000 kw)	698.66
建筑业总产值	（万元）	Gross Output Value of Construction	(10 000 yuan)	172725363
竣工产值	（万元）	Output Value of Completed Projects	(10 000 yuan)	67434971
房屋建筑施工面积	（万平方米）	Floor Space of Buildings under Construction	(10 000 sq.m)	65040
房屋建筑竣工面积	（万平方米）	Floor Space of Buildings Completed	(10 000 sq.m)	18710
利润总额	（万元）	Total Profits	(10 000 yuan)	6370039
税金总额	（万元）	Total Tax	(10 000 yuan)	3922149
利税总额	（万元）	Total Pre-Tax Profits	(10 000 yuan)	10292188
按总产值计算的劳动生产率	（元/人）	Overall Labor Productivity	(yuan/person)	408653
技术装备率	（元/人）	Value of Machinery per Laborer	(yuan/person)	3510
动力装备率	（千瓦/人）	Power of Machinery per Laborer	(kw/person)	1.65
房屋建筑面积竣工率	(%)	Rate of Floor Space of Buildings Completed	(%)	28.77
产值利润率	(%)	Ratio of Profit to Gross Output Value	(%)	3.69
产值利税率	(%)	Ratio of Pre-tax Profit to Gross Output Value	(%)	5.96

Main Indicators of Construction Enterprises by Registered Statistical Categories(2023)

内资企业 Domestic Invested Enterprises	港澳台投资企业 Enterprises with Investment from Hong Kong, Macao and Taiwan	外商投资企业 Foreign Invested Enterprises
10050	3	2
422.59	0.05	0.03
14082369	3198	6613
8113977	1831	2950
1482795		780
174442		110
698.46		0.20
172695392	21468	8503
67426053	416	8503
65040		
18710		
6365810	3549	680
3921185	489	475
10286995	4038	1155
408658	461677	264891
3509		24299
1.65		6.33
28.77		
3.69	16.53	8.00
5.96	18.81	13.58

15-3 各市(州)建筑业企业个数
Number of Construction Enterprises by Region

单位：个 (unit)

市(州)	Region	2013	2014	2015	2016	2017	2018	2019	2020	2021	2022	2023
全省	**Sichuan**	**4271**	**3965**	**3952**	**4333**	**5191**	**5860**	**6043**	**7405**	**8453**	**9214**	**10055**
成都市	Chengdu	1478	1200	1206	1408	1733	1801	1772	2108	2348	2441	2434
自贡市	Zigong	133	129	121	116	136	135	115	157	175	202	230
攀枝花市	Panzhihua	91	78	80	80	90	93	89	100	115	125	136
泸州市	Luzhou	164	159	175	199	257	310	361	418	489	546	614
德阳市	Deyang	255	242	240	235	256	271	251	326	352	374	408
绵阳市	Mianyang	386	411	402	404	426	448	446	577	770	825	993
广元市	Guangyuan	172	165	168	179	190	216	247	300	341	364	388
遂宁市	Suining	148	143	139	169	176	177	166	240	261	282	377
内江市	Neijiang	119	111	103	107	113	115	106	135	147	163	178
乐山市	Leshan	147	152	160	169	191	201	199	222	229	269	296
南充市	Nanchong	249	243	241	249	280	330	317	449	563	637	686
眉山市	Meishan	134	135	126	119	126	117	160	221	287	343	408
宜宾市	Yibin	213	197	188	211	300	464	576	664	715	762	847
广安市	Guangan	99	110	109	123	140	187	202	219	243	305	341
达州市	Dazhou	124	118	119	125	140	161	158	276	334	386	409
雅安市	Yaan	52	44	44	51	53	58	70	101	116	123	163
巴中市	Bazhong	97	133	139	139	181	243	215	251	261	250	262
资阳市	Ziyang	122	110	98	60	61	69	54	64	70	108	128
阿坝藏族羌族自治州	Aba	27	28	29	31	82	127	145	148	174	197	207
甘孜藏族自治州	Ganzi	26	22	24	26	32	55	81	89	97	99	103
凉山彝族自治州	Liangshan	35	35	41	133	228	282	313	340	366	413	447

15-4 各市(州)按登记注册统计类别分建筑业企业个数(2023年)
Number of Construction Enterprises by Region and Registered Statistical Categories(2023)

单位：个 (unit)

市(州)及分组	Region and Group	企业个数 Number of Enterprises	内资企业 Domestic Invested Enterprises	港澳台投资企业 Enterprises with Investment from Hong Kong, Macao and Taiwan	外商投资企业 Foreign Invested Enterprises
全省	**Sichuan**	**10055**	**10050**	**3**	**2**
按市(州)分	**Grouped by Region**				
成都市	Chengdu	2434	2430	3	1
自贡市	Zigong	230	230		
攀枝花市	Panzhihua	136	136		
泸州市	Luzhou	614	614		
德阳市	Deyang	408	408		
绵阳市	Mianyang	993	993		
广元市	Guangyuan	388	388		
遂宁市	Suining	377	377		
内江市	Neijiang	178	177		1
乐山市	Leshan	296	296		
南充市	Nanchong	686	686		
眉山市	Meishan	408	408		
宜宾市	Yibin	847	847		
广安市	Guangan	341	341		
达州市	Dazhou	409	409		
雅安市	Yaan	163	163		
巴中市	Bazhong	262	262		
资阳市	Ziyang	128	128		
阿坝藏族羌族自治州	Aba	207	207		
甘孜藏族自治州	Ganzi	103	103		
凉山彝族自治州	Liangshan	447	447		
按资质等级分	**Grouped by Qualification Grade**				
总承包企业	The General Contractor	8351	8350	1	
特级企业	The Special Grade	37	37		
一级企业	The First Grade	824	824		
二级企业	The Second Grade	2283	2283		
三级企业	The Third Grade	5207	5206	1	
专业承包企业	The Specialized Contractor	1704	1700	2	2
一级企业	The First Grade	299	297	1	1
二级企业	The Second Grade	893	891	1	1
三级企业及其他	The Third Grade & Others	512	512		

注：自2023年起，按照《关于市场主体统计分类的划分规定》（国统字〔2023〕14号）执行新的登记注册统计类别。
a) Implement new registration and statistical categories in accordance with the "Regulations on the Classification of Market Entity Statistics" (Guotongzi〔2023〕No. 14) since 2023.

15−5 各市(州)建筑业企业就业人员
Number of Employed Persons in Construction Enterprises by Region

单位：万人 (10 000 persons)

市(州)	Region	2013	2014	2015	2016	2017	2018	2019	2020	2021	2022	2023
全省	**Sichuan**	**262.65**	**241.79**	**244.23**	**291.82**	**377.99**	**382.56**	**351.62**	**395.12**	**364.57**	**341.05**	**341.73**
成都市	Chengdu	90.10	72.91	69.93	94.29	112.91	118.22	102.81	113.06	97.34	93.55	104.18
自贡市	Zigong	9.44	8.98	9.59	8.56	10.44	12.91	10.41	11.52	11.48	11.96	9.17
攀枝花市	Panzhihua	7.65	4.26	4.22	3.97	7.30	5.19	4.16	4.11	3.76	3.52	5.49
泸州市	Luzhou	21.99	23.05	24.33	31.53	41.03	40.76	43.90	42.15	45.56	35.62	32.45
德阳市	Deyang	12.87	10.00	8.35	8.65	9.40	11.25	10.39	10.51	9.03	9.07	12.56
绵阳市	Mianyang	15.00	15.83	18.28	20.02	23.77	22.79	20.71	23.27	24.01	23.24	32.84
广元市	Guangyuan	5.09	4.83	5.24	6.08	7.82	9.63	8.83	8.85	8.48	8.70	8.25
遂宁市	Suining	8.90	8.74	8.51	10.45	11.29	10.26	11.00	15.36	15.69	15.10	14.46
内江市	Neijiang	8.48	8.47	9.40	9.24	10.90	10.26	7.67	9.84	9.31	8.29	7.32
乐山市	Leshan	5.42	5.79	6.05	6.39	8.10	9.78	6.94	8.92	7.94	7.82	8.92
南充市	Nanchong	15.44	15.02	14.28	18.73	23.14	28.30	20.72	35.30	34.45	32.22	30.28
眉山市	Meishan	8.31	8.39	8.59	10.55	11.93	11.50	14.39	17.24	17.88	15.33	12.75
宜宾市	Yibin	10.57	10.42	10.61	11.62	15.56	19.82	22.55	24.00	21.52	20.44	20.38
广安市	Guangan	11.54	12.20	11.79	12.81	13.79	15.08	13.13	11.72	11.77	13.12	12.30
达州市	Dazhou	10.94	10.72	10.32	10.56	12.20	13.58	14.89	18.17	19.49	19.52	12.50
雅安市	Yaan	1.22	1.54	1.68	1.82	2.98	3.06	2.45	2.65	2.37	2.47	2.29
巴中市	Bazhong	9.08	10.20	12.82	16.04	21.91	22.82	20.55	22.87	10.87	7.44	5.46
资阳市	Ziyang	7.68	7.74	7.45	6.21	6.84	7.79	6.39	6.34	6.47	7.09	3.39
阿坝藏族羌族自治州	Aba	0.67			0.67	0.79	1.32	1.64	1.60	1.21	1.13	1.35
甘孜藏族自治州	Ganzi		0.50	0.57	0.53	0.60	1.02	1.19	1.05	0.97	0.93	0.91
凉山彝族自治州	Liangshan	1.84	1.71	1.78	3.11	25.28	7.22	6.90	6.58	4.96	4.47	4.49

15-6 各市(州)按登记注册统计类别分建筑业企业就业人员(2023年)
Number of Employed Persons in Construction Enterprises by Region and Registered Statistical Categories (2023)

单位：万人 (10 000 persons)

市(州)及分组	Region and Group	合计 Total	内资企业 Domestic Invested Enterprises	港澳台投资企业 Enterprises with Investment from Hong Kong, Macao and Taiwan	外商投资企业 Foreign Invested Enterprises
全省	**Sichuan**	**341.73**	**341.69**	**0.03**	**0.01**
按市(州)分	**Grouped by Region**				
成都市	Chengdu	104.18	104.14	0.03	0.01
自贡市	Zigong	9.17	9.17		
攀枝花市	Panzhihua	5.49	5.49		
泸州市	Luzhou	32.45	32.45		
德阳市	Deyang	12.56	12.56		
绵阳市	Mianyang	32.84	32.84		
广元市	Guangyuan	8.25	8.25		
遂宁市	Suining	14.46	14.46		
内江市	Neijiang	7.32	7.32		
乐山市	Leshan	8.92	8.92		
南充市	Nanchong	30.28	30.28		
眉山市	Meishan	12.75	12.75		
宜宾市	Yibin	20.38	20.38		
广安市	Guangan	12.30	12.30		
达州市	Dazhou	12.50	12.50		
雅安市	Yaan	2.29	2.29		
巴中市	Bazhong	5.46	5.46		
资阳市	Ziyang	3.39	3.39		
阿坝藏族羌族自治州	Aba	1.35	1.35		
甘孜藏族自治州	Ganzi	0.91	0.91		
凉山彝族自治州	Liangshan	4.49	4.49		
按资质等级分	**Grouped by Qualification Grade**				
总承包企业	The General Contractor	315.07	315.07	0.01	
特级企业	The Special Grade	33.02	33.02		
一级企业	The First Grade	114.88	114.88		
二级企业	The Second Grade	73.50	73.50		
三级企业	The Third Grade	93.67	93.67	0.01	
专业承包企业	The Specialized Contractor	26.66	26.62	0.02	0.01
一级企业	The First Grade	8.00	7.97	0.02	0.01
二级企业	The Second Grade	11.54	11.54		
三级企业及其他	The Third Grade & Others	7.12	7.12		

注：自2023年起，按照《关于市场主体统计分类的划分规定》（国统字〔2023〕14号）执行新的登记注册统计类别。
a) Implement new registration and statistical categories in accordance with the "Regulations on the Classification of Market Entity Statistics" (Guotongzi〔2023〕No. 14) since 2023.

15-7 各市(州)建筑业企业施工、竣工房屋面积(2023年)

Floor Space of Buildings under Construction and Completed of Construction Enterprises by Region(2023)

市(州)及分组	Region and Group	房屋建筑施工面积(万平方米) Floor Space of Buildings under Construction (10 000 sq.m)	#本年新开工 Newly-started Buildings	房屋建筑竣工面积(万平方米) Floor Space of Buildings Completed (10 000 sq.m)	#住宅 Residential Housing	房屋面积竣工率(%) Rate of Floor Space Completed (%)
全省	**Sichuan**	**65039.52**	**19296.13**	**18709.60**	**11667.65**	**28.77**
按市(州)分	**Grouped by Region**					
成都市	Chengdu	36418.20	8595.86	7392.84	4543.55	20.30
自贡市	Zigong	1327.70	592.23	517.62	383.00	38.99
攀枝花市	Panzhihua	686.50	258.08	99.86	53.30	14.55
泸州市	Luzhou	4722.47	1835.51	1885.30	730.72	39.92
德阳市	Deyang	2172.82	702.46	589.28	358.09	27.12
绵阳市	Mianyang	2461.85	746.49	1110.03	715.33	45.09
广元市	Guangyuan	530.09	173.60	164.95	101.74	31.12
遂宁市	Suining	1778.09	548.23	788.02	411.84	44.32
内江市	Neijiang	1316.28	453.39	557.83	382.50	42.38
乐山市	Leshan	1110.36	388.31	513.68	386.67	46.26
南充市	Nanchong	3696.64	1913.89	1790.67	1477.20	48.44
眉山市	Meishan	1403.97	490.05	467.49	295.75	33.30
宜宾市	Yibin	2479.49	831.70	869.53	516.05	35.07
广安市	Guangan	871.84	386.48	454.48	328.03	52.13
达州市	Dazhou	2081.16	580.46	758.12	534.40	36.43
雅安市	Yaan	352.98	111.81	92.71	53.55	26.26
巴中市	Bazhong	308.83	107.15	175.41	120.70	56.80
资阳市	Ziyang	331.02	133.54	71.86	52.10	21.71
阿坝藏族羌族自治州	Aba	69.91	32.58	35.04	16.31	50.12
甘孜藏族自治州	Ganzi	83.11	33.01	25.20	4.35	30.32
凉山彝族自治州	Liangshan	836.20	381.30	349.69	202.47	41.82
按资质等级分	**Grouped by Qualification Grade**					
总承包企业	The General Contractor	63561.07	18566.47	17742.35	11089.75	27.91
特级企业	The Special Grade	19273.43	4844.39	3401.23	1891.13	17.65
一级企业	The First Grade	28256.56	6853.09	7407.72	4830.59	26.22
二级企业	The Second Grade	9541.54	3780.36	4008.76	2690.53	42.01
三级企业	The Third Grade	6489.54	3088.63	2924.64	1677.49	45.07
专业承包企业	The Specialized Contractor	1478.45	729.67	967.24	577.90	65.42
一级企业	The First Grade	388.97	159.15	346.84	207.72	89.17
二级企业	The Second Grade	513.51	241.78	425.05	271.24	82.77
三级企业及其他	The Third Grade & Others	575.96	328.74	195.35	98.94	33.92

15-8 各市(州)建筑业企业房屋施工面积
Floor Space under Construction of Construction Enterprises by Region

单位：万平方米 (10 000 sq.m)

市(州)	Region	2013	2014	2015	2016	2017	2018	2019	2020	2021	2022	2023
全省	**Sichuan**	**47377.67**	**53362.63**	**52795.35**	**54048.32**	**60593.38**	**63481.47**	**61742.99**	**67655.15**	**72351.79**	**76212.61**	**65039.52**
成都市	Chengdu	22115.29	22463.04	23852.51	23327.39	25294.66	26083.82	28378.91	29193.84	30146.12	32177.87	36418.20
自贡市	Zigong	1337.10	1689.31	1807.44	2030.35	2462.64	2562.71	2613.71	2948.89	2207.04	2541.74	1327.70
攀枝花市	Panzhihua	543.93	546.12	443.54	504.24	543.15	599.40	575.66	211.34	578.55	655.08	686.50
泸州市	Luzhou	3652.50	4250.37	4063.63	4493.66	4923.93	5062.74	4742.86	4531.16	5383.94	9781.20	4722.47
德阳市	Deyang	2124.82	2440.91	1979.12	1969.73	1970.44	2179.28	2317.19	2714.32	2426.65	3212.23	2172.82
绵阳市	Mianyang	2149.56	2675.96	2788.66	2696.52	3123.88	3728.64	3207.36	4019.49	3645.15	3402.97	2461.85
广元市	Guangyuan	591.40	740.49	860.18	1085.02	1106.73	1180.89	1004.49	842.38	661.29	554.75	530.09
遂宁市	Suining	1115.87	1293.20	1470.14	1608.21	2022.84	1795.05	1753.44	2322.71	5549.76	5648.68	1778.09
内江市	Neijiang	1041.99	1336.58	1372.57	1507.44	1446.66	1352.94	943.09	1390.95	2094.02	1122.37	1316.28
乐山市	Leshan	897.37	829.18	1000.99	1128.86	1513.57	1664.44	1227.64	1622.44	2570.06	1342.41	1110.36
南充市	Nanchong	2936.77	3123.15	3026.20	3110.31	3730.38	4430.21	4516.28	4887.93	5828.20	4369.63	3696.64
眉山市	Meishan	1154.33	1334.19	1447.88	1639.34	1891.08	1597.53	1440.50	1507.49	1667.61	1618.40	1403.97
宜宾市	Yibin	1281.63	3255.42	1420.49	1524.87	1849.88	2343.11	1857.05	3840.86	2973.87	3258.79	2479.49
广安市	Guangan	1373.97	1640.87	1467.11	1505.44	1615.21	1511.37	1087.66	918.59	975.66	987.87	871.84
达州市	Dazhou	1925.55	2183.50	2158.90	2258.85	2337.79	2485.36	2219.69	2744.77	3150.16	3083.37	2081.16
雅安市	Yaan	133.09	179.48	211.84	269.22	478.77	424.96	360.05	438.75	456.69	512.69	352.98
巴中市	Bazhong	1693.16	1851.24	1798.07	2038.10	2602.17	2827.20	2111.35	2173.29	814.21	532.26	308.83
资阳市	Ziyang	983.24	1100.23	1235.57	694.24	860.17	772.02	608.78	596.06	482.47	511.03	331.02
阿坝藏族羌族自治州	Aba	47.42	56.58	46.64	50.43	95.24	83.24	67.95	74.14	60.69	75.51	69.91
甘孜藏族自治州	Ganzi	37.99	34.95	28.50	36.73	37.82	90.54	51.76	36.29	94.11	43.82	83.11
凉山彝族自治州	Liangshan	240.71	337.88	135.36	569.37	686.35	706.03	657.57	639.45	585.53	779.97	836.20

15-9 各市(州)建筑业企业房屋竣工面积
Floor Space Completed of Construction Enterprises by Region

单位：万平方米 (10 000 sq.m)

市(州)	Region	2013	2014	2015	2016	2017	2018	2019	2020	2021	2022	2023
全省	**Sichuan**	**18211.86**	**19544.25**	**20666.78**	**20977.99**	**22598.10**	**24876.82**	**20355.93**	**22572.79**	**23250.76**	**22389.91**	**18709.60**
成都市	Chengdu	5787.99	5870.98	5985.54	6242.71	5837.70	6813.06	5437.82	6126.16	6504.34	6380.41	7392.84
自贡市	Zigong	460.45	563.04	608.37	609.66	870.07	747.26	682.82	913.79	1207.37	1493.57	517.62
攀枝花市	Panzhihua	277.10	175.66	94.59	185.45	161.63	146.61	113.75	122.45	137.97	249.31	99.86
泸州市	Luzhou	1704.97	1964.55	2177.22	2262.69	2372.83	2646.46	2680.60	2619.62	2275.46	1968.09	1885.30
德阳市	Deyang	843.84	765.54	864.30	706.88	737.00	513.15	512.35	867.94	873.17	820.18	589.28
绵阳市	Mianyang	703.27	825.47	943.77	1018.21	1300.32	1770.05	1304.46	1148.58	1450.64	1472.04	1110.03
广元市	Guangyuan	203.92	247.81	225.87	283.04	292.84	340.35	268.54	234.07	261.66	208.18	164.95
遂宁市	Suining	707.89	793.49	889.56	906.57	1201.15	1339.96	1094.60	1231.92	1397.53	1211.49	788.02
内江市	Neijiang	500.13	658.18	792.71	837.86	865.03	802.04	671.46	841.99	1015.06	691.62	557.83
乐山市	Leshan	387.70	342.87	568.18	482.82	595.52	520.96	375.60	493.24	490.24	600.08	513.68
南充市	Nanchong	1897.44	1925.93	2035.27	2030.84	2278.22	2710.07	1760.87	2675.17	2878.67	2273.17	1790.67
眉山市	Meishan	670.15	641.74	729.00	808.22	866.09	1025.82	925.65	885.55	751.55	655.55	467.49
宜宾市	Yibin	675.72	776.92	805.03	818.39	949.52	905.97	800.56	786.92	807.92	1416.20	869.53
广安市	Guangan	737.57	848.59	845.74	842.39	872.56	884.42	679.35	486.63	590.61	560.81	454.48
达州市	Dazhou	807.62	1106.82	1022.08	1039.44	1131.75	1248.45	988.47	1104.18	1325.78	1223.13	758.12
雅安市	Yaan	75.33	104.85	118.05	169.13	181.95	197.51	197.00	164.12	162.92	137.96	92.71
巴中市	Bazhong	1034.10	1233.37	1147.90	1153.05	1504.32	1629.38	1265.92	1278.03	519.57	404.63	175.41
资阳市	Ziyang	545.93	528.08	581.06	279.48	215.99	274.15	282.33	215.71	236.93	230.13	71.86
阿坝藏族羌族自治州	Aba	31.21	41.76	38.24	34.71	58.30	51.77	41.16	41.02	34.35	39.82	35.04
甘孜藏族自治州	Ganzi	15.63	14.22	15.54	19.99	22.37	36.49	36.73	35.44	33.59	21.25	25.20
凉山彝族自治州	Liangshan	143.90	114.40	178.75	246.45	282.94	272.87	235.89	300.25	295.42	332.30	349.69

15-10 各市(州)建筑业企业动力装备情况(2023年)

Power of Machinery and Equipment Owned of Construction Enterprises by Region(2023)

市(州)及分组	Region and Group	自有机械设备总台数(台) Number of Machinery and Equipment Owned (unit)	自有机械设备总功率(万千瓦) Total Power of Machinery and Equipment Owned (10 000 kw)	自有机械设备净值(万元) Net Value of Machinery and Equipment Owned (10 000 yuan)	技术装备率(元/人) Value of Machinery per Laborer (yuan/person)	动力装备率(千瓦/人) Power of Machinery per Laborer (kw/person)
全省	**Sichuan**	**174552**	**698.66**	**1483575**	**3510**	**1.65**
按市(州)分	**Grouped by Region**					
成都市	Chengdu	86889	495.89	885863	5625	3.15
自贡市	Zigong	5159	8.56	19417	2048	0.90
攀枝花市	Panzhihua	6418	21.83	54803	10425	4.15
泸州市	Luzhou	4123	12.74	50764	1352	0.34
德阳市	Deyang	5708	20.29	41589	2704	1.32
绵阳市	Mianyang	5418	10.73	32612	1209	0.40
广元市	Guangyuan	3380	9.17	18688	2147	1.05
遂宁市	Suining	3898	7.89	34632	2439	0.56
内江市	Neijiang	5104	8.19	8753	1040	0.97
乐山市	Leshan	7000	9.53	39818	4297	1.03
南充市	Nanchong	9035	18.35	78815	1936	0.45
眉山市	Meishan	6387	21.70	33644	2314	1.49
宜宾市	Yibin	5434	9.81	25981	1066	0.40
广安市	Guangan	4862	13.01	32856	2439	0.97
达州市	Dazhou	4646	11.32	48446	3734	0.87
雅安市	Yaan	1683	2.73	10778	3731	0.94
巴中市	Bazhong	6059	7.18	35812	6223	1.25
资阳市	Ziyang	1088	3.39	10336	2785	0.91
阿坝藏族羌族自治州	Aba	210	0.69	1273	785	0.43
甘孜藏族自治州	Ganzi	727	1.03	3193	2581	0.83
凉山彝族自治州	Liangshan	1324	4.64	15503	1783	0.53
按资质等级分	**Grouped by Qualification Grade**					
总承包企业	The General Contractor	155948	664.71	1393104	3558	1.70
特级企业	The Special Grade	44878	331.05	574252	8708	5.02
一级企业	The First Grade	53857	189.32	388110	2798	1.36
二级企业	The Second Grade	35427	76.90	236464	2763	0.90
三级企业及其他	The Third Grade & Other	21779	67.44	194183	1919	0.67
专业承包企业	The Specialized Contractor	18604	33.95	90472	2902	1.09
一级企业	The First Grade	7094	11.69	17710	1827	1.21
二级企业	The Second Grade	8398	17.79	28197	2148	1.36
三级企业及其他	The Third Grade & Other	3112	4.48	44565	5337	0.54

15-11 各市(州)按登记注册统计类别和构成分建筑业企业总产值(2023年)

单位：万元

市(州)及分组	Region and Group	建筑业总产值 Total Output Value	内资企业 Domestic Invested Enterprises	港澳台投资企业 Enterprises with Investment from Hong Kong, Macao and Taiwan	外商投资企业 Foreign Invested Enterprises
全省	**Sichuan**	**172725362.8**	**172695392**	**21468**	**8503**
按市(州)分	**Grouped by Region**				
成都市	Chengdu	79572907	79543134	21468	8305
自贡市	Zigong	3517538	3517538		
攀枝花市	Panzhihua	3442488	3442488		
泸州市	Luzhou	12283895	12283895		
德阳市	Deyang	5233332	5233332		
绵阳市	Mianyang	8769875	8769875		
广元市	Guangyuan	2769977	2769977		
遂宁市	Suining	5146972	5146972		
内江市	Neijiang	3403816	3403618		198
乐山市	Leshan	3297720	3297720		
南充市	Nanchong	14857342	14857342		
眉山市	Meishan	5456347	5456347		
宜宾市	Yibin	8410001	8410001		
广安市	Guangan	4487007	4487007		
达州市	Dazhou	3792289	3792289		
雅安市	Yaan	995441	995441		
巴中市	Bazhong	1512979	1512979		
资阳市	Ziyang	1230205	1230205		
阿坝藏族羌族自治州	Aba	664747	664747		
甘孜藏族自治州	Ganzi	501149	501149		
凉山彝族自治州	Liangshan	3379334	3379334		
按新资质等级分	**Grouped by Qualification Grade**				
总承包企业	The General Contractor	161041992	161041536	456	
特级企业	The Special Grade	44261930	44261930		
一级企业	The First Grade	54946170	54946170		
二级企业	The Second Grade	29434873	29434873		
三级企业	The Third Grade	32399020	32398564	456	
专业承包企业	The Specialized Contractor	11683371	11653855	21012	8503
一级企业	The First Grade	4988263	4959361	20596	8305
二级企业	The Second Grade	4488587	4487974	416	198
三级企业及其他	The Third Grade & Others	2206521	2206521		

注：自2023年起，按照《关于市场主体统计分类的划分规定》（国统字〔2023〕14号）执行新的登记注册统计类别。

Gross Output Value of Construction Enterprises by Region, Registered Statistical Categories and Composition(2023)

(10 000 yuan)

建筑工程产值 Output Value of Construction	安装工程产值 Output Value of Installation	其他产值 Other Output Value	房屋工程和土木工程 Output Value of Building & Civil Engineering
152520577	**12941360**	**7263425**	**162919449**
69623882	6132070	3816955	75092521
3189014	233171	95354	3362875
3091913	165803	184772	3361717
10728151	832682	723063	11882575
4619940	435217	178176	4878243
8036789	537822	195265	8035657
2571652	142895	55431	2703549
4455452	518774	172746	4855280
2922689	371289	109838	3360789
2871081	342371	84268	3003543
13245612	1076020	535710	13675111
4731554	512998	211796	5105844
7719766	383135	307100	7627270
3668618	728430	89959	4216537
3356027	193947	242315	3730413
919362	50993	25086	982250
1346755	116776	49449	1483705
1131955	70135	28115	1188128
617232	15345	32171	609465
460610	4034	36506	491277
3212526	77454	89354	3272701
144785244	9486634	6770114	156844835
41374919	1439826	1447186	43756512
48648439	3282365	3015366	53547957
26367610	2174530	892733	28359248
28394277	2589913	1414830	31181118
7735333	3454726	493311	6074614
2935622	1837893	214748	2695250
3095562	1205490	187536	2008001
1704149	411344	91028	1371363

a) Implement new registration and statistical categories in accordance with the "Regulations on the Classification of Market Entity Statistics" (Guotongzi〔2023〕No. 14) since 2023.

15-11 续表 continued

单位：万元 (10 000 yuan)

市(州)及分组	Region and Group	#房屋工程建筑业 Building	#土木工程建筑业 Civil Engineering	建筑安装业产值 Output Value of Installation	建筑装饰、装修和其他建筑业产值 Output Value of Ornament, Decoration and Other Construction	竣工产值 Output Value of Completed Construction
全省	**Sichuan**	**104583994**	**58335455**	**5303458**	**4502456**	**67434971**
按市(州)分	**Grouped by Region**					
成都市	Chengdu	34159128	40933393	2409284	2071103	30462315
自贡市	Zigong	3196064	166811	147217	7446	1705013
攀枝花市	Panzhihua	2904219	457499	60852	19918	1738864
泸州市	Luzhou	10551553	1331022	259788	141533	4553558
德阳市	Deyang	3405736	1472507	180642	174447	1892539
绵阳市	Mianyang	6158220	1877437	311446	422772	4049112
广元市	Guangyuan	1944855	758694	21537	44892	1196258
遂宁市	Suining	3918331	936950	80739	210952	2048046
内江市	Neijiang	2914208	446581	16311	26716	1790887
乐山市	Leshan	2664568	338975	233041	61136	1463354
南充市	Nanchong	10582130	3092981	648019	534213	5200051
眉山市	Meishan	4270969	834875	279194	71309	1843050
宜宾市	Yibin	5831649	1795621	270463	512269	3294600
广安市	Guangan	2762385	1454152	218274	52197	1650912
达州市	Dazhou	3264045	466368	27534	34343	1661765
雅安市	Yaan	636429	345821		13191	342937
巴中市	Bazhong	1066186	417519	7112	22162	558626
资阳市	Ziyang	627446	560682	29757	12320	326365
阿坝藏族羌族自治州	Aba	465227	144239	50229	5054	283581
甘孜藏族自治州	Ganzi	294662	196614	6574	3299	254478
凉山彝族自治州	Liangshan	2965985	306716	45447	61186	1118660
按新资质等级分	**Grouped by Qualification Grade**					
总承包企业	The General Contractor	102094850	54749985	2402901	1794256	62219971
特级企业	The Special Grade	18735169	25021343		505418	15416464
一级企业	The First Grade	38765794	14782163	965815	432398	23244457
二级企业	The Second Grade	21801320	6557928	714486	361140	12528563
三级企业	The Third Grade	22792567	8388551	722601	495301	11030488
专业承包企业	The Specialized Contractor	2489144	3585470	2900557	2708199	5215000
一级企业	The First Grade	621526	2073725	1179596	1113417	2411108
二级企业	The Second Grade	1182187	825814	1262210	1218376	1880545
三级企业及其他	The Third Grade & Others	685432	685931	458752	376407	923347

15-12 各市(州)建筑业企业总产值
Gross Output Value of Construction Enterprises by Region

单位：万元 (10 000 yuan)

市(州)	Region	2014	2015	2016	2017	2018	2019	2020	2021	2022	2023
全省	**Sichuan**	**81485208**	**88475906**	**100441634**	**119962154**	**137522652**	**146681509**	**156126956**	**173511928**	**178456122**	**172725363**
成都市	Chengdu	38792821	40953808	44314587	49595545	56958394	58743793	62270111	68246762	73861180	79572907
自贡市	Zigong	1782088	2033489	2432486	3112290	4088151	3902789	4647211	5406506	4931596	3517538
攀枝花市	Panzhihua	1632167	1752843	2001219	2193364	2450241	2603344	1218687	2874504	3138553	3442488
泸州市	Luzhou	5220235	5786230	7615767	10261744	10447970	15901090	14258058	17331105	16222150	12283895
德阳市	Deyang	2566878	2644426	3034254	3617901	4350052	4457886	4272336	4811922	5318164	5233332
绵阳市	Mianyang	3521134	3975714	4407795	5686736	7212475	7087793	8183961	9522685	10080451	8769875
广元市	Guangyuan	1074803	1255189	1458403	1783979	2242770	2298774	2373689	2720904	2649845	2769977
遂宁市	Suining	1825481	2105375	2481006	3308825	3025877	4055024	5139208	6013871	6065522	5146972
内江市	Neijiang	1878608	2074803	2559424	2641133	2962726	2769287	3355281	3966443	3687784	3403816
乐山市	Leshan	1259091	1510509	1795349	2360367	2811028	2317748	2863582	3119416	3325394	3297720
南充市	Nanchong	4965352	5312236	6028991	7663298	10596612	9002105	13874144	16877901	15203248	14857342
眉山市	Meishan	1996535	2407274	3037935	3436698	3434996	4335658	4501611	5186390	5606434	5456347
宜宾市	Yibin	1948325	2231710	2673171	3605742	4882438	6135580	6958595	7604993	8646974	8410001
广安市	Guangan	3322882	3705093	4439155	5251317	5487875	5584670	3054711	3643081	4425187	4487007
达州市	Dazhou	2760362	2895431	3466774	4027765	4616833	5082648	5831298	7203926	6903012	3792289
雅安市	Yaan	244349	281120	337592	454729	543237	691939	770912	1012423	997222	995441
巴中市	Bazhong	3791359	4194525	4815169	6441841	6401113	6599724	7149588	2207169	1820627	1512979
资阳市	Ziyang	1891727	2173625	1875901	2219734	1906140	1677739	1697997	1985223	1594240	1230205
阿坝藏族羌族自治州	Aba	93986	111016	122475	193296	378084	599587	694069	594744	528787	664747
甘孜藏族自治州	Ganzi	96289	89581	94817	141019	236058	331629	369879	393574	416206	501149
凉山彝族自治州	Liangshan	820736	981910	1449368	1964831	2489581	2502703	2642030	2788389	3033547	3379334

15-13 各市(州)建筑业企业主要财务指标(2023年)
Major Financial Indicators of Construction Enterprises by Region(2023)

单位：万元 (10 000 yuan)

市(州)及分组	Region and Group	资产合计 Total Assets	负债合计 Total Liabilities	所有者权益合计 Total Owners' Equities	利润总额 Total Profits	税金总额 Total Tax	利税总额 Total Pre-tax Profits
全省	**Sichuan**	**245077354**	**181940631**	**63136723**	**6370039**	**4141479**	**10511518**
按市(州)分	**Grouped by Region**						
成都市	Chengdu	142503108	111505003	30998106	3363037	1601904	4964941
自贡市	Zigong	3463795	2537713	926083	93975	120640	214615
攀枝花市	Panzhihua	4721613	3848073	873540	114204	52424	166628
泸州市	Luzhou	9004322	5842152	3162170	422297	351118	773415
德阳市	Deyang	6106488	4672615	1433873	129057	128673	257731
绵阳市	Mianyang	13311392	8871402	4439989	282104	250284	532388
广元市	Guangyuan	3085991	2049785	1036205	30200	96451	126650
遂宁市	Suining	3991823	2408151	1583672	155506	146809	302315
内江市	Neijiang	4202902	2457807	1745095	143807	149632	293438
乐山市	Leshan	4612925	2778727	1834198	152813	110943	263756
南充市	Nanchong	7774041	5308195	2465845	510832	377993	888825
眉山市	Meishan	8405551	5750618	2654933	140776	127378	268155
宜宾市	Yibin	12411875	9877918	2533958	284827	170464	455292
广安市	Guangan	5633184	3667942	1965242	156095	162152	318247
达州市	Dazhou	3456529	2138035	1318494	175618	123185	298803
雅安市	Yaan	4010846	2251478	1759368	45052	26579	71631
巴中市	Bazhong	1766592	1186558	580034	20696	28860	49556
资阳市	Ziyang	2587537	1809489	778048	65628	31942	97570
阿坝藏族羌族自治州	Aba	609778	386917	222861	890	15948	16838
甘孜藏族自治州	Ganzi	363351	186988	176363	5596	14293	19889
凉山彝族自治州	Liangshan	3053712	2405066	648647	77029	53807	130836
按资质等级分	**Grouped by Qualification Grade**						
总承包企业	The General Contractor	230477073	171398847	59078226	5974135	3814163	9788298
特级企业	The Special Grade	66617286	54553737	12063549	1908950	611551	2520501
一级企业	The First Grade	82625739	62921252	19704487	1968939	1340818	3309757
二级企业	The Second Grade	40692616	26605666	14086951	886404	927103	1813506
三级企业	The Third Grade	40541432	27318192	13223240	1209842	934692	2144534
专业承包企业	The Specialized Contractor	14600281	10541784	4058497	395904	327315	723219
一级企业	The First Grade	7079393	5371309	1708085	181736	131974	313709
二级企业	The Second Grade	5013271	3453962	1559308	111522	118104	229625
三级企业及其他	The Third Grade & Others	2507617	1716513	791104	102646	77238	179885

15-14 各市(州)总承包和专业承包建筑业企业资产和负债(2023年)

Assets and Liabilities of General and Professional Contractor Construction Enterprises by Region(2023)

单位：万元 (10 000 yuan)

市(州)及分组	Region and Group	年末资产 合计 Total Assets (year-end)	#流动资产 Current Assets	年末负债 合计 Total Liabilities (year-end)	#流动负债 Current Liabilities
全省	**Sichuan**	**245077354**	**182641892**	**181940631**	**144352105**
按市(州)分	**Grouped by Region**				
成都市	Chengdu	142503108	110100974	111505003	98951450
自贡市	Zigong	3463795	2640092	2537713	1513307
攀枝花市	Panzhihua	4721613	3122849	3848073	3344408
泸州市	Luzhou	9004322	6558436	5842152	4189113
德阳市	Deyang	6106488	5438451	4672615	3144709
绵阳市	Mianyang	13311392	8380870	8871402	5139816
广元市	Guangyuan	3085991	2228955	2049785	1175431
遂宁市	Suining	3991823	2904034	2408151	1112433
内江市	Neijiang	4202902	2493714	2457807	1316795
乐山市	Leshan	4612925	2834735	2778727	1970043
南充市	Nanchong	7774041	5154885	5308195	2591287
眉山市	Meishan	8405551	6430007	5750618	3586345
宜宾市	Yibin	12411875	9731186	9877918	7275853
广安市	Guangan	5633184	3985266	3667942	2484751
达州市	Dazhou	3456529	2129876	2138035	1014685
雅安市	Yaan	4010846	1874198	2251478	1187993
巴中市	Bazhong	1766592	1235986	1186558	481353
资阳市	Ziyang	2587537	1906196	1809489	1495489
阿坝藏族羌族自治州	Aba	609778	495487	386917	301657
甘孜藏族自治州	Ganzi	363351	327627	186988	132300
凉山彝族自治州	Liangshan	3053712	2668069	2405066	1942887
按资质等级分	**Grouped by Qualification Grade**				
总承包企业	The General Contractor	230477073	170562826	171398847	136088088
特级企业	The Special Grade	66617286	49822587	54553737	48690842
一级企业	The First Grade	82625739	65822395	62921252	54024930
二级企业	The Second Grade	40692616	29020519	26605666	17858510
三级企业	The Third Grade	40541432	25897326	27318192	15513806
专业承包企业	The Specialized Contractor	14600281	12079066	10541784	8264017
一级企业	The First Grade	7079393	6429623	5371309	4897472
二级企业	The Second Grade	5013271	3618852	3453962	2255608
三级企业及其他	The Third Grade & Others	2507617	2030590	1716513	1110937

15-15 各市(州)总承包和专业承包建筑业企业所有者权益和利税(2023年)
Owners' Equities and Pre-tax Profits of General and Professional Contractor Construction Enterprises by Region(2023)

单位：万元 (10 000 yuan)

市(州)及分组	Region and Group	所有者权益 Owners' Equities	利税总额 Total Pre-tax Profits	利润总额 Total Profits	税金总额 Total Taxes	#主营业务税金及附加 Taxes and Extra Charges on Project Settlement Accounts
全省	**Sichuan**	**63136723**	**10511518**	**6370039**	**4141479**	**681974**
按市(州)分	**Grouped by Region**					
成都市	Chengdu	30998106	4964941	3363037	1601904	207220
自贡市	Zigong	926083	214615	93975	120640	23741
攀枝花市	Panzhihua	873540	166628	114204	52424	8475
泸州市	Luzhou	3162170	773415	422297	351118	61047
德阳市	Deyang	1433873	257731	129057	128673	23878
绵阳市	Mianyang	4439989	532388	282104	250284	33607
广元市	Guangyuan	1036205	126650	30200	96451	25061
遂宁市	Suining	1583672	302315	155506	146809	26632
内江市	Neijiang	1745095	293438	143807	149632	47083
乐山市	Leshan	1834198	263756	152813	110943	16026
南充市	Nanchong	2465845	888825	510832	377993	97803
眉山市	Meishan	2654933	268155	140776	127378	15454
宜宾市	Yibin	2533958	455292	284827	170464	23141
广安市	Guangan	1965242	318247	156095	162152	25843
达州市	Dazhou	1318494	298803	175618	123185	20843
雅安市	Yaan	1759368	71631	45052	26579	4082
巴中市	Bazhong	580034	49556	20696	28860	5535
资阳市	Ziyang	778048	97570	65628	31942	3760
阿坝藏族羌族自治州	Aba	222861	16838	890	15948	2711
甘孜藏族自治州	Ganzi	176363	19889	5596	14293	1357
凉山彝族自治州	Liangshan	648647	130836	77029	53807	8674
按资质等级分	**Grouped by Qualification Grade**					
总承包企业	The General Contractor	59078226	9788298	5974135	3814163	629892
特级企业	The Special Grade	12063549	2520501	1908950	611551	93762
一级企业	The First Grade	19704487	3309757	1968939	1340818	181557
二级企业	The Second Grade	14086951	1813506	886404	927103	169550
三级企业	The Third Grade	13223240	2144534	1209842	934692	185024
专业承包企业	The Specialized Contractor	4058497	723219	395904	327315	52082
一级企业	The First Grade	1708085	313709	181736	131974	12994
二级企业	The Second Grade	1559308	229625	111522	118104	25095
三级企业及其他	The Third Grade & Others	791104	179885	102646	77238	13994

15−16 各市(州)按登记注册统计类别分建筑业企业劳动生产率(2023年) Labor Productivity of Construction Enterprises by Region and Registered Statistical Categories(2023)

单位：元/人 (yuan/person)

市(州)及分组	Region and Group	按总产值计算的劳动生产率 Overall Labor Productivity in Terms of Total Output Value	内资企业 Domestic Invested Enterprises	港澳台投资企业 Enterprises with Investment from Hong Kong, Macao and Taiwan	外商投资企业 Foreign Invested Enterprises
全省	**Sichuan**	**408653**	**408658**	**4226696**	**4225910**
按市(州)分	**Grouped by Region**				
成都市	Chengdu	505252	505304	1574915	1574164
自贡市	Zigong	371064	371064	94796	94796
攀枝花市	Panzhihua	654889	654889	52566	52566
泸州市	Luzhou	327275	327275	375339	375339
德阳市	Deyang	340284	340284	153793	153793
绵阳市	Mianyang	325149	325149	269719	269719
广元市	Guangyuan	318183	318183	87056	87056
遂宁市	Suining	362417	362417	142018	142018
内江市	Neijiang	404455	404600	84158	84123
乐山市	Leshan	355860	355860	92669	92669
南充市	Nanchong	364989	364989	407063	407063
眉山市	Meishan	375285	375285	145392	145392
宜宾市	Yibin	345113	345113	243688	243688
广安市	Guangan	333101	333101	134704	134704
达州市	Dazhou	292281	292281	129748	129748
雅安市	Yaan	344550	344550	28891	28891
巴中市	Bazhong	262907	262907	57548	57548
资阳市	Ziyang	331502	331502	37110	37110
阿坝藏族羌族自治州	Aba	410161	410161	16207	16207
甘孜藏族自治州	Ganzi	405133	405133	12370	12370
凉山彝族自治州	Liangshan	388670	388670	86946	86946
按资质等级分	**Grouped by Qualification Grade**				
总承包企业	The General Contractor	411347	411353	3914992	3914926
特级企业	The Special Grade	671165	671165	659479	659479
一级企业	The First Grade	396150	396150	1387005	1387005
二级企业	The Second Grade	343917	343917	855871	855871
三级企业	The Third Grade	319958	319974	1012002	1011936
专业承包企业	The Specialized Contractor	374823	374741	311704	310984
一级企业	The First Grade	514562	515146	96942	96271
二级企业	The Second Grade	341964	342045	131259	131210
三级企业及其他	The Third Grade & Others	264245	264245	83503	83503

主要统计指标解释

建筑业统计单位 指从事房屋、构筑物建造和设备安装活动的法人企业。建筑业法人企业应具有建筑业资质并能够独立核算，同时还应具备以下条件：①依法成立，有自己的名称、组织机构和场所，能够承担民事责任；②独立拥有和使用资产，承担负债，有权与其他单位签订合同；③独立核算盈亏，能够编制资产负债表。

建筑业总产值 是以货币形式表现的建筑业企业在一定时期内生产的建筑业产品和提供服务的总和。建筑业总产值包括：

(1)建筑工程产值：指列入建筑工程预算内的各种工程价值。

(2)安装工程产值：指设备安装工程价值以及将预制部品部件安装成建筑工程产品的价值，不包括被安装设备本身的价值。

(3)其他产值：指建筑业总产值中除建筑工程、安装工程以外的产值。包括房屋构筑物修理产值、非标准设备制造产值、总包企业向分包企业收取的管理费以及不能明确划分的施工活动所完成的产值。

建筑业增加值 指建筑业企业在报告期内以货币形式表现的从事建筑业生产经营活动的最终成果。

房屋施工面积 指在报告期内施工的全部房屋建筑面积，包括本期新开工的房屋建筑面积、上期跨入本期继续施工的房屋建筑面积、上期停缓建在本期恢复施工的房屋建筑面积、本期竣工的房屋建筑面积及本期施工后又停缓建的房屋建筑面积。

房屋竣工面积 指报告期内房屋建筑按照设计要求已全部完工，达到住人和使用条件，经验收鉴定合格或达到竣工验收标准，可正式移交使用的各栋房屋建筑面积的总和。

Explanatory Notes on Main Statistical Indicators

Statistical Units in the Construction Industry refer to corporate enterprises engaged in the construction of buildings and structures and in the installation of equipment. A corporate construction enterprise should have qualification certificates with independent accounting system, and should meet the following 3 requirements: a) being set up in line with relevant legal basis, having its full name, organization and location, and capable of taking civil liabilities; b) independently possessing and using its assets and assuming its liabilities, and entitled to sign contracts with other institutions; c) making independent accounts of its profits and losses, and capable of compiling its own balance sheet.

Gross Output Value of Construction refers to total of construction products and services, expressed in monetary terms, produced or rendered by construction and installation enterprises during a given period of time. It includes:

1) Output value of construction projects: the value of projects covered by the project budgets;

2) Output value of installation projects: the value of the installation of equipment, and the value of installing prefabricated components into construction engineering products (excluding the value of the equipment to be installed);

3) Other output values: the output value of construction industry apart from that of construction projects and installation projects. It includes: output value of repair of buildings and structures; output value of manufacturing of non-standard equipment; overhead expenses received by contracted enterprises from the sub-contracted enterprises, and the completed output value of construction activities for which there is no clear definition.

Value-added of Construction refers to the final result of the activities of production and management of construction industry in monetary terms in the reference period.

Floor Space of Buildings under Construction refers to the total floor space area of buildings under construction in the reference period. It includes buildings new started; buildings started earlier and continued during the reference period; buildings suspended earlier but restarted during the reference period; buildings completed during the reference period; and buildings under construction but suspended during the reference period.

Floor Space of Buildings Completed refers to the total floor space area of buildings that have been completed in the reference period in accordance with the requirements of the design, up to the standard for accommodation or putting into use, and have been checked and accepted by departments concerned as qualified or up to the standard of buildings completed and can be handed over for putting into use.

16 交通运输和邮电业

Chapter 16 Transportation and Post

16−1 交通运输业情况
Conditions of Transport

指标		Item		2010	2015	2020	2021	2022	2023
运输线路长度		**Length of Transport Routes**							
铁路营业里程	(公里)	Railways in Operation	(km)	3549	4442	5312	5687	5937	6471
公路里程	(万公里)	Highways	(10 000 km)	26.6	31.6	39.4	39.9	40.5	41.8
内河航道里程	(万公里)	Navigable Inland Waterways	(10 000 km)	1.1	1.1	1.1	1.1	1.1	1.1
航空里程	(万公里)	Civil Aviation	(10 000 km)	56.1	97.2	145.6	131.5	123.3	146.3
客运量总计	**(万人)**	**Total Passenger Traffic**	**(10 000 persons)**	**242732**	**140044**	**61738**	**64837**	**42949**	**66243**
铁路		Railways		6829	9078	11210	13890	9453	20533
公路		Highways		230988	124014	45258	45349	29816	37977
水路		Waterways		2733	2748	954	864	726	1108
民用航空		Civil Aviation		2182	4204	4316	4734	2954	6625
旅客周转量总计	**(亿人公里)**	**Total Passenger-Kilometers**	**(100 million passenger-km)**	**1391.7**	**1663.0**	**1202.7**	**1303.3**	**846.3**	**1841.9**
铁路		Railways		221.5	271.8	254.3	310.7	214.5	508.9
公路		Highways		802.2	671.6	289.8	270.3	168.6	227.0
水路		Waterways		2.3	2.6	1.0	1.0	0.9	1.0
民用航空		Civil Aviation		365.7	717.0	657.8	721.3	462.3	1105.0
货运量总计	**(万吨)**	**Total Freight Traffic**	**(10 000 tons)**	**133364**	**153270**	**170038**	**182699**	**184766**	**199404**
铁路		Railways		7093	5893	5860	5865	6343	6372
公路		Highways		121017	138622	157598	171377	172329	185814
水路		Waterways		5218	8688	6527	5400	6049	7148
民用航空		Civil Aviation		36	67	53	57	45	70
货物周转量总计	**(亿吨公里)**	**Total Freight Ton-kilometers**	**(100 million ton-km)**	**1710.8**	**2289.5**	**2733.3**	**2940.8**	**3052.1**	**3279.7**
铁路		Railways		642.8	613.8	811.1	871.8	905.5	988.1
公路		Highways		985.1	1480.6	1617.7	1789.8	1858.0	1983.9
水路		Waterways		75.1	183.5	291.8	261.7	275.6	291.0
民用航空		Civil Aviation		7.8	11.7	12.8	14.5	13.0	16.7
民用汽车拥有量	**(万辆)**	**Possession of Civil Motor Vehicles**	**(10 000 units)**	**355.0**	**768.5**	**1292.2**	**1382.0**	**1458.4**	**1542.5**
#私人汽车		Private Vehicles		281.0	677.3	1141.2	1218.4	1288.6	1363.0
载客汽车拥有量	**(万辆)**	**Possession of Buses and Cars**	**(10 000 units)**	**281.6**	**674.0**	**1158.6**	**1239.2**	**1313.6**	**1392.0**
载货汽车拥有量	**(万辆)**	**Possession of Trucks**	**(10 000 units)**	**70.4**	**89.6**	**124.6**	**136.8**	**140.5**	**143.9**
其他机动车拥有量	**(万辆)**	**Possession of Other Motor Vehicles**	**(10 000 units)**	**5.9**	**5.0**	**5.8**	**6.0**	**6.2**	**6.5**
公路部门营运车辆	**(万辆)**	**Number of Motor Vehicles Owned by Highway Departments**	**(10 000 units)**	**62.0**	**57.1**	**54.4**	**57.8**	**58.7**	**54.9**
民用运输船舶拥有量	**(艘)**	**Possession of Civil Transport Vessels**	**(unit)**	**8414**	**7489**	**4718**	**4495**	**4262**	**3935**
机动船		Motor Vessels		7350	6435	4024	3806	3486	3202
驳船		Barges		1064	1054	694	689	776	733

注：①从2014年开始，公路货运量和货物周转量由抽样调查改为根据高速公路计重收费数据推算，公路客运量和旅客周转量中的出租车和公交车统计范围作了较大调整，故2014年相关数据与往年不可比；②2023年起，航空货运量及货物周转量数据由原4家航空公司增加为7家提供，故数据与往年不可比；③公路数据由四川省交通运输厅道路运输管理局提供，铁路数据由成都铁路局提供，水运数据由四川省交通运输厅航务管理局提供，航空数据由四川航空公司、国航西南分公司、东航四川分公司、成都航空公司提供。

a) Since 2014, freight traffic and ton-kilometers of highways are changed from the sample survey to highway toll collection data, statistics range of taxi and bus in highway passenger traffic and passenger-kilometers made a big adjustment, so data of 2014 are not comparable with previous years; b) Since 2023, the data on air cargo volume and cargo turnover has been provided by 7 airlines instead of the original 4 airlines ,making the data incomparable to previous years; c) Highway data are provided by Road Transport Administration of Sichuan Provincial Transportation Bureau, railway data are provided by Chengdu Railway Bureau, waterway data are provided by the Shipping Administration of Sichuan Provincial Communications Department, air data are provided by Sichuan Airlines, Air China Southwest branch, Sichuan branch of China Eastern Airlines and Chengdu airlines.

16-2 各市(州)公路运输情况(2023年)
Main Indicators of Highway Transportation by Region(2023)

市(州)	Region	公路总里程(公里) Total Length of Highways (km)	#等级公路里程 Expressway and Class I to IV Highways	#高速公路 Expressway	民用汽车拥有量(万辆) Possession of Civil Motor Vehicles (10 000 units)	#私人汽车 Private Vehicles	公路旅客周转量(万人公里) Passenger-kilometers of Highways (10 000 passenger-km)	公路货物周转量(万吨公里) Freight Ton-kilometers of Highways (10 000 ton-kilometers)
全省	**Sichuan**	**418254**	**409359**	**9806**	**1542.53**	**1363.02**	**2270346**	**19839274**
成都市	Chengdu	29213	29202	1248	650.17	541.97	455427	4175616
自贡市	Zigong	10342	10133	287	35.57	33.01	46158	670742
攀枝花市	Panzhihua	5383	4771	231	25.17	22.82	34754	658645
泸州市	Luzhou	21820	21480	601	59.90	54.97	162043	1369454
德阳市	Deyang	10729	10641	374	65.12	59.59	84798	842502
绵阳市	Mianyang	24992	23825	709	95.59	89.34	149388	839035
广元市	Guangyuan	24526	22817	575	36.77	34.71	49731	657902
遂宁市	Suining	14586	14347	386	38.39	36.09	49587	526723
内江市	Neijiang	14464	14373	387	37.14	34.05	90760	539341
乐山市	Leshan	16994	16893	512	57.23	51.88	138159	1313763
南充市	Nanchong	32378	32273	570	74.52	68.24	159111	1425645
眉山市	Meishan	9754	9344	460	50.53	46.86	35769	833250
宜宾市	Yibin	27241	26435	591	62.36	57.73	93432	755996
广安市	Guangan	17577	17531	436	36.77	34.39	44260	308232
达州市	Dazhou	30297	29948	534	51.62	47.44	145204	1334890
雅安市	Yaan	8549	8268	377	25.90	22.92	41468	748285
巴中市	Bazhong	26219	26103	429	34.12	32.08	103797	506812
资阳市	Ziyang	14215	14129	378	25.38	23.48	59231	355932
阿坝藏族羌族自治州	Aba	15863	15345	312	13.37	11.87	83452	486022
甘孜藏族自治州	Ganzi	33201	32730	45	11.48	10.10	86218	244780
凉山彝族自治州	Liangshan	29911	28769	364	53.36	49.39	157599	1245708

注：“民用汽车拥有量”全省合计包括省本级数，故各市州之和不等于全省。
a) Data of Possession of Civil Motor Vehicles include provincial data, therefore, the sum of cities and states is not equal to the whole province.

16-3 邮电业务情况
Conditions of Postal and Telecommunication Services

指标	Item	2018	2019	2020	2021	2022	2023
邮政业务	**Postal Services**						
邮政业务总量 (亿元)	Business Volume of Postal Services (100 million yuan)	348.4	447.8	537.7	374.2	403.0	469.6
营业网点 (处)	Number of Offices (unit)	6114	6132	28160	29649	29998	31829
邮路长度 (万公里,单程)	Length of Postal Routes (10 000 km, one way)	15.88	17.61	43.90	28.44	37.30	
邮运汽车 (辆)	Postal Cars (unit)	886	964	1075	1051	884	882
函件 (万件)	Number of Letters (10 000 pcs)	2776	2638	2254	1994	2167	2373
包裹 (万件)	Number of Parcels (10 000 pcs)	89	79	70	69	62	85
报刊期发数 (万份)	Issue of Newspapers and Magazines (10 000 copies)	688	735	669	661	665	663
快递业务量 (万件)	Pieces of Express Mail Services (10 000 pcs)	145992	179105	215159	278270	286918	349484
电信业务	**Telecommunication Services**						
电信业务总量 (亿元)	Business Volume of Telecommunication Services (100 million yuan)	3295.4	5155.0	7525.9	935.1	950.2	997.0
年末固定电话用户 (万户)	Number of Fixed Telephone Subscribers at Year-end (10 000 subscribers)	1721	1872	1885	1919	1954	1943
城市固定电话 (万户)	Urban Fixed Telephone Subscribers (10 000 subscribers)	1041	1219	1220	1130	1069	1130
农村固定电话 (万户)	Rural Fixed Telephone Subscribers (10 000 subscribers)	680	653	665	789	885	813
年末移动电话用户 (万户)	Number of Mobile Telephone Subscribers at Year-end (10 000 subscribers)	9069	9444	9125	9339	9623	9671
互联网宽带接入用户数 (万户)	Number of Broad Band Subscribers of Internet (10 000 subscribers)	2625	2812	2976	3221	3566	3768

注：①邮政业务总量2016-2020年按2010年不变单价计算，2021年按2020年不变单价计算，同比增长按可比口径计算；电信业务总量2016-2020年按2015年不变单价计算，2021年按2020年不变单价计算，同比增长按可比口径计算。②2010年起邮路长度不含邮政速递公司自营邮路；2023年《邮政行业统计调查制度》取消邮路长度指标；特快专递包括邮政公司和其他快递公司数据。③邮政业务数据由四川省邮政管理局、中国邮政集团四川省分公司提供；电信业务数据由四川省通信管理局提供。

a) The data of Business Volume of Postal Services from 2016 to 2020 are calculated by the constant unit price in 2010, the data in 2020 are calculated by the constant unit price in 2020, the year-on-year growth is calculated by the comparable standard; The data of Business Volume of Telecommunication Services from 2016 to 2020 are calculated by the constant unit price in 2015, the data in 2020 are calculated by the constant unit price in 2020, the year-on-year growth is calculated by the comparable standard; b)Postal routes exclude express delivery company's own length postman since 2010.The Postal Industry Statistical Survey System has abolished the postal route length indicator since 2023. The data of pieces of express mail services comes from the post offices and other express delivery companies; c)Data of the postal service are provided by the Sichuan Provincial Post Office and China Post Group's Sichuan branch. Data from the telecommunication services are provided by the Sichuan Provincial Communications Administration Bureau.

主要统计指标解释

铁路营业里程 又称营业长度，指投入客货运输营业或临时营业的线路长度。

公路里程 指报告期末公路的实际长度。统计范围：包括城间、城乡间、乡（村）间能行驶汽车的公共道路，公路通过城镇街道的里程，公路桥梁长度、隧道长度、渡口宽度。不包括城市街道里程，断头路里程，农（林）业生产用道路里程，工（矿）企业等内部道路里程。统计原则：按已竣工验收或交付使用的实际里程计算；两条或多条公路共同经由同一路段的重复里程，只计算一次。

内河航道里程 指在一定时期内，能通航运输船舶及排筏的天然河流、湖泊水库、运河及通航渠道的长度。包括全年季节性通航累计三个月以上的航道，不包括仅供零散流放竹、木排的河道。两省以河为界的航道里程，双方均按一半计算，以免重复。

定期航班航线里程 指定期航班营运里程的总长度，以万公里为计算单位。航线里程的统计分为按重复距离计算和按不重复距离计算两种形式。“按重复距离计算”是指不同航线的相同航段距离可以重复累加；“按不重复距离计算”则不同航线相同航段只统计一次。

货(客)运量 指在一定时期内，各种运输工具实际运送的货物重量(旅客数量)。货运按吨计算，客运按人计算。货物不论运输距离长短、货物类别，均按实际重量统计。旅客不论行程远近或票价多少，均按一人一次客运量统计；半价票、小孩票也按一人统计。

货物(旅客)周转量 指在一定时期内，由各种运输工具运送的货物(旅客)数量与其相应运输距离的乘积之总和。该指标可以反映运输业生产的总成果，也是编制和检查运输生产计划，计算运输效率、劳动生产率以及核算运输单位成本的主要基础资料。计算货物周转量通常按发出站与到达站之间的最短距离，也就是计费距离计算。计算公式为：

货物(旅客)周转量=Σ〔货物(旅客)运输量×运输距离〕

民用汽车拥有量 指报告期末，在公安交通管理部门按照《机动车注册登记工作规范》，已注册登记领有民用车辆牌照的全部汽车数量。汽车拥有量统计的主要分类：根据汽车结构分为载客汽车、载货汽车及其他汽车；根据汽车所有者不同分为个人(私人)汽车、单位汽车；根据汽车的使用性质分为营运汽车、非营运汽车；根据汽车大小规格不同，载客汽车分为大型、中型、小型和微型，载货汽车分为重型、中型、轻型和微型。

邮政、电信业务总量 指以货币形式表示的邮政、电信通信企业为社会提供各类邮政、电信通信服务的总数量。计算方法为各类业务的实物量分别乘以相应的不变单价，求出各类业务的货币量加总求得。没有不变单价的业务按其业务收入直接相加。

移动电话用户 指在电信运营企业营业网点办理开户登记手续，通过移动电话交换机进入移动电话网，占用移动电话号码的各类电话用户。包括各类签约用户、智能网预付费用户、无线上网卡用户。

固定电话用户 指在电信企业营业网点办理开户登记手续并已接入固定电话网上的全部电话用户。

住宅电话用户 指私人付费或安装在居民住宅并按照私人或住宅电话用户登记注册和收费的各类电话用户。

Explanatory Notes on Main Statistical Indicators

Length of Railways in Operation refers to the total length of the trunk line for passenger and freight transportation in full operation or temporary operation.

Length of Highways refers to the actual length of highways at the end of reference period. It covers public roads running vehicles between cities, between urban and rural areas, and between townships (villages), as well as highways passing through streets at small cities and towns, length of bridges and tunnels, width of ferry piers. It does not include the length of streets in cities, dead end highways, the length of streets built for agricultural (forest) production and inside factories (mines). Mileage can only be included when the road is completed, checked and accepted or put into operation. If two or more highways use the same section, the length of the section is counted only once.

Length of Navigable Inland Waterways refers to the length of natural rivers, lakes, reservoirs and canals that are open to navigation for ships and rafts during a given period. It includes the channels with annual seasonal navigation for more than three months, excluding waterways for scattered bamboo and wooden rafts. If two provinces share one river as the border, the length of waterways will be equally divided for each province to avoid duplication.

Length of Regular Civil Aviation Routes refers to the total length of all routes for scheduled flights, which is calculated using 10,000 kilometres as the measuring unit. There are usually two ways to calculate the route length: duplicated calculation and non-duplicated calculation. Duplicated calculation means that the same segment of different routes can be added with duplication, while the non-duplicated calculation allows the same segment of different routes to be counted only once.

Freight (Passenger) Traffic refers to the weight of freight (number of passengers) transported with various means within a specific period of time. Freight transport is calculated in tons and passenger traffic is calculated in terms of number of persons. Freight transport is calculated in terms of the actual weight of the goods, irrespective of the type of freight and distance of transport. Passenger traffic is calculated by the principle that one person can be counted only once in one trip, irrespective of travelling distance and ticket price. The passengers who travel with a discounted ticket or a children ticket is also calculated as one person.

Freight Ton-kilometers (Passenger-kilometers) refers to the sum of the product of the volume of transported cargo (passengers) multiplied by the transport distance. As an indicator to reflect the achievement of the transportation industry, this is an important indicator to show the total results of the transport industry; to prepare and examine the transport plan; and to serve as the main basic data for calculating the efficiency, labour productivity and unit cost of transport. Normally, the shortest distance between the departure station and the destination station (i.e., the payable distance) is the basis in calculating the freight ton-kilometres. The formula is as follows:

$$\begin{matrix}\text{Freight ton-kilometres}\\ \text{(passenger-kilometres)}\end{matrix} = \sum\left[\begin{matrix}\text{freight}\\ \text{(passenger)traffic}\end{matrix} \times \begin{matrix}\text{distance of}\\ \text{transportation}\end{matrix}\right]$$

Possession of Civil Motor Vehicles refer to the total numbers of vehicles at the end of the reference period that are registered and received vehicles license according to the Working Regulations for Motor Vehicle Registration formulated by the transport management offices. Motor vehicles are classified into different categories. By the structure of motor vehicles, they are divided into passenger vehicles, trucks and others; by ownership, into private vehicles and vehicles for the unit's use; by usage, into business vehicles and non-business vehicles; and by size of vehicles, into large passenger vehicles, medium-sized passenger vehicles, small passenger vehicles and mini passenger vehicles, heavy trucks, light-heavy trucks, light trucks and mini-trucks.

Business Volume of Post and Telecommunications refers to the total amount of postal and telecommunication services, expressed in value terms, provided by the post and telecommunications departments for the society. Business volume of post and telecommunications is the sum of each service in kind multiplying with its correspondent unit price (constant price). For business activities without constant price, the business revenue is added up directly.

Mobile Phone Subscribers refer to persons who have gone through registration procedures in the operation outlets of enterprises engaged in telecommunications and are hence connected with the mobile phone communication network through the mobile phone switchboards and occupy mobile phone numbers. Included are various types of contracted subscribers, prepaid users for intelligent network and wireless network card users.

Fixed Telephone Subscribers refer to all subscribers who have gone through registration procedures in the operation outlets of enterprises engaged in telecommunications and are hence connected to the local telecommunications service provider through fixed line network.

Household Telephone Subscribers refer to all kinds of subscribers with telephone sets paid privately or installed in the dwelling units of residents, and registered with payment as private subscribers or residence subscribers.

17 国内贸易

Chapter 17 Domestic Trade

17-1 社会消费品零售总额
Total Retail Sales of Consumer Goods

单位：亿元 (100 million yuan)

年份 Year	社会消费品零售总额 Total Retail Sales of Consumer Goods	年份 Year	社会消费品零售总额 Total Retail Sales of Consumer Goods
1990	348.60	2007	4114.77
1991	399.85	2008	4956.13
1992	470.63	2009	5789.67
1993	572.09	2010	6888.84
1994	741.93	2011	8282.82
1995	958.52	2012	9606.44
1996	1136.62	2013	10976.63
1997	1291.47	2014	12353.94
1998	1408.05	2015	13834.40
1999	1514.96	2016	15519.69
2000	1669.30	2017	17404.45
2001	1877.55	2018	19340.75
2002	2066.85	2019	21342.98
2003	2289.71	2020	20824.87
2004	2621.15	2021	24133.21
2005	3010.66	2022	24104.64
2006	3480.55	2023	26313.40

17-2 按各项分组的社会消费品零售总额
Total Retail Sales of Consumer Goods by the Grouping

单位：亿元 (100 million yuan)

指标	Item	2016	2017	2018	2019	2020	2021	2022	2023
全省	**Sichuan**	**15519.69**	**17404.45**	**19340.75**	**21342.98**	**20824.87**	**24133.21**	**24104.64**	**26313.40**
按销售单位所在地分	Grouped by Location of Retailers								
城镇	Town	12595.56	14124.67	15652.47	17225.38	17138.83	19936.22	20122.50	21994.04
乡村	Rural	2924.13	3279.78	3688.28	4117.60	3686.04	4197.00	3982.14	4319.35
按消费形态分	Grouped by Consumption Patterns								
餐饮收入	Catering Revenue	1900.13	2137.98	2418.61	2727.82	2482.46	3349.61	3011.54	3597.41
商品零售	Retail Sale	13619.56	15266.47	16922.14	18615.16	18342.41	20783.61	21093.10	22715.99
按行业分	Grouped by Industry of Retailers								
批发业	Wholesale Trade	3170.11	3541.58	3931.16	4323.88	4128.19	4742.46	4888.56	5274.47
零售业	Retail Trade	10459.34	11741.77	13018.14	14231.37	14186.29	16010.09	16174.01	17408.15
住宿业	Lodge Trade	143.48	156.88	174.25	199.27	165.68	200.85	179.74	210.90
餐饮业	Catering Trade	1746.76	1964.22	2217.20	2588.46	2344.71	3179.81	2862.33	3419.88

17−3 各市(州)社会消费品零售总额
Total Retail Sales of Consumer Goods by Region

单位：亿元 (100 million yuan)

市(州)	Region	2013	2014	2015	2016	2017	2018	2019	2020	2021	2022	2023
全省	**Sichuan**	**10976.63**	**12353.94**	**13834.40**	**15519.69**	**17404.45**	**19340.75**	**21342.98**	**20824.87**	**24133.21**	**24104.64**	**26313.40**
成都市	Chengdu	4348.80	4944.42	5507.76	6124.00	6853.05	7561.92	8313.40	8118.53	9251.81	9096.48	10001.63
自贡市	Zigong	326.14	359.74	400.12	441.06	490.86	540.35	598.88	583.37	691.04	712.14	746.71
攀枝花市	Panzhihua	143.23	155.32	170.10	185.00	201.33	218.22	240.55	235.14	278.29	285.73	315.86
泸州市	Luzhou	482.59	546.08	626.51	720.14	820.96	926.24	1032.13	1013.81	1204.28	1244.41	1316.16
德阳市	Deyang	446.81	498.37	562.57	638.71	720.67	808.07	893.99	851.19	1010.06	1014.81	1114.07
绵阳市	Mianyang	704.11	788.64	893.63	1010.20	1138.88	1277.27	1419.47	1394.26	1652.16	1635.00	1822.36
广元市	Guangyuan	221.54	246.33	276.35	308.94	346.22	385.44	425.27	419.24	495.42	474.59	501.98
遂宁市	Suining	251.71	279.39	313.37	352.44	390.43	432.63	479.06	467.37	548.70	562.16	623.96
内江市	Neijiang	302.84	336.73	377.97	426.60	473.03	523.15	577.33	558.93	660.51	641.81	703.84
乐山市	Leshan	390.18	432.18	488.04	551.56	620.42	692.21	766.51	748.31	891.12	904.29	994.37
南充市	Nanchong	602.96	679.92	766.08	868.75	987.19	1114.75	1241.09	1217.57	1448.73	1484.36	1653.11
眉山市	Meishan	287.35	320.17	359.93	406.13	450.38	503.06	556.05	543.26	629.72	639.75	645.21
宜宾市	Yibin	520.59	585.86	660.40	748.12	844.75	946.33	1045.06	1026.99	1209.95	1209.98	1245.07
广安市	Guangan	289.10	321.98	361.49	409.32	456.16	509.16	564.31	549.40	651.38	617.41	684.08
达州市	Dazhou	533.13	600.10	683.08	777.90	880.14	989.70	1098.89	1085.01	1281.49	1318.18	1462.71
雅安市	Yaan	144.66	161.56	181.57	202.56	224.42	245.97	271.14	263.80	301.01	306.17	335.88
巴中市	Bazhong	245.34	276.70	318.00	364.39	415.47	469.74	507.47	482.00	485.10	493.39	542.17
资阳市	Ziyang	226.09	251.96	258.01	284.66	317.71	352.40	387.05	377.34	445.23	446.58	470.86
阿坝藏族羌族自治州	Aba	64.85	73.06	82.06	91.28	93.78	95.28	101.03	96.81	107.89	104.93	117.30
甘孜藏族自治州	Ganzi	65.83	73.48	78.93	87.43	97.73	108.84	119.43	114.31	127.66	129.52	143.52
凉山彝族自治州	Liangshan	378.77	421.95	468.43	520.52	580.86	640.02	704.87	678.23	761.66	782.95	872.55

17-4 限额以上批发和零售业法人企业情况
Conditions of Incorporated Enterprises above Designated Size in Wholesale and Retail Trades

指标		Item		2016	2017	2018	2019	2020	2021	2022	2023
批发和零售业		**Wholesale and Retail Trades**									
法人企业数	(个)	Number of Corporation Units	(unit)	6819	6637	6930	8004	9333	10734	12829	15063
从业人员期末人数	(人)	Number of Employees at the End of the Period	(person)	479270	452861	463018	475239	506951	542399	561420	602603
商品购进额	(亿元)	Total Purchases	(100 million yuan)	11883.4	12218.5	14258.8	16884.6	19112.8	24355.9	28119.9	32600.6
商品销售额	(亿元)	Total Sales	(100 million yuan)	13313.8	13702.9	15626.9	18970.0	20928.3	26416.5	30204.8	34786.2
期末商品库存额	(亿元)	Total Stock at Year-end	(100 million yuan)	851.8	885.7	943.7	1132.6	1344.2	1439.3	1686.8	2134.4
批发业		**Wholesale Trade**									
法人企业数	(个)	Number of Corporation Units	(unit)	2330	2305	2545	3364	4281	5269	6643	8033
从业人员期末人数	(人)	Number of Employees at the End of the Period	(person)	151524	150874	153857	168574	189730	205652	228264	259384
商品购进额	(亿元)	Total Purchases	(100 million yuan)	6694.2	7345.0	8960.0	11131.3	13003.3	17368.3	20807.3	24658.1
商品销售额	(亿元)	Total Sales	(100 million yuan)	7437.9	8211.4	9522.5	12405.5	14146.7	18672.3	22346.4	26202.1
期末商品库存额	(亿元)	Total Stock at Year-end	(100 million yuan)	458.4	473.3	516.6	688.1	871.1	967.8	1187.6	1594.9
零售业		**Retail Trade**									
法人企业数	(个)	Number of Corporation Units	(unit)	4489	4332	4385	4640	5052	5465	6186	7030
从业人员期末人数	(人)	Number of Employees at the End of the Period	(person)	327746	301987	309161	306665	317221	336747	333156	343219
商品购进额	(亿元)	Total Purchases	(100 million yuan)	5189.3	4873.5	5298.7	5753.2	6109.5	6987.6	7312.5	7942.5
商品销售额	(亿元)	Total Sales	(100 million yuan)	5875.9	5491.5	6104.3	6564.5	6781.5	7744.2	7858.4	8584.1
期末商品库存额	(亿元)	Total Stock at Year-end	(100 million yuan)	393.3	412.4	427.1	444.5	473.0	471.5	499.3	539.5

17-5 限额以上批发零售贸易、住宿餐饮业法人企业情况(2023年)

Conditions of Incorporated Enterprises above Designated Size in Wholesale and Retail Trades, Lodging and Catering Services (2023)

单位：个、人 (unit, person)

指标	Item	法人企业数 Number of Corporation	从业人员期末人数 Persons Engaged
总计	**Total**	**21020**	**933088**
一、批发业合计	**Wholesale Trades**	**8033**	**259384**
内资企业	Domestic-Funded Enterprises	7969	251643
国有独资公司	State Sole-proprietorship Corporations	87	3382
私营有限责任公司	Private Limited Liability Corporations	5792	124700
其他有限责任公司	Other Limited Liability Corporations	1912	96140
私营股份有限公司	Private Share-holding Corporations Ltd.	28	5191
其他股份有限公司	Other Share-holding Corporations Ltd.	32	7682
全民所有制企业（国有企业）	Enterprises Owned by the Whole people	36	13311
集体所有制企业（集体企业）	Collective Ownership Enterprises	10	210
股份合作企业	Cooperative Stock Enterprises	3	203
个人独资企业	Sole Proprietorship Enterprises	59	722
合伙企业	Partnership Enterprises	9	102
港、澳、台商投资企业	Enterprises with Investment from Hong Kong,Macao and Taiwan	25	2249
外商投资企业	Foreign Invested Enterprises	29	4823
二、零售业合计	**Retail Trades**	**7030**	**343219**
内资企业	Domestic-Funded Enterprises	6917	308801
国有独资公司	State Sole-proprietorship Corporations	32	752
私营有限责任公司	Private Limited Liability Corporations	5012	177304
其他有限责任公司	Other Limited Liability Corporations	1259	94591
私营股份有限公司	Private Share-holding Corporations Ltd.	9	4975
其他股份有限公司	Other Share-holding Corporations Ltd.	28	20967
全民所有制企业（国有企业）	Enterprises Owned by the Whole people	14	190
集体所有制企业（集体企业）	Collective Ownership Enterprises	16	272
股份合作企业	Cooperative Stock Enterprises	11	264
个人独资企业	Sole Proprietorship Enterprises	506	9073
合伙企业	Partnership Enterprises	29	400
港、澳、台商投资企业	Enterprises with Investment from Hong Kong,Macao and Taiwan	57	15967
外商投资企业	Foreign Invested Enterprises	45	18212
三、住宿餐饮业合计	**Lodging and Catering Trades**	**5957**	**330485**
内资企业	Domestic-Funded Enterprises	5916	300007
国有独资公司	State Sole-proprietorship Corporations	23	1873
私营有限责任公司	Private Limited Liability Corporations	4241	213779
其他有限责任公司	Other Limited Liability Corporations	891	66089
私营股份有限公司	Private Share-holding Corporations Ltd.	8	368
其他股份有限公司	Other Share-holding Corporations Ltd.	2	206
全民所有制企业（国有企业）	Enterprises Owned by the Whole people	12	1384
集体所有制企业（集体企业）	Collective Ownership Enterprises	4	127
股份合作企业	Cooperative Stock Enterprises	6	1381
个人独资企业	Sole Proprietorship Enterprises	688	13776
合伙企业	Partnership Enterprises	40	987
港、澳、台商投资企业	Enterprises with Investment from Hong Kong,Macao and Taiwan	25	23819
外商投资企业	Foreign Invested Enterprises	16	6659

17-6 各市(州)限额以上批发零售贸易、住宿餐饮业法人企业情况(2023年)

Conditions of Incorporated Enterprises above Designated Size in Wholesale and Retail Trades, Lodging and Catering Services by Region(2023)

单位：个、人 (unit, person)

市(州)	Region	合计 Total		批发业 Wholesale Trade		零售业 Retail Trade		住宿业 Lodging Trade		餐饮业 Catering Trade	
		法人企业数 Number of Incorporated Enterprises	从业人员期末人数 Number of Employees at the End of the Period	法人企业数 Number of Incorporated Enterprises	从业人员期末人数 Number of Employees at the End of the Period	法人企业数 Number of Incorporated Enterprises	从业人员期末人数 Number of Employees at the End of the Period	法人企业数 Number of Incorporated Enterprises	从业人员期末人数 Number of Employees at the End of the Period	法人企业数 Number of Incorporated Enterprises	从业人员期末人数 Number of Employees at the End of the Period
全省	**Sichuan**	**21020**	**933088**	**8033**	**259384**	**7030**	**343219**	**2258**	**100088**	**3699**	**230397**
成都市	Chengdu	5504	470870	2549	109748	1369	170656	674	39348	912	151118
自贡市	Zigong	777	21184	222	6737	355	6959	63	3968	137	3520
攀枝花市	Panzhihua	540	17245	327	6481	121	6410	43	2019	49	2335
泸州市	Luzhou	1747	48163	864	23700	491	13936	122	4024	270	6503
德阳市	Deyang	685	24540	406	11729	166	6526	39	1671	74	4614
绵阳市	Mianyang	1616	51731	560	16360	482	16464	171	7358	403	11549
广元市	Guangyuan	456	12972	120	3337	197	5193	72	2913	67	1529
遂宁市	Suining	683	23547	194	6702	258	8910	62	2041	169	5894
内江市	Neijiang	669	19464	273	6391	218	7177	53	1899	125	3997
乐山市	Leshan	839	27057	353	7948	288	12218	100	4010	98	2881
南充市	Nanchong	1024	29352	253	6087	455	13089	88	3265	228	6911
眉山市	Meishan	521	19215	188	4365	213	8631	54	2868	66	3351
宜宾市	Yibin	1514	37639	560	10914	553	15216	126	4148	275	7361
广安市	Guangan	765	17483	120	2589	388	9057	50	1651	207	4186
达州市	Dazhou	1161	32904	289	6980	506	15996	140	4547	226	5381
雅安市	Yaan	446	9879	177	2863	124	3551	66	2207	79	1258
巴中市	Bazhong	568	16282	109	2764	290	7928	47	1968	122	3622
资阳市	Ziyang	257	8882	105	3249	107	3752	26	732	19	1149
阿坝藏族羌族自治州	Aba	164	5140	8	286	64	1606	79	2977	13	271
甘孜藏族自治州	Ganzi	164	3963	11	800	77	1163	62	1774	14	226
凉山彝族自治州	Liangshan	920	35576	345	19354	308	8781	121	4700	146	2741

17-7 分行业限额以上批发零售贸易法人企业商品购、销、存总额(2023年)
Total Purchases, Sales and Inventory of Incorporated Enterprises above Designated Size in Wholesale and Retail Trades by Sector(2023)

单位：万元　　(10 000 yuan)

指标	Item	购进总额 Total Purchases	销售总额 Total Sales	年末库存总额 Inventory (year-end)
总计	**Total**	**326005774**	**347861865**	**21343763**
一、批发企业合计	**Wholesale Trades**	**246580957**	**262020659**	**15949166**
食品、饮料、烟草批发业	Food, Beverages and Tobaccos	40083067	46009812	7807757
#米、面制品及食用油批发	Rice, Flour and Edible Oil	4893790	5011492	671217
烟草制品批发	Tobaccos	7733030	11278012	917770
纺织、服装及家庭用品批发	Textiles, Garments and Household Articles	6582310	7108962	328618
#服装批发	Garments	621370	663002	59226
文化、体育用品及器材批发业	Cultural, Sports Appliances and Equipments	1941152	2089973	171785
医药及医疗器材批发业	Medicines and Medical Appliances	20088152	22155274	1822136
矿产品、建材及化工产品批发	Mineral Products, Building Marerials and Chemical Products	140194683	146171199	3423247
#煤炭及制品批发业	Coal and Related Products	12088274	12507208	141420
石油及制品批发业	Petroleum and Related Products	18675162	20672192	413660
金属及金属矿批发业	Metal Materials and Mineral	57874092	59367068	1620042
建材批发业	Building Materials	17620742	18300393	488931
化肥批发业	Chemical Fertilizers	6224274	6497694	213734
机械设备、五金产品及电子产品批发	Machinery, Hardware and Electronic Equipment	15530952	15787258	1234547
#汽车、摩托车及零配件批发	Motor Vehicles, Motorcycles and Their Parts	3744584	3903040	356928
电气设备批发	Electrical Equipment	544162	594243	27811
计算机、软件及辅助设备	Computers, Software and Assistant Equipment	5333496	5231705	409270
贸易经纪与代理	Trade Broker and Agency	2354	2264	96
其他批发业	Others not Classified	9016854	9505740	253103
二、零售企业合计	**Retail Trades**	**79424817**	**85841206**	**5394597**
综合零售业	General Retail	10759836	12527706	715800
#百货零售业	General Merchandise	3805295	4835700	173532
超级市场零售业	Supermarkets	6273080	6898098	469525
食品、饮料及烟草制品专门零售	Special Retail of Food, Beverages and Tobaccos	2932087	3384205	194621
纺织、服装及日用品专门零售业	Special Retail of Textiles, Garments and Daily	1504531	1892369	228975
#服装零售业	Garments	790589	969117	133096
文化、体育用品及器材专门零售	Special Retail of Cultural, Sports Appliances and Equipments	1240389	1634546	175606
医药及医疗器材专门零售业	Special Retail of Medicines and Medical Appliances	2989489	3483038	329094
汽车、摩托车燃料及零配件	Motor Vehicles, Motorcycles, Fuel and Parts	43960055	45184829	3059408
#汽车新车零售业	Retail of New Motor Vehicles	27621547	27665630	2591610
机动车燃油零售业	Retail of Motor Vehicle Fuel	15631016	16761833	393829
家用电器及电子产品专门零售	Special Retail of Household Appliance and Electronic Product	3187449	3587179	240572
五金、家具室内装饰材料专门零售	Special Retail of Hardware, Furniture and Domestic Decoration Material	590611	698202	50659
货摊、无店铺及其他零售业	Stalls, Non-Shop and Other Retail Trades	12260371	13449133	399862

17-8 各市(州)限额以上批发零售贸易法人企业商品购、销、存总额(2023年)

Total Purchases, Sales and Inventory of Incorporated Enterprises above Designated Size in Wholesale and Retail Trades by Region(2023)

单位：万元 (10 000 yuan)

市(州)	Region	购进总额 Total Purchases	销售总额 Total Sales			年末库存总额 Inventory (year-end)
				批发 Wholesale Trade	零售 Retail Trade	
全省	**Sichuan**	**326005774**	**347861865**	**261267787**	**86594078**	**21343763**
成都市	Chengdu	169815137	180742922	134664148	46078775	11527296
自贡市	Zigong	5368669	5780016	4288441	1491575	200105
攀枝花市	Panzhihua	8508914	9388669	8396390	992279	295474
泸州市	Luzhou	27287563	28853354	22602954	6250400	2083252
德阳市	Deyang	14592224	15632796	12832807	2799989	402008
绵阳市	Mianyang	19784796	20689240	16031602	4657639	1017527
广元市	Guangyuan	3321744	3627916	2479629	1148288	147844
遂宁市	Suining	3948269	4579753	2760874	1818880	280212
内江市	Neijiang	9534565	10073234	8560340	1512895	219147
乐山市	Leshan	7926966	8558932	5685496	2873436	285640
南充市	Nanchong	5437081	5920210	2499089	3421121	316586
眉山市	Meishan	5327893	5762978	4266336	1496642	242276
宜宾市	Yibin	19482750	20166442	17683388	2483054	2849149
广安市	Guangan	3000766	3377445	2026153	1351292	120867
达州市	Dazhou	6059511	6297791	2932219	3365573	340172
雅安市	Yaan	3742952	4061762	3373236	688525	113454
巴中市	Bazhong	1905193	2100537	919107	1181430	145717
资阳市	Ziyang	2385223	2550932	1985513	565418	212363
阿坝藏族羌族自治州	Aba	357824	442094	226190	215904	16704
甘孜藏族自治州	Ganzi	439644	597441	333533	263908	22899
凉山彝族自治州	Liangshan	7778089	8657402	6720346	1937056	505074

17-9 限额以上批发零售贸易法人企业主要财务指标(2023年)
Main Financial Indicators of Incorporated Enterprises above Designated Size in Wholesale and Retail Trades(2023)

单位：万元 (10 000 yuan)

指标	Item	资产合计 Total Assets	#流动资产 Current Assets	#固定资产净额 Net Value of Fixed Assets	负债合计 Total Liabilities	所有者权益 Total Owners' Equities	主营业务收入 Revenue from Principal Business
总计	**Total**	**195994437**	**142798509**	**9950769**	**131983083**	**64012341**	**307848024**
一、批发企业合计	**Wholesale Trades**	**159276577**	**119521388**	**5897543**	**106342072**	**52935388**	**230841672**
#国有控股	State-holding Majority Shares	89632045	63702692	3707526	57216195	32415850	108751834
按登记注册类型分	Grouped by Registration						
内资企业	Domestic-Funded Enterprises	152759106	114825218	5650493	101964414	50795576	223614974
国有独资公司	State Sole-proprietorship Corporations	14709524	7839992	724589	8032222	6677303	8305026
私营有限责任公司	Private Limited Liability Corporations	31662603	24606177	1285538	21681792	9981695	64699797
其他有限责任公司	Other Limited Liability Corporations	93254439	72377808	3035931	66111143	27143296	127546685
私营股份有限公司	Private Share-holding Corporations Ltd.	3365792	2526213	78253	2287391	1078402	3296057
其他股份有限公司	Other Share-holding Corporations Ltd.	4951756	3499924	239626	2451406	2500350	8474010
全民所有制企业(国有企业)	Enterprises Owned by the Whole people	4519437	3734188	264318	1164785	3354652	10717390
集体所有制企业(集体企业)	Collective Ownership Enterprises	100443	85436	4353	89929	10514	253221
股份合作企业	Cooperative Stock Enterprises	9768	5904	3581	8602	1166	18408
个人独资企业	Sole Proprietorship Enterprises	88555	66665	10073	52090	36466	178611
合伙企业	Partnership Enterprises	88840	74974	4220	78156	10684	117542
港澳台商投资企业	Enterprises with Investment from Hong Kong, Macao and Taiwan	1981489	1733610	27922	1360437	621052	4205810
外商投资企业	Foreign Invested Enterprises	4520709	2952219	215180	3014489	1506221	2981130
二、零售企业合计	**Retail Trades**	**36717859**	**23277121**	**4053227**	**25641010**	**11076952**	**77006352**
#国有控股	State-holding Majority Shares	9216181	4286045	1215498	4870390	4345792	16122651
按登记注册类型分	Grouped by Registration						
内资企业	Domestic-Funded Enterprises	31705211	20831304	3278942	22466096	9239218	67212591
国有独资公司	State Sole-proprietorship Corporations	1116503	388461	39727	509210	607293	206779
私营有限责任公司	Private Limited Liability Corporations	11866409	8743002	1259873	8437343	3429169	29904868
其他有限责任公司	Other Limited Liability Corporations	13896218	9372525	1157834	11200269	2695948	26210124
私营股份有限公司	Private Share-holding Corporations Ltd.	908995	603205	93721	401553	507442	333604
其他股份有限公司	Other Share-holding Corporations Ltd.	3551077	1506436	614464	1740248	1810829	9571550
全民所有制企业(国有企业)	Enterprises Owned by the Whole people	41946	27724	8188	27821	14125	14024
集体所有制企业(集体企业)	Collective Ownership Enterprises	20711	17127	1838	7158	13553	44618
股份合作企业	Cooperative Stock Enterprises	13304	8836	2200	6045	7260	45778
个人独资企业	Sole Proprietorship Enterprises	274898	153480	98344	132412	142485	823927
合伙企业	Partnership Enterprises	14067	9630	2551	3631	10436	54469
港澳台商投资企业	Enterprises with Investment from Hong Kong, Macao and Taiwan	1480623	1093312	171635	1021377	459246	3222611
外商投资企业	Foreign Invested Enterprises	3524502	1346106	601806	2147503	1376999	6558487

注：自2023年起，按照《关于市场主体统计分类的划分规定》（国统字〔2023〕14号）执行新的登记注册统计类别。
a) Implement new registration and statistical categories in accordance with the "Regulations on the Classification of Market Entity Statistics" (Guotongzi〔2023〕No. 14) since 2023.

17-9 续表 continued

单位：万元 (10 000 yuan)

指标	Item	营业成本 Cost of Operation	税金及附加 Tax and Extra	管理费用 Cost of Management	财务费用 Cost of Finance	营业利润 Business Profits	利润总额 Total Profits
总计	**Total**	**284745080**	**1849086**	**4355468**	**1112658**	**9570996**	**9667386**
一、批发企业合计	**Wholesale Trades**	**214922622**	**1632161**	**2600565**	**788974**	**7792988**	**7831256**
#国有控股	State-holding Majority Shares	102320881	1404696	902401	389529	3215533	3226676
按登记注册类型分	Grouped by Registration						
内资企业	Domestic-Funded Enterprises	208175328	1619311	2517281	761515	7582218	7621133
国有独资公司	State Sole-proprietorship Corporations	8065875	23504	69194	37643	104884	112824
私营有限责任公司	Private Limited Liability Corporations	59897922	122353	1046880	228955	2485672	2505320
其他有限责任公司	Other Limited Liability Corporations	120800745	216308	935511	571345	3217121	3236416
私营股份有限公司	Private Share-holding Corporations Ltd.	3091649	3757	26069	3743	146974	148303
其他股份有限公司	Other Share-holding Corporations Ltd.	8053444	10813	45849	3591	305725	308097
全民所有制企业（国有企业）	Enterprises Owned by the Whole people	7734369	1241114	385521	-87691	1298993	1287347
集体所有制企业（集体企业）	Collective Ownership Enterprises	247040	256	2298	2931	-1052	-877
股份合作企业	Cooperative Stock Enterprises	15748	46	404	9	947	943
个人独资企业	Sole Proprietorship Enterprises	155817	902	4287	538	13281	13242
合伙企业	Partnership Enterprises	104977	257	1263	455	9606	9449
港澳台商投资企业	Enterprises with Investment from Hong Kong, Macao and Taiwan	4080935	5151	26628	17454	51608	51413
外商投资企业	Foreign Invested Enterprises	2635632	7691	55617	9967	152691	152238
二、零售企业合计	**Retail Trades**	**69822458**	**216925**	**1754903**	**323685**	**1778008**	**1836130**
#国有控股	State-holding Majority Shares	14996795	22373	229000	13064	601918	603960
按登记注册类型分	Grouped by Registration						
内资企业	Domestic-Funded Enterprises	60972173	179755	1523210	272973	1669907	1738052
国有独资公司	State Sole-proprietorship Corporations	196528	293	6283	1824	2218	4583
私营有限责任公司	Private Limited Liability Corporations	26676245	87550	734762	143171	879813	910794
其他有限责任公司	Other Limited Liability Corporations	24231305	63864	591733	128366	258065	286883
私营股份有限公司	Private Share-holding Corporations Ltd.	263638	1955	17117	-2078	55265	59620
其他股份有限公司	Other Share-holding Corporations Ltd.	8802538	21546	133505	-2235	389913	390661
全民所有制企业（国有企业）	Enterprises Owned by the Whole people	11608	140	2014	96	-377	428
集体所有制企业（集体企业）	Collective Ownership Enterprises	38267	148	2385	4	2045	2152
股份合作企业	Cooperative Stock Enterprises	40786	181	1788	71	453	394
个人独资企业	Sole Proprietorship Enterprises	663599	3866	31151	3657	79144	79152
合伙企业	Partnership Enterprises	45235	210	2293	91	3299	3321
港澳台商投资企业	Enterprises with Investment from Hong Kong, Macao and Taiwan	2870546	22484	100055	6888	53273	37613
外商投资企业	Foreign Invested Enterprises	5969421	14682	131154	43765	53383	59016

17−10 各市(州)限额以上批发零售贸易法人企业主要财务指标(2023年)
Main Financial Indicators of Incorporated Enterprises above Designated Size in Wholesale and Retail Trades by Region(2023)

单位：万元 (10 000 yuan)

市(州)	Region	资产合计 Total Assets	负债合计 Total Liabilities	主营业务收入 Revenue from Principal Business	营业成本 Cost of Operation	销售费用 Selling Expenses	税金及附加 Tax and Extra	营业利润 Business Profits
全省	**Sichuan**	**195994437**	**131983083**	**307848024**	**284745080**	**10578037**	**1849086**	**9570996**
成都市	Chengdu	87081412	61016405	160024942	150489490	5799263	649075	3083094
自贡市	Zigong	1877696	1286333	4980368	4771090	121611	43770	209776
攀枝花市	Panzhihua	4040942	2641907	6109121	5579519	201970	28538	306245
泸州市	Luzhou	17482717	12811161	25985015	23523482	991635	131064	1159275
德阳市	Deyang	10502896	6650198	13987449	12789283	681613	79849	374923
绵阳市	Mianyang	15312454	8542019	18408126	17079367	421908	98487	613400
广元市	Guangyuan	1954010	1434292	3314505	3056987	76890	39407	117901
遂宁市	Suining	3304621	2077934	4184401	3480959	229453	48306	366027
内江市	Neijiang	5358131	3865616	9102535	8306184	122882	65432	534882
乐山市	Leshan	8152587	5343634	7631370	6711725	206608	65904	569134
南充市	Nanchong	2775173	1938760	5353282	4687660	147088	100754	330704
眉山市	Meishan	4025332	2721295	5313422	4885091	161782	52626	161066
宜宾市	Yibin	17228098	11169527	18070439	16398496	571809	126732	832383
广安市	Guangan	1598688	1060753	3067665	2770788	90475	39298	117291
达州市	Dazhou	2301668	1368104	5681255	5006323	224657	72766	248407
雅安市	Yaan	2350246	1431103	3756005	3509155	126410	28387	63973
巴中市	Bazhong	1742999	838986	1889432	1641654	91751	36351	65876
资阳市	Ziyang	2665757	2006904	2317715	2142224	66485	31861	50085
阿坝藏族羌族自治州	Aba	162772	91538	392422	327593	19786	14339	22514
甘孜藏族自治州	Ganzi	231143	130071	527540	461138	26080	15413	16954
凉山彝族自治州	Liangshan	5845097	3556543	7751016	7126873	197884	80730	327087

17-11 限额以上住宿餐饮法人企业主要财务指标(2023年)
Main Financial Indicators of Incorporated Enterprises above Designated Size in Lodging and Catering Services(2023)

单位：万元 (10 000 yuan)

指标	Item	资产合计 Total Assets	#流动资产 Current Assets	#固定资产净额 Net Value of Fixed Assets	负债合计 Total Liabilities	所有者权益 Total Owners' Equities	主营业务收入 Revenue from Principal Business
总计	**Total**	**14603661**	**6621403**	**4273596**	**11365129**	**3238613**	**8131612**
#国有控股	State-holding Majority Shares	2915095	1281779	899654	2165213	749882	617763
按登记注册类型分	Grouped by Registration						
内资企业	Domestic-Funded Enterprises	12747054	5613509	4010112	10338391	2408745	7355929
国有独资公司	State Sole-proprietorship Corporations	285775	102300	68472	165929	119846	57003
私营有限责任公司	Private Limited Liability Corporations	6288108	2725036	2231063	5260921	1027279	5082273
其他有限责任公司	Other Limited Liability Corporations	5560876	2587707	1389883	4566617	994258	1718610
私营股份有限公司	Private Share-holding Corporations Ltd.	25772	11391	7466	17798	7974	8589
其他股份有限公司	Other Share-holding Corporations Ltd.	41935	32499	5013	8353	33582	2917
全民所有制企业(国有企业)	Enterprises Owned by the Whole people	159516	22867	117987	189148	-29632	34779
集体所有制企业(集体企业)	Collective Ownership Enterprises	1553	684	504	256	1296	3074
股份合作企业	Cooperative Stock Enterprises	52702	35031	10105	15936	36767	45542
个人独资企业	Sole Proprietorship Enterprises	305520	85977	169051	101962	203548	373115
合伙企业	Partnership Enterprises	24730	9768	10528	10952	13778	29466
港澳台商投资企业	Enterprises with Investment from Hong Kong, Macao and Taiwan	419106	138364	94433	243440	175666	554841
外商投资企业	Foreign Invested Enterprises	1437500	869530	169051	783299	654202	220841

注：自2023年起，按照《关于市场主体统计分类的划分规定》（国统字〔2023〕14号）执行新的登记注册统计类别。
a) Implement new registration and statistical categories in accordance with the "Regulations on the Classification of Market Entity Statistics" (Guotongzi〔2023〕No. 14) since 2023.

17-11 续表 continued

单位：万元 (10 000 yuan)

指标	Item	营业成本 Cost of Operation	税金及附加 Tax and Extra	管理费用 Cost of Management	财务费用 Cost of Finance	营业利润 Business Profits	利润总额 Total Profits
总计	**Total**	**4307043**	**42287**	**1164989**	**149020**	**733365**	**761307**
#国有控股	State-holding Majority Shares	383512	6009	132413	24649	-16522	-13290
按登记注册类型分	Grouped by Registration						
内资企业	Domestic-Funded Enterprises	3918181	39526	1064418	144005	405209	432543
国有独资公司	State Sole-proprietorship Corporations	28731	373	9429	1480	8225	8137
私营有限责任公司	Private Limited Liability Corporations	2601929	21913	656857	76378	352231	359200
其他有限责任公司	Other Limited Liability Corporations	964561	13088	333808	58436	4839	22929
私营股份有限公司	Private Share-holding Corporations Ltd.	4942	35	1239	-187	-575	-500
其他股份有限公司	Other Share-holding Corporations Ltd.	1855	30	728	99	343	86
全民所有制企业（国有企业）	Enterprises Owned by the Whole people	14110	274	16819	4637	-13503	-13402
集体所有制企业（集体企业）	Collective Ownership Enterprises	2188	55	183	13	500	517
股份合作企业	Cooperative Stock Enterprises	26180	380	5927	-160	2196	3658
个人独资企业	Sole Proprietorship Enterprises	255247	3090	34781	3021	47895	48800
合伙企业	Partnership Enterprises	18159	286	4408	286	3016	3071
港澳台商投资企业	Enterprises with Investment from Hong Kong, Macao and Taiwan	240578	493	40140	2928	55928	57079
外商投资企业	Foreign Invested Enterprises	148284	2268	60431	2087	272228	271685

17-12 各市(州)限额以上住宿餐饮法人企业主要财务指标(2023年)

Main Financial Indicators of Incorporated Enterprises above Designated Size in Lodging and Catering Services by Region(2023)

单位：万元 (10 000 yuan)

市(州)	Region	资产合计 Total Assets	负债合计 Total Liabilities	主营业务收入 Revenue from Principal Business	营业成本 Cost of Operation	销售费用 Selling Expenses	税金及附加 Tax and Extra	营业利润 Business Profits
全省	**Sichuan**	**14603661**	**11365129**	**8131612**	**4307043**	**2152269**	**42287**	**733365**
成都市	Chengdu	7137970	5789278	4724313	2177960	1692424	15855	469035
自贡市	Zigong	257633	183155	159198	97293	18882	845	12519
攀枝花市	Panzhihua	233187	199046	80665	47396	18264	860	537
泸州市	Luzhou	468357	265929	311251	189393	34860	2783	47548
德阳市	Deyang	240928	193843	126207	77716	21850	951	-1957
绵阳市	Mianyang	908156	601391	512436	308281	69024	4432	74356
广元市	Guangyuan	335488	272522	103458	80933	15709	1103	3375
遂宁市	Suining	481783	371167	197919	123924	20250	1322	23449
内江市	Neijiang	408589	252065	152111	94967	14002	908	25261
乐山市	Leshan	348561	259112	188365	107142	28704	1011	16360
南充市	Nanchong	408956	321105	289010	184472	30118	2388	31465
眉山市	Meishan	262106	193070	118669	64389	26932	940	1922
宜宾市	Yibin	518850	384374	233793	159324	27218	738	3439
广安市	Guangan	178501	144220	149542	101652	16220	899	15055
达州市	Dazhou	273606	147641	307185	213386	29631	2439	26636
雅安市	Yaan	339079	266741	79420	55809	10405	674	-1404
巴中市	Bazhong	281846	241603	105171	67239	14484	1254	771
资阳市	Ziyang	81512	75697	34194	18069	7228	516	-1043
阿坝藏族羌族自治州	Aba	695494	663643	64759	23757	27129	803	-17781
甘孜藏族自治州	Ganzi	232331	153951	44104	20858	6471	622	-792
凉山彝族自治州	Liangshan	510730	385576	149841	93085	22464	943	4614

主要统计指标解释

社会消费品零售总额 指企业（单位、个体户）通过交易直接售给个人、社会集团非生产、非经营用的实物商品金额，以及提供餐饮服务所取得的收入金额。个人包括城乡居民和入境人员，社会集团包括机关、社会团体、部队、学校、企事业单位、居委会或村委会等。

批发业 指向其他批发或零售单位（含个体经营者）及其他企事业单位、机关团体等批量销售生活用品、生产资料的活动，以及从事进出口贸易和贸易经纪与代理的活动，包括拥有货物所有权，并以本单位(公司)的名义进行交易活动，也包括不拥有货物的所有权，收取佣金的商品代理、商品代售活动；还包括各类商品批发市场中固定摊位的批发活动，以及以销售为目的的收购活动。

零售业 指百货商店、超级市场、专门零售商店、品牌专卖店、售货摊等主要面向最终消费者（如居民等）的销售活动，以互联网、邮政、电话、售货机等方式的销售活动，还包括在同一地点，后面加工生产，前面销售的店铺（如面包房）；谷物、种子、饲料、牲畜、矿产品、生产用原料、化工原料、农用化工产品、机械设备（乘用车、计算机及通信设备除外）等生产资料的销售不作为零售活动；多数零售商对其销售的货物拥有所有权，但有些则是充当委托人的代理人，进行委托销售或以收取佣金的方式进行销售。

批发和零售业商品购进、销售、库存额 指各种登记注册类型的批发和零售业企业以本企业为总体的，从国内、国外市场购进的商品总价、销售和出口的商品总价、库存的商品总价等情况。该指标可以反映商品流转过程中商品购进、销售、库存之间的比例关系和存在的问题。

商品购进额 指从本企业以外的单位和个人购进(包括从国外直接进口)作为转卖或加工后转卖的商品金额（含增值税）。

商品销售额 指对本单位以外的单位和个人出售的商品金额（包括售给本单位消费用的商品，含增值税）。

期末商品库存额 对于批发和零售业法人单位和个体经营户，是指报告期末取得所有权的全部商品金额（含增值税）；对于批发和零售业产业活动单位，是指报告期末实际在库且归属法人具有所有权的全部商品金额（含增值税）。

住宿业 指为旅行者提供短期留宿场所的活动，有些单位只提供住宿，也有些单位提供住宿、饮食、商务、娱乐一体的服务，不包括主要按月或按年长期出租房屋住所的活动。

餐饮业 指通过即时制作加工、商业销售和服务性劳动等，向消费者提供食品和消费场所及设施的服务。

营业额 指住宿和餐饮业单位在经营活动中因提供服务或销售商品等取得的全部收入（含增值税），收入主要来源于提供客房、餐费服务、商品销售和其他服务，如商务服务。不包括多产业法人企业附营的其他行业产业活动单位的餐费收入、商品销售收入等各项收入。其中，客房收入指住宿和餐饮业单位在经营活动中因提供住宿服务取得的收入（含增值税）。不包括多产业法人企业附营的其他行业产业活动单位的客房收入。餐费收入指本单位为顾客提供就餐服务取得的收入（含增值税），包括：经烹饪、调制加工后出售的各种食品，如主食、炒菜、凉拌菜等的收入。不包括多产业法人企业附营的其他行业产业活动单位的餐费收入。

限额以上批发和零售业统计单位 指年主营业务收入2000万元及以上的批发业统计单位和年主营业务收入500万元及以上的零售业统计单位。

限额以上住宿和餐饮业统计单位 指年主营业务收入200万元及以上的住宿和餐饮业统计单位。

Explanatory Notes on Main Statistical Indicators

Total Retail Sales of Consumer Goods refer to the revenue received by enterprises (units, self-employed individuals) through direct sales of non-production and non-business physical commodities to individuals and social institutions, and revenue from providing catering services. Individuals include rural and urban households, population from abroad, social institutions include government agencies, social organizations, military units, schools, institutions, neighbourhood (village) committees, etc.

Wholesale Trade refers to the activities of selling wholesale commodities for daily use and capital goods to other enterprises of wholesale and retail trades (including self-employed individuals) and other enterprises, institutions and government agencies and organizations, and the activities of engaging in import and export and acting as a trade agent. The wholesaler may have the ownership of the commodities for wholesale and trade in the name of its own (a company), and the wholesaler can act as commission agent or commodity broker without the ownership of commodities. Also included are the wholesale activities at the fixed stalls in wholesale market and the acquisition for sales purpose.

Retail Trade refers to the activities of department stores, supermarkets, franchised stores, brand stores, retail stalls and on-the-spot-making-selling stores selling commodities to the final consumers (residents) by any means, including internet, post, telephone, sales machine. It also includes shops with sales and production located in the same places (such as bakeries). Retail trade excludes the activities of sales of capital goods such as grain, seed, feed, livestock, mineral products, raw material for production, industrial chemicals, chemical products for agricultural use, machine and equipment (excluding vehicles, computers and communication equipment). Most retailers have the ownership of commodities to sell, but some are acting as agents or brokers to make transactions for a commission.

Purchase, Sales and Stock of Commodities by Wholesale and Retail Trades refer to the total volume of commodities purchased, total volume of sales and exports, and the stock of commodities by wholesale and retail enterprises of different status of registration from domestic and overseas markets. This indicator reflects the relationship among purchase, sales and stock of commodities in the circulation of goods and reveals the existing problems.

Total Purchases of Commodities refer to the total value of purchases of commodities by enterprises (establishments) from other establishments or individuals (including direct import from abroad) for the purpose of re-selling, either with or without further processing of the commodities purchased.

Total Sales of Commodities refer to value of commodities sold by the establishments to other establishments and individuals (including goods sold for self consumption, including VAT).

Total Stock of Commodities at End of Period For corporate units and self-employed individuals engaged in wholesale and retail trade, it refers to total value (including VAT) of commodities possessed at the end of the reference period; and for wholesale and retail establishments, it refers to the value (including VAT) of all commodities actually in stock and owned by their corporate units at the end of reference period.

Hotel Services refer to short-term accommodation services provided to visitors. Some units may provide only accommodation while others provide a combination of accommodation, meals, business services and recreational facilities. It excludes activities related to the provision of long-term primary residences, typically leased on a monthly or annual basis.

Catering Services refer to the activities of providing foods, serving locations and facilities to customers through instant processing, commercial sales and service-type labor.

Business Revenue refers to total revenue (including VAT) of hotels and catering services received from providing services or selling commodities through business activities. Revenue comes mainly from providing hotels, catering services, selling of commodities and other services, such as commodity services. It does not include revenue from providing meals or selling of commodities by establishments affiliated to other multi-industrial corporate enterprises. Income from hotel rooms refers to income (including VAT) of hotels and catering services by providing lodging services through business activities. Income from meals refers to income (including VAT) from providing catering services, including selling of cooked or prepared foods, such as staple food, cooked dishes, or cold dishes. It does not include income from meals provided by establishments affiliated to other multi-industrial corporate enterprises.

The Criteria for Wholesale and Retail Sale Trades above Designated Size refer to wholesale trade with annual principal business sales over 20 million yuan; and retail trade, with annual principal business sales over 5 million yuan.

The Statistical Units of the Enterprises of Hotel and Catering Services above the Designated Size refer to those with an annual income from main business at and over 2 million yuan.

18 对外经济贸易和旅游

Chapter 18 Foreign Trade and Economic Cooperation and Tourism

18-1 对外经济贸易
Foreign Trade and Economic Cooperation

指标	Item	2017	2018	2019	2020	2021	2022	2023
进出口总额(万元人民币)	**Total Imports and Exports (RMB 10 000)**	**46058562**	**59467108**	**67659210**	**80818566**	**95136019**	**100767282**	**95749128**
出口总额	Total Exports	25384899	33326526	38923204	46543256	57086659	62151778	60339130
进口总额	Total Imports	20673663	26140582	28736006	34275310	38049360	38615504	35409998
进出口差额	Balance	4711236	7185944	10187198	12267946	19037299	23536274	24929132
进出口总额 (万美元)	**Total Imports and Exports (USD 10 000)**	**6810677**	**8993788**	**9805150**	**11680195**	**14732165**	**15105920**	**13611377**
出口总额	Total Exports	3755394	5039827	5638075	6724817	8840867	9302994	8580779
进口总额	Total Imports	3055283	3953961	4167075	4955378	5891298	5802926	5030598
进出口差额	Balance	700111	1085866	1471000	1769439	2949569	3500068	3550181
进出口总额 (万美元)	**Total Imports and Exports of Goods (USD 10 000)**	**6810677**	**8993788**	**9805150**	**11680195**	**14732165**	**15105920**	**13611377**
出口总额	Total Exports	3755394	5039827	5638075	6724817	8840867	9302994	8580779
初级产品	Primary Goods	80380	87334	88206	74185	105501	143553	118225
工业制成品	Manufactured Goods	3675014	4952493	5549869	6650632	8735366	9159441	8462554
进口总额	Total Imports	3055283	3953961	4167075	4955378	5891298	5802926	5030598
初级产品	Primary Goods	204725	260025	270328	240100	470266	827019	1041784
工业制成品	Manufactured Goods	2850558	3693936	3896747	4715278	5421032	4975907	3988814
外商直接投资 (万美元)	**Foreign Direct Investment (USD 10 000)**	**617751**	**630972**	**1033698**	**1203947**	**973316**	**352590**	**348986**
对外承包工程 (万美元)	**Foreign Contracted Projects (USD 10 000)**							
新签合同额	Value of Newly Signed Contracts	791610	1026598	1851000	624000	904000	729551	1413322
完成营业额	Completed Turnover	393093	610791	637200	518056	647000	657716	585153

注：①进出口统计资料由成都海关提供。②外商投资统计资料由四川省经济合作局提供，由商务部统计反馈；自2019年起，将原“外商直接投资”指标中“外商投资性公司投资”“外商投资企业再投资”等子项指标调入“外商其他投资”，故与往年不可比。

a) Import and export statistics are provided by Chengdu Customs; b) Statistics on foreign investment are provided by Sichuan Province Bureau of Economic Cooperation, collected and fed back by the Ministry of Commerce; "Investment by Foreign Investment Company" and "Reinvestment by Foreign Investment Company"of "Foreign Direct Investment" were altered to "Other Foreign Investment" since 2019, and are not comparable with those in previous years.

18−2 出口商品分类金额
Exports Value by Category of Commodities

单位：万美元 (USD 10 000)

商品类别	Category of Commodities	2017	2018	2019	2020	2021	2022	2023
总额	**Total Value**	**3755394**	**5039827**	**5638075**	**6724817**	**8840867**	**9302994**	**8580779**
初级产品	**Primary Goods**	**80380**	**87334**	**88206**	**74185**	**105501**	**143553**	**118225**
食品及活动物	Food and Live Animals	29115	26076	27909	26826	32986	59698	60454
饮料及烟类	Beverages and Tobacco	15801	24523	20124	14695	13342	13767	11216
非食用原料(燃料除外)	Nonedible Raw Materials(Except Fuels)	26337	27142	29270	20509	26729	24001	24954
矿物燃料、润滑油及有关原料	Mineral Fuels, Lubricants and Related Materials	3920	2162	865	371	46	315	6300
动植物油、脂及蜡	Animal and Vegetable Oils, Fats and Waxes	5207	7431	10038	11784	32398	45772	15301
工业制成品	**Manufactured Goods**	**3675014**	**4952493**	**5549869**	**6650632**	**8735366**	**9159441**	**8462554**
化学成品及有关产品	Chemicals and Related Products	267795	328608	309436	307708	512635	851017	751410
按原料分类的制成品	Manufactured Goods Classified by Material	282485	326069	342855	272028	526988	758011	827185
机械及运输设备	Machinery and Transport Equipment	2771439	3836523	4354846	5578891	6693438	6253926	5338489
杂项制品	Miscellaneous Products	330687	440159	512901	477159	959320	1190514	1422169
未分类的商品	Products Not Classified	22608	21134	29831	14846	42985	105973	123301

18−3 进口商品分类金额
Imports Value by Category of Commodities

单位：万美元 (USD 10 000)

商品类别	Category of Commodities	2017	2018	2019	2020	2021	2022	2023
总额	**Total Value**	**3055283**	**3953961**	**4167075**	**4955378**	**5891298**	**5802926**	**5030598**
初级产品	**Primary Goods**	**204725**	**260025**	**270328**	**240100**	**470266**	**827019**	**1041784**
食品及活动物	Food and Live Animals	30550	36635	45694	52528	76447	90747	109473
饮料及烟类	Beverages and Tobacco	2359	3574	4169	3350	2523	4525	7526
非食用原料(燃料除外)	Nonedible Raw Materials(Except Fuels)	163806	203331	186262	156549	256712	592412	773643
矿物燃料、润滑油及有关原料	Mineral Fuels, Lubricants and Related Materials	7347	14607	28405	22859	121082	111917	106518
动植物油、脂及蜡	Animal and Vegetable Oils, Fats and Waxes	663	1878	5798	4814	13502	27418	44624
工业制成品	**Manufactured Goods**	**2850558**	**3693936**	**3896747**	**4715278**	**5421032**	**4975907**	**3988814**
化学成品及有关产品	Chemicals and Related Products	67747	84755	109395	135245	167837	222395	187204
按原料分类的制成品	Manufactured Goods Classified by Material	79124	93306	123614	92929	107208	131961	241279
机械及运输设备	Machinery and Transport Equipment	2516806	3284124	3431754	4228047	4861397	4304804	3308879
杂项制品	Miscellaneous Products	163404	219553	203274	250438	261589	288958	242179
未分类的商品	Products Not Classified	23477	12198	28710	8619	23001	27789	9273

18-4 各市(州)进出口总额
Total Imports and Exports by Region

单位：万元人民币 (RMB 10 000)

市(州)	Region	2014	2015	2016	2017	2018	2019	2020	2021	2022	2023
全省	**Sichuan**	**43147490**	**31902213**	**32630378**	**46058562**	**59467108**	**67659210**	**80818566**	**95136019**	**100767282**	**95749128**
成都市	Chengdu	34298302	24513092	27133815	39418475	49823510	58226928	71542077	82219702	83464154	74897925
自贡市	Zigong	412591	303508	259504	307496	325207	308382	318105	422338	525056	597348
攀枝花市	Panzhihua	185183	159454	138750	262429	305871	317230	304255	414719	531041	545646
泸州市	Luzhou	169416	195502	209070	1393313	835559	843142	897790	1295311	1922054	2208773
德阳市	Deyang	2385243	1899038	1160506	1040093	1265732	1411486	1163887	1436944	1834700	2268935
绵阳市	Mianyang	1791396	1625042	1165475	1149688	2600377	2090541	2162726	2505470	2690134	2857781
广元市	Guangyuan	259383	42767	14793	16918	50498	63279	26464	100663	148392	182842
遂宁市	Suining	386979	390192	271032	235705	252456	362023	368764	493810	832192	1089093
内江市	Neijiang	193672	87705	87095	95890	141499	141361	197898	297193	398145	1124794
乐山市	Leshan	681727	546668	584625	697908	736496	586738	495554	919211	1104438	701316
南充市	Nanchong	172118	68353	107715	195969	100503	648004	356178	520743	611616	1144767
眉山市	Meishan	204016	127244	137185	186721	438084	352722	395132	802731	1192424	1349517
宜宾市	Yibin	546618	589678	614223	576008	968599	1411234	1830371	2365333	3168554	3641885
广安市	Guangan	680505	662364	338901	200650	269160	343926	142160	238396	381748	472728
达州市	Dazhou	199874	229028	106078	46741	57110	199229	265998	515357	722992	1034990
雅安市	Yaan	47297	49780	30546	30027	41966	72155	65825	129372	540666	720416
巴中市	Bazhong	102641	117112	79903	26509	52700	60745	24870	53941	90953	130676
资阳市	Ziyang	342331	210613	131618	114626	128776	154607	188871	274079	397077	518438
阿坝藏族羌族自治州	Aba	29215	22333	23322	22670	21548	13721	17901	28642	29457	32927
甘孜藏族自治州	Ganzi	8202	9166	6088	8027	12944	15605	12353	16216	21158	25592
凉山彝族自治州	Liangshan	50781	53576	30134	32701	38512	36150	41386	85849	160332	202737

18-4 续表 continued

单位：万美元 (USD 10 000)

市(州)	Region	2014	2015	2016	2017	2018	2019	2020	2021	2022	2023
全省	**Sichuan**	**7020297**	**5118856**	**4934941**	**6810677**	**8993788**	**9805150**	**11680195**	**14732165**	**15105920**	**13611377**
成都市	Chengdu	5592156	3942361	4102173	5830149	7536217	8439640	10338866	12731504	12527409	10629357
自贡市	Zigong	67150	49015	39353	45378	49364	44824	45988	65424	78331	84886
攀枝花市	Panzhihua	30128	25643	20993	38706	46691	45972	44015	64185	79217	77590
泸州市	Luzhou	27563	31343	31331	205717	276333	122010	130105	200951	283520	312111
德阳市	Deyang	388352	305107	176354	153574	191518	204313	168325	222727	273401	322101
绵阳市	Mianyang	291780	262710	176907	169832	391266	302895	312011	387534	405008	405309
广元市	Guangyuan	42146	6953	2262	2522	7620	9194	3841	15570	21708	25661
遂宁市	Suining	62808	63078	41029	34830	38169	52498	53548	76707	118551	155532
内江市	Neijiang	31495	14115	13253	14204	21524	20531	28703	46080	59161	159136
乐山市	Leshan	111031	88223	88772	102967	111977	85398	71548	142379	167507	99866
南充市	Nanchong	28088	11044	16090	29065	15291	92397	50894	80658	90492	162099
眉山市	Meishan	33376	20517	20812	27580	66267	51261	57655	124206	177319	192207
宜宾市	Yibin	88989	95163	93128	84923	146859	204126	265101	366441	473983	518739
广安市	Guangan	110634	106776	50852	29648	41154	50376	20405	36805	57196	67569
达州市	Dazhou	32610	37078	15983	6909	8660	28693	38487	79852	108869	147620
雅安市	Yaan	7696	7907	4645	4428	6356	10508	9607	19992	80579	102456
巴中市	Bazhong	16680	19043	12151	3988	7860	8803	3626	8351	13586	18548
资阳市	Ziyang	43254	19068	19780	16909	19614	22241	27124	42487	58778	93651
阿坝藏族羌族自治州	Aba	4758	3600	3534	3337	3263	1996	2581	4440	4438	4671
甘孜藏族自治州	Ganzi	1334	1469	919	1193	1929	2231	1804	2520	3068	3595
凉山彝族自治州	Liangshan	8263	8642	4622	4817	5852	5244	5960	13355	23799	28676

18－5 各市(州)出口总额
Total Exports by Region

单位：万元人民币 (RMB 10 000)

市(州)	Region	2014	2015	2016	2017	2018	2019	2020	2021	2022	2023
全省	**Sichuan**	**27540270**	**20564533**	**18475606**	**25384899**	**33326526**	**38923204**	**46543256**	**57086659**	**62151778**	**60339130**
成都市	Chengdu	20766302	14802901	14504563	20649286	27447777	33098374	41068498	48412141	50050937	45386373
自贡市	Zigong	189768	164647	148063	175476	216357	230629	233124	306432	371752	456306
攀枝花市	Panzhihua	104604	136110	91254	112078	125988	133543	119121	171283	362531	409707
泸州市	Luzhou	153851	177375	186047	1330566	691476	409881	453087	698687	1144295	1505913
德阳市	Deyang	1903885	1449135	885378	708276	927477	1101669	823883	1136463	1254160	1595726
绵阳市	Mianyang	1272154	1186529	681538	613788	654625	705827	782831	1108895	1722546	2035157
广元市	Guangyuan	256237	40067	12193	12927	33320	30243	24457	96187	123208	150227
遂宁市	Suining	257874	267961	166537	119841	138961	202735	183829	380651	658400	489392
内江市	Neijiang	170821	73085	66798	76379	115742	101059	132548	210751	351725	1008286
乐山市	Leshan	515569	425790	449886	512786	579394	453078	369924	740111	952854	541924
南充市	Nanchong	168751	61106	104334	187427	67536	631783	335949	479947	567713	1101962
眉山市	Meishan	128111	108014	124286	149372	187836	157203	224029	594830	793354	964562
宜宾市	Yibin	372790	393379	364023	320064	607498	906454	1239113	1674766	2040140	2292718
广安市	Guangan	661020	659763	336659	190706	255195	323795	130870	227043	364172	418155
达州市	Dazhou	168583	207824	104446	43484	54502	194497	232540	468958	664900	992541
雅安市	Yaan	42896	44429	24161	25286	31869	32219	48151	78939	145854	246026
巴中市	Bazhong	102641	117009	79896	26382	44558	51842	22703	43445	88084	118003
资阳市	Ziyang	229141	170405	92070	74143	81743	97446	54022	131340	290136	400564
阿坝藏族羌族自治州	Aba	16486	16464	17288	16009	14876	11228	11629	24115	24759	22653
甘孜藏族自治州	Ganzi	8193	9163	6088	8027	12944	15603	12348	16212	21067	25588
凉山彝族自治州	Liangshan	50595	53378	30097	32596	36852	34097	40599	85464	159191	177350

18-5 续表 continued

单位：万美元 (USD 10 000)

市(州)	Region	2014	2015	2016	2017	2018	2019	2020	2021	2022	2023
全省	**Sichuan**	**4483913**	**3309290**	**2795498**	**3755394**	**5039827**	**5638075**	**6724817**	**8840867**	**9302994**	**8580779**
成都市	Chengdu	3390833	2390406	2193971	3055922	4150657	4795450	5932997	7496518	7502094	6437797
自贡市	Zigong	30902	26611	22496	25889	32863	33545	33745	47496	55129	64864
攀枝花市	Panzhihua	17032	21923	13806	16537	19202	19395	17194	26513	53623	58220
泸州市	Luzhou	25028	28422	27874	196438	254813	59388	65806	108525	166714	213151
德阳市	Deyang	310129	234883	134598	104493	139943	159349	119302	176289	188193	226196
绵阳市	Mianyang	207234	192082	103517	90760	99016	102093	112798	171738	258972	287826
广元市	Guangyuan	41635	6522	1865	1928	5049	4390	3555	14875	17942	21036
遂宁市	Suining	42014	43312	25257	17715	20929	29410	26565	59180	92956	70040
内江市	Neijiang	27778	11755	10173	11316	17614	14701	19266	32664	52139	142817
乐山市	Leshan	83959	68796	68273	75750	88169	65989	53346	114666	144811	77142
南充市	Nanchong	27541	9868	15574	27789	10222	90050	47922	74337	83816	156057
眉山市	Meishan	20865	17414	18861	22082	28504	22803	32867	91992	118989	137602
宜宾市	Yibin	60693	63571	55226	47176	91780	131062	179570	259525	304575	326320
广安市	Guangan	107457	106355	50512	28184	39064	47459	18782	35045	54585	59826
达州市	Dazhou	27439	33469	15738	6427	8265	28014	33613	72658	100117	141604
雅安市	Yaan	6982	7043	3670	3726	4820	4676	7059	12188	21929	35102
巴中市	Bazhong	16680	19026	12126	3969	6629	7513	3296	6721	13173	16735
资阳市	Ziyang	27459	15097	13807	10946	12504	13976	7800	20386	42824	76492
阿坝藏族羌族自治州	Aba	2685	2655	2622	2352	2248	1633	1680	3739	3728	3227
甘孜藏族自治州	Ganzi	1332	1468	919	1193	1929	2231	1803	2519	3055	3594
凉山彝族自治州	Liangshan	8233	8610	4615	4802	5606	4947	5849	13295	23630	25133

18-6 各市(州)进口总额
Total Imports by Region

单位：万元人民币 (RMB 10 000)

市(州)	Region	2014	2015	2016	2017	2018	2019	2020	2021	2022	2023
全省	**Sichuan**	**15607220**	**11337680**	**14154772**	**20673663**	**26140582**	**28736006**	**34275310**	**38049360**	**38615504**	**35409998**
成都市	Chengdu	13532000	9710191	12629252	18769189	22375733	25128554	30473579	33807561	33413217	29511553
自贡市	Zigong	222823	138861	111441	132020	108850	77753	84981	115906	153304	141042
攀枝花市	Panzhihua	80579	23344	47496	150351	179883	183687	185134	243436	168510	135939
泸州市	Luzhou	15565	18127	23023	62747	144083	433261	444703	596624	777759	702859
德阳市	Deyang	481358	449903	275128	331817	338255	309817	340004	300481	580540	673210
绵阳市	Mianyang	519242	438513	483937	535900	1945752	1384714	1379895	1396575	967588	822625
广元市	Guangyuan	3146	2700	2600	3991	17178	33036	2007	4476	25184	32615
遂宁市	Suining	129105	122231	104495	115864	113495	159288	184934	113159	173792	599701
内江市	Neijiang	22851	14620	20297	19511	25757	40302	65351	86442	46420	116509
乐山市	Leshan	166158	120878	134739	185122	157102	133660	125630	179100	151584	159392
南充市	Nanchong	3367	7247	3381	8542	32967	16221	20229	40796	43903	42806
眉山市	Meishan	75905	19230	12899	37349	250248	195519	171103	207901	399070	384955
宜宾市	Yibin	173828	196299	250200	255944	361101	504780	591258	690567	1128414	1349167
广安市	Guangan	19485	2601	2242	9944	13965	20131	11290	11353	17576	54573
达州市	Dazhou	31291	21204	1632	3257	2608	4732	33457	46399	58092	42450
雅安市	Yaan	4401	5351	6385	4741	10097	39936	17674	50433	394812	474390
巴中市	Bazhong		103	7	127	8142	8903	2167	10496	2869	12674
资阳市	Ziyang	113190	40208	39548	40483	47033	57161	134849	142739	106941	117874
阿坝藏族羌族自治州	Aba	12729	5869	6034	6661	6672	2493	6272	4527	4698	10274
甘孜藏族自治州	Ganzi	9	3				2	5	4	91	5
凉山彝族自治州	Liangshan	186	198	37	105	1660	2053	787	385	1141	25387

18-6 续表 continued

单位：万美元 (USD 10 000)

市(州)	Region	2014	2015	2016	2017	2018	2019	2020	2021	2022	2023
全省	**Sichuan**	**2536384**	**1809566**	**2139443**	**3055283**	**3953961**	**4167075**	**4955378**	**5891298**	**5802926**	**5030598**
成都市	Chengdu	2201323	1551955	1908202	2774227	3385560	3644190	4405869	5234986	5025315	4191560
自贡市	Zigong	36248	22404	16857	19489	16501	11279	12243	17928	23202	20022
攀枝花市	Panzhihua	13096	3720	7187	22169	27489	26577	26821	37672	25594	19370
泸州市	Luzhou	2535	2921	3457	9279	21520	62622	64299	92426	116806	98960
德阳市	Deyang	78223	70224	41756	49081	51575	44964	49023	46438	85208	95905
绵阳市	Mianyang	84546	70628	73390	79072	292250	200802	199213	215796	146036	117483
广元市	Guangyuan	511	431	397	594	2571	4804	285	695	3766	4625
遂宁市	Suining	20794	19766	15772	17115	17240	23088	26983	17527	25595	85492
内江市	Neijiang	3717	2360	3080	2888	3910	5830	9437	13416	7022	16319
乐山市	Leshan	27072	19427	20499	27217	23808	19409	18202	27713	22696	22724
南充市	Nanchong	547	1176	516	1276	5069	2347	2972	6321	6676	6042
眉山市	Meishan	12511	3103	1951	5498	37763	28458	24788	32214	58330	54605
宜宾市	Yibin	28296	31592	37902	37747	55079	73064	85532	106916	169408	192419
广安市	Guangan	3177	421	340	1464	2090	2917	1622	1760	2611	7743
达州市	Dazhou	5171	3609	245	482	395	679	4873	7194	8752	6016
雅安市	Yaan	714	864	975	702	1536	5832	2548	7804	58650	67354
巴中市	Bazhong		17	25	19	1234	1290	330	1630	413	1813
资阳市	Ziyang	15795	3971	5973	5963	7110	8265	19324	22101	15954	17159
阿坝藏族羌族自治州	Aba	2073	945	912	985	1015	363	901	701	710	1444
甘孜藏族自治州	Ganzi	2	1					1	1	13	1
凉山彝族自治州	Liangshan	30	32	7	15	246	297	112	60	169	3543

18-7 旅游发展情况
Development of Tourism

指标		Item		2020	2021	2022	2023
旅行社数	**（个）**	**Number of Travel Agencies**	**(unit)**	**1336**	**1422**	**1519**	**1966**
星级饭店数	**（个）**	**Number of Star-rated Hotels**	**(unit)**	**356**	**347**	**339**	**348**
入境游客	**（万人次）**	**Number of Overseas Visitor Arrivals**	**(10 000 person-times)**	**24.61**			
外国人		Foreigners		20.10			
港澳同胞		Chinese Compatriots From Hong Kong and Macao		3.20			
台湾同胞		Chinese Compatriots From Taiwan Province		1.31			
国内游客	**（万人次）**	**Number of Domestic Visitors**	**(10 000 person-times)**	**45107.41**		**63641.06**	**104660.46**
旅游收入	**（亿元）**	**Tourism Earnings**	**(100 million yuan)**	**7173.29**			
国际旅游(外汇)收入	（万美元）	Foreign Exchange Earnings from International Tourism	(USD 10 000)	4679.05			
国内旅游收入	（亿元）	Earnings from Domestic Tourism	(100 million yuan)	7170.07		7059.94	12782.95

注：旅行社个数为登记数。
a)The number of travel agencies is the registered number.

18-8 接待入境游客情况
Basic Conditions of Overseas Visitor Arrivals

单位：万人次 (10 000 person-times)

项目	Item	2005	2010	2015	2018	2019	2020
总计	**Total**	**106.28**	**104.93**	**273.20**	**369.82**	**414.78**	**24.61**
外国人	**Foreigners**	**68.27**	**74.97**	**193.44**	**276.47**	**313.09**	**20.10**
亚洲	Asia	47.50	40.95	83.83	104.64	133.31	9.46
日本	Japan	15.45	20.23	17.18	24.69	30.45	2.90
马来西亚	Malaysia	6.80	3.18	12.62	14.46	19.69	0.78
新加坡	Singapore	7.39	3.62	12.37	18.72	17.63	0.54
泰国	Thailand	5.80	2.13	6.45	17.73	21.02	0.84
欧洲	Europe	9.50	17.44	53.30	86.39	93.14	4.05
英国	United Kingdom	1.86	5.24	17.41	27.35	24.44	0.52
德国	Germany	1.95	2.42	9.70	15.43	19.95	1.26
法国	France	1.77	2.80	7.47	7.47	9.69	0.53
意大利	Italy	0.80	0.72	2.72	4.26	4.17	0.22
北美洲	North America	8.49	11.93	39.83	48.34	50.21	3.84
加拿大	Canada	1.12	2.20	7.12	8.84	7.35	3.19
美国	United States	6.99	8.91	28.78	33.02	38.04	0.45
澳大利亚	Australia	1.02	2.31	8.95	15.89	16.07	0.46
非洲	Africa	0.29	0.40	2.29	3.55	2.57	0.18
其他	Others	1.18	1.09	2.73	11.03	12.72	1.90
港澳同胞	**Chinese Compatriots From Hong Kong and Macao**	**13.99**	**15.11**	**43.49**	**49.65**	**52.86**	**3.20**
台湾同胞	**Chinese Compatriots from Taiwan Province**	**24.02**	**14.85**	**36.27**	**43.70**	**48.83**	**1.31**

18−9 各市(州)旅游发展情况(2023年)
Development of Tourism by Region(2023)

市(州)	Region	星级饭店数 (个) Number of Star-rated Hotels (unit)	国内旅游人数 (万人次) Number of Domestic Visitors (10 000 person-times)	国内旅游收入 (亿元) Earnings from Domestic Tourism (100 million yuan)
全省	**Sichuan**	**348**	**104660.46**	**12782.95**
成都市	Chengdu	72	28831.84	3710.07
自贡市	Zigong	11	5187.81	519.62
攀枝花市	Panzhihua	13	763.18	69.87
泸州市	Luzhou	20	5544.58	738.24
德阳市	Deyang	12	5708.15	504.66
绵阳市	Mianyang	23	9391.42	819.94
广元市	Guangyuan	23	3610.16	488.50
遂宁市	Suining	12	1480.20	222.06
内江市	Neijiang	10	5818.68	701.69
乐山市	Leshan	12	11764.64	1206.08
南充市	Nanchong	21	7215.61	701.69
眉山市	Meishan	5	3269.14	273.24
宜宾市	Yibin	4	8901.22	804.78
广安市	Guangan	10	2896.71	242.87
达州市	Dazhou	13	1966.15	352.87
雅安市	Yaan	16	2353.85	226.56
巴中市	Bazhong	16	1799.39	374.05
资阳市	Ziyang	11	1947.33	93.91
阿坝藏族羌族自治州	Aba	11	1607.78	203.38
甘孜藏族自治州	Ganzi	13	1129.72	225.57
凉山彝族自治州	Liangshan	20	8408.89	602.95

注：国内旅游人数全省合计对重复统计人数进行了剥离，故各市州加总不等于全省合计。

a) The data of domestic visitors stripped the number of repeated statistics, so the sum number of cities and states is not equal to the total of the province.

主要统计指标解释

货物进出口总额 指实际进出我国关境的货物总金额。包括对外贸易实际进出口货物，来料加工装配进出口货物，国家间、联合国及国际组织无偿援助物资和赠送品，华侨、港澳台同胞和外籍华人捐赠品，租赁期满归承租人所有的租赁货物，进料加工进出口货物，边境地方贸易及边境地区小额贸易进出口货物，中外合资企业、中外合作经营企业、外商独资经营企业进出口货物和公用物品，到、离岸价格在规定限额以上的进出口货样和广告品(无商业价值、无使用价值和免费提供出口的除外)，从保税仓库提取在中国境内销售的进口货物，以及其他进出口货物。该指标可以观察一个国家在对外贸易方面的总规模。我国规定出口货物按离岸价格统计，进口货物按到岸价格统计。

实际利用外资 指批准的合同外资金额的实际执行数，外国投资者根据批准外商投资企业的合同(章程)的规定实际缴付的出资额和企业投资总额内外国投资者以自己的境外自有资金实际直接向企业提供的贷款。

外商投资 指国外及港澳台地区的法人和自然人在中国大陆地区以现金、实物、无形资产、股权等方式进行投资。其中，外商直接投资是指国外及港澳台地区投资者在非上市公司中的全部投资及在单个外国投资者所占股权比例不低于 10%的上市公司中的投资。

对外承包工程 根据《对外承包工程管理条例》，对外承包工程是指中国的企业或者其他单位承包境外建设工程项目的活动。

对外劳务合作 指组织劳务人员赴其他国家或地区为国外的企业或机构工作的经营性活动。

入境游客 指报告期内来中国（大陆）观光、度假、探亲访友、就医疗养、购物、参加会议或从事经济、文化、体育、宗教活动的外国人、港澳台同胞等游客（即入境旅游人数）。统计时，入境游客按每入境一次统计 1 人次。入境游客包括入境过夜游客和入境一日游游客。

国内游客 指报告期内在中国（大陆）观光游览、度假、探亲访友、就医疗养、购物、参加会议或从事经济、文化、体育、宗教活动的中国（大陆）居民人数，其出游的目的不是通过所从事的活动谋取报酬。统计时，国内游客按每出游一次统计 1 人次。

国际旅游收入 指入境游客在中国（大陆）境内旅行、游览过程中用于交通、参观游览、住宿、餐饮、购物、娱乐等全部花费。

国内旅游收入(旅游总花费) 指国内游客在国内旅行、游览过程中用于交通、参观游览、住宿、餐饮、购物、娱乐等全部花费。

Explanatory Notes on Main Statistical Indicators

Import and Export of Goods refer to the value of commodities actually imported or exported across the border of China. They include the actual imports and exports through foreign trade, imported and exported goods under the processing and assembling trades and materials, supplies and gifts as aid given gratis between governments and by the United Nations and other international organizations, and contributions donated by overseas Chinese, compatriots in Hong Kong and Macao and Chinese with foreign citizenship, leasing commodities owned by tenant at the expiration of leasing period, the imported and exported commodities processed with imported materials, commodities trading in border areas, the imported and exported commodities and articles for public use of the Sino-foreign joint ventures, cooperative enterprises and ventures with sole foreign investment. Also included are import or export of samples and advertising goods for which CIF or FOB value are beyond the permitted ceiling (excluding goods of no trading or use value and free commodities for export), imported goods sold in China from bonded warehouses and other imported or exported goods. The indicator of the total imports and exports at customs can be used to observe the total size of external trade in a country. In accordance with the stipulation of the Chinese government, exports are calculated at FOB, while imports are calculated at CIF.

The actual utilization of foreign capital refers to the actual number of execution of the approved contractual foreign capital amount, the actual amount of foreign investment paid by foreign investors in accordance with the provisions of the contract (articles of association) for the approval of foreign-funded enterprises, and the total amount of enterprise investment actually provided by foreign investors to enterprises directly with their own overseas funds.

Foreign Investment refers to investment in China by legal or natural persons of foreign countries and of Hong Kong, Macao and Taiwan, in the form of cash, physical assets, intangible assets and equity and others. Foreign direct investment refers to investment by investors from foreign countries and from Hong Kong, Macao and Taiwan in a non-listed company, or the investment of over 10 percent or more in a listed company.

Overseas Contracted Projects refer to activities of contracting overseas construction projects by Chinese enterprises or any other units, which are stipulated in the Regulations on Administration of Foreign Contracted Project.

Overseas Labor Services refer to operational activities of organizing labour force to go abroad providing services to foreign enterprises or agencies.

Overseas Visitor Arrivals refer to the number of tourists of foreigners, Chinese compatriots from Hong Kong, Macao and Taiwan who come to China (mainland) within the reference period for sight-seeing, vacation, visiting relatives, medical treatment, shopping, attending conference, or to engage in economic, cultural, sports and religious activities (namely the number of overseas visitor arrivals). In compiling statistics, each arrival is counted as one person-time. Overseas visitor arrivals includes inbound overnight tourists and one-day tourists.

Number of Domestic Tourists refers to the number of Chinese (mainland) residents who travel within China (mainland) for sight-seeing, vacation, visiting relatives, medical treatment, shopping, attending conference, or to engage in economic, cultural, sports and religious activities. In compiling statistics, each travel is counted as one person-time.

Foreign Exchange Earnings from International Tourism refer to the total expenditure of overseas visitors during their stay in the mainland of China on transportation, sighting, accommodation, food, shopping and entertainment.

Income from Domestic Tourism refer to expenditure of domestic tourists on transportation, sighting, accommodation, food, shopping and entertainment while they travel.

19 金融业

Chapter 19 Financial Intermediation

19—1 金融机构(含外资)本外币信贷收支表(资金来源)
Balance Sheet of Local and Foreign Credit Funds of Financial Institutions (Funds Sources)

单位：亿元 (100 million yuan)

项目	Item	2023	比年初增减数 amount over the beginning of the year
资金来源总计	**All Sources**	**130827.62**	**12321.62**
各项存款	Deposits	122980.74	11312.47
非金融企业存款	Deposits of Non-financial Enterprises	28091.39	1668.37
住户存款	Deposits of Households	71978.80	8415.07
#活期存款	Demand Deposits	18577.30	655.51
机关团体存款	Deposits of Organizations and Communities	16777.74	920.56
财政性存款	Deposits of Fiscal	2240.99	74.38
非银行业金融机构存款	Deposits of Non-banking Financial Institutions	3786.97	224.32
金融债券	Financial Bonds	632.51	63.26
卖出回购资产	Assets Sold for Repurchase	9.59	-15.55
借款及非银行业金融机构拆入	Borrowing and Non-banking Financial Institutions Borrowing	18.18	-1.28
联行往来(净)	Inter-branched Exchange (net)		
应付及暂收款	Account Payable and Temporary Collection	3345.90	441.99
各项准备	Reserves	3083.07	132.76
所有者权益	Owners' Equities	5290.91	604.61
其他	Others	-4533.28	-216.64

注：本表金融机构包括中国人民银行、中资全国性大型银行、中资全国性中小型银行、中资区域性中小型银行、城市信用社、农村信用社、财务公司、信托投资公司、租赁公司、外资金融机构和汽车金融公司(以下有关各表同)。

a) Financial institution of balance sheet includes the People’s Bank of China, large, small and medium-sized Chinese-funded national banks, small and medium-sized regional and Chinese-funded banks, urban and rural credit cooperative banks, finance companies, financial trust and investment companies, financial leasing companies, Foreign financial institutions and auto finance company (the same as the following related tables) .

19—2 金融机构(含外资)本外币信贷收支表(资金运用)

Balance Sheet of Local and Foreign Credit Funds of Financial Institutions (Funds Uses)

单位：亿元 (100 million yuan)

项目	Item	2023	比年初增减数 amount over the beginning of the year
资金运用总计	**All Uses**	**130827.62**	**12321.62**
各项贷款	Loans	105790.59	13409.85
住户贷款	Loans of Households	32742.92	3188.52
短期贷款	Shot-term Loans	5278.67	699.94
中长期贷款	Medium-term & Long-term Loans	27464.25	2488.58
企（事）业单位贷款	Loans of Enterprises (Institutions)	72422.26	10216.35
短期贷款	Shot-term Loans	14538.31	2416.04
中长期贷款	Medium-term & Long-term Loans	54629.54	8011.33
票据融资	Bill Financing	3146.50	-183.23
各项垫款	Various Money Paid Back Later	30.11	-19.89
债券投资	Bond Investment	15024.29	1735.03
股权及其他投资	Equity and Other Investment	3840.27	-58.49
买入返售资产	Redemptory Capital for Sale	309.93	-41.36
存放非银行业金融机构款项	Due from Non-banking Financial Institutions	47.13	0.35
联行往来(净)	Inter-branched Exchange (net)	4137.44	-2777.85
应收及预付款	Account Receivable and Advanced Payment	1094.61	61.25
固定资产	Fixed Assets	579.41	-7.66
外汇占款	Position for Foreign Purchase		
投资性房地产	Investment Property	3.95	0.48

注：“企（事）业单位贷款”原为“非金融企业及机关团体贷款”，统计口径未变。

a) The indicator "loans of Enterprises (Institutions)" was originally the indicator "Loans of Non-financial Enterprises & Government", and the statistical caliber has not changed.

19-3 各市(州)金融机构各项存款和贷款(2023年底)

Deposits and Loans of Financial Institutions by Region at Year-end of 2023

单位：亿元 (100 million yuan)

市(州)	Region	本外币 各项存款 RMB and Foreign Currency Deposits	人民币 各项存款 RMB Deposits	#住户存款 Household Savings	本外币 各项贷款 RMB and Foreign Currency Loans	人民币 各项贷款 RMB Loans	#短期贷款 Short-term Loans	#中长期贷款 Medium and Long-term Loans
全省	**Sichuan**	**122980.74**	**121920.96**	**71745.14**	**105790.59**	**104692.52**	**19234.32**	**81926.72**
成都市	Chengdu	58435.76	57488.41	25822.95	61191.15	60111.08	9677.21	48954.08
自贡市	Zigong	2986.78	2983.49	2146.40	1995.88	1995.04	447.67	1483.99
攀枝花市	Panzhihua	1383.82	1381.81	1037.34	1014.13	1012.85	260.21	664.34
泸州市	Luzhou	4310.03	4302.09	2926.04	3617.28	3617.11	793.51	2672.29
德阳市	Deyang	4527.32	4514.17	3115.25	2894.01	2885.04	654.46	1977.96
绵阳市	Mianyang	7040.65	7026.98	4248.24	4412.83	4412.08	1225.49	3011.27
广元市	Guangyuan	2257.18	2256.31	1764.92	1456.18	1456.05	290.16	1089.95
遂宁市	Suining	2786.43	2782.87	2079.69	1950.38	1949.42	494.94	1354.09
内江市	Neijiang	2726.48	2722.68	2204.02	1709.16	1709.14	497.02	1107.38
乐山市	Leshan	3936.34	3927.10	2939.39	2668.54	2668.29	546.84	1923.17
南充市	Nanchong	5260.45	5256.06	4258.00	3849.03	3848.71	778.31	2925.28
眉山市	Meishan	3498.08	3493.85	2700.78	2646.36	2646.15	484.81	2063.85
宜宾市	Yibin	5281.72	5247.42	2641.11	4593.25	4589.98	767.71	3607.65
广安市	Guangan	2978.26	2977.17	2466.56	1483.05	1483.04	304.45	1077.56
达州市	Dazhou	4868.39	4866.24	3826.95	3070.62	3070.59	663.85	2307.41
雅安市	Yaan	1745.99	1740.07	1268.63	1326.17	1325.42	315.93	949.37
巴中市	Bazhong	1949.04	1948.65	1656.11	1328.96	1328.95	195.93	1097.47
资阳市	Ziyang	2097.60	2096.55	1684.65	1467.89	1467.87	304.89	1136.88
阿坝藏族羌族自治州	Aba	819.92	819.86	434.01	545.53	545.53	68.02	464.20
甘孜藏族自治州	Ganzi	943.31	943.25	409.39	581.33	581.32	53.95	510.99
凉山彝族自治州	Liangshan	3147.20	3145.94	2114.69	1988.87	1988.85	408.94	1547.54

注：成都市数据包含四川省本部数据(以下有关各表同)。

a) The data of Chengdu includes the data of Sichuan provincial headquarters (the same as the following related tables).

19-4 各市(州)金融机构人民币各项存款(年底余额)
Deposits of Financial Institutions by Region at Year-end(RMB)

单位：亿元 (100 million yuan)

市(州)	Region	2013	2014	2015	2016	2017	2018	2019	2020	2021	2022	2023
全省	**Sichuan**	**47667.28**	**53282.03**	**59184.83**	**65638.43**	**71591.42**	**76088.75**	**81783.68**	**90350.48**	**98645.13**	**110284.84**	**121920.96**
成都市	Chengdu	23662.21	26797.50	29474.92	31597.50	34581.17	36820.23	38777.88	42500.12	46905.62	52240.47	57488.41
自贡市	Zigong	974.97	1075.20	1319.76	1524.05	1723.67	1708.76	2068.48	2375.19	2500.42	2737.79	2983.49
攀枝花市	Panzhihua	784.18	802.87	856.81	938.59	981.36	1041.79	1080.64	1113.02	1173.64	1272.26	1381.81
泸州市	Luzhou	1409.46	1611.60	1829.88	2179.23	2459.19	2634.80	2802.82	3100.75	3423.87	3841.86	4302.09
德阳市	Deyang	1793.35	1918.54	2066.30	2307.72	2455.34	2694.37	2911.79	3288.48	3602.09	4046.82	4514.17
绵阳市	Mianyang	2410.27	2621.72	2882.91	3181.69	3588.52	3848.78	4457.80	5082.30	5618.92	6246.74	7026.98
广元市	Guangyuan	933.80	1005.82	1134.41	1302.22	1417.40	1478.55	1559.34	1684.63	1822.50	2065.42	2256.31
遂宁市	Suining	893.29	989.44	1187.12	1376.76	1554.82	1571.98	1650.51	1873.72	2109.41	2427.68	2782.87
内江市	Neijiang	1077.59	1134.36	1202.20	1366.90	1512.92	1649.36	1799.07	2019.52	2196.82	2472.57	2722.68
乐山市	Leshan	1524.56	1709.12	1723.96	1858.89	2080.04	2217.55	2477.86	2731.04	2985.75	3450.96	3927.10
南充市	Nanchong	1916.56	2154.46	2561.43	3047.30	3216.07	3292.66	3540.73	3947.52	4201.43	4770.79	5256.06
眉山市	Meishan	1115.04	1253.85	1432.08	1670.36	1961.14	2087.24	2322.95	2645.29	2827.25	3184.07	3493.85
宜宾市	Yibin	1573.67	1685.23	1911.25	2322.47	2646.64	2976.12	3366.80	3712.05	4124.40	4636.03	5247.42
广安市	Guangan	1114.68	1265.03	1424.65	1662.73	1828.89	1867.48	1981.73	2196.21	2339.97	2667.44	2977.17
达州市	Dazhou	1588.05	1752.37	2086.42	2624.98	2801.93	2927.09	3187.16	3519.48	3838.62	4332.93	4866.24
雅安市	Yaan	842.89	974.25	1008.95	1042.06	1104.51	1125.73	1206.49	1315.71	1397.89	1562.02	1740.07
巴中市	Bazhong	678.61	777.13	921.73	1145.80	1247.67	1247.59	1298.15	1432.52	1595.86	1792.34	1948.65
资阳市	Ziyang	1083.87	1245.84	1377.85	1673.02	1355.97	1418.75	1469.41	1598.65	1682.31	1885.14	2096.55
阿坝藏族羌族自治州	Aba	435.15	473.60	535.36	568.00	594.92	652.71	664.59	738.32	729.48	759.37	819.86
甘孜藏族自治州	Ganzi	442.28	499.03	588.24	595.64	631.30	698.35	705.51	787.96	805.62	908.88	943.25
凉山彝族自治州	Liangshan	1271.89	1386.67	1490.66	1652.53	1847.95	2128.87	2453.94	2688.01	2763.26	2983.25	3145.94

19−5 各市(州)金融机构人民币住户存款(年底余额)
Household Deposits of Financial Institutions by Region at Year-end(RMB)

单位：亿元 (100 million yuan)

市(州)	Region	2013	2014	2015	2016	2017	2018	2019	2020	2021	2022	2023
全省	**Sichuan**	**22956.68**	**25731.62**	**28575.90**	**31950.42**	**34800.89**	**38402.77**	**43214.16**	**49289.28**	**54849.24**	**63336.46**	**71745.14**
成都市	Chengdu	8408.79	9280.25	9922.18	10831.38	11995.87	13168.73	14931.89	17121.44	19063.70	22451.41	25822.95
自贡市	Zigong	639.49	718.51	819.38	923.57	1033.62	1145.90	1301.29	1555.06	1705.15	1920.05	2146.40
攀枝花市	Panzhihua	411.91	431.79	462.44	522.97	575.92	658.90	712.86	778.82	850.90	942.80	1037.34
泸州市	Luzhou	880.83	1000.65	1140.17	1313.47	1475.96	1631.83	1833.05	2080.07	2318.37	2618.86	2926.04
德阳市	Deyang	1074.21	1188.39	1292.47	1425.36	1531.40	1703.84	1903.96	2148.38	2394.51	2748.12	3115.25
绵阳市	Mianyang	1328.09	1479.82	1640.86	1838.25	2028.73	2242.62	2524.03	2874.84	3221.01	3724.84	4248.24
广元市	Guangyuan	557.47	641.05	733.00	811.44	891.97	979.68	1099.24	1238.67	1379.96	1582.45	1764.92
遂宁市	Suining	577.96	649.28	788.08	910.44	1005.90	1117.10	1244.53	1417.71	1602.73	1841.05	2079.69
内江市	Neijiang	749.61	836.39	935.67	1045.62	1144.95	1265.67	1411.39	1581.66	1741.58	1976.64	2204.02
乐山市	Leshan	931.54	1057.43	1161.20	1277.37	1407.65	1574.30	1789.68	2035.55	2254.74	2591.48	2939.39
南充市	Nanchong	1306.68	1467.24	1723.13	2009.68	2175.10	2397.37	2668.48	3064.68	3373.76	3837.18	4258.00
眉山市	Meishan	778.44	907.67	1020.38	1156.75	1275.28	1467.72	1651.38	1869.09	2078.81	2390.66	2700.78
宜宾市	Yibin	770.04	886.63	1010.17	1150.62	1277.47	1424.08	1597.13	1814.39	2029.70	2330.15	2641.11
广安市	Guangan	795.90	902.15	1061.78	1198.60	1316.29	1398.36	1534.74	1743.07	1915.63	2196.09	2466.56
达州市	Dazhou	1139.67	1304.62	1505.90	1739.52	1917.50	2055.08	2329.22	2656.88	2966.39	3401.63	3826.95
雅安市	Yaan	379.84	447.05	505.29	543.35	596.13	669.47	764.67	871.61	980.56	1124.86	1268.63
巴中市	Bazhong	482.26	557.00	634.06	741.94	828.99	913.97	1016.36	1155.90	1304.97	1492.55	1656.11
资阳市	Ziyang	806.05	938.20	1060.43	1211.38	884.28	967.07	1069.81	1188.39	1329.82	1507.85	1684.65
阿坝藏族羌族自治州	Aba	148.26	164.64	186.67	215.71	233.12	257.07	277.37	315.71	347.14	390.15	434.01
甘孜藏族自治州	Ganzi	139.72	163.93	186.06	209.67	226.66	247.36	265.66	299.19	322.72	369.81	409.39
凉山彝族自治州	Liangshan	627.81	687.43	764.83	873.33	978.10	1116.65	1287.43	1478.18	1667.08	1897.85	2114.69

19-6 各市(州)金融机构人民币各项贷款(年底余额)
Loans of Financial Institutions by Region at Year-end(RMB)

单位：亿元 (100 million yuan)

市(州)	Region	2013	2014	2015	2016	2017	2018	2019	2020	2021	2022	2023
全省	**Sichuan**	**29542.74**	**33884.06**	**38011.83**	**42828.13**	**48124.44**	**54097.84**	**61089.01**	**69504.94**	**78963.92**	**91104.80**	**104692.52**
成都市	Chengdu	17617.51	19778.93	21970.64	25522.23	28870.55	32057.77	35766.59	40376.89	45768.93	52632.13	60111.08
自贡市	Zigong	449.33	520.81	614.57	708.35	825.98	1010.40	1198.43	1401.81	1600.48	1825.82	1995.04
攀枝花市	Panzhihua	608.93	658.19	697.15	738.63	795.54	804.70	826.33	705.59	764.11	865.47	1012.85
泸州市	Luzhou	766.70	919.42	1092.70	1281.64	1451.30	1714.16	2001.09	2366.98	2688.39	3079.85	3617.11
德阳市	Deyang	956.40	1065.81	1075.92	1190.04	1292.54	1442.31	1650.09	1911.01	2193.54	2554.61	2885.04
绵阳市	Mianyang	1252.78	1398.50	1532.85	1667.43	1864.71	2167.25	2476.18	2812.66	3275.09	3751.75	4412.08
广元市	Guangyuan	406.87	472.32	531.18	610.20	703.84	795.37	903.16	1001.20	1116.91	1275.23	1456.05
遂宁市	Suining	499.02	615.01	740.81	820.20	922.72	1040.67	1171.96	1308.89	1430.35	1665.49	1949.42
内江市	Neijiang	514.11	608.07	688.15	731.65	782.70	901.69	1020.70	1179.73	1302.39	1464.07	1709.14
乐山市	Leshan	931.75	1086.79	1230.91	1308.83	1431.65	1558.88	1726.36	1917.68	2125.28	2401.30	2668.29
南充市	Nanchong	824.66	1038.07	1293.89	1479.68	1684.34	1961.17	2268.61	2606.19	2951.50	3381.05	3848.71
眉山市	Meishan	531.99	625.17	683.76	747.19	864.31	1042.89	1257.19	1537.92	1831.21	2215.72	2646.15
宜宾市	Yibin	760.64	900.79	1054.48	1223.82	1390.60	1636.91	1971.69	2510.24	3053.21	3745.74	4589.98
广安市	Guangan	424.53	514.94	582.13	639.09	725.86	809.57	930.22	1027.34	1150.15	1309.37	1483.04
达州市	Dazhou	655.58	801.71	929.32	1077.62	1277.93	1502.91	1713.16	1949.66	2239.52	2617.04	3070.59
雅安市	Yaan	412.44	474.98	510.09	527.85	594.84	657.82	764.79	853.94	977.50	1157.92	1325.42
巴中市	Bazhong	264.93	345.03	457.83	542.50	641.40	716.43	804.30	932.73	1051.71	1182.59	1328.95
资阳市	Ziyang	525.02	642.08	716.90	735.29	597.15	706.89	817.62	1017.77	1128.52	1303.65	1467.87
阿坝藏族羌族自治州	Aba	186.44	205.68	221.63	252.47	269.70	299.56	336.97	375.46	417.34	475.70	545.53
甘孜藏族自治州	Ganzi	167.60	194.05	230.49	273.62	317.17	353.62	418.25	470.09	490.34	523.64	581.32
凉山彝族自治州	Liangshan	575.47	655.43	700.41	749.78	819.60	916.87	1065.32	1241.16	1407.46	1676.67	1988.85

19-7 金融机构人民币存款基准利率
Benchmark Interest Rates of Deposits of Financial Institutions

单位：年利率% (Annual Interest Rate %)

项目	Item	2014.11.22 Nov.22 2014	2015.03.01 Mar.1 2015	2015.05.11 May.11 2015	2015.06.28 June.28 2015	2015.08.26 Aug.26 2015	2015.10.24 Oct.24 2015
活期存款	**Demand Deposits**	**0.35**	**0.35**	**0.35**	**0.35**	**0.35**	**0.35**
定期存款(整存整取)	**Time Deposits(Lump-sum Time Deposit)**						
三个月	3 Months	2.35	2.10	1.85	1.60	1.35	1.10
半年	6 Months	2.55	2.30	2.05	1.80	1.55	1.30
一年	1 Year	2.75	2.50	2.25	2.00	1.75	1.50
二年	2 Years	3.35	3.10	2.85	2.60	2.35	2.10
三年	3 Years	4.00	3.75	3.50	3.25	3.00	2.75

19-8 金融机构人民币贷款基准利率
Benchmark Interest Rates of Loans of Financial Institutions

单位：年利率% (Annual Interest Rate %)

项目	Item	2014.11.22 Nov.22 2014	2015.03.01 Mar.1 2015	2015.05.11 May.11 2015	2015.06.28 June.28 2015	2015.08.26 Aug.26 2015	2015.10.24 Oct.24 2015
短期贷款	**Short-term Loans**						
一年以内(含一年)	1-Year Or Less	5.60	5.35	5.10	4.85	4.60	4.35
中长期贷款	**Mediun-term & Long-time Loans**						
一至五年(含五年)	1-5-Year(including 5-Year)	6.00	5.75	5.50	5.25	5.00	4.75
五年以上	Longer than 5-Year	6.15	5.90	5.65	5.40	5.15	4.90

19-9 人民币对外主要外币年平均汇价(中间价)
Annual Average RMB Exchange Rate against Major Foreign Currencies (Middle Rate)

单位：人民币元 (RMB yuan)

年份 Year	100美元 $100	100日元 100 yen	100港元 HK $ 100	100欧元 € 100
1987	372.21	2.5799	47.74	
1988	372.21	2.9082	47.70	
1989	376.51	2.7360	48.28	
1990	478.32	3.3233	61.39	
1991	532.33	3.9602	68.45	
1992	551.46	4.3608	71.24	
1993	576.20	5.2020	74.41	
1994	861.87	8.4370	111.53	
1995	835.10	8.9225	107.96	
1996	831.42	7.6352	107.51	
1997	828.98	6.8600	107.09	
1998	827.91	6.3488	106.88	
1999	827.83	7.2932	106.66	
2000	827.84	7.6864	106.18	
2001	827.70	6.8075	106.08	
2002	827.70	6.6237	106.07	800.58
2003	827.70	7.1466	106.24	936.13
2004	827.68	7.6552	106.23	1029.00
2005	819.17	7.4484	105.30	1019.53
2006	797.18	6.8570	102.62	1001.90
2007	760.40	6.4632	97.46	1041.75
2008	694.51	6.7427	89.19	1022.27
2009	683.10	7.2986	88.12	952.70
2010	676.95	7.7279	87.13	897.25
2011	645.88	8.1050	82.97	900.11
2012	631.25	7.9037	81.38	810.67
2013	619.32	6.3323	79.85	822.19
2014	614.28	5.8196	79.22	816.51
2015	622.84	5.1543	80.34	691.41
2016	664.23	6.1243	85.58	734.26
2017	675.18	6.0244	86.64	763.03
2018	661.74	5.9890	84.43	780.16
2019	689.85	6.3347	88.05	772.55
2020	689.76	6.4626	88.93	787.55
2021	645.15	5.8735	83.00	762.93
2022	672.61	5.1261	85.89	707.21
2023	704.67	5.0350	90.02	764.25

19–10 保险业务经济技术指标
Economic and Technical Indicators of Insurance Business

单位：万元 (10 000 yuan)

项目	Item	2017	2018	2019	2020	2021	2022	2023
保费收入合计	**Premium Income Total**	**19393937**	**19580848**	**21486588**	**22735688**	**22049053**	**22977901**	**24835080**
财产保险	**Property Insurance**	**4963608**	**5424358**	**5835613**	**6393823**	**6539641**	**7151125**	**7758616**
企业财产保险	Enterprise Property Insurance	124654	130097	150880	156205	175623	165856	178118
机动车辆保险	Automobile Insurance	3923080	3073062	3833437	3945521	3882642	4092582	4309384
货物运输保险	Cargo Transportation Insurance	13923	16629	17020	19891	30992	69090	107643
责任保险	Liability Insurance	218753	285056	409698	497651	538072	573804	591302
信用保证保险	Credit and Guarantee Insurance	32972	39561	17633	24250	26047	18489	40770
其他财产保险	Others	650227	1249953	1406946	1750305	1886266	2231304	2531399
人身保险	**Life Insurance**	**14430329**	**14156489**	**15650974**	**16341865**	**15509412**	**15826776**	**17076464**
人寿保险	Life Insurance Business							
非分红产品	Non-participating	7480289	5158949	5359186	6259995	6338874	7646722	9632227
分红产品	Participating	4090501	6344701	6903222	6280889	5350268	4420659	3477038
投资连接产品	Unit-link	543	540	607	728	631	560	546
万能产品	Universal	44849	45017	45260	42225	39032	38607	39574
健康险	Health Insurance							
短期健康险	Short-term Health Insurance	744711	873179	1294255	1618574	1588951	1717641	992026
长期健康险	Long-term Health Insurance	1603716	1725761	2188912	2470089	2551576	2609066	2731297
意外伤害险	Personal Accident Insurance	465720	511860	561815	581979	606398	564204	203757
赔款给付支出合计	**Claim Total**	**5833192**	**6327362**	**6347551**	**6877491**	**7929963**	**7639003**	**9744933**
财产保险	**Property Insurance**	**2411127**	**3103449**	**3416508**	**3675059**	**4226426**	**4398946**	**5230550**
企业财产保险	Enterprise Property Insurance	50036	99156	77395	106054	141212	79268	95771
机动车辆保险	Automobile Insurance	1973086	2215797	2276536	2369671	2615979	2571834	2853952
货物运输保险	Cargo Transportation Insurance	6850	7016	6647	8002	13069	36153	62113
责任保险	Liability Insurance	82785	110996	140322	210007	261823	295669	363825
信用保证保险	Credit and Guarantee Insurance	16584	11151	5459	12931	5627	14957	70111
其他财产保险	Others	281785	659333	910150	968394	1188715	1401064	1784778
人身保险	**Life Insurance**	**3422065**	**3224724**	**2931043**	**3202891**	**3704103**	**3240057**	**4514383**
人寿保险	Life Insurance Business							
非分红产品	Non-participating	566454	594569	567437	542477	682697	594228	524794
分红产品	Participating	2129803	1994973	1545693	1588210	1384944	1394456	2750093
投资连接产品	Unit-link	125	102	69	661	1848	422	268
万能产品	Universal	10418	10505	9586	9418	10038	9217	11672
健康险	Health Insurance							
短期健康险	Short-term Health Insurance	459970	572261	787484	902640	1066142	1207364	1565860
长期健康险	Long-term Health Insurance	132634	191031	251277	453273	923179	552706	431450
意外伤害险	Personal Accident Insurance	122660	71601	149933	172205	190620	187983	217941

注：因部分机构目前处于风险处置阶段，数据口径暂时调整为不包含风险处置机构，直至相关机构风险处置结束(以下有关表同)。

a) As some institutions are currently in the risk disposal stage, the data caliber is temporarily adjusted to exclude risk disposal institutions until the risk disposal of relevant institutions is completed(the same as the following related tables).

19-11 各财产保险公司和人身保险公司四川省分公司保费收入
Premium Income of Property Insurance Companies (Sichuan Branch) and Life Insurance Companies (Sichuan Branch)

单位：万元 (10 000 yuan)

公司名称	Company Name	2022	2023
财产保险公司	**Property Insurance Companies**	**7151125**	**7758616**
中国人民财产保险股份有限公司	PICC Property&Casualty Insurance Company Limited	2355059	2492043
中国太平洋财产保险股份有限公司	China Pacific Insurance (Group) Co.,Ltd.	628997	733010
中国平安财产保险股份有限公司	Ping An Insurance (Group) Company of China,Ltd.	1602191	1673310
永安财产保险股份有限公司	Yong An Insurance Co.,Ltd.	46823	32886
华泰财产保险股份有限公司	Huatai Insurance Co., Ltd.	45478	49907
中华联合财产保险股份有限公司	China United Property Insurance Company	411309	464193
太平保险有限公司	TaiPing Insurance Company Ltd.	218709	257336
中国大地财产保险股份有限公司	China Continent Property & Casualty Insurance Company	187188	206131
华安财产保险股份有限公司	Sinosafe Insurance	59789	62719
中航安盟财产保险有限公司	Groupama-Avic PropertyInsurance Co.,Ltd.	94183	99029
中国出口信用保险公司	China Export & Credit Insurance Corporation (SINOSURE)	10873	29294
大家财产保险股份有限公司	Dajia Property & Casualty Insurance Co.,Ltd.	35104	30070
永诚财产保险股份有限公司	Alltrust Insurance Company of China,Ltd.	33845	33957
安盛天平财产保险股份有限公司	AXA Tianping P&C Insurance Co.,Ltd.	17965	16663
阳光财产保险股份有限公司	Sunshine Property & Casualty Insurance Company of China,Ltd.	187636	164204
都邦财产保险股份有限公司	Dubang Property & Casualty Insurance Company of China,Ltd.	17689	20288
渤海财产保险股份有限公司	Bohai Property & Casuatly Insurance Company of China,Ltd.	2462	4640
中银保险有限公司	China Bank Property & Casualty Insurance Company of China,Ltd.	19958	19362
华农财产保险股份有限公司	Huanong Property & Casualty Insurance Co.,Ltd.	40881	48077
安诚财产保险股份有限公司	Ancheng Property & Casualty Insurance Co.Ltd.	18333	19335
亚太财产保险有限公司	Asia Pacific Property Insurance Company Limited	19088	20701
浙商财产保险股份有限公司	Zheshang Property & Casualty Insurance Co.,Ltd.	7362	8834
鼎和财产保险股份有限公司	Dinghe Property & Casualty Insurance Company of China,Ltd.	12104	16015
英大泰和财产保险股份有限公司	Yingda Taihe Property & Casualty Insurance Co.,Ltd.	56800	63541
锦泰财产保险股份有限公司	JinTai Property Insurane Co.,Ltd.	175867	212408
紫金财产保险股份有限公司	Zijin Property and Casualty Insurance Co.,Ltd.	22739	24915
中国人寿财产保险股份有限公司	China Life Property & Casualty Insurance Co.,Ltd.	354960	391053
信达财产保险股份有限公司	Cinda Property Insurance Co.,Ltd.	37030	40812
国泰财产保险有限责任公司	Cathay Insurance Co., Ltd.	26540	35561
富德财产保险股份有限公司	Fund Property & Casualty Insurance Co.,Ltd.	3884	4600
安华农业保险股份有限公司	Anhua Agricultural Insurance Co.,Ltd.	8926	8850

19-11 续表 1 continued

单位：万元 (10 000 yuan)

公司名称	Company Name	2022	2023
中意财产保险有限公司	Generali China Insurance Co.,Ltd.	12362	14725
鑫安汽车保险股份有限公司	Sanguard Automobile Insurance Co., Ltd.	15770	17544
利宝保险有限公司	Liberty Insurance Co.,Ltd.	10928	12770
诚泰财产保险份有限公司	Cheng Tai Property Insurance Company Limited	15272	15839
富邦财产保险有限公司	Fubon Property Insurance Co.,Ltd.	2283	4988
珠峰财产保险股份有限公司	Everest Property Insurance Co.,Ltd.	10170	11828
中煤财产保险股份有限公司	China Coal Property Insurance Co.,Ltd.	10191	10449
长江财产保险股份有限公司	Changjiang Property Insurance Co.,Ltd.	3522	5150
前海联合财产保险股份有限公司	Qianhai United Property & Casualty Insurance Co.,Ltd.	9752	13394
恒邦财产保险股份有限公司	Hengbang Property Insurance Co.,Ltd.	7762	9611
京东安联	Allianz JD Property Insurance Co., Ltd.	36050	65765
泰山财产保险股份有限公司	Taishan Property Insurance Co., Ltd	27183	27450
现代财产保险（中国）有限公司	Hyundai Insurance(china) Company Limited	2056	4240
北部湾财产保险股份有限公司	Beibu Gulf Property Insuiance CO.,Ltd	587	9073
众安在线财产保险股份有限公司	Zhongan Online Property Insurance Co.,Ltd.	166123	188863
中国铁路财产保险自保有限公司	China Railway Property Insurance Holding Co.,Ltd.	1136	2328
阳光渝融信用保证保险股份有限公司	Sunshine Yurong Credit and Guarantee Insurance Co.,Ltd.	4	3
泰康在线财产保险股份有限公司	Taikang Online Property Insurance Co.,Ltd.	60165	60745
安心财产保险有限责任公司	Answern Property & Casualty Insurance Co.,Ltd.		
众惠相互	Public Mutual Insurance Co.,Ltd.	38	107
人身保险公司	**Life Insurance Companies**	**15826776**	**17076464**
中国人寿保险股份有限公司	China Life Insurance(Group) Company	3019198	3169006
中国太平洋人寿保险股份有限公司	China Pacific Insurance(group) Co.,Ltd.	882078	739520
中国平安人寿保险股份有限公司	Ping An Insurance (Group) Company of China,Ltd.	1466911	1574755
新华人寿保险股份有限公司	New China Insurance Co.,Ltd.	604953	526243
泰康人寿保险股份有限公司	Taikang Life Insurance Company	1019881	1152132
太平人寿保险有限公司	Taipjng Life Insurance Co.,Ltd.	1399845	1534417
民生人寿保险股份有限公司	Minsheng Life Insurance Co.,Ltd.	74129	74443
中英人寿保险有限公司	Aviva Cofco Life Insurance Co.,Ltd.	221069	249636
富德生命人寿保险股份有限公司	Sino Life Insurance Co.,Ltd.	277875	297854
北大方正人寿保险有限公司	Founder Meiji Yasuda Life Insurance Co.,Ltd.	47395	47984
长城人寿保险股份公司	Great Wall Life Insurance Co.,Ltd.	107044	157659
中宏人寿保险股份公司	Manulife-Sinochem Insurance Co.,Ltd.	139093	181334
中德安联人寿保险有限公司	Allianz China Life Insurance Co.,Ltd.	34818	39505
农银人寿保险股份有限公司	ABC Life Insurance Co.,Ltd.	238640	190314
中国人民人寿保险股份有限公司	PICC Life Insurance Co.,Ltd.	894031	872183
华泰人寿保险有限公司	Huatai Life Insurance Co.,Ltd.	44467	41856
人保健康保险有限公司	PICC Health Insurance Co.,Ltd.	48128	59240
恒安标准人寿保险有限公司	Heng'an Standard Life Co.,Ltd.	28369	35883

19-11 续表 2 continued

单位：万元 (10 000 yuan)

公司名称	Company Name	2022	2023
招商信诺保险有限公司	CIGNA&CMC Insurance Co.,Ltd.	60140	73725
合众人寿保险有限公司	Union Life Insurance Co.,Ltd.	91972	67993
阳光人寿保险有限公司	Sunshine Life Insurance Co.,Ltd.	200203	207090
中意人寿保险有限公司	General China Insurance Co.Ltd.	78136	100617
中国平安养老保险股份有限公司	Ping An Insurance (Group) Company of China,Ltd.	74684	74561
太平养老保险股份有限公司	TaiPing Pension Company Limited	31598	39470
恒大人寿保险有限公司	Evergrande Life Insurance Company Limited	710982	
中邮人寿保险有限公司	China Post Lift Insurance Co.,Ltd.	627067	711337
幸福人寿保险有限公司	Happy Life Insurance Co.,Ltd.	104079	95032
中美联泰大都会人寿保险有限公司	Sino-US United Metlife Insurance Co.,Ltd.	47525	49069
国华人寿保险股份有限公司	Guohua Life Insurance Co.,Ltd.	299509	278084
和谐健康保险股份有限公司	Harmony Health Insurance Company Limited	209004	395299
安邦人寿保险股份有限公司	Anbang Life Insurance Co.,Ltd.	510179	689453
光大永明人寿保险有限公司	Sun Life Everbright Life Insurance Co.,Ltd.	55711	57063
工银安盛人寿保险有限公司	ICBC-AXA Assurance Co.,Ltd.	208548	188520
百年人寿保险股份有限公司	Aeon Life Insurance Co.,Ltd.	291674	287471
中融人寿保险股份有限公司	Zhongrong Life Insurance Co.,Ltd.	99701	49036
英大泰和人寿保险股份有限公司	Yingda Taihe Life Insurance Co.,Ltd.	20308	22009
中银三星人寿保险有限公司	BOC Samsung Life Insurance Company Limited	160529	224448
建信人寿保险有限公司	CCB Life Insurance Company Limited	238942	158760
泰康养老保险股份有限公司	Taikang Pension Insurance Co.,Ltd.	76850	111366
同方全球人寿保险有限公司	Aegon THTF Life Insurance Co.,Ltd.	25525	29165
东吴人寿保险股份有限公司	SooChow Life Insurance Company Limited	78537	104009
利安人寿保险股份有限公司	Lian Life Insurance Co.,Ltd.	137780	163969
交银康联人寿保险有限公司	Bocomm Life Insurance Co.,Ltd.	28967	41250
前海人寿保险股份有限公司	Foresea Life Insurance Co.,Ltd.	244554	477281
长生人寿保险有限公司	Great Wall Changsheng Life Insurance Co.,Ltd.	74835	74389
安邦养老保险股份有限公司	Ampang Pension Insurance Co.,Ltd.	878	10874
陆家嘴国泰人寿保险有限责任公司	Cathay Lujiazui Life Insurance Company Limited	27922	37308
太保安联健康保险股份有限公司	CPIC Allianz Health Insurance Co.,Ltd.	1831	2779
平安健康保险股份有限公司	Ping An Health Insurance Company of China,Ltd.	70186	87067
中信保诚人寿保险有限公司	CITIC Prudential Life Insurance Company Limited	50879	52564
国宝人寿保险股份有限公司	Guobao Life Insurance Co.,Ltd.	133195	193015
复星联合健康保险股份有限公司	Fosun United Health Insurance Co.,Ltd.	31993	41493
中华联合人寿保险股份有限公司	China United Life Insurance Co.,Ltd.	148628	127214
复星保德信人寿保险有限公司	Pramerica Fosun Life Insurance Co.,Ltd.	10752	34942
友邦人寿保险有限公司	AIA Life Insurance Co.,Ltd.	12934	22637

主要统计指标解释

金融机构信贷收支表 金融机构信贷收支表的统计范围包括中国人民银行、银行业存款类金融机构、银行业非存款类金融机构。银行业存款类金融机构包括银行、信用社和财务公司；银行业非存款类金融机构包括信托投资公司、金融租赁公司、汽车金融公司和贷款公司。中国人民银行总行根据金融机构的基层单位全面填报、并按各自系统汇总的资料，进行归并和汇总，最后得到金融机构的信贷收支表。

各项存款 金融机构资金来源的主要项目，包括住户存款、非金融企业存款、机关团体存款、财政性存款、非银行业金融机构存款和境外存款。

各项贷款 金融机构资金运用的主要项目，包括住户贷款、企（事）业单位贷款、非银行金融机构贷款和境外贷款。

保险公司 在中国境内的、经过保险监督管理部门批准设立，并依法登记注册的各类商业保险公司。

保险金额 指保险人承担赔偿或者给付保险金责任的最高限额。

保费 指投保人为取得保险人在约定范围内所承担赔偿责任而支付给保险人的费用。

赔款 指保险人根据保险合同的规定，向被保险人支付的赔偿保险责任损失的金额。

给付 包括死伤医疗给付和满期给付。死伤医疗给付是指保险人根据人寿保险及长期健康保险合同的规定，因被保险人在保险期内发生保险责任范围内的保险事故支付给被保险人(或受益人)的金额。满期给付是指被保险人生存期满，保险人按人寿保险合同规定支付给被保险人的满期保险金额。

Explanatory Notes on Main Statistical Indicators

Statistical scope of balance sheet of credit funds of financial institutions and data on cash income and expenditure cover the People's Bank of China, banking depository financial institutions, banking non-depository financial institutions. Banking depository financial institutions include banks, credit cooperatives and finance companies; Banking non-depository financial institutions include financial trust and investment companies, financial leasing companies, auto financing companies and loan companies. The grassroots units of the above financial institutions fill out the questionnaires and report to the higher authority. The higher authorities tabulate the data level by level. Finally, the Head Office of the People's Bank of China tabulates the data to obtain the national total.

Total Deposits are the main items of financial sources of financial institutions, which include deposits of households, deposits of non-financial enterprises, deposits of government departments & organizations, fiscal deposits, deposits of non-banking financial institutions and overseas deposits.

Total Loans are the main items of financial uses of financial institutions, which include loans to households, loans to non-financial enterprises and government departments & organizations, loans to non-banking financial institutions and overseas loans.

Insurance Companies refers to commercial insurance companies of various forms registered by law and established in China with the approval of insurance regulatory agencies.

Amount Insured refers to the maximum that the insurance will get for the claim of the case insured.

Premium is the fee paid by the insurance to the insurer to obtain the obligation of compensation from the insurance within the agreed terms.

Settled Claim is the compensation paid by the insurer to the insurance in accordance with the insurance contract.

Payment includes payment for death, injury or medical treatment and payment at maturity. Payment for death, injury or medical treatment refers to the money paid to the insurance (or the beneficiary) in accordance with the life or health insurance contract when the insurance encounters accidents within the insured period covered in the contract. Payment at maturity refers to the payment to the insurance in accordance with the life insurance contract at the end of the insured period.

20 教育、科技和专利

Chapter 20 Education, Science, Technology and Patents

20-1 各类学校数
Number of Schools by Type

单位：所 (unit)

年份 Year	普通高等学校 Regular Institutions of Higher Education	中等职业学校 Secondary Vocational Schools	普通中学 Regular Secondary Schools	小学 Primary Schools	幼儿园 Kindergartens	特殊教育学校 Special Education Schools
1952	10		306	35373	609	
1957	13		488	43665	612	
1962	17		866	44683	305	
1965	20		3693	108974	1349	5
1970	18		2769	70263	687	3
1975	17		3287	86254	2397	3
1978	28		4605	72563	35306	3
1980	29		4524	67659	24814	3
1985	39		4017	61953	13280	9
1990	40		4332	55047	13831	22
1995	42		4578	55799	12485	53
1996	42		4506	48911	11602	59
1997	42		4420	46917	11223	55
1998	43		4448	46092	11385	62
1999	43		4375	45133	12016	63
2000	42		4321	43326	12780	63
2001	49		5154	31447	7875	69
2002	59		5093	25972	7935	68
2003	62		5000	24573	8388	70
2004	68		4965	21935	7602	73
2005	72		4995	19305	8875	83
2006	76		5181	17372	8596	88
2007	76		5093	15834	8580	88
2008	78		4937	13993	8425	93
2009	92		4809	12437	8562	95
2010	93	679	4738	9282	9483	100
2011	94	656	4704	8847	10162	107
2012	99	630	4643	8586	10794	113
2013	103	595	4630	7257	11759	119
2014	107	568	4633	6959	12111	122
2015	109	550	4590	6487	12365	124
2016	109	526	4555	5981	12903	125
2017	109	520	4476	5721	13243	127
2018	119	508	4484	5730	13396	128
2019	126	497	4513	5725	13568	129
2020	132	493	4469	5679	13752	132
2021	134	482	4328	5443	13407	135
2022	134	463	4162	5213	12869	137
2023	137	442	4050	5119	12387	138

注：普通高等学校包括普通本科学校和高等职业学校；中等职业学校包括技工学校。各类学校基本情况由四川省教育厅提供(以下相关表同)。
a) Regular Institutions of Higher Education include ordinary undergraduate schools and higher vocational schools; Secondary vocational schools include Technical Schools. The basic statistics of schools is provided by Sichuan Provincial Department of Education (the same as the following tables).

20−2 各类学校专任教师数

Number of Full-time Teachers of Schools by Type

单位：人 (person)

年份 Year	普通高等学校 Regular Institutions of Higher Education	中等职业学校 Secondary Vocational Schools	普通中学 Regular Secondary Schools	小学 Primary Schools	幼儿园 Kindergartens	特殊教育学校 Special Education Schools
1952	1228		5953	111229	1556	
1957	3238		11873	132141	4679	
1962	5675		18597	146639	4523	
1965	6125		29097	225914	4720	35
1970	6414		55788	213151	3992	53
1975	7487		92015	334794	1858	20
1978	9047		167540	342661	39245	25
1980	10562		152660	343175	39028	44
1985	14577		145715	340164	32284	115
1990	16058		176179	321087	43573	322
1995	16439		190184	320923	55420	728
1996	16799		193942	323713	56052	730
1997	16786		196636	330212	56107	837
1998	17228		199357	334999	57738	987
1999	17891		207305	336356	58165	1148
2000	18418		217039	331551	58128	1113
2001	21984		227035	325123	30956	942
2002	26852		237425	321193	30591	973
2003	31372		247098	316029	32515	994
2004	39306		253358	307940	33997	1068
2005	44854		258924	307113	36654	1174
2006	52211		265540	306886	37530	1318
2007	55903		269967	306149	39337	1407
2008	59174		273559	307687	41827	1478
2009	61772		279414	306528	45136	1572
2010	64991	44051	284962	305741	51909	1711
2011	67448	48873	285755	305508	57528	1784
2012	73137	48186	290366	304899	65403	1941
2013	76795	45952	292629	305619	77336	2055
2014	81404	46767	292967	304909	86414	2211
2015	84430	46869	293165	308059	96885	2355
2016	85832	46621	294676	314406	105592	2503
2017	83949	46314	298805	325016	117052	2798
2018	86997	46046	304586	329927	122972	2970
2019	89796	45835	312867	337840	128724	3094
2020	95395	46606	321354	344855	132068	3220
2021	99025	52086	330723	349448	158076	3427
2022	104901	53266	335249	349535	164187	3607
2023	112171	55345	339750	352007	160865	3957

20-3 各类学校在校学生数
Number of Enrollments of Formal Education by Type

单位：人 (person)

年份 Year	普通高等学校 Regular Institutions of Higher Education	中等职业学校 Secondary Vocational Schools	普通中学 Regular Secondary Schools	小学 Primary Schools	幼儿园 Kindergartens	特殊教育学校 Special Education Schools
1952	9104		155252	3807776		
1957	19565		320254	4574044		
1962	36587		324216	3962046		
1965	28236		669901	7859341	127921	398
1970			1481952	6341703	95325	503
1975	21203		2085366	11013460	199412	345
1978	35715		3838846	10745859	1389229	339
1980	48497		2974390	11441551	957632	347
1985	72812		2516824	10418664	833754	623
1990	91866		2892023	6873322	1062885	1422
1995	126280		2705466	7350179	1777728	509
1996	131459		2765730	7797611	1793653	7400
1997	140451		2748214	8270885	1779648	9444
1998	151905		2908894	8438446	1860762	10104
1999	180256		3364576	8270859	1923949	10771
2000	235470		3919813	8026506	1892626	8224
2001	316701		4282666	7948490	1658864	14616
2002	412357		4568419	7785414	1595534	13390
2003	512663		4810712	7554308	1588575	15839
2004	637340		4909216	7365754	1527298	17354
2005	775436		4855390	7145093	1526827	24788
2006	860640		5014951	7217750	1562466	28621
2007	918438		5054691	6965306	1560935	39900
2008	991072		5026261	6488221	1597919	41739
2009	1035934		4990033	6170471	1707263	41767
2010	1086215	1399557	4900896	5921080	1887545	41839
2011	1139316	1407636	4778133	5798017	2110148	40898
2012	1223680	1398563	4558398	5607407	2192890	44287
2013	1270818	1302260	4233225	5259536	2314907	43731
2014	1328329	1195396	4073109	5313193	2407717	42289
2015	1387889	1107828	3934438	5417353	2481681	43251
2016	1446559	1019183	3895408	5495234	2593131	47780
2017	1499715	973974	3904323	5518361	2625168	53461
2018	1564710	941636	4007635	5554589	2608595	56851
2019	1661737	926504	4135256	5557731	2644188	61072
2020	1800903	946700	4206686	5529052	2652303	64979
2021	1920825	1027419	4236307	5489827	2617586	65981
2022	2051526	1082668	4240293	5450163	2539742	64476
2023	2164130	1035888	4255807	5490451	2315634	64055

注：普通高等学校学生数为普通本专科学生数；特殊教育在校生数含随班就读、送教上门等人数(以下有关各表同)。

a) Number of students in regular institutions of higher education is the number of ordinary college students; Number of students in special education schools includes the number of students enrolled in the class(the same as the following related tables).

20-4 各类学校招生数

Number of Entrants of Formal Education by Type

单位：人 (person)

年份 Year	普通高等学校 Regular Institutions of Higher Education	中等职业学校 Secondary Vocational Schools	普通中学 Regular Secondary Schools	小学 Primary Schools	特殊教育学校 Special Education Schools
1952	2353		81221		
1957	4823		116364	128678	
1962	4895		121261	1544971	
1965	6570		316756	2302127	
1970			747057	1899719	
1975	7569		1200679	2800872	33
1978	14916		1609352	2649457	34
1980	11610		1106948	2519225	87
1985	26069		943009	1455993	281
1990	26962		1019786	999538	485
1995	41714		1041585	1479126	1423
1996	43774		948623	1412690	1210
1997	46196		964969	1397645	1386
1998	49035		1176141	1293404	1232
1999	65481		1427007	1240217	1163
2000	95565		1527602	1256880	1182
2001	119470		1595486	1338908	2676
2002	152754		1717062	1320396	2157
2003	180308		1746751	1223734	2550
2004	215243		1696131	1169163	2726
2005	267198		1684360	1092214	3916
2006	266491		1767927	1151856	4503
2007	297566		1758759	1083015	6169
2008	328341		1754692	1006479	6333
2009	307127		1692325	945131	6483
2010	337892	575964	1641724	1231433	6684
2011	351846	575321	1593466	996827	6767
2012	381519	543472	1510249	1009618	8398
2013	376806	531212	1390078	950346	8230
2014	408941	482493	1332203	929667	8014
2015	436467	441280	1297254	934786	8096
2016	439286	414212	1322169	930103	9579
2017	460776	395511	1335486	911391	10361
2018	484148	376168	1385397	952217	10298
2019	525622	377015	1427850	933467	10914
2020	589288	399935	1405459	881239	11867
2021	603662	421504	1421976	896387	10919
2022	674407	412729	1426496	884407	11870
2023	696653	363115	1422224	953281	12571

20−5 各类学校毕业生数
Number of Graduates of Formal Education by Type

单位：人 (person)

年份 Year	普通高等学校 Regular Institutions of Higher Education	中等职业学校 Secondary Vocational Schools	普通中学 Regular Secondary Schools	小学 Primary Schools	特殊教育学校 Special Education Schools
1952	2742				
1957	1773		75254	739606	
1962	5317		80499	303087	
1965	8489		104984	399595	
1970	4796		142279	829050	
1975	5701		626880	1279795	35
1978	5884		1268232	1782504	35
1980	7130		934730	1603760	82
1985	13592		728872	1446826	57
1990	27672		746250	1408170	66
1995	40915		644932	1018463	336
1996	37872		719950	897863	445
1997	35658		818628	875741	552
1998	36672		868089	1069005	1036
1999	35465		804529	1327862	943
2000	40104		818595	1397579	1190
2001	44602		992309	1347390	1824
2002	52405		1224114	1361854	1677
2003	74307		1299710	1324117	2090
2004	100998		1385780	1221872	2131
2005	139328		1510287	1187842	2160
2006	173287		1527428	1221708	2953
2007	228028		1554082	1247914	4565
2008	247707		1575017	1253417	5312
2009	252214		1571659	1166577	5933
2010	278577	357279	1587603	1113444	5817
2011	289165	387422	1606332	1042069	5486
2012	286756	405599	1571830	1001656	7969
2013	318407	447222	1512136	886816	9191
2014	338643	498424	1422928	830744	9004
2015	361510	452593	1379237	803044	8634
2016	362127	433944	1329596	842414	8192
2017	386145	386220	1293825	869517	9557
2018	393689	363828	1262078	919381	10094
2019	402922	345110	1298731	935545	11408
2020	433106	320695	1324237	922320	13123
2021	451644	297714	1377819	929839	12054
2022	510447	306969	1408731	924554	14259
2023	552236	331214	1389557	911654	16877

20-6 普通高等学校情况(2023年)
Statistics on Regular Institutions of Higher Education(2023)

单位：所、人 (unit, person)

项目	Item	学校数 Number of Institutions	毕业生数 Graduates	招生数 Entrants	在校学生数 Enrollment	教职工数 Educational Personnel
合计	**Total**	**137**	**552236**	**696653**	**2164130**	**155115**
#女	Female		293252	353137	1085899	82995
综合大学	Comprehensive University	43	193021	245917	743778	50878
理工院校	Science and Engineering College	47	177830	228374	717051	53071
农业院校	Agriculture College	3	13842	16626	58310	4654
医药院校	Medicine College	12	36185	44775	141102	10870
师范院校	Teacher Training College	12	60991	71001	228393	16012
财经院校	Economics and Finance College	6	20897	31324	86497	5590
政法院校	Politics and Law College	2	2843	3838	10846	773
体育院校	Physical Culture College	2	2464	2842	10108	1422
艺术院校	Art Institutes	6	22178	25499	81432	6642
民族院校	College of Nationalities	2	9370	10918	39610	2759
语文院校	Chinese College	2	12615	15539	47003	2444

20-7 普通高等学校专任教师情况(2023年)
Full-time Teachers of Regular Higher Education Institutions(2023)

单位：所、人 (unit, person)

项目	Item	专任教师数 Full-time Teachers	正高级 Senior	副高级 Sub-senior	中级 Middle	初级 Junior	未定职称 No Rank
合计	**Total**	**110182**	**10934**	**27378**	**40010**	**21171**	**10689**
#女	Female	60144	3467	13160	22807	13819	6891
综合大学	Comprehensive University	35530	3195	8852	11972	6933	4578
理工院校	Science and Engineering College	37249	3878	9570	13398	7351	3052
农业院校	Agriculture College	3566	475	815	1590	384	302
医药院校	Medicine College	8039	1018	2079	2828	1549	565
师范院校	Teacher Training College	12349	1265	3064	5017	2179	824
财经院校	Economics and Finance College	4113	435	1021	1467	792	398
政法院校	Politics and Law College	487	57	135	193	66	36
体育院校	Physical Culture College	749	99	189	328	117	16
艺术院校	Art Institutes	4210	212	730	1600	1197	471
民族院校	College of Nationalities	1953	258	563	947	116	69
语文院校	Chinese College	1937	42	360	670	487	378

注：普通本（专）科学校附设中职班的专任教师未单独统计职称情况。
a) The professional titles of full-time teachers in secondary vocational classes attached to regular undergraduate (junior) Institutions are not counted separately.

20-8 普通本科分学科学生数(2023年)
Number of Regular Students for Normal Courses in Higher Education Institutions by Discipline(2023)

单位：人 (person)

项目	Item	毕业生数 Graduates	招生数 Entrants	在校学生数 Enrollment
合计	**Total**	**265688**	**324925**	**1142291**
#女	Female	147364	174594	606876
哲学	Philosophy	41	141	468
经济学	Economics	9226	8597	34262
法学	Law	8003	8900	33663
教育学	Education	16061	25265	75751
文学	Literature	27157	28253	111492
历史学	History	1378	1694	6390
理学	Science	16187	18849	71985
工学	Engineering	84726	108487	379783
农学	Agriculture	3272	4700	15209
医学	Medicine	17013	23930	84769
管理学	Management	48234	54468	176308
艺术学	Art	34390	41641	152211

20-9 分学科研究生数(2023年)
Number of Postgraduates by Academic Field(2023)

单位：人 (person)

项目	Item	毕业生数 Graduates	#攻读博士学位 Study in Doctor Degree	招生数 Entrants	#攻读博士学位 Study in Doctor Degree	在校学生数 Enrollment	#攻读博士学位 Study in Doctor Degree
合计	**Total**	**45483**	**3374**	**55437**	**5959**	**166999**	**22967**
#女	Female	23594	1435	27426	2366	81812	9028
哲学	Philosophy	166	30	163	55	595	204
经济学	Economics	2207	161	2297	196	6310	994
法学	Law	2373	99	2735	184	7821	781
教育学	Education	2524	32	2850	76	8743	262
文学	Literature	1734	81	1865	134	5611	630
历史学	History	244	29	400	70	1097	255
理学	Science	3004	457	3753	629	11294	2477
工学	Engineering	17504	1437	22042	3035	67343	11656
农学	Agriculture	2351	115	2962	222	9004	798
医学	Medicine	5408	728	6799	1027	20203	3465
军事学	Strategics						
管理学	Management	6732	194	7796	283	24224	1320
艺术学	Art	1127	10	1508	10	4233	47
交叉学科	Interdisciplinary	109		267	38	521	78
专业学位	**Professional Degree**	**25963**	**430**	**32420**	**1534**	**93740**	**4506**

注：不含在职人员攻读硕士学位人数。
a) Data in this table does not include the number of on-the-job personnel studying for master's degree.

20−10　中等职业学校情况(2023年)
Statistics on Secondary Vocational Schools(2023)

单位：人　　(person)

项目	Item	毕业生数 Graduates	招生数 Entrants	在校学生数 Enrollment	专任教师数 Full-time Teachers
合计	**Total**	**283033**	**299764**	**867123**	**45091**
#女	Female	127767	134619	393050	26812
#专业课	Specialty Course				
农林牧渔大类	Farming, Forestry, Animal Husbandry and Fishery	8848	8771	27950	700
资源环境与安全大类	Resources, Environment and Security	1528	2937	5949	108
能源动力与材料大类	Energy, Power and Materials	374	786	2302	114
土木建筑大类	Civil Engineering	14290	8874	28578	901
水利大类	Water Conservancy	77	119	200	16
装备制造大类	Equipment Manufacture	24942	32163	86931	2417
生物和化工大类	Biological and Chemical engineering	682	1078	2699	135
轻工纺织大类	Light industry and Textile	3219	2187	6421	199
食品药品与粮食大类	Food, Medicine and Grain	627	2386	5273	151
交通运输大类	Transportation	43995	42271	128889	2607
电子与信息类	Electronics and Information	61414	68327	193849	5140
医药卫生大类	Medicine and Sanitation	32349	29745	96499	2269
财经商贸大类	Financial Business	18469	21177	59633	1817
旅游大类	Tourism Service	19797	22994	61151	1847
文化艺术大类	Culture and Art	7462	14674	37827	2436
新闻传播大类	News communication	1011	885	3277	96
教育与体育大类	Education and Sports	34085	26620	88050	3155
公安与司法大类	Public Security and Justice	582	315	1261	37
公共管理与服务大类	Public Management and Service	9282	13455	30384	827
实习指导课	Practice Guidance Section				4322
#文化基础课	Basic Courses				20119

注：数据不包含技工学校。
a) Statistics exclude technical schools.

20−11 技工学校情况
Statistics on Technical Schools

单位：所、人 (unit, person)

年份 Year	学校数 Number of Schools	毕业生数 Graduates	招生数 Entrants	在校学生数 Enrollment	教职工数 Educational Personnel	培训社会人员数 Number of Training for Social Personnel	#失业人数 Unemployed	#农村劳动者 Rural Laborers
1990	387	37673	46334	119125	25778	23049		
1995	407	60392	54438	130896	26504			
2000	186	20177	16753	40147	9843	54335	6830	
2005	121	28326	47042	101037	8992	141836	14470	36156
2006	122	37684	53857	120462	9821	129603	19098	36935
2007	112	40946	65242	136395	9671	131459	18164	49701
2008	120	40816	68771	144608	10080	153200	16114	53324
2009	121	43214	64335	162614	10404	227563	18741	66781
2010	116	46910	52019	141407	10136	181246	12921	57617
2011	115	46500	42362	136347	9368	204035	19838	58244
2012	92	33009	41243	107175	8064	181758	9923	63233
2013	87	30804	39157	113406	8354	180313	14542	39216
2014	85	30337	38651	116168	8324	132163	9752	33996
2015	83	29507	40500	120337	9589	130328	11112	29498
2016	81	30136	39632	106669	10480	117333	14350	36776
2017	84	32730	46180	113961	10775	127922	7561	29794
2018	89	35994	50395	121576	11694	137377	9921	28713
2019	90	37221	53160	130413	11713	105419	8693	25329
2020	96	38653	63194	148400	12144	130122	3913	21362
2021	99	42077	70109	165389	13249	131554	7049	20794
2022	100	44998	67101	174717	13413	166878	4465	16052
2023	101	48181	63351	168765	13298	163803	5612	22030

注：①本表由四川省人力资源和社会保障厅提供；②1996年以前的数据包括重庆市部分；③2009年开始，原指标“培训社会人员结业数”调整为“培训社会人员数”。

a) Data of the table are provided by Sichuan Provincial Department of Human Resources and Social Security; b)The data before 1996 included Chongqing; c) Since 2009, indicator "number of training personnel exit" is adjusted to indicator "number of training for social personnel".

20−12 成人教育情况(2023年)
Statistics on Adult Education(2023)

单位：所、人 (unit, person)

项目	Item	学校数 Number of Schools	毕(结)业生数 Graduates	招生数 Entrants	在校学生数 Enrollment	教职工数 Educational Personnel	#专任教师 Full-time Teachers
成人高等教育	**Adult Education Schools**	**78**	**80425**	**72610**	**171964**	**912**	**563**
职工高等学校	Schools of Higher Education for Staff and Workers	10	5356	4768	9471	330	237
广播电视大学	Radio and TV Universities	2	6757	8575	19900	582	326
普通高校成人教育	Adult Higher Education	66	68312	59267	142593		
成人技术培训学校	**Technical training school for adults**	**1890**	**837587**		**1078247**	**9010**	**5977**
职工技术培训学校	Technical Training Schools for Staff and Workers	99	227291		199619	2895	2444
农村成人文化技术培训学校(机构)	Technical Training Schools for Peasants	1467	535630		804392	3655	1736
教育部门办	Sponsored by Education Department	1432	468457		734226	3572	1670
其他部门办	Sponsored by other Department	32	58161		61524	44	30
民办	Sponsored by Private	3	9012		8642	39	36
其他培训机构	Other Training Schools for Adults	324	74666		74236	2460	1797
教育部门办	Sponsored by Education Department	16	39581		31807	545	378
其他部门办	Sponsored by other Department	30	6831		6807	142	93
民办	Sponsored by Private	278	28254		35622	1773	1326

注：成人技术培训学校数据中含其他培训机构数据。
a) Data of adult technical training schools include data of other training institutions.

20−13 各类学校女学生和女教师数
Number of Female Students and Teachers of School by Type

单位：人 (person)

指标	Item	2017	2018	2019	2020	2021	2022	2023
女学生	**Number of Female Students**							
普通本(专)科学校	Regular Institutions of Higher Education	801108	834748	882046	940347	985927	1034583	1085899
中等职业学校	Secondary Vocational Schools	417361	383349	365796	368100	390005	410706	393050
普通中学	Regular Secondary Schools	1915578	1968154	2028436	2065193	2084753	2091860	2099586
高中	Senior	724463	714093	719517	726030	741591	754870	768687
初中	Junior	1191115	1254061	1308919	1339163	1343162	1336990	1330899
小学	Primary Schools	2648104	2669666	2671156	2660856	2643187	2625849	2647229
特殊教育	Special Schools	20171	21984	23553	25197	25367	24868	24830
女教师	**Number of Female Teachers**							
普通本(专)科学校	Regular Institutions of Higher Education	40966	42924	43148	48818	51730	56420	61769
中等职业学校	Secondary Vocational Schools	19253	19485	19712	20328	22847	24669	26812
普通中学	Regular Secondary Schools	145893	151549	158665	165888	173794	179537	187095
高中	Senior	45644	47370	48947	50495	53411	57149	61376
初中	Junior	100249	104179	109718	115393	120383	122388	125719
小学	Primary Schools	202473	210586	220222	227676	233123	236502	243614
特殊教育	Special Schools	2042	2168	2278	2395	2542	2815	3022

注：中等职业学校中不包括技工学校。
a) Female teachers in secondary vocational schools don't include technical schools.

20-14 各市(州)普通本(专)科学校情况(2023年)
Statistics on Regular Higher Education Institutions by Region(2023)

单位：所、人 (unit, person)

市(州)	Region	学校数 Number of Schools	毕业生数 Graduates	招生数 Entrants	在校学生数 Enrollment	专任教师数 Full-time Teachers
全省	**Sichuan**	**137**	**552236**	**696653**	**2164130**	**112171**
成都市	Chengdu	58	274664	327574	1071864	58967
自贡市	Zigong	3	15453	16025	54688	2810
攀枝花市	Panzhihua	3	6721	8396	28250	1339
泸州市	Luzhou	7	21560	31401	93456	4217
德阳市	Deyang	9	29646	48402	140284	6568
绵阳市	Mianyang	11	53916	63527	187797	8719
广元市	Guangyuan	3	6920	8379	22798	997
遂宁市	Suining	4	4141	11412	23996	1032
内江市	Neijiang	4	12450	15500	44128	2166
乐山市	Leshan	3	13130	14653	51777	2772
南充市	Nanchong	7	29668	36565	114339	5897
眉山市	Meishan	6	17738	31480	82599	3544
宜宾市	Yibin	2	10257	11828	39103	2231
广安市	Guangan	1	5548	4685	13961	729
达州市	Dazhou	3	11723	14496	42572	1964
雅安市	Yaan	2	14790	15084	54899	3581
巴中市	Bazhong	1	3234	4430	11869	391
资阳市	Ziyang	3	4976	12647	25448	1243
阿坝藏族羌族自治州	Aba	2	3702	4324	13793	735
甘孜藏族自治州	Ganzi	2	2492	4956	14443	560
凉山彝族自治州	Liangshan	3	9507	10889	32066	1709

20–15 各市(州)中等职业教育情况(2023年)
Statistics on Secondary Vocational Schools by Region(2023)

单位：所、人 (unit, person)

市(州)	Region	学校数 Schools	毕业生数 Graduates	招生数 Entrants	在校学生数 Enrollment	教职工数 Educational Personnel	#专任教师 Full-time Teachers
全省	**Sichuan**	**341**	**283033**	**299764**	**867123**	**52626**	**45091**
成都市	Chengdu	74	63693	62620	176699	12465	10526
自贡市	Zigong	8	9759	11571	35804	1728	1512
攀枝花市	Panzhihua	4	4288	4386	12082	726	583
泸州市	Luzhou	15	23358	25092	75757	3344	3176
德阳市	Deyang	16	8300	11600	30732	2077	1635
绵阳市	Mianyang	21	15598	15790	48214	2857	2526
广元市	Guangyuan	10	6637	9231	26932	1625	1381
遂宁市	Suining	10	5717	8033	21180	1540	1312
内江市	Neijiang	15	11154	9393	28199	1806	1510
乐山市	Leshan	18	10892	13608	37246	2274	1869
南充市	Nanchong	29	20912	21561	66007	4230	3273
眉山市	Meishan	15	12068	17588	40664	2752	2144
宜宾市	Yibin	16	20361	22506	62893	3863	3513
广安市	Guangan	23	19349	11105	38692	2276	1873
达州市	Dazhou	25	15843	19478	57283	3221	2808
雅安市	Yaan	7	3840	4142	12339	786	653
巴中市	Bazhong	9	10542	10879	32494	1711	1645
资阳市	Ziyang	7	6515	7916	23756	1056	1225
阿坝藏族羌族自治州	Aba	2	1259	678	2690	222	211
甘孜藏族自治州	Ganzi	3	2259	2238	6670	342	272
凉山彝族自治州	Liangshan	14	10689	10349	30790	1725	1444

注：以上数据不含技工学校。
a) Data in this table exclude technical schools.

20-16 各市(州)普通高中情况(2023年)
Statistics on Regular Senior Secondary Schools by Region(2023)

单位：所、人 (unit, person)

市(州)	Region	学校数 Number of Schools	毕业生数 Graduates	招生数 Entrants	在校学生数 Enrollment	专任教师数 Full-time Teachers
全省	**Sichuan**	**817**	**470064**	**510643**	**1500614**	**115660**
成都市	Chengdu	180	74389	96223	266875	22607
自贡市	Zigong	23	13239	14256	42738	2952
攀枝花市	Panzhihua	13	7093	7973	23613	1986
泸州市	Luzhou	30	37192	34451	108118	7134
德阳市	Deyang	27	15538	16210	49381	4040
绵阳市	Mianyang	36	33194	37140	108775	8096
广元市	Guangyuan	24	14470	16799	48332	3845
遂宁市	Suining	30	17034	19299	54547	4253
内江市	Neijiang	40	20510	20323	62595	4342
乐山市	Leshan	29	14357	15667	45388	4117
南充市	Nanchong	53	37563	33933	105037	7368
眉山市	Meishan	29	15117	15276	45979	4111
宜宾市	Yibin	43	27420	33816	94636	7249
广安市	Guangan	41	22526	23205	69343	5641
达州市	Dazhou	54	42497	40411	122305	8204
雅安市	Yaan	17	7366	7639	23732	1991
巴中市	Bazhong	42	18961	18858	54944	5374
资阳市	Ziyang	33	16375	18626	56486	3770
阿坝藏族羌族自治州	Aba	17	4572	4608	13804	1454
甘孜藏族自治州	Ganzi	14	5497	5552	16779	1369
凉山彝族自治州	Liangshan	42	25154	30378	87207	5757

20−17 各市(州)普通初中情况(2023年)
Statistics on Regular Junior Secondary Schools by Region(2023)

单位：所、人 (unit, person)

市(州)	Region	学校数 Number of Schools	毕业生数 Graduates	招生数 Entrants	在校学生数 Enrollment	专任教师数 Full-time Teachers
全省	**Sichuan**	**3233**	**919493**	**911581**	**2755193**	**224090**
成都市	Chengdu	463	155075	171245	489367	40721
自贡市	Zigong	109	29940	26916	85413	6738
攀枝花市	Panzhihua	39	12574	11761	35508	3064
泸州市	Luzhou	178	68572	52119	171961	13527
德阳市	Deyang	101	31095	31469	95352	7860
绵阳市	Mianyang	130	53504	50352	155252	11899
广元市	Guangyuan	115	25891	25998	78616	6814
遂宁市	Suining	107	28823	30083	90361	7150
内江市	Neijiang	122	37922	32869	105282	8268
乐山市	Leshan	130	29075	29754	89266	7452
南充市	Nanchong	319	62370	58597	183029	16544
眉山市	Meishan	119	27334	28590	83927	7174
宜宾市	Yibin	224	64129	61628	191233	14641
广安市	Guangan	204	39133	38250	119596	11315
达州市	Dazhou	300	68843	62669	200019	16946
雅安市	Yaan	45	14344	13752	41446	3659
巴中市	Bazhong	170	33240	31675	98097	9691
资阳市	Ziyang	160	32938	26775	87797	7186
阿坝藏族羌族自治州	Aba	34	8852	9519	28075	2968
甘孜藏族自治州	Ganzi	38	15298	18950	48770	3441
凉山彝族自治州	Liangshan	126	80541	98610	276826	17032

20-18 各市(州)普通小学情况(2023年)
Statistics on Primary Schools by Region(2023)

单位：所、人 (unit, person)

市(州)	Region	学校数 Number of Schools	毕业生数 Graduates	招生数 Entrants	在校学生数 Enrollment	专任教师 Full-time Teachers
全省	**Sichuan**	**5119**	**911654**	**953281**	**5490451**	**352007**
成都市	Chengdu	647	169497	257479	1270137	75064
自贡市	Zigong	102	26856	23436	143942	9378
攀枝花市	Panzhihua	55	10761	13344	68283	4447
泸州市	Luzhou	194	51338	49214	293848	17534
德阳市	Deyang	201	31356	31906	178162	11526
绵阳市	Mianyang	331	48102	51035	285933	17236
广元市	Guangyuan	253	26181	22149	131493	11308
遂宁市	Suining	163	29948	28689	175435	11657
内江市	Neijiang	200	32944	29442	176114	11604
乐山市	Leshan	203	30127	31874	186794	12114
南充市	Nanchong	271	58244	52962	326754	23876
眉山市	Meishan	174	28058	31558	175708	11529
宜宾市	Yibin	286	61510	53773	338031	20781
广安市	Guangan	153	38892	34380	216445	14730
达州市	Dazhou	258	62643	50589	330078	24697
雅安市	Yaan	125	13797	16622	87781	6307
巴中市	Bazhong	173	31633	28959	183478	15254
资阳市	Ziyang	143	26377	21415	136950	8822
阿坝藏族羌族自治州	Aba	183	10532	10066	62702	6198
甘孜藏族自治州	Ganzi	293	20345	17745	115852	7911
凉山彝族自治州	Liangshan	711	102513	96644	606531	30034

20−19 各市(州)幼儿园情况(2023年)
Statistics on Kindergartens by Region(2023)

单位：所、个、人 (unit, person)

市(州)	Region	园数 Number of Kindergartens	班数 Number of Classes	幼儿数 Children Enrollment	教职工数 Educational Personnel	#教师 Teachers
全省	**Sichuan**	**12387**	**85455**	**2315634**	**279488**	**160865**
成都市	Chengdu	2840	22314	616773	103815	50051
自贡市	Zigong	425	2043	53601	6463	3847
攀枝花市	Panzhihua	168	1135	31915	4329	2464
泸州市	Luzhou	691	4006	110514	11184	6460
德阳市	Deyang	382	2751	76467	8661	5486
绵阳市	Mianyang	730	4676	124402	15311	9785
广元市	Guangyuan	290	2284	61317	5270	3912
遂宁市	Suining	428	2642	72087	8419	5279
内江市	Neijiang	511	2672	68988	7080	4514
乐山市	Leshan	592	2990	76623	9608	6099
南充市	Nanchong	607	5085	130670	12282	9190
眉山市	Meishan	389	2935	78031	9477	5974
宜宾市	Yibin	855	4503	127864	17144	9491
广安市	Guangan	533	3148	86118	12112	7001
达州市	Dazhou	613	5229	132473	10110	7733
雅安市	Yaan	271	1519	41533	5398	3054
巴中市	Bazhong	288	2618	68004	5436	4723
资阳市	Ziyang	383	1933	51449	5084	3224
阿坝藏族羌族自治州	Aba	228	1046	26901	2894	2071
甘孜藏族自治州	Ganzi	348	1423	38139	4631	2294
凉山彝族自治州	Liangshan	815	8503	241765	14780	8213

20-20 研究与试验发展(R&D)情况
Basic Statistics on Research and Development by Region

年份 Year	R&D人员折合全时人员 (人年) Full-time Equivalent of R&D Personnel (man-year)	#研究人员 Researchers	R&D经费内部支出 (万元) Internal Expenditure on R&D (10 000 yuan)	#日常性支出 Routine Expenses
2001	48180	35325	574712	506285
2002	61312	44957	619233	571565
2003	57867	43995	794211	736462
2004	60201	46373	780066	713398
2005	65747	51403	962450	894850
2006	67932	53552	1075659	984546
2007	78452	62595	1391130	1273338
2008	87557	63130	1622607	1537790
2009	85921	48786	2144590	1755258
2010	83506	45205	2706452	2031519
2011	82485	44005	2941010	2371221
2012	98010	52059	3508589	2747195
2013	109708	57956	3999702	3133297
2014	119676	62756	4493285	3577596
2015	116842	67516	5028761	4274116
2016	124614	70834	5614193	4857028
2017	144821	77241	6378500	5546985
2018	158847	81071	7370813	6483823
2019	170777	91965	8709515	7720356
2020	189828	99173	10552846	9328686
2021	197143	103746	12145209	10896817
2022	227141	112489	12150136	10770864
2023	250058	124353	13578026	11867730

注：R&D人员折合全时人员中的研究人员，在2009年及以前为科学家和工程师。
a) Indicator of researchers in the full-time equivalent of R&D personnel is the indicator of scientists and engineers before 2009.

20-21 研究与试验发展(R&D)经费构成情况
Basic Statistics on Composition of Research and Development Expenditure

指标	Item	2010	2015	2020	2021	2022	2023
研究与试验发展(R&D)经费 (万元)	Funds for R&D (10 000 yuan)	2706452	5028761	10552846	12145209	12150136	13578026
地区生产总值(GDP) (亿元)	GDP (100 million yuan)	17224.78	30342.01	48501.64	54087.98	56610.20	60132.88
R&D经费与地区生产总值(GDP)之比 (%)	Ratio of Expenditure on R&D to GDP (%)	1.57	1.66	2.17	2.25	2.14	2.26
R&D经费按执行部门分组(万元)	**Grouped by Executive Departments(10 000 yuan)**						
科研机构	Scientific Research Institutions	1239870	2116421	4165591	4717718	3536833	4262035
高等院校	Institutions of Higher Education	363509	465250	851926	954977	1052181	1157687
企业	Enterprises	1061086	2402691	5474433	6350920	7327081	7955958
#工业企业	Industrial Enterprises	879858	2238051	4276383	4801710	5300775	5718223
其他	Others	41987	44399	60897	121593	234042	202345
R&D经费按资金来源分组(万元)	**Grouped by Funding Sources (10 000 yuan)**						
政府资金	Government Appropriation Funds	1512528	2302223	4201990	5131656	3913968	4558687
企业资金	Funds Raised by Enterprises	1136088	2439994	5707215	6516310	7604377	8277143
境外资金	Foreign Funds	5958	12915	26565	4229	8223	11775
其他资金	Other Funds	51878	273629	617076	493014	623568	730420

注：R&D经费与地区生产总值之比，根据地区生产总值最新核实数据作了修正。
a) Ratio of expenditure on R&D to GDP was revised by use of lastest updated data of GDP.

20－22 各市(州)研究与试验发展(R&D)经费支出情况
Basic Statistics on Research and Development Expenditure by Region

市(州)	Region	R&D经费内部支出(万元) Internal Expenditure on R&D (10 000 yuan)		R&D经费内部支出与地区生产总值之比(%) Ratio of Internal Expenditure on R&D to GDP (%)	
		2022	2023	2022	2023
全省	**Sichuan**	**12150136**	**13578026**	**2.14**	**2.26**
成都市	Chengdu	7332591	8241224	3.52	3.73
自贡市	Zigong	156775	142230	0.96	0.81
攀枝花市	Panzhihua	147323	176151	1.21	1.35
泸州市	Luzhou	295670	313233	1.14	1.15
德阳市	Deyang	509144	537652	1.81	1.78
绵阳市	Mianyang	2041392	2362496	5.63	5.85
广元市	Guangyuan	50720	52554	0.45	0.45
遂宁市	Suining	124136	124488	0.77	0.73
内江市	Neijiang	136034	161371	0.82	0.89
乐山市	Leshan	164956	166105	0.71	0.68
南充市	Nanchong	200043	201204	0.74	0.74
眉山市	Meishan	221812	247304	1.36	1.42
宜宾市	Yibin	424572	456365	1.24	1.20
广安市	Guangan	55675	60383	0.39	0.40
达州市	Dazhou	105484	105843	0.42	0.40
雅安市	Yaan	85665	119369	0.95	1.18
巴中市	Bazhong	26481	28071	0.35	0.36
资阳市	Ziyang	28048	32074	0.30	0.31
阿坝藏族羌族自治州	Aba	11399	11774	0.25	0.23
甘孜藏族自治州	Ganzi	4527	4739	0.10	0.09
凉山彝族自治州	Liangshan	27687	33395	0.13	0.15

20－23　各市(州)规模以上工业企业研究与试验发展(R&D)及专利情况(2023年)

Basic Statistics on Research and Development and Patent of Industrial Enterprises above Designated Size by Region (2023)

市(州)	Region	R&D人员全时当量（人年）Full-time Equivalent of R&D Personnel (man-year)	R&D经费（万元）Expenditure on R&D (10 000 yuan)	专利申请数（件）Number of Patent Application (piece)	#发明专利 Invention	有效发明专利数（件）Number of Valid Invention Patents (piece)
全省	**Sichuan**	**128074**	**5718223**	**41770**	**17184**	**62570**
成都市	Chengdu	53897	2416497	21721	10597	34681
自贡市	Zigong	2238	117226	809	255	1502
攀枝花市	Panzhihua	2310	144202	729	274	1139
泸州市	Luzhou	4924	257855	920	264	1188
德阳市	Deyang	9698	469903	2443	876	3930
绵阳市	Mianyang	16841	813768	4284	1867	8033
广元市	Guangyuan	1259	47216	402	76	353
遂宁市	Suining	2878	117015	1071	267	1372
内江市	Neijiang	3125	139617	610	201	982
乐山市	Leshan	3505	145488	931	248	1543
南充市	Nanchong	2790	118384	810	223	629
眉山市	Meishan	5955	231237	1796	598	2240
宜宾市	Yibin	9432	401512	2081	532	1865
广安市	Guangan	2493	56362	590	152	444
达州市	Dazhou	2924	92135	809	160	712
雅安市	Yaan	1361	78676	503	196	567
巴中市	Bazhong	744	19544	216	38	203
资阳市	Ziyang	1225	20443	460	115	403
阿坝藏族羌族自治州	Aba	52	4970	87	30	89
甘孜藏族自治州	Ganzi	20	387	79	43	24
凉山彝族自治州	Liangshan	402	25787	419	172	671

20−24 各市(州)科学研究与技术服务机构人员数、经费收入和支出总额(2023年)

Personnel、Income and Expenditure of Scientific Research and Technology Service Institution by Region(2023)

市(州)	Region	机构（个）Institution (unit)	从业人员（人）Personnel (person)	经费总收入（万元）Total Income (10 000 yuan)	#科技活动收入 Income from Scientific and Technological Activities	经费总支出（万元）Total Expenditure (10 000 yuan)	#科技活动支出 Expenditure on Scientific and Technological Activities
全省	**Sichuan**	**339**	**42606**	**2395794**	**2113652**	**2210961**	**1900589**
成都市	Chengdu	198	32739	2065905	1873534	1891036	1672646
自贡市	Zigong	8	1022	31311	13353	31583	13180
攀枝花市	Panzhihua	7	437	14418	10358	13588	11261
泸州市	Luzhou	6	324	11923	11512	10459	9023
德阳市	Deyang	5	667	25422	18141	24928	17149
绵阳市	Mianyang	4	251	14902	13396	13702	11758
广元市	Guangyuan	4	128	4121	3553	3752	3699
遂宁市	Suining						
内江市	Neijiang	9	629	23852	18698	23581	17818
乐山市	Leshan	8	1092	27432	20796	26620	16497
南充市	Nanchong	12	1087	36233	28021	37006	29466
眉山市	Meishan						
宜宾市	Yibin	18	1238	44263	28442	44028	29522
广安市	Guangan						
达州市	Dazhou	15	814	25859	16185	24771	15102
雅安市	Yaan	4	177	4244	4048	4181	3162
巴中市	Bazhong	14	189	4484	2571	4664	2112
资阳市	Ziyang						
阿坝藏族羌族自治州	Aba	9	271	12231	11790	12246	11683
甘孜藏族自治州	Ganzi	5	211	6688	6674	5721	5502
凉山彝族自治州	Liangshan	6	1078	29121	21223	28153	20838

20−25 高等学校科技活动情况(2023年)
Science and Technology Activities of Higher Education (2023)

项目 市(州)	Item Region	研究机构数 (个) Number of Research Institutions (unit)	R&D人员 (人) R&D Personnel (person)	R&D人员折合全时当量 (人年) R&D Personnel Equivalent to Full-time Equivalent (man-year)	R&D经费内部支出 (万元) Internal Expenditure on R&D (10 000 yuan)	#基础研究 Fundamental Research	项目(课题)数 (项) Number of Projects (unit)
合计	**Total**	**1004**	**93431**	**38179**	**1157687**	**493515**	**92886**
理科	Science	582	47606	28611	998162	449104	47812
文科	Liberal arts	422	45825	9567	159524	44411	45074
成都市	Chengdu	622	60624	25113	906513	401100	58728
自贡市	Zigong	30	1978	695	20399	596	2802
攀枝花市	Panzhihua	12	1103	343	8884	2112	1299
泸州市	Luzhou	42	4275	2345	30962	19880	3733
德阳市	Deyang	23	2086	1074	16496	2201	1579
绵阳市	Mianyang	62	4168	1670	34059	19141	5902
广元市	Guangyuan		306	77	429	41	379
遂宁市	Suining	4	226	51	427	194	156
内江市	Neijiang	12	1635	525	9709	2244	2069
乐山市	Leshan	50	1285	495	8358	3704	1449
南充市	Nanchong	70	6147	2089	50711	18194	6671
眉山市	Meishan		403	112	635	127	274
宜宾市	Yibin	24	1675	766	17135	2019	1819
广安市	Guangan						
达州市	Dazhou	15	1517	416	4389	2423	1038
雅安市	Yaan	14	3190	1632	38697	15172	2840
巴中市	Bazhong		107	26	74	3	81
资阳市	Ziyang		156	40	211	172	93
阿坝藏族羌族自治州	Aba						
甘孜藏族自治州	Ganzi	6	537	114	1202	722	429
凉山彝族自治州	Liangshan	16	1063	372	5451	1770	999

20−26　科技成果水平及应用情况(2023年)
Level and Utility of Achievement in Scientific and Technical Research(2023)

单位：项　　　　(item)

指标	Item	合计 Total	科研机构 Research Institutions	大专院校 Universities and Colleges	企业 Enterprises	其他 Others
基本情况	**Basic Condition**	**4087**	**388**	**1872**	**1291**	**536**
登记项目数	Number of Projects Registered	4087	388	1872	1291	536
奖励项目数	Number of Projects Praised					
成果计划	**Achievements Plan**	**4087**	**388**	**1872**	**1291**	**536**
国家计划项目	Projects of Country Plans	34	10	10	7	7
部门计划项目	Projects of Department	7	1		5	1
地方计划项目	Projects of Local Government	3546	357	1808	912	469
部门基金项目	Projects of Department Foundation	3		1		2
地方基金项目	Projects of Local Government Foundation	35	3	20	4	8
其他	Others	462	17	33	363	49
成果类别	**Achievements Type**	**4087**	**388**	**1872**	**1291**	**536**
基础理论	Basic Theory	1148	114	842	23	169
应用技术	Applied Technology	2869	268	996	1262	343
软科学	Soft Science	70	6	34	6	24
成果水平	**Achievements Level**	**1430**	**130**	**316**	**828**	**156**
国际领先	International Original	56	5	14	34	3
国际先进	International Advanced	288	22	90	163	13
国内领先	Domestic Original	686	42	117	448	79
国内先进	Domestic Advanced	400	61	95	183	61
应用项目	**Projects Applied**	**2869**	**268**	**996**	**1262**	**343**
农、林、牧、渔业	Farming, Forestry, Animal Husbandry and Fishery	488	92	124	235	37
工业	Industry	773	32	170	562	9
建筑业	Construction	61	1	20	40	
交通运输、邮电通讯业	Transportation, Postal and Telecommunication Services	130	8	69	50	3
信息传输、计算机服务和软件业	Information Transmission, Computer Services and Software	326	17	117	179	13
批发和零售业	Wholesale and Retail Trades	6		1	5	
住宿和餐饮业	Hotels and Catering Services	6		2	4	
金融、保险业	Banking and Insurance	4		4		
房地产业	Real Estate	5		2	3	
租赁和商务服务业	Leasing And Business Services	2			2	
科学研究、技术服务和地质勘查业	Scientific Research, Technic Services and Geological Prospecting	320	72	149	69	30
水利、环境和公共设施管理业	Management of Water Conservancy, Environment and Public Facilities	113	14	54	38	7
居民服务和其他服务业	Residential Service And Others	4		1	2	1
教育	Education	16		4	12	
卫生、社会保障和社会福利业	Health Care, Social Security and Social Welfare	584	26	272	47	239
文化、体育和娱乐业	Culture, Sports and Entertainment	11	2	3	6	
公共管理和社会组织	Public Management and Social Organizations	19	3	4	8	4
其他行业	Others	1	1			
未应用项目	**Projects not Applied**	**818**	**102**	**542**	**57**	**117**

注：科技成果水平及应用资料由四川省科学技术厅提供。
a) Data of achievement and application of information technology are provided by Sichuan Provincial Science and Technology Department.

20-27 专利授权量
Patent Granted

单位：项 (item)

项目	Item	2016	2017	2018	2019	2020	2021	2022	2023
全省	**Sichuan**	**62445**	**64006**	**87372**	**82066**	**108386**	**146937**	**135507**	**113073**
1．发明	I. Creations and Inventions	10350	11367	11697	12053	14187	19337	25458	33339
实用新型	Utility Models	31813	33613	53121	51521	73927	105328	89368	63767
外观设计	Designs	20282	19026	22554	18492	20272	22272	20681	15967
2．个人	II. Individuals	12097	11274	13232	13450	18775	20952	16238	10824
大专院校	Universities and Colleges	6297	8165	10102	10858	14285	17441	17076	13865
科研单位	Research Institutions	1854	2133	2370	2471	2865	3285	4351	3915
工矿企业	Industrial and Mineral Enterprises	41064	41097	60199	53278	68699	96721	92283	79012
机关团体	Government Agencies and Organizations	1133	1337	1469	2009	3762	8537	5559	5457

注：专利资料由四川省市场监督管理局提供。
a) The data of patent information is provided by Administration for Market Regulation of Sichuan Province.

20-28 各类技术合同签订及执行情况
Concluded and Fulfilled Technical Contracts

单位：项、万元 (item, 10 000 yuan)

项目	Item	合同数 Number of Contracts		合同成交额 Value of Contracts		技术交易额 Technology Business Value	
		2022	2023	2022	2023	2022	2023
全省	**Sichuan**	**23620**	**28396**	**16497724**	**19515775**	**10759799**	**12542840**
技术开发	Technical Development	10419	12335	3220476	5146670	2871657	4626404
技术转让	Technical Transfer	1284	1049	638228	752867	552140	726224
技术咨询	Technical Consultation	2465	2527	122128	333979	111677	175550
技术服务	Technical Services	9366	12127	12459608	13099287	7169999	6859498
技术许可	Technical License	86	358	57283	182972	54324	155164

注：各类技术合同签定及执行情况由四川省科学技术厅提供。
a) Data of various types of technology and the implementation of the contract signed are provided by Sichuan Provincial Science and Technology Department.

主要统计指标解释

普通、职业高等学校 指国家依法审批的，实施高等学历教育的全日制大学、独立设置的学院、独立学院、本科层次职业学校、高等专科学校、高等职业学校及其他普通高教机构。

大学、独立设置的学院主要实施本科及本科层次以上的教育。独立学院主要实施本科层次的教育。本科层次职业学校主要实施本科层次职业教育。高等专科学校、高等职业学校实施专科层次的教育。其他普通高教机构是指承担国家普通招生计划任务不计校数的机构，包括普通高等学校分校、大专班等。

成人高等学校 指国家依法审批的，招收具有高中毕业或同等学力的人员为主要培养对象，利用函授、业余、脱产等多种形式，对其实施高等学历教育的学校。包括：职工高等学校、农民高等学校、管理干部学院、教育学院、独立函授学院、广播电视大学、其他成人高教机构等。其他成人高教机构是指承担国家成人招生计划任务不计校数的机构。

科技活动 统计资料范围为全社会有研究与试验发展（R&D）活动的企事业单位，具体包括工业法人单位、地级及以上独立核算的政府属科学研究与技术开发机构及科技信息与文献机构、全日制普通高等学校及附属医院以及研究与试验发展（R&D）活动相对密集行业（包括农、林、牧、渔业，建筑业，交通运输、仓储和邮政业，信息传输、软件和信息技术服务业，金融业，租赁和商务服务业，科学研究和技术服务业，水利、环境和公共设施管理业，卫生和社会工作，文化、体育和娱乐业等）中从事研究与试验发展（R&D）活动的企事业单位。创新活动统计资料范围为规模以上工业法人单位。

研究与试验发展(R&D) 指为增加知识存量（也包括有关人类、文化和社会的知识）以及设计已有知识的新应用而进行的创造性、系统性工作，包括基础研究、应用研究和试验发展三种类型。国际上通常采用R&D活动的规模和强度指标反映一国的科技实力和核心竞争力。

R&D人员 指报告期R&D活动单位中从事基础研究、应用研究和试验发展活动的人员。包括直接参加上述三类R&D活动的人员，以及与上述三类R&D活动相关的管理人员和直接服务人员，即直接为R&D活动提供资料文献、材料供应、设备维护等服务的人员。不包括为R&D活动提供间接服务的人员，如餐饮服务、安保人员等。

R&D人员全时当量 指报告期R&D人员按实际从事R&D活动时间计算的工作量，以“人年”为计量单位。为国际上比较科技人力投入而制定的可比指标。

R&D经费支出 指报告期调查单位内部为实施R&D活动而实际发生的全部经费，按支出性质分为日常性支出和资产性支出。不包括调查单位委托其他单位或与其他单位合作开展R&D活动而转拨给其他单位的全部经费。

R&D项目（课题）数 R&D项目（课题）是进行R&D活动的基本组织形式，通常由R&D活动执行单位依据项目立项书或合同书等形式明确项目任务、目标、人员和经费等。

专利 是专利权的简称，是对发明人的发明创造经审查合格后，由国家知识产权局依据专利法授予发明人和设计人对该项发明创造享有的专有权。包括发明、实用新型和外观设计。反映拥有自主知识产权的科技和设计成果情况。

发明(专利) 指对产品、方法或者其改进所提出的新的技术方案。是国际通行的反映拥有自主知识产权技术的核心指标。

实用新型(专利) 指对产品的形状、构造或者其结合所提出的适于实用的新的技术方案。反映具有一定技术含量的技术成果情况。

外观设计(专利) 指对产品的形状、图案、色彩或者其结合所作出的富有美感并适于工业上应用的新设计。反映拥有自主知识产权的外观设计成果情况。

Explanatory Notes on Main Statistical Indicators

Regular and Vocational Higher Education Institutions refer to full-time universities, independently established schools, independent colleges, undergraduate level vocational schools, higher professional colleges, higher vocational colleges and other regular higher education institutions approved by the state according to law and implementing higher academic education.

Universities and independently established schools primarily provide normal courses at undergraduate and higher levels. Independent colleges mainly provide normal undergraduate courses. Undergraduate level vocational schools primarily provide undergraduate level vocational courses. Higher professional colleges and higher vocational colleges primarily provide undergraduate of short-cycle courses. Other regular higher education institutions refer to educational establishments, which are responsible for enrolling higher education students under the State Plan but not enumerated in the total number of schools, including: branch schools of regular higher education institutions and junior colleges.

Adults Higher Education Institutions refer to educational establishments approved by the state according to law, enrolling personnel graduated from senior secondary school or with equivalent education, and providing higher education courses in forms of correspondence, spare time or full time, for adults. Adults higher education institutions include schools of higher education for staff and workers, schools of higher education for peasants, institutions of administration, educational colleges, independent correspondence colleges, radio and television universities and other educational establishments of higher education for adult. Other educational establishments of higher education for adult refer undertakings to enrol adult students under the State Plan but not enumerated in the number of schools.

Scientific and Technological Activities (S&T Activities) Data on scientific and technological activities cover research and experimental development (R&D) activities of enterprises and institutions of whole society, mainly including industrial corporate units above designated size, industrial corporate units below designated size, scientific research and technological development institutions and scientific and technological information and literature institutions of prefecture level and above under the government with independent accounting, full-time universities and colleges, affiliated hospitals, and enterprises and institutions engaged in R&D activities in relatively R&D-intensive industries (such as agriculture, forestry, animal husbandry, fishery, construction, transport, storage and post, information transmission, software and information technology service, finance, leasing and business services, scientific research and technical services, management of water conservancy, environment and public facilities, health and social service, culture, sports and entertainment). Data on innovation activities cover industrial corporate units above designated size.

Research and Experimental Development (R&D) refers to creative and systematic work undertaken in order to increase the stock of knowledge (including knowledge of humankind, culture and society) and to devise new applications of available knowledge. R&D includes 3 categories of activities: basic research, applied research and experimental development. The scale and intensity of R&D are widely used internationally to reflect the strength of S&T and the core competitiveness of a country in the world.

R&D Personnel refer to persons of R&D activities units engaged in basic research, applied research, and experimental development at the reference period, including persons of directly participating in the three activities above, as well as management and direct service staff related to R&D activities, such as literature provision, material supply, equipment maintenance staff, it excludes persons providing indirect support and ancillary services, such as canteen and security staff.

Full-time Equivalent of R&D Personnel refers to the ratio of working hours actually spent on R&D during a specific reference period (usually a calendar year) divided by the total number of hours conventionally worked in the same period by an individual or by a group. The measurement unit of the ratio is "man-years". This is an internationally comparable indicator of S&T manpower input.

Expenditure on R&D refers to the real expenditure of surveyed units on their own R&D activities in reporting period. It is divided into current expenditures and gross fixed capital expenditures for R&D according to the nature of expenditure. It doesn't include the fees transferred to cooperated or entrusted agencies on R&D activities.

Number of R&D Projects (subjects) R&D Projects (subjects) are the basic forms of R&D activities, The project task, target, personnel and expenditure are usually defined by R&D activity execution unit according to project approval specification or contract document.

Patent is an abbreviation for the patent right and refers to the exclusive right of ownership by the inventors or designers for the creation or inventions, given from the China National Intellectual Property Administration after due process of assessment and approval in accordance with the Patent Law. Patents are granted for inventions, utility models and designs. This indicator reflects the achievements of S&T and design with independent intellectual property.

Patented Inventions refer to the new technical proposals to the products or methods or their modifications. This is universal core indicator reflecting the technologies with independent intellectual property.

Patented Utility Models refer to the practical and new technical proposals on the shape and structure of the product or the combination of both. This indicator reflects the condition of technological results with certain technical content.

Designs refer to the aesthetics and industrially applicable new designs for the shape, pattern and colour of the product, or their combinations. This indicator reflects the appearance design achievements with independent intellectual property.

21 文化、体育和卫生

Chapter 21 Culture, Sports and Public Health

21-1 文化艺术、文物事业机构数
Number of Institutions for Culture, Art and Cultural Relics

单位：个 (unit)

年份 Year	艺术表演团体 Art Performance Troupes	公共图书馆 Public Libraries	文化馆 Cultural Centers	文化站 Cultural Stations	博物馆 Museums
1952	126	4	148	146	1
1957	148	21	163	115	2
1962	205	36	161	76	11
1965	198	36	167	31	13
1970	169	36	171	16	13
1975	190	36	178	13	13
1978	193	57	178	8	12
1980	183	71	177	656	11
1985	148	82	172	5196	24
1990	109	109	168	4957	34
1991	106	112	168	4973	37
1992	105	117	169	4329	37
1993	103	117	169	3745	37
1994	101	118	170	3634	42
1995	101	123	171	3613	42
1996	101	125	172	3384	44
1997	101	127	170	3574	44
1998	100	129	170	3689	47
1999	99	129	171	3666	47
2000	98	129	171	3667	50
2001	89	129	174	3720	51
2002	89	131	173	3525	51
2003	89	132	181	3722	51
2004	84	137	180	3701	54
2005	85	141	180	4515	54
2006	81	146	202	3600	59
2007	84	151	202	3795	62
2008	83	154	203	3873	85
2009	84	156	203	4019	89
2010	82	161	204	4448	108
2011	75	169	205	4593	144
2012	63	188	205	4595	152
2013	52	197	207	4595	188
2014	51	198	207	4601	206
2015	52	203	207	4578	225
2016	50	203	207	4574	239
2017	52	204	207	4578	255
2018	52	204	207	4574	252
2019	49	206	207	4410	256
2020	46	207	207	4231	258
2021	48	207	206	4089	267
2022	49	209	206	4083	316
2023	47	209	206	4063	272

注：文化艺术、图书馆、博物馆等资料由四川省文化和旅游厅提供；艺术表演团体为文化和旅游部门所属。

a) Data of culture and art, libraries, museums and other information are provided by Sichuan Provincial Department of Culture and Tourism; Artistic performance groups belong to the cultural and tourism departments

21−2 各市(州)文化艺术、文物事业机构和人员数(2023年)
Institutions and Personnel of Culture, Art and Cultural Relics by Region(2023)

单位：个、人、万册 (unit, person, 1 0000 volumes)

市(州)	Region	艺术表演团体 Art Performance Troupes		公共图书馆 Public Libraries			文化馆 Cultural Centers		博物馆 Museums	
		机构数 Institutions	从业人员 Employed Persons	机构数 Institutions	从业人员 Employed Persons	藏书量 Collections	机构数 Institutions	从业人员 Employed Persons	机构数 Institutions	从业人员 Employed Persons
全省	**Sichuan**	**47**	**3167**	**209**	**2543**	**5343**	**206**	**3234**	**272**	**6773**
成都市	Chengdu	6	562	22	615	1503	22	434	59	1907
自贡市	Zigong	6	269	7	65	86	7	74	10	356
攀枝花市	Panzhihua	2	125	6	47	103	6	74	5	105
泸州市	Luzhou	1	13	9	84	237	8	94	12	215
德阳市	Deyang	1	17	7	74	140	7	86	11	459
绵阳市	Mianyang	2	114	10	97	288	10	212	17	387
广元市	Guangyuan	2	21	8	79	168	8	86	17	265
遂宁市	Suining	1	41	7	88	112	6	76	6	178
内江市	Neijiang	5	101	6	91	114	6	113	7	104
乐山市	Leshan	2	132	12	85	127	12	117	13	212
南充市	Nanchong	2	188	10	84	286	10	129	12	395
眉山市	Meishan	1	36	7	66	93	7	92	6	69
宜宾市	Yibin	2	191	12	98	245	11	178	16	281
广安市	Guangan			7	98	249	7	168	4	263
达州市	Dazhou	2	172	8	113	184	8	234	7	204
雅安市	Yaan			9	69	131	9	92	13	175
巴中市	Bazhong	2	50	6	82	121	6	125	18	388
资阳市	Ziyang	2	17	4	50	91	4	78	2	127
阿坝藏族羌族自治州	Aba	1	97	14	77	106	14	104	22	224
甘孜藏族自治州	Ganzi	1	66	19	88	135	19	349	7	92
凉山彝族自治州	Liangshan	1	114	18	143	223	18	226	7	133
省本级	Provincial level	5	841	1	250	602	1	93	1	234

注：全省合计中含省直属单位数。
a) The provincial data includes those of unites directly under the province.

21-3 各市(州)文化站情况(2023年)

Statistics on Cultural Stations by Region(2023)

市(州)	Region	文化站(个) Cultural Stations (unit)	#乡镇文化站 Township Cultural Stations	从业人员(人) Employed Persons (person)	举办展览(个) Number of Exhibitions (unit)	组织文艺活动次数(次) Art Performances & Cultural Sessions (time)	藏书量(千册) Collections (1 000 copies)
全省	**Sichuan**	**4063**	**524**	**8545**	**7978**	**50467**	**17190**
成都市	Chengdu	335	183	1348	1345	18539	2562
自贡市	Zigong	99	25	167	88	993	225
攀枝花市	Panzhihua	61	17	166	60	726	247
泸州市	Luzhou	126	26	243	143	1165	695
德阳市	Deyang	118	12	216	165	1218	971
绵阳市	Mianyang	289	17	584	467	2253	1336
广元市	Guangyuan	199	7	322	486	1766	990
遂宁市	Suining	124	20	216	186	1329	523
内江市	Neijiang	120	14	291	135	861	422
乐山市	Leshan	200	11	616	105	1536	708
南充市	Nanchong	426	57	920	1784	3736	1273
眉山市	Meishan	133	21	270	88	1808	429
宜宾市	Yibin	186	20	367	407	2354	896
广安市	Guangan	179	18	324	199	1232	535
达州市	Dazhou	229	19	443	673	1455	991
雅安市	Yaan	133	14	290	258	1251	447
巴中市	Bazhong	185	17	277	787	2285	1378
资阳市	Ziyang	122	9	307	187	1908	383
阿坝藏族羌族自治州	Aba	174		304	133	930	397
甘孜藏族自治州	Ganzi	293		299	62	1476	406
凉山彝族自治州	Liangshan	332	17	575	220	1646	1376

21 4 文化馆、文化站业务活动及经费情况(2023年)

Basic Statistics on Activities and Expenditures of Cultural Centers and Cultural Stations(2023)

项目		Item		总计 Total	文化馆 Cultural Centers	文化站 Cultural Stations
单位数	(个)	Number of Units	(unit)	4269	206	4063
举办展览	(个)	Number of Exhibitions	(unit)	9423	1429	7994
组织文艺活动	(次)	Art Performances and Cultural Sessions	(time)	62855	12276	50579
举办训练班		Training Courses				
班次	(次)	Number of Classes	(time)	31692	7340	24352
培训人次	(万人次)	Number of Persons Completing Courses	(10 000 person-times)	119.1	27.6	91.5
群众业余演出团(队)	(个)	Part-time Art Groups	(unit)	24343	3893	20450
总支出	(万元)	Total Expenses	(10 000 yuan)	123341	72995	50346
#基本支出	(万元)	Basic Expenses	(10 000 yuan)	65780	46773	19007

注：本表各项指标仅指文化部门系统内的。
a) Data in this table only refers to those under the administration of cultural departments.

21-5 公共图书馆业务活动及经费情况(2023年)
Business Activities and Expenditures of Public Libraries(2023)

项目		Item		总计 Total	省级公共图书馆 Public Libraries at Provincial Level	市(州)级公共图书馆 Public Libraries at Prefecture Level	县级公共图书馆 Public Libraries at County Level
总藏量	(万册、件)	Total Collections	(10 000 volumes)	5343	602	1588	3153
实际持证活跃读者数	(人)	Actual Number of Documented Active Readers		4507068	647433	1697779	2161856
书刊外借情况		Condition of Books Borrowed by the Readers					
人次	(万人次)	Total Number of Circulation	(10 000 person-times)	1310	17	342	951
册次	(万册次)	Number of Books Borrowed by the Readers	(10 000 volume-times)	2381	67	621	1694
为读者举办各种活动		Service Activities Provided for Readers					
次数	(次、个)	Number of Activities	(time, unit)	8349	107	1578	6664
参加人数	(万人次)	Number of Readers Involved	(10 000 person-times)	555	36	249	272
总支出	(万元)	Total Expenditures	(10 000 yuan)	99338	11907	24753	62679
基本支出	(万元)	Basic Expenses	(10 000 yuan)	67082	5153	11811	50118
#新增藏量购置费	(万元)	Purchase of New Reserves	(10 000 yuan)	5174	950	2118	2106
本年新增藏量	(万册)	New Reserves this Year	(10 000 copies)	287	13	63	211
阅览室座席	(千位)	Seating Capacity of Reading Rooms	(1 000 seats)	91894	2958	21460	67476

注：总藏量从2013年起不包括电子图书。因部门报表制度调整，自2023年起，原“书架总长度”指标不再进行统计。

a) Total collections don't include electronic books since 2013. Due to the adjustment of departmental reporting system, the original "total length of bookshelves" indicator will no longer be counted since 2023.

21-6 博物馆、文物机构业务活动及经费情况(2023年)
Business Activities and Expenditures of Museums and Cultural Relic Agencies(2023)

项目		Item		博物馆 Museums	文物保护管理机构 Cultural Relic Agencies
藏品	(件/套)	Number of Collections	(piece/set)	1359230	129273
#一级品	(件/套)	Grade One	(piece/set)	3255	563
本年支出	(万元)	Total Expenses	(10 000 yuan)	233388	75986
#基本支出	(万元)	Basic Expense	(10 000 yuan)	62699	25158

注：2023年博物馆统计口径发生变化，不再包含民营博物馆。

a) The statistical caliber of museums has changed and no longer includes private museums since 2023.

21-7 图书、杂志和报纸出版情况

Number of Books, Magazines and Newspapers Published

年份 Year	图书 Books Published				杂志 Magazines Published				报纸 Newspapers Published			
	种数(种) Kind of Publi-cations (kind)	#新出版 New Publi-cations	总印数(万册) Total Printed Copies (10 000 copies)	总印张数(万印张) Total Printed Sheets (10 000 sheets)	种数(种) Kind of Publi-cations (kind)	每期平均印数(万册) Average Printed Copies per Issue (10 000 copies)	总印数(万册) Total Printed Copies (10 000 copies)	总印张数(万印张) Total Printed Sheets (10 000 sheets)	种数(种) Kind of News-paper Publi-shed (kind)	每期平均印数(万份) Average Printed Copies per Issue (10 000 copies)	总印数(万份) Total Printed Copies (10 000 copies)	总印张数(万印张) Total Printed Sheets (10 000 sheets)
1952	53	20	1481	3195	25	45	565	540	14	34	6799	5150
1957	52		909	1783					15	35	8109	6005
1962	86		2484	5256								
1965	65		6280	15006								
1970	24		4225	10677								
1975	292	233	17184	48499								
1978	277	241	24993	83916	13	57	562	1173	15	170	51889	43758
1980	549	502	31370	119063	71	341	3036	8699	22	214	50627	42305
1985	1273	1151	28023	99516	224	690	5532	17810	69	859	92878	64138
1990	2676	1896	21152	82360	226	324	3257	9149	66	818	94657	64642
1995	3017	1876	15438	83894	287	487	4993	14898	93	710	100500	122632
1996	3833	2256	27975	138772	289	409	4339	12025	95	680	109084	138292
1997	4510	2005	33272	153193	289	405	4336	12484	95	763	126818	227065
1998	4436	2369	31491	151112	284	403	4508	13211	100	757	124922	235944
1999	4306	2254	29852	147862	287	419	4754	14944	100	782	127708	240359
2000	3855	2134	27315	157672	275	451	4950	16238	91	711	133590	366840
2001	3820	2104	26032	158031	334	362	4172	16233	84	671	136737	394553
2002	3895	2244	25932	165312	256	440	5572	20688	92	654	135163	319004
2003	4131	2315	25889	170470	267	352	4767	21421	93	634	139266	357423
2004	4059	1911	21690	154980	225	293	5269	32515	107	651	155972	498494
2005	4836	2975	23643	193903	330	459	7502	60933	130	659	155865	671830
2006	4873	3070	19643	149609	335	509	8215	59996	136	618	155800	685570
2007	5150	3287	19591	146591	335	496	9514	74788	136	660	168638	656104
2008	5021	2885	19490	142562	336	475	8237	53222	136	670	164273	737694
2009	6719	3878	17492	127321	336	494	8303	52759	136	613	155286	797707
2010	6645	3396	19493	147325	340	498	10593	74892	136	687	170176	999545
2011	8081	3951	24787	179489	343	471	9293	67424	136	670	174021	1019233
2012	7794	4235	23587	176618	343	470	9066	63236	136	661	172573	865664
2013	8554	4946	23416	186771	346	417	7499	54658	137	687	170457	833132
2014	9095	5252	19623	156848	349	376	6382	44033	136	653	167699	752920
2015	10097	6074	24805	193337	352	330	5655	35616	134	642	162781	647618
2016	10878	6332	24264	196767	354	316	5045	29000	132	636	162153	646976
2017	13329	8287	29195	224165	355	282	5128	28702	130	551	141828	368846
2018	14456	8746	32520	254859	356	278	4997	28352	84	520	132695	327090
2019	13885	7305	36565	286394	358	282	5231	28804	79	476	120448	260286
2020	12891	6781	34996	271096	358	273	5131	28499	78	422	104858	207613
2021	14406	7190	41931	319411	354	251	5077	28040	71	410	99971	189102
2022	12944	6613	40882	315029	354	252	5079	27939	69	409	98258	174107
2023	14226	6709	43714	351618	356	228	4589	25252	65	379	90530	156818

注：图书、杂志、报纸、音像制品出版资料由中共四川省委宣传部提供。

a) Data of books, magazines, newspapers, audio-visual products published are provided by Propaganda Department of the Sichuan Provincial Party Committee of the Communist Party in China.

21−8 录像和录音制品出版情况
Publication of Video and Audio Recordings

年份 Year	录像制品 Video Recordings		录音制品 Audio Recordings	
	种数 (种) Kind of Recordings (Kind)	数量 (万盒、万张) Volume (10 000 pieces)	种数 (种) Kind of Recordings (Kind)	数量 (万盒、万张) Volume (10 000 pieces)
2000	172	97.72	92	64.03
2001	260	391.98	114	93.53
2002	446	501.51	210	95.39
2003	490	310.23	158	127.27
2004	241	198.36	42	61.96
2005	294	171.80	177	88.20
2006	542	240.82	139	70.45
2007	491	164.01	164	71.73
2008	343	153.23	72	25.40
2009	250	124.30	75	40.58
2010	191	108.46	47	28.38
2011	96	73.13	32	25.77
2012	91	80.35	12	5.03
2013	77	45.54	35	19.70
2014	54	47.85	38	17.34
2015	48	67.45	15	8.65
2016	73	54.52	14	1.77
2017	53	61.25	17	3.80
2018	91	54.23	11	3.20
2019	43	2.92	9	0.53
2020	64	3.02	10	3.31
2021	40	2.75	18	2.00
2022	41	4.77	13	1.84
2023	39	3.59	9	1.91

21-9 广播电视事业发展情况
Basic Statistics on Development of Broadcasting and Television

年份 Year	中短波发射台及转播台（座）Transmission Stations and Relaying Stations of Medium and Short Wave (set)	中波发射机功率（部/千瓦）Power of Transmitters of Medium Wave (unit / kw)	调频、电视发射台及转播台（座）FM, TV Transmitting and Relaying Stations (set)	电视发射机功率（部/千瓦）Power of Television Transmission (unit / kw)	广播综合人口覆盖率(%) Comprehensive Population Coverage Rate of Broadcasting (%)	电视综合人口覆盖率(%) Comprehensive Population Coverage Rate of Television (%)	广播电视台（个）Broadcasting and Television Stations of County Level (set)
1952	2	2 / 2			20.06		
1957	1	2 / 2			20.06		80
1962	4	3 / 23.8	1	1 / 1	30.18	3.87	129
1965	4	3 / 123.8	1	1 / 1	30.09	3.87	141
1970	4	5 / 260.6	1	1 / 1	35.28	5.29	150
1975	9	10 / 327.6	14	15 / 5.50	43.13	18.73	157
1978	9	11 / 413.3	82	76 / 6.74	46.91	38.60	165
1980	11	15 / 488.0	208	235 / 21.39	49.91	45.69	168
1985	13	20 / 442.5	865	921 / 73.05	52.37	58.70	169
1990	18	29 / 453.0	2100	2577 / 183.38	64.46	71.46	166
1995	27	43 / 515.1	3114	4036 / 218.38	80.40	85.50	134
1996	27	40 / 521.1	3303	3952 / 207.09	84.47	83.57	161
1997	27	48 / 556.1	3227	3959 / 230.62	86.34	87.37	162
1998	29	48 / 556.1	3264	4009 / 235.94	88.90	88.97	44
1999	30	47 / 654.2	2626	3244 / 185.04	91.05	91.98	46
2000	28	52 / 673.1	4779	5636 / 266.82	92.85	93.61	42
2001	35	68 / 482.5	4839	5598 / 267.37	93.66	94.46	42
2002	34	69 / 558.0	4428	5353 / 260.53	94.07	95.08	110
2003	34	69 / 558.0	4385	5696 / 263.36	94.83	95.54	111
2004	34	69 / 558.0	4308	4546 / 250.77	95.34	96.39	111
2005	35	96 / 658.0	3849	5044 / 262.29	95.41	96.74	113
2006	35	96 / 658.0	2471	5524 / 280.14	95.70	96.77	113
2007	37	112 / 711.0	2469	5757 / 376.57	95.92	97.05	114
2008	37	114 / 710.0	4434	5644 / 505.59	95.97	97.10	119
2009	37	96 / 680.0	3944	5323 / 600.38	96.19	97.27	152
2010	37	101 / 687.0	3482	4810 / 587.11	96.22	97.33	156
2011	37	102 / 787.0	3001	4121 / 628.24	96.60	97.69	158
2012	36	96 / 747.0	3056	4173 / 644.52	96.78	97.75	159
2013	36	96 / 747.0	2187	2906 / 661.39	96.98	97.89	165
2014	40	104 / 701.5	566	944 / 638.77	97.04	98.07	165
2015	36	95 / 659.2	403	942 / 1260.95	97.14	98.24	165
2016	36	104 / 774.0	338	934 / 978.76	97.19	98.29	165
2017	39	108 / 645.0	345	1059 / 656.74	97.42	98.54	165
2018	42	109 / 780.0	303	969 / 623.81	97.84	98.79	171
2019	42	109 / 688.0	312	992 / 616.83	98.23	98.95	171
2020	51	102 / 560.0	325	773 / 491.00	98.87	99.33	173
2021	42	101 / 568.3	331	1429 / 484.65	99.16	99.57	170
2022	44	94 / 524.6	322	1824 / 492.38	99.39	99.72	170
2023	43	100 / 542.6	309	1748 / 381.72	99.53	99.77	162

注：广播电视资料由四川省广播电视局提供。
a) Data of radio and TV broadcast information are provided by Broadcasting and Television Bureau of Sichuan Provincial.

21-10 广播电视播放情况(2023年)
Statistics on Broadcasting and Television(2023)

项目	Item	节目套数(套) Number of Programs (set)	公共广播(电视)节目播出时间(小时) Broadcasting Hours of Public Broadcasting (Television) (hour)	新闻资讯类节目 News and Referrence Programs	专题服务类节目 Special Subject and Services Programs	综艺类节目 Omnibus Entertainment Programs	广播(影视)剧类节目 Broadcast Movies And TV	广告类节目 Advertisement	其他类节目 Others
广播播出合计	**All Radio Broadcasting**	**146**	**738880**	**183276**	**146163**	**119315**	**49587**	**46868**	**193671**
省级广播电台	Provincial Level	8	61138	8438	15896	16454	1916	6947	11487
市(州)级广播电台	Prefecture Level	45	282342	62517	67707	43126	17824	22571	68596
县级广播电视台	County Level	93	395400	112321	62560	59735	29846	17350	113588
电视播出合计	**All Television Broadcasting**	**209**	**1188695**	**181031**	**123999**	**51636**	**575523**	**84232**	**172274**
省级电视台	Provincial Level	8	69414	10586	12706	3572	25063	13535	3952
市(州)级电视台	Prefecture Level	48	306237	47886	49687	10098	132614	35053	30898
县级广播电视台	County Level	153	813044	122559	61606	37966	417846	35643	137424

21-11 各市(州)有线广播电视情况(2023年)
Statistics on Cable Broadcasting and Television by Region(2023)

单位：户、皮长 (households, kilometer)

市(州)	Region	有线广播电视实际用户 Actual Users of Cable Broadcasting and Television	#数字电视实际用户 Actual Users of Digital Television	#付费数字电视实际用户 Actual Users of Pay Digital Television	有线广播电视传输干线总长 Total Length of Main Link of Cable Broadcasting and Television Transmission
全省	**Sichuan**	**9437238**	**8643256**	**4498909**	**34197**
成都市	Chengdu	3447492	2988601	1327519	13193
自贡市	Zigong	247286	247286	114298	999
攀枝花市	Panzhihua	56526	55790	53376	320
泸州市	Luzhou	365332	364742	131487	896
德阳市	Deyang	610359	610359	232262	485
绵阳市	Mianyang	402109	399368	284314	1981
广元市	Guangyuan	329393	255916	143988	880
遂宁市	Suining	660632	635987	326246	450
内江市	Neijiang	234268	231026	124391	750
乐山市	Leshan	374248	374248	158487	752
南充市	Nanchong	445709	427247	335695	1840
眉山市	Meishan	137236	137236	107991	530
宜宾市	Yibin	325157	320806	183867	1146
广安市	Guangan	456560	391233	189603	466
达州市	Dazhou	608491	489348	341094	660
雅安市	Yaan	204336	190093	73912	685
巴中市	Bazhong	174629	174629	173644	697
资阳市	Ziyang	184336	183959	138563	536
阿坝藏族羌族自治州	Aba	27639	25841	1900	2088
甘孜藏族自治州	Ganzi	30247	26819	4681	1107
凉山彝族自治州	Liangshan	115253	112722	51591	3736

21-12 各市(州)农村广播电视有线传输情况(2023年)
Basic Statistics on Rural Radio and Television Cable Transmission by Region(2023)

单位：户、% (households, %)

市(州)	Region	农村有线广播电视实际用户数 Actual Users of Rural Cable radio and Television	农村有线广播电视入户率 Rural Households on Cable TV Rate	农村广播综合覆盖率 Comprehensive Coverage Rate of Rural Broadcasting	农村电视综合覆盖率 Comprehensive Coverage Rate of Rural Television
全省	**Sichuan**	**2691879**	**14.54**	**99.37**	**99.70**
成都市	Chengdu	348062	5.78	100.00	100.00
自贡市	Zigong	72464	14.55	100.00	100.00
攀枝花市	Panzhihua	14371	7.50	99.97	100.00
泸州市	Luzhou	112175	15.60	99.48	99.49
德阳市	Deyang	237169	30.12	100.00	100.00
绵阳市	Mianyang	262120	20.76	100.00	100.00
广元市	Guangyuan	170068	34.84	99.48	99.66
遂宁市	Suining	339944	40.74	100.00	100.00
内江市	Neijiang	125714	16.67	100.00	100.00
乐山市	Leshan	94242	14.43	99.68	99.72
南充市	Nanchong	122300	6.37	99.98	99.99
眉山市	Meishan	60794	12.67	100.00	100.00
宜宾市	Yibin	168360	25.35	98.69	99.48
广安市	Guangan	149809	23.12	99.79	99.79
达州市	Dazhou	157115	18.58	100.00	100.00
雅安市	Yaan	28834	9.99	98.86	100.00
巴中市	Bazhong	86260	14.01	100.00	100.00
资阳市	Ziyang	100033	14.85	98.70	99.15
阿坝藏族羌族自治州	Aba	7001	3.24	91.79	99.41
甘孜藏族自治州	Ganzi	2248	1.12	98.56	98.48
凉山彝族自治州	Liangshan	32796	3.11	96.25	98.26

21-13 体育事业情况(2023年)
Basic Conditions of Sports Cause(2023)

项目		Item		2023
国家级青少年体育俱乐部	(所)	Youth Sports Clubs of National Level	(unit)	264
国家级高水平体育后备人才基地	(个)	National High Level Sports Talented Reserve Bases	(unit)	40
四川省高水平体育后备人才基地	(个)	Provincial High Level Sports Talented Reserve Bases	(unit)	72
城市街道体育组织累计	(个)	Sports Organizations in the Urban Streets	(unit)	3678
#本年度新增	(个)	Newly Added at the Current Year	(unit)	190
农村乡镇体育组织累计	(个)	Sports Organizations in the Rural Villages and Towns	(unit)	4701
健身站(点)累计	(个)	Fitness Stations (points)	(unit)	16697
#本年度新增	(个)	Newly Added at the Current Year	(unit)	335
社区体育健身俱乐部累计	(个)	Community Sports Fitness Clubs	(unit)	1984
行政村农民体育健康工程累计	(个)	Farmer Sports Health Projects in Administrative Village	(unit)	47391
本年度举办全民健身科学知识宣传讲座次数	(次)	Number of Lectures on Scientific Knowledge of National Fitness	(time)	1173
本年度编印科学健身知识书籍册数	(册)	Copies of Books Published Scientific Knowledge of Fitness	(volume)	30000
审批社会体育指导员人数累计	(人)	Approval of the Number of Social Sports Instructors	(unit)	284000
本年度培训社会体育指导员人数	(人)	Number of People Receiving Social Sports Instructor Training	(unit)	22000
世界级比赛获得奖牌数	(枚)	Number of Medals Won in the World Competition	(piece)	10
#金牌	(枚)	Gold Medals	(piece)	6
亚洲级比赛获得奖牌数	(枚)	Number of Medals Won in Asian Games	(piece)	63
#金牌	(枚)	Gold Medals	(piece)	40
全国比赛获得奖牌数	(枚)	Number of Medals Won in the National Competition	(piece)	96
#金牌	(枚)	Gold Medals	(piece)	33

注：体育事业情况由四川省体育局提供。

a) Data in the table are provided by the Sports Bureau of Sichuan Province.

21-14 各市(州)体育彩票发行情况(2023年)
Sports Lottery Distribution by Region(2023)

单位：万元 (10 000 yuan)

市(州)	Region	当年体育彩票发行额 Sports Lottery Issuance in Current Year	#足彩 Soccer Betting	#竞彩 Race Lottery	#即开型 Open-Type	当年提取公益金 Public Welfare Fund Drawn from Sports Lottery
全省	**Sichuan**	**1947104**	**54770**	**1252523**	**253318**	**463831**
成都市	Chengdu	874075	26873	531424	139176	208515
自贡市	Zigong	51057	1957	34326	4912	12134
攀枝花市	Panzhihua	35453	575	23029	3536	8634
泸州市	Luzhou	65368	1798	45517	6257	15415
德阳市	Deyang	79631	1499	56825	6377	18872
绵阳市	Mianyang	94684	2976	62386	11120	22493
广元市	Guangyuan	36975	1042	25028	4518	8677
遂宁市	Suining	43201	571	30913	3122	10314
内江市	Neijiang	47254	1573	33352	3828	11151
乐山市	Leshan	78889	2041	50011	8661	19153
南充市	Nanchong	76395	1944	51192	8203	18185
眉山市	Meishan	59520	1553	38238	7977	14163
宜宾市	Yibin	94084	2166	69409	7325	21920
广安市	Guangan	43432	909	34583	2176	9958
达州市	Dazhou	61701	2202	41744	4460	14880
雅安市	Yaan	32276	1503	20463	4078	7672
巴中市	Bazhong	40682	971	26692	3556	9903
资阳市	Ziyang	29171	1203	19930	2688	6902
阿坝藏族羌族自治州	Aba	13969	79	8033	2739	3366
甘孜藏族自治州	Ganzi	13755	110	5277	4889	3360
凉山彝族自治州	Liangshan	75530	1224	44150	13719	18164

注：当年提取公益金合计中含中央、省级提取数据。
a) Pubic welfare funds drawn from sport lottery include state and provincial data.

21-15 医疗卫生机构情况(2023年)
Statistics on Health Institutions(2023)

机构类别	Item	机构数(个) Health Institutions (unit)	实有床位数(张) Beds (bed)	人员合计(人) Personnel (person)	#卫生技术人员 Medical Technical Personnel	#管理人员 Administrative Personnel
全省	**Total**	**74980**	**708592**	**926060**	**740317**	**54475**
医院合计	Total Number of Hospitals	2479	533181	544845	448973	35994
综合医院	General Hospitals	1423	300191	347391	291318	21961
中医医院	Hospitals of Chinese Medicine	277	81366	83117	71536	4836
中西医结合医院	Hospital Combining Traditional Chinese and Western Medicine	38	10542	11792	10079	675
民族医院	Minority Nationality Hospital	43	2283	2448	1988	189
专科医院	Specialized	676	136721	99173	73508	8240
#口腔	Stomatological	61	976	5395	3739	661
眼科	Ophthalmological	69	3439	5832	3800	757
耳鼻喉	Otolaryngology	9	719	797	498	76
肿瘤	Oncological	13	3819	4861	4110	212
心血管病	Cardiovascular System Diseases	2	626	906	791	46
胸科	Chest	1	65	45	35	1
妇产(科)	Gynecological and Obstetrical	1	60	58	47	7
血液病	Hematology	40	2111	5084	3317	475
儿童	Pediatrics	7	782	1489	1194	100
精神病	Psych iatrical	182	88432	30190	23925	1959
传染病	Epidemiological	8	2422	2480	2134	147
皮肤病	Dermatology	11	468	609	432	70
麻风病	Leprological	2	8	16	12	2
职业病	Occupational disease	2	907	1028	845	181
骨科	Orthopedics	54	6795	6753	5462	504
康复	Recuperation	48	6260	5144	4137	508
整形外科	Orthopedic Survey	3	190	425	258	46
美容	Beauty	36	735	5943	2326	581
其他专科	Other Specialized	127	17907	22118	16446	1907
护理院(中心)	Nursing Home (center)	22	2078	924	544	93
康复疗养机构	Rehabilitation and Convalescent Institution	13	1580	866	546	119
社区卫生服务中心	Community Health Care Centre	545	22955	35086	30152	1779
社区卫生服务站	Community Health Service Stations	559	377	3574	3213	355
卫生院	Sanitation Station	2778	135249	115684	100380	5288
门诊部	Outpatient Department	1681	230	29339	20980	2441
诊所	Clinics	22872		71539	66239	2731
卫生所、医务室	Healthy Centre	809		2669	2432	95
村卫生室	Village Clinics	42301		57459	17582	
护理站	Nursing Station	36		346	141	51
急救中心(站)	First-aid Centre	23	56	634	416	89
采供血机构	Blood Collection and Supply Institution	57		3725	2742	395
妇幼保健院(所、站)	Maternity and Child Care Centre	201	14345	33403	28189	2300
专科疾病防治院(所、站)	Specialized Prevention Station	20	619	531	302	83
疾病预防控制中心(防疫站)	Epidemic Prevention and Control Centre	211		15190	11636	1106
卫生监督所	Sanitary Supervision Station	161		2352	1938	150
医学科学研究机构	Research Institution of Medical Sciences	5		453	195	56
医学在职培训机构	Medical On the Job Training Institution	9		75	22	24
健康教育所(站、中心)	Healthy Education Centre	9		144	26	42
其他卫生机构	Other Health Care Institutions	211		8146	4213	1377

注：卫生机构资料由四川省卫生健康委员会提供。
a) Data of health agencies are provided by Health Commission of sichuan provincial.

21-16 卫生机构数
Number of Health Institutions

单位：个 (unit)

年份 Year	机构数 Number of Health Care Institutions	#医院 Hospitals	#社区卫生服务中心 Community Health Care Centers	#卫生院 Sanitation Stations	#疾病预防控制中心 Epidemic Prevention and Control Centers	#妇幼保健院(所、站) Maternity and Child Care Centers
2002	72768	1173	44	6280	214	200
2003	72810	1164	50	6048	208	198
2004	70944	1144	63	5369	209	196
2005	72399	1155	68	5179	207	197
2006	75262	1178	213	5012	207	202
2007	72862	1162	214	4845	208	201
2008	71195	1143	234	4817	208	201
2009	72907	1187	257	4745	207	202
2010	74311	1260	306	4688	207	203
2011	75814	1393	344	4619	206	203
2012	76555	1542	361	4607	204	200
2013	80039	1716	379	4595	207	202
2014	81081	1822	397	4575	207	202
2015	80114	1942	397	4511	206	202
2016	79516	2067	412	4493	206	202
2017	80480	2219	417	4476	206	203
2018	81539	2343	424	4437	206	201
2019	83757	2417	433	4421	208	201
2020	82793	2435	459	4317	210	202
2021	80249	2481	498	3687	212	202
2022	74041	2465	548	2811	211	202
2023	74980	2479	545	2778	211	201

21-17 各市(州)医疗卫生机构数
Number of Health Institutions by Region

单位：个 (unit)

市(州)	Region	2014	2015	2016	2017	2018	2019	2020	2021	2022	2023
全省	**Total**	**81081**	**80114**	**79516**	**80480**	**81539**	**83757**	**82793**	**80249**	**74041**	**74980**
成都市	Chengdu	8190	8481	9853	10183	10755	12121	11954	12497	12333	13329
自贡市	Zigong	2409	2346	2274	2333	2245	2238	2162	2143	2127	2219
攀枝花市	Panzhihua	1079	1064	1060	1064	1056	1113	1009	1077	1070	1059
泸州市	Luzhou	4619	4566	4560	4628	4616	4711	4727	4556	4513	4536
德阳市	Deyang	2774	2717	2708	2738	2819	2822	2450	2251	2149	2224
绵阳市	Mianyang	4494	4417	4371	4449	4674	4856	4857	4556	4493	4607
广元市	Guangyuan	3554	3545	3460	3557	3540	3544	3370	3210	2736	2652
遂宁市	Suining	3762	3735	3846	3822	3779	3725	3984	3907	3790	3657
内江市	Neijiang	3228	3195	3096	3259	3297	3303	3579	3764	3787	3759
乐山市	Leshan	3277	3098	3100	3206	3259	3251	3224	3237	3152	3186
南充市	Nanchong	8780	8712	8703	8696	8583	8457	8248	8302	5347	5653
眉山市	Meishan	2107	2057	2044	2068	2040	2139	2136	2247	2151	2196
宜宾市	Yibin	5136	4963	5025	5062	5260	5120	4993	4867	4899	4870
广安市	Guangan	3561	3500	3447	3446	3446	3443	3353	2333	2365	2487
达州市	Dazhou	4397	4413	4172	4191	4293	4514	4548	4223	3685	3602
雅安市	Yaan	1518	1494	1334	1426	1456	1573	1544	1365	1265	1207
巴中市	Bazhong	3299	3164	3234	3218	3274	3348	3344	3366	3021	3087
资阳市	Ziyang	4956	4902	3485	3460	3438	3432	3367	3225	2888	2686
阿坝藏族羌族自治州	Aba	1683	1649	1642	1656	1683	1756	1728	1620	1546	1531
甘孜藏族自治州	Ganzi	2776	2725	2706	2719	2777	2825	2813	2528	2585	2494
凉山彝族自治州	Liangshan	5482	5371	5396	5299	5249	5466	5403	4975	4139	3939

21-18 各市(州)各类医疗卫生机构数(2023年)
Number of Health Institutions by Region(2023)

单位：个 (unit)

市(州)	Region	机构数 Number of Health Care Institutions	#医院 Hospitals	#社区卫生服务中心 Community Health Care Centers	#卫生院 Sanitation Stations	#疾病预防控制中心 Epidemic Prevention and Control Centers	#妇幼保健院(所、站) Maternity and Child Care Centers
成都市	Chengdu	13329	671	161	147	25	21
自贡市	Zigong	2219	67	19	71	7	7
攀枝花市	Panzhihua	1059	27	14	37	6	6
泸州市	Luzhou	4536	146	31	104	8	8
德阳市	Deyang	2224	89	21	74	7	6
绵阳市	Mianyang	4607	139	24	152	12	10
广元市	Guangyuan	2652	81	13	137	8	7
遂宁市	Suining	3657	68	15	84	6	6
内江市	Neijiang	3759	80	13	73	6	6
乐山市	Leshan	3186	92	17	126	12	12
南充市	Nanchong	5653	176	53	211	10	10
眉山市	Meishan	2196	84	20	69	8	7
宜宾市	Yibin	4870	137	16	124	11	11
广安市	Guangan	2487	86	16	110	7	7
达州市	Dazhou	3602	146	25	186	8	8
雅安市	Yaan	1207	48	7	89	9	9
巴中市	Bazhong	3087	79	30	135	6	6
资阳市	Ziyang	2686	50	12	91	4	3
阿坝藏族羌族自治州	Aba	1531	43	10	171	14	14
甘孜藏族自治州	Ganzi	2494	45	2	295	19	19
凉山彝族自治州	Liangshan	3939	125	26	292	18	18

21–19 医疗卫生机构床位数
Number of Beds in Health Institutions

单位：张 (unit)

年份 Year	床位数 Number of Beds	#医院 Hospitals	#社区卫生服务中心 Community Health Care Centers	#卫生院 Sanitation Stations	#妇幼保健院（所、站） Maternity and Child Care Centers
2002	187179	119976	206	56467	4289
2003	187741	120173	144	56671	4501
2004	191523	123995	304	56945	4786
2005	194940	127129	1053	57460	5016
2006	201854	130677	2270	59707	5301
2007	214329	136757	3149	66063	5838
2008	244119	149289	4526	80697	6390
2009	275555	167271	5170	92403	7050
2010	302061	185459	6812	98252	7843
2011	335151	212282	8299	102544	7892
2012	390122	257333	8636	111550	8759
2013	426378	289022	9003	114412	9682
2014	459588	319155	9046	117090	10152
2015	488719	345791	8995	119156	10681
2016	519149	375708	9388	120387	11122
2017	563419	411911	10135	127419	11794
2018	598842	442215	10649	131644	12499
2019	631707	469814	11192	135840	12857
2020	649658	484823	12959	135807	13273
2021	662018	497531	15483	132305	13398
2022	683873	516961	20013	130412	13610
2023	708592	533181	22955	135249	14345

21-20 各市(州)医疗卫生机构床位数
Number of Beds in Health Institutions by Region

单位：张 (unit)

市(州)	Region	2014	2015	2016	2017	2018	2019	2020	2021	2022	2023
全省	**Total**	**459588**	**488719**	**519149**	**563419**	**598842**	**631707**	**649658**	**662018**	**683873**	**708592**
成都市	Chengdu	108031	114726	128058	134507	143248	148941	153663	160833	167231	176143
自贡市	Zigong	16396	17644	18832	20064	22014	23776	23646	23224	23857	25026
攀枝花市	Panzhihua	9599	10097	9867	10004	10398	10453	10389	10538	10781	11131
泸州市	Luzhou	22666	24548	26612	29256	31839	34561	34608	35014	37369	38719
德阳市	Deyang	19118	19968	21190	22570	24254	26352	26377	27194	28120	29852
绵阳市	Mianyang	30756	32110	33708	36322	38559	40316	40666	41878	43453	44746
广元市	Guangyuan	16753	18211	19778	21233	22091	23892	24125	22137	21252	20436
遂宁市	Suining	15825	17197	18174	19543	20139	21404	22752	20965	21578	22061
内江市	Neijiang	19825	20326	20769	22605	24106	25859	25896	26436	26759	27747
乐山市	Leshan	18979	19290	20553	22390	24063	25329	25834	26280	26490	27840
南充市	Nanchong	29670	32634	36222	40193	41694	43726	45514	47009	47103	48821
眉山市	Meishan	15830	16296	16687	19170	19693	19943	20370	21019	21561	24275
宜宾市	Yibin	25061	26408	29437	32122	33454	35242	36215	36472	37380	38963
广安市	Guangan	13213	14729	15940	18186	19777	21310	22242	21796	21790	22393
达州市	Dazhou	22495	23998	25447	29915	32943	35862	39834	41557	44555	45501
雅安市	Yaan	10812	11759	11861	12382	12344	13230	13818	14553	14851	14807
巴中市	Bazhong	14608	15546	16767	19174	21769	22651	22687	22809	22829	24497
资阳市	Ziyang	20847	22269	16302	17815	19004	20226	20687	21639	22700	20551
阿坝藏族羌族自治州	Aba	4272	4435	4447	4551	4899	5121	5381	5288	5472	5832
甘孜藏族自治州	Ganzi	5063	4918	5054	4955	5207	5381	5606	5506	8135	7180
凉山彝族自治州	Liangshan	19769	21610	23444	26462	27347	28132	29348	29871	30607	32071

21-21 各市(州)各类医疗卫生机构床位数(2023年)
Number of Beds in Health Institutions(2023)

单位：张 (unit)

市(州)	Region	床位数 Number of Beds	#医院 Hospitals	#社区卫生服务中心 Community Health Care Centers	#卫生院 Sanitation Stations	#妇幼保健院(所、站) Maternity and Child Care Centers
成都市	Chengdu	176143	145995	9477	16878	3472
自贡市	Zigong	25026	19364	607	4225	688
攀枝花市	Panzhihua	11131	10129	13	708	245
泸州市	Luzhou	38719	27999	1561	8293	862
德阳市	Deyang	29852	20107	1177	7877	594
绵阳市	Mianyang	44746	30427	623	12942	725
广元市	Guangyuan	20436	15665	225	4001	525
遂宁市	Suining	22061	15617	675	5224	305
内江市	Neijiang	27747	20467	110	6686	460
乐山市	Leshan	27840	19833	839	5892	872
南充市	Nanchong	48821	38368	1575	7756	1044
眉山市	Meishan	24275	16113	1511	6058	575
宜宾市	Yibin	38963	29191	1073	8203	487
广安市	Guangan	22393	17303	458	4270	362
达州市	Dazhou	45501	30088	1090	12401	646
雅安市	Yaan	14807	12654	255	1832	63
巴中市	Bazhong	24497	16260	695	6918	590
资阳市	Ziyang	20551	14184	208	5793	266
阿坝藏族羌族自治州	Aba	5832	4644	66	957	151
甘孜藏族自治州	Ganzi	7180	4527	4	2181	463
凉山彝族自治州	Liangshan	32071	24246	713	6154	950

21−22 医疗卫生机构人员数
Number of Persons Engaged in Health Institutions

单位：人 (Person)

年份 Year	人员合计 Total	#卫生技术人员 Medical Technical Personnel	#执业医师 Licensed Physicians	#执业助理医师 Licensed Assistant Physicians	#注册护士 Licensed Nurses	#管理人员 Administrative Personnel
2002	378830	248470	86978	33378	60098	20070
2003	373628	245326	86101	34124	59494	17960
2004	363179	242255	84785	34531	60871	17392
2005	362014	244367	86205	35832	61237	15825
2006	378374	255140	87944	41446	63730	15903
2007	388644	264206	91273	34848	73485	19467
2008	400248	277112	96460	25324	78062	18500
2009	437758	303050	109090	29594	91164	18456
2010	467774	323915	114734	29843	104930	23288
2011	505113	353561	122525	31489	121319	25632
2012	549866	389001	130106	33272	139811	26850
2013	595645	426597	139037	34805	157459	29675
2014	627159	451747	145026	34494	175522	32091
2015	647577	472816	149101	33110	190643	30778
2016	671305	496343	153859	32171	207691	31480
2017	710787	530935	162995	32590	228608	32747
2018	747160	563086	171554	34056	247322	34910
2019	794282	602428	185247	36000	270616	36742
2020	826989	633275	195693	39598	286010	37515
2021	865444	672722	209833	40564	306685	42532
2022	887493	698209	216016	42148	318267	44357
2023	926060	740317	234510	44927	335453	54475

21-22 续表 continued

单位：人 (Person)

年份 Year	人员合计 Total	#医院 Hospitals	#社区卫生服务中心 Community Health Care Centers	#卫生院 Sanitation Stations	#疾病预防控制中心 Epidemic Prevention and Control Centers	#妇幼保健院(所、站) Maternity and Child Care Centers
2002	378830	144086	556	79247	11219	10053
2003	373628	142945	509	77447	10944	8672
2004	363179	142017	709	72939	10518	8674
2005	362014	142955	1487	70403	10410	8648
2006	378374	147122	2672	69172	10491	8856
2007	388644	167432	5918	73729	10450	10588
2008	400248	175472	7813	76405	10444	11188
2009	437758	195099	9370	82778	10352	11950
2010	467774	215902	11658	84200	10431	13153
2011	505113	243520	13773	88075	10638	14297
2012	549866	277344	14393	93287	11035	15656
2013	595645	309129	15091	95886	11307	16950
2014	627159	336694	15532	97671	11552	18096
2015	647577	359411	16003	100127	11593	20071
2016	671305	383958	17788	104809	12307	22440
2017	710787	412759	18699	109238	12697	24678
2018	747160	438202	19684	112784	12812	26133
2019	794282	463045	20847	116012	13127	28309
2020	826989	482747	23597	116090	13453	30084
2021	865444	508955	27195	115361	14007	31705
2022	887493	522712	33278	113450	14975	32822
2023	926060	544845	35086	115684	15190	33403

21-23 各市(州)医疗卫生机构人员数
Number of Persons Engaged in Health Institutions by Region

单位：人 (Person)

市(州)	Region	2014	2015	2016	2017	2018	2019	2020	2021	2022	2023
全省	**Total**	**627159**	**627159**	**671305**	**710787**	**747160**	**794282**	**826989**	**865444**	**887493**	**926060**
成都市	Chengdu	164273	164273	190236	200739	215863	237668	249639	270698	277488	294912
自贡市	Zigong	21570	21570	22799	23899	24861	25651	25790	26411	27045	27636
攀枝花市	Panzhihua	12683	12683	12776	12901	13130	13396	13426	14102	14381	14456
泸州市	Luzhou	29513	29513	31196	34524	36642	40101	42218	42998	44264	45616
德阳市	Deyang	25826	25826	28024	29404	30425	32032	32424	33454	34453	35510
绵阳市	Mianyang	37303	37303	38265	39971	42343	44639	46252	48034	50062	53958
广元市	Guangyuan	21006	21006	21979	22924	24382	25387	26713	26829	26512	26781
遂宁市	Suining	19830	19830	21174	22718	23256	24397	26345	26402	26809	26867
内江市	Neijiang	23486	23486	24017	25305	26184	27538	28703	29264	30459	31638
乐山市	Leshan	23516	23516	24523	25762	26858	28270	29463	30234	31268	31832
南充市	Nanchong	41401	41401	44833	47840	49793	50950	51263	53214	52260	53342
眉山市	Meishan	20432	20432	20639	22705	23026	24013	24849	26213	27382	28445
宜宾市	Yibin	31183	31183	33793	36343	38141	38967	40778	42421	46003	48179
广安市	Guangan	18917	18917	20942	22295	22957	24811	25622	25623	26384	27741
达州市	Dazhou	33415	33415	33435	36205	37522	39900	42378	45890	46238	45428
雅安市	Yaan	12470	12470	13269	13983	14723	15809	16105	16509	17043	17011
巴中市	Bazhong	21328	21328	21820	22523	23551	23760	24118	24126	24365	25193
资阳市	Ziyang	25470	25470	18478	19138	19756	20352	21631	22327	22862	22795
阿坝藏族羌族自治州	Aba	7736	7736	8498	8774	9228	9481	9726	9733	9980	10593
甘孜藏族自治州	Ganzi	8711	8711	9387	9622	9931	10129	10563	10558	10854	11110
凉山彝族自治州	Liangshan	27090	27090	31222	33212	34588	37031	38983	40404	41381	47017

21−24 各市(州)各类医疗卫生机构人员数(2023年)
Number of Persons Engaged in Health Institutions(2023)

单位：人 (Person)

市(州)	Region	人员合计 Total	#卫生技术人员 Medical Technical Personnel	#执业医师 Licensed Physicians	#执业助理医师 Licensed Assistant Physicians	#注册护士 Licensed Nurses	#管理人员 Administrative Personnel
成都市	Chengdu	294912	230246	78779	6913	109204	22401
自贡市	Zigong	27636	22841	6722	1291	10398	1551
攀枝花市	Panzhihua	14456	12135	4018	375	5718	756
泸州市	Luzhou	45616	36306	11050	2324	17319	1756
德阳市	Deyang	35510	28832	9234	1820	12830	2075
绵阳市	Mianyang	53958	44600	14232	2866	19910	4621
广元市	Guangyuan	26781	21612	6419	1390	9410	1242
遂宁市	Suining	26867	21349	7325	1167	9138	1567
内江市	Neijiang	31638	25603	7743	1883	11832	2104
乐山市	Leshan	31832	25381	7709	1738	11897	1770
南充市	Nanchong	53342	42483	14324	2949	18478	2986
眉山市	Meishan	28445	23280	7660	1995	9988	907
宜宾市	Yibin	48179	39824	10977	3114	18604	2748
广安市	Guangan	27741	21665	6404	1337	9942	1089
达州市	Dazhou	45428	36637	10658	3213	16799	1581
雅安市	Yaan	17011	14344	4301	905	6362	785
巴中市	Bazhong	25193	19875	5829	1956	8355	805
资阳市	Ziyang	22795	18438	5228	1810	8084	1089
阿坝藏族羌族自治州	Aba	10593	7775	2118	704	2738	498
甘孜藏族自治州	Ganzi	11110	7948	1577	1002	2654	454
凉山彝族自治州	Liangshan	47017	39143	12203	4175	15793	1690

21-24 续表 continued

单位：人 (Person)

市(州)	Region	人员合计 Total	#医院 Hospitals	#社区卫生服务中心 Community Health Care Centers	#卫生院 Sanitation Stations	#疾病预防控制中心 Epidemic Prevention and Control Centers	#妇幼保健院(所、站) Maternity and Child Care Centers
成都市	Chengdu	294912	188663	16223	12127	3247	8657
自贡市	Zigong	27636	16895	822	3794	570	1571
攀枝花市	Panzhihua	14456	9379	701	1031	291	598
泸州市	Luzhou	45616	25949	1729	6279	543	1316
德阳市	Deyang	35510	20420	1231	5474	619	1292
绵阳市	Mianyang	53958	31828	1195	8559	837	2037
广元市	Guangyuan	26781	15262	627	4959	433	1131
遂宁市	Suining	26867	14186	659	4326	460	755
内江市	Neijiang	31638	16861	362	5070	551	1234
乐山市	Leshan	31832	17965	870	4259	578	1693
南充市	Nanchong	53342	32563	2037	7166	656	2206
眉山市	Meishan	28445	15157	1467	4612	509	1615
宜宾市	Yibin	48179	26672	1338	7687	778	1444
广安市	Guangan	27741	15036	1151	5212	581	941
达州市	Dazhou	45128	24871	1445	8633	776	1352
雅安市	Yaan	17011	11567	388	2221	495	339
巴中市	Bazhong	25193	13075	780	4990	390	1093
资阳市	Ziyang	22795	11754	633	5047	385	800
阿坝藏族羌族自治州	Aba	10593	5433	217	2190	591	541
甘孜藏族自治州	Ganzi	11110	4695	50	2777	575	586
凉山彝族自治州	Liangshan	47017	26614	1161	9271	1325	2202

21−25 前十大类病伤死亡原因及构成(2023年)
Death Rate of 10 Major Diseases Categories(2023)

顺位 No.	病伤死亡原因	Causes of Deaths	死亡率(1/10万) Death Rate (per 100 000 persons)	构成(%) As of Total Deaths (%)
1	循环系统疾病	Diseases of the Circulatory System	276.51	35.41
2	肿瘤	Tumor	182.11	23.32
3	呼吸系统疾病	Diseases of the Respiratory System	169.75	21.74
4	伤害	Trauma	55.42	7.10
6	内分泌营养代谢	Endocrine Nutrition Metabolism	30.09	3.85
7	消化系统疾病	Diseases of the Digestive System	23.35	2.99
5	神经系统疾病	Nervous System Diseases	12.32	1.58
8	传染病和寄生虫病	Infectious Disease and Parasitic Disease	9.01	1.15
9	泌尿生殖系统疾病	Diseases of the Genitourinary System	8.60	1.10
10	精神和行为障碍	Mental and Behavioral Disorders	3.45	0.44

21−26 前十位单病种死亡原因及构成(2023年)
Death Rate of 10 Single-species Major Diseases(2023)

顺位 No.	前十位单病种类目	10 Single-species Major Diseases	死亡率(1/10万) Death Rate (per 100 000 persons)	构成(%) As of Total Deaths (%)
1	脑血管病	Cerebrovascular Disease	133.97	17.16
2	慢性阻塞性肺疾病	Chronic Obstructive Pulmonary Disease	125.43	16.06
3	缺血性心脏病	Ischemic Heart Disease	105.67	13.53
4	肺癌	Malignant Tumor	54.77	7.01
5	肝癌	Malignant Liver Tumor	34.88	4.47
6	糖尿病	Diabetes mellitus	27.12	3.47
7	跌倒	Fall	25.31	3.24
8	食管癌	Malignant Esophagus Tumor	20.99	2.69
9	高血压及并发症	Hypertension and Complications	19.82	2.54
10	结直肠癌	Colorectal Cancer	18.31	2.35

21−27 国家免疫规划疫苗基础免疫接种率(2023年)
Basis Inoculability Rate of National Immunization Vaccine Planning(2023)

种类	Item	常规报告接种率(%) Inoculability Rate of Conventional Reports (%)
卡介苗	Bcg Vaccine	97.30
脊灰疫苗	Poliomyelitis Vaccine	94.99
百白破三联	Chin cough, Diphtheria and Tetanus Joint Vaccine	94.01
麻疹疫苗	Measles Vaccine	91.70
乙肝疫苗全程	Hepatitis-B Vaccine Full Process	94.10

21–28 传染病报告发病及死亡情况(2023年)
Incidence and Death from Infectious Diseases(2023)

病种	Item	发病率(1/10万) Incidence Diseases Rate (per 100 000 persons)	死亡率(1/10万) Death Rate (per 100 000 persons)	病死率(%) Mortality Rate per 100 Infectious Disease Patients(%)
甲乙丙合计	**Total of Category A, B and C**	**1970.17**	**5.43**	**0.28**
一、甲乙类合计	**I. Total of Category A and B**	**614.04**	**5.42**	**0.88**
鼠疫	The Plague			
霍乱	Cholera			
传染性非典型肺炎	SARS			
艾滋病	AIDS	13.21	4.90	37.08
HIV	HIV	13.83	3.77	27.25
病毒性肝炎	Hepatitis	130.93	0.30	0.23
甲肝	A	1.22		
乙肝	B	105.54	0.03	0.03
丙肝	C	21.58	0.27	1.25
丁肝	D	0.02		
戊肝	E	2.31		
肝炎(未分型)	Hepatitis (Not Classified)	0.26		
脊髓灰质炎	Poliomyelitis			
人感染高致病性禽流感	People Avian Flu			
麻疹	Measles	0.04		
流行性出血热	Hemorrhage Fever	0.26		
狂犬病	Hydrophobia			100.00
流行性乙型脑炎	Encephalitis B	0.03		
登革热	Dengue Fever	0.22		
炭疽	Anthrax	0.08		
细菌性和阿米巴性痢疾	Dysentery	3.37		
肺结核	Pulmonary Tuberculosis	54.21	0.17	0.32
伤寒和副伤寒	Typhoid and Paratyphoid Fever	0.38		
流行性脑脊髓膜炎	Epidemic Encephalitis	0.01		
百日咳	Pertussis	0.81		
白喉	Diphtheria			
新生儿破伤风 *	Newborn Baby Tetanus			
猩红热	Scarlet Fever	1.44		
布鲁氏菌病	Brucellosis	0.50		
淋病	Gonorrhea	4.93		
梅毒	Syphilis	54.97	0.01	0.02
钩端螺旋体病	Leptospirosis	0.01		
血吸虫病	Schistosomiasis	0.01		
疟疾	Malaria	0.19		
人感染H7N9禽流感	Human Infection with H7N9 Avian Influenza			
新型冠状病毒肺炎	Novel Coronavirus Pneumonia	348.41	0.03	0.01
二、丙类合计	**Ⅱ. Total of Category C**	**1356.13**		
流行性感冒	Influenza	1133.92		
流行性腮腺炎	Epidemic Mumps	7.51		
风疹	Rubella	0.03		
急性出血性结膜炎	Acute Hemorrhagic Conjunctivitis	0.76		
麻风病	Leprosy	0.02		
流行性和地方性斑疹伤寒	Typhus Fever	0.23		
黑热病	Kala-Azar	0.02		6.67
包虫病	Echinococcosis	0.67		
丝虫病	Filariasis	0.67		
其他感染性腹泻病	Other Infectious Diarrheal diseases	94.16		
手足口病	Hand-foot-mouth Disease	118.81		

注：新生儿破伤风发病率＝当年发病数÷当年0岁组人口数×1000‰；新生儿破伤风死亡率＝当年死亡数÷当年0岁组人口数×1000‰。
a) Incidence diseases rate of newborn baby tetanus=Number of incidence diseases in current year ÷ Number of population of 0 age group in current year×1000‰; Death rate of newborn baby tetanus=Number of death in current year ÷ Number of population of 0 age group in current year×1000‰.

主要统计指标解释

艺术表演团体 指由文化部门主办或实行行业管理(经文化行政部门审批并领取营业性演出许可证),专门从事表演艺术等活动的各类专业艺术表演团体,含民间职业剧团。不包括群众业余文艺表演团体。

广播/电视节目综合人口覆盖率 指根据原国家广播电视总局制定的《广播电视人口覆盖率统计技术标准和方法》进行统计调查的,在对象区内能接收到由中央、省、地市或县通过无线、有线或卫星等各种技术方式转播的各级广播/电视节目的人口数占对象区总人口数的百分比。

医疗卫生机构 指从卫生健康行政部门取得《医疗机构执业许可证》,或从民政、工商行政、机构编制管理部门取得法人单位登记证书,为社会提供医疗保健、疾病控制、卫生监督服务或从事医学科研和医学在职培训等工作的单位。医疗卫生机构包括医院、基层医疗卫生机构、专业公共卫生机构、其他医疗卫生机构。

医院 包括综合医院、中医医院、中西医结合医院、民族医院、各类专科医院和护理院,不包括专科疾病防治院、妇幼保健院和疗养院。

卫生人员 指在医院、基层医疗卫生机构、专业公共卫生机构及其他医疗卫生机构工作的职工,包括卫生技术人员、乡村医生和卫生员、其他技术人员、管理人员和工勤人员。一律按支付年底工资的在岗职工统计,包括各类聘任人员(含合同工)及返聘本单位半年以上人员,不包括临时工、离退休人员、退职人员、离开本单位仍保留劳动关系人员、本单位返聘和临聘不足半年人员。

卫生技术人员 包括执业医师、执业助理医师、注册护士、药师(士)、检验技师(士)、影像技师、卫生监督员和见习医(药、护、技)师(士)等卫生专业人员。不包括从事管理工作的卫生技术人员(如院长、副院长、党委书记等)。

执业医师 指《医师执业证》"级别"为"执业医师"且实际从事医疗、预防保健工作的人员,不包括实际从事管理工作的执业医师。执业医师类别分为临床、中医、口腔和公共卫生四类。

执业助理医师 指《医师执业证》"级别"为"执业助理医师"且实际从事医疗、预防保健工作的人员,不包括实际从事管理工作的执业助理医师。执业助理医师类别分为临床、中医、口腔和公共卫生四类。

床位数 指年末医疗卫生机构实有床位,又称实有床位数、病床数。实有床位包括正规床、简易床、监护床、超过半年的加床、正在消毒和修理的床位、因扩建或大修而停用的床位。不包括产科新生儿床、接产室待产床、库存床、观察床、临时加床和病人家属陪待床。

甲乙类法定报告传染病发病率 指某年某地区每10万人口中甲乙类法定报告传染病发病数。即甲乙类法定传染病发病率=甲乙类法定报告传染病发病数/人口数×100000。

甲乙类法定报告传染病死亡率 指某年某地区每10万人口中甲乙类法定报告传染病死亡数。即甲乙类法定报告传染病死亡率=甲乙类法定报告传染病死亡数/人口数×100000。

Explanatory Notes on Main Statistical Indicators

Arts Performance Troupes refer to the various professional performing arts groups, sponsored by the cultural departments or guided by the cultural societies (approved by the cultural administration authority, or permitted with the commercial performance certificate), including non-public troupes. The mass amateur arts performance troupes are not included.

Population Coverage Rate of Radio/Television Programs refers to the percentage of population in the target region who can receive radio/television programmes transmitted by national, provincial, municipal or county stations through wireless, cable or satellite techniques, according to Statistical Standard and Method on Television and Radio Coverage of Population established by the State Administration of Radio and Television.

Health Care Institutions refer to the units which have been qualified with the Certification of Health Care Institution, or qualified with the Certification of Corporate Unit by the civil affairs, administration for industry and commerce, and engaging in medical care services, disease control services, health supervision services, or medicine research and on-job training, etc., including: hospitals, health care institutions at grass-root level, specialized public health institutions, and other health care institutions.

Hospitals include general hospitals, traditional Chinese medicine hospitals, hospitals of integrated traditional Chinese and western medicine, nationalities hospitals, specialized hospitals and nursing hospitals, as well as affiliated hospitals of medical colleges, excluding specialized disease prevention and treatment institutes, maternal and child health centers and convalescent hospitals.

Health Personnel refer to all employees engaged in the health care institutions, such as hospitals, health care institutions at grass-root level, specialized public health institutions, and other health care institutions, including health technical personnel, village doctors and assistants, other technical personnel, administrative staffs and logistics technical workers. Data are based on the year end payroll, including personnel employed (including contract workers) and re-employed after retirement by the institution for more than 6 months, excluding temporary workers, retired personnel, resigned personnel, personnel who have left the institution but kept the contract relation and personnel who are re-employed after retirement or temporarily employed for less than 6 months.

Health Technical Personnel refer to the professional staff engaged in health care, including licensed physicians and physician assistants, registered nurses, pharmacists, laboratory and imaging technicians, health care supervisors and intern doctors, pharmacists, nurses, and technical personnel, excluding health technical personnel engaged in management (e.g. president, vice president and secretary of the party committee etc).

Licensed Physicians refer to the medical workers with licenses of qualified doctors and are employed in medical treatment, disease prevention or healthcare institutions, excluding the licensed doctors engaged in management. The physicians are divided into 4 categories: clinician, Chinese medicine, stomatology and public health.

Licensed Physician Assistants refer to the medical workers with licenses of qualified assistant doctors and are employed in medical treatment, disease prevention or healthcare institutions, excluding the licensed assistant doctors engaged in management. Physician assistants are divided into 4 categories: clinician, Chinese medicine, stomatology and public health.

Number of Beds refer to the actual number of beds in health care institutions at year-end, also known as the actual number of beds or hospital beds, including regular beds, simple beds, monitoring beds, extra bed over 6 months, beds under disinfection or repairing, beds deactivated due to expansion or overhaul, not including neonatal beds, pre-delivery beds, inventory beds, observation beds, temporary beds and family accompany beds.

Morbidity Rate of Class A and B Notifiable Infectious Diseases refers to the number of cases of Class A and B notifiable infectious diseases per 100 thousand population in the reference year. The formula is:

Morbidity rate of Class A and B notifiable infectious diseases = number of cases of Class A and B notifiable infectious diseases / population × 100000

Mortality Rate of Class A and B Notifiable Infectious Diseases refers to the number of deaths of Class A and B notifiable infectious diseases per 100 thousand population in the reference year. The formula is:

Mortality rate of Class A and B notifiable infectious diseases= number of deaths of Class A and B notifiable infectious diseases / population × 100000

22 其他社会活动

Chapter 22 Other Social Activities

SICHUAN STATISTICAL YEARBOOK

22-1 收养类单位基本情况
Statistics on Adoption Units

项目		Item		2023
单位数	(个)	Number of Units	(unit)	2859
工商部门登记	(个)	Registered in Business Administration	(unit)	517
编制部门登记	(个)	Registered in Establishment Departments	(unit)	1681
民政部门登记	(个)	Registered in Civil Administration	(unit)	491
一个机构多个牌子	(个)	One unit with more the one name	(unit)	170
床位数	(张)	Number of Beds	(unit)	356431
工商部门登记	(张)	Registered in Business Administration	(unit)	70205
编制部门登记	(张)	Registered in Establishment Departments	(unit)	199467
民政部门登记	(张)	Registered in Civil Administration	(unit)	67026
一个机构多个牌子	(张)	One unit with more the one name	(unit)	19733
工作人员	(人)	Persons Engaged	(person)	39175
工商部门登记	(人)	Registered in Business Administration	(person)	9885
编制部门登记	(人)	Registered in Establishment Departments	(person)	19092
民政部门登记	(人)	Registered in Civil Administration	(person)	8243
一个机构多个牌子	(人)	One unit with more the one name	(person)	1955

注：收养类单位情况由四川省民政厅、四川省退役军人事务厅提供。
a) Data of adoption units are provided by Sichuan Provincial Civil Affairs Department and Sichuan Department of Veterans Affairs.

22-2 收养类单位床位数及收(供)养人员数
Number of Beds and Persons Housed in Adoption Units

项目	Item	床位数(张) Number of Beds (unit)		收(供)养人数(人) Person Housed (person)	
		2022	2023	2022	2023
合计	**Total**	**56613**	**55040**	**32187**	**32846**
优抚事业单位	Units for Arranging the Family Members of Martyrs and Disabled Veterans	2850	3741	419	393
荣誉军人休养院	Convalescent Homes for Honored Ex-servicemen	1060	1090	145	156
复员退伍军人(精神病)医院	Mental Hospitals for Ex-servicemen	310	800	29	28
光荣院	Homes for Disabled Veterans	1480	1851	245	209
福利收养性单位	Welfare Adoption Units	53763	51299	31768	32453
社会福利院	Social Welfare Homes	30380	27694	15053	14497
儿童福利院	Children Welfare Homes	6853	6179	2489	2131
社会福利医院	Psychopathy Welfare Homes	16530	17426	14226	15825

22-3 社区服务机构和设施情况
Statistics on Community Service Organizations and Facilities

项目		Item		2023
社区服务机构单位数	(个)	Number of Community Service Organizations	(unit)	35550
#农村社区服务机构	(个)	Rural Community Service Organization	(unit)	19224
#可以为居民提供便民办事服务的机构	(个)	Institutions to Provide Convenience Services for Residents	(unit)	19002
#可以为居民提供活动场所的机构	(个)	Mechanism for Providing Active Sites for Residents	(unit)	3440
#可以为居民提供养老等服务的机构	(个)	Institutions to Provide Pension Services for Residents	(unit)	10904
年末职工人数	(人)	Number of Employees at the end of this Year	(person)	137499
#女性	(人)	Female	(person)	53906
机构床位数	(张)	Number of Beds in Organizations	(unit)	93645
日间照料床位数	(张)	Day Care Beds	(unit)	43751
#农村	(张)	Countryside	(unit)	
住宿收养床位数	(张)	Residential Adoption Beds	(unit)	49894
#农村	(张)	Countryside	(unit)	
年末收养人数	(人)	Number of Adoption at the end of this Year	(person)	13318
#农村	(人)	Countryside	(person)	7487

22-4 婚姻登记和离婚情况
Statistics on Marriages and Divorces

项目		Item		2010	2015	2020	2021	2022	2023
按居住地分		**By Residence**							
内地居民登记结婚	(对)	Registered Marriages of Mainland	(couple)	713263	740186	535913	511063	463249	478311
#涉外及华侨、港澳台居民登记结婚	(对)	Registered Marriages with Foreigner, overseas Chinese and the Citizen of Hong Kong, Macao, Taiwan	(couple)	1580	1340	617	546	659	1847
按婚前状况分		**By Premarital Situation**							
初婚	(人)	First Marriages	(person)	1197122	1138435	766332	729011	673113	702862
再婚	(人)	Remarriages	(person)	232564	344617	306728	294207	254703	257457
#再婚中恢复结婚	(对)	Remarriages of Divorced Couple	(couple)	8594	29669	29484	25599	19728	19451
内地居民离婚数	(对)	Registered Divorces of Mainland	(couple)	173824	241133	261983	147285	155406	176805

22-5 各市(州)内地居民婚姻登记和离婚情况
Statistics on Marriage and Divorces of Mainland by Region

单位：对 (couple)

市(州)	Region	内地居民登记结婚 Registered Marriages of Mainland						内地居民登记离婚 Registered Divorces of Mainland					
		2010	2015	2020	2021	2022	2023	2010	2015	2020	2021	2022	2023
全省	**Sichuan**	**713263**	**740186**	**535913**	**511063**	**463249**	**478311**	**173824**	**241133**	**261983**	**147285**	**155406**	**176805**
成都市	Chengdu	119408	125085	108875	112097	111841	134056	43236	52726	61214	37669	41767	49778
自贡市	Zigong	24959	24349	15417	14147	12545	11761	6369	9259	9044	5106	5386	5966
攀枝花市	Panzhihua	9780	10064	6827	6240	5880	6090	3946	4344	3826	2193	2376	2577
泸州市	Luzhou	38260	35798	25321	23489	21939	21982	8331	11388	12354	6725	7067	8006
德阳市	Deyang	26303	30978	19427	19044	17114	17141	10157	12165	11377	6327	6316	7183
绵阳市	Mianyang	46778	43988	28803	27565	24401	24518	13033	15931	16040	8009	8543	9125
广元市	Guangyuan	19400	23257	16292	14841	12152	12699	4462	5735	6841	3363	3331	4268
遂宁市	Suining	25423	31339	18981	17882	15746	14924	4552	9395	9735	5043	5257	6176
内江市	Neijiang	36061	32677	20899	18810	15821	15429	8898	14161	13617	7147	7190	7840
乐山市	Leshan	27988	29105	21018	19155	17426	17253	9547	11438	12338	7121	7722	8129
南充市	Nanchong	60430	57118	38344	35170	30177	28663	9612	14884	17516	9620	9480	11133
眉山市	Meishan	37337	30658	20584	19804	16920	16207	10337	11454	10801	6948	7374	8207
宜宾市	Yibin	40138	45466	32982	30234	27043	26627	10830	15171	18231	9741	9967	10847
广安市	Guangan	33873	34607	24953	23130	19545	19687	5533	10169	11692	5974	5761	6979
达州市	Dazhou	55942	56163	32874	30499	26934	25412	7964	13322	14401	7093	6780	6997
雅安市	Yaan	12715	13400	10338	9135	8235	7947	3731	5371	5325	3125	3309	3380
巴中市	Bazhong	40540	33497	21167	21974	18285	16648	2757	5585	6896	3216	3775	4305
资阳市	Ziyang	37014	35376	15732	14061	12384	11851	7502	12479	8803	4822	4792	5573
阿坝藏族羌族自治州	Aba	6145	7648	6389	6199	4649	5073	381	1138	1529	923	958	1128
甘孜藏族自治州	Ganzi	3949	12516	9403	8702	7472	6760	458	1171	1787	1180	1397	1383
凉山彝族自治州	Liangshan	10820	27097	41287	38885	36740	37583	2188	3847	8616	5940	6858	7825

注：婚姻登记情况由四川省民政厅提供。全省合计数包括涉外及华侨、港澳台居民登记结婚、离婚数。离婚数不包括法院判决数。

a) Data of marriage registration are provided by Sichuan Provincial Civil Affairs Department. The total of the province includes registered marriages and divorces with foreigners, overseas Chinese, and the citizen of Hong Kong, Macao, Taiwan. The number of divorces mediated by the count are not included in that of divorces.

22-6 律师、公证、调解工作基本情况
Basic Statistics on Lawyers, Notarization and Mediation

项目		Item		2005	2010	2015	2020	2021	2022	2023
律师工作		**Lawyers**								
律师事务所	(所)	Number of Law Offices	(unit)	615	802	1130	1718	1842	1965	2117
律师工作者	(人)	Number of Lawyers	(person)	6331	9297	15526	28011	30137	33936	37959
#专职律师	(人)	Full-time Lawyers	(person)	6025	8504	14519	22281	24415	27242	29641
担任法律顾问的单位	(家)	Number of Units with Permanent Legal Advisors	(unit)	12704	15530	35510	41184	48023	42709	50197
民事诉讼代理	(件)	Agent of Civil Cases	(case)	35310	49772	96880	181837	265119	274756	308772
刑事案件辩护及代理	(件)	Defender and Agent of Criminal Cases	(case)	15852	33845	41613	44359	50353	48937	57275
非诉讼法律事务	(件)	Agent of Non-Litigious Legal Affairs	(case)	44558	42463	39122	58428	52137	52859	49691
咨询和代写法律文书	(次)	Agent of Advise and Legal Documents Written for Others	(copy)	283976	502229	315901	194358	166918	174117	148676
公证工作		**Notarization**								
公证处	(个)	Number of Notary Offices	(unit)	207	205	208	209	210	210	210
公证人员	(人)	Notarial Personnel	(person)	1165	1720	2221	2686	2665	2499	2757
#公证员	(人)	Notaries	(person)	679	723	839	938	989	983	1031
受理国内公证	(件)	Internal Notarization	(case)	150854	732398	832457	1160722	1085978	1003966	1281376
受理涉外公证	(件)	Foreign-related Notarization	(case)	18322	65775	101597	88269	96116	80704	120469
受理涉台、港、澳公证	(件)	Notarization of Hong Kong Macao & Taiwan	(case)	2366	6886	6087	2216	2329	3200	5517
出证	(件)	Number of Notarized Documents	(copy)	170028	802173	943074	1251207	1184423	1087870	1407362
人民调解工作		**People's Mediation**								
专职司法助理员	(人)	Number of Full-time Judicial Assistants	(person)	1053	2739	3862	4713	4728	4650	4448
人民调解委员会	(个)	Number of People's Mediation Committees	(unit)	64879	63912	63587	42566	40745	40557	40299
调解员	(人)	Number of Mediators	(person)	524428	429763	376748	236167	223031	222276	200177
基层法律服务所调解纠纷	(件)	Mediation of Grassroots Legal Service	(case)	42060	39282	44755	368094	366186	365321	423480

注：律师、公证和调解资料由四川省司法厅提供。

a) Data of lawyers, notarization and mediation information are provided by Sichuan Provincial Department of Justice.

22−7 调解民间纠纷情况
Statistics on Mediation of Civil Disputes

项目	Item	调解纠纷（件）Mediation of Disputes (case)		各类纠纷所占比重（%）Percentage of Disputes (%)	
		2022	2023	2022	2023
合计	**Total**	**365321**	**423480**	**100.0**	**100.0**
婚姻家庭纠纷	Marriage and Family Disputes	71382	80982	19.5	19.1
邻里纠纷	Neighborhood Disputes	101965	127027	27.9	30.0
房屋宅基地纠纷	Homestead Housing Disputes	7636	8030	2.1	1.9
合同纠纷	Contracts Disputes	18311	20215	5.0	4.8
生产经营纠纷	Production and Management Disputes	6086	5933	1.7	1.4
损害赔偿	Damage Disputes	29808	31391	8.2	7.4
劳动争议	Labor Disputes	17548	23160	4.8	5.5
山林土地纠纷	Forest Land Disputes	15612	19473	4.3	4.6
征地拆迁纠纷	Land Acquisition and Resettlement Disputes	3527	4292	1.0	1.0
环境保护	Environmental Protection	1872	2088	0.5	0.5
道路交通事故	Road Traffic Accidents	33062	32909	9.1	7.8
物业纠纷	Property Disputes	7323	9087	2.0	2.2
医疗纠纷	Medical Malpractice	2476	2880	0.7	0.7
其他纠纷	Other Disputes	48713	56013	13.3	13.2

22-8 各市(州)检察机关审查批准、决定逮捕犯罪嫌疑人和提起公诉被告人情况

Criminal Suspects Approved and Arrested and Defendants Prosecuted by People's Procuratorate by Region

案件分类 市(州)	Case Item Region	批捕、决定逮捕合计 Total of Approval and Arrest 2022 件 (case)	2022 人 (person)	2023 件 (case)	2023 人 (person)	决定起诉合计 Total of Public Prosecutions 2022 件 (case)	2022 人 (person)	2023 件 (case)	2023 人 (person)
合计	**Total**	**13651**	**19365**	**19588**	**27582**	**46170**	**70596**	**51826**	**78894**
公安、安全、监狱机关提请小计	**Sub-total of Requests by Departments of State and Public Security and Prisons**	**13631**	**19339**	**19567**	**27563**	**45250**	**69497**	**50859**	**77758**
危害国家安全、公共安全案	Offences Against State Security	373	430	497	557	13795	14160	15569	15905
破坏社会主义市场经济秩序案	Offences Against Socialist Economic Order	552	922	855	1578	2144	4771	1955	4864
侵犯公民人身、民主权利案	Offences Against Citizens' Personal and Democratic Rights	2683	3038	3361	3802	4636	5598	5172	6373
妨害社会管理秩序案	Offences Against Social Management Order	4398	7349	6030	9750	14128	29066	15412	31328
侵犯财产案	Offences Against Properties	5625	7600	8818	11869	10536	15889	12744	19277
危害国防利益案	Offences Against National Defense	5	6	6	7	11	13	7	11
检察机关直接立案侦查案件小计	**Sub-total of Cases Handled Directly by Procuratorate Offices**	**15**	**20**	**19**	**19**	**920**	**1099**	**967**	**1113**
贪污贿赂案	Offences on Corruption and Bribery	7	10	6	6	878	1035	928	1052
渎职侵权案	Offences on Abuse and Dereliction of Duty	8	10	13	13	42	64	39	61
按市(州)分	**Grouped by Region**								
四川省人民检察院	Provincial Procuratorate								
成都市	Chengdu	3331	4473	6429	8509	11301	15732	13597	18716
自贡市	Zigong	521	645	640	882	1788	2504	1896	2767
攀枝花市	Panzhihua	242	358	262	411	1126	1685	1015	1508
泸州市	Luzhou	638	890	895	1487	2337	3440	2299	3744
德阳市	Deyang	416	516	705	926	1699	2324	2133	3102
绵阳市	Mianyang	511	732	755	1099	2508	4005	3066	4817
广元市	Guangyuan	319	487	367	561	1333	2354	1374	2310
遂宁市	Suining	489	641	623	857	1585	2215	1760	2604
内江市	Neijiang	649	960	884	1240	1520	2402	2180	3374
乐山市	Leshan	420	590	625	938	1765	2651	2045	3354
南充市	Nanchong	876	1404	1245	1736	3252	5804	3819	6324
眉山市	Meishan	467	618	605	825	1407	2167	1483	2543
宜宾市	Yibin	967	1330	1145	1526	2669	4124	3052	4550
广安市	Guangan	364	530	625	937	1451	2590	1684	2832
达州市	Dazhou	718	992	872	1251	2249	3561	2054	3339
雅安市	Yaan	341	555	364	620	875	1678	934	1801
巴中市	Bazhong	311	429	402	526	1543	2339	1489	2140
资阳市	Ziyang	391	520	404	577	1448	2069	1524	2228
阿坝藏族羌族自治州	Aba	133	210	166	257	592	966	573	879
甘孜藏族自治州	Ganzi	251	412	189	261	837	1221	691	1029
凉山彝族自治州	Liangshan	1242	1997	1321	2080	2762	4551	3050	4757
四川省人民检察院成都铁路运输分院	Procuratorate of Chengdu Railroad Bureau	55	76	65	76	123	214	108	176

22-9 人民法院审理各类案件受理结案情况
Trial Cases Accepted and Settled by Courts

单位：件 (case)

项目	Item	受理 Cases Accepted		结案 Cases Settled	
		2022	2023	2022	2023
合计	**Total**	**1667277**	**1894821**	**1587885**	**1733202**
一审	**First Trial**	**974621**	**1100610**	**927073**	**1029330**
刑事	Criminal	47904	54894	45969	52566
民事	Civil	913646	1031642	869094	964567
行政	Administrative	12278	13365	11299	11608
行政赔偿	Administrative compensation	793	709	711	589
二审	**Second Trial**	**93095**	**107842**	**84455**	**92889**
刑事	Criminal	5211	5813	4946	5278
民事	Civil	79731	94320	72065	80702
行政	Administrative	7566	7145	6906	6417
行政赔偿	Administrative compensation	587	564	538	492
审判监督	**Trial Oversight**	**2761**	**2688**	**1800**	**1687**
刑事	Criminal	181	210	152	174
民事	Civil	2542	2332	1614	1375
行政	Administrative	35	140	31	132
行政赔偿	Administrative compensation	3	6	3	6
再审审查	**Retrial review**	**19122**	**5520**	**17611**	**5202**
国家赔偿与司法救助	**State Compensation and Judicial Assistance**	**5850**	**554310**	**5550**	**485160**
执行案件	**Enforcement cases**	**477707**	**19562**	**459839**	**17855**
刑罚与执行变更审查	**Punishment and Execution change review**	**22360**	**24444**	**22174**	**24134**
其他案件	**Other Cases**	**71761**	**79845**	**69383**	**76945**

注：人民法院审理案件等情况由四川省高级人民法院提供。受理案件中包括上年旧存。

a) People's court cases are prepared and provided by Sichuan Provincial Higher People's Court. Trial cases include the last year left.

22-10 人民法院执行案件标的和减、免、缓诉讼费情况
Subjects Implemented and Litigation Costs Reduced, Exempted and Deferred by Courts

项目		Item		2022	2023
首次执行申请执行标的	(亿元)	Subject matter of application for the first execution	(100 million yuan)	3430.68	3523.22
首次执行到位标的	(亿元)	Subject matter of the first execution in place	(100 million yuan)	1085.85	1021.69
减、免、缓诉讼费案件	(件)	Cases of Litigation Costs Reduced, Exempted and Deferred	(case)	2613	1726
减、免、缓诉讼费	(万元)	Litigation Costs Reduced, Exempted and Deferred	(10 000 yuan)	2312.40	2278.91
减交	(万元)	Reduction	(10 000 yuan)	286.39	185.02
免交	(万元)	Exemption	(10 000 yuan)	403.89	1133.93
缓交	(万元)	Deferral	(10 000 yuan)	1622.12	959.96

22-11　公安机关受理查处治安案件情况(2023年)
Offense Cases Against Public Order Handled by Public Security Organs(2023)

单位：起　　　　(case)

案件类别	Category of Cases	受理 Cases Accepted to be Treated	查处 Cases Investigated and Treated
合计	**Total**	**333046**	**225625**
扰乱公共秩序	Disrupt Public Order	19155	16846
#扰乱单位秩序	Disrupt Unit Order	1652	1246
#扰乱公共场所秩序	Disrupt Public Place Order	1205	978
#扰乱公共交通工具秩序	Disrupt Public Transport Order	133	102
#妨碍交通工具正常行驶	Impedes Normal Conditions of Transport	163	110
#扰乱大型群众性活动秩序	Disrupt the order of large scale mass activities	5	5
妨害公共安全	Prejudice Public Safety	3736	3030
#违反危险物质管理规定 非法携带枪支、弹药、管制刀	Violation of Hazardous Material Regulations Illegal Possession of Firearms. Ammunition. Knife Control	700	563
#盗窃、损毁公共设施	Theft and Damage to Public Facilities	661	371
侵犯他人人身权利、财产权利	Infringe upon the Personal and Property Rights to others	243160	146368
#强迫他人劳动	Forced Labor		
#侮辱、诽谤、诬告陷害	Insult, Libel, Calumniation	1136	569
#发送信息干扰正常生活	Send Information Interfered with the Normal Life	168	80
#殴打他人	Assault	74329	50977
#盗窃	Theft	76190	32257
妨害社会管理	Prejudice and Social Management	66995	59381
#阻碍执行职务	Impeding the Implementation of Duties	1242	1097
#违反旅馆业管理	Hotel Management Violation	2257	2044
#卖淫、嫖娼	Prostitution, Whoring	6021	5530
#毒品违法活动	Drug-related activities	14821	14164

注：治安情况、火灾事故和交通事故资料由四川省公安厅提供。
a) Data of law and order, fire and accident are provided by Sichuan Provincial Public Security Bureau.

22-12 各市(州)查处治安案件和刑事案件立案数

Number of Offense Cases Against Public Order Investigated and Prosecuted and Criminal Case Filed by Region

单位：起 (case)

市(州)	Region	治安案件 Offense Cases Against Public Order				刑事案件立案 Criminal Case Filed	
		发现 Discovered		查处 Investigated and Prosecuted			
		2022	2023	2022	2023	2022	2023
全省	**Sichuan**	**475206**	**333046**	**326728**	**225625**	**272555**	**190974**
成都市	Chengdu	191194	168340	107060	103560	135304	86030
自贡市	Zigong	12452	9201	6959	5153	8060	5994
攀枝花市	Panzhihua	7986	2284	6326	1138	3454	2294
泸州市	Luzhou	16152	10989	15071	9938	8569	7015
德阳市	Deyang	16186	9523	9013	4893	11266	7325
绵阳市	Mianyang	26034	13474	16691	7844	9277	7303
广元市	Guangyuan	14443	6346	11258	4592	6411	5554
遂宁市	Suining	16814	9082	14196	7855	6708	4554
内江市	Neijiang	11148	7244	10047	5330	7437	6358
乐山市	Leshan	14265	9333	14210	9313	7577	5565
南充市	Nanchong	30809	13155	24374	10278	11126	9413
眉山市	Meishan	10453	8692	7595	6850	6180	4423
宜宾市	Yibin	21717	14078	9215	5478	13847	10542
广安市	Guangan	15561	7265	15562	7329	6117	5059
达州市	Dazhou	16951	8629	15658	8185	6978	5090
雅安市	Yaan	4118	3101	3474	2576	3122	2356
巴中市	Bazhong	11070	5058	10691	4549	5758	4597
资阳市	Ziyang	14550	6919	8498	3638	5966	3716
阿坝藏族羌族自治州	Aba	1926	1329	1803	1170	1344	1234
甘孜藏族自治州	Ganzi	2365	1323	2272	1227	1277	885
凉山彝族自治州	Liangshan	19012	17681	16755	14729	6777	5667

22-13 火灾事故情况
Statistics on Fire Accidents

指标	Item	合计 Total		特大事故 Extraordinarily		重大事故 Serious		较大事故 major		一般事故 Ordinary	
		2022	2023	2022	2023	2022	2023	2022	2023	2022	2023
火灾事故发生起数 (起)	Number of Fires (case)	45630	47249					6	2	45624	47247
死亡人数 (人)	Number of Deaths (person)	119	115					13	8	106	107
受伤人数 (人)	Number of Injuries (person)	132	114					2	3	130	111
损失金额 (万元)	Losses Converted into Cash (10 000 yuan)	29314	29809					4853	1191	24462	28617
平均每起事故损失 (万元)	Losses per Case(10 000 yuan)	0.64	0.63					808.79	595.68	0.54	0.61

22-14 各市(州)火灾事故情况
Statistics on Fire Accidents by Region

市(州)	Region	火灾事故(起) Number of Fire Accidents (case)		火灾伤亡人数(人) Number of Casualties (person)		火灾损失金额(万元) Losses Converted into Cash (10 000 yuan)	
		2022	2023	2022	2023	2022	2023
全省	**Sichuan**	**45630**	**47249**	**251**	**229**	**29314.4**	**29808.5**
成都市	Chengdu	14924	13480	70	54	7550.3	6210.7
自贡市	Zigong	1991	2274	6	10	651.3	709.1
攀枝花市	Panzhihua	700	720	5	4	1616.5	414.8
泸州市	Luzhou	2922	2614	25	24	4928.4	2243.4
德阳市	Deyang	1769	2232	7	10	860.2	1155.7
绵阳市	Mianyang	2941	3809	8	9	1058.9	962.8
广元市	Guangyuan	1054	1074	16	6	963.2	1082.9
遂宁市	Suining	2525	2151	5	14	759.4	1550.5
内江市	Neijiang	1257	1396	10	6	790.1	860.1
乐山市	Leshan	1066	825	10	5	1702.8	1256.4
南充市	Nanchong	3536	4236	22	17	1467.7	1789.5
眉山市	Meishan	1442	1762	6	5	476.8	1921.2
宜宾市	Yibin	2425	2049	11	7	1776.9	2621.2
广安市	Guangan	1457	1928	9	9	687.9	1493.2
达州市	Dazhou	1919	1278	2	6	582.2	614.0
雅安市	Yaan	583	785	1	8	475.5	556.9
巴中市	Bazhong	915	1038	17	13	618.1	705.1
资阳市	Ziyang	1049	2069	8	18	759.6	1015.8
阿坝藏族羌族自治州	Aba	288	354	1		321.4	620.6
甘孜藏族自治州	Ganzi	228	173	3	1	887.5	994.2
凉山彝族自治州	Liangshan	639	1002	9	3	379.7	1030.6

22−15 交通事故情况(2023年)
Statistics on Traffic Accidents(2023)

项目		Item		合计 Total	特大事故 Extraordinarily	重大事故 Serious	较大事故 Major	其他 Others
发生数	(起)	Number of Traffic Accidents	(case)	7122			33	7089
死亡人数	(人)	Number of Deaths	(person)	2328			120	2208
受伤人数	(人)	Number of Injuries	(person)	7288			63	7225
损失折款	(万元)	Losses Converted into Cash	(10 000 yuan)	7444			560	6885
平均每起事故损失	(元)	Losses Converted per Case	(yuan)	10453			169636	9712

22−16 各市(州)交通事故情况(2023年)
Statistics on Traffic Accidents by Region(2023)

市(州)	Region	发生数 (起) Number of Traffic Accidents (case)	死亡人数 (人) Number of Deaths (person)	受伤人数 (人) Number of Injuries (person)	损失折款 (万元) Losses Converted into Cash (10 000 yuan)
全 省	**Sichuan**	**7122**	**2328**	**7288**	**7446**
成都市	Chengdu	1326	478	814	443
自贡市	Zigong	207	46	193	47
攀枝花市	Panzhihua	131	24	145	21
泸州市	Luzhou	202	69	186	91
德阳市	Deyang	67	53	32	21
绵阳市	Mianyang	425	201	334	161
广元市	Guangyuan	375	76	512	124
遂宁市	Suining	69	36	63	27
内江市	Neijiang	80	23	71	5
乐山市	Leshan	611	177	614	314
南充市	Nanchong	172	102	153	253
眉山市	Meishan	107	62	86	29
宜宾市	Yibin	527	124	583	209
广安市	Guangan	32	23	21	6
达州市	Dazhou	185	73	217	86
雅安市	Yaan	518	69	591	394
巴中市	Bazhong	63	25	66	51
资阳市	Ziyang	113	79	77	13
阿坝藏族羌族自治州	Aba	299	71	444	314
甘孜藏族自治州	Ganzi	260	62	505	472
凉山彝族自治州	Liangshan	960	219	1032	379
其它					
省管高速公路公安局	Provincial Expressway Public Security Bureau	367	236	512	3953
机场公安局	Airport Public Security Bureau	25		36	23
成铁公安局	Chengdu Railway Public Security Bureau	1		1	10

主要统计指标解释

社区服务机构和设施数 具有面向老人及其家庭的商品递送、医疗保健、家庭保洁、日间照料、陪伴服务等为社区居家养老服务的设施和突出综合服务的职能。指报告期末设立的社区服务指导中心、社区服务中心、社区服务站、未登记的农村特困人员救助供养机构、社区养老照料机构和设施、社区互助型养老服务机构、其他社区服务机构的总数。

公证（出证） 指公证处根据当事人申请，依照事实和法律，按照法定程序制作的，具有法律效力的司法证明文书。

批准逮捕 指人民检察院对公安机关、国家安全机关、监狱管理机关提出逮捕的犯罪嫌疑人进行审查，根据事实，依法做出逮捕决定。该指标主要反映人民检察院对提请逮捕犯罪嫌疑人进行审查后依法做出批准逮捕决定的情况。

决定逮捕 指人民检察院对直接立案侦查的案件，认为需要逮捕犯罪嫌疑人时，依据法律做出的逮捕决定。该指标主要反映人民检察院对直接受理的案件行使决定逮捕权的情况。

受理 指人民法院对符合诉讼法规定立案条件，决定立案审理的案件。受理包括上期“旧存”和本期“新收”案件两部分。

结案 指人民法院依照诉讼法规定审理案件，案件审理结束已作出处理决定的案件。

特大火灾 指造成 30 人以上死亡，或者 100 人以上重伤，或者 1 亿元以上直接财产损失的火灾。

重大火灾 指造成 10 人以上 30 人以下死亡，或者 50 人以上 100 人以下重伤，或者 5000 万元以上 1 亿元以下直接财产损失的火灾。

较大火灾 指造成 3 人以上 10 人以下死亡，或者 10 人以上 50 人以下重伤，或者 1000 万元以上 5000 万元以下直接财产损失的火灾。

一般火灾 指造成 3 人以下死亡，或者 10 人以下重伤，或者 1000 万元以下直接财产损失的火灾。

特大交通事故 指一次造成死亡 3 人以上，或者重伤 11 人以上，或者死亡 1 人，同时重伤 8 人以上，或者死亡 2 人，同时重伤 5 人以上，或者财产损失 6 万元以上的交通事故。

重大交通事故 指一次造成死亡 1 至 2 人，或者重伤 3 人以上 10 人以下，或者财产损失 3 万元以上不足 6 万元的交通事故。

Explanatory Notes on Main Statistical Indicators

Number of Service Institutions and facilities in Communities refer to the community institutions and integrated facilities offer the commodity delivery, health care, cleaning, adult day care, companion and others for the elderly. Including the total number of community service guidance centers, community service centers, community service stations, unregistered rural assistance and support institutions for the needy, community elderly care institutions and facilities, community mutual aid pension institutions for the elderly and other community service institutions at the end of the reporting period.

Notarization (certification) refer to legally binding judicial notary documents, developed at the request of the interested party based on facts and the law following certain legal proceedings.

Approval for Arrest refers to the decision made by people's procuratorate office, in accordance with law and relevant facts, to approve the arrest of the suspects as proposed by the public security departments, state security departments or prisons authority. This indicator reflects approved arrests made by people's procuratorate offices that are proposed by related departments.

Decision on Arrest refers to the decision made by people's procuratorate office, in accordance with law, to arrest the suspects in the cases that are accepted and to be investigated by the procurators office. This indicator mainly reflects the implementation of the decision on arrest by people’s procuratorate office.

Acceptance of Case refers to People's Court decide to accept in accordance with the Provisions of Procedural law. The cases include two parts: cases turned over from previous year and cases accepted this year.

Settlement of Case refers to People's Court decide to accept the case and make decision in accordance with the Provisions of Procedural law.

Extraordinarily Serious Fire Case refers to a case which has caused over 30 deaths; or over 100 serious injuries; or a direct property loss over 100 million yuan(RMB).

Serious Fire Case refers to a case which has caused over 10 to 30 deaths; or over 50 to 100 serious injuries; or a direct property loss over 50 million to 100 million yuan(RMB).

Comparatively Serious Fire Case refers to a case which has caused over three to ten deaths; or over 10 to 50 serious injuries; or a direct property loss over 10 million to 50 million yuan(RMB).

Ordinary Fire Case refers to a case which has caused less than three deaths; or less than 10 serious injuries; or a direct property loss less than 10 million yuan(RMB).

Extraordinarily Serious Traffic Accident refers to an accident which has caused three or more deaths; or over 11 serious injuries; or one death and over 8 serious injuries; or two deaths and over 5 serious injuries; or a loss over 60 thousand yuan(RMB).

Serious Traffic Accident refers to an accident which has caused one or two deaths, or three to ten serious injuries; or a loss over 30 thousand yuan to 60 thousand yuan(RMB).